Sustainable Digitalization Strategies in Business and Healthcare

Durmuş Çağrı Yıldırım
Tekirdag Namık Kemal University, Turkey

Seda Yıldırım
Tekirdag Namık Kemal University, Turkey

Vinay Kandpal
Graphic Era University, Dehradun, India

IGI Global
Scientific Publishing
Publishing Tomorrow's Research Today

Vice President of Editorial	Melissa Wagner
Director of Acquisitions	Mikaela Felty
Director of Book Development	Jocelynn Hessler
Production Manager	Mike Brehm
Cover Design	Jose Rosado

Published in the United States of America by
IGI Global Scientific Publishing
701 East Chocolate Avenue
Hershey, PA, 17033, USA
Tel: 717-533-8845
Fax: 717-533-7115
Website: https://www.igi-global.com E-mail: cust@igi-global.com

Library of Congress Cataloging-in-Publication Data

Names: Yildirim, Durmus Çagri, 1981- editor. | Yıldırım, Sedat, 1983- editor. | Kandpal, Vinay editor.
Title: Sustainable digitalization strategies in business and healthcare / edited by Durmuş Çağrı Yıldırım, Seda Yıldırım, and Vinay Kandpal.
Description: Hershey, PA : IGI Global Scientific Publishing, [2025] | Includes bibliographical references and index. | Summary: "This book explores topics related to digitalization and sustainability"-- Provided by publisher.
Identifiers: LCCN 2025026199 (print) | LCCN 2025026200 (ebook) | ISBN 9798337350875 hardcover | ISBN 9798337350882 paperback | ISBN 9798337350899 ebook
Subjects: LCSH: Sustainable development--Technological innovations--Case studies. | Industrial management--Technological innovations--Case studies. | Medical care--Technological innovations--Case studies. | COVID-19 Pandemic, 2020-2023--Economic aspects--Case studies.
Classification: LCC HC79.E5 S86155 2026 (print) | LCC HC79.E5 (ebook)
LC record available at https://lccn.loc.gov/2025026199
LC ebook record available at https://lccn.loc.gov/2025026200

British Cataloguing in Publication Data
A Cataloguing in Publication record for this book is available from the British Library.

Table of Contents

Detailed Table of Contents

This chapter investigates the impact of digitalization on business development at global level. It focusses on establishing the relationship between various metrics of digitalization and revenue growth of the business sector. It uses secondary data that is taken from World Bank Reports on Trends and Progress 2024. Accordingly, it finalizes four crucial variables (digital adoption rate, mobile broadband subscription, e-commerce penetration, and investment in digital infrastructure) to achieve chapter's objectives. It transforms a business development metric at global level. This metric investigates the impact of digital adoption, integration of digital transformation and technological integration on revenue of the business sector at global level. It employs a simple linear regression model to examine the impact of the afore-mentioned independent variables on the revenue growth of the business sector. It develops a quantitative approach to obtain the magnitude and numeric impact of digitalization on business development.

Digitalization is greatly supportive to increase the entrepreneurial ecosystem. Therefore, this chapter provides the impact of digitalization on entrepreneurship promoting indicators as giving more focus on the Indian economy. It also investigates the dynamic linkages of digitalization with job creation, government backing, and entrepreneurial ecosystem in India. It used a log-linear regression model for the mentioned investigation. It finds a high positive relationship between digitalization and employment growth. It noted a modest positive correlation between digitalization and government support. It also showed a strong favorable influence of employment levels on government assistance. It provides an understanding towards India's entrepreneurial ecosystem as emphasizing the catalytic impact of digitalization on driving employment and creating appropriate entrepreneurship. The findings have implications for policymakers, entrepreneurs, and stakeholders working to build a vibrant entrepreneurial ecosystem in India.

Tanzania's economic progress and efforts to reduce poverty require sustainable rural entrepreneurship. However, the accessibility of critical information technology resources is still a significant obstacle. Although rural entrepreneurs can benefit from e-government services, the existing studies have failed to consider their experiences and challenges. Therefore, to address this gap, this chapter assesses the role of e-government services in encouraging rural entrepreneurship in Tanzania. Semi-structured interviews were conducted in 2024 with fifteen rural entrepreneurs using a qualitative methodology based on the Technology Acceptance Model (TAM). While e-government services can improve business operations and compliance, the study highlights that barriers to digital literacy and connectivity are still present. This research demonstrates the pressing need for measures that will enhance access and functionality of e-government while also increasing rural economic development through sustainable entrepreneurship.

There has been a sea change in retail with the new wave of consumers who are looking to get instant access to products, which is leading to Q-commerce. Q-commerce can be defined as Quick Commerce, a means through which retailers/retailing can attempt to be different by delivering products within a minute. This chapter is an elaboration of how Q-commerce affects consumer behaviour and retail strategies. The COVID-19 pandemic really speeded up the transition from traditional retail to e-commerce and placed convenience at a new standard that challenges traditional retailing practices.In that regard, technological developments are the bedrock of Q-commerce, but at the same time, operational efficiency is enhanced through artificial intelligence, real-time analytics, and well-improved logistics. While delivery becomes faster through innovations, increasing customer loyalty, it creates ethical and sustainability concerns. The section highlights how the retailers should align rapid growth with responsible practices to manage the adverse environmental effects caused by fast delivery.

The shift to a circular economy will probably happen more quickly than in the past. Additionally, there is increasing social pressure on businesses to go carbon neutral, in contrast to earlier changes that frequently faced opposition from the general population. In the 2030s, the circular economy would become not only the dominant economic sector but also the exclusive one. A model approach to sustainability and the circular economy is required due to the excessive consumption of fashion, which has led to the unsustainable use of energy and natural resources (primarily fibres and water). This has resulted in millions of tons of textile waste annually. Natural resources are limited, and while the Earth begs for attention, humanity has long been recklessly consuming them. Circular business models are necessary because most currently operating companies are constructed on linear models. Although numerous studies have been conducted, more consumer knowledge is still needed. The current study focuses on how conscious consumers are of sustainable fashion.

The integration of green investments and corporate social responsibility (CSR) into core business strategies should be given top priority in future hotel management guidelines. To establish credibility, hotels ought to prioritize augmenting their utilization of renewable energy sources, augmenting their endeavours to reduce waste and conserve water, and pursuing green certifications. Managers can investigate government incentives and partnerships that support sustainability initiatives in order to overcome financial challenges. Hotels ought to make a point of highlighting to visitors the benefits of their sustainability initiatives and how they enhance their overall stay. In a market that is becoming more environmentally conscious, hotels can stay competitive and promote long-term success by closely observing the results of their green investments and fine-tuning their CSR strategies in response to feedback from guests and industry trends.

The rapid advancement of technology reshaped sectors, and the concept of digital health encompasses a broad spectrum of innovations, including telemedicine, technologies engagement and provided critical support systems around the world faced unprecedented challenges, digital health solutions emerged as vital tools for maintaining the continuity of care, improving accessibility, and enhancing the overall efficiency of health services. The COVID-19 pandemic catalyzed a massive shift towards digital health, as physical severely limited facilities. Telemedicine platforms surged in popularity, allowing safety shifts was ongoing management. Digital technologies, could maintain regular contact with these patients, adjusting treatment plans and offering support. Moreover, digital health tools facilitated rapid data collection and analysis, enabling more of the evolving crisis. For instance, played a crucial symptom tracking contact tracing, helping to identify outbreaks and manage community spread. Additionally, allowed policymakers to inform resource allocation public health strategies.

Digital transformation has emerged as a pivotal force in healthcare, particularly during health crises like the COVID-19 pandemic. As traditional systems faced unprecedented challenges, the rapid adoption of digital solutions became essential for ensuring patient care continuity and safety. Telemedicine surged, enabling remote consultations and reducing the burden on healthcare facilities. Electronic health records (EHRs) were optimized for better data sharing, facilitating coordinated responses among care teams. Wearable health technology gained traction, empowering individuals to monitor their health in real-time. Furthermore, data analytics and AI played crucial roles in predicting outbreaks and personalizing treatment plans.

Preface

The COVID-19 crisis has been a turning point that has accelerated digitalization in the 21st century. Sustainability and the healthcare sector have gone through major stages in digitalization. In this edited volume, " Sustainable Digitalization Strategies in Business and Healthcare," we aim to collect original, and review studies related to digital health issues and sustainability.

It is thought that this book will provide useful information for both academics and professionals, especially for teachers and students. It is thought that this book, which has contributions from international authors, will provide a global perspective.

CHAPTER OVERVIEW

Chapter 1: A Global Perspective on Impact of Digitalization on Business Development

This chapter investigates the impact of digitalization on business development at global level. It focusses on establishing the relationship between various metrics of digitalization and revenue growth of the business sector. It uses secondary data that is taken from World Bank Reports on Trends and Progress 2024. Accordingly, it finalizes four crucial variables (digital adoption rate, mobile broadband subscription, e-commerce penetration, and investment in digital infrastructure) to achieve chapter's objectives. It transforms a business development metric at global level. This metric investigates the impact of digital adoption, integration of digital transformation and technological integration on revenue of the business sector at global level. It employs a simple linear regression model to examine the impact of the afore-mentioned independent variables on the revenue growth of the business sector. It develops a quantitative approach to obtain the magnitude and numeric impact of digitalization on business development.

Chapter 2: Impact of Digitalization on Entrepreneurship Promoting Indicators in India

Digitalization is greatly supportive to increase the entrepreneurial ecosystem. Therefore, this chapter provides the impact of digitalization on entrepreneurship promoting indicators as giving more focus on the Indian economy. It also investigates the dynamic linkages of digitalization with job creation, government backing, and entrepreneurial ecosystem in India. It used a log-linear regression model for the mentioned investigation. It finds a high positive relationship between digitalization and employment growth. It noted a modest positive correlation between digitalization and government support. It also showed a strong favorable influence of employment levels on government assistance. It provides an understanding towards India's entrepreneurial ecosystem as emphasizing the catalytic impact of digitalization on driving employment and creating appropriate entrepreneurship. The findings have implications for policymakers, entrepreneurs, and stakeholders working to build a vibrant entrepreneurial ecosystem in India.

Chapter 3: Assessing e-Government Services for Sustainable Rural Entrepreneurship in Tanzania

Tanzania's economic progress and efforts to reduce poverty require sustainable rural entrepreneurship. However, the accessibility of critical information technology resources is still a significant obstacle. Although rural entrepreneurs can benefit from e-government services, the existing studies have failed to consider their experiences and challenges. Why? Therefore, to address this gap, this chapter assesses the role of e-government services in encouraging rural entrepreneurship in Tanzania. Semi-structured interviews were conducted in 2024 with fifteen rural entrepreneurs using a qualitative methodology based on the Technology Acceptance Model (TAM). While e-government services can improve business operations and compliance, the study highlights that barriers to digital literacy and connectivity are still present. This research demonstrates the pressing need for measures that will enhance access and functionality of e-government while also increasing rural economic development through sustainable entrepreneurship.

Chapter 4: The Rise of Quick Commerce - Redefining Retail through Digital Innovation and Sustainable Practices

There has been a sea change in retail with the new wave of consumers who are looking to get instant access to products, which is leading to Q-commerce. Q-commerce can be defined as Quick Commerce, a means through which retailers/

retailing can attempt to be different by delivering products within a minute. This chapter is an elaboration of how Q-commerce affects consumer behaviour and retail strategies. The COVID-19 pandemic really speeded up the transition from traditional retail to e-commerce and placed convenience at a new standard that challenges traditional retailing practices.In that regard, technological developments are the bedrock of Q-commerce, but at the same time, operational efficiency is enhanced through artificial intelligence, real-time analytics, and well-improved logistics. While delivery becomes faster through innovations, increasing customer loyalty, it creates ethical and sustainability concerns. The section highlights how the retailers should align rapid growth with responsible practices to manage the adverse environmental effects caused by fast delivery.

Chapter 5: Consumer Awareness on Sustainable Fashion: Sustainable Fashion

The shift to a circular economy will probably happen more quickly than in the past. Additionally, there is increasing social pressure on businesses to go carbon neutral, in contrast to earlier changes that frequently faced opposition from the general population. In the 2030s, the circular economy would become not only the dominant economic sector but also the exclusive one. A model approach to sustainability and the circular economy is required due to the excessive consumption of fashion, which has led to the unsustainable use of energy and natural resources (primarily fibres and water). This has resulted in millions of tons of textile waste annually. Natural resources are limited, and while the Earth begs for attention, humanity has long been recklessly consuming them. Circular business models are necessary because most currently operating companies are constructed on linear models. Although numerous studies have been conducted, more consumer knowledge is still needed. The current study focuses on how conscious consumers are of sustainable fashion.

Chapter 6: Corporate Social Responsibility and Green Investments: A New Paradigm for Hotel Management

The integration of green investments and corporate social responsibility (CSR) into core business strategies should be given top priority in future hotel management guidelines. To establish credibility, hotels ought to prioritize augmenting their utilization of renewable energy sources, augmenting their endeavours to reduce waste and conserve water, and pursuing green certifications. Managers can investigate government incentives and partnerships that support sustainability initiatives in order to overcome financial challenges. Hotels ought to make a point of highlighting to visitors the benefits of their sustainability initiatives and how they enhance their overall stay. In a market that is becoming more environmentally conscious, hotels can stay competitive and promote long-term success by closely observing the results of their green investments and fine-tuning their CSR strategies in response to feedback from guests and industry trends.

Chapter 7: Health Crises and Digitalization Digital Health

The rapid advancement of technology reshaped sectors, and the concept of digital health encompasses a broad spectrum of innovations, including telemedicine, technologies engagement and provided critical support systems around the world faced unprecedented challenges, digital health solutions emerged as vital tools for maintaining the continuity of care, improving accessibility, and enhancing the overall efficiency of health services. The COVID-19 pandemic catalyzed a massive shift towards digital health, as physical severely limited facilities. Telemedicine platforms surged in popularity, allowing safety shifts was ongoing management. Digital technologies, could maintain regular contact with these patients, adjusting treatment plans and offering support. Moreover, digital health tools facilitated rapid data collection and analysis, enabling more of the evolving crisis. For instance, played a crucial symptom tracking contact tracing, helping to identify outbreaks and manage community spread. Additionally, allowed policymakers to inform resource allocation public health strategies.

Chapter 8: Digital Transformation in Response to Health Crises

Digital transformation has emerged as a pivotal force in healthcare, particularly during health crises like the COVID-19 pandemic. As traditional systems faced unprecedented challenges, the rapid adoption of digital solutions became essential for ensuring patient care continuity and safety. Telemedicine surged, enabling remote consultations and reducing the burden on healthcare facilities. Electronic health records (EHRs) were optimized for better data sharing, facilitating coordinated responses among care teams. Wearable health technology gained traction, empowering individuals to monitor their health in real-time. Furthermore, data analytics and AI played crucial roles in predicting outbreaks and personalizing treatment plans. The shift towards a more digital-first approach not only addressed immediate needs but also laid the groundwork for a more resilient healthcare system. Stakeholders now recognize that embracing technology is critical for future-proofing healthcare against potential crises, enhancing overall healthcare delivery, and improving patient outcomes.

Chapter 9: Breaking Barriers How Artificial Intelligence Is Revolutionizing Healthcare

This paper aims at exploring AI integration and its impact on the healthcare industry in terms of having a way around conventional limitations and offer better service quality. Artificial intelligence and automation, features of machine learning, and natural language processing are stepping into diagnostics, treatment, and patient management. From early diagnoses, individualized treatment, and robot-assisted surgeries, it provides customers with better results, with minimal human intervention. AI is also improving the process of identifying new drugs and allowing telemedicine to deliver healthcare to those that have none. This has the potential of yielding explosive results for the field, although it also identified some existing limitations such as data privacy concerns, regulatory constraints, and the need for competent workforce. The paper describes how healthcare will change with the help of AI making it more efficient, fair and revolutionizing the approach to patients.

Chapter 10: Digital Health Navigating Digital Transformation and Digital Stress: Understanding Digital Health in the Era of Transformation

This chapter will discuss the topic of Digital Health, Digital Stress and Digital Transformation focusing on how digital tools and platforms are employed to enhance the employee's wellness and productivity. The application of Digital Health solutions helps to a great extent to remove barriers that prevent employees from being healthy and actively involved in the discussion of the problem since the overload of the working capacities of not only employees but also managers is observed nowadays, the issue of burnout and stress, fatigue coming from an insufficient number of digital breaks and digital exhaustion. The chapter will explain how organizations can leverage digital solutions to support initiatives connected with Sustainable Development Goals 3 (Good Health and Wellbeing) and Sustainable Development Goals 8 (Decent Work and Economic Growth) by decreasing the load created by constant connectivity and improving work environments.

Chapter 11: The Digital Footprint of COVID-19 On Women Health and the Indian Digital Space: Bridging Health and Equity Gaps

The present paper examines the "Whisper Presents Keep Girls in School" advertisement as a socio-cultural artifact highlighting the lacuna regarding the awareness and education surrounding menstrual health and hygiene in India. By asserting the difficulties and challenges young girls and women face, the advertisement argues for the requirement of extensive menstrual health education. The prevalent socio-cultural understanding is built on the restriction of the agency of women, and the associated dismissal attitude acts as a contributing factor towards a plethora of health risks, including reproductive tract infections and cervical cancer. Insufficient knowledge, shortage of convenient mobility, and lack of quality sanitary facilities are the predominant factors that make menstrual health and hygiene a challenging issue in India. The arrival of the COVID-19 epidemic further exacerbated these issues. The paper advocates for accessible, affordable healthcare and supportive cultures for young women. Prioritizing menstrual health promotes gender equality (SDG-3) and overall well-being.

Chapter 12: Beyond Bias: 'Hichki' as a Lens for Disability and Gender Equality in Education

This paper examines the text 'Hichki' as a cultural artifact reflecting the intersections of quality education and the SDGs, focusing on disability and gender equity in Indian society. The study focuses on Tourette syndrome, perceptions of disability, societal biases' that hinder access to education, and Covid-19 pedagogical practices. The analysis highlights the crucial role of female teachers in fostering inclusivity and nurturing student talent in the classroom. The media's portrayal of the protagonist as a female educator underscores the importance of empowering women in education and breaking down gender stereotypes that often limit their professional opportunities. Additionally, the "guru" concept is explored as a central pillar of Indian education, emphasizing mentorship, respect, and the transformative power of learning. By situating 'Hichki' within the broader SDG framework, this study notes the importance of addressing disability, supporting female teachers, and promoting gender equality to achieve comprehensive educational outcomes in India.

As editors, we would like to thank all our authors who collaborated internationally and hope that our book will be useful.

Durmus Çagri Yildirim
Tekirdag Namık Kemal University, Turkey

Seda Yildirim
Tekirdag Namık Kemal University, Turkey

Vinay Kandpal
Graphic Era University, Dehradun, India

Acknowledgment

We would like to thank the authors and referees who supported us in the hope that this book will contribute to the green economy and sustainable development literature and provide useful information to researchers and readers. Since the responsibility of the book chapters belongs to the corresponding author and co-authors of each chapter, you can contact the chapter authors for information.

Durmus Çagri Yildirim
Tekirdag Namık Kemal University, Turkey

Seda Yildirim
Tekirdag Namık Kemal University, Turkey

Vinay Kandpal
Graphic Era University, Dehradun, India

Chapter 1
A Global Perspective on Impact of Digitalization on Business Development

Dhitasmita De
https://orcid.org/0009-0008-2735-960X
Department of Humanities and Social Sciences, Graphic Era University, Dehradun, India

Ajay Kumar Singh
https://orcid.org/0000-0003-0429-0925
Department of Humanities and Social Sciences, Graphic Era University, Dehradun, India

ABSTRACT

This chapter investigates the impact of digitalization on business development at global level. It focusses on establishing the relationship between various metrics of digitalization and revenue growth of the business sector. It uses secondary data that is taken from World Bank Reports on Trends and Progress 2024. Accordingly, it finalizes four crucial variables (digital adoption rate, mobile broadband subscription, e-commerce penetration, and investment in digital infrastructure) to achieve chapter's objectives. It transforms a business development metric at global level. This metric investigates the impact of digital adoption, integration of digital transformation and technological integration on revenue of the business sector at global level. It employs a simple linear regression model to examine the impact of the afore-mentioned independent variables on the revenue growth of the business sector. It develops a quantitative approach to obtain the magnitude and numeric impact of digitalization on business development.

DOI: 10.4018/979-8-3373-5087-5.ch001

INTRODUCTION

Recently, the impact of digitalization and digital transformation on various sectors of the economy are increasing consistency across counties (Leviäkangas, 2016; Jyoti & Singh, 2023). Mostly digitalization and digital infrastructure are working as a significant driver to enhance business operations and management. The process of digitalization is also known as digital transformation. While digital transformation is referred to as a process for using available and emerging digital technologies (DTs) in digital forms to solve different purposes of humanities in all fields (Singh et al., 2024). It is also referred to the utilization of DTs to enhance the existing processes, operations and business models. It also leverages the potential that digital tools and raw data possess augment competence, potency, associativity, and clientele experience in the business sector and entrepreneurial activities. Currently digitalization is the most significant technological tool that has a significant impact on sustainability aspects of individuals, communities and organization in a nation (Leviäkangas, 2016; Singh et al., 2024a). Computerisation of systems began in the 1980s in most countries. Thereafter, its involvement in economic and social sectors increased progressively worldwide (Singh, 2025a). Foster (1986) projected that the manufacturing sectors and a significant portion of the service industries would undergo a significant technological shift in the 2000s.

Digitization involves the conversion of analog information into digital format (Chae, 2022). Further, it converts analog data into a series of numbers (i.e., binary codes) (Gradillas & Thomas, 2023). Thereupon, it can be used for further processes in different sectors. Digitalization includes wide and broad transformations of information in digital forms. It also helps to increase the usability of available raw data and digital tools for enhancing proficiency, potency, associativity, and customer experience in a business organization. However, digitalization and digitization can be used together in place of each other. Numerous research studies, academicians and researchers have tried to observe that how digitalization is a term far more diverse than digitization? Despite that, existing literature could provide the significant diversity between digitalization and digitization. Digitization refers to the conversion of analog information into digital format. This process more or less involves conversion of analog data into a series of numbers, i.e., binary codes. This form of data can be easily stored using digital technologies (DTs) and further utilization of it for different purposes. The process of digitization often includes scanning, capturing or encrypting data into physical format and binary codes that can be easily readable and understandable by computers (Gradillas & Thomas, 2023). Thus, it makes processing and transforming of available information in digital forms for increasing its accessibility and usability of large group of communities in diversified fields.

While digitalization doesn't remain limited to conversions of available data and information in digital format. Digitalization mostly involved the collection, processing, and analysing of data for innovative purposes in business and other sectors. Thus, it also creates and adds value to the use of DTs in the innovative process (Lanzolla et al., 2021). DTs are also playing a positive role to increase the process of incubation centres in research organizations (Chan et al., 2022). Incubators are a crucial driver to increase entrepreneurial innovation (Chan et al., 2022). Therefore, research institutions and organizations are introducing technology business incubators and business development centres to increase business ecosystem in many countries. Although, in practice, there is no clear consensus on how to conceptualise digitization and digitalization terms are applied by the researchers? Consequently, the same construct has been employed to refer to several occurrences in innovation management research (Gradillas & Thomas, 2023). But the differences between digitization and digitalization are pretty huge. The advancements in information technology (IT) began with the early use of computers in the 19th century. At present, applications of IT in different sectors including business are on the progressive path worldwide.

Nowadays sophisticated applications like virtual reality, augmented reality, artificial intelligence, robotics, cloud computing, internet of things, etc. are the revolution in IT and digital fields (Nadkarni & Prügl, 2021). Recently, almost all fields have been also impacted by the adoption of DTs. In the healthcare sector, the concept of 'digital health' has been streamlined for identifying diagnosis, scanning, patient care and medicine dispensing (Piccolo, 2024; Singh et al., 2025b). Surgeries for curing different diseases are being optimized through machine learning algorithms, electronic health records, telesurgery and telemedicine, etc. (Jain et al., 2024). The movement of education sector is drastically changing due to introduction of digital libraries, online books, online classrooms, proctored exam conducting platforms to create. It also exhibits a real at-home virtual classroom which saw the use of its full potential during the covid 19 pandemic (Timotheou, et al., 2022).

Finance and banking sectors are adopting DTs for improving digital banking. Therefore, the banking sector is given more focus for using banking apps, blockchain technology, fraud detection technologies, mobile payment apps and UPI payments (Kapadia & Madhav, 2020). These technologies are making transactions faster and reducing cash transactions every day (Kapadia & Madhav, 2020). Transportation and logistics with the efficient use of GPS Tracking, automated warehousing and predictive analysis have been improved significantly. DTs is also changing the dynamics of supply chains and inventory management systems (Herold et al., 2021). The impacts of digitalization have been observed beneficial for businesses and its related sectors and industries in the last decade. Over the last decade, the adoption of DTs across all sectors and spectrums of a business model have become both a want and a need. The adoption of DTs in business sector have transformed their entire face and its related industries (Chae, 2022). This new emergence and adoption of DTs, especially in business models, have been significant in bringing about various improvements like operation transformation, efficiency improvement, and putting forward new opportunities for businessman and common people. It is helping to rationalize processes, augment customer exposure or experience and drive innovation.

DTs have transformed the way in which business-to-business firms can grow effectively and efficiently (Ritter & Pederson, 2019). This form of digitalization has been beneficial for not only the businessman and customers as well. Use of internet technology, mobile phones, social media, Artificial Intelligence and AI Chatbots are helping to increase efficiency and creating easier ways for consumers. Social media is also positive to increase the digital transformation of business (Dwivedi et al., 2021). Social media is also helps to increase progress of manufacturing sector (Singh et al., 2024b). Thus, social media and DTs may be crucial to increase social sustainability (Singh, 2025b). DTs technologies are also increasing the connection of customers and businessmen across the globe. Customers have also benefited from this simple access to businesses worldwide as using different DTs. Firms and organisations have also benefited even more as digitalization is changing the businesses operation and its impact. For instance, it is playing a significant role for improving connectivity and popularity in the market. E-commerce platforms, social media marketing, customer relation management, mobile apps, and remote work and collaboration are helping business communities and customers to satisfy their needs (Wengler et al., 2021). There is a significant confusion between two terms that have been simultaneously used instead of one another for estimating their impact on business development in the literature.

The enormous growth in businesses is reported due to application of digitalization and DTs in the last 5 years. The growth of the business sector could be continued due to use of DTs during Covid-19 pandemic. Most economies were shut down due to Covid-19. Covid -19 showed the adverse effects on jobs creation and production of different sectors. Despite that, DTs could be helpful for businessmen to increase their progress during this pandemic. There was a bankruptcy and shutdown of numerous businesses, while one the other a significant number of new businesses were created during Covid-19 due to use of DTs in business sector. Thus, there is also a newfound growth in sales and customer connectivity during this time period. The organizational and industrial levels in various businesses and their operations witnesses' dramatic changes in lieu of Digitalization or digital adoption. Therefore, this chapter provides the overview of global perspectives on impact of digitalization on business development after Covid-19. Accordingly, this chapter has following specific objectives:

- To assess the determinants of digitalization in the context of the business sector as per the existing literature.
- To establish the relationship between digital adoption rate (DAR) and business development after Covid-19 at global level.
- To provide specific policy suggestions for increasing the application of DTs in the business sector for its better growth.

LITERATURE REVIEW

Nowadays, the progress of the business sector can be worked without digitalization and digital technologies (DTs). It is, therefore, important to establish a structural framework among the relationship between digitalization and business development (Millan et al., 2017). Digitalization and innovation management are interrelated to each other in a most complex way. There lies a constant challenge for developing and establishing the framework that encompasses the same as there lies immense vagueness surrounding the systematic construction among the digitalization and business sector (Gradillas & Thomas, 2023). Albukhitan (2020) described digital transformation as an important research topic in the area of business development and its creation. Digital transformation is basically the amalgamation of digital technologies (DTs) into new business models. It is existing operations that help to make dramatic changes and alterations to the ways industry's function and deliver value to their clientele. The impact of digitalization as stated by Chae (2022) and this study has been witnessed by businesses to an extent that digital business research has become a newfound concept that maps the impact of digital innovation. While digital innovation helps to create an innovative entrepreneurship ecosystem (Kreiterling, 2023; Singh & Jyoti, 2023a).

Entrepreneurship ecosystem is working as catalysts for increasing innovation, and social and economic changes (Alfehaid et al., 2024). Digital innovation may be effective to create new start-ups (Kitsios & Kamariotou, 2023; Singh et al., 2025a). Further, it is crucial to increase economic development (Singh & Jyoti, 2023b). Digital innovation is also changing the livelihood of peoples in multidimensional aspects. Findings of previous literature also claimed that adoption of DTs have a significant contribution for creation of new products and services. The line of digital business research has also brought about significant DTs to the foreground of business innovation management (Chae, 2022). Leviäkangas (2016) argued that a great deal in a business can be sensed and monitored at any time and at anywhere as using the Internet of Everything (IoE), intelligent sensor production, economies of scale, and platforms like consumer electronics, mobile devices, and urban infrastructures.

The development and transformation in the process of business production and operations, the advent of digital adoption has symmetrically boosted the emergence and creation of digital ventures. It is also found a significant boost of digital business entrepreneurships due to application of DTs in different countries (Singh & Jyoti, 2023a). Kollmann et al. (2022) was undertaken as study on fundamentals of e-entrepreneurships and company founding. Kollmann (2006) described how the emerging digital ventures capitalize electronic information via data networks to generate value of new business models? This digital business research field consists of more than just this, the concept of digital platform (supply chain or industry platform) has significantly emerged as an important strategy for business entrepreneurs in industrial innovation and management (Chae, 2022). The role of digital technologies in business and management, Calderon-Monge and Ribeiro-Soriano (2024) explained how social networks work provide market visibility to firms and organizations. It also established a broader and meaningful connection between DTs and business organization. Chan et al. (2022) emphasised on the importance of clouds in bringing accessibility, storage and relevant information exchange, flow of work and its monitoring and facilitating remote collaborations in the business sector.

While establishing a relationship between digital adoption and business development, Zare and Persaud (2024) mentioned the existence of a mutually complementary relationship reinforcing between the two but there still lies the lack of clear understanding in the current phase between digital technologies (DT) and business model innovation (BMI). A study by Unruh and Kiron (2017) on digital transformation, highlighted that how DTs and transformations are operators of the corporate world as they not only establish new technologies for new innovations and operations, but also take efficient care of their implications on the society as a whole. Westerman et al. (2011) described digitalization as an indicator of change in both the organization and its business model due to a dramatic increase in the amalgamation and adoption of DTs to revamp the performance purview of the businesses. The advent of digital technologies (DTs) has enabled the emergence of new business models (for e.g., platform-based and subscription-based). Taeuscher and Laudien (2018) discussed platform-based business models and explained how recent technological advances have enabled the emergence of new business models based digital platforms. In accordance with the above studies, Parker et al. (2016) explained how marketplaces and platforms like Airbnb, Uber, Ola, Rapido, OYO, etc., have brought about radical changes in the organization of various economic activities through the introduction of new businesses. It primarily focused on accessibility enhancement, increase in convenience of users thereby creating new opportunities for income. DTs also provide another scope for business entrepreneurs (Singh & Jyoti, 2023a). Lindström et al. (2023) provided discussion on subscription-based business models. Further, it establishes how tech firms have modernized the subscription-based businesses like newspaper subscription or milk delivery subscription with the businesses. It stated that interlinkages of digital services via subscription platforms in the business.

Nadkarni and Prügl (2021) described the importance of both digital possibilities and skilled execution to work in accordance and parallel to one another to realize the true transformative power of digital adoption and technological transformation in business models. Avalos et al. (2024) investigated that the firm digitalization during covid 19, drew a stark contrast between two forms of impacts, while on one hand, the pandemic compelled and drove firms, industries and various businesses, to invest more in digital platforms. It focuses on digital adoption in their respective organizations to keep their businesses and ventures afloat and connected to their existing and new customers. The other viewpoint of this study is to increase digital divide across several dimensions which have led to significant differences digitally between small and large firms. Calderon-Monge and Ribeiro-Soriano (2024) discussed the role of digitalization in businesses. Åström et al. (2022) detected the view on how DTs are playing a significant role for creating and reinforcing disruptions in the society as well as at many levels of the industry.

The theoretical framework on business development and digitalization, scholars like Fichman et al. (2014) suggested that how digitalization is about both the technological adoption through means of social media, analytics and "big data," intelligent autonomous systems, etc., along with the paradigm shift in operational and management paired with organizational strategy. Andzulis et al. (2012) examined the contribution of social media in the sales process of the business sector. Barneya et al. (2001) stated that how resources controlled by a firm and can be viewed as both tangible and intangible assets as stating, and how digital capabilities are a firm's strength in building a strong and sustainable base for their operations for the long run. Christopher (2016) explained how digitalization has completely redefined the business sector through tons and tons of integration like automation, communication enhancement etc. It is leading to certain improvements like supply chain management due to real-time tracking systems and predictive analysis.

In mapping the impact of digitalization on business development, Dwivedi et. al. (2021) conducted a systematic literature review on social media's contribution in business development. Social media is defined by Andzulis et. al. (2012) as "the technological component of the communication, transaction and relationship building functions of a business which leverages the network of customers and prospects to promote value co-creation." Social media has seemingly changed the way customers and sellers interact with one another. Consumers are free to compare the same product across different prices and select the best deals out of them using social media. Social media also allows businesses to personally connect with their customers, and build and enhance quality of products (Dwivedi et. al., 2021). Singh et al. (2024) also highlighted a positive role of social media in small scale enterprises.

Despite all the various benefits of DTs, the advent of such a major technological transformation has brought several challenges in the business sector. Kreiterling (2023) mentioned and described four different challenges that entrepreneurs face due to digitalization or technological transformation, such as regulatory barriers that include lack of resource fundings, high costs of innovations, various regulations that hinder the entrepreneurial growth, difficulty in securing efficient and prolonged funding, use of outdated or obscure technologies and most importantly socio-political considerations. It also justified the threats in various other dimensions like cybersecurity, digital divide and workplace displacement due to an increase in automation of mundane tasks. The report by McKinsey & Company (2020) also stated the constant need to upskill and reskill to be relevant in the job market and even for new and all existing entrepreneurs and businesses. Kapadia and Madhav (2020) explored the role of digitalization for improving the quality of services in the Indian banking industry. Alfehaid et al. (2024) investigated the role of ICT in entrepreneurship in Saudi Arabia. Gupta and Singh (2025) also specified the significant contribution of social media and technologies in women entrepreneurship in India.

RESEARCH METHODOLOGY

Study Area

The study area has been chosen based on the availability of data for the variables that have been chosen by the researchers. The researchers have conducted a global overview analysis on the impact of digitalization on the development of business operations and management based on the reports available on the Global context on the World Bank Report (2024), and World Bank Group (2024). This report basically provides the global overview of the various metrics of digitalization.

Research Design

This study uses a quantitative research design to analyse the impact of digitalization on business development. The study tries to understand how different technological transformations have an impact on business operations and management over the last decade. In this study, the aim of researchers is to examine the magnitude and direction of impact that the various metric of digital technologies (DTs) has an impact on business sectors at global level.

Data Source

The secondary data is taken from the World Bank Group statistics on Digital Progress and Trends Report, Digital 2024: Global Overview Report, Digital 2022: Digital Adoption. These reports provide an extensive yearly data on all the variables as chosen by the researchers that aided the researcher in mapping the impact of digitalization on the business development. This research article also used secondary data that has been collected through extensive review of published articles (from over 30 journals), conference proceedings, books and various reports published by international organizations.

Data Collection Technique

The data is collected from various sources like research articles, books, conference proceedings and World Bank Trends and Progress Report 2024. The report is used to generate a list of dependent and independent variables. These variables mentioned have strictly been chosen due to extensive availability of yearly data and their relevance with the objectives of this chapter. The scattered data had been compiled into a structured dataset for further statistical analysis.

Finalization of Variables

To map the development of businesses in terms of revenue, i.e., quantitative terms, the researcher chose the following variables like revenue growth of businesses, digital adoption rate, mobile broadband subscription, E-commerce penetration and investment in digital infrastructure. The description of the variables is provided in Table 1.

Table 1. Description of the variables

Name of the Variable	Measured by	Code name
Revenue growth of businesses	Annual percentage growth in revenue of businesses	*RGB*
Digital adoption rate	Percentage of the population using the internet	*DAR*
Mobile broadband subscription	Number of mobile broadband subscriptions per 100 people.	*MBS*
E-Commerce penetration	Percentage of retail sales conducted online	*ECP*
Investment in digital infrastructure	Annual investment in digital infrastructure as a percentage of GDP	*IDI*

Source: Finalized by the authors.

DATA ANALYSIS AND RESULTS

The data collected from the reports have been transformed in a structured format (Table 2). A simple regression analysis is conducted to map the impact of individual independent variables on dependent variables. Table 2 explores the progress in revenue growth of the business sector due to adoption of various digital technologies (DTs), e-commerce penetration and investment in digital infrastructure.

Table 2. Revenue growth of business due to digital transformations (2015-2022)

Year	Revenue growth of businesses (in%) (y) (RGB)	Digital adoption rate (%) (x_1) (DAR)	Mobile broadband subscription (per 100 people) (x_2) (MBS)	E-commerce penetration (%) (x_3) (ECP)	Investment in digital infrastructure (% of GDP) (x_4) (IDI)
2015	3.5	43	47	7.4	1.2
2016	3.8	45	50	8.6	1.3
2017	4.1	48	54	9.4	1.4
2018	4.3	51	58	11.2	1.5
2019	4.0	54	62	12.8	1.6
2020	-2.5	57	66	16.4	1.8
2021	5.5	60	70	18.0	2.0
2022	4.7	63	74	19.6	2.2
2023	4.2	66	78	20.8	2.3
2024	4.5	68	82	21.5	2.4

Sources: World Bank Group (2024).

This paper is desired to mapping the impact of all the independent variables on the dependent variables. Thus, it conducts separate regression analysis for assessing the impact of individual independent variables (i.e., like *DAR*, *MBS*, *ECP*, and *IDI*) on *RGB* (i.e., revenue growth of businesses). Firstly, it tries to map the impact of $\mathbf{x}_1$ on **y** through a simple linear regression. In order to examine the impact of *DAR* on *RGB*, it uses simple regression equation as:

$$RGB= \propto_1+\propto_2 (DAR) + e \qquad (1)$$

Here, *RGB* is revenue growth of businesses; *DAR* is digital adoption rate; *e* is error-term; and ${}_1$ and ${}_2$ are intercept term and coefficient of *DAR* with *RGB*, respectively in equation (1). It develops simple linear regression to find the value of intercept and coefficient. ${}_1$ and ${}_2$ are estimated as using bellow equations:

$\propto_{1} = yi - \propto_{2} xi$ (2)

$\propto_{2} =$

$\frac{\sum (X1Y)}{\sum (X1)^2}$ (3)

Table 3. Summary of estimated values of $\propto_1$ *and* $\propto_2$

Year	Revenue growth of businesses (in%) (y) (RGB)	Digital adoption rate (%) (x_1) (DAR)	Y (y-yi)	X_1 (x_1-x_1i)	X_1Y	$(X_1)^2$
2015	3.5	43	-0.11	-12.5	1.375	156.25
2016	3.8	45	0.19	-10.5	-1.995	110.25
2017	4.1	48	0.49	-7.5	-3.675	56.25
2018	4.3	51	0.39	-4.5	-1.755	20.25
2019	4	54	0.39	-1.5	-0.585	2.25
2020	-2.5	57	-6.11	1.5	-9.165	2.25
2021	5.5	60	1.89	4.5	8.505	20.25
2022	4.7	63	1.09	7.5	8.175	56.25
2023	4.2	66	0.59	10.5	6.195	110.25
2024	4.5	68	0.89	12.5	11.125	156.25
Average	yi= 3.61	xi = 55.5				
Sum			-0.3	0	18.2	690.5

Source: Estimated by authors.

Table 3 shows the process that is used to estimate the values of $_1$ and $_2$. The values of $_1$ and $_2$ is given bellow:

$\propto_{2} = \frac{\sum (X1Y)}{\sum (X1)^2}$ $\propto_{1} = yi - \propto_{2} xi$

$\propto_{2} = \frac{18.2}{690.5}$ $\propto_{1} = 3.61 - (0.02635771*55.5)$

$\propto_{2} = 0.02635771$ $\propto_{1} = 2.14714699$

Therefore, the linear association of *DAR* with *RGB* is found as:

RGB = 2.14714699+ 0.02635771 (*DAR*) + e(4)

Accordingly, it repeats the similar process for assessing the other independent variables on revenue growth of businesses. It applied following equation to examine the impact of *MBS* on revenue growth of businesses:

$$RGB = \partial_1 + \partial_2 (MBS) + e \qquad (5)$$

Here, *MBS* is mobile broadband subscription; ∂_1 and ∂_2 are intercept term and coefficient of *MBS* with *RGB* in equation (5). The values of ∂_1 and ∂_2 are estimated as:

$$\partial_1 = yi - \partial_2 xi \qquad (6)$$

$$\partial_2 =$$

$$\frac{\sum (X1Y)}{\sum (X1)^{\wedge}2} \qquad (7)$$

Table 4 explore the statistical technique that is used to computed the values of ∂_1 and ∂_2.

Table 4. Summary of estimated values of$\partial_1$and∂_2

Year	Revenue Growth of Businesses (in%) (y) (RGB)	Mobile Broadband Subscription (per 100 people) (x2) (MBS)	Y (y-yi)	X_2 (x_2- x_2i_1	X_2Y	$(X_2)^2$
2015	3.5	47	-0.11	-17.1	1.881	292.41
2016	3.8	50	0.19	-14.1	-2.679	198.81
2017	4.1	54	0.49	-10.1	-4.949	102.01
2018	4.3	58	0.39	-6.1	-2.379	37.21
2019	4	62	0.39	-2.1	-0.819	4.41
2020	-2.5	66	-6.11	1.9	-11.609	3.61
2021	5.5	70	1.89	5.9	11.151	34.81
2022	4.7	74	1.09	9.9	10.791	98.01
2023	4.2	78	0.59	13.9	8.201	193.21
2024	4.5	82	0.89	17.9	15.931	320.41

continued on following page

Table 4. Continued

Year	Revenue Growth of Businesses (in%) (y) (RGB)	Mobile Broadband Subscription (per 100 people) (x2) (MBS)	Y (y-yi)	X_2 (x_2-x_2i_1	X_2Y	$(X_2)^2$
Average	yi =3.61	xi = 64.1				
Sum			-0.3	0	25.52	1284.9

Source: Estimated by authors.

The values of ∂_1 and ∂_2 are finalized as:

$$\partial_2 = \frac{\sum (X2Y)}{\sum (X2)^\wedge 2} \partial_{1\,=}\ yi - \partial_2 xi$$

$$\partial_2 = \frac{25.52}{1284.9} \partial_{1\,=}\ 3.61 - (0.01986147 * 64.1)$$

$$\partial_2 = 0.01986147\ \partial_{1\,=}\ 2.33687991$$

Therefore, the linear association of *MBS* with *RGB* is noted as:

RGB= 2.33687991 +0.01986147 (*MBS*) + *e* (8)

Following form of simple regression is developed to estimate the impact of *ECP* on *RGB*:

$$RGB = \xi_1 + \xi_2(ECP) + e \qquad (9)$$

Here, ξ_1 and ξ_2 are the intercept-term and coefficient of *ECP* with *RGB*, respectively in equation (9). While The values of ξ_1 and ξ_2 are computed as:

$$\xi_{1\,=}\ yi - \xi_2 xi \qquad (10)$$

$$\xi_2 =$$

$$\frac{\sum (X3Y)}{\sum (X3)^\wedge 2} \qquad (11)$$

Table 5 explore the statistical technique that is used to computed the values of ξ_1 and ξ_2.

The values of ξ_1 and ξ_2 are finalized as:

$$\xi_2 = \frac{\sum (\mathbf{X3Y})}{\sum (\mathbf{X3})^\wedge 2} \quad \xi_1 = \text{yi} - \xi_2\text{xi}$$

$$\xi_2 = \frac{5.744}{255.521} \quad \xi_1 = 3.61 - (0.02247956 * 14.57)$$

$$\xi_2 = 0.02247956 \quad \xi_1 = 3.28247279$$

Therefore, the linear association of *ECP* with *RGB* is noted as:

RGB= 3.28247279+0.02247956 (ECP) + e(12)

Table 5. Summary of estimated values of ξ_1 and ξ_2

Year	Revenue Growth of Businesses (in%) (y) (RGB)	E-commerce Penetration (%) (x_3) (ECP)	Y (y-yi)	X_3 (x_3-x_3i)	X_3Y	$(X_3)^2$
2015	3.5	7.4	-0.11	-7.17	0.7887	51.4089
2016	3.8	8.6	0.19	-5.97	-1.1343	35.6409
2017	4.1	9.4	0.49	-5.17	-2.5333	26.7289
2018	4.3	11.2	0.39	-3.37	-1.3143	11.3569
2019	4	12.8	0.39	-1.77	-0.6903	3.1329
2020	-2.5	16.4	-6.11	1.83	-11.1813	3.3489
2021	5.5	18	1.89	3.43	6.4827	11.7649
2022	4.7	19.6	1.09	5.03	5.4827	25.3009
2023	4.2	20.8	0.59	6.23	3.6757	38.8129
2024	4.5	21.5	0.89	6.93	6.1677	48.0249
Average	yi =3.61	xi = 14.57				
Sum			-0.3	0	5.744	255.521

Source: Estimated by authors.

Following simple regression is adopted to estimate the impact of *IDI* on *RGB*:

$RGB = \psi_1 + \psi_2$ (IDI)+e (13)

Here, ψ_1 and ψ_2 are intercept-term and coefficient of *IDI* with *RGB* in equation (13). While ψ_1 and ψ_2 are estimated as:

$$\psi_1 = yi - \psi_2 xi \tag{14}$$

$$\psi_2 = \frac{\sum (X3Y)}{\sum (X3)^2} \tag{15}$$

Table 6 implies the process for estimating the values of ψ_1 and ψ_2.

$$\psi_2 = \frac{\sum (X4Y)}{\sum (X4)^2} \quad \psi_1 = yi - \psi_2 xi$$

$$\psi_2 = \frac{1.214}{1.701} \quad \psi_1 = 3.61 - (0.71369782*1.77)$$

$$\psi_2 = 0.71369782 \quad \psi_1 = 2.34675485$$

Therefore, the linear association of *IDI* with *RGB* is detected as:

$RGB = 2.34675485 + 0.71369782\ (IDI) + e$(16)

Table 6. Summary of estimated values of ψ_1 and ψ_2

Year	Revenue Growth of Businesses (in%) (y) (RGB)	Investment in Digital Infrastructure (% of GDP) (x4) (IDI)	Y (y-yi)	X_2 (x_4-x_4i)	X_4Y	$(X_4)^2$
2015	3.5	1.2	-0.11	-0.57	0.0627	0.3249
2016	3.8	1.3	0.19	-0.47	-0.0893	0.2209
2017	4.1	1.4	0.49	-0.37	-0.1813	0.1369
2018	4.3	1.5	0.39	-0.27	-0.1053	0.0729
2019	4	1.6	0.39	-0.17	-0.0663	0.0289
2020	-2.5	1.8	-6.11	0.03	-0.1833	0.0009
2021	5.5	2	1.89	0.23	0.4347	0.0529

continued on following page

Table 6. Continued

Year	Revenue Growth of Businesses (in%) (y) (RGB)	Investment in Digital Infrastructure (% of GDP) (x4) (IDI)	Y (y-yi)	X_2 (x_4-x_4i)	X_4Y	$(X_4)^2$
2022	4.7	2.2	1.09	0.43	0.4687	0.1849
2023	4.2	2.3	0.59	0.53	0.3127	0.2809
2024	4.5	2.4	0.89	0.63	0.5607	0.3969
Average	yi =3.61	xi = 1.77				
Sum			-0.3	0	1.214	1.701

Source: Estimated by authors.

DISCUSSION ON DESCRIPTIVE AND EMPIRICAL RESULTS

Descriptive Results

The statistical data for this study is taken from various sources like World Bank Group reports, Digital 2024: Global Overview Data, Digital 2022: Digital Adoption. This data spans includes during 2015 – 2024. It includes almost all the countries as per the World Bank Reports published in 2024. This data comprises metrics that are important to study the impact of digitalization on business development. These metrics are such as revenue growth of businesses (RGB) which is considered as a dependent variable. While revenue growth of businesses depends on four independent variables like digital adoption rate (*DAR*), mobile broadband subscription (*MBS*), E-commerce penetration (*ECP*), and investment in digital infrastructure (*IDI*). Although, there are numerous metrics and factors that can be considered for examining the impact of the digital transformation and digital technologies (DTs) on businesses and their developing drivers. While the researchers could select only the above-mentioned four variables to conduct a quantitative analysis. The aim of this chapter is to describe the trends and patterns in all the variables individually over the course of a decade.

Revenue Growth of Businesses (RGB):*RGB* which has been considered as a dependent variable, which depicts the quantitative growth in numerous businesses across the globe and shows a general upward trend from 2015 to 2019. *RGB* is increasing by almost 0.3% every year till 2018. BGR is witnessed to peak at 4.3% in 2018. There is also a slight fall from 2018 to 2019 by 0.3% when *RGB* fell from 4.3% to 4% between 2018-19. This dip took a significant fall in 2020, where RGB fell to -2.5%, due to sudden lockdown and halt in all economic activities. However, after 2020, i.e., from 2021, *RGB* recovers, reaching its highest peak ever recorded at 5.5% in almost a year, and later on stabilizing around 4.2% to 4.7% in the subsequent years.

Digital Adoption Rate (*DAR*):*DAR* is steadily increasing from 43% in 2015 to 68% in 2024 without any fall or decrease during the undertaken time period. It depicts that despite all problems in the economic sector in the global arena, the digital adoption rate across all businesses and organizations continued to rise. The rise in *DAR* can be considered to be an aftermath of several factors like advancements in technology, rise in internet availability, dramatic increase in the importance of digital knowledge and early access to internet technology in the world.

Mobile Broadband Subscription (*MBS*): With an increase in digital tools and technology, an increase in the availability of MBS is rather given. Therefore, MBS also shows a steady increase, from 47 subscriptions per 100 people in 2015 to 82 subscriptions in 2024. This steady growth is a clear indication that there has been an increasing reach and accessibility of Mobile Internet Services due to the use of smartphones and affordable data packages by telecommunication services industries across countries.

E-commerce Penetration (*ECP*): E-commerce penetration which basically means the invasion of e-commerce, i.e., the buying and selling of goods and services through online platform. Over the last decade or so, the penetration of E-commerce has a significant importance in the operating of business. The available data show a significant rise in the *ECP* between 2015 to 2024 with a HeadStart of 7.4% in 2015 to 21.5% in 2024. It is almost thrice the rate a decade ago. Further, it is also emphasizing the importance of e-commerce in the business landscape. Nowadays, most customers are preferring online shopping and digital transactions for time saving and unwillingness to carry a wallet everywhere. It is also providing a suitable online ecosystem for customers to be engaged in shopping as per their convenient and favourable time at home. Therefore, E-commerce is also helping to increase a cashless economy. It is also and reducing financial risk in trading of goods and services as compared to physical presence of customers in the market. Therefore, E-commerce is also found favourable to increase financial security of customers. However, it has been also observed that brands that solely depended on real-time buying and selling of goods and services now have had to shift to a more digitized version of trade and commerce.

Investment in Digital Infrastructure (*IDI*):*IDI* which is the fourth independent variable in mapping the impact of digitalization on *BGR*. *IDI* refers to the investments in the area of digital infrastructure across various businesses. The data shows an increase in *IDI* from 1.2% of GDP in 2015 to 2.4% in 2024. It underscores the importance of investing in digital infrastructure and depicts how much investment has been made to support the growing digital economy. This investment could be in the form of any of the following: high-speed internet, data centres, and digital platforms (Singh & Singh, 2025).

This descriptive analysis of this chapter is aimed to explain the trends and patterns of all the variables that have been taken into consideration by the researchers, while mapping the impact of digitalization on business development. All the metrics like digital adoption rate, mobile broadband subscription, e-commerce penetration and investment in digital infrastructure and the kind of impact and the magnitude of their impact on revenue growth of business has been further discussed using regression models.

Empirical Results

Simple linear regression equations are adopted to observe the impact of digital adoption rate (*DAR*), mobile broadband subscription (*MBS*), E-commerce penetration (*ECP*) and investment in digital infrastructure (*IDI*) on Revenue Growth of Businesses in this chapter. For this investigation, the researchers conducted individual simple regression analysis which results are given as:

Impact of *DAR* on *RGB*:

Regression Model: $RGB = \propto_1 + \propto_2$ (DAR) + e

Calculated coefficients:

Intercept ($\propto_1$): 2.14714699

Slope ($\propto_2$): 0.02635771

Regression Equation: $RGB = 2.14714699 + 0.02635771(DAR) + \mathrm{e}$

Impact of *MBS* on *RGB*:

Regression Model: $RGB = \partial_1 + \partial_2 (MBS) + \mathrm{e}$

Calculated coefficients:

Intercept (∂_1): 2.33687991

Slope (∂_2): 0.01986147

Regression Equation: $RGB = 2.33687991 + 0.01986147(MBS) + \mathrm{e}$

Impact of *ECP* on *RGB*:

Regression Model: $RGB = \xi_1 + \xi_2$ (ECP) + e

Calculated coefficients:

Intercept (ξ_1) = 3.28247279

Slope (ξ_2): 02247956

Regression Equation: $RGB = 3.28247279 + 0.02247956(ECP) + \mathrm{e}$

Impact of *IDI* on *RGB*:

Regression Model: $RGB = \psi_1 + \psi_2 (IDI) + \mathrm{e}$

Calculated coefficients:

Intercept (ψ_1): 2.34675485

Slope (ψ_2): 0.71369782

Regression Equation: *RGB* = 2.34675485+ 0.71369782(*IDI*) + e

Digital Adoption Rate (DAR): While conducting a simple linear regression between *RGB* and *DAR*, the regression coefficient of *DAR* with *RGB* is reported 0.02635771. It indicates a positive relationship between *DAR* and *RGB*. Further, it claimed that 1% increase in *DAR* may cause to increase *RGB* by 0.026%. This suggests that high digital adoption rates would be positive for increasing business revenue growth. But with even less than 1% growth, the regression coefficient maps that while digital adoption is beneficial. Thus, it may need to be complemented by other factors that may also play a major role in increasing the revenue growth of businesses. There is found a significant diversity in the digital adoption rate in various regions of the world (World Bank Group, 2024). Accordingly, the global countries should increase the digital adoption rate to increase the uniformity in the digital infrastructure for further growth of business sector.

Mobile Broadband Subscription (MBS): While conducting a simple linear regression between *RGB* and *MBS*, the regression coefficient of *MBS* with *RGB* is noted 0.01986147. It implies a positive relationship between *MBS* and *RGB*. The positive coefficient (0.01986147) of *MBS* with *RGB*, suggests that mobile broadband subscriptions would be positive and significant for increasing *RGB*. It is aligning with the idea that is a better, efficient and affordable access to mobile internet, business operations and customer engagement enhance thereby ultimately leading to higher revenue growth of business sector.

E-commerce Penetration (ECP): While conducting a simple linear regression between *RGB* and *ECP*, the regression coefficient of *ECP* with *RGB* is detected as 0.2247956. The result specifies a positive relationship between *ECP* and *RGB*. The positive coefficient (0.02247956) of *ECP* with *RGB* indicates that penetration of E-Commerce has a significant impact on business growth. E-commerce is effective for increasing the involvement of people in business activities and making significant changes in the business sector. E-commerce also creates a conducive ecosystem for customers and businessmen to make the price variation in the goods and services. Hence, it helps to increase decision making capacity of customers in the product market. The use of digital payment is also helping for customers to make online payment and their willingness to be engaged in online businesses.

Investment in Digital Infrastructure (*IDI*): After conducting a simple linear regression between *RGB* and *IDI*, the regression coefficient of *IDI* with *RGB* is found 0.71369782. It indicates a positive relationship between *IDI* and *RGB*. The positive and relatively large coefficient of *IDI* with *RGB* infer that investment in digital infrastructure has a large and wide impact on development of businesses. A 1% increase in investment in digital infrastructure may be useful to increase the revenue growth of businesses by 0.714%. Thus, investment in digital infrastructure is very important for increasing the growth pattern of the business sector. The global economies should invest more in digital infrastructure like high-speed internet, affordable mobile data connection, and digital tools and devices for improving the growth of business sector.

LIMITATIONS AND SCOPE FOR FUTURE STUDY

The following points compute the limitations of this chapter:

- **Data Collection and Availability**: Due to unavailability of yearly data for numerous independent variables, the researcher had to stick to 4 independent variables and calculate their impact on revenue growth of businesses. These independent variables are digital adoption rate, mobile broadband subscription, e-commerce penetration and investment in digital infrastructure. Whereas there are other variables that have crucial impact on business development due to digital transformation.
- **Data Credibility and Verification:** As there is no other sources that presented yearly data of the independent variables, the researcher had to stick to the reports presented by World Bank groups in 2022 and 2024.
- **Temporal scope:** The data available to the researcher through the World Bank group 2024 and 2022 report, this study is based on a specific time period. Thus, it leads to increase a limitation as digitalisation transforms rapidly and the data of one time period may not be similar to the available time period between 2015 to 2024.
- **Industry Specificity**: The researchers conducted a quantitative analysis for assessing the impact of digitalisation on business development. This data is solely based on the global impact of digitalisation on the revenue growth of businesses and is not an industry specific study. This again leads to another limitation as digitalisation varies across different industries. This study may also not account for all the industry specific factors that specifically influence that progress of a specific industry.
- **Technological Advancements**: This study may not be able to account for constant, technological changes and advancements that have been brought about in the recent past. There are other factors that have an impact on business development.
- **External factors**: This study does not account for any external factor that may have any sort of impact on business development. This study solely focuses on the impact of digital adoption rate, mobile broadband subscription, e-commerce penetration and investment in digital infrastructure on revenue growth of businesses. While it excludes may factors like regulatory frame-

work, competition, market demand and supply, technology transfer, and other macro level indicators like foreign direct investment, R&D expenditure, bank rate, inflation, ICT imports and exports, per capita income, level of employment, etc.

- Based on the above-mentioned limitations, the future studies may keep in mind the following scope while studying the impact of digitalization on business development:
- **Qualitative Research:** This study solely focused on mapping the impact of digitalisation on the revenue growth of businesses. More qualitative study can be considered for estimating the impact of digitalisation on business development. Future studies can also take into account variables like digital skills and competencies and digital literacy.
- **Case Studies**: Incorporating various qualitative methods of research like case study, and focus and groups discussion would be able to provide a deep understanding on the impact of digitalisation on business development. It would involve the proper analysis of mechanisms that actually leads to increase digitalisation impacting indicators in business development.
- **Cross Country Comparison**: Further studies can also take into account cross country comparison and map the impact of digital transformation on business development. A comparative analysis of the impact of digitalisation on business development across nations would also provide the insightful idea among the relationship between digitalization and business growth.
- **Consumer Behaviour**: Through a primary survey, researchers can map the change in the trend of consumer behaviour while interacting with businesses online and analyse. This survey can also be used to understand the impact of social media on business development.
- **Sustainable Business Ecosystem (SBE):** DTs may be conducive to increase the SBE. While this chapter does not provide an ample relationship on how digitalization would be beneficial to increase the SBE? Future researchers can also focus on analysing how different policies and recommendations could lead to a better integration of businesses into the digital platform and how government policies can encourage and ensure to remove hindrance of digital adoption. Further, how digital adoption may be helpful to increase SBE.

POLICY IMPLICATIONS

To achieve long-term revenue growth, firms should prioritise boosting digital adoption rates, expanding mobile broadband availability, improving e-commerce capabilities, and investing in strong digital infrastructure. Policy makers should also contribute to the above-mentioned efforts by fostering an enabling environment for digital transformation and offering incentives for digital infrastructure investments (Empoli & Massaro, 2021). Therefore, following suggestions can be favourable for increase the business growth as using DTs, digitalization and digital transformation in global countries:

- **Enhance Digital Literacy Programs, and Mobile and Internet Accessibility:** It is very important for every individual, customers or business owner to have proper digital knowledge for meeting their wants and needs in different prospects. Thus, the Government should pay more attention towards imparting digital literacy among all its citizens, irrespective of gender, age, cast, etc. In order to enhance digital literacy, the government can also introduce new programmes or schemes that provide individuals from all walks of life with an easy access to digital knowledge which would provide them ample guidance and knowledge on digital tools and services. A GSMA report published in 2021 emphasised the importance of governments in all nations to bridge the digital divide between the demand and the supply side (Groenestege et al., 2021). Thus, the government should also increase the mobile and internet accessibility for the people to increase digital infrastructure.
- **Increased Accessibility of Mobile Broadband Connections:** As witnessed in the data presented above, there is a positive relation between mobile broadband subscription and revenue growth of businesses. It is, therefore, necessary for governments to ensure affordable access to mobile broadband connections for the common people. It would lead to increase efficiency and ease of connectivity to all businesses across the globe.
- **E-commerce Promotion:** The government policies must be devoted to increasing online businesses. The government should also increase customer's intention and trust in online trading of goods and services. It would reduce real time trade-in commerce and improve digital payments. Business owners and entrepreneurs must be imparted proper knowledge as setting their businesses online and reaching a larger audience through the internet and its various tools like social media advertisements. It is recommended that digital skills and training would be supportive for enhancing digital inclusion and economic opportunities (Group, 2021; Singh, 2025b).

- **Encourage Public-Private Partnerships:** As most private enterprises or businesses focus solely on profit maximisation. Therefore, public private partnerships can enhance digital transformation effectively. Private sector can increase their consistency to adopt DTs and digital transformation in their business. Private sector can also make huge investments in digital infrastructure. A collaboration between public and private sectors would not only encourage digital transformation, but it would also ensure the digital divide among public and private partners across countries.
- **Provision of Tax Incentives for Digital Investments:** If the businesses that are focusing on increasing, their digital investments are provided with tax, relaxation, or tax incentives for investing in digital transformation. This can also encourage other businesses to opt for more investments in digital integration. Further, it would increase the movement of businesses towards the digital platform and stimulate the digital economic growth in the world. It would also increase digital business ecosystem.
- **Scope and Support for Research and Development (R&D):** With an increase in digital integration across all sectors, there is an also need for research and development in this field. Thus, the governments should increase the scope for R&D in digital tech technologies. The government should also provide ample support in the form of financial aid to drive, growth and development of the digital sector.
- **Data Privacy and Security:** The advent of digital tech technologies and digitalisation in all fields has put forward personal information of all individuals on an open platform. A strong data privacy and security policy can thereby enhance trust among individuals indulging themselves in digital technologies (DTs). The importance of a secured digital infrastructure has been mentioned by the European commission, while focusing on digital transformation (Lynn et al., 2022).

INNOVATION AND SIGNIFICANCE OF THE CHAPTER

This chapter has a significant contribution in theoretical literature due to following reasons: This chapter provides the summary of existing literature which already explored the association of digitalization with the business sector in different dimensions. This chapter also examines the numerical impact of digitalisation on business development. It includes four independent variables like digital adoption rate, mobile broadband subscription, e-commerce penetration and investment in digital infrastructure, and revenue growth of businesses as dependent variables in the regression equations. This study shows the dramatic change in revenue growth of businesses globally due to digital integration across various businesses and enterprises. There is a need to encourage businesses to move towards digital platforms to promote digital adoption and increase its growth pattern. Finally, this study suggests how the business sector needs to adopt DTs, digital transformation and digital infrastructure to increase their sales, growth and development in sustainable ways in the long run. Most specifically, this chapter also highlights multiple areas in which further studies can be considered.

CONCLUSION

This study explored the impact of digital transformation on business development and its operations and management. It focuses on how various aspects of technological integration into the business sector influence the revenue growth of businesses worldwide. This study uses secondary data from Reports published by the World Bank such as the World Bank's Groups' "Global Overview 2024" and "Global Overview 2022" reports to assess the impact of independent variables on dependent variable. This study finalized four key independent variables i.e., digital adoption rate, mobile broadband subscriptions, e-commerce penetration, and investment in digital infrastructure. In order to map the impact of the independent variable, the dependent variable is kept to be revenue growth of businesses globally. The simple regression analysis is conducted to assess the impact of all the four variables on *RGB*. The empirical analysis revealed that *DAR*, *MBS*, *ECP*, and *IDI* have a positive impact on revenue growth of businesses. Investment in digital infrastructure (*IDI*) has a most significant impact, followed by digital adoption rate (*DAR*) and mobile broadband subscription (*MBS*), while e-commerce penetration (*ECP*) had the least impact on *RGB*. As per the findings of this study, it can be stated that there is an urgency for increasing extensive investment in digital infrastructure to increase the progress of business sector worldwide.

REFERENCES

Albukhitan, S. (2020). Developing digital transformation strategy for manufacturing. *Procedia Computer Science, 170*(1), 664–671. DOI: 10.1016/j.procs.2020.03.173

Alfehaid, F., Omri, A., & Altwaijri, A. (2024). Impact of ICT diffusion and opportunity entrepreneurship on environmental sustainability in Saudi Arabia. *Heliyon, 10*(19), 1–10. DOI: 10.1016/j.heliyon.2024.e39009 PMID: 39430546

Andzulis, J. M., Panagopoulos, N. G., & Rapp, A. (2012). A review of social media and implications for the sales process. *Journal of Personal Selling & Sales Management, 32*(1), 305–316. DOI: 10.2753/PSS0885-3134320302

Åström, J., Reim, W., & Parida, V. (2022). Value creation and value capture for AI business model innovation: A three-phase process framework. *Review of Managerial Science, 16*(1), 2111–2213. DOI: 10.1007/s11846-022-00521-z

Avalos, E., Cirera, X., Cruz, M., Iacovone, L., Medvedev, D., Nayyar, G., & Ortega, S. R. (2024). Firms' digitalization during the COVID-19 pandemic: A tale of two stories. *Science & Public Policy, 51*(6), 1241–1256. DOI: 10.1093/scipol/scae022

Barneya, A., Wrightb, M., David, J., & Ketchen, J. (2001). The resource-based view of the firm: Ten years after 1991. *Journal of Management, 27*(6), 625–641. DOI: 10.1177/014920630102700601

Calderon-Monge, E., & Ribeiro-Soriano, D. (2024). The role of digitalization in business and management: A systematic literature review. *Review of Managerial Science, 18*(1), 449–491. DOI: 10.1007/s11846-023-00647-8

Chae, B. K. (2022). Mapping the evolution of digital business research: A bibliometric review. *Sustainability (Basel), 14*(12), 1–17. DOI: 10.3390/su14126990

Chan, Y., Krishnamurthy, R., & Sadreddin, A. (2022). Digitally-enabled university incubation processes. *Technovation, 118*(1), 1–10. DOI: 10.1016/j.technovation.2022.102560

Christopher, M. (2016). *Logistics and supply chain management.* Pearson Education. https://old.mu.ac.in/wp-content/uploads/2021/02/Logistics-and-Supply-Chain-Management-Martin-Christopher.pdf

Digital 2022: Digital Adoption Doubles Over the Past Decade. (2022). [Online]. https://datareportal.com/reports/digital-2022-digital-adoption-doubled-over-the-past-decade

Digital 2024: Global Overview Report. (2024). [Online]. https://datareportal.com/reports/digital-2024-global-overview-report

Dwivedi, Y. K., Ismagilova, E., & Raman, N. P. (2021). Social media adoption, usage and impact in business-to-business (B2B) context: A state-of-the-art literature review. *Information Systems Frontiers*, *25*(1), 971–993. DOI: 10.1007/s10796-021-10106-y

Empoli, S. D., & Massaro, G. (2021). [Online]. https://www.transatlantic.org/

Fichman, R. G., Santos, B. L. D., & Zheng, Z. (E.) (2014). Digital innovation as a fundamental and powerful concept in the information systems curriculum. *MIS Quarterly*, 38(2), 329-354. https://www.jstor.org/stable/26634929

Foster, R. N. (1986). *Innovation: The Attackers Advantage.* https://fs.blog/richard-foster-the-attackers-advantage/

Gradillas, M., & Thomas, L. D. (2023). Distinguishing digitization and digitalization: A systematic review and conceptual framework. *Journal of Product Innovation Management.* Advance online publication. DOI: 10.1111/jpim.12690

Groenestege, M. T., Bowman, K., Cruz, G., Delaporte, A., Jackson, N., Lopez, M., Manimohan, M., & Sibthorpe, C. (2021). *Accelerating mobile internet adoption: Policy considerations to bridge the digital divide in low- and middle-income countries.* GSMA Head Office., https://www.gsma.com/solutions-and-impact/connectivity-for-good/mobile-for-development/wp-content/uploads/2021/05/Accelerating-Mobile-Internet-Adoption-Policy-Considerations.pdf

Group, D. I. (2021). [Online]. https://www.fcc.gov/.https://www.fcc.gov/sites/default/files/acdde-digital-empowerment-wg-digital-inclusion-rec-06242021.pdf

Gupta, M., & Singh, A. K. (2025). Factors influencing the sustainability of women micro-entrepreneurship in Jammu and Kashmir. In Bayram, G., Bayram, A., & Sak, M. (Eds.), *Examining Barriers and Building Resiliency for Rural Women Entrepreneurs* (pp. 129–162). IGI Global Scientific Publishing., DOI: 10.4018/979-8-3693-9178-5.ch005

Herold, D. M., Ćwiklicki, M., Pilch, K., & Mikl, J. (2021). The emergence and adoption of digitalization in the logistics and supply chain industry: An institutional perspective. *Journal of Enterprise Information Management*, *34*(6), 1917–1938. DOI: 10.1108/JEIM-09-2020-0382

Jain, M., Shakdwipee, D. P., & Bhatia, T. K. (2024). Digitalization and healthcare quality. *Educational Administration: Theory and Practice*, *30*(5), 6240–6243. DOI: 10.53555/kuey.v30i5.3923

Jyoti, B., & Singh, A. K. (2023). Does digitalization have a causal relationship with economic development? an experience from a country-wise panel data statistical analysis. In R. Sine Nazlı & G. Sari (Eds.), *Handbook of Research on Perspectives on Society and Technology Addiction* (pp. 34-61). IGI Global. DOI: 10.4018/978-1-6684-8397-8.ch003

Kapadia, S., & Madhav, V. (2020). The impact of digitization on banking and financial services industry in India. *The IUP Journal of Bank Management*, *19*(2), 24–31.

Kitsios, F., & Kamariotou, M. (2023). Digital innovation and entrepreneurship transformation through open data hackathons: Design strategies for successful start-up settings. *International Journal of Information Management*, *69*(1), 1–13. DOI: 10.1016/j.ijinfomgt.2022.102472

Kollmann, T. (2006). *What is e-entrepreneurship? – fundamentals of company founding in the net economy*. Elgaeonline., DOI: 10.1504/IJTM.2006.009247

Kollmann, T., Kleine-Stegemann, L., & Cruppe, K. (2022). Eras of digital entrepreneurship. *Business & Information Systems Engineering*, *64*(1), 15–31. DOI: 10.1007/s12599-021-00728-6

Kreiterling, C. (2023). Digital innovation and entrepreneurship: A review of challenges in competitive markets. *Journal of Innovation and Entrepreneurship*, *12*(1), 1–13. DOI: 10.1186/s13731-023-00320-0

Lanzolla, G., Pesce, D., & Tucci, C. L. (2021). The digital transformation of search and recombination in the innovation function: tensions and an integrative framework. *Journal of Product Innovation Management*, 38(), 90-113. 90-113. DOI: 10.1111/jpim.12546

Leviäkangas, P. (2016). Digitalisation of Finland's transport sector. *Technology in Society*, *47*(1), 1–15. DOI: 10.1016/j.techsoc.2016.07.001

Lindström, C. W., Vishkaei, B. M., & Giovanni, P. D. (2023). Subscription-based business models in the context of tech firms: Theory and applications. *International Journal of Industrial Engineering and Operations Management*, *6*(3), 256–274. DOI: 10.1108/IJIEOM-06-2023-0054

Lynn, T., Rosati, P., Conway, E., Curran, D., & O'Gorman, G. F. (2022). Infrastructure for digital connectivity. In *Digital Towns* (pp. 109–132). Springer., DOI: 10.1007/978-3-030-91247-5_6

MicKinsy & Company. (2020). How covid-19 has pushed companies over the technology tipping point-and transformed business sector. [Online]. https://www.mckinsey.com/capabilities/strategy-and-corporate-finance/our-insights/how-covid-19-has-pushed-companies-over-the-technology-tipping-point-and-transformed-business-forever

Millan, M. M., Claudia, D. R., & Sepúlveda. (2017). *Structural Change, Fundamentals, and Growth A Framework and Case Studies.* World Bank Group. worldbank.org

Nadkarni, S., & Prügl, R. (2021). Digital transformation: A review, synthesis and opportunities for future research. *Management Review Quarterly*, *71*(1), 233–341. DOI: 10.1007/s11301-020-00185-7

Parker, G. G., Alstyne, M. W., & Choudary, S. P. (2016). *Platform revolution: how networked markets are transforming the economy and how to make them work for you.* W. W. Norton & Company.

Piccolo, R. (2024). Digitisation, health literacy and health empowerment of older people. *The International Entrepreneurship and Management Journal*, *20*(1), 3001–3034. DOI: 10.1007/s11365-024-00980-8

Ritter, T., & Pederson, C. L. (2019). Digitization capability and the digitalization of business models in business-to-business firms: Past, present, and future. *Industrial Marketing Management*, *68*(1), 180–190. DOI: 10.1016/j.indmarman.2019.11.019

Singh, A. K. (2025a). Causality of digitalization with social sustainability in selected countries. In Siyal, S. (Ed.), *Impact of Digitalization on Education and Social Sustainability* (pp. 39–78). IGI Global., DOI: 10.4018/979-8-3693-1854-6.ch002

Singh, A. K. (2025b). Importance of digital technologies in economic sector of selected countries. In Ahmadi, A., Mna, A., & Slimani, A. (Eds.), *Renewable Energy and the Economic Welfare of Society* (pp. 335–370). IGI Global Scientific Publishing., DOI: 10.4018/979-8-3693-7580-8.ch015

Singh, A. K. (2025c). Causality of digitalization with social sustainability in selected countries. In Siyal, S. (Ed.), *Impact of Digitalization on Education and Social Sustainability* (pp. 39–78). IGI Global., DOI: 10.4018/979-8-3693-1854-6.ch002

Singh, A. K., Ashraf, S. N., & Gupta, M. (2025a). Association between start-up entrepreneurship and economic development across countries. In Popescu, C. (Ed.), *Building Inclusive Global Knowledge Societies for Sustainable Development* (pp. 471–504). IGI Global Scientific Publishing., DOI: 10.4018/979-8-3693-6298-3.ch018

Singh, A. K., & Jyoti, B. (2023a). Does digitalization have a bi-directional causal relationship with the entrepreneurship ecosystem? Evidence from a country-wise panel data analysis. In Yanamandra, R., & Indiran, L. (Eds.), *Handbook of Research on Designing Sustainable Strategies to Develop Entrepreneurial Intention* (pp. 178–172). IGI Global., DOI: 10.4018/978-1-6684-8781-5.ch007

Singh, A. K., & Jyoti, B. (2023b). Empirical evidence from different income group countries on the interdependency between digitalization and economic development. In Patricia Ordóñez de Pablos and Xi Zhang (Eds.), 5G, Artificial Intelligence, and Next Generation Internet of Things: Digital Innovation for Green and Sustainable Economies, (pp. 44-85). IGI Global. DOI: DOI: 10.4018/978-1-6684-8634-4.ch003

Singh, A. K., Kumar, S., & Gupta, M. (2024a). Relationship between digitalization and environmental sustainability in selected countries. In Yıldırım, S., Yıldırım, D., Demirtaş, I., & Kandpal, V. (Eds.), *Green Transition Impacts on the Economy, Society, and Environment* (pp. 83–107). IGI Global., DOI: 10.4018/979-8-3693-3985-5.ch006

Singh, A. K., & Singh, R. (2025). Digital infrastructure and sustainable development goals in G20 countries. In Popescu, C. (Ed.), *Building Inclusive Global Knowledge Societies for Sustainable Development* (pp. 363–408). IGI Global Scientific Publishing., DOI: 10.4018/979-8-3693-6298-3.ch014

Singh, A. K., Singh, S., & Gupta, M. (2024b). A literature review for the association of social media with micro and small enterprises in India. In Hossain, S. (Ed.), *Cases on Social Media and Entrepreneurship* (pp. 38–62). IGI Global., DOI: 10.4018/979-8-3693-1781-5.ch003

Singh, A. K., Srinivasan, S., & Jyoti, B. (2025b). Implications of digitalization on public health sector across countries. In Wickramasinghe, N. (Ed.), *Digitalization and the Transformation of the Healthcare Sector* (pp. 359–394). IGI Global Scientific Publishing., DOI: 10.4018/979-8-3693-9641-4.ch013

Taeuscher, K., & Laudien, S. (2018). Understanding platform business models: A mixed methods study of marketplaces. *European Management Journal, 38*(3), 319–329. DOI: 10.1016/j.emj.2017.06.005

Timotheou, S., Miliou, O., Dimitriadis, Y., Sobrino, S. V., Giannoutsou, N., Cachia, R., Monés, A. M., & Ioannou, A. (2022). Impacts of digital technologies on education and factors influencing schools' digital capacity and transformation: A literature review. *Education and Information Technologies, 28*(1), 6695–6726. DOI: 10.1007/s10639-022-11431-8 PMID: 36465416

Unruh, G., & Kiron, D. (2017). Digital transformation on purpose. *MIT Sloan Management Review, 10*(1), 1–13. https://sloanreview.mit.edu/article/digital-transformation-on-purpose/

Wengler, S., Hildmann, G., & Vossebein, U. (2021). Digital transformation in sales as an evolving process. *Journal of Business and Industrial Marketing, 36*(4), 599–614. DOI: 10.1108/JBIM-03-2020-0124

Westerman, G., Calmejane, C., Bonnet, D., Ferraris, P., & McAfee, A. (2011). Digital transformation: a road-map for billion-dollar organizations. *MIT Center for Digital Business and Capgemini Consulting*. https://www.capgemini.com/wp-content/uploads/2017/07/Digital_Transformation__A_Road-Map_for_Billion-Dollar_Organizations.pdf

World Bank Group. (2024). *Digital Progress and Trends Report: Interactive Charts – Digital Adoption*. [Online]. https://www.worldbank.org/en/data/interactive/2024/03/04/digital-progress-and-trends-report-interactive-charts

Zare, J., & Persaud, A. (2024). Digital transformation and business model innovation: A bibliometric analysis of existing research and future perspectives. *Management Review Quarterly, x*(x), x–x. DOI: 10.1007/s11301-024-00426-z

KEY TERMS AND DEFINITIONS

Digitization: It is a process that used different technologies for transforming the analog information into digital format for increasing the accessibility and usability of available information among the large users.

Digital Business Ecosystem (DBE): It is a highly innovative business that extensively uses digital tools and entities like the internet, mobile apps, software, digital platform, digital devices and hardware for trading of goods and services.

Digital Technologies (DTs): DTs are the digital and electronic devices that increase the communication among the customers and producers in diverse fields and sectors.

Digital Infrastructure: It is a technology-based ecosystem that promotes use of digital technologies in business, communication, education, skill development, technology transfer, marketing, etc.

Digital Economy: It involves also economic activities that have their dependence on digital technologies, digital devices, digital platform and web-based server to enhance the communication of economic agents in different sectors including business, marketing, technology, advertisement, agricultural, supply chain, etc.

Entrepreneurship Ecosystem: It an integration of all stakeholders (i.e., government, businessman, entrepreneurs, customers and research institutions) who take favourable actions to nurture appropriate business ecosystem.

Sustainable Business Ecosystem (SBE): It is an integration of all stakeholders including businessmen, entrepreneurs, customers, and government who work together to resolve the environmental concern in the business and industrial sector. These also take conducive actions to increase the sustainability of all dimensions related to sustainable development and SDGs.

Chapter 2
Impact of Digitalization on Entrepreneurship Promoting Indicators in India

Vaishnavi Sharma
https://orcid.org/0009-0003-8436-8514
Department of Humanities and Social Sciences, Graphic Era University, Dehradun, India

Ajay Kumar Singh
https://orcid.org/0000-0003-0429-0925
Department of Humanities and Social Sciences, Graphic Era University, Dehradun, India

ABSTRACT

Digitalization is greatly supportive to increase the entrepreneurial ecosystem. Therefore, this chapter provides the impact of digitalization on entrepreneurship promoting indicators as giving more focus on the Indian economy. It also investigates the dynamic linkages of digitalization with job creation, government backing, and entrepreneurial ecosystem in India. It used a log-linear regression model for the mentioned investigation. It finds a high positive relationship between digitalization and employment growth. It noted a modest positive correlation between digitalization and government support. It also showed a strong favorable influence of employment levels on government assistance. It provides an understanding towards India's entrepreneurial ecosystem as emphasizing the catalytic impact of digitalization on driving employment and creating appropriate entrepreneurship. The findings have implications for policymakers, entrepreneurs, and stakeholders working to build a

DOI: 10.4018/979-8-3373-5087-5.ch002

vibrant entrepreneurial ecosystem in India.

INTRODUCTION

The introduction of digital technologies (DTs) has transformed many aspects of human life, including communication channels, business, education, and the source of multiple entertainment as well (Gupta et al., 2025). DTs are creating a favorable path of digitalization (Singh et al., 2025a). While digitalization is playing an active role to increase livelihood security for people, businessmen, entrepreneurs and other stakeholders (Singh & Jyoti, 2023b). The business ecosystem is also leading to increase digitalization (Singh & Jyoti, 2023b). Digital technologies are contributing to increasing the efficiency of marketing, and reducing cost and enhancing personalization marketing (Archi et al., 2023). The rapid advancement of DTs has resulted in significant transformations across a variety of disciplines, including entrepreneurship ecosystem (Felicetti et al., 2023). The Internet is facilitating multiple opportunities for entrepreneurs and businessman to build and create new businesses, ventures and start-ups (Gupta et al., 2025). Other DTs are also nurturing a conducive ecosystem to increase business opportunities (Singh & Jyoti, 2023b). Hence, DTs have generated a dynamic and imaginative entrepreneurial ecosystem (Singh & Jyoti, 2023b). DTs are also increasing the contribution of other activities like advertisement, supply chain, product quality, innovation, technological upgradation, marketing, and online market that help to create entrepreneurship ecosystem (Singh & Ashraf, 2020). Furthermore, digitalization is also playing a positive role to increase the communication of producers and consumers in online marketing (Jyoti & Singh, 2023). Digitalization is also supportive to provide multiple information to the customers and producers through online websites (Singh & Jyoti, 2023c). Hence, digitalization appears to be an appropriate driver to increase the entrepreneurial ecosystem (Singh & Ashraf, 2020). Furthermore, digitalization is a driver for transforming industries, economies, and social conventions of the people to a greater extent.

The advancement of digital technologies (DTs) has resulted in a revolution in corporate structures, communication methods, operations, and cultural dynamics (Singh & Jyoti, 2023b). The entrepreneurial ecosystem refers to the collective collection of persons, organizations, and assets that collaborate to promote entrepreneurial activity in a certain region or industry (Acs et al., 2017). Singh and Jyoti (2023a) also noticed that entrepreneurial behaviour is necessary to increase the entrepreneurship ecosystem. Entrepreneurial activities, therefore, include multiple indicators that help to nurture an appropriate entrepreneurship ecosystem (Singh & Jyoti, 2023a). Appropriate entrepreneurship ecosystem also depends on triple helix models (Singh et al., 2024a). The Triple helix model includes businessmen, research organizations and governments (Singh et al., 2024a). There are other activities like customers, digital transformation, digitalization, technological advancement, human resources, availability of raw materials and ecosystem services, R&D ecosystem, technology transfer, commercialization of technologies, market feasibility, availability of finance, financial inclusion, etc. that also promote entrepreneurship ecosystem (Singh et al., 2023). These indicators are also helpful to increase the growth of manufacturing sector (Singh et al., 2020).

Entrepreneurial ecosystems have a complicated association with many actors, including investors, government agencies, academic institutions, and support organizations (Singh et al., 2020). For instance, technology business incubators (TBIs) are helping new entrepreneurs to develop new business in different sectors (Singh et al., 2024a). TBIs in agricultural universities are providing various technical facilities to the farmers to increase their economic return in the farming sector. Therefore, integration of above-mentioned stakeholders would be active to meet the requirements of innovation, finance, knowledge transfer, infrastructure, marketing, raw material etc. of the business sector (Singh & Jyoti, 2023b). Further, entrepreneurial success has always been tied to area resources such as physical infrastructure, human networks, and market accessibility (Singh et al., 2024a).

Digitalization has upset these traditions, bringing new opportunities and challenges for the entrepreneurship ecosystem (Singh & Jyoti, 2023b). For instance, the incorporation of digital technologies (DTs) into entrepreneurial ecosystems affects a number of factors such as market penetration, resource availability, and value creation (Singh & Jyoti, 2023b). Also, traditional business models have been altered by digital platforms such as social media, blockchain, cloud computing, and Artificial Intelligence (AI) (Roundy, 2022; Cheng et al., 2022; Singh et al., 2024b). Social media is also an effective platform to increase the progress of online marketing (Singh et al., 2024b). Moreover, social media and digital marketing have made it possible for small businesses to compete with bigger, more established companies by connecting them to a larger audience at a lesser cost (Singh et al., 2024b). Nowadays, an increasing number of business owners are utilizing the above-mentioned resources to develop innovative products, increase marketing, and increase output. Also, digitalization is helping to reduce most barriers for entrepreneurship (Hein et al., 2024). For example, online marketplaces such as Shopify and Amazon allow entrepreneurs to start a business with minimal financial investment. Cloud-based platforms also enable entrepreneurs with little financial investment to access cutting-edge technologies.

One important area where digitalization has altered the entrepreneurial environment is financing (Singh et al., 2024d). Previously, business owners could only obtain money from banks, angel investors, or venture capitalists. Acquiring these sources of funding can be challenging for many aspiring business owners, particularly those from underserved areas. They often need personal connections and wide networks. Digitalization could also increase the business communication of entrepreneurs and customers in rural and urban areas in many countries (Singh & Kumar, 2022). Therefore, digitalization has fundamentally altered this perspective with the advent of new financial methods. Crow-funding (a way to raise capital for a business/project by collecting small amounts of money from a large number of people could be successful due to expansion of social media (Singh et al., 2024b). Initial Coin Offerings (ICOs) (way for a company to raise capital/money by selling a new cryptocurrency to investors, similar to IPOs in the stock market, but for the cryptocurrencies) system is also growing very fast due to digitalization and DTs.

Crowdfunding websites like Kickstarter and Indiegogo allow business owners to directly expose their ideas to the public by circumventing traditional gatekeepers (Hoque 2024). It also enhancing the online platform for entrepreneurs to develop new products (Hoque 2024). Concepts, venture capital companies are increasing their dependence on Artificial Intelligence (AI) and big data to evaluate the potential of businesses. Consequently, the efficiency of entrepreneurial ecosystems has increased and it is allowing for quicker decision-making and a decrease in the risks involved with early-stage investment (Hoque 2024). At present, a greater number of people may now access finance, allowing entrepreneurs from different backgrounds to raise capital for their initiatives due to digitalization and digital infrastructure (Singh & Singh, 2025). Peer-to-peer lending platforms also provide alternative funding options that are more flexible and have lower interest rates than traditional banks (Dömötör et al., 2023). Additionally, digitalization has altered how investors evaluate firms. Using algorithms that took at market trends, consumer demand, and business sustainability (Beaulieu & Sarker, 2015).

Digitalization has numerous advantages, but it also presents new challenges that entrepreneurial ecosystems must overcome. One of the main issues is the digital divide, which could exacerbate disparities in access and commercial performance (Dimoso & Utonga, 2024). In places, with limited access to digital tools, high-speed internet, and digital literacy, entrepreneurs could find it challenging to reap the new rewards of digitalization (Singh et al., 2024c). This divide may lead to differences in entrepreneurial success between developed and developing countries, as well as urban and rural locations. Cybersecurity is another important problem in the entrepreneurial ecosystems that have been digitally altered (Wibisono, 2023). The frequency of financial fraud is also increasing due to the application of digitalization. Because more and more of their operations are being carried out online, businesses are especially vulnerable to cyberattacks (Wibisono, 2023). Hackers may find startups particularly attractive targets because they lack the resources and expertise to implement robust cybersecurity measures (Wibisono, 2023). Serious financial and brand damage brought on by data breaches can be extremely detrimental to a startup. Additionally, the speed at which digital innovation is developing could pose challenges for current legal systems. Regulation gaps may exist because lawmakers and governments occasionally struggle to keep up with the rapid changes brought forth by digitalization, which worries businesses (Kreiterling, 2023). For instance, governments are dealing with regulatory challenges as they attempt to balance financial stability, consumer protection, and innovation in the wake of the rise of digital currencies.

Digitalization is changing entrepreneurship-supporting ecosystems, opening up new opportunities for innovation, market access, and business expansion (Singh et al., 2024b). By reducing obstacles to entry, increasing resource accessibility, and creating new funding sources, digital technologies are democratizing entrepreneurship. However, these opportunities are not without challenges, the digital divide, the dangers to cyber security, and legal gaps (Wibisono, 2023). Institutions, policymakers, and entrepreneurs must collaborate to establish a friendly, secure, and supportive environment for digital entrepreneurship. The ongoing digitalization revolution will bring with it unprecedented opportunities and challenges, and will undoubtedly define future entrepreneurial environments (Fernandes et al., 2023). Entrepreneurs who can adapt to this rapidly changing environment will be well-positioned to lead innovation and economic growth in the ensuing decades. Earlier researchers have examined the impact of digital technologies (DTs) on entrepreneurship and entrepreneurial ecosystems in different countries (Dabbous et al., 2023; Felicetti et al., 2023; Singh et al., 2024b; Dimoso & Utonga, 2024). However, limited studies could observe the digitalization of the entrepreneurial ecosystem in India. Hence, this chapter analyzes how digitalization affects entrepreneurship promoting indicators as giving extensive focus on the Indian economy. For this investigation, it uses previous literature and available secondary data. It includes entrepreneurial ecosystem promoting indicators like innovation, market access, funding, and networking for creating business ecosystem in India.

LITERATURE REVIEW

Past literature has highlighted the implications of digitalization, digital technologies and digital infrastructure, and digital tools in entrepreneurship and entrepreneurial ecosystems in different countries (Peng, 2000; Singh & Jyoti, 2023a). Ries (2011) specified the importance of digitalization for promoting innovation in the entrepreneurship ecosystem. Bouncken et al. (2015) investigated the role of digitalization for assessing the finance for entrepreneurs through crowdfunding. Crowdfunding business model includes six categories (Beaulieu & Sarker, 2015). Beaulieu et al. (2014) highlighted that crowdfunding is a fast-expanding technology-enabled procedure with the potential to disrupt the finance markets. To ensure efficiency, it is critical to understand the roles of founders, investors, and technology providers. Beaulieu et al. (2014)'s study examines the research and identifies six crowdfunding business models: private equity, royalties, microfinance, peer-to-peer lending, rewards, and donations. It also presents a conceptual research framework based on these models and makes recommendations for future research areas.

Acs et al. (2017) proposed that an ecosystem is a biotic community that includes its physical environment and interactions with living and nonliving components. Economies and entrepreneurship studies have frequently disregarded the role of entrepreneurship in economic systems. The entrepreneurial ecosystem method, which has roots in regional development and strategy literature, provides insights into the interconnectedness of community actors in creating new value (Singh & Ashraf, 2020). However, research on regional development and strategic management has mainly overlooked entrepreneurs' role in creating new value. This paper discusses contributions to the entrepreneurial ecosystem concept and recommends a new area of research. Singh and Jyoti (2023b) also claimed that digitalization is effective to increase the entrepreneurship ecosystem. The entrepreneurship ecosystem is also helpful to increase digitalization.

Dabbous et al. (2023) considered a comparative investigation for assessing the influence of digitalization on entrepreneurial activity and competitiveness in 34 countries. The findings suggested that digitalization improves entrepreneurial activity and competitiveness, with connection, internet use, and digital integration being the most important drivers. However, this study is also argued that digital skills and public services are not as vital in entrepreneurial activities. Therefore, digital skills and public services must be promoted to increase entrepreneurial activities (Singh & Jyoti, 2023a). It also recommends that governments and politicians encourage new firms, increase internet usage, and promote digital integration in order to boost long-term competitiveness. Awaliyah et al. (2023) detected the implications of financial technology in the banking sector.

Singh and Ashraf (2020) developed entrepreneurship ecosystem index (EEI) to assess the progress of the entrepreneurship ecosystem in 34 selected economies between 2000 and 2017. The index contains 12 measures of entrepreneurial activity, such as finance, government support, taxation, and infrastructure. The EEI is created using the composite Z-score technique, and it was then evaluated for its relationship with socio-economic, science and technology (S&T), and intellectual property rights (IPR) aspects. It is highlighted that India is rated 8th in the EEI, with a broad range of efficiency, factor, and innovation-driven economies. This study also used linear, non-linear regression models to look at the causal relationship between EEI and per capita GDP. The findings revealed a significant link between the entrepreneurship ecosystem, socio economic development, and indices linked to science and technology and intellectual property (Singh et al., 2024e).

Satalkina and Steiner (2020) suggested that digital transformation affects socio-economic systems by altering corporate processes, resource demands, networking, and communication technologies. Digital transformation also has an impact on the societal system, including competitiveness, resilience, and the viability of the innovation system. The underlying innovation system circumstances drive digital entrepreneurship, which can occur as a process or as an outcome. Satalkina and Steiner (2020)'s study intends to present a theory-based systematization of performance indicators that define digital entrepreneurship. A collection of ten determinants of digital entrepreneurship, which include aspects such as individual patterns, organizational management processes, and external infrastructure, define the phenomena in three dimensions: the entrepreneur, the entrepreneurial process, and the applicable ecosystem. The researchers also delineated the interrelationships between the subindices of the selected compound indicators and factors of digital entrepreneurship.

Tandon et al. (2020) investigated the influence of digitalization on India's entrepreneurial ecosystem, namely start-ups. It focuses on understanding entrepreneurial and digital ecosystems. Digital entrepreneurship and government assistance are necessary for the entrepreneurial sector. It also examines the implications for Indian entrepreneurs who are seeking to launch successful technology-based start-ups, and emphasizing the need to understand the junction of various industries. It reported a crucial impact of digitalization on entrepreneurial ecosystem of India. Halida and Wilantini (2022) pointed out that digitalization is helping entrepreneurs to increase accessibility of the market. Fernandes et al. (2023) also considered Scopus data to examine the progress of scientific research in the area of digital entrepreneurship and sustainability. It identifies three thematic clusters: innovation, digital transformation strategy, business models, and sustainability and development objectives. The study conducts bibliometric analysis on 58 publications and it presents the most significant contributions for each cluster. The paper proposes a future research agenda that has important implications for the theory and practice of various aspects of digital entrepreneurship and its sustainability.

Felicetti et al. (2023) compiled the most recent scholarly studies on the nexus of innovation and entrepreneurship published in the last two decades. A thorough literature evaluation of 185 papers was done Felicetti et al. (2023) for identification of relevant subjects in the research domain. This study reported six key determinants i.e., start-up collaboration networks, business model innovation, digital platforms, digital ventures, the digital entrepreneur profile, and digital innovation ecosystems for promoting the growth of the business sector. It also suggests three major study avenues for the future research: multi-level examination of digital innovation in entrepreneurial enterprises, multidisciplinary approaches, and the development of theories for digital innovation. This study also provides a framework for studying the role of innovation in entrepreneurial enterprises. It suggests a reference model for scholars in entrepreneurship and innovation management.

RESEARCH METHODOLOGY

Data Sources

The data for this research article is collected through secondary sources, including research journals, Government e-Marketplace (Ge-M), Government of India, Ministry of Commerce and Industry, Department of Promotion of Industry and Internal Trade, Start-Up India website, International Telecommunication Union (ITU), World Telecommunication/ ICT Indicators Database. Entrepreneurial ecosystem related indicators are taken from GEM. This study examines how digitalization (as an independent variable/regressor/explanatory variable/exogenous variable) affects entrepreneurial promoting indicators (i.e., explained as a dependent variable/explained variable/endogenous variable). Additionally, independent variables such as Internet Penetration, Digital Literacy, E-Commerce Adoption, Increase in Employment Level, Community Development, Refined Infrastructure (Tandon et al., 2020), Financing for Entrepreneurs, and Governmental Support and Policies (Singh & Ashraf, 2020) are also used. The econometric model is developed using only three independent variables i.e., digitalization, Increase in Employment Level (IEL), and Government Support and Policies (GS) through funds. The variables are also selected as per available data. The variables are derived from the official websites of the World Bank, UNDP, Ge-M, GOI, MCI, DPIIT, ITU, and ICT database. Table 1 provides the summary of undertaken variables.

Table 1. Summary of the variables

Year	Individuals using the Internet/Digitalization (% of the total population of India) [DL]	Increase in Employment Level (IEL)	Government Support (in billion US dollars) [GS]
2018	20	88147	10.8
2019	30	132804	13.41
2020	43	161796	11.37
2021	56	198762	38

Source: World Bank, UNDP, Ge-M, GOI, MCI, DPIIT, ITU, and ICT database.

Formulation of Log-linear Regression Model

This article assumes that Entrepreneurial Ecosystem (EE) is a function of digitalization (DL), increase in employment level (IEL), and government support and policies (GS). The data for all these explanatory variables are mentioned in Table 1. Accordingly, the functional relationship between the independent variables and dependent variables can be demonstrated as:

$$EE = f\{DL, IEL, GS\} \quad (1)$$

The equation (1) represents that EE is dependent on DL, IEL and GS. The explanation of the equation can be done by transforming it into the log-linear regression model-

$$\ln(EE)_t = \alpha_o + \alpha_1 \ln(DL)_t + \alpha_2 \ln(IEL)_t + \alpha_3 \ln(GS)_t + \mu \quad (2)$$

In the equation (2), $(EE)_t$ represents the entrepreneurial ecosystem at the time *t*, $(DL)_t$ represents the digitalization or individuals using the Internet at time *t*, $(IEL)_t$ represents the increase in the employment level at time *t* and $(GSP)_t$ represents the government support at time *t*, respectively. Also, α_o represents the constant terms or coefficients, α_1 indicates the regression coefficient of digitalization at time *t*, α_2 represents the regression coefficient of increase in the employment level at time *t*, α_3 represents the regression coefficient of government support, and *ln* represents the logarithmic respectively.

HISTORICAL PERSPECTIVE OF ENTREPRENEURIAL ECOSYSTEM

The evolution of entrepreneurial ecosystems from traditional localized ecosystems to digitally driven, worldwide networks is highlighted by the historical perspective on these ecosystems. At first, local elements such as knowledge, financial resources, local markets, physical infrastructure, and legal frameworks largely influenced entrepreneurial ecosystems (Singh & Ashraf, 2020). It also helps to establish and grow their companies and entrepreneurs, and depended on local contacts with banks, academic institutions, government regulations, and labor markets.

- **Early Stages of Entrepreneurial Ecosystems:** It is originally proposed in the late 20th century, the idea of entrepreneurial ecosystems was primarily inspired by regional economic development ideas that emphasized innovation clusters and localized economic growth. Ecosystems were largely characterized by closeness throughout this stage. Silicon Valley, Route 128 in Boston, and Israel's "Startup Nation" are just a few early examples of how spatially concentrated ecosystems facilitated the expansion of new businesses. Universities, government-supported incubators, regional venture capital firms, and research institutions were important players in these ecosystems (Singh et al., 2024b). Dense networks of in-person contacts and the local flow of talent and information are beneficial to entrepreneurs (O'Connor et al., 2018). The borders of cities or regions limited ecosystems, and geographic clustering emerged as a key tactic for promoting innovation.

- **Digitalization and Shifting in Global Networks:** The traditional ecosystems started to change in the late 1990s and early 2000s as digital technologies gained popularity. Advances in computing, e-commerce, and the internet enabled firms to expand outside their local areas. Digitalization made it easier to connect globally and improve access to markets, capital, and expertise regardless of one's physical location (Singh & Jyoti, 2023b). It also completely changed the operating way of business ecosystems. With the transition to a digital entrepreneurial ecosystem, new businesses were no longer restricted by geographic boundaries and could utilize resources like cloud computing, digital marketing platforms, e-commerce tools, and virtual networks (O'Connor et al., 2018; Cheng et al., 2022; Wibisono, 2023). This change not only increased accessibility but also called into question the established dominance of local ecosystems. Instead of requiring physical closeness, entrepreneurs from rural or undeveloped countries might work with remote teams, connect with foreign financiers, or access global markets (Singh & Jyoti, 2023b). Innovation could come from anywhere in the world with access to basic infrastructure of digitalization, which also made entrepreneurship more decentralized and inclusive (O'Connor et al., 2018).
- **Digital Platforms and the Emergence of a New Ecosystem Model:** Platforms like Amazon, Google, and Alibaba became essential to the operation of entrepreneurial ecosystems due to expansion of digitalization and digital infrastructure (Wibisono, 2023). These platforms, which included cloud-based solutions, payment gateways, and hosting services, offered the digital infrastructure required to enable new endeavors. Additionally, social networking sites like Facebook, Instagram, and LinkedIn gave business owners the means to communicate with clients around the world and promote their goods. The nature of rivalry and cooperation has also changed as a result of the digital entrepreneurial environment. Direct rivalry within local marketplaces was emphasized in traditional ecosystems (O'Connor et al., 2018).

Digital ecosystems, on the other hand, promoted a more cooperative strategy. Startups might interact with APIs, take advantage of alliances with bigger tech platforms, and even get money or guidance from digital incubators and accelerators (Singh et al., 2025b). By creating new channels for capital raising, crowdfunding websites like Kickstarter and Indiegogo further democratized financial access.

Entrepreneurial ecosystems have changed dramatically due to application of digitalization (Singh & Jyoti, 2023b). It is evolving from local networks to global due to digitally driven activities. Several opportunities have also increased and resource access has been more accessible to all, but there are drawbacks as well, such as the digital divide, cybersecurity threats, and complicated regulations (Peng, 2000). These ecosystems' survival rests on their capacity to adjust to these realities while striking a balance between inclusive access, solid regulatory frameworks, and global connectedness. The development of digital ecosystems emphasizes how crucial it is to support innovation at the nexus of market access, policy, and technology (Peng, 2000).

DIGITALIZATION AND ENTREPRENEURIAL ECOSYSTEM

The intersection of technology and economics has been an exciting path, with revolutionary advances that have transformed industries, civilizations, and global economies. Digitalization and DTs are great drivers to increase the entrepreneurship and entrepreneurial ecosystem. Both have interconnection and high dependence on digitalization and DTs (Singh & Jyoti, 2023b).

- **Mechanical Computing and Industrial Revolution:** The invention of mechanical computing in the 17th and 18th centuries paved the way for automation and efficiency in a variety of industries. The Industrial Revolution of the 19th century, typified by mechanization, steam power, and mass production, signaled a substantial transition from rural to industrial economies, resulting in greater productivity and economic expansion (Collier & MacLachlan, 1998).
- **The Digital Age from Transistors to the Internet:** The transistor transformed electronics in the mid-20th century, allowing for the creation of tiny and powerful computers. Mainframe computers first appeared in the 1950s and 1960s and were employed by governments and enterprises to perform sophisticated calculations (Floud & Johnsom, 2008). Personal computers evolved in the 1970s and 1980s, making computing power available to in-

dividuals and small enterprises, thus encouraging innovation and economic growth. The Internet, which emerged in the 1960s, revolutionized communication, commerce, and information exchange, making the World Wide Web more user-friendly and accessible to the general public (Floud & Johnsom, 2008).

- **A New Paradigm of Digital Economy:** The Internet has transformed retail and customer behavior with E-commerce, the Dot-com Boom, and the Mobile Revolution. E-commerce increased market reach and decreased transaction costs, while the Dot-com Boom resulted in the fast rise of internet-based business (Leiner & Cerf, 2000). Smartphones and mobile internet access proliferated throughout the mobile revolution, changing consumer behavior and company models forever. Big data and AI have also created new potential for innovation and economic growth, propelling progress in a variety of industries like healthcare and finance (Leiner & Cerf, 2000).
- **Digitalization and Current Entrepreneurship Ecosystem:** Digitalization has revolutionized business ecosystems by increasing access to information, broadening market reach, and lowering entry barriers (Singh & Jyoti, 2023c). The Internet, automation, and data analytics are now critical components of entrepreneurial success. At present entrepreneurship ecosystems include entrepreneurs, investors, institutions, and the government, and these are getting significant benefits from digital tools such as cloud computing, e-commerce platforms, and social media, DTs also enable entrepreneurs to scale operations and engage with global markets without requiring significant physical infrastructure (Sayabek et al., 2020; Cheng et al., 2022). Digitalization entails increasing connection, developing human capital through digital education, and integrating technology into company processes (Singh et al., 2024c). Widespread internet connection has transformed business operations by enabling online transactions, global marketing, and new client acquisition (Kotarba, 2018). E-commerce, fintech, and digital marketing are examples of digital tools that have increased the efficiency of small firms in the global market (Singh & Jyoti, 2023c). Digitalization has fueled innovation by creating new business models and collaborative platforms for startups (Singh et al., 2025b). Technologies such as AI, big data, and IoT enable entrepreneurs to develop creative solutions. The adaptability of digital platforms permits rapid market changes, which is critical for managing competitive contexts (Kotarba, 2018). Digitalization is critical for long-term competitiveness, and it is promoting economic growth, social sustainability, and environmental responsibility (Singh, 2025a,b). Entrepreneurs who integrate digital technologies can enhance production, maximize resources, and lessen their environmental effects. The governments are recognizing the necessity of policies

that facilitate these transactions, particularly in ICT infrastructure, digital literacy, and technical innovation. However, the impact of digitalization differs by the economy, with industrialized nations frequently benefiting more than developing ones (Dimoso & Utonga, 2024). The impact of digitalization is determined by technical adoption, human capital, and regulatory frameworks (Singh & Singh, 2025). Despite this, digitalization has had a huge impact on entrepreneurial ecosystems, allowing companies to develop, scale, and compete in a quickly changing global landscape. It has given entrepreneurs the tools they need to flourish in a digitally transformed world, resulting in a more integrated, competitive, and sustainable economy (Dimoso & Utonga, 2024).

DIGITALIZATION AND ENTREPRENEURIAL ECOSYSTEM PROMOTING INDICATORS

Digitalization is affecting economies, industries, and entrepreneurial ecosystems on a worldwide scale. With the fast use of digital technologies (DTs), entrepreneurs are embracing new tools and platforms to innovate, get market access, secure investment, and extend their networks. This section of the study investigates how digitalization affects four critical aspects of the entrepreneurial ecosystem i.e., innovation, market access, funding, and networking (Singh et al., 2025b). It also looks at the benefits and problems that digitalization brings for entrepreneurs and the entrepreneurship ecosystem.

- **Digitalization and Innovation:** Digitalization has transformed how entrepreneurs innovate, allowing them to develop new business models and disrupt established industries. Platforms such as Uber and Airbnb show how digital technologies (DTs) may connect supply and demand more efficiently, bypassing traditional intermediaries (Ries, 2011). Cloud computing, big data, and Artificial Intelligence (AI) have enabled entrepreneurs to innovate without making significant infrastructure expenditures, decreasing operational costs and time-to-market (Cheng et al., 2022). The digital revolution has accelerated the innovation cycle, allowing for speedier prototyping and iterative development (Ries, 2011). Tools such as 3D printing and digital twin technology help to reduce product creation risks. Agile methodology and collaborative technology accelerated invention and market responsiveness. Digitalization has democratized access to innovation tools, allowing entrepreneurs of all backgrounds to participate in the startup ecosystem (Ries, 2011). Open-source software, low-code platforms, and online learning tools such as Udemy and Coursera allow anybody to develop regardless of their location or financial position. However, rapid technological improvements can render inventions obsolete, and digital innovation frequently encounters governmental barriers, particularly data protection and intellectual property (Ries, 2011).

- **Digitalization and Market Access:** Digitalization has transformed businesses by allowing them to reach worldwide markets via E-commerce platforms such as Amazon, eBay, and Alibaba, as well as social media platforms like Instagram and TikTok (Singh et al., 2024b). Digital tools enable entrepreneurs to acquire and analyze client data, revealing previously unreachable insights (Halida & Wilantini, 2022). Big data analytics and artificial intelligence enable product customization, which increases consumer pleasure and loyalty. Netflix uses AI algorithms to provide tailored content. However, digitalization created barriers to market access, such as intense online rivalry, expensive advertising costs, cybersecurity concerns, and compliance with international regulations such as The General Data Protection Regulation (Halida & Wilantini, 2022).
- **Digitalization and Funding:** Digitalization has transformed the financial industry, allowing enterprises to raise financing via crowdfunding sites such as Kickstarter and Indiegogo (Bouncken et al., 2015). These platforms bypass traditional banking institutions and harness user interest to validate company proposals. They also increase venture capital access through platforms such as AngelList, which allows venture capitalists to evaluate company potential using AI and machine learning (Roundy, 2022;). FinTech advancements such as peer-to-peer lending and blockchain-based fundraising provide businesses with new financial opportunities (Awaliyah et al., 2023). Initial Coin Offerings (ICOs) and Security Token Offerings (STOs) enable businesses to raise cash by issuing digital tokens, giving them flexibility and worldwide accessibility for investors. However, digital financing platforms come with hazards, such as crowdfunding initiatives failing to accomplish their objectives and growing regulatory scrutiny of blockchain-based fundraising (Beaulieu & Sarker, 2015).
- **Digitalization and Networking:** Entrepreneurs can interact with colleagues, mentors, and investors around the world via digital platforms such as LinkedIn, Meetup, and Slack (Felicetti et al., 2023; Gupta et al., 2025). The COVID-19 pandemic has accelerated the move to virtual gatherings and conferences, allowing entrepreneurs to participate in webinars, pitch competitions, and industry events from anywhere. Digital platforms such as Reddit, artificial intelligence, Quora, and GitHub make it easier to share information and collaborate in the entrepreneurial environment, boosting creativity and

collective learning (Roundy, 2022). However, digital networking has limitations, such as creating long-term relationships online and dealing with information overload, making it difficult for entrepreneurs to locate significant connections and possibilities.

DIGITAL ENTREPRENEURIAL ECOSYSTEM IN INDIA

India's business environment supports the emergence of digital entrepreneurs. The economists refer to these characteristics as "growth vehicles," which combine traditional and digital components. In an entrepreneurial environment, the first factor, "open source," is crucial for digital entrepreneurs seeking growth. Customizable software eliminates the need for entrepreneurs to design proprietary software, saving time and money when translating ideas into operational enterprises. The rise of a shared economy in India has created a peer-to-peer community for sharing ideas, products, and services. The market has seen a surge in demand for digital services, leading to the development of more dynamic business models. Governmental support through "The National Skill Development Council," "Atal Incubation Centre," and "Make in India" initiatives have also contributed to the adoption of digital entrepreneurship (Tandon et al., 2020). More educational institutions, corporations, and incubators are promoting entrepreneurship by launching mentorship programs and co-working spaces in India (Singh et al., 2024c). Venture capital firms have been instrumental in supporting Indian entrepreneurs by providing both money and mentoring (Singh et al., 2024a). However, various issues impede the consolidation of India's entrepreneurial activities. One obstacle in today's labor market is the absence of specialized skill sets (Tandon et al., 2020). Entrepreneurs often lack expertise in how to strategically implement a business strategy due to restricted education in most educational institutions. Entrepreneurs encounter challenges in sustaining their ventures, including over-reliance on overseas markets, under-penetration of domestic markets, and inadequate marketing capabilities (Singh et al., 2024a).

Many start-ups fail after a short period of operation, and Indian entrepreneurs struggle to scale up their businesses (Singh et al., 2024a). Other factors affecting a digital entrepreneur may include- unstable internet and communication technology infrastructure, as well as limited access to traditional financial credit (Tandon et al., 2020). An aspiring entrepreneur meets a harsh reality in terms of the opportunity cost of entrepreneurship and the costs of conducting a company in India. This increases their susceptibility, leading to fear of failure. In a society that prioritizes material achievement, government jobs, and stability, these factors can hinder entrepreneurial activity. Entrepreneurs confront significant opportunity costs and business costs, making it challenging to succeed in India. This increases their susceptibility, leading to fear of failure. In a society that places high value on material accomplishment, government jobs and a sense of well-settledness are substantial barriers to entrepreneurial engagement (Tandon et al., 2020).

Figure 1. Growth vehicles and bottleneck of entrepreneurial activities

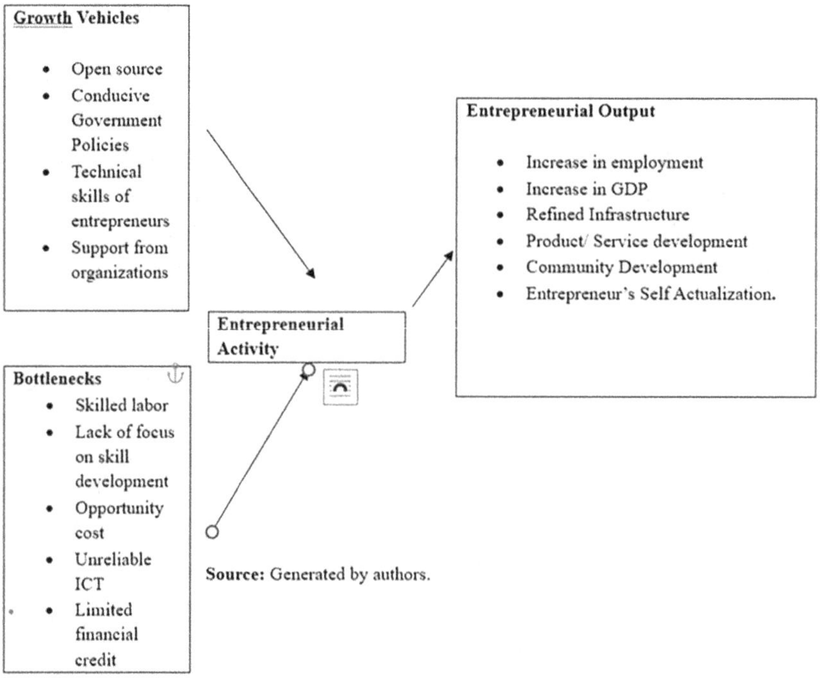

Source: Generated by authors.

Emerging economies can greatly benefit from productive entrepreneurship and ecosystem services due to their market orientation and rising economic growth. Peng (2020) claimed that business research findings from economies such as the US and Europe may not be applicable to emerging markets due to their diverse settings. Despite academic research on entrepreneurship, there is still a need to better understanding of it in the context of emerging economies (Bruton et al., 2008). Emerging countries including Brazil, Russia, India, and China are expected to outperform as compared to developed economies like the USA, Japan, and the UK (Marquis & Raynard, 2015). Jain et al. (2015) noted that the Indian economy has grown significantly since its liberalization. According to IBM (2016), there were 100,000 new company registrations in the 2010s and investment for start-ups increased by doubling between 2014-2015. Between 2010 and 2014, an estimated US $1,818 million was invested in Indian start-ups via venture capital and private equity.

Recent economic benefits include employment creation, new company models, market disruptions, and technological advancements due to DTs (Thornton, 2018). Limited research on the Indian entrepreneurial landscape highlights the region's distinct entrepreneurial activity. Earlier researchers have identified three types of innovation i.e., Jugaad, Reverse, and Gandhian (Prahalad & Mashelkar, 2010; Prabhu & Jain, 2015). India's entrepreneurial ecosystem is evolving and struggles to support start-ups, with over 90% failing within the first year (Singh et al., 2024a). According to the GEM, there is a correlation between low opinions about entrepreneurship as a viable career path and high prestige for entrepreneurs. To promote sustainable growth for entrepreneurs in India, it is important to study the performance of the forces that drive the economy (Singh et al., 2024a). Figure 1 explores the growth vehicles and bottleneck of the entrepreneurial and entrepreneurship ecosystem.

Role of Government in Entrepreneurship Ecosystem

The government's role initiatives play a key role in promoting entrepreneurial development (). Benefits to Indians include job creation and financial support for those in need. The government has implemented initiatives to encourage entrepreneurship in India (Amit, 2014; Jindal & Bhaedwaj, 2016). Dhaliwal (2016) suggested that these activities can explore how available resources can be used to support economic development. These initiatives include the Pradhan Mantri Employment Generation Program, credit-linked capital subsidy scheme for technological upgrades, micro and small firm cluster development program, Rajiv Gandhi Udyami Mitra Yojana, and the Atal Innovation Model. The government is promoting India's entrepreneurial ecosystem by establishing Mudra Bank and introducing special economic zones. India also implemented The Micro, Small, and Medium Enterprises Act, 2006, and the Ministry of Skill Development and Entrepreneurship in 2014. These initiatives also aim to develop and train Indian youngsters for long-term employment and self-sufficiency. The Indian Government's Start-up India and Make in India initiatives have had a substantial impact on the entrepreneurship ecosystem in India (Jindal & Bhaedwaj, 2016). Several measures are also being taken to increase the entrepreneurship ecosystem in India. Transform India into a knowledge-based economy fueled by digital technologies (DTs). The Digital India program has successfully integrated rural and urban populations to establish an e-governance platform that gives equal access to government services for all individuals. The goal is to foster inclusive growth by improving the manufacture of electronic products and services. The Start-up India project supports poor, youth, and female entrepreneurs by offering bank finance and incentives (Jyoti & Singh, 2020). The start-up India portal connects small entrepreneurs and provides financing, credit guarantees, and loans for greenfield manufacturing services (Jyoti & Singh, 2020).

Supporting the Government: Agencies, Financial Institutions, and Universities

Several public and commercial bodies, as well as educational institutions, are supporting the government's entrepreneurial initiatives. Several organizations, including the National Skill Development Council (NSDC), Allied Sector Skill Councils (SSCs), Niti Aayog, MSME Technology Centers, National Institute for Entrepreneurship and Small Business Development (NIESBUD), National Institute for Micro Small and Medium Enterprises (NIMSME), and Indian Institute for Entrepreneurship (IIE), aim to enhance India's entrepreneurial ecosystem (Jindal & Bhaedwaj, 2016). The government has established specialized funds to facilitate corporate operations and promote growth. Since 2015, the Indian government has introduced various programs to support innovation and entrepreneurship, including the India Aspiration Fund, National Skill Development Fund, and Electronics Development Fund (Sunita & Srija, 2016). Over the last five years, India has seen a significant increase in entrepreneurial activity, ranking among the top five countries in the world for start-ups (Thornton, 2018). According to the survey, over 43% of India's 10,000 start-ups are technology-based, primarily in e-commerce, finance, health, and B2B markets. According to Thornton (2018), India's tech start-ups are expected to increase from 4300 in 2015 to over 11,500 by 2020. The Indian Government has partnered with the National Institute of Construction Management and Research (NICMAR), the Indian Institute of Foreign Trade (IIFT), the Institute of Company Secretaries of India (ICSI), and the Institute of Chartered Accountants of India to improve the ease of doing business in the country and boost its global ranking. The success of these projects could lead to a significant shift in market structures and operations, propelling the Indian economy to higher levels of development.

EMPIRICAL RESULT

The regression analysis is carried out to determine the relationship between the dependent and independent variables and to evaluate the model's efficacy and statistical significance (Table 2). The correlation coefficient shows a strong positive association between the dependent and independent variables (Table 3). The value of R^2 (=0.9993) depicts that the independent variables explain 99.93% of the variance in the dependent variable. It is also implying that the model is highly effective in predicting the outcome. The value of the adjusted R^2 (=0.9979) compensated for the limited sample size and number of predictors. It demonstrates that the model maintains a high level of explanatory power while limiting overfitting. The value of the standard error is found 0.9273 and measures the average distance that observed data points fall from the regression line. A low number suggests a close fit between the model and the data. The number of observations, i.e., 4, that is used in the model is a very small sample size, while the results are technically accurate. However, their generalizability may be limited due to the small sample size.

From the data, the residual sum of squares (RSS) is reported 1255.89. It demonstrates the variation explained by the model's independent variables (Figure 2). Whereas the residual sum of squares (RSS= 0.86) shows the model's unexplained variation. The F-statistic (730.21) determines the overall significance of the regression model. A high F-statistic shows that the independent variables together account for a considerable amount of variance in the dependent variable, and the p-value for the F-test is less than the customary threshold of 0.05. It indicates the regression model is significant. The results demonstrate the contributions of each independent variable and the intercept. Firstly, taking deep insights into the intercept, the coefficient (-31.28) is the anticipated value of the dependent variable when all independent variables are zero. Due to this tiny dataset, this value is unlikely to be of practical consequence. The values of T-statistic (-13.91) and p-value (0.0457) show that the intercept is statistically significant ($p < 0.05$). It indicates its impact on the model. Secondly, talking about the variable (88147), the coefficient value, i.e. (0.00048), depicts that for each unit increase in this predictor, the dependent variable increases by 0.00048, while the other variables remain unchanged. The T-statistic value (31.33) and the P-value (0.0203) demonstrate that this variable is highly statistically significant ($p< 0.05$), indicating a strong positive influence on the dependent variable. Lastly, analysing the variable 10.8, the coefficient value (-0.1903) indicates that for each unit increase in this predictor, the dependent variable reduces by 0.1903, while the other variables remain unchanged. The T-statistic value (-3.35) and the P-value (0.1848) depict that the variable is not statistically significant ($p>0.05$), indicating that its impact on the dependent variable is insignificant in this model.

Figure 2. Regression results

Summary Output

Regression Statistics	
Multiple R	0.999658
R Square	0.999316
Adjusted R Square	0.997947
Standard Error	0.927334
Observations	4

ANOVA

	df	*SS*	*MS*	*F*	*Significance F*
Regression	2	1255.89	627.945	730.2129	0.026158
Residual	1	0.859948	0.859948		
Total	3	1256.75			

	Coefficients	*Standard Error*	*t Stat*	*P-value*	*Lower 95%*	*Upper 95%*	*Lower 95.0%*	*Upper 95.0%*
Intercept	-31.2777	2.2486	-13.909	0.0456	-59.8499	-2.705	-59.849	-2.7055
88147	0.000476	1.52E-	31.332	0.0203	0.000283	0.000	0.0002	0.0006
10.8	-0.1903	0.0568	-3.3482	0.1847	-0.91246	0.531	-0.9124	0.5318

Source: Author's estimation.

The overall regression model is statistically significant ($p<0.05$) and effectively explains the variance in the dependent variable. The variable 88147 is statistically significant, with a strong positive association with the dependent variable, and the variable 10.8 is not statistically significant, indicating that it does not make a major contribution to the dependent variable in this model. The extremely high R square value and adjusted R square value suggest that the model explains almost all of the variance in the dependent variable. Table 2 represents the correlation matrix, including pairwise correlation coefficients for the variables (the variables are DL, IEL, and GS).

Table 2. Correlation coefficient among the variables

	Column 1	*Column 2*	*Column 3*
Column 1	1		
Column 2	0.987648	1	
Column 3	0.670328	0.707957	1

Source: Author's estimation.

There is a significant positive association between Column 1 (DL) and Column 2 (IEL). This implies that as digitalization mechanisms increase, the level of employment in the country also increases proportionately in a fairly comparable ratio. There is a moderately favourable association between Column 1 (DL) and Column 3 (GS). This implies that increases in Column 1 are modestly correlated with increases in Column 3. Also, there is a significant positive relationship between Column 2 (IEL) and Column 3 (GS). This shows that increases in Column 2 are closely correlated with increases in Column 3, and the diagonal values (1) represent the perfect correlation between each variable and itself.

LIMITATIONS AND SCOPE OF FURTHER STUDY

This study discovered a substantial positive association between digitalization and employment levels. It also implies that as digitalization mechanisms progress, employment levels are likely to rise proportionally. A moderate positive connection is found between digitalization and government support and policies. A substantial connection is found between employment levels and government support. It shows a strong relationship between these variables. Despite a small sample size, the regression model proved statistically significant ($p<0.05$), explaining 99.93% of the variance in the entrepreneurial ecosystem. Policymakers and stakeholders should consider digitalization as a critical driver for job creation and entrepreneurial ecosystem development. Investing in digital infrastructure and encouraging digital literacy can have a favourable economic impact. The strong positive relationship between IEL and GS shows that government assistance is more effective when it is combined with employment creation programs. Tailoring policies to promote job creation have a significant impact on the entrepreneurial ecosystem.

The study's main limitation is its tiny sample size. Future research should prioritize dataset expansion to increase the generalizability of findings and generate more robust conclusions. While this study concentrated on three essential characteristics, the creation of a strong entrepreneurial ecosystem necessitates a multidimensional approach that includes aspects such as education, innovation, and financing (Singh et al., 2024c). The further study of this article can include extra data points to validate the findings and improve model generalizability, investigate the impact of additional possible influencers on the entrepreneurial ecosystem, such as educational efforts, innovation hubs, and financial inclusion programs. Conduct cross-national or cross-regional research to uncover best practices and contextual variances in the interaction between digitalization, employment, government support, and entrepreneurial ecosystems. Use supplement quantitative analysis with qualitative research to acquire a better understanding of the mechanisms and stakeholders that shape the entrepreneurial ecosystem. This study helps to better comprehend the complex links that exist between digitalization, employment, government support, and India's entrepreneurial ecosystem. While admitting the sample size limitations, the findings have important implications for policymakers, entrepreneurs, and stakeholders striving to maintain a healthy entrepreneurial ecosystem. Future research can give comprehensive direction for cultivating thriving entrepreneurial settings by addressing identified knowledge gaps and building on existing insights.

CONCLUSION

This study has investigated the impact of digitalization on entrepreneurial ecosystems as giving emphasis on the Indian economy. The study's historical perspective on entrepreneurial ecosystems emphasizes the shift from traditional regional networks to globally interconnected, digitally driven systems. The impact of digitalization on innovation, market assessment, funding, and networking in entrepreneurial ecosystems exposes both potential and obstacles. Digital entrepreneurship is still in its early phases in emerging economies like India, and there is a need for researchers and academicians to study the variables of the entrepreneurial ecosystem that support or hinder its growth. The focus should not only be on new digital firms or start-ups (Ngoasong, 2015), but also how digitalization affects current MSMEs and small businesses in India (Autio & Levie, 2017). There will be a need to analyse the conceptual components of the business model in the digital era (Standing & Mattsson, 2016). The role of public policy in developing sustainable entrepreneurial initiatives must be promoted (Hall et al., 2010).

This chapter used a log-linear regression model to investigate the associations between digitalization (DL), employment levels (IEL), government assistance and policies (GS), and the entrepreneurial ecosystem (EE). Despite having a small sample size of only four observations, the empirical research shows a substantial positive association between digitalization, employment, and government support for the entrepreneurial ecosystem. The findings indicate that digitalization is a crucial driver of entrepreneurial growth, with a large beneficial influence on employment levels. However, the absence of statistical significance of government support in the model calls into doubt the efficacy of present policy initiatives. In conclusion, this study adds to our understanding of digitalization in shaping entrepreneurial ecosystems, particularly in India. The findings underscore the importance of governments, businesses, and stakeholders realizing digitalization's potential while tackling its obstacles. Prioritizing digital literacy, infrastructure development, and inclusive policies is crucial for fostering a thriving entrepreneurial ecosystem in India.

This section of the study involves the measures that the institution or any economy can take to nourish its ongoing and future outcomes so that inclusive growth and development can occur. It is potential for digital and technology advancements to offer competitive advantages in niche markets. For this, the government should prioritize investments in digital infrastructure, such as high-speed internet, data centers, and cloud computing (Cheng et al., 2022). Implement digital literacy programs to provide entrepreneurs, small company owners, and employees with the skills they need to succeed in the digital economy. Indian startups, such as Infosys and Wipro, have paved the way for new techniques in Silicon Valley and other start-up hotspots. Start-ups like HealthifyMe, Quantta, and TerraBlue XT have followed in their footsteps and achieved global success. Advancements in ICT and digital ecosystems have led to a rapid transformation of the corporate landscape. Digitalization is no longer an option. Conglomerates and huge enterprises are spending considerably on technology. To maintain a competitive advantage, start-ups with traditional business models must implement novel digital interventions. Indian entrepreneurs face dynamic changes in the business environment, including the impact of demonetization, new GST laws, and support for innovation, self-employment, and entrepreneurship. Despite the unpredictable and uncertain climate for Indian entrepreneurs, there are chances for localized innovation to drive disruption. Thus, the use of digital breakthroughs, combined with inventive disruptions will prepare entrepreneurs to survive in the new era.

The government's focus on digitizing the population presents an opportunity to connect rural entrepreneurs with metropolitan marketplaces. Urban entrepreneurs with tech skills could be placed to bridge the gap between rural and urban areas. AS mentors for rural entrepreneurs, consolidating entrepreneurial networks has an ability to boost rural entrepreneurs by developing skills and establishing new job opportunities. Developing an entrepreneurial culture and abilities in the country is crucial for promoting self-employment and entrepreneurship as a career path. The government can also implement policies that encourage inclusive digitalization, ensuring that the benefits reach all parts of society, especially rural areas, women, and marginalized people. The government should also implement policies that offer targeted assistance to MSMEs, such as finance, mentorship, and digital resources. Furthermore, governments can create a more streamlined regulatory environment that promotes innovation, entrepreneurship, and digitalization while protecting data privacy and security and giving tax breaks to start-ups, MSMEs, and firms that invest in digitalization, innovation, and R&D. The central agencies can also foster public-private collaborations to encourage entrepreneurship, technological advancements, and innovation by using the knowledge and resources of both the sectors and by encouraging international cooperation and knowledge sharing to keep up with global best practices in digitalization and entrepreneurship. By implementing these policy consequences, the government may boost entrepreneurial growth, innovation, and digitalization, hence fostering economic development and job creation in India.

REFERENCES

Acs, Z. J., Stam, E., Audretsch, D. B., & O'Connor, A. (2017). The lineages of the entrepreneurial ecosystem approach. *Small Business Economics*, *49*(1), 1–10. DOI: 10.1007/s11187-017-9864-8

Amit, R. (2014). Entrepreneurship development in India: role of economic growth, foreign investment and financial development. *AIMA Journal of Management & Research*, 8(3/4), 1-9. https://apps.aima.in/ejournal_new/articlespdf/342-amit.pdf

Archi, Y. E., Benbba, B., Kabil, M., & Dávid, L. D. (2023). Digital technologies for sustainable tourism destinations: State of the art and research agenda. *Administrative Sciences*, *13*(1), 1–21. DOI: 10.3390/admsci13080184

Autio, E., & Levie, J. (2017). Management of entrepreneurial ecosystems. In Ahmetoglu, G., Chamorro-Premuzic, T., Klinger, B., & Karcisky, T. (Eds.), *The Wiley Handbook of Entrepreneurship*., DOI: 10.1002/9781118970812.ch19

Awaliyah, T., Safitri, N., Hartaty, S., Felani, F., & Judijanto, L. (2023). The impact of financial technology innovation on banking service transformation: A case study in the FinTech Industry. *Global International Journal of Innovative Research*. https://www.researchgate.net/publication/377355013_The_Impact_of_Financial_Technology_Innovation_on_Banking_Service_Transformation_A_Case_Study_in_the_FinTech_Industry

Beaulieu, T., Sarker, S., & Sarker, S. (2015). A conceptual framework for understanding crowdfunding. *Communications of the Association for Information Systems*, *37*(1), 1–12. DOI: 10.17705/1CAIS.03701

Bouncken, R. B., Komorek, M., & Kraus, S. (2015). Crowdfunding: The current state of research. *The International Business & Economics Research Journal*, *14*(3), 407–416. https://www.researchgate.net/publication/275657510_Crowdfunding_The_Current_State_Of_Research. DOI: 10.19030/iber.v14i3.9206

Bruton, G. D., Ahlstrom, D., & Obloj, K. (2008). Entrepreneurship in emerging economies: Where are we today and where should research go in the future. *Entrepreneurship Theory and Practice*, *32*(1), 1–12. DOI: 10.1111/j.1540-6520.2007.00213.x

Cheng, M., Qu, Y., Jiang, C., & Zhao, C. (2022). Is cloud computing the digital solution to the future of banking. *Journal of Financial Stability*, *63*(1), 1–20. DOI: 10.1016/j.jfs.2022.101073

Collier, B., & MacLachlan, J. (1998). *Charles Babbage and the engine of perfection*. Oxford University Press.

Dabbous, A., Barakat, K. A., & Kraus, S. (2023). The impact of digitalization on entrepreneurial activity and sustainable competitiveness: A panel data analysis. *Technology in Society*, *73*(1), 1–13. DOI: 10.1016/j.techsoc.2023.102224

Dhaliwal, A. (2016). Role of entrepreneurship in economic development. *International Journal of Scientific Research and Management*, *30*(1), 4262–4269. https://www.krmangalam.edu.in/blog/role-of-entrepreneurship-in-economic-development/

Dimoso, R. L., & Utonga, D. (2024). A systematic review of digital technology adoption in small and medium-sized enterprises: Implications for performance in developing countries. *International Journal of Development and Management Review*, *19*(1), 1–16. https://www.ajol.info/index.php/ijdmr/article/view/273499

Dömötör, . (2023). Peer-to-peer lending: Legal loan sharking or altruistic investment? Analyzing platform investments from a credit risk perspective. *Journal of International Financial Markets, Institutions and Money*, *86*(1), 1–14.

Felicetti, A. M., Corvello, V., & Ammirato, S. (2023). Digital innovation in entrepreneurial firms: A systematic literature review. *Review of Managerial Science*, *18*(1), 315–362. DOI: 10.1007/s11846-023-00638-9

Fernandes, C., Pires, R., & Alves, M.-C. G. (2023). Digital entrepreneurship and sustainability: The state of the art and research agenda. *Economies*, *11*(1), 1–13.

Floud, R., & Johnson, P. (2008). *The Cambridge Economic History of the Industrial Revolution*. Cambridge University Press.

Gupta, M., Sharma, B., & Singh, A. K. (2025). Impact of digital technologies on tourist arrival in selected economies. In Lytras, M., Alkhaldi, A., & Ordóñez de Pablos, P. (Eds.), *Harnessing AI, Blockchain, and Cloud Computing for Enhanced e-Government Services* (pp. 441–474). IGI Global Scientific Publishing., DOI: 10.4018/979-8-3693-7678-2.ch014

Halida, U. M., & Wilantini, C. (2022). The role of digitalization in expanding MSME market access. *Quantitative Economics and Management Studies*, *3*(1), 1–10. DOI: 10.35877/454RI.qems861

Hall, J., Daneke, G., & Lenox, M. (2010). Sustainable development and entrepreneurship: Past contributions and future directions. *Journal of Business Venturing*, *25*(5), 439–448. DOI: 10.1016/j.jbusvent.2010.01.002

Hein, A., Schreieck, M., Riasanow, T., Setzke, D. S., Wiesche, M., Böhm, M., & Krcmar, H. (2019). Digital platform ecosystem. *Electronic Markets*, *30*(1), 87–98. DOI: 10.1007/s12525-019-00377-4

Hoque, M. M. (2024). Crowdfunding for innovation: a comprehensive empirical review. *Future Business Journal*, 10(102).

Jain, S., Nair, A., & Ahlstrom, D. (2015). Towards a theoretical understanding of innovation and entrepreneurship in India. *Asia Pacific Journal of Management*, *32*(4), 835–841. DOI: 10.1007/s10490-015-9444-x

Jindal, M., & Bhaedwaj, A. (2016). Entrepreneurship development in India: a new paradigm. *Proceedings of the World Congress on Engineering*, 2. https://www.iaeng.org/publication/WCE2016/WCE2016_pp724-726.pdf

Jyoti, B., & Singh, A. K. (2020). Characteristics and determinants of new start-ups in Gujarat, India. *Entrepreneurship Review*, *1*(2), 1–25. DOI: 10.38157/entrepreneurship-review.v1i2.154

Jyoti, B., & Singh, A. K. (2023). Does digitalization have a causal relationship with economic development? an experience from a country-wise panel data statistical analysis. In R. Sine Nazlı & G. Sari (Eds.), *Handbook of Research on Perspectives on Society and Technology Addiction* (pp. 34-61). IGI Global. DOI: 10.4018/978-1-6684-8397-8.ch003

Kotarba, M. (2018). Digital transformation of business models. *Foundations of Management,* 10(1), 123-142. https://intapi.sciendo.com/pdf/10.2478/fman-2018-0011

Kreiterling, C. (2023). Digital innovation and entrepreneurship: A review of challenges in competitive markets. *Journal of Innovation and Entrepreneurship*, *69*(1), 1–10. DOI: 10.1186/s13731-023-00320-0

Leiner, B. M., & Cerf, V. G. (2000). *A brief history of the Internet.*https://www.usg.edu/galileo/skills/unit07/internet07_02.phtml

Marquis, C., & Raynard, M. (2015). Institutional strategies in emerging markets. *The Academy of Management Annals*, *9*(1), 1–13. DOI: 10.5465/19416520.2015.1014661

Ngoasong, M. Z. (2015). Digital entrepreneurship in emerging economies: the role of ICTs and local contexts. *AIB-UKI Conference*, 16-18.

O'Connor, A., Stam, E., Sussan, F., & Audretsch, D. B. (2018). Entrepreneurial Ecosystems: The Foundations of Place-based Renewal. In O'Connor, A., Stam, E., Sussan, F., & Audretsch, D. (Eds.), *Entrepreneurial Ecosystems. International Studies in Entrepreneurship* (Vol. 38). Springer., DOI: 10.1007/978-3-319-63531-6_1

Peng, M. W. (2000). *Business strategies in transition economies. Sage Publications.* https://us.sagepub.com/en-us/nam/business-strategies-in-transition-economies/book9311

Prabhu, J., & Jain, S. (2015). Innovation and entrepreneurship in India: Understanding jugaad. *Asia Pacific Journal of Management, 32*(1), 843–868. DOI: 10.1007/s10490-015-9445-9

Prahalad, C., & Mashelkar, R. (2010). Innovation's holy grail. *Harvard Business Review, 88*, 132–141. https://hbr.org/2010/07/innovations-holy-grail

Ries, E. (2011). *The lean startup: how today's entrepreneurs use continuous innovation to create radically succesful businesses.* Crown. https://books.google.co.in/books/about/The_Lean_Startup.html?id=tvfyz-4JILwC&redir_esc=y

Roundy, P. T. (2022). Artificial intelligence and entrepreneurial ecosystems: Understanding the implications of algorithmic decision-making for startup communities. *Journal of Ethics in Entrepreneurship and Technology, 2*(1), 23–38. DOI: 10.1108/JEET-07-2022-0011

Satalkina, L., & Steiner, G. (2020). Digital Entrepreneurship: A theory-based systematization of core performance indicators. *Sustainability (Basel), 12*(10), 1–10. DOI: 10.3390/su12104018

Sayabek, Z., Suieubayeva, S., & Utegenova, A. (2020). *Digital transformation in business.* Springer International Publishing. https://www.springerprofessional.de/en/digital-transformation-in-business/17010220

Singh, A. K. (2025a). Importance of digital technologies in economic sector of selected countries. In Ahmadi, A., Mna, A., & Slimani, A. (Eds.), *Renewable Energy and the Economic Welfare of Society* (pp. 335–370). IGI Global Scientific Publishing., DOI: 10.4018/979-8-3693-7580-8.ch015

Singh, A. K. (2025b). Causality of digitalization with social sustainability in selected countries. In Siyal, S. (Ed.), *Impact of Digitalization on Education and Social Sustainability* (pp. 39–78). IGI Global., DOI: 10.4018/979-8-3693-1854-6.ch002

Singh, A. K., & Ashraf, S. N. (2020). Association of entrepreneurship ecosystem with economic growth in selected countries: An empirical exploration. *Journal of Entrepreneurship. Business Economics (Cleveland, Ohio), 8*(2), 36–92. http://scientificia.com/index.php/JEBE/article/view/138

Singh, A. K., Ashraf, S. N., & Singh, S. (2024a). A policy direction from review of literature for determinants and problems of the start-up ecosystem in India. In Sharma, R., Mehta, K., & Yu, P. (Eds.), *Fostering Innovation in Venture Capital and Startup Ecosystems* (pp. 306–326). IGI Global., DOI: 10.4018/979-8-3693-1326-8.ch015

Singh, A. K., Gupta, M., & Kumar, S. (2025b). Empirical association of start-up ecosystems with economic development in different income countries. In Popescu, C. (Ed.), *Building Inclusive Global Knowledge Societies for Sustainable Development* (pp. 107–140). IGI Global Scientific Publishing., DOI: 10.4018/979-8-3693-6298-3.ch006

Singh, A. K., & Jyoti, B. (2023a). Empirical investigation for assessing the causality of entrepreneurship ecosystem with entrepreneurial behavior and attitudes across countries. In Abe, E., & Abe, I. (Eds.), *Cases on the Interplay Between Family, Society, and Entrepreneurship* (pp. 315–353). IGI Global., DOI: 10.4018/978-1-6684-8748-8.ch012

Singh, A. K., & Jyoti, B. (2023b). Does digitalization have a bi-directional causal relationship with the entrepreneurship ecosystem? Evidence from a country-wise panel data analysis. In Yanamandra, R., & Indiran, L. (Eds.), *Handbook of Research on Designing Sustainable Strategies to Develop Entrepreneurial Intention* (pp. 178–172). IGI Global., DOI: 10.4018/978-1-6684-8781-5.ch007

Singh, A. K., & Jyoti, B. (2023c). Empirical evidence from different income group countries on the interdependency between digitalization and economic development. In Patricia Ordóñez de Pablos and Xi Zhang (Eds.), 5G, Artificial Intelligence, and Next Generation Internet of Things: Digital Innovation for Green and Sustainable Economies, (pp. 44-85). IGI Global. DOI: DOI: 10.4018/978-1-6684-8634-4.ch003

Singh, A. K., Jyoti, B., & Mishra, V. K. (2023). Policy implications from selected countries for a sustainable future of the society through green entrepreneurship and economic development. In Mohammed El Amine, A., Ul-Durar, S., & Hattab, H. (Eds.), *Entrepreneurship Ecosystems and Their Opportunities and Challenges* (pp. 129–162). IGI Global., DOI: 10.4018/978-1-6684-7140-1.ch006

Singh, A. K., & Kumar, S. (2022). Factors influencing entrepreneurship ecosystem and economic development: Evidence from cross-sectional country-wise imbalanced panel data analysis. *The IUP Journal of Entrepreneurship Development*, *19*(3), 24–47.

Singh, A. K., Kumar, S., & Gupta, M. (2024e). Relationship between digitalization and environmental sustainability in selected countries. In Yıldırım, S., Yıldırım, D., Demirtaş, I., & Kandpal, V. (Eds.), *Green Transition Impacts on the Economy, Society, and Environment* (pp. 83–107). IGI Global., DOI: 10.4018/979-8-3693-3985-5.ch006

Singh, A. K., Singh, B., & Ashraf, S. N. (2020). Implications of intellectual property protection, and science and technological development in the manufacturing sector in selected economies. *Journal of Advocacy. Research in Education*, *7*(1), 16–35. https://oaji.net/articles/2021/1704-1615668997.pdf

Singh, A. K., Singh, R., & Singh, Richa (2024d). Impact of digitalization on sustainable development in G20 countries. In E. Ahmed (Ed.), *Developing Digital Inclusion Through Globalization and Digitalization* (pp. 287-335). IGI Global, International Academic Publisher, United States. DOI: 10.4018/979-8-3693-4111-7.ch013

Singh, A. K., & Singh, R. (2025). Digital infrastructure and sustainable development goals in G20 countries. In Popescu, C. (Ed.), *Building Inclusive Global Knowledge Societies for Sustainable Development* (pp. 363–408). IGI Global Scientific Publishing., DOI: 10.4018/979-8-3693-6298-3.ch014

Singh, A. K., Singh, S., & Gupta, M. (2024b). A literature review for the association of social media with micro and small enterprises in India. In Hossain, S. (Ed.), *Cases on Social Media and Entrepreneurship* (pp. 38–62). IGI Global., DOI: 10.4018/979-8-3693-1781-5.ch003

Singh, A. K., Singh, S., & Sharma, S. K. (2024c). Importance and challenges of online learning in higher educational institutions during COVID-19 in Uttarakhand State of India. In Hossain, S. (Ed.), *Cases on Social Media and Entrepreneurship* (pp. 193–212). IGI Global., DOI: 10.4018/979-8-3693-1781-5.ch012

Singh, A. K., Srinivasan, S., & Jyoti, B. (2025a). Implications of digitalization on public health sector across countries. In Wickramasinghe, N. (Ed.), *Digitalization and the Transformation of the Healthcare Sector* (pp. 359–394). IGI Global Scientific Publishing., DOI: 10.4018/979-8-3693-9641-4.ch013

Standing, C., & Mattsson, J. (2016). Fake it until you make it: Business model conceptualization in digital entrepreneurship. *Journal of Strategic Marketing*, *26*(5), 385–399. DOI: 10.1080/0965254X.2016.1240218

Sunita, S., & Srija, A. (2016). *Entrepreneurship development in India- the focus on start-ups*. Laghu Udyog Samachar. http://164.100.94.191/niti/writereaddata/files/document_publication/MSME%20January%202016_0.pdf

Tandon, A., Gupta, A., Goel, P., & Singh, V. K. (2020). Impact of digitalization on entrepreneurial ecosystems: An Indian perspective. *International Journal of Business and Globalisation*, *25*(2), 154–169. DOI: 10.1504/IJBG.2020.107887

Thornton, G. (2018). *Startups India- an Overview*. Global Assets. https://data.worldbank.org/indicator/IT.NET.USER.ZS?locations=1W-IN

Wibisono, E. (2023). The digital entrepreneurial ecosystem in the European Union: Evidence from the digital platform economy index. *European Planning Studies*, *31*(6), 1270–1292. DOI: 10.1080/09654313.2023.2202683

KEY TERMS AND DEFINITIONS

Entrepreneurial Activities: These includes training and skills programs that motivate people to start new business.

Entrepreneurship Ecosystem: It is a set of activities that lead to increased business opportunities for the people.

Digital Technologies (DTs): DTs help to create an online platform for achieving different tasks of people.

Digital Entrepreneurship: It includes the trading of goods and services through online or digital platform.

Innovation: It is helpful for the organizations, businessmen and entrepreneurs to develop new products.

Chapter 3
Assessing e-Government Services for Sustainable Rural Entrepreneurship in Tanzania

James Morrice Maghori
https://orcid.org/0009-0002-6491-3952
The Institute of Rural Development Planning, Tanzania

Galinoma Gahele Lubawa
https://orcid.org/0000-0001-9198-4495
The Institute of Rural Development Planning, Tanzania

ABSTRACT

Tanzania's economic progress and efforts to reduce poverty require sustainable rural entrepreneurship. However, the accessibility of critical information technology resources is still a significant obstacle. Although rural entrepreneurs can benefit from e-government services, the existing studies have failed to consider their experiences and challenges. Therefore, to address this gap, this chapter assesses the role of e-government services in encouraging rural entrepreneurship in Tanzania. Semi-structured interviews were conducted in 2024 with fifteen rural entrepreneurs using a qualitative methodology based on the Technology Acceptance Model (TAM). While e-government services can improve business operations and compliance, the study highlights that barriers to digital literacy and connectivity are still present. This research demonstrates the pressing need for measures that will enhance access and functionality of e-government while also increasing rural economic development through sustainable entrepreneurship.

DOI: 10.4018/979-8-3373-5087-5.ch003

INTRODUCTION

Sustainable rural entrepreneurship has a valuable contribution to promoting economic development and reducing poverty in developing countries, including Tanzania (Adenutsi, 2023; Majenga et al.,2024; Manzoor et al., 2021). This study defines sustainable rural entrepreneurship as creating and managing business activities that promote economic growth while promoting social inclusion and resilience to challenges. This definition emphasises the previous experience of entrepreneurs, their competence, and family and government support (e.g. the provision of electronic services) as building stones of business sustainability and contributing to the country's economy (Barth and Zalkat, 2021). Despite the broad scope of its importance, rural sustainable entrepreneurship is still affected by several challenges, such as limited access to resources, financial factors, poor infrastructure, production factors (labour and capital) and limited integration with formal economic systems (Alassaf et al., 2020; Stewart, 2022; Odeyemi et al., 2024). One of the solutions to overcome obstacles is through electronic government(e-government) services, which can facilitate access to essential government functions like tax registration and online payment (Ishengoma & Shao, 2025). However, the extent to which rural entrepreneurs use and benefit from e-government services has yet to be explored, making this an important area of research. This chapter assesses the effects of e-government services on sustainable rural entrepreneurship in Tanzania, using a qualitative approach to identify benefits and obstacles for improving e-government service delivery.

Electronic government, also referred to as "e-government," has multiple definitions that reflect its diverse nature. According to Gordon (2002), e-government is the utilisation of ICTs such as blockchains, robotics and the Internet of Things to enhance government processes, as well as artificial intelligence and Big Data. It is also defined by Yildiz (2016) as "the electronic communication between the governments, their clients (*including businesses, other government entities, and citizens*) and suppliers". Thus, the definition of e-government emphasises the importance of ICTs in enhancing public service delivery, strengthening governance, and encouraging communication between government and stakeholders (Sagarik, 2023). According to the Tanzania E-Government Act 10 of 2019, e-government means the government uses or applies information and communication technology to provide public services. Thus, this chapter adopts this definition (United Republic of Tanzania-URT, 2019). This Tanzanian law also defined "*e-government services*" as all services provided electronically by public institutions (URT, 2019).

Globally, e-government projects have become increasingly significant as methods for fostering socioeconomic development, improving public service quality, availability of services 24/7 and accountability (Hans & Rutenge, 2024; Ishengoma &

Shao, 2025; United Nations, 2024). Such initiatives, which are particularly relevant in rural areas (Hans & Rutenge, 2024; Omweri, 2024), address issues such as isolation, inadequate infrastructure and technology, and limited access to services and information. Even with these efforts, however, about 1.9 billion people are still at the mercy of the digital divide, and the most significant gaps are located in regions such as Africa and Oceania (United Nations, 2024). The use of information and communication technologies (e.g. e-government) can help rural communities and public administration become more connected, resulting in inclusive and equitable access to essential services that can be provided through e-government (Dhaoui, 2019; United Nations, 2020).

Tanzania has made several initiatives to achieve progress in the use of e-government. The Tanzania e-Government Strategy 2022 (URT, 2022), the National ICT Policy (2016), and the Financial Sector Development Plan (2020–2029/30) are just a few of the e-government initiatives that the government has prioritised to enhance service delivery. Such initiatives seek to solve ICT-related issues across the country, such as increased ICT capability, encouragement of cost-effective delivery methods, and demand-driven financial products. However, existing studies on e-government services in Tanzania have mainly focused on perspectives from government agencies and urban stakeholders, which may differ from those of rural stakeholders (Hans & Rutenge, 2024; Mushi, 2024). Therefore, Tanzania's rural areas continue to receive little attention, highlighting the need for specific study into their potentials, problems and the intersection of e-governance (Lubis et al., 2024; Lubawa & Kandpal, 2024). It is, therefore, essential to assess the effects of e-government services in rural areas where 65.6% of Tanzania's population lives (URT, 2024).

Through semi-structured interviews and qualitative research design, the study examined the effects of e-government services on sustainable rural entrepreneurship in Tanzania. The Technology Acceptance Model guided the study. The study's findings hold the potential to promote further e-government adoption, not only in Tanzania but also in other emerging economies.

E-government Initiatives in Tanzania

Since the government of Tanzania started using the e-government, several improvements have been made to increase its efficiency and reach more users to get better services. The journey began with the adoption of the National IT Policy in 2003, revised in 2016, which laid the foundation for integrating ITC into government operations. Thus, to enhance the effectiveness of online service delivery, the Tanzania government established the e-Government Agency (eGA) in 2012 to coordinate online projects and subsequently developed an e-Government Strategy in 2016, which was also reviewed in 2022, aiming to digitise public services and improve citizen access (URT, 2022). The Government Electronic Payment Gateway(GePG) is an example of an e-government service that has been used to collect payments. The GePG System has made it simpler for all parties involved to pay for public services (Hans & Rutenge, 2024; Sausi et al., 2021). Public institutions can also use it to create invoices and track income reports. This GePG system has strengthened government revenue collection, reduced revenue loss, improved government financial control, and has succeeded in satisfying users with its effectiveness (Sausi et al., 2021).

Although the use of e-government in Tanzania has contributed to improving communication between the government and citizens as well as achieving the delivery of public services more efficiently (Hans & Rutenge, 2024; Ishengoma & Shao, 2025), other studies showed that the way people think it is easy to use e-government systems does not affect their openness or willingness to use those systems (Mushi, 2024). Thus, the easy-to-use e-government systems do not make the systems more transparent or encourage individuals to use the systems. Therefore, improving trust, participation, and transparency may be more important than ease of use in increasing people's willingness to adopt e-government systems.

Tanzania's journey to enhance e-government services continued, as evidenced by the score of 0.4054 available from the E-Government Development Index (EGDI), which is still lower than the global average of 0.6102[1]. The EGDI uses three components to measure e-government progress, namely, the Human Capital Index, the Telecommunication Infrastructure Index, and the Online Service Index[2]. Additionally, Tanzania has dropped from its 2022 ranking of 128th to 137th out of 193 UN member states with an E-Participation Index (EPI) score of 0.2877[3]. These findings highlight Tanzania's ongoing struggles to improve its digital government infrastructure and better engage its populace. Although Tanzania is showing progress in e-government services, however, significant gaps remain, especially in rural areas with limited digital access (TCRA, 2023; Mushi et al., 2024). With a low EGDI and a drop in the EPI, this study assumes that rural entrepreneurs may face challenges in accessing online government services and engaging with digital platforms. Issues such as poor internet infrastructure, low digital literacy, and limited opportunities for rural communities to interact with government initiatives may hinder progress (TCRA, 2023).

THEORETICAL ANALYSIS

This qualitative study examines the Tanzanian rural entrepreneurs' experiences with using e-government services by focusing on the benefits and challenges they face to attain sustainable entrepreneurship. Studies recognised e-government initiatives for reducing transaction costs, enhancing transparency for citizens and businesses, offering continuous access, enhancing accountability, and ensuring 24/7 service availability (Ishengoma & Shao, 2025; Lyulyov et al., 2024). Davis's Technology Acceptance Model (TAM) (1989) has been used as the foundation of this study. The TAM posits that the behaviour, as the outcome, predicted by perceived ease of use and perceived usefulness collectively predict an individual's actual system use (Davis, 1989).

Mooya and Phiri (2021) suggest that attitudes toward technology are shaped by learning and experience, with education enhancing perceptions of ease of use and benefits. Thus, this study posits that rural entrepreneurs can learn technology from experienced colleagues if the systems are user-friendly and they are willing to learn (Kelly & Palaniappan, 2023; Sheppard & Vibert, 2019). Therefore, due to its effectiveness in evaluating the adoption of technology, the TAM is used in this study (Ilyas et al., 2023; Wilson et al., 2020). E-government, therefore, can reduce operational costs for rural entrepreneurs by saving time otherwise spent visiting government offices and dealing with queues. Hence, it is essential to comprehend how technology improves productivity, financial performance, income, and resource efficiency by making use of it (Anum et al., 2024; Parente, 2020). While rural businesses face challenges, the availability of e-government services can foster sustainable rural entrepreneurship. A theoretical analysis is depicted in Figure 1.

Figure 1. Theoretical Analysis

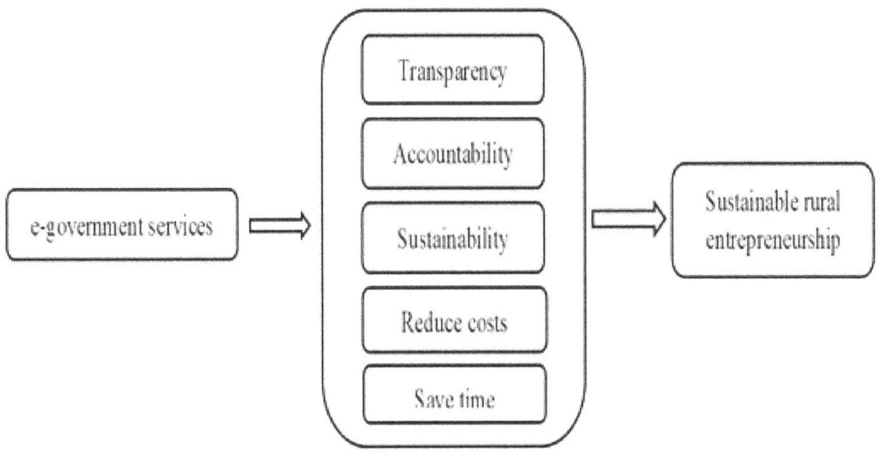

Source: Figure by authors

E-government and sustainable rural business practices

In the digital world, e-government has been used as a strategic tool that increases management efficiency and public participation to promote sustainable business practices (Cassaro et al., 2024; Dhaoui, 2022). It has been suggested that e-government programs contribute significantly to economic development, especially in rural areas, by simplifying processes, reducing bureaucratic obstacles and thus, enhancing access to resources and information for local businesses (Lubis et al., 2024; Kiviaho & Einolander, 2023). E-government has also improved public services and government accountability as essential indicators of governance effectiveness (Ishengoma & Shao, 2025; Sagarik, 2023). The introduction of online business registration platforms has simplified bureaucratic procedures, fostering entrepreneurship, economic growth and innovation (Cassaro et al.,2024). Beyond the service delivery improvements, e-governance has promoted inclusivity, enabling greater public participation in development processes (Castro & Lopes, 2022).

Additionally, it is acknowledged that e-government is a driving force behind the attainment of the Sustainable Development Goals (SDGs), specifically in the areas of poverty alleviation (SDG 1), institutional transparency (SDG 16), and inequality reduction (SDG 10). E-government has also enabled rural communities to be involved in the decision-making process that affects their lives by promoting participatory governance (Pougel et al., 2018). To maximise their influence on sustainable rural business practices, however, issues like the digital divide and disparities in technology use need to be resolved (Dhaoui, 2022). Ensuring accessibility, user-friendly technology, and productivity-enhancing tools (with tangible benefits) are essential to long-term success, which drives sustainable development in rural areas.

STUDY DESIGN, DATA COLLECTION AND ANALYTICAL APPROACH

In-depth interviews with rural entrepreneurs from Tanzania's diverse rural locations were engaged in this qualitative study from October to December 2024 by visiting them at their business premises. The qualitative approach was used since it typically explores people's thoughts and feelings, or at least what they say about them, to gain an understanding of their reality (Lubawa and Osabuohien, 2024). Since most literature on e-government usage by entrepreneurs focuses on urban areas, a qualitative approach is deemed suitable as a starting point for rural studies (Coombs et al., 2022). Therefore, to gather sufficient qualitative data, this qualitative study ensured that the day chosen for the interview considered the availability of the respondents to give them enough time to connect with the interviewer and answer the questions competently (Rutledge et al., 2020). (Rutledge et al., 2020).

Semi-structured interviews were used to collect information after developing an interview outline with a thematic approach (Monda et al., 2023; Lubawa and Osabuohien, 2024). Each interview lasted between forty and fifty-five minutes. In reaching a sample of 15 qualified respondents, the study employed purposive sampling to select rural entrepreneurs who participated voluntarily after being informed of the clear objectives of the research and understanding them. These respondents were chosen due to their knowledge of e-government services in Tanzania and having operated businesses in rural environments for at least five years. The sample size of 15 respondents was reached after determining that the volume of information was sufficient to answer the research questions (Hennink et al., 2019; Gill, 2020).

Following more than three times listening to the audio recording, the data was subjected to qualitative conventional content analysis. This method entails identifying and comprehending patterns or themes in the data without the pre-existing categories of patterns, themes or theories (Lubawa and Osabuohien, 2024). Thereafter, it followed the scientific steps of conventional content analysis: after the entire script of the collected data is made from the reordered data, the first step is to read all the data to get a general understanding, similar to reading a novel. Subsequently, a second and third reading were conducted, scrutinising every word to identify distinctive codes. A final, iterative reading was then carried out. During this time, notes were examined to record first impressions, ideas, and preliminary assessments. The discovered codes were then labelled as found, and themes were produced (Lubawa & Osabuohien, 2024).

RESULTS AND DISCUSSION

Respondents' Profile

Table 1 presents the characteristics of 15 rural entrepreneurs who voluntarily participated in the interviews. These characteristics include age, gender, level of education, business activities, and years of experience. Understanding these characteristics has ensured data collection was done from the intended respondents. The study findings show that both genders, male and female, use technology in Tanzania's rural environment. Although a gender gap exists in technology usage (Mwaseba et al. 2025), this study suggests that e-government adoption is not inherently restricted by gender. Historically, rural women's responsibilities were limited to domestic work such as fetching water, collecting firewood and cooking for the family. This study, however, shows that women are actively involved in various business activities, such as selling forest products, running retail shops, and managing small food processing businesses(e.g., sunflower oil processing and grains mills). With these results, one can say that Tanzania's use of digital tools for all genders supports economic empowerment and gender equality in rural Tanzania, aligning with SDG-5(Gender Equality) and SDG-8(Decent Work and Economic Growth).

The findings also show that the respondents are 33 to 62 years old and are actively engaged in rural entrepreneurship at various stages of life. This age range suggests that middle-aged and older adults contribute significantly to the rural economy. Their entrepreneurship generates personal income, drives rural economic growth, and enhances the availability of goods and services in rural areas. Thus, e-government service is vital for this age to strengthen their entrepreneurship. Furthermore, the information indicates that most respondents have completed secondary education, showing the importance of formal education in providing rural entrepreneurs with the necessary business skills. The existence of entrepreneurs with a university education shows that higher education is increasingly essential for rural businesses, unlike the perception that those with higher education like to seek opportunities only in cities. Along with sufficient education, entrepreneurs also have adequate business experience between 5 to 26 years. This experience helps them to understand the challenges and opportunities of e-government.

Table 1. Profile of rural entrepreneurs in Tanzania

Respondent	Business activity	Gender	Age	Education level	business experience (Years)
1	Money agency business (M-Pesa, Halo-Pesa, Airtel money)	Male	38	University	5
2	Selling forest products	Female	35	Secondary education	8
3	Wine Processing Factory	Male	62	Secondary education	24
4	Grain milling	Female	48	Secondary education	16
5	Small-Scale Bread Bakery	Female	47	Secondary education	18
6	Small rice mill owner	Male	50	Secondary education	26
7	Maise Flour Milling Factory	Male	54	Secondary education	22
8	Retail Shop	Female	33	Secondary education	7

continued on following page

Table 1. Continued

Respondent	Business activity	Gender	Age	Education level	business experience (Years)
9	Furniture and Aluminum Products Factory	Male	42	Secondary education	12
9	Home Utensils Shop (e.g., cups, plates, spoons, etc.)	Female	36	Secondary education	10
10	Grain Storage Warehouse (e.g., rice, maise, beans, peanuts)	Male	52	Secondary education	18
11	Sunflower Oil Processing Factory	Male	39	Secondary education	12
12	Wholesale Liquor Shop	Male	49	Secondary education	12
13	Building materials store	Male	46	Secondary education	9
14	Maise Flour Milling Factory	Male	48	Secondary education	16
15	Microfinance	Male	55	University	10

Source: The Authors'

Rural entrepreneurs' perspectives on e-Government

This chapter has used a thematic analysis approach (Braun and Clarke (2006) to create a thematic map that includes quotation extracts, code sets, and final themes. The analysis led to the identification of seven main themes: e-readiness, efficiency and ease of digital platforms in business activities, ways to access e-government services, digital transformation of business processes in rural areas, and accessibility barriers to digital use, improving accessibility and usability and building capacity and support (Table 2).

Table 2. Extracted quotations, coding, and themes from responses to e-government questions

Extracted quotation	Coding	Theme
• I have been using tax registration services (e.g. filing returns, access to the Tanzania Revenue Authority (TRA) tax information, utility payments, and registering businesses) and applying for business licenses from our district council. • As an entrepreneur, I have used services such as business registration and the Tax Information website of the Tanzania Revenue Authority (TRA) to simplify my operations and ensure compliance with government tax procedures. • I used the TAUSI website to register my sunflower oil processing plant. The platform provided a clear step-by-step guide that facilitated the registration process and payment of the service levy efficiently. • I used an online payment platform linked to the local government website for business license and service tax payments.	• Access to tax and licensing services. • Business registration, tax services, online payment. • Access to e-Government Services (Types of e-government services available). • Availability of service, though there is an internet challenge • Evidence of E-Government Utilization Among Rural Entrepreneurs in Tanzania. • Online tax registration, filing, and payment services. • The list of online e-government services available for entrepreneurs in Tanzania: *(i) Business registration.* *(ii) Tax registration and filing returns* *(iii) Service levy payments.* *(iv) Business license renewal.* *(v) Access to the Tanzania Revenue Authority (TRA) tax information.* *(vi) Online payment of various government fees.*	Utilisation of E-Government services for business operations and compliance (e-Preparedness)

continued on following page

Table 2. Continued

Extracted quotation	Coding	Theme
• The portal enabled me to calculate and pay service tax directly from my village while here at my business, thus eliminating the need for travel. This significantly reduced my time consumption and travel-related costs. • In fact, this online government service has made it easier to register my business and submit taxes. • I can say with certainty that online government services have made it easier to register my business and file taxes, thus saving me time. • The most important thing is to know the legal requirements, procedures, and tax rates, especially from TRA. • I was able to renew my business license online without having to wait in long queues. • E-government has helped me register my business officially and understand my tax obligations. • E-government makes it easier for businesses to register and pay taxes. For example, instead of filling out a lot of paperwork and visiting many offices, you can now register your business online and pay taxes using the phone.	• Easier registration; tax filing • Efficiency and Cost Savings through E-Government • Benefits of e-Government Services • Time-saving benefits • Online renewal; time-saving. • Efficiency Gains from e-Government Services. • Benefits of Online Services • Streamlined processes. • Efficiency in operations.	Efficiency and convenience of digital platforms in business operations.
• I primarily use my smartphone and occasionally visit an internet café. • Using my smartphone, I was able to access the website of the Business Registration and Licensing Agency (BRELA). The phone has also enabled me to pay for the business license online instead of physically going to the city council. • Given the nature of my grain processing business, having a Smartphone was essential for searching for markets online. When it came to using e-government services, I continued to utilise my phone for tasks like paying service levies and renewing business licenses. Furthermore, I have a computer and laptop for business use.	• Smartphone usage: internet café, mobile phones • Access to e-government platforms. • Digital transformation of business processes. • Smartphone, computer/ laptop.	• Channels for Accessing e-Government Services. • Digital transformation of business processes in rural areas.

continued on following page

Table 2. Continued

Extracted quotation	Coding	Theme
• It's difficult because I struggle with the language, and I don't have enough knowledge of using digital tools. • I face delays in registering documents and meeting regulations because I don't have the digital tools or skills needed to apply. • I often need help from someone knowledgeable to fill in the information, which sometimes causes delays. • The lack of local language options can be unhelpful for some users. • The main barriers are poor internet connectivity, language, and limited skills. • My experience has been mixed; while I can access some services online, connectivity issues often hinder my ability to use them effectively. • Poor internet connection and hard-to-use platforms are challenges. • Connectivity issues often hinder my ability to use e-government services effectively.	• Language barriers, digital literacy. • Delays in registration • Digital Skills Barriers • Language barriers • Barriers to e-government Access. • Language barriers • Barriers (connectivity, language, skills) • Platform usability challenges • Mixed experience; connectivity issues. • Impact of Barriers on Business Operations.	• Barriers to digital accessibility (barriers to e-Government Use)

continued on following page

Table 2. Continued

Extracted quotation	Coding	Theme
• I suggest providing training sessions on using e-government services. • The online registration feature is helpful, but it lacks local language support. • The online registration feature is helpful, but the website's design could be more user-friendly. • Increasing accessibility, improving website usability, and offering services in Kiswahili[4] would help. • The government could create local help centres (Help desks, support). • Improving internet infrastructure and providing digital literacy training in the community would help. • Training on digital skills and services in Kiswahili would make the e-government service provisional more effective. • I think the platform would be easier to use if it was easier to navigate. Also, having more material in Kiswahili would help a lot of people like me. • Improving internet infrastructure and providing digital literacy training would significantly help. • The government could establish mobile service units to assist rural entrepreneurs. • The government should enhance internet connectivity and provide training on these platforms. • E-government services have a positive impact but need better accessibility and usability. • Saving time by getting online services has given me more time to focus on my business and expand my activities.	• Digital skills training • Language barriers • Usability issues • Accessibility and usability • Support infrastructure • Internet infrastructure, Digital literacy • Training, Language support • Platform usability, Language support • Internet infrastructure, Digital literacy • Mobile service units • Connectivity, Digital skills • Service impact and accessibility. • Time-saving benefits	• Improving Accessibility and Usability *(Perceived Ease of Use)* • Capacity Building and Support.

E-preparedness

The study confirms the use of e-government for rural entrepreneurs to access government services online for business registration, tax filing, and license renewal. These results dispel the notion that the use of e-government is in urban rather than rural areas. Therefore, it shows the readiness of rural entrepreneurs to use the e-government system (*e-preparedness*). Rural entrepreneurs have been getting various services related to e-government from different public institutions such as the Tanzania Revenue Authority (TRA), BRELA and local government portal (e.g. TAUSI), which simplify compliance processes and promote formalisation of business operations. This trend highlights the vital role of digital government initiatives in reducing bureaucratic obstacles and improving access to essential services (Thomas et al., 2015), in line with SDG-8 (Dignified Work and Economic Growth) and SDG-9 (Industry, Innovation, and Infrastructure). During the interview, one of the respondents said,

> *... when it came time to renew the license and get a new tax estimate, I received instructions from the government authorities that these services are now available online. So, using my phone, I joined and applied for a new license and paid the estimated tax. I also received a new permit online (he shows the image of the license on his mobile phone). I was happy because it saved my time doing business. Previously, I would have had to travel to the district council and the TRA office in town to queue up to get the same services.*

The acceptance of e-government by Tanzanian rural entrepreneurs may be influenced by demographic factors such as age, income and education (Magomana & Maireva, 2021; Nyagango et al., 2023), which contribute to understanding the importance of e-government for their business sustainability. These results confirm the growing use of technology for rural entrepreneurs in Tanzania to access government services. This trend aligns with global discussions on the significance of e-government in encouraging compliance and operational efficiency (United Nations, 2024; Xie et al., 2022).

Efficiency and convenience of digital platforms in business operations

The results have shown the benefits of e-government for rural entrepreneurs, which include saving time and costs in paying taxes, renewing licenses and avoiding disruptions to business operations. These results confirm that e-government has saved time for rural entrepreneurs by eliminating the need to travel many kilometres to access financial services. However, this research used a qualitative method with a small sample of rural entrepreneurs. Therefore, it is still likely to get rural entrepreneurs who can walk more than five kilometres to reach financial services (FinScope Tanzania, 2023). The results support the perceived importance of e-government systems from the TAM perspective by indicating the potential for increased efficiency and convenience for users (Davis, 1989; Ishengoma, 2024). One of the rural entrepreneurs shared this information during the interview;

> *... before adopting e-government services, I had to temporarily close my business to visit the local council and renew my license. The process was entirely manual, and the high volume of applications meant it took several days to obtain a new license. This lengthy process consumed valuable time that could have been used to focus on the business and increase productivity.*

The quotes above demonstrate the advantages users gain from utilising e-government services to enhance business efficiency and compliance. Additionally, the quoted passages indicate common sense regarding the TAM model's perceived effectiveness. Therefore, online services facilitate the efficiency of service delivery and ensure business continuity (Wahed and Ismail, 2022; Yang et al., 2024). Thus, e-government systems provide convenient and cost-effective solutions that cater to rural entrepreneurs' needs while improving government performance.

Channels for accessing e-government services

Regarding the digital tool types used to access e-government services, the findings show that rural entrepreneurs mainly use smartphones, computers, and laptops. This reliance is because these digital tools are widely available in Tanzania at affordable prices (Ishengoma & John, 2024). According to the report "*Communications Statistics Quarterly for the Year Ending June 2024*, Version 1.1" (TCRA, 2024), the use of mobile phones for online financial transactions has increased significantly among Tanzanians in recent years, indicating increasing adoption of technology. The report states that mobile money subscriptions reached 56 million accounts by June 2024 (TCRA, 2024), indicating increasing adoption of digital finance among Tanzanians. Therefore, the outcomes suggest that the availability of smartphones (and other digital tools) in rural areas has made it easier for entrepreneurs to access e-government and improve their compliance with regulations while simplifying their business operations. The study's outcomes underscore the crucial role of low-cost digital tools in enhancing rural entrepreneurs' access to e-government in Tanzania, leading to compliance and operational efficiency through the increased use of digital finance. One of the respondents shared this information during the interview.

> *... "I use my smartphone, but I also have a laptop here in my office, as you can see..." (pointing to the laptop on the office desk).*

Digital transformation of rural business models

Although this study focused on e-government services, it also revealed that rural entrepreneurs are undergoing digital transformation in their business processes. In the past, they bought smartphones to access e-government services more efficiently. However, they discovered additional benefits such as simplified business processes, including storing market and financial information from banks and facilitating the application of digital platforms like M-KOBA[5]. This development shows that technological development contributes to economic growth and rural development. One of the respondents shared the following information during the interview:

In my grain processing business (corn flour, rice), owning a smartphone is essential to find markets outside our village. The phone also helps to manage my young workers if I am away, or rather to manage the factory operations in general. This device is used as a database to store customer communications and facilitate communication with crop farmers to monitor price trends. Mobile phones are essential in transforming business models by engaging in customer-supplier interactions, providing market access, and supporting daily operations. Smartphones are the engine that drives business.

Therefore, one can argue that rural entrepreneurs in Tanzania have successfully implemented a simple business model to seize technological opportunities to sustain their business (Shepherd et al., 2024).

Barriers to e-government services

Although e-government in Tanzania has been successfully implemented, the study has identified some problems. The problems that plague rural entrepreneurs are poor internet connectivity, language barriers and low digital literacy. These findings align with the Tanzania Communications Regulatory Authority (TCRA) report that states limited connectivity hinders rural enterprises from effectively using e-government services (TCRA, 2023). In a developing nation like Tanzania, where communication infrastructure is still proving problematic, digital challenges are bound to arise (Mwantimwa, 2019). The 2023 report by the Tanzania Communications Regulatory Authority highlights that mobile service providers, including Airtel, Viettel, MIC, Tigo, Zantel and TTCL, continue to face infrastructural issues that lead to internet connectivity outages. A village entrepreneur who owns a grain mill said the following;

...for the environment of our village, sometimes the internet is not very reliable, and you cannot send any requests until it is improved. Moreover, technical language is often difficult to understand. So... it would be better if e-government services were available in simple Kiswahili, the national language and widely understood.

It is suggested that the e-government implementation has faced various obstacles, including limited ICT skills, incomplete infrastructure, and a digital divide between the rural poor and the emerging urban middle class (Mohale, 2024; Mwaseba et al. 2025; Rarhoui, 2024). Other challenges include the lack of access to the internet, electricity, or computers (Rangarirai Matavire, 2010; Samsor, 2021). However, the identified problems have helped other countries improve e-government systems to make the government more efficient and provide better quality services. Enhanced services and reliability of the e-government system will result in better user satisfaction and system usage growth (Sausi et al., 2021; Owusu et al., 2022).

Therefore, the problems highlighted in this study call for action to overcome these hindrances so that rural entrepreneurs in Tanzania can get the quality services that e-government s can provide.

Improving accessibility and usability

Rural entrepreneurs have suggested that they need simple systems, better internet infrastructure and content in local languages like "*Kiswahili*". Accessibility can be made easier by utilising simplified navigation and responsive support services. One of the rural business owner's responses has been captured as follows:

> *..."I suggest providing training sessions on using e-government services," and "the platform would be easier to use if it was easier to navigate and offered more material in Kiswahili."*

Therefore, rural entrepreneurs have been advised to consider the importance of convenience, language support, and usability in improving user experience and encouraging the adoption of e-government services. These results are consistent with the concept of ease of use (PEoU) of the TAM model, emphasising the use of Kiswahili as a mother tongue improves and facilitates understanding for users of the e-government system, increases user satisfaction, and promotes confidence in accessing services from the e-government (Hooda et al., 2023; Sausi et al.,2021). To effectively reach rural entrepreneurs, e-government systems should prioritise local content, perceived ease of use (PEoU), context, personal initiatives, trust, infrastructure, affordability, mobility, compatibility, and observability since these are key drivers of technology adoption in Tanzania (Ishengoma and John, 2024). Although accessibility can improve user satisfaction and adoption in rural areas (Sausi et al., 2021), other scholars, such as Mushi (2024), caution that ease of use alone does not guarantee transparency or increase willingness to use e-government systems. Even simple systems require governments to prioritise accountability, transparent reporting, and consumer benefits to enhance transparency and utility.

Therefore, rural entrepreneurs in Tanzania have emphasised the importance of convenience, language support, and usability in adopting e-government services. Aligning with the TAM model, studies suggest that Kiswahili should enhance user experience, satisfaction, and confidence (Hooda et al., 2023; Sausi et al., 2021). Effective communication should also prioritise local content and ease of use (Ishengoma & John, 2024). While accessibility improves adoption (Sausi et al., 2021), Mushi (2024) cautions that transparency and willingness to use digital services depend on more than ease of use.

Capacity building and support

The study reveals that rural entrepreneurs in Tanzania need help adapting to and succeeding in the e-government age. Although descriptive analysis indicates that rural entrepreneurs have access to secondary education, which meets the fundamental requirement for understanding the e-government system, practical training is still essential. Technological systems, such as artificial intelligence(AI), are not yet integrated into the formal education curriculum in Tanzania. For example, in terms of secondary education, which is fundamental for everyone, the country is facing a shortage of resources, especially in technology equipment and qualified teachers in the field of technology (Hamoud & Nzilano, 2024). Accordingly, most people in Tanzania learn to use technology informally through life experiences and after school. Thus, addressing the digital skills gap among rural entrepreneurs through practical training programs can enhance technology adoption, as they currently lack such training (Majenga et al., 2024). One of the rural entrepreneur's responses to e-government is:

> *... I learnt to use e-government services through the help of my fellow entrepreneurs, as at first, I struggled to understand the necessary steps and how to complete them. I advise the government to provide education on these systems, especially for users like us who are not familiar with them and are still new to technology. We do not study e-government in secondary school. As TRA provides education to taxpayers, the government should also provide education on e-government to help us.*

It is suggested that practical training programs can close knowledge gaps and increase digital confidence among rural entrepreneurs, thus promoting entrepreneurship in rural environments (Magomana & Maireva, 2021). Likewise, research shows that educating entrepreneurs improves their ability to adhere to government regulations; for example, tax education increases compliance with tax laws among Tanzanian SMEs (Abjadi et al., 2023). In addition, implementing community-based training and support services via mobile phones can alleviate isolation and foster connections to online communities (Ismail, 2023).

CONCLUSION

This study examined the effects of e-government services on sustainable rural entrepreneurship in Tanzania, highlighting successes, challenges, and recommendations for improving the delivery of digital services. The results show that e-government increases business operations, compliance, efficiency and digital transformation. However, the study revealed the presence of barriers to the use of e-government, including language barriers, limited digital skills and access to services. Therefore, to address these issues, research recommendations include expanding internet access, providing digital literacy training, and providing capacity-building programs. Additionally, smartphones, computers and laptops are valuable tools for accessing government services online.

Thus, to strengthen the access of rural entrepreneurs to e-government services, this study suggests several measures to be implemented. First, governments must improve the accessibility of the system by providing content in the mother tongue, which is Kiswahili. Second, it is recommended that there be practical programs, including digital skills training, to equip rural entrepreneurs with the necessary skills in e-government. The third recommendation is for the government to strengthen the internet infrastructure in rural areas to provide reliable digital services. Finally, the study recommends strengthening Tanzania's National IT Policy and e-Government Strategy to establish sustainable e-government initiatives for rural areas. These initiatives will foster rural entrepreneurship, enhance public service delivery, and improve compliance with government regulations (Rwabunywenge et al., 2024).

REFERENCES

Abjadi, A. I., Wiketye, E. J., & Mpogole, H. (2023). Factors Contributing to Tax Compliance among Small and Medium Sized Enterprises: A Case of Selected SMEs in Iringa Municipality. *International Journal of Finance and Accounting*, *2*(1), 94–105. DOI: 10.37284/ijfa.2.1.1559

Adenutsi, D. (2023). Entrepreneurship, Job Creation, Income Empowerment and Poverty Reduction in Low-Income Economies. *Theoretical Economics Letters*, *13*(6), 1579–1598. DOI: 10.4236/tel.2023.136089

Alassaf, P., Zaien, S., & Oláh, J. (2020). Factors affecting e-government implementation developing countries e-opportunities. *Acta Oeconomica Universitatis Selye*, *9*(1), 7–23. DOI: 10.36007/Acta.2020.9.1.1

Anum, N., Fatima, N., Ifrah, N., Lyba, N., & Sajjad, J. (2024). Leveraging digitalisation and servitisation to improve Financial Performance: An Empirical analysis. *Journal of Policy Research*, *10*(2), 75–89. DOI: 10.61506/02.00209

Barth, H., & Zalkat, G. (2021). Refugee entrepreneurship in the agri-food industry: The Swedish experience. *Journal of Rural Studies*, *86*, 189–197. DOI: 10.1016/j.jrurstud.2021.06.011

Braun, V., & Clarke, V. (2006). Using thematic analysis in psychology. *Qualitative Research in Psychology*, *3*(2), 77–101. DOI: 10.1191/1478088706qp063oa

Cassaro, E., Oro, I. M., Begnini, S., & Georges, M. R. R. (2024). The influence of digital transformation and implementation barriers on innovation in Brazilian micro, small, and medium enterprises. *Small Business International Review*, *8*(2), e660. DOI: 10.26784/sbir.v8i2.660

Castro, C., & Lopes, C. (2022). Digital government and sustainable development. *Journal of the Knowledge Economy*, *13*(2), 880–903. DOI: 10.1007/s13132-021-00749-2

Coombs, N. C., Campbell, D. G., & Caringi, J. (2022). A qualitative study of rural healthcare providers' views of social, cultural, and programmatic barriers to healthcare access. *BMC Health Services Research*, *22*(1), 438. Advance online publication. DOI: 10.1186/s12913-022-07829-2 PMID: 35366860

Davis, F. D. (1989). Perceived usefulness, perceived ease of use, and user acceptance of information technology. *Management Information Systems Quarterly*, *13*(3), 319–340. DOI: 10.2307/249008

Dhaoui, I. (2019). Good governance for sustainable development. MPRA Paper No. 92544.UN (2020) The Impact of COVID-19 on the Arab Region: An Opportunity to Build Back Better. *Policy Brief.*

Dhaoui, I. (2022). E-Government for Sustainable Development: Evidence from MENA Countries. *Journal of the Knowledge Economy*, *13*(3), 2070–2099. DOI: 10.1007/s13132-021-00791-0

FinScope Tanzania. (2023). *FinScope Tanzania: Insights that drive innovation.* Financial Sector Deepening Tanzania. Retrieved January 12, 2025, from https://www.fsdt.or.tz/finscope/

Gill, S. (2020). Qualitative Sampling Methods. *Journal of Human Lactation*, *36*(4), 579–581. DOI: 10.1177/0890334420949218 PMID: 32813616

Gordon, F.T. (2002). E-government-introduction. ERCIM News 48.

Hamoud, S. S., & Nzilano, J. L. (2024). Exploring Science Teachers' Beliefs and Practices of ICT integration in secondary school teaching: A Mixed Method approach. *University of Dar es Salaam Library Journal*; https://journals.udsm.ac.tz/index.php/lj/article/view/6584

Hans, N., & Rutenge, M. M. (2024). Evaluation of the opportunities presented by the adoption of E-Government in enhancing Local Government Authority performance at Kinondoni Municipal Council in Tanzania. *African Journal of Empirical Research*, *5*(4), 479–488. DOI: 10.51867/ajernet.5.4.38

Hennink, M. M., Kaiser, B. N., & Weber, M. B. (2019). What influences saturation? Estimating sample sizes in focus group research. *Qualitative Health Research*, *29*(10), 1483–1496. DOI: 10.1177/1049732318821692 PMID: 30628545

Hooda, A., Gupta, P., Jeyaraj, A., & Dwivedi, Y. (2023). Clarifying the Role of E-Government Trust in E-Government Success Models: A Meta-analytic Structural Equation Modeling Approach. *AJIS. Australasian Journal of Information Systems*, *27*. Advance online publication. DOI: 10.3127/ajis.v27i0.4079

Ilyas, M., Din, A. U., Haleem, M., & Ahmad, I. (2023). Digital entrepreneurial acceptance: An examination of technology acceptance model and do-it-yourself behavior. *Journal of Innovation and Entrepreneurship*, *12*(1), 15. Advance online publication. DOI: 10.1186/s13731-023-00268-1

Inakefe, G. I., Bassey, V. U., Ikeanyibe, O. M., Nwagboso, C. I., Agbor, U. I., Ebegbulem, J., Mbonu, F. I., & Ike, G. U. (2023). Digital Literacy and E-Governance adoption for service delivery in Cross River State Civil Service. *International Journal of Electronic Government Research*, *19*(1), 1–23. DOI: 10.4018/IJEGR.328327

Ishengoma, F. and John, E. (2024), “Factor” influencing the adoption of mobile-based AI services in Tanzanian manufacturing SMEs”, *Vilakshan - XIMB Journal of Management*, Vol. ahead-of-print No. ahead-of-print. DOI: 10.1108/XJM-11-2023-0214

Ishengoma, F. and Shao, D. (2025), “A framework for aligning e-government initiatives with the sustainable development goals”, *Journal of Innovative Digital Transformation*, Vol. ahead-of-print No. ahead-of-print. DOI: 10.1108/JIDT-09-2024-0025

Ismail J. Ismail (2023) Seeing through digitalisation! The influence of entrepreneurial networks on market participation among smallholder farmers in Tanzania. The mediating role of digital technology, *Cogent Food & Agriculture,* 9:1, 2171834, DOI: DOI: 10.1080/23311932.2023.2171834

Kelly, A. E., & Palaniappan, S. (2023). Using a technology acceptance model to determine factors influencing continued usage of mobile money service transactions in Ghana. *Journal of Innovation and Entrepreneurship*, *12*(1), 34. Advance online publication. DOI: 10.1186/s13731-023-00301-3

Kiviaho, A., & Einolander, J. (2023). Digital transformation, well-being and shrinking communities: Narrowing the divides between urban and rural. *Heliyon*, *9*(8), e18801. DOI: 10.1016/j.heliyon.2023.e18801 PMID: 37600410

Lubawa, G. G., & Kandpal, D. V. (2024). Advancing Financial Inclusion through Digital Finance Innovations in Tanzania. In Editor(s) (s): Ernesto. D.R. Santibanez Gonzalez, Vinay Kandpal, Peterson K. Ozili, Prasenjit Chatterjee. Fintech for ESG and the Circular Economy.(pp.255-287), John Wiley & Sons, Inc; DOI: 10.1002/9781394234035.ch14

Lubawa, G. G., & Osabuohien, E. S. (2024). Developing Sustainable Tourism in Tanzania: Perspective from Wine Stakeholders. In Martínez-Falcó, J., Marco-Lajara, B., Sánchez-García, E., & Millán-Tudela, L. A. (Eds.), *Wine Tourism and Sustainability*. Palgrave Macmillan., DOI: 10.1007/978-3-031-48937-2_3

Lubis, S., Purnomo, E. P., Lado, J. A., & Hung, C.-F. (2024). Electronic governance in advancing sustainable development goals through systematic literature review. *Discover Global Society*, *2*(1), 77. Advance online publication. DOI: 10.1007/s44282-024-00102-3

Lyulyov, O., Pimonenko, T., Saura, J. R., & Barbosa, B. (2024). How do e-governance and e-business drive sustainable development goals? *Technological Forecasting and Social Change*, *199*, 123082. DOI: 10.1016/j.techfore.2023.123082

Magomana, N. R., & Maireva, C. (2021). Information Technology and entrepreneurship development in Africa. *East African Journal of Education and Social Sciences, Issue 2 (April to June 2021)*, 239–242. DOI: 10.46606/eajess2021v02i02.0095

Majenga, A. K., Namabira, J., & Justine, E. K. (2024). Promoting Rural Entrepreneurship in Tanzania Through Empowering Voluntary Financial Saving Groups. *African Journal of Applied Research, 10*(1), 275–294. DOI: 10.26437/ajar.v10i1.688

Manzoor, F., Wei, L., & Sahito, N. (2021). The role of SMEs in rural development: Access of SMEs to finance as a mediator. *PLoS One, 16*(3), e0247598. DOI: 10.1371/journal.pone.0247598 PMID: 33684146

Matavire, R., Chigona, W., Roode, D., Sewchurran, E., Davids, Z., Mukudu, A., & Abu, C. B. (2010). Challenges of eGovernment project implementation in a South African context. *Electronic Journal of Information Systems Evaluation, 13*(2), 153–164.

Mohale, C. (2024). The Role of E-Government in the Promotion of Municipal Service Delivery in South Africa. *International Journal of Social Science Research and Review, 7*(3), 1–19. DOI: 10.47814/ijssrr.v7i3.1992

Monda, A., Feola, R., Parente, R., Vesci, M., & Botti, A. (2023). Rural development and digital technologies: A collaborative framework for policy-making. *Transforming Government, 17*(3), 328–343. DOI: 10.1108/TG-12-2022-0162

Mooya, N., & Phiri, J. (2021). Factors hindering the adoption of E-marketing among cable manufacturers in Zambia, based on the technology acceptance model (TAM). *Technology and Investment, 12*(2), 51–65. DOI: 10.4236/ti.2021.122004

Mushi, G. E., Burgi, P., & Di Marzo Serugendo, G. (2024). State of Agricultural E-Government Services to Farmers in Tanzania: Toward the Participatory Design of a Farmers Digital Information System (FDIS). *Agriculture, 14*(3), 475. DOI: 10.3390/agriculture14030475

Mushi, R. M. (2024). Assessing the factors influencing intention to use e-government in Tanzania: The perspective of trust, participation and transparency. *Journal of Electronic Business & Digital Economics, 3*(2), 156–169. DOI: 10.1108/JEBDE-08-2023-0017

Mwantimwa, K. (2019). ICT usage to enhance firms' business processes in Tanzania. *Journal of Global Entrepreneurship Research, 9*(1), 46–58. DOI: 10.1186/s40497-019-0170-6

Mwaseba, S. L., Mwang'onda, E. S., & Ngwilizi, D. (2025). Exploring the Roots of Gender Inequality in Digital Payments Utilisation in Tanzania. In FinTech and Financial Inclusion (1st Edition, p. 18). Routledge. https://doi.org/https://doi.org/10.4324/9781003514114-17

Nyagango, A. I., Sife, A. S., & Kazungu, I. (2023). Factors influencing the use of mobile phone for accessing agricultural marketing information by grape smallholder farmers in Tanzania. *Cogent Business & Management, 10*(3), 2257865. Advance online publication. DOI: 10.1080/23311975.2023.2257865

Odeyemi, N. O., Oyewole, N. A. T., Adeoye, N. O. B., Ofodile, N. O. C., Addy, N. W. A., Okoye, N. C. C., & Ololade, N. Y. J. (2024). Entrepreneurship in Africa: A Review of Growth and Challenges. *International Journal of Management & Entrepreneurship Research, 6*(3), 608–622. DOI: 10.51594/ijmer.v6i3.874

Omweri, F. S. (2024). A Systematic Literature Review of E-Government Implementation in Developing Countries: Examining Urban-Rural Disparities, Institutional Capacity, and Socio-Cultural Factors in the Context of Local Governance and Progress towards SDG 16.6. *International Journal of Research and Innovation in Social Science, VIII*(VIII), 1173–1199. DOI: 10.47772/IJRISS.2024.808088

Owusu, A., Akpe-Doe, C. E., & Taana, I. H. (2022). Assessing the effectiveness of E-government services in Ghana: A case of the registrar general's department. [IJEGR]. *International Journal of Electronic Government Research, 18*(1), 1–23. DOI: 10.4018/IJEGR.289827

Parente, R. (2020). Digitalization, consumer social responsibility, and humane entrepr President's good news from the future? *Journal of the International Council for Small Business, 1*(1), 56–63. DOI: 10.1080/26437015.2020.1714368

Pougel, F., Bonnel, S., & Beier, G. (Socioeconomicnd sustainability: a literature review. *Journal of Innovations and Sustainability, 4*(1), 9–54. https://doi.org/DOI: 10.51599/is.2018.04.01.09

Rarhoui, K. (2024, February 1). *E-government in Africa: challenges and prospects.* https://hal.science/hal-04450951v1

Rutledge, P. B., & Hogg, J. L. C. (2020). In-depth interviews. The International Encyclopedia of Media Psychology, 1–7. DOI: 10.1002/9781119011071.iemp0019

Sagarik, D. (2023). Enhancing Digital Competitiveness Through the Lens of Digital Government Among Asian Economies. *In International Journal of Public Administration in the Digital Age* (Vol. 10, Issue 1, p. 1). IGI Global. DOI: 10.4018/IJPADA.326122

Samsor, A. M. (2021). Challenges and Prospects of e-Government implementation in Afghanistan. *International Trade, Politics and Development*, *5*(1), 51–70. DOI: 10.1108/ITPD-01-2020-0001

Sausi, J. M., Mtebe, J. S., & Mbelwa, J. (2021). Evaluating user satisfaction with the e-payment gateway system in Tanzania. *South African Journal of Information Management*, *23*(1). Advance online publication. DOI: 10.4102/sajim.v23i1.1430

Shepherd, D. A., Patzelt, H., & Breugst, N. (2024). 66 *Simple Rules for Entrepreneurs*. httpConsumers'g/DOI: 10.1007/978-3-031-62032-4

Sheppard, M., & Vibert, C. (2019). Re-examining the relationship between ease of use and usefulness for the next generation. *Education and Information Technologies*, *24*(5), 3205–3218. DOI: 10.1007/s10639-019-09916-0

Stewart, T. M. (2022). *Recommendations for implementing an e-government system: A generic qualitative study*. [Doctoral dissertation, Capella University]. ProQuest Dissertations Publishing.

TCRA. (Tanzania Communications Regulatory Authority, 2023): Quality of Service Result for Mobile Communication Services in Tanzania for the period of April to June 2023, https://www.tcra.go.tz/pages/reports

TCRA. (Tanzania Communications Regulatory Authority, 2024): Communications Statistics Quarter ending June 2024 Version 1.1, https://www.tcra.go.tz/pages/reports

The United Republic of Tanzania. (2020). *Financial Sector Development Masterplan (FSDMP), (2020/21–2029/30)*. Ministry of Finance and Planning.

Thomas, G., Botha, R. A., & Van Greunen, D. (2015). Understanding the problem of coordination in a large scale distributed environment from a service lens view — Towards the South African public sector e-Administration criteria for coordination support. *Government Information Quarterly*, *32*(4), 526–538. DOI: 10.1016/j.giq.2015.08.002

United Nations. (2020). The Impact of COVID-19 on the Arab Region: An Opportunity to Build Back Better. *Policy Brief*.

United Nations. (2024). E-government survey 2024: *Accelerating digital transformation for sustainable development with the addendum on artificial intelligence*. Department of Economic and Social Affairs. https://publicadministration.un.org/egovkb/en-us/

United Republic of Tanzania. (URT, 2016). Tanzania National ICT Policy. Ministry of Works, Transport and Communication.

United Republic of Tanzania (URT,2024), Ministry of Finance, Tanzania National Bureau of Statistics and President's Office - Finance and Planning, Office of the Chief Government Statistician, Zanzibar. The 2022 Population and Housing Census: Basic Demographic and Socioeconomic Profile; Tanzania Mainland, April 2024.

United Republic of Tanzania (URT). (2019). *E-Government Act, 2019* (Act No. 10 of 2019). ISSN 0856-0331X.

United Republic of Tanzania[URT] (2022): Tanzania e-Government Strategy 2022. President's Office - Public Service Management. Retrieved on 15th October 2024 from the website www.utumishi.go.tz

Wahed, M. M. A., & Ismail, T. S. (2022). An online system for issuing building permits in light of e-government in Egypt. In Journal, H. B. R. C. (Ed.), *Issue 1* (Vol. 18, p. 53). Taylor & Francis., DOI: 10.1080/16874048.2021.2019447

Wilson, N., Keni, K., & Tan, P. H. P. (2021). The Role of Perceived Usefulness and Perceived Ease-of-Use toward Satisfaction and Trust Which Influence Computer Consumers' Loyalty in China. *Gadjah Mada International Journal of Business, 23*(3), 262. DOI: 10.22146/gamaijb.32106

Xie, G., Huang, L., Bin, H., Apostolidis, C., Jiang, Y., Li, G., & Cai, W. (2022). Sustainable Entrepreneurship in Rural E-Commerce: Identifying Entrepreneurs in Practitioners by Using Deep Neural Networks Approach. *Frontiers in Environmental Science, 10*, 840479. DOI: 10.3389/fenvs.2022.840479

Yang, C., Gu, M., & Albitar, K. (2024). Government in the digital age: Exploring the impact of digital transformation on governmental efficiency. *Technological Forecasting and Social Change, 208*, 123722. DOI: 10.1016/j.techfore.2024.123722

Yildiz, M. (2016). E-Government: Informatisation of Government and Politics. In Farazmand, A. (Ed.), *Global Encyclopedia of Public Administration, Public Policy, and Governance. In Springer eBooks* (pp. 1–7)., DOI: 10.1007/978-3-319-31816-5_2450-1

ENDNOTES

1 https://africa-digital.com/2024/e-government-for-africa/?utm_source=chatgpt.com

2 https://www.statista.com/statistics/421580/egdi-e-government-development-index-ranking/?utm_source=chatgpt.com

3 https://publicadministration.un.org/egovkb/en-us/Data/Country-Information/id/183-United-Republic-of-Tanzania?utm_source=chatgpt.com

4 Kiswahili is Tanzania's national language, used for communication across the country. It unites people from different cultures and backgrounds.

5 M-Koba is a digital platform developed by Vodacom Tanzania to modernize traditional savings groups by enhances the convenience, security, cost-effectiveness, and transparency of group savings by digitizing all traditional savings.

Chapter 4
The Rise of Quick Commerce:
Redefining Retail Through Digital Innovation and Sustainable Practices

Aryan Gupta
Christ University, India

Deepak Jha
https://orcid.org/0009-0002-3815-8666
Christ University, India

ABSTRACT

There has been a sea change in retail with the new wave of consumers who are looking to get instant access to products, which is leading to Q-commerce. Q-commerce can be defined as Quick Commerce, a means through which retailers/retailing can attempt to be different by delivering products within a minute. This chapter is an elaboration of how Q-commerce affects consumer behaviour and retail strategies. The COVID-19 pandemic really speeded up the transition from traditional retail to e-commerce and placed convenience at a new standard that challenges traditional retailing practices.In that regard, technological developments are the bedrock of Q-commerce, but at the same time, operational efficiency is enhanced through artificial intelligence, real-time analytics, and well-improved logistics. While delivery becomes faster through innovations, increasing customer loyalty, it creates ethical and sustainability concerns. The section highlights how the retailers should align rapid growth with responsible practices to manage the adverse environmental effects caused by fast delivery.

DOI: 10.4018/979-8-3373-5087-5.ch004

INTRODUCTION

The retail sector is experiencing significant changes because of the rise of Quick commerce, an innovative concept that offers ultra-fast delivery of products, often within minutes. Q-commerce caters to the increasing demand for prompt and satisfactory service from customers, unlike traditional e-commerce, which usually involves lengthy delivery wait times.

The definition and application of Quick commerce are explored in this chapter which also charts its development from traditional retail to e-commerce and ultimately to the quick delivery model. The shift has been sped up considerably by the covid-19 pandemic, especially in urban areas where customers have pressing time constraints.

The changing behaviour of consumers, the need to have an easier and quicker experience in purchasing, has fuelled a rise in impulsive buying driven by Q-commerce. The following section describes the population demographics of changing millennials and young professionals living in cities, which are fuelling these trends. We will also look at the creative operational approaches that underpin Q-commerce, like improvements inlets minute delivery logistics and technology integration. In the light of the above changes, typical retail businesses are now exposed to additional pressure in shaving competitive landscapes as they try to adjust themselves to Q-commerce. Section seeks to demystify how Q-commerce is changing the strategy and the expectations of the customer by a closer look at these dynamics. (Eunhye, S. O. N., & KWON, K. H.) (Krainik, P. (2023))

As Quick Commerce continues to boom, the influence of this on the purchasing behaviour of its customers becomes more apparent. People have transformed their purchasing behaviors into an easier, immediate manner in favour of easy access to products as opposed to old retailing experiences in which speed and ease were given more importance. There will be more urban dwellers as users of Q-commerce as they will be busier than all the other schedules. This shift brings spontaneous buying and raises the bar regarding excellent customer service and convenient access to products. Companies must adjust to such changed customer demands such as seamless online and mobile shopping experiences and swift deliveries. (Holma, M., & Junestrand, A. (2024) (Luna Sanchez, P. (2024))

Quick Commerce is changing how businesses operate as well as how customers behave. The astute application of dark stores and micro-fulfilment centres is one of the main concepts of Q-commerce. BSince these small, localized facilities allow businesses to maintain products closer to the customer, deliveries may be quicker and the general cost of logistics may be lower.(Schorung, M. (2023)) (Pache, G. (2023, September))

These local centers, located in urban centers close to customers, focus on products that are used and sold on a regular basis, such as grocery and other household items. In addition to these tenets of high customer expectations of receiving reliable and prompt services, this local inventory management increases profitability.

In addition, the optimization of Q-trade operations depends on technological development. Companies are increasingly using real-time analytics, artificial intelligence and machine learning to optimize their supply chains and create more accurate demand forecasts. The use of AI-based algorithms can enable retailers to pick which goods are likely to be in demand at what time so that such stocks can be prepositioned at the micro-fulfilment centers, and real-time data analytics can monitor delivery performance against potential bottlenecks that could delay or slow down the delivery process. By incorporating these technologies, the core of the logistics industry has changed, and firms can now provide quicker delivery services to customers while not compromising on quality..(Abdul-Yekeen, A. M., Rasaq, O., Ayinla, M. A., Sikiru, A., Kujore, V., & Agboola, T. O. (2024).)

However, there are many challenges affecting the explosive growth of Q-commerce. The question of scalability is the most important challenge. When companies grow in demand to cater to customers who want faster delivery, they would need to further develop their infrastructural base. This can at times lead to costly drop-off locations and dark stores. These establishments are located in cities, closer to the consumer markets, and concentrate on leading lines of product categories and commoditized products, including basic necessities in the home and everyday provisions. In addition to capacity in the manufacturing plant, this localization of the distribution network also addresses customers' demanding needs for reliable and time-sensitive service.

As stated earlier, the environmental factor relating to Q-commerce makes this a third challenge the companies have to face. Quick delivery is said to carry a large quantity of fuel and carbon footprints, especially in small and frequent deliveries. The growing environmental awareness among consumers has forced the Q-commerce industry to adopt sustainable practices at higher rates. In an effort to reduce the environmental impact of their business, companies are beginning to explore the use of electric cars, bicycle carriers and environmentally friendly packaging options. However, adopting environmentally friendly methods may be expensive and time-consuming, which is a big issue for businesses attempting to strike a balance between environmental responsibility and productivity.

(Son, E., & Kwon, K. H. (2024)) (Paché, G. (2022)) (Huang, M., & Yen, B. P. (2021))

Customer loyalty takes center stage in Q-Commerce. When speed and loyalty to a brand are the order of the day in a market, the most innovative way of retaining customers is required. Offering personalized service, loyalty programs and special promotions are just some of the strategies companies use to build long-term relationships with their customers. With a high level of competition as the industry attracts more competitors, loyalty from the customers becomes quite hard to maintain. Businesses are thus compelled to innovate and improve on their services since consumers have always been interested in services that offer fast delivery, convenience, or even best value for money, for Q-commerce, it all boils down to finding a fine balance between satisfying immediate consumer needs and enduring relationships. In the post-covid scenario, the industry will need to change day by day as they can see what business is nearly looking at to stay ahead of the competition.

Quick Commerce is transforming the retail landscape because consumers increasingly need fast and easily accessible access to it. This new model of doing things has changed how consumers shop, for urban millennials and young professionals who require quick access to goods. The advantages of Q-commerce are that operations become more efficient through dark stores and with more advanced technology but then it presents issues like scalability and environmental concerns. Businesses will have to react to such dynamics by offering seamless experiences and sustainable practices that will ascertain customer loyalty. Therefore, in effect, the future of retail is more about how companies operate effectively in this new world of post-pandemic.(Fornari, E., Negri, F., & Iuffmann Ghezzi, A. (2022)) (Ranjekar, G., & Roy, D. (2023)) (Mukherjee, S., & Michael, H. (2016)) (Ganapathy, V., & Gupta, C. (2023)) (Chien, A. W., Kurnia, S., & von Westarp, F. (2003))

LITERATURE REVIEW

Q-commerce, short for Quick Commerce, is a rapid delivery model that has been underlined and emphasizes the delivery of products to consumers in minutes or hours after their order has been placed. This is seen as the third generation of e-commerce, with ultra-fast delivery and convenience being its major focus. Originally launched in 2011 with the entry of Postmates, Q-commerce was especially sidetracked during 2017, and it accelerated rapidly over the COVID-19 period. Consumers continued to look to online shopping for grocery items that required immediate deliveries. Q-commerce eventually spilled over from its origins in food deliveries into grocery deliveries, medicines, or apparel, capturing a broader general trend in consumer expectations concerning speed and convenience (Tahrim, 2024).

Q-commerce has fundamentally changed the behavior of the consumer and a monumental shift has been noticed in the way of the consumers about speed and convenience while shopping. As it has been researched that consumers expect delivery on the same day and even instantly and it has been surveyed that 70% of U.S. consumers prefer fast fulfillment when they shop online (Harter et al., 2024). The great need for speed of Q-commerce platforms, which holds impulse buying and essential needs close to themselves, has, therefore impacted the dynamics of traditional retailing to be profound.

- **Operational and Supply Chain Innovations**

Q-commerce requires agile operations, and innovative supply chain strategies are required. Companies opt for local warehouses or "dark stores" to help them have shorter delivery times, and these can be much shorter compared to traditional means (Yang et al., 2024). Advanced logistics management systems in conjunction with AI-driven inventory management also allow them to optimize their operations to have the appropriate inventory on hand to dispatch quickly. The deliveries get faster because of this hyper-local approach, and customer satisfaction becomes strong since their demands are met right away.

- **Technological Advancements and Innovations**

The third critical aspect of Q-commerce is technology adoption. Using mobile applications, location-based services, and real-time analytics order processing efficiency and real-time tracking are guaranteed, thus providing avenues for better customer-retailer communication and shipping processes with AI technology, adoption also helps in the prediction of consumer patterns of demand, which ensures businesses are at perfect levels of stock in addition to improved quality of service.Q-commerce, while very fast-growing in the marketplace, is still inherently tough. A system that positions itself on the basis of fast delivery tends to over-stretch the supply chain when the occasion calls for it or when there occurs a shock and surprise in a system. A number of Q-commerce companies are also finding it difficult to stay profitable with such extremely low margins. The business model also gets complicated with a need for continuous investment in technology and infrastructure for sustainability. (Mukherjee, S., & Michael, H. (2022)) (Fornari, E., Negri, F., & Iuffmann Ghezzi, A. (2022))

- **Sustainability and Environmental Impact**

The rapid model of Q-commerce has a faster delivery nature, a key factor that leads to high carbon emission; this is because a courier makes short-distance trips. However, some Q-commerce companies are now embracing sustainability in setting up green packaging and carbon-neutral delivery to change this aspect. Balancing speed with sustainability presents an especially challenging imperative for the industry as it seeks to catch up with increasing consumer demand for environmentally responsible practices.(Krainik, P. (2023)) (Cano, J. A., Londoño-Pineda, A., & Rodas, C. (2022))

Q-commerce has grown exponentially, but the model is far from free of a list of major challenges. The pressure of delivering fast can be very demanding on supply chains, particularly in high-demand times or even when unexpected disruptions occur. And in an environment characterized more or less by thin margins, efforts to stay profitable promise to be quite a tall order for many Q-commerce companies.

Q-commerce is redefining the traditional retail landscape as companies focus on adopting omnichannel strategies to outdo others in the game. Retailers are "interweaving" their online services with their physical-channel ones to make shopping easier for all possible targets for such a product. For example, in addition to speedy delivery, curbside pickups are now part of the game.(George, 2024).

- **Key Development: Business Models and Profitability in Q-commerce**

• The other great value for Q-commerce's development is the innovative business models. Q-commerce bases them on extreme convenience and ultra-fast delivery as a value proposition. It mainly depends on hyper-localized delivery services with low-inventory storage, which allows faster turnaround time for consumers. The Q-commerce firms, unlike e-commerce firms, largely avoid large central warehouses and instead rely on micro-fulfillment centers or "dark stores," all strategically located near more-demanding areas, says It helps the corporations to satisfy the request of the customer for immediate or same-day delivery. Although this mode of operation is beneficial to hasten numerous issues crop up regarding profitability. (Sharma Giri, A. (2023))

Massive attention to the speed makes Q-commerce businesses keep running through razor-thin margins as the cost of delivery, inventory management, and logistical complexities is expensive to keep. Profitability therefore becomes a tightrope between efficiency and scalability, often at the cost of huge investments in technology, workforce, and delivery infrastructure (Jones & Williams, 2024). Most firms in the sector survive by leveraging venture capital financing but remain doubtful for sustainability in the long term. Some corporations have managed to survive by adapting to an alternative source of income through premium membership, subscription service, and other ventures in collaboration with other industries, such as health and beauty.

(Manani, J. (2022))

Impact on Traditional Retail and Omnichannel Strategies

Q-commerce is convenient and speedy, but it has forced legacy players to rethink their strategies. Many brick-and-mortar companies, especially grocery chains, have begun embracing the omnichannel strategy for many reasons-mostly to make the game of Q-commerce more balanced. Omnichannel retailing is an integration of both online and offline channels where consumers can seamlessly shop across the two. Curbside pickup and click-and-collect services, not to mention same-day delivery, have become part of the traditional operations of many retailers as they try to give an experience akin to Q-commerce (Smith & Weber, 2024).

(Foresti, L., Perotti, S., Ekren, B. Y., & Prataviera, L. B. (2022, October))

This flexibility allows retailers to be competitive in a Q-commerce-dominated world while at the same time holding on to the physical presence that consumers demand from many. Operatively, they sidestep the costs associated with the construction of individual micro-fulfillment centers by using the existing structure and, for example, in-store inventory. In this way, blending physical and digital retail allows traditional companies to reach a wider customer base while appealing to customers who may demand different delivery speeds and different kinds of convenience.

Jiang, P., & Rosenbloom, B. (2005). Yeo, V. C. S., Goh, S. K., & Rezaei, S. (2017).

- **Consumer Behavior and Role of Impulse Buying**

Consumer behavior in Q-commerce is proportional to the convenience it offers in terms of time. As above, Q-commerce is a huge trigger for impulse buying. The minute-long delivery gets into the brains of the consumers, especially with fastidious product categories such as food and beverages and personal care products (Ali & Thompson, 2023). The retailers targeting impulse purchases emphasize targeted promotions, dynamic pricing, and customized recommendations to speed up real-time sales. Therefore, Q-commerce platforms have emerged as a necessary tool for tapping into last-minute purchasing decisions.

This, however, brought a focus on quick, impulse consumption at a cost in terms of overconsumption and waste.Instant gratification may encourage overspending and augment waste streams, which further burdens the environment. The increased expectation from consumers to ultimately lead toward more sustainable consumption patterns will be one of the greatest challenges business groups in this space have to deal with.Bharathithasan, S., & Srinivasan, K. S. (2024).

Challenges in Q-commerce

The future of Q-commerce is bright but threatening. When companies continue to grow and expand, increasing operational pressure drives companies into profitability while catering to the consumer demands about achieving both speed and sustainability. Over time, the logistics and technology expenses overwhelmed businesses' capacity; in turn, they could not pass this on into customers' checks without losing competitive advantage. Second, regulatory issues more so in urban areas may mean that micro-fulfillment centers do not have accessible real estate, as it complicates expansion efforts. (Albshaier, L., Almarri, S., & Hafizur Rahman, M. M. (2024)).

A further area of development for Q-commerce will be the way in which it should relate to its autonomous delivery systems, such as drones and robots, so that delivery can be significantly speeded up and per-unit operating costs would be the minimum, especially for small items like food and pharmaceuticals. Other areas where it could scale operations are with AI-driven inventory management systems that enable the projection of demand based on real-time data, further chiseling down operations to a scalable extent.

(Odeyemi, O., Elufioye, O. A., Mhlongo, N. Z., & Ifesinachi, A. (2024))

Q-commerce will also witness a rising need for environmental practices by consumers. As sustainability increasingly gains the character of an ever-important selection criterion, businesses that provide green delivery, for example through electric vehicles and 'ecological' packaging, will probably win at the markets. Businesses that can manage to control speed and are environmentally conscious will probably emerge victorious in the long run.

(Timothy, O. T., Fisayo, A. A., Thiru, R., Raji, M. A., & Olodo, H. B. (2024))

Indeed, Q-commerce revolutionized the retailing industry by turning its focus to speed and convenience. It came like a storm and transformed consumer behavior, operational models, and led traditional retailers to reassess their strategies. Despite this, major issues are yet to be faced regarding profit concerns, issues of sustainability, and the long-term viability of the Q-commerce business model. In the light of further and accelerating technological changes in the business and industry, firms will be better positioned for success in this changing market when they get the right balance between operational efficiency, customer satisfaction, and environmental responsibility.

{(Pache, G. (2023, September)) (Luna Sanchez, P. (2024)) (Schorung, M. (2023)) (Ranjekar, G., & Roy, D. (2023)) (Cano, J. A., Londoño-Pineda, A., & Rodas, C. (2022)) (Ganapathy, V., & Gupta, C. (2023))(Stojanov, M. (2022). Q-commerce}

The last decade has witnessed a lot of changes in the retail industry, mainly due to changing market dynamics, changing customer behavior, and technological breakthroughs. One such change is the faster version of e-commerce, which is called

Quick Commerce (Q-commerce). It delivers goods within 10–30 minutes using gig economy-based delivery networks, AI-based inventory management, and micro-fulfillment centers (Mukherjee & Michael, 2022). New consumer demand patterns created by huge cravings for Q-commerce due to the customers' need for speed and convenience have increased because of the COVID-19 pandemic, according to recent literature by Harter et al., 2024. Although this has much revolutionary power, problems concerning scalability, sustainability, and profitability issues still arise from Q-commerce. To this paper, the conceptual framework was created by building on existing theories and incorporating recent literature regarding the exploration of dynamics, implications, and the future of Q-commerce.

Theoretical Foundation

Consumer Behavior Theory

According to Oliver's Expectancy-Disconfirmation Theory of 1980, Q-commerce performance is positively correlated with customer happiness and behavior. The concept states that a customer is satisfied when they perceive that their performance is beyond their expectations just before the time of purchase. Ali and Thompson (2023) explain the speed-based satisfaction of customers who are using Ultra-Fast delivery in Q-commerce. Research shows that buyers are more likely to remain loyal if the delivery takes place immediately as compared to the traditional methods of e-commerce (Bharathidasan & Srinivasan, 2024).

The theories of impulse purchase further explain why Q-commerce has appeal. Contextual marketing and time-bound offers exploit emotional cues from the customers to provoke impulsive response (Choi et al., 2023).

In addition, behavioral economics explains how convenience affects the decision, especially an urban time-constrained consumer who will pay more to use for convenience (Kumar & Sharma, 2023).

Innovation Diffusion Theory

Technological resources include real-time analytics, predictive algorithms, and hyper-localized dark stores. Such resources are the primary strength of Q-commerce (Mukherjee & Michael, 2022). Utilizing these resources efficiently enables companies to develop unique products for their customers, which results in customer loyalty and efficient operation. One of the most significant competitive advantages that Gorillas has is the application of AI-based inventory systems that eliminate waste and increase service dependability (Al Bashaier et al., 2024).

Value accruable to shopping experiences has increased substantially as Q-commerce promises to ensure immediacy, which most probably will disseminate across diverse demographic groups.

The Resource-Based View (Barney, 1991) states that firms can derive an advantage from specific and inimitable resources. The first resources in the Q-commerce domain are technological capabilities such as real-time analytics, predictive algorithms, and hyper-localized dark stores (Mukherjee & Michael, 2022). Proper utilization of such resources allows businesses to create unique products for clients, and this leads to customer loyalty along with operational effectiveness. One of Gorillas' primary competitive advantages is its use of AI-based inventory systems, which reduce waste and increase service dependability (Al Bashaier et al., 2024).

Resource-Based View (RBV)

The Resource-Based View (Barney, 1991) states that firms can derive an advantage from specific and inimitable resources. The first resources in the Q-commerce domain are technological capabilities such as real-time analytics, predictive algorithms, and hyper-localized dark stores (Mukherjee & Michael, 2022). Proper utilization of such resources allows businesses to create unique products for clients, and this leads to customer loyalty along with operational effectiveness. One of Gorillas' primary competitive advantages is its use of AI-based inventory systems, which reduce waste and increase service dependability (Al Bashaier et al., 2024).

Conceptual Framework

Redefining Speed and Convenience

Q-commerce is a response to an increasing desire of consumers to have immediate satisfaction. For the choice of platform, 78% of the online customers choose delivery speed, according to a research in recent times (Harter et al., 2024). Q-commerce deploys a hyper-localized strategy as against traditional e-commerce, which depends upon the centralised distribution centres. Micro-fulfillment centers and dark stores in urban neighborhoods allow for delivery within under 30 minutes.

For example, In India, Swiggy Instamart and Zepto have strategically placed the dark stores in metropolitan cities so that the order could be processed and delivered relatively faster (Bharathithasan & Srinivasan, 2024). This reduces order delivery times and also consumer satisfaction, as it matches the urgency of grocerying or immediate medical supplies among others.

Implications of this model go beyond consumer satisfaction. It opens opportunities for business to penetrate the underdeveloped markets of Tier-2 and Tier-3 cities, where the traditional retail channels are not developed. However, with such high fixed costs involved in maintaining decentralized infrastructure, it is a highly scalability-intensive business, particularly for the smaller players (Jones & Williams, 2024).

Operational Innovations: Bridging Technology and Logistics

Q-commerce is very dependent on advanced logistics and high-tech integration. Predictive algorithms help to optimize the levels of inventory in such a way that fast-moving items are always available. Real-time analytics are used for dynamic pricing and demand forecasting, thereby improving operational efficiency further (Yang et al., 2024).

Technological innovations in the form of autonomous delivery systems are starting to transform last-mile logistics. Companies such as Amazon and JD.com are looking at drones and robotic deliveries in an effort to reduce costs and improve reliability (Odeyemi et al., 2024). In addition, AI-based route optimization tools help delivery drivers to reduce their travel times and fuel consumption, which resonates with the Q-commerce value proposition of speed.

Though these improvements increase efficiency, there is high capital investment at the start. Small firms lack competitiveness with well-endowed giants; thus, markets experience consolidation. Too much dependence on technology also leaves weaknesses, like cyber risks and system downtimes that bring operations to a halt (Choi et al., 2023).

Sustainability: Balancing Speed with Responsibility

Because the Q-commerce concept involves frequent, small-scale delivery, it has been criticized for environmental concerns. Among the growing ecological footprints of the industry are carbon emissions from delivery trucks and more packaging waste. (Cano et al., 2022). Because these trips are shorter and more frequent, Q-commerce deliveries emit 50% more emissions per order compared to standard e-commerce, according to the study (Krainik, 2023).

These have led to businesses embracing such sustainable activities. The urban areas now begin to witness the electric vehicles and bicycle delivery which are a relief effort towards reducing pollutants. For instance, Zapp, a Q-commerce firm based in the UK, has pledged to use only electric vehicles for delivery (Smith & Weber, 2024). As part of efforts to reduce waste, several sites have also resorted to recyclable and biodegradable packaging.

On the other hand, sustainable operations reduce profit margins and are expensive.

The challenge is to balance the speed with sustainability, and this calls for innovation in carbon offset programs and circular packaging systems (Yang et al., 2024). Governments and regulatory bodies have a role to play in incentivizing green initiatives with tax benefits or subsidies.

- **Profitability: The Tightrope Between Efficiency and Scale**

Because of such slim profit margins, the growth of Q-commerce has to rely on venture financing. Most players are out of luck when it comes to profitability because of too much cost in running an operation: labor, technology, and infrastructure (Jones & Williams, 2024). To ensure sustainable income, several platforms are now using subscription-based models, like Deliveroo, while others want to be partnered with FMCG companies where sponsorships and advertising support offset some of the operational costs.

However, the fear of lack of profitability may push business ventures into hybrid models. In that case, blending Q-commerce with traditional e-commerce or brick-and-mortar stores can minimize the risks and spread the business streams. For example, Walmart has integrated curbside pickup with same-day delivery to enhance operational efficiencies and give customers multiple alternatives to access their services, according to Smith & Weber (2024).

Applications of the Conceptual Model

Retail Transformation

The Q-commerce concept can transform retailing strategies. Traditional merchants can opt for omnichannel strategies, where the online and offline experiences are smoothly combined. Tesco grocery shops, for example, have used the "click-and-collect" model, in which online orders are picked from actual locations, to bridge the gap between e-commerce and physical retailing(Al Bashaier et al., 2024).

- **Policy Development**

This conceptual framework enables the government to come up with policies that would make Q-commerce sustainable. For instance, policies could enforce electric vehicles and regulate packaging waste. Subsidies on green infrastructure like charging stations for electric vehicles might be other options for boosting its use across all corners.

- **Consumer Education**

Educating consumers on the impact of their purchasing decisions is very important. Platforms can reward sustainable behaviors, such as combining orders or choosing eco-friendly delivery options, with discount or loyalty rewards. All these initiatives make consumer behavior align with sustainability goals for long-term environmental benefits (Kumar & Sharma, 2023).

- **Challenges**

1. Infrastructure and Scalability

In urban regions, the availability of real estate is the major restriction in micro-fulfillment centers. Possible alternative uses would be shared logistics hubs or collaborations with existing retailers (Mukherjee & Michael, 2022).

2. Advances in Technology

They may be promising, but budding technologies, like autonomous delivery systems, also pose safety and regulatory hurdles.

Further research and pilot programs are needed to evaluate their feasibility and scalability (Odeyemi et al., 2024).

3. Sustainability

Next-generation Q-commerce models should focus on the principles of a circular economy. Collaborations with renewable energy companies and innovations in green packaging will be critical to reducing this sector's environmental footprint (Cano et al., 2022).

While posing a serious threat to sustainability and profitability, Q-commerce is a disruptor in the retail industry as it changes the concept of speed and convenience. Using this conceptual model can serve as a guide for businesses, legislators, and researchers to navigate the complexity that Q-commerce presents and, therefore, realize its potential for transformation. Further research would have to occur as the industry matures to examine the relationship between technology, customer behaviour, and environmental sustainability in order to ensure a balanced approach to growth and innovation.

IMPLICATIONS OF THE CONCEPTUAL MODEL

Q-commerce is a disruptor for the retail industry in terms of speed and convenience but challenges its sustainability and profitability. This conceptual model would help businesses, policymakers, and researchers find their ways in this complexity and unlock its transformative potential as the industry moves forward.. Future research must be made on the interactions of technology, consumer behavior, and environmental sustainability, hence balancing growth and innovation.

- **Impact on Consumer Behavior and Expectations:**

Q-commerce would hence be that critical disruptive element in retail-a new term for defining quickness with convenience that causes great and severe sustainability concerns and would also become profit-unfriendly. The road map with respect to conceptual developments in understanding what Q-commerce holds for firms, policymakers, or researchers while trying to explain the difficulties in harnessing the transformed potential would still be highly required for making the firm understand where innovation and growth could come within the frame.

- **Operational and Technological Innovations:**

Quick-commerce has disrupted the retail and e-commerce world by shifting consumer expectations and corporate strategies entirely. Q-commerce is an area that offers a paradigm shift toward lightning-fast delivery, personalized customer experiences, and efficiency in operations, all covered in this chapter. Its impact spans across all sorts of enterprises and consumers alike as well as the broader socioeconomic and environmental environments within which they operate.

- **Sustainability Considerations:**

Even though Q-commerce has delivered much convenience to consumers, it also offers new problems, mainly on environmental concerns. The rapid model of delivering goods involves many trips that cut short distances between the final destination and hence emit higher carbon and influence the environment.(Krainik, 2023). Although there is already an indication in the Q-commerce market that sustainability should come as part of the entity, companies are positioning themselves along with consumer expectations for sustainability to align by adopting green packaging, carbon-neutral delivery systems, and other environmentally friendly practices (Cano et al., 2022; Timothy et al., 2024). Increased consumer demand for environmentally-friendly practices can leave companies at a competitive disadvantage in a Q-commerce market if they remain behind.

- **Impact on Traditional Retailers:**

Q-commerce has caused a significant amount of stress on brick and mortar shops, mainly in the food and grocery sectors. Omnichannel strategies, combining both the physical and digital channels to provide more flexible shopping experiences, have been adopted by many heritage businesses to deliver curbside pickups and same-day delivery options to customers (Smith & Weber, 2024). This change allows conventional stores to remain relevant in a marketplace dominated increasingly by Q-commerce. Traditional retail has the need for continuous investment in infrastructure, logistics, and technology for survival and meeting the constant changing needs of customers.

- **Profitability and Business Model Sustainability:**

One of the major implications of Q-commerce is the problem of maintaining profitability. As discussed, the business model of Q-commerce is characterized by razor-thin margins, necessitating continuous investment in infrastructure, technology, and delivery capabilities (Jones & Williams, 2024). Reliance on venture capital funding and increasing costs for logistics and inventory management leave Q-commerce companies at considerable risk for long-term sustainability. Companies that successfully balance operational efficiency with scalability and profitability, perhaps through subscription services or alternative revenue streams, may have the best prospects for long-term success (Manani, 2022).

FUTURE RESEARCH DIRECTIONS

Quite numerous opportunities for further research have been created by the swift development of Q-commerce, especially in areas that remain less known or unexplored. The conceptual framework established in this chapter outlines some of the most important subjects of study that will assist in better understanding how Q-commerce impacts business and society.

1. **Consumer Behavior and Impulse Buying in Q-commerce:** The impact of Q-commerce on consumer behavior has been explored, but much more research is required to understand the underlying psychological factors that drive impulse buying in this context. How do the instantaneous gratification and convenience of Q-commerce influence consumer purchasing patterns? How much do cus-

tomers think Q-commerce encourages impulsive behaviour as opposed to more deliberate shopping? These kinds of studies can help businesses better customize their marketing strategies to increase sales (Choi et al., 2023; Ali & Thompson, 2023).

2. **Technological Innovations and AI in Q-commerce:** In logistics and inventory management, some of the regions to which AI and machine learning have been quite extensively explored include Q-commerce. Future possible studies can focus on ways in which Q-commerce businesses will deploy drones, driverless delivery vehicles, as well as predictive analytics into their future operations to advance their functionality even more. Potential studies include examining how it manages to reduce the operating costs and faster delivery while keeping errors lower (Odeyemi et al., 2024; Fornari et al., 2022).
3. **Sustainability and Environmental Impact:** As Q-commerce scales, it raises pressing issues related to the environmental dimensions of a rapid delivery model. For future research, development of sustainable delivery methods and carbon-neutral packaging and green logistics solutions will be relevant. Further studies may be oriented toward exploring consumer attitudes in terms of sustainability in Q-commerce and how these consumer attitudes drive purchasing decisions in the platform. This research would be very important to businesses that want to link their activities to the increased need for environmentally conscious practices (Krainik, 2023; Timothy et al., 2024).
4. **Profitability and Business Models in Q-commerce:** Although Q-commerce has witnessed explosive growth, its business model is a problem because of operational costs, which are rather high and margins are pretty thin. Future research studies may assess whether Q-commerce business models could be sustainable over the long term, focusing on profit. Scholars might investigate if Q-commerce companies could sustain their financial stability by implementing new revenue streams, such as premium membership programs. The potential of Q-commerce in developing nations, where consumer behaviour and cost structures may differ greatly from those in developed markets, can be investigated in further research (Jones & Williams, 2024; Sharma Giri, 2023).
5. **Regulatory Challenges and Urban Expansion:** There is bound to be a regulatory matter involving zoning, transportation, and labor as Q-commerce companies start moving in urban locations. Future study may focus on the Q-commerce regulatory environment, such as in cities where room for micro-fulfillment centers is scarce. Such business operations that want to scale in densely populated areas, therefore, need to see if city governments can help or restrict the growth of Q-commerce (Al Bashaier et al., 2024).

6. **Omnichannel Strategies in Traditional Retail:** That has shifted the omnichannel strategy of traditional retailers. Further research might be tracing the evolution of omnichannel retailing and how it reacts to Q-commerce. Which methods of integrating physical stores in the online channels are more efficient? How do the retailers balance the speed to fulfill the demands with the hindrances that a physical presence provides? These questions, in turn, would perfect the strategies for businesses as they continue to compete with an increasingly digital and on-demand retail environment (Smith & Weber, 2024; Foresti et al., 2022).

CONCLUSION

In short, Q-commerce reflects a fundamental shift in the behavior of consumers, the structures of businesses, and the strategies of operation. It impacts many retail areas, including environmental concerns such as rapid logistics that pollute the environment, coupled with the customer's expectations for faster deliveries. As the dynamics of Q-commerce are continually evolving, businesses must become responsive, innovative, and sustainable. F Future prospects for Q-commerce will be on the basis of technical advancement, environmental consciousness, and the need for profitability. In addition to the expansion of academic understanding of Q-commerce, more research in these fields will provide businesses hope for success in this dynamic and cutthroat business environment.

- **Key Insights and Contributions**

One of the key takeaways from the book is that Q-commerce signifies a dramatic shift in what customers demand, where ease and speed are now the foremost imperatives. Businesses, due to this need of near-instant delivery, had to develop new models: micro-fulfilment centres and dark shopfronts, which improve operational efficiencies and reduce delivery times further.

The integration of AI, machine learning, and real-time analytics further empowers businesses to meet the demands of hyper-localized and rapid delivery, thereby improving customer experience and logistical performance. Thus, Q-commerce is not a passing fad but rather a necessary evolution of retail in the digital age.

In addition, this chapter examines the operational challenges and the sustainability of the business model with Q-commerce. Explosive growth within the sector comes with great financial and logistic challenges, particularly regarding profitability. Companies in Q-commerce are often caught between a dilemma of having to pursue fast delivery and scalability that come with a very heavy cost in terms of running an efficient supply chain. Businesses are considering newer options such as subscription-based models and alternative revenue streams, which would help in securing long-term financial viability, considering these challenges that many are confronted with.

One major input of this chapter has been related to the examination of Q-commerce about the environmental effects. These services, even though speedy for consumers, pose grave issues of sustainability in delivering more frequently short distances and adding extra carbon emissions into the air. This paper points to a need where Q-commerce needs to practice more environment-friendly ways for its sustainability like eco-packaging materials, carbon neutral delivery models. The rising demand for sustainable business practices among consumers is further emphasizing the integration of environmental responsibility into the heart of Q-commerce operations.

Moreover, the chapter shows the broader impact of Q-commerce on traditional retail. Since the Q-commerce companies keep shaking the market, brick-and-mortar retailers have no choice but to evolve with omnichannel strategies. The strategy, which integrates the online and offline platforms, makes traditional retailers competitive while responding to consumer demands for speed and convenience. The interplay between Q-commerce and traditional retail leaves signals of entering a new era in retail, agility, technological integration, and customer-centric approaches.

Broader Relevance to the Discipline

The ideas and insights presented in this chapter have high relevance to the broad field of business, marketing, and supply chain management. Rising Q-commerce is not merely a challenge for retailers; instead, it holds much broader implications of how businesses in any given industry will think about logistics, customer engagement, and sustainability into the future. Q-commerce will seriously affect consumer culture, the logistics of cities, and in the organization of traditional shopping.

This chapter is meant to serve as a starting point for further research into the operational, technological, and social aspects of Q-commerce by scholars and practitioners.

According to these results, businesses need to slow down to meet the demands of their changing and eco-conscious customers. Q-commerce is an interesting subject for further academic research because of the vast scope for innovation that it offers in areas such as artificial intelligence, logistics, and customer behavior analysis.

In conclusion, the chapter brings out that Q-commerce is not an innovation merely in delivery but rather represents the reflection of a bigger change concerning consumer behavior regarding the retail industry. The future of Q-commerce will be dependent on how a company is able to integrate these leading-edge technologies with sustainable and customer-centric ways of creating services. This should continue looking into these dynamics for better understanding about how Q-commerce will transform the future of retail in a digital-physical manner, along with its implications on the bigger global marketplace.

The chapter has elaborately explored Q-commerce as an emerging force in the digital retail sector. In view of its evolution, the operational innovations, changes to consumer behavior, and issues of sustainability, this chapter contributes a comprehensive framework towards understanding the nuances of a rapidly growing industry. In doing so, we've highlighted how there's interconnection among the factors like technological progress, consumer expectation, business strategies, and sustainability practice; it therefore gives an idea about Q-commerce present situation and potential future scenario.

REFERENCES

Albshaier, A., Han, L., & Jeong, D. (2024). AI-powered logistics in Q-commerce: Innovations and challenges.

Albshaier, L., Almarri, S., & Hafizur Rahman, M. M. (2024). A review of blockchain's role in E-Commerce transactions: Open challenges, and future research directions. *Computers, 13*(1), 27. DOI: 10.3390/computers13010027

Ali, S., & Thompson, M. (2023). The impact of fast delivery on consumer behavior in Q-commerce. *Systematic Reviews.*

Barney, J. B. (1991). Firm resources and sustained competitive advantage. *Journal of Management, 17*(1), 99–120. DOI: 10.1177/014920639101700108

Bharathithasan, K., & Srinivasan, R. (2024). The role of dark stores in quick commerce logistics.

Bharathithasan, S., & Srinivasan, K. S. (2024). Unpacking the impact of rapid delivery and product uniqueness on quick commerce business success using PLS SEM. *International Journal of Process Management and Benchmarking, 17*(2), 153–166. DOI: 10.1504/IJPMB.2024.138351

Cano, F., Martínez, M., & González, R. (2022). Environmental implications of last-mile delivery in Q-commerce: An empirical analysis.

Cano, J. A., Londoño-Pineda, A., & Rodas, C. (2022). Sustainable logistics for e-commerce: A literature review and bibliometric analysis. *Sustainability (Basel), 14*(19), 12247. DOI: 10.3390/su141912247

Chien, A. W., Kurnia, S., & von Westarp, F. (2003). The acceptance of online grocery shopping.

Choi, T. M., Li, X., & Liu, T. (2023). Behavioral economics of impulse buying in the Q-commerce industry.

Foresti, L., Perotti, S., Ekren, B. Y., & Prataviera, L. B. (2022, October). E-Grocery challenges and a solution approach from multi-objective perspectives. In *Global Joint Conference on Industrial Engineering and Its Application Areas* (pp. 10-21). Springer.

Fornari, E., Negri, F., & Iuffmann Ghezzi, A. (2022). The Wheel of Retailing is still spinning: Promises, Compromises, and Pitfalls of Quick-Commerce. In Next Generation Marketing. People, Planet, Place: cooperation & shared value for a new era of critical marketing (Proceedings) (pp. 1-12).

Ganapathy, V., & Gupta, C. (2023). Critical success factors for quick commerce grocery delivery in India: An exploratory study. Sustainability, Agri, Food and Environmental Research-DISCONTINUED, 12(1).

George, A. S., Baskar, T., & Pandey, D. (2024). Rocket-powered E-commerce: Exploring the feasibility and implications of suborbital package delivery. *Partners Universal Innovative Research Publication*, *2*(2), 56–70.

Harter, A., Stich, L., & Spann, M. (2024). The effect of delivery time on repurchase behavior in quick commerce. *Journal of Service Research*, •••, 10946705241236961.

Harter, S., Johnson, K., & Wang, L. (2024). Consumer preferences in the age of quick commerce: A global survey.

Holma, M., & Junestrand, A. (2024). How far are you willing to go when the prices are so low?: A mixed-method study on how ultra-fast e-commerce marketing strategies affect consumers' sustainability beliefs.

Huang, M., & Yen, B. P. (2021). Driving forces for digital transformation–Case studies of Q-commerce.

Jiang, P., & Rosenbloom, B. (2005). Customer intention to return online: Price perception, attribute-level performance, and satisfaction unfolding over time. *European Journal of Marketing*, *39*(1/2), 150–174. DOI: 10.1108/03090560510572061

Jones, R., & Williams, J. (2024). The profitability challenges of Q-commerce startups. *Critical Review*.

Krainik, P. (2023). Has the future of retail arrived? An empirical analysis of drivers for the adoption of Q-commerce in the consumer durables segment (Doctoral dissertation).

Krainik, T. (2023). The carbon footprint of quick commerce: How sustainable is fast delivery? Kumar, P., & Sharma, R. (2023). Understanding consumer preferences in Q-commerce.

Luna Sanchez, P. (2024). An analysis of the drivers of consumers' purchasing behavior in quick commerce platforms.

Manani, J. (2022). Sentimental analysis on quick commerce platform based on customer reviews in Google Play Store.

Mucowska, M. (2021). Trends of environmentally sustainable solutions of urban last-mile deliveries on the e-commerce market—A literature review. *Sustainability (Basel)*, *13*(11), 5894. DOI: 10.3390/su13115894

Mukherjee, A., & Michael, J. (2022). Technology-driven logistics in Q-commerce: A review of operational innovations.

Mukherjee, S., & Michael, H. (2021). Modern trends, challenges and opportunity of e-commerce in India–An overview.

Odeyemi, A., Patil, R., & Jackson, B. (2024). Autonomous delivery systems in quick commerce: Prospects and challenges.

Odeyemi, O., Elufioye, O. A., Mhlongo, N. Z., & Ifesinachi, A. (2024). AI in E-commerce: Reviewing developments in the USA and their global influence. *International Journal of Science and Research Archive, 11*(1), 1460–1468. DOI: 10.30574/ijsra.2024.11.1.0232

Oliver, R. L. (1980). A cognitive model of the antecedents and consequences of satisfaction decisions.

Paché, G. (2022). The impact of logistics on product assortment policy: An illustration with Q-Commerce. *Journal of Supply Chain Management: Research and Practice, 16*(2), 1–10.

Pache, G. (2023, September). Q-commerce logistical networks: A shift in digital retail towards "going dark"? In EMNet 2023 (pp. 1-12).

Ranjekar, G., & Roy, D. (2023). *Rise of quick commerce in India: Business models and infrastructure requirements.* Centre for Transportation and Logistics.

Rogers, E. M. (2003). Diffusion of innovations.

Schorung, M. (2023). Quick commerce: Will the disruption of the food retail industry happen? Investigating the quick commerce supply chain and the impacts of dark stores (Doctoral dissertation, Université Gustave Eiffel).

Sharma Giri, A. (2023). E-commerce supply chain risk mitigation and online sales performance.

Smith, P., & Weber, J. (2024). The evolution of Q-commerce business models: From delivery startups to integrated retail solutions.

Son, E., & Kwon, K. H. (2024). Sustainable spatial strategies for mitigating air pollution in quick commerce environments. *Environmental Research and Technology, 7*(1), 131–139. DOI: 10.35208/ert.1367863

Stojanov, M. (2022). Q-commerce–The next generation e-commerce. Бизнес управление (Business Management), (1), 17-34.

Tahrim, S. (2022). Challenges & opportunities of Q-commerce grocery stores: A study on Pandamart.

Timothy, O. T., Fisayo, A. A., Thiru, R., Raji, M. A., & Olodo, H. B. (2024). Impact of AI chatbots on youth consumer behavior in e-commerce: Evidence from Southwest Nigeria.

Yang, Y., Lee, S., & Kim, H. (2024). The future of Q-commerce: Exploring market trends and consumer demand.

Yeo, V. C. S., Goh, S. K., & Rezaei, S. (2017). Consumer experiences, attitude and behavioral intention toward online food delivery (OFD) services. *Journal of Retailing and Consumer Services*, *35*, 150–162. DOI: 10.1016/j.jretconser.2016.12.013

Chapter 5
Consumer Awareness on Sustainable Fashion

Saba Inamdar
https://orcid.org/0000-0001-5917-4070
Presidency University, India

Sameera Afroze
https://orcid.org/0000-0002-9162-1712
St. Joseph's Degree and PG College, India

ABSTRACT

The shift to a circular economy will probably happen more quickly than in the past. Additionally, there is increasing social pressure on businesses to go carbon neutral, in contrast to earlier changes that frequently faced opposition from the general population. In the 2030s, the circular economy would become not only the dominant economic sector but also the exclusive one. A model approach to sustainability and the circular economy is required due to the excessive consumption of fashion, which has led to the unsustainable use of energy and natural resources (primarily fibres and water). This has resulted in millions of tons of textile waste annually. Natural resources are limited, and while the Earth begs for attention, humanity has long been recklessly consuming them. Circular business models are necessary because most currently operating companies are constructed on linear models. Although numerous studies have been conducted, more consumer knowledge is still needed. The current study focuses on how conscious consumers are of sustainable fashion.

DOI: 10.4018/979-8-3373-5087-5.ch005

INTRODUCTION

The three leading players in environmental conservation and sustainable development are people, the economy, and society. Since society is the cornerstone of sustainable development, it is responsible for identifying and achieving a sustainable balance across the system. In an industrial setting, ethical and value debates are intricate and frequently challenging to put into practice when designers and fashion firms select the best available environmental and social answer at a given time, which is the embodiment of best practice. The phrase "sustainable fashion" has been defined and interpreted in several ways in the currently available literature. The slow fashion movement includes sustainable fashion, which has changed recently. It frequently uses other synonyms and similar terms, such as ethical fashion and eco-fashion (Carrey & Survellon 2014). The fashion business is undeniably one of the major polluters in the world today, even though sustainable fashion has no universally accepted definition. (UN Alliance for sustainable fashion n. d). According to estimates, the entire fashion industry will be worth around USD 2.5 trillion (1012) in 2020, accounting for roughly 4% of the market share (Fashion United website on "Global Fashion Industry Statistics" n.d).

The abundance of fashion goods makes people hungrier and widens the divide between their perceptions of sustainable fashion and their natural purchasing habits. The amount of clothing purchased and the time consumed must be limited to minimise fashion waste and its detrimental effects on the environment. It is imperative to increase public knowledge of the green aspects of fashion. For firms to effectively assess the situation and spread awareness of sustainable fashion, it is critical to understand the current state of the market. Customers' growing worry over fashion businesses' unethical activities has been demonstrated, yet this concern is not always evident in their actions (Bray et al., 2010). Although they worry about pollution and climate change, most consumers do not purchase clothing from sustainable brands.

There is an attitude-behaviour divide because, although they think their environmentally conscious consumption benefits the environment, it still has little influence on their apparel purchases (Soyer & Dittrich, 2021). According to research, many consumers are interested in sustainable fashion and care about the environment, yet fast fashion—which typically consists of cheaper goods—continues to rule the market (Paco et al., 2020). If sustainable clothing meets customer requirements and educates them about sustainability in fashion, the gap between consumer mindset and real-life behaviours can be narrowed (Jeong & Ko 2021). It appears that the continued production and sale of garments run counter to environmental preservation and sustainability (Henninger et al., 2016).

CONCEPT OF CIRCLAR ECONOMY AND CIRCULAR BUSINESS MODEL

When waste and pollution are taken into account during the design process, special attention is paid to the use of sustainable raw materials and renewable resources in the production of goods. For instance, the materials used to make the products are of a higher caliber. In that situation, they will be considerably easier to recycle, resulting in a more dependable end product, making them much more likely to circulate back through the fashion pipeline. This necessitates spending money on more environmentally friendly raw material procurement and increasing the use of renewable energy sources. The Ellen MacArthur Foundation has identified the following as the main tenets of a circular fashion economy:

- Circulate goods and materials at their best value; Eliminate waste and pollution
- Restore nature

Instead of merely aiming to recycle after the customer journey, the circular fiber effort seeks to address the problems created by the fashion industry at the outset of the pipeline (*How to Build a Circular Economy | Ellen Macarthur Foundation*, n.d.). The fashion industry as a whole should become more restorative and sustainable if fashion brands commit to a circular economy throughout their supply chain. Reducing the flow of new materials makes sense from an environmental standpoint, and even while developing technologies still require additional planning and funding, they will continue to show promise for expanding closed-loop systems. Brands and retailers have the opportunity to decouple revenue from resource consumption and production by switching to circular and sharing business models. The resale and rental markets for apparel are expanding quickly, and consumer study revealed that among UK residents who purchase at least two things each month, nearly two-thirds already do so (Herold & Prokop, 2023). There are conflicting findings regarding the industry life cycle affects and business model innovation, whether in early industry life cycles or at later stages. Managing business model development includes understanding the industry development and the effect of industry structure, which is that business model innovation occurs in larger firms to a greater extent (Giesen et al., 2007; Massa & Tucci, 2014; Waldner et al., 2015).

Services have been viewed as a potential growth avenue for businesses that sell items and may also produce those things (Jacob & Ulaga, 2008; Kindström, 2010). The process of generating services, quality and loyalty, network collaboration, as well as technological advancement, are just a few of the aspects of developing products that include services (Kindström & Kowalkowski, 2009; Tambo, 2014).

An organisation that can drive change, including a governance framework to combine assets and rearrange these resources, is needed to make the move to a business model that offers more services (Teece, 2010). A company model must also vary to reflect changes in the corporate landscape. Globalisation, ICT, and emerging market strategies were noted by Casadesus-Masanell & Ricart (2010) as significant variables influencing change in business model creation. Sustainability has been mentioned as a phenomenon to take into account while developing new business models by Massa & Tucci (2014). Several challenges to developing a circular business model are highlighted by Hvass & Pedersen (2019) in their empirical case study, namely divergent viewpoints on value, ambiguous success criteria, poor alignment with restricted internal capabilities, little consumer interest, and the current approach. In a study nine categories were used to categorise the barriers to circular supply chains. These categories included management and decision-making, design difficulties, material issues, rules and regulations, lack of knowledge and awareness, and a lack of integration and collaboration (Kazancoglu et al., 2020).

Business model innovation involves "creating new methods to collect, produce, and deliver value and expands beyond more narrowly defined categories, such as product development," according to Pedersen et al. (2018). Business model innovation stands out for its holistic approach, which takes into account an organisation's whole structure rather than being limited, for example, to only a technical innovation (Pedersen et al., 2018). It should be highlighted that modifying the income stream, synchronising the time horizons, or incorporating incentives are examples of business model innovation rather than developing new goods, technologies, or markets (Veleva, 2021). Most existing firms are built on linear models; hence a shift to circular business models is required (Salvador et al., 2020). There are two forms of business model innovation: incremental and radical, and it is also feasible to combine the two (Nußholz, 2018Pedersen & Netter, 2015). Innovations can alter an organisation and its value network produce, deliver, and capture value (i.e., create economic value) or alter the value propositions in a way that has a major positive or significantly reduced negative impact on the environment and/or society (Bocken et al., 2014). Using a recently discovered significant lack of clarity in theoretical conceptualisation as a starting point, Geissdoerfer et al. (2020) provide a thorough definition of circular business models as business models that are cycling, extending, intensifying, and/or dematerialising material and energy loops to reduce the resource inputs into and the waste and emission leakage out of an organisational system. This entails methods for recycling, lengthening the use period, increasing the use phase, and replacing items with services and technology. Leading circular business models include, circular supply, which substitutes recycled or renewable materials for virgin ones, resource recovery, which turns waste into secondary raw materials, product life extension, which extends the useful life of current products, sharing models and product service system models that provide services rather than products, such as those that enable the sharing of unused items (International Energy Agency, 2018). Reselling, renting, repairing, and remaking are the main circular business strategies (Moro, 2021; Ramírez-Escamilla et al., 2024).

The circular economy is viewed as a different economic structure that enables global sustainability in sustainable practices (De Los Rios & Charnley, 2017; Murray et al., 2017). In contrast to the existing economic model, it proposes a circularity logic to reconstruct the link between human economic activity and the environment (Geissdoerfer et al., 2017). Businesses of different sizes and market categories can use the circular economy as a strategy (Murray et al., 2017). When a new business model is implemented, there may be conflicts with the old business model, such as an increased risk of losing current clients or internal competition between various components of an established business model (Waldner et al., 2015). Adopting a circular business model is like moving from a linear business model that entails a make-and-dispose process to a sustainable one that establishes closed-loop supply chains through cooperative engagement with outside partners. By connecting the building blocks to the value creation in closed-loop supply chains, such as a circular collaborative business model, circular communication, and circular awareness, the foundation for the idea of implementing a circular business model in the value network framework (Aarikka-Stenroos et al., 2022).

Even though the underlying beliefs of consumers as a driving factor are not clearly and frequently represented, a new study of fashion shoppers' perceptions of collaborative consumption reveals support for more sustainable consumption of clothes (Becker-Leifhold, 2018). Because of quick fashion trends, clothing is not worn as long as it could be, which contributes to the significant environmental effect of clothing production (Niinimäki & Hassi, 2011; Zamani et al., 2017). Agyemang et al. (2018) suggest the possible benefits of implementing the circular economy as internal drivers, such as monetary advantages from greater profitability and market share, a result of the circular economy's capability to draw customers, increased consumer loyalty, and improvements in product quality. The following elements could be identified as external drivers: politics and economics (regulations, economic growth), human and animal health, environment issues (global warming and reduced environmental impact), society (consumer con), international competition, companies' social responsibility, and stakeholders' pressure, government support, legislation, and geographic proximity. The idea of circular business models is presented and described as "business models that create, capture and deliver value to improve resource efficiency by extending the lifespan of products and parts, thereby realising environmental, social, and economic benefits" to make circular economy more easily implementable in businesses (Frishammar & Parida, 2019). It has been difficult to shift the focus of business toward circular economy because of managerial resistance, a lack of consumer and government backing, and difficulties procuring the necessary technology (Saha et al., 2021).

Lehtimäki et al. (2020) give the example of a waste management company that, despite having a revolutionary circular economy solution that was inventive, was unable to commercialise it due to client reluctance. As per Da Giau et al. (2016) make the argument that the web has taken over as the primary medium for communicating sustainability measures. The most popular methods for reaching a larger audience are social media platforms, which allow businesses to get in touch with customers who have previously demonstrated an interest in certain topics, including sustainability (Han et al., 2017). According to a previous study by Singhal et al. (2019) several factors affect consumers' intentions toward remanufactured items, with perceived risk and advantages being the most prevalent influencing factors.

A comprehensive framework that provides an acceptable balance between economic, environmental, and social factors is required by circular business model, which also demands organisational reform to achieve sustainability (Wang & Hazen, 2016). It is desired for organisations to embrace circular business model in a phased manner. The framework must also include a diagnostic stage to evaluate the supply chain, as well as numerous problems, opportunities, and difficulties with the targeted performance goals.

CONSCIOUS CONSUMERISM

Conscious consumerism is the practice of making educated and responsible purchase decisions that consider the social, environmental, and ethical consequences of products and services. This movement originated in the 1960s and 1970s when consumers began to question huge firms' ethics and the environmental effect of mass manufacturing. However, it wasn't until the 2000s that conscious consumption gained steam, thanks to the advent of social media and increased awareness of environmental concerns like climate change and sustainable living. Fashion is frequently recognised as one of the most polluting and ecologically damaging industries, as well as a resource-intensive industry with several opportunities to mitigate environmental consequences (Colucci & Vecchi, 2021). In recent decades, overconsumption of trendy clothing has become a significant issue, intimately linked to global economic development. Furthermore, the life cycle of fashion items is growing shorter because of the "fast fashion" business and client demands rather than necessities leading to rarely worn clothing, laundered frequently, and abandoned quickly. (Marques et al., 2020). The existing apparel industry may not be as sustainable as it is because of the linear economy, commonly known as a manner of conducting business. In a linear economy, raw materials are taken out of nations with abundant resources, mass-produced goods are sold to consumers, who finally discard them. This refers to popular quick fashion apparel made primarily of polyester derived from oil that ends up being discarded after being worn just seven times on average (Claudio, 2007). Put another way, humans are ruthlessly taking advantage of nature as a resource. The manufacture of virgin textile fibres consumes a lot of non-renewable resources and has an enormous impact on the environment, whether natural or artificial (Marques et al., 2020). As the second-largest polluter after the oil industry, the apparel industry is currently coming under more international attention and is still expanding. By 2050, it may use up 26% of the world's carbon budget if the current trend continues (Herold & Prokop, 2023).

In the era of the VUCA world, there are concerns over the environmental effects of production and consumption. A linear economic model is developing on the social, academic, and governmental levels. As per Ghisellini et al., (2016) and Korhonen et al., (2018), this model's environmental and socioeconomic implications, such as the drop in biodiversity and the global climate crisis, have resulted in the verdict that it is not sustainable. The fashion business exists in a complicated, fragmented global chain that affects the economic, social, and environmental sustainability grounds (Wren, 2022). The industry faces difficulties related to unethical work practises, such as the exploitation of child and slave labour and production under subpar working conditions, as a result of the outsourcing of production processes, the practise of offshore production, especially in developing countries, and the use of intensive labour (Turker & Altuntas, 2014).

Businesses classified as "born green" or "born sustainable" are developed on the principles of innovation and collaboration and are guided by sustainability principles from the outset (Todeschini et al., 2017). Its techniques and products are developed with sustainability and creativity in mind from the inception. The environment is impacted by actors in the garment sector during the production process, product transportation, and product disposal. Recycling materials and using resources wisely lessen the environmental impact of production (Lieder & Rashid, 2016; Niinimäki & Hassi, 2011). A circular economy prioritises the equity and rights of every person working in the fashion sector and will open up fresh, inclusive, distributed growth opportunities. Sectors of the economy that creates goods can be created as:

- Utilise more
- Made to be repeated
- Made with secure, recyclable, or renewable materials

By making the fashion industry circular, the underlying causes of problems like pollution, biodiversity loss, and climate change can be effectively combated. This shift promotes sustainability, reduces waste, and encourages more responsible consumption and production patterns within the industry.

BUSINESS APPROACHES TOWARDS A CIRCULAR FASHION

Sporadically studies have focussed on the actual uptake of circular business model. Advancements and learning are thought to be necessary for sustainable business strategies in general (Teece, 2010). A conceptual paper provides a road-map for the business model transformation process of incumbent firms, but it does not address the actual capabilities needed to implement the change (Frishammar & Parida, 2019). Customers drive the industry business model, which places ongoing pressure on producers to cut manufacturing costs to compete globally. Entry barriers are greater at the stages of design, distribution, branding, advertising, and market research than in manufacturing. Therefore, the large brand owners, distributors, and retailers have the most negotiating leverage. MNCs may therefore greatly influence their value chain without having to participate. Consumers are the most important aspect of the success of a circular business model as they may either encourage or hinder the adoption of the new circular fashion model through their purchase, usage and discarding decisions (Musova et al., 2021). Consumers like the notion of reusing textile waste to make new garments. Thus, circular businesses should be the "new normal." (Vehmas et al., 2018). Consumers want more visible and factual information on circular apparel and the impact of their actions (Vehmas et al., 2018). Organisations are making information more visible to customers by including it on garment labels, giving consumers more power. The tag of the garment contains information on the sustainable raw materials used in its production. Customers desire to support innovative circular models in the fashion sector is greater than their comprehension of the idea (Musova et al., 2021).

Rethinking the design process in the production of sustainable products is a significant challenge for the fashion industry (Mesa, 2023). A barrier for businesses that do not yet understand the benefits of using organic materials in the creation of product is the option to reduce, and reuse, and they are given strategic precedence (Sgambaro et al., 2024). Most companies today design their products based on client demands for functionality and aesthetics, and they manufacture them with cost efficiency in mind. Once the products are sold and leave the company's premises, the company's responsibility typically ends. However, circular products are designed with radically different parameters (Aguiar et al., 2021). More time is spent during the design phase, reducing time and cost at the end of the product's life, resulting in a more efficient, cost-effective, and environmentally friendly product throughout its lifecycle. The design phase and the waste management phase are integrated into a single process (Tan et al., 2024). An ideal circular product starts similarly to a conventional one, addressing the client's needs and expectations. However, the next consideration involves assessing which elements of the product are truly necessary (D'Itria & Aus, 2023). In a zero-waste economy, the first step is to reduce materials as much as possible (Shahbazi & Jönbrink, 2020).

The next step involves identifying resources that can be sourced from existing streams in the economy, using non-virgin resources (Bocken et al., 2014). This might involve choosing recycled paper, upcycled office furniture, or fixed IT equipment by default. Ensuring that the processes to support these choices are in place is essential. It is important to determine how these resources will be utilized in the manufacturing process. Following that, it is important to consider that the product will perform throughout its life. Identifying potential parts that may degrade and creating solutions to replace them, rather than manufacturing entirely new products, adds value without unnecessary waste. When the product becomes unusable, its end-of-life processing should be planned, with recycling considered as a last resort in the waste hierarchy (Hapuwatte & Jawahir, 2021).

Since sustainability begins with product design, fashion design courses should incorporate ecological practices into their curricula so that new professionals may become aware of them (Sgambaro et al., 2024). However, the fashion educational system continues to use conventional design techniques, which proves to be a significant barrier to introducing circular economy standards inside the industry. Countries like Turkey, and Italy are leading the way in developing sustainable practices in the fashion sector by integrating circular economy principles into fashion design programs. By teaching students to prioritize resource efficiency, waste reduction, and material reuse, these programs prepare future designers to create fashion with minimal environmental impact. This shift encourages innovative methods in manufacturing, consumption, and disposal, ensuring that the next generation of designers can meet the growing demand for eco-friendly products, reduce carbon footprints, and achieve sustainability goals (Atalay Onur, 2020; Spreafico & Landi, 2022). According to Chi's (2015) research, social and emotional variables are crucial but secondary to price and clothing quality when making a purchasing decision.

Colucci and Vecchi (2021) conducted interviews with several fashion companies to learn about the problems they confront while implementing circular business models and classified the issues as technical, operational, and consumer-related. Recycling methods that are unable to achieve the appropriate level of quality, difficulties recycling mixed fabrics, research and development that takes a long time to create, untrustworthy certificates, and durable denim fabric that is difficult to make with a low environmental effect are all technical concerns. The requirement to properly integrate take-back systems, the complexity in forming partnerships owing to the complex dynamics among different enterprises, and the need for innovations to be expandable at the industrial level so that they are not too expensive to execute are all operational challenges. Fast-fashion mentality, the problem of recognising the rental model, and the inflated cost of sustainable clothes are all consumer-related issues. Hvass & Pedersen (2019) identified two key issues: value proposition and consumer interaction. The study found two significant issues connected to the value proposition element of an organization's business model: recognizing the circular value proposition and implementing it into an organization's business model's present value proposition. The study discovered three key issues with consumer interaction in the circular business concept. These include a lack of consumer knowledge and acceptability, as well as the ability to effectively convey the program to customers and engage and encourage them to recycle and reuse clothing. Another point to be noted is the consumption of remanufactured clothes. Consumers must not only return worn things but also purchase remanufactured items, to develop the circular economy (Colucci & Vecchi, 2021). According to studies, customers in general have a negative perception of remanufactured clothes and are often unwilling to accept them (Hazen et al., 2017). Different perspectives on circular business model have been offered by several studies that address circular economy for the fashion industry. Brydges (2021) examined circular economy practices as implemented and integrated into all supply chains in the fashion industry. The authors identified several issues and chances for business models in sustainable fashion, and looked at consumer values and intents about notions of circular fashion consumption. It makes sense to examine the link between fashion and sustainability from three angles: the demand side (consumers), the regulator side (fast fashion firms), and the supply side (governments and industrial organisations) (Todeschini et al., 2017; Kim et al., 2021).

LITERATURE REVIEW

Customer Awareness Towards Sustainable Fashion

Most people in the fashion business agree that it is one of the world's most resource-intensive and polluting industries, with severe environmental consequences (Centobelli et al., 2022). The manufacture of textiles, the use of chemicals, the use of water, the creation of trash, and carbon emissions greatly influence its environmental footprint (Claudio, 2007). Many environmental issues need immediate attention and intervention during the apparel life cycle, from raw material extraction through production, distribution, use, and disposal (Rathinamoorthy, 2019). The growing worldwide awareness of the environmental effects of clothing has resulted in a significant rise in research based on fashion sustainability, notably between 2010 and 2020. Despite the availability of research, many studies require more consistency and coherence due to disparities in study aims, regions of concentration, and techniques (Bick et al., 2018; Rahman et al., 2023)

Various initiatives and strategies have been conceived to mitigate the detrimental impact of the fashion industry on the environment (Saricam et al., 2017). Instances of sustainable fashion methodologies encompass the utilisation of eco-conscious materials such as recycled polyester and organic cotton, the integration of circular economy paradigms promoting reuse, repair, and recycling, and the adoption of sustainable manufacturing techniques along with measures to enhance transparency within the supply chain. Nonetheless, notwithstanding these strides, impediments hindering these remedies' widespread embrace and expansion necessitate earnest attention and resolution (Pucker, 2022; Oliveira et al., 2024). A first-ever study to explore consumer awareness of the sustainable fashion construct by Shen & Richards (2013) described four critical aspects of sustainable fashion: recycling/vintage, fair trade/local manufacture, organic/vegan, and artisan/custom. Further, the study indicated three unique customer groups based on their attitudes toward sustainable fashion. In agreement is the study by Shen (2024), which revealed that consumer awareness of sustainable fashion varies annually, with an overall improvement. Consumers are more knowledgeable about concepts like recycling, Vintage, and Organic, and the connection between Veganism and sustainable fashion. However, awareness levels still need to be higher for Artisan, Custom, Fair Trade, and Locally Made. The pandemic has positively influenced awareness of these concepts. Another study by Jimenez-Fernandez et al. (2023) on the relationship between awareness and positive attitudes toward the fashion industry's environmental and social damage, alongside additional factors such as benefits and facilitation methods, identified that people who understand and value these concepts are more likely to have positive views. Furthermore, the study looks at the impact of Gender on people's opinions of sustainable fashion. The fast fashion industry has a significant influence on young people because of its allure and cost. Fast fashion appeals to teenagers in particular since they have tight finances and value the opportunity to wear stylish clothing at extremely inexpensive costs. Fast fashion manufacturers employ a variety of strategies to keep clothing prices low, enabling youngsters to switch up their looks often without breaking the bank. Because of this, the fast fashion industry as a whole, with the help of targeted marketing, primarily targets young people. Young people must thus assume responsibility and spread knowledge about the negative effects of rapid fashion on the environment, especially the production and handling of consumer textile waste (Polajnar Horvat & Šrimpf Vendramin, 2021).

Consumers Decisions Towards Sustainable Fashion Purchase

The growth of fast fashion has fostered an excessive consumer culture within the fashion sector (Schor, 2013). Rapid turnover and low costs attract consumers, which encourages impulsive purchases, fashion obsolescence, and the disposable nature of apparel, which is influenced by psychological, social, and economic reasons, which feed a vicious cycle of overconsumption that worsens environmental damage and the build-up of textile waste (Joy et al., 2012). In contrast to hopes for a shift towards sustainable fashion, the industry has transitioned from pre-made clothing to fast fashion. However, fast fashion is challenged by even faster trends rather than sustainable practices gaining ground as anticipated. Despite concerns from stakeholders, ultra-fast fashion companies are thriving financially, expanding through acquisitions of established fast fashion brands (Dzhengiz et al., 2023). Consumers are becoming more cognizant of the environmental and social impacts of the fashion industry, leading to shifts in their purchasing behaviours (Jimenez-Fernandez et al., 2023). A study by Tran et al. (2022) examined the influence of social media on Vietnamese Gen Z consumers' buying intentions and devotion to eco-friendly fashion goods. It concluded that social media is a substantial means of communicating eco-friendly fashion information and that existing knowledge and attitudes must be revised to encourage young customers to invest in environmentally friendly items. The survey suggested that firms emphasise service and product quality above green marketing methods for Vietnamese Generation Z. It also advocated for government involvement to promote high-quality, environmentally responsible fashion businesses.

Globalisation, consumerism, and income inequality shape fashion consumption and production patterns worldwide. Economic incentives, such as corporate governance, taxation policies, regulatory frameworks, and subsidies, influence the garment industry's sustainability outcome, underscoring the need to adopt holistic ways to tackle environmental concerns. Creating and transporting clothing generates much waste and pollution, sometimes at the expense of low wages in developing nations. People are becoming aware of its impact on human rights and the environment. Businesses are pressured to take actions that benefit the environment and treat employees properly (Abbate et al., 2023).

Consumer Perception Towards Sustainable Fashion Products

The confluence of environmental, social, and economic variables emphasises the complexities of sustainability challenges in the fashion business (Čiarnienė & Vienažindienė, 2014; Wren, 2022; Webster, 2023). While progress has been made in identifying solutions and possibilities like artificial intelligence offers various uses in the fashion sector, supporting sustainable initiatives in data analysis, supply chain management, creative design, sales and promotion, and waste reduction, critical gaps remain in grasping the overall consequences of suggested interventions and their transformational potential (Casciani et al., 2022; Ramos et al., 2023).

A study revealed a disparity in buyers' awareness and attitudes towards sustainable fashion and a lack of action when purchasing. It highlights differences in comprehension regarding fashion sustainability and related factors, particularly between genders, which could influence customer behaviour. Understanding these characteristics can assist in adopting appropriate fashion industry strategies and enhance customer behaviour toward sustainable fashion items (Mandarić et al., 2021). Another study on two southern Indian cities revealed that urban consumers' attitudes towards sustainable fashion are influenced by environmental knowledge, attitude, and perceived consumer effectiveness revealing that these factors drive consumers' intentions to purchase sustainable clothing (Tryphena & Aram, 2023).

STATEMENT OF PROBLEM

Fashion is widely acknowledged as a resource-intensive, most polluting, and ecologically harmful business. However, this sector also has much potential to reduce its adverse environmental effects (Colucci & Vecchi, 2021). The excessive consumption of fashionable apparel has grown to be a severe problem in recent decades and is closely related to the advancement of the world economy.

OBJECTIVES OF THE STUDY

- To investigate customer awareness towards sustainable fashion.
- To determine how consumers make decisions towards the purchase of sustainable fashion.
- To understand how consumers feel about fashion products with sustainable features.

METHODOLOGY

An online questionnaire using the Google Forms platform was used as a tool for this quantitative study. The questionnaire was distributed by email, social media, and personal connections using the snowball method. The questionnaire was based on two previously published articles, Shen et al. (2013) and Ceylan (2019), that looked at a comparable topic because there are no standardised questions for this kind of research. The first part of the questionnaire includes questions related to the socio-demographic profile of the respondents. The second part of the questionnaire had three constructs: feeling about sustainability, knowledge about sustainability, and decision-making. The obtained data is analysed using two statistical methods. While the second technique uses regression analysis to identify a causal relationship between numerous factors (individual attributes) and the three attitude components, the first technique uses descriptive analysis to summarise the current condition of the customer's attitude toward sustainability. Likert scale is used in the questionnaire, i.e. (1) Strongly agree (2) Agree (3) Neutral (4) Disagree (5) Strongly Disagree. A total of 130 responses were used for the analysis.

Table 1. Demographic Profile of Respondents

		Frequency	Percent
Gender	Male	63	48
	Female	67	52
Age	(20-25yrs)	39	30
	(25-30 yrs)	33	25
	(30-35yrs)	31	24
	(35-40 yrs)	27	21
Educational Qualifications	Undergraduate	49	38
	Graduate	39	30
	Post Graduate	27	21
	Doctorate	15	12
Employment Status	Student	41	31
	Self Employed	18	14
	Private Employee	49	38
	Unemployed	22	17
Annual Income	3-5Lakhs PA	27	21
	5-7 Lakhs PA	43	33
	7-10 Lakhs PA	39	30
	Above 10 Lakhs PA	21	16
Budget Expenditure on Clothing	>25%	9	7
	>20-25%	44	34
	>10-20%	69	53
	<10%	8	6

Source: Primary Data

Amongst the 130 respondents as characterized in **Table 1**, 48% were males and 52% were females, and they were 20-40 years old. 49% were undergraduates, 39% were graduates, and 15% were doctorates. The annual income of the respondents ranged from 3 to 10 lakhs. Looking at the budget expenditure, 6% spend less than 10%, 53% spend in the range of 10-20%

34% of fashion consumers spend >20-25%, and 7% spend more than 25% of their annual income.

Both regression analysis and descriptive statistics are employed to determine the awareness and knowledge about sustainability among fashion consumers.

The first question on sustainability knowledge forms the cognitive component of consumers' attitudes.

- I know child labour issues in the global supply chain of fashion apparel.
- Be aware of the waste and pollution caused by the excessive fashion apparel production in the fashion industry.

Table 2. Cross Tabulation of Cognitive Questions by Gender

	Q10			Q11		
SCALE	MALE	FEMALE	ALL	MALE	FEMALE	ALL
1	0.81%	0.00%	0.81%	0.00%	0.00%	0.00%
2	6.42%	5.32%	11.74%	3.43%	6.73%	10.16%
3	13.68%	10.89%	24.57%	7.23%	9.65%	16.88%
4	19.86%	14,36%	34.22%	17.56%	26.54%	44.1%
5	19.24%	15.72%	34.96%	27.65%	31.24%	58.89
MEAN	4.82	4.05	4.65	3.87	4.82	4.32

Source: Primary Data

Table 3. Correlation coefficient matrix for cognitive questions

i	Q11	Q12	Q13	Q14
Q11	1			
Q12	0.0367*	1		
Q13	0.0425*	0.0014*	1	
Q14	0.143*	0.276*	0.365*	1

Significance Level *10%
Source: Primary Data

The findings in **Table 2** and **Table 3** are based on descriptive statistics of variables. A regression model was used to capture the relationship among the variables of circular business. The dependent variables (Q10, Q11) are ordinal and categorical (Ordinal Probit); the Oprobit model was used to determine awareness of sustainable fashion.

Table 4. Oprobit Regression Results for Cognitive Questions

	Regressors	**Q11**	**Q12**
Q1	Female	-0.56	0.29
Q2	Age	0.04	0.00
	Self employed	-0.56	-0.33
Q3	Government Employee Private Employee	0.087 -0.675	-0.345 0.097
	Students	0.057	-0.64
Q4	Budget share	-0.876	-0.735
Q8	Friends	0.324	0.231
Q9	Social media	0.465	0.043
No: of observations=128			
	AIC	387.34	317.654
	BIC	343.219	387.114

Source: Primary Data

Table 4 shows that females pay more attention to child labour issues, and males are more aware of environmental issues; as the fashion budget of the consumer increases, the awareness level goes down.

Behavioral Questions: The purchase decisions depend on the income and preferences of the individual buyers. In order to determine the behavioural aspects, regression analysis was used to identify factors driving the decision. The three questions related to sustainability are as follows.

Q5. What is the percentage of sustainable clothing from all your purchase?

(a) Above 50% (b) 40-50% (c) 30-40% (d) 20-30% (e) 10-20%

Table 5. Distribution of Sustainable purchase By Gender

	Above 50%	40-50%	30-40%	20-30%	10-20%
Male	8	14	22	33	53
Female	6	13	20	30	58

No: of Observations=130
Source: Primary Data

Table 5 displays the distribution of sustainable purchases is quite similar for males and females, consistent with the findings in cognitive questions.

Q6. How much extra would you like to spend for fashion products with sustainability features?

Above 50% (b) 25-50% (c) 15-25% (d) 5-15% (e) < 5%

Table 6. Distribution of Sustainable Purchase By Gender

	Above 50%	25-50%	15-25%	5-15%	< 5%
Male	6	20	28	33	43
Female	4	10	35	30	39

No: of Observations=130
Source: Primary Data

Table 6 shows the distribution of sustainable purchases is quite similar for males and females, consistent with the findings in cognitive questions.

Q7. How much extra would you like to spend for fashion products with sustainability features?

Above 50% (b) 25-50% (c) 15-25% (d) 5-15% (e) < 5%

Table 7. Expenditure on Sustainable Fashion by Gender

	Above 50%	25-50%	15-25%	5-15%	< 5%
Male	5	20	28	33	42
Female	3	22	34	30	41

No: of Observations=130
Source: Primary Data

Table 7 reveals willingness of more males to pay more to purchase fashion with sustainable features. Females are less sensitive to price while buying fashion.

Q.8 How much extra income is required to buy fashion products with sustainability features?

(a) Above 50% (b) 25-50% (c) 15-25% (d) 5-15% (e) < 5%

Table 8. Income Sensitivity of Sustainable Purchase by Gender

	Above 50%	25-50%	15-25%	5-15%	< 5%
Male	45	24	20	34	5
Female	40	32	19	30	4

No: of Observations=128
Source: Primary Data

Table 8 concludes that males are ready to increase their purchase of sustainable fashion, which is consistent with findings in sustainable awareness.

Table 9 represents cognitive questions (C=Average of cognitive Questions 11-12) and affective factor (A=Simple average of affective questions 15-18).

Table 9. Oprobit Regression Results for Behavioural Questions

	Regressors	Q6	Q7	Q8
Q1	Female	-0.39	0.43	0.24
Q2	Age	0.05	-0.089	0.00
	British	0.06	0.49	0.07
Q3	American European	0.859 0.07	0.37 -0.43	0.10 -0.44
	Others	-0.245	-0.291	0.00
	Self employed	0.312	1.342	0.312
Q4	Government Employee Private Employee	0.324 -0.425	5.345 -1.297	1.683 -0.157
	Students	0.029	-0.74	0.478
Q5	Budget share	-0.695	-0.815	-0.587
Q9	Friends	0.203	0.314	0.012
Q10	Social Media	0.675	0.023	0.027
C	Cognitive Index	0.069	-0.017	-0.127
A	Affective Index	0.276	0.019	-0.341
	No of Observations	128	128	128
	AIC	436.518	473.297	432.543
	BIC	398.127	502.388	426.312

Source: Primary Data

Below are the key findings on the behavioural aspects of sustainability

- Females are more inclined to use social media /friends when compared to males when consuming fashion with sustainable features.
- The buying behaviour of employed people is different from that of students.
- Social media influences the buying behaviour.
- Females are less sensitive to price and income than males.

Affective: The affective dimensions of fashion products are studied below using Oprobit regression results

Table 10. Oprobit Regression Results for Affective Questions

	Regressors	Q15	Q16	Q17	Q18
Q1	Female	-0.213	-0.29	0.073	-0.271
Q2	Age	0.025	-0.069	-0.077	-0.031
	British	0.053	0.049	-0.02	-0.197
Q3	American European	0.054 0.063	0.057 0.057	-0.982 -0.4	-0.693 -0.192
	Others	0.195	0.29	0.65	0.049
	Self employed	3.112	4.342	-0.912	0.416
Q4	Government Employee Private Employee	2.642 -0.395	4.095 0.97	-0.793 -1.057	0.429 0.294
	Students	-0.758	-0.834	0.798	0.412
Q5	Budget share	0.56	0.035	-0.087	-0.072
C	Cognitive Index	0.969	0.713	0.295	0.564
	No: of Observations	125	125	125	125
	AIC	294.003	356.976	398.541	592.312
	BIC	312.029	298.712	473.628	594.463

Source: Primary Data

Table 10 draws the following conclusion:

- Males and females share similar patterns in the affective component of sustainability.
- Culture plays a significant role in determining the buying behaviour of sustainable products
- Economic status also plays a significant role in the feelings of sustainable purchase.

First, it was found that among buyers of fast fashion goods, claimed knowledge of sustainability is likely greater than actual knowledge due to overconfidence; hence, the attitude toward sustainability may be overestimated. Consumers should renew their knowledge regularly to avoid falling victim to false marketing. Second, fashion product makers must be mindful that consumers, particularly working-class women, are open to quick fashion goods with sustainability features. Given that female, young working-class consumers dominate the fashion sector, this has enormous marketing ramifications for clothing makers.

Finally, policymakers must acknowledge that, despite widespread public awareness of sustainability, this understanding does not necessarily transfer into prudent economic action. As a result, government policies must include appropriate levies and subsidies to promote a more long-term sustainable fast fashion industry. The study's quantitative findings are consistent with Chi's research, which found that pricing and garment quality are essential to customer behavior in the fashion business.

Careful integration of new technology with the preservation of local and cultural values is necessary to acknowledge the varied effects of global trends and to encourage mindful production and consumption. This balance is demonstrated by ideas like eco-fashion and slow fashion, which emphasize environmentally friendly production methods that honour regional customs. A comprehensive eco-humanistic vision combined with scientific and technical breakthroughs can lead to a sustainable development system on a global scale (Bonelli et al., 2024). Studies on sharing and/or circular economies are becoming more popular, and the apparel and fashion sector is one of them (Pedersen & Netter, 2015; Zamani et al., 2017). The creation of clothing is known to have a significant detrimental influence on the environment (Niinimäki & Hassi, 2011). Although the underlying beliefs of customers as a driving factor are not obvious and consistent, a recent survey of fashion buyers' opinions on collaborative consumption reveals support for more sustainable consumption of clothes (Becker-Leifhold, 2018). Businesses in the garment sector must use fewer resources, particularly energy, raw materials, water, and chemicals, to meet future difficulties and keep creating societies with lower environmental impact (Tukker, 2004; Schaltegger et al., 2016). Lessening the use of these resources will have a positive effect on the environment. Producing less and producing more effectively are the two main effects.

While developing business models the important factor is to take into account the external environment, which is crucial for sustainable consumption to grow and prosper as a substitute for traditional consumption, taking into account trends like increased urbanisation (Florida et al., 2008) and the effects of climate change. The company's capacity to make enough money for long-term survival and maintain enough financial strength must be considered while redesigning its existing business model to incorporate more sustainable alternatives. When used in full collections rather than merely pilot projects, the extraction of raw materials and the fabrication of textiles become selling factors. Large shops try to inform their customers about selecting products made of easily recyclable, less harmful materials (Dragomir & Dumitru, 2022). Additionally, higher-quality materials last longer, providing the client with long-lasting delight. Researchers have discovered that using organic cotton, recycled cotton, and recycled cotton can greatly lessen total environmental impact, including the potential for acidification, water depletion, and climate change, especially during the manufacturing stage (Moazzem et al., 2021).

CONCLUSION

The questionnaire was based on a conceptual framework of consumer attitudes toward purchasing sustainable products, which includes the emotional, behavioural, and cognitive components (or "ABCs" of consumer attitudes). The collected data is then examined using both descriptive statistics and regression analysis. Age is never shown to significantly impact any of the three components, indicating that the millennial generation is fairly represented in sample. In contrast, work position explains a considerable percentage of the variation in attitudes toward sustainability. Furthermore, while the cognitive and behavioural elements are generally stable across age groups, the emotional aspect varies. When forecasting customer behaviour for fashion goods with sustainability features, emotional factors trump cognitive ones.

Due to overconfidence, it was found that fashion customers' reported knowledge of sustainability is likely higher than their actual knowledge, influencing their attitude toward purchasing fashion goods with sustainability characteristics. Considering the discussion above the study concludes that consumers should renew their knowledge regularly to avoid falling victim to false marketing. Further, fashion product makers must know that consumers, particularly women, are interested in something other than fast fashion goods with sustainability features. To encourage adoption of circular economy by consumers, customers must be made aware of the possibility of rapid access to services like exchange and repair for product life extension. Offering customers cost-saving benefits can encourage them to participate in the circular economy. Customers should be aware of their options for speedy access to extended product life, such as exchange and repair services, at the time of purchase. Customers still mainly focus their judgments on price and quality, even if knowledge is expanding quickly.

Moreover, in the developing circularity practice, the role of the state as a regulator, NGOs as pressure organisations for social and economic well-being, and trade associations as the industrial lobby force are all obvious. Designing waste out is the first step. Everything is built to be disassembled, reassembled, and reused repeatedly.

These short component cycles set them apart from normal recycling, which typically results in significant energy and labour losses. The second is to distinguish between a product's durable and consumable components. While the durables are made to be reused and retained in technological loops, a growing percentage of non-toxic, biodegradable components are safely disposed of into the environment. Third, the energy needed to power the cycles is renewable, which lessens the dependency on finite resources and increases the robustness of the energy systems. Additionally, the circular economy transforms customers into users of goods requiring access and not ownership.

REFERENCES

Aarikka-Stenroos, L., Chiaroni, D., Kaipainen, J., & Urbinati, A. (2022). Companies' Circular Business Models Enabled by Supply Chain Collaborations: An Empirical-Based Framework, Synthesis, and Research Agenda. *Industrial Marketing Management*, *105*, 322–339. DOI: 10.1016/j.indmarman.2022.06.015

Abbate, S., Centobelli, P., Cerchione, R., Nadeem, S. P., & Riccio, E. (2023). Sustainability Trends and Gaps in the Textile, Apparel and Fashion Industries. *Environment, Development and Sustainability*, *26*(2), 2837–2864. DOI: 10.1007/s10668-022-02887-2 PMID: 36788931

Aguiar, M. F., Mesa, J. A., Jugend, D., Pinheiro, M. A. P., & Fiorini, P. D. C. (2021). Circular Product Design: Strategies, Challenges and Relationships with New Product Development. *Management of Environmental Quality*, *33*(2), 300–329. DOI: 10.1108/MEQ-06-2021-0125

Agyemang, M., Kusi-Sarpong, S., Khan, S. A., Mani, V., Rehman, S. T., & Kusi-Sarpong, H. (2019). Drivers and Barriers to Circular Economy Implementation: An Explorative Study in Pakistan's Automobile Industry. *Management Decision*, *57*(4), 971–994. DOI: 10.1108/MD-11-2018-1178

Atalay Onur, D. (2020). Integrating Circular Economy, Collaboration and Craft Practice in Fashion Design Education in Developing Countries: A Case from Turkey. *Fashion Practice*, *12*(1), 55–77. DOI: 10.1080/17569370.2020.1716547

Becker-Leifhold, C. V. (2018). The Role of Values in Collaborative Fashion Consumption—A Critical Investigation Through the Lenses of The Theory of Planned Behavior. *Journal of Cleaner Production*, *199*, 781–791. DOI: 10.1016/j.jclepro.2018.06.296

Bick, R., Halsey, E., & Ekenga, C. C. (2018). The Global Environmental Injustice of Fast Fashion. *Environmental Health : A Global Access Science Source*, *17*(1), 92. DOI: 10.1186/s12940-018-0433-7 PMID: 30591057

Bocken, N. M. P., Short, S. W., Rana, P., & Evans, S. (2014). A Literature and Practice Review to Develop Sustainable Business Model Archetypes. *Journal of Cleaner Production*, *65*, 42–56. DOI: 10.1016/j.jclepro.2013.11.039

Bonelli, F., Caferra, R., & Morone, P. (2024). In Need of a Sustainable and Just Fashion Industry: Identifying Challenges and Opportunities Through a Systematic Literature Review in a Global North/Global South Perspective. *Discover Sustainability*, *5*(1), 186. DOI: 10.1007/s43621-024-00400-5

Brydges, T. (2021). Closing the Loop on Take, Make, Waste: Investigating Circular Economy Practices in The Swedish Fashion Industry. *Journal of Cleaner Production, 293*, 126245. DOI: 10.1016/j.jclepro.2021.126245

Casadesus-Masanell, R., & Ricart, J. E. (2010). From Strategy to Business Models and Onto Tactics. *Long Range Planning, 43*(2–3), 195–215. DOI: 10.1016/j.lrp.2010.01.004

Casciani, D., Chkanikova, O., & Pal, R. (2022). Exploring the Nature of Digital Transformation in the Fashion Industry: Opportunities for Supply Chains, Business Models, and Sustainability-Oriented Innovations. *Sustainability: Science. Sustainability, 18*(1), 773–795. DOI: 10.1080/15487733.2022.2125640

Centobelli, P., Abbate, S., Nadeem, S. P., & Garza-Reyes, J. A. (2022). Slowing the Fast Fashion Industry: An All-Round Perspective. *Current Opinion in Green and Sustainable Chemistry, 38*, 100684. DOI: 10.1016/j.cogsc.2022.100684

Chi, T. (2015). Consumer Perceived Value of Environmentally Friendly Apparel: An Empirical Study of Chinese Consumers. *Journal of the Textile Institute, 106*(10), 1038–1050. DOI: 10.1080/00405000.2014.985879

Čiarnienė, R., & Vienažindienė, M. (2014). Management of Contemporary Fashion Industry: Characteristics and Challenges. *Procedia: Social and Behavioral Sciences, 156*, 63–68. DOI: 10.1016/j.sbspro.2014.11.120

Claudio, L. (2007). Waste Couture: Environmental Impact of the Clothing Industry. *Environmental Health Perspectives, 115*(9). Advance online publication. DOI: 10.1289/ehp.115-a449 PMID: 17805407

Colucci, M., & Vecchi, A. (2021). Close the Loop: Evidence on the Implementation of The Circular Economy from The Italian Fashion Industry. *Business Strategy and the Environment, 30*(2), 856–873. https://ideas.repec.org//a/bla/bstrat/v30y2021i2p856-873.html. DOI: 10.1002/bse.2658

D'Itria, E., & Aus, R. (2023). Circular Fashion: Evolving Practices in A Changing Industry. *Sustainability: Science. Practice and Policy, 19*(1), 2220592. DOI: 10.1080/15487733.2023.2220592

Da Giau, A., Macchion, L., Caniato, F., Caridi, M., Danese, P., Rinaldi, R., & Vinelli, A. (2016). Sustainability Practices and Web-Based Communication: An Analysis of The Italian Fashion Industry. *Journal of Fashion Marketing and Management, 20*(1), 72–88. DOI: 10.1108/JFMM-07-2015-0061

De Los Rios, I. C., & Charnley, F. J. S. (2017). Skills and Capabilities for A Sustainable and Circular Economy: The Changing Role of Design. *Journal of Cleaner Production*, *160*, 109–122. DOI: 10.1016/j.jclepro.2016.10.130

Dragomir, V. D., & Dumitru, M. (2022). Practical Solutions for Circular Business Models in The Fashion Industry. *Cleaner Logistics and Supply Chain*, *4*, 100040. DOI: 10.1016/j.clscn.2022.100040

Dzhengiz, T., Haukkala, T., & Sahimaa, O. (2023). (Un)Sustainable Transitions towards Fast and Ultra-Fast Fashion. *Fashion and Textiles*, *10*(1), 19. DOI: 10.1186/s40691-023-00337-9

Florida, R., Gulden, T., & Mellander, C. (2008). The Rise of The Mega-Region. *Cambridge Journal of Regions, Economy and Society*, *1*(3), 459–476. DOI: 10.1093/cjres/rsn018

Frishammar, J., & Parida, V. (2019). Circular Business Model Transformation: A Roadmap for Incumbent Firms. *California Management Review*, *61*(2), 5–29. DOI: 10.1177/0008125618811926

Geissdoerfer, M., Pieroni, M. P. P., Pigosso, D. C. A., & Soufani, K. (2020). Circular Business Models: A Review. *Journal of Cleaner Production*, *277*, 123741. DOI: 10.1016/j.jclepro.2020.123741

Geissdoerfer, M., Savaget, P., Bocken, N. M. P., & Hultink, E. J. (2017). The Circular Economy – A New Sustainability Paradigm? *Journal of Cleaner Production*, *143*, 757–768. DOI: 10.1016/j.jclepro.2016.12.048

Ghisellini, P., Cialani, C., & Ulgiati, S. (2016). A Review on Circular Economy: The Expected Transition to A Balanced Interplay of Environmental and Economic Systems. *Journal of Cleaner Production*, *114*, 11–32. DOI: 10.1016/j.jclepro.2015.09.007

Giesen, E., Berman, S. J., Bell, R., & Blitz, A. (2007). Three Ways to Successfully Innovate your Business Model. *Strategy and Leadership*, *35*(6), 27–33. DOI: 10.1108/10878570710833732

Han, S.-C., Henninger, C. E., Apeagyei, P., & Tyler, D. (2017). *Determining Effective Sustainable Fashion Communication Strategies*. Palgrave Macmillan., https://eprints.whiterose.ac.uk/139287/ DOI: 10.1007/978-3-319-51253-2_7

Hapuwatte, B. M., & Jawahir, I. S. (2021). Closed-Loop Sustainable Product Design for Circular Economy. *Journal of Industrial Ecology*, *25*(6), 1430–1446. DOI: 10.1111/jiec.13154

Hazen, B. T., Mollenkopf, D. A., & Wang, Y. (2017). Remanufacturing for the Circular Economy: An Examination of Consumer Switching Behavior. *Business Strategy and the Environment*, *26*(4), 451–464. DOI: 10.1002/bse.1929

Herold, P. I., & Prokop, D. (2023). Is Fast Fashion Finally Out of Season? Rental Clothing Schemes as A Sustainable and Affordable Alternative to Fast Fashion. *Geoforum*, *146*, 103873. DOI: 10.1016/j.geoforum.2023.103873

How to Build a Circular Economy | Ellen Macarthur Foundation. (n.d.). Retrieved 18 January 2025, from https://www.ellenmacarthurfoundation.org/

Hvass, K. K., & Pedersen, E. R. G. (2019). Toward Circular Economy of Fashion: Experiences from a Brand's Product Take-Back Initiative. *Journal of Fashion Marketing and Management*, *23*(3), 345–365. DOI: 10.1108/JFMM-04-2018-0059

International Energy Agency. (2018). *Renewables Information 2018*. OECD., DOI: 10.1787/renew-2018-

Jacob, F., & Ulaga, W. (2008). The Transition from Product to Service in Business Markets: An Agenda for Academic Inquiry. *Industrial Marketing Management*, *37*(3), 247–253. DOI: 10.1016/j.indmarman.2007.09.009

Jimenez-Fernandez, A., Aramendia-Muneta, M. E., & Alzate, M. (2023). Consumers' Awareness and Attitudes in Circular Fashion. *Cleaner and Responsible Consumption*, *11*, 100144. DOI: 10.1016/j.clrc.2023.100144

Joy, A., Sherry, J. F.Jr, Venkatesh, A., Wang, J., & Chan, R. (2012). Fast Fashion, Sustainability, and the Ethical Appeal of Luxury Brands. *Fashion Theory*, *16*(3), 273–295. DOI: 10.2752/175174112X13340749707123

Kazancoglu, I., Kazancoglu, Y., Yarimoglu, E., & Kahraman, A. (2020). A Conceptual Framework for Barriers of Circular Supply Chains for Sustainability in The Textile Industry. *Sustainable Development (Bradford)*, *28*(5), 1477–1492. DOI: 10.1002/sd.2100

Kim, I., Jung, H. J., & Lee, Y. (2021). Consumers' Value and Risk Perceptions of Circular Fashion: Comparison Between Secondhand, Upcycled, And Recycled Clothing. *Sustainability (Basel)*, *13*(3), 1208. DOI: 10.3390/su13031208

Kindström, D. (2010). Towards a Service-Based Business Model – Key Aspects for Future Competitive Advantage. *European Management Journal*, *28*(6), 479–490. DOI: 10.1016/j.emj.2010.07.002

Kindström, D., & Kowalkowski, C. (2009). Development of Industrial Service Offerings: A Process Framework. *Journal of Service Management*, *20*(2), 156–172. DOI: 10.1108/09564230910952753

Korhonen, J., Honkasalo, A., & Seppälä, J. (2018). Circular Economy: The Concept and its Limitations. *Ecological Economics*, *143*, 37–46. DOI: 10.1016/j.ecolecon.2017.06.041

Lehtimäki, H., Piispanen, V.-V., & Henttonen, K. (2020). Strategic Decisions Related to Circular Business Model in A Forerunner Company: Challenges due to Path Dependency and Lock-in. *South Asian Journal of Business and Management Cases*, *9*(3), 402–412. DOI: 10.1177/2277977920957957

Lieder, M., & Rashid, A. (2016). Towards Circular Economy Implementation: A Comprehensive Review in Context of Manufacturing Industry. *Journal of Cleaner Production*, *115*, 36–51. DOI: 10.1016/j.jclepro.2015.12.042

Mandarić, D., Hunjet, A., & Kozina, G. (2021). Perception of Consumers' Awareness about Sustainability of Fashion Brands. *Journal of Risk and Financial Management*, *14*(12), 594. DOI: 10.3390/jrfm14120594

Marques, A. D., Marques, A., & Ferreira, F. (2020). Homo Sustentabilis: Circular Economy and New Business Models in Fashion Industry. *SN Applied Sciences*, *2*(2), 306. DOI: 10.1007/s42452-020-2094-8

Massa, L., & Tucci, C. (2014). Business Model Innovation. *Oxford Handbook of Innovation Management*, 420–441. https://infoscience.epfl.ch/handle/20.500.14299/106759

Mesa, J. A. (2023). Design for Circularity and Durability: An Integrated Approach from DFX Guidelines. *Research in Engineering Design*, *34*(4), 443–460. DOI: 10.1007/s00163-023-00419-1

Moazzem, S., Wang, L., Daver, F., & Crossin, E. (2021). Environmental Impact of Discarded Apparel Landfilling and Recycling. *Resources, Conservation and Recycling*, *166*, 105338. DOI: 10.1016/j.resconrec.2020.105338

Moro, D. S. (2021, May 3). *Resale, Rental and Repair: The 3 Rs-that-are-Changing-Fashion*. Cikis Studio. http://www.cikis.studio/en/article/resale-rental-and-repair-the-3-Rs-that-are-changing-fashion

Murray, A., Skene, K., & Haynes, K. (2017). The Circular Economy: An Interdisciplinary Exploration of the Concept and Application in a Global Context. *Journal of Business Ethics*, *140*(3), 369–380. DOI: 10.1007/s10551-015-2693-2

Musova, Z., Musa, H., Drugdova, J., Lazaroiu, G., & Alayasa, J. (2021). Consumer Attitudes Towards New Circular Models in the Fashion Industry. *Journal of Competitiveness*, *13*(3), 111–128. DOI: 10.7441/joc.2021.03.07

Niinimäki, K., & Hassi, L. (2011). Emerging Design Strategies in Sustainable Production and Consumption of Textiles and Clothing. *Journal of Cleaner Production, S0959652611001569*. Advance online publication. DOI: 10.1016/j.jclepro.2011.04.020

Nußholz, J. L. K. (2018). A Circular Business Model Mapping Tool for Creating Value from Prolonged Product Lifetime and Closed Material Loops. *Journal of Cleaner Production*, *197*, 185–194. DOI: 10.1016/j.jclepro.2018.06.112

Oliveira, R. C., de Alencar Nääs, I., & Garcia, S. (2024). Clothes Consumption and Disposal Practices: A Look at The Profile of Brazilian Apparel Consumers. *Journal of Responsible Production and Consumption*, *1*(1), 107–126. DOI: 10.1108/JRPC-01-2024-0006

Pedersen, E. R. G., Gwozdz, W., & Hvass, K. K. (2018). Exploring the Relationship Between Business Model Innovation, Corporate Sustainability, and Organisational Values Within the Fashion Industry. *Journal of Business Ethics*, *149*(2), 267–284. DOI: 10.1007/s10551-016-3044-7

Pedersen, E. R. G., & Netter, S. (2015). Collaborative Consumption: Business Model Opportunities and Barriers for Fashion Libraries. *Journal of Fashion Marketing and Management*, *19*(3), 258–273. DOI: 10.1108/JFMM-05-2013-0073

Polajnar Horvat, K., & Šrimpf Vendramin, K. (2021). Issues Surrounding Behavior Towards Discarded Textiles and Garments in Ljubljana. *Sustainability (Basel)*, *13*(11), 6491. DOI: 10.3390/su13116491

Pucker, K. P. (2022, January 13). The Myth of Sustainable Fashion. *Harvard Business Review*. https://hbr.org/2022/01/the-myth-of-sustainable-fashion

Rahman, O., Hu, D., & Fung, B. C. M. (2023). A Systematic Literature Review of Fashion, Sustainability, and Consumption Using a Mixed Methods Approach. *Sustainability (Basel)*, *15*(16), 12213. DOI: 10.3390/su151612213

Ramírez-Escamilla, H. G., Martínez-Rodríguez, M. C., Padilla-Rivera, A., Domínguez-Solís, D., & Campos-Villegas, L. E. (2024). Advancing Toward Sustainability: A Systematic Review of Circular Economy Strategies in The Textile Industry. *Recycling*, *9*(5), 95. DOI: 10.3390/recycling9050095

Ramos, L., Rivas-Echeverría, F., Pérez, A. G., & Casas, E. (2023). Artificial Intelligence and Sustainability in the Fashion Industry: A Review from 2010 to 2022. *SN Applied Sciences*, *5*(12), 387. DOI: 10.1007/s42452-023-05587-2

Rathinamoorthy, R. (2019). Consumer's Awareness on Sustainable Fashion. In Muthu, S. S. (Ed.), *Sustainable Fashion: Consumer Awareness and Education* (pp. 1–36). Springer Singapore., DOI: 10.1007/978-981-13-1262-5_1

Saha, K., Dey, P. K., & Papagiannaki, E. (2021). Implementing Circular Economy in The Textile and Clothing Industry. *Business Strategy and the Environment*, *30*(4), 1497–1530. DOI: 10.1002/bse.2670

Salvador, R., Barros, M. V., Luz, L. M. D., Piekarski, C. M., & De Francisco, A. C. (2020). Circular Business Models: Current Aspects That Influence Implementation and Unaddressed Subjects. *Journal of Cleaner Production*, *250*, 119555. DOI: 10.1016/j.jclepro.2019.119555

Saricam, C., Erdumlu, N., Silan, A., Dogan, B. L., & Sonmezcan, G. (2017). Determination of Consumer Awareness about Sustainable Fashion. *IOP Conference Series. Materials Science and Engineering*, *254*, 172024. DOI: 10.1088/1757-899X/254/17/172024

Schaltegger, S., Hansen, E. G., & Lüdeke-Freund, F. (2016). Business Models for Sustainability: Origins, Present Research, and Future Avenues. *Organization & Environment*, *29*(1), 3–10. DOI: 10.1177/1086026615599806

Schor, J. B. (2013). From Fast Fashion to Connected Consumption: Slowing Down the Spending Treadmill. In Osbaldiston, N. (Ed.), *Culture of the Slow* (pp. 34–51)., DOI: 10.1057/9781137319449_3

Sgambaro, L., Chiaroni, D., & Urbinati, A. (2024). The Design and Servitization of Products According to The Circular Economy Principles: An Ecosystem Perspective in The Building Industry. *Journal of Cleaner Production*, *454*, 142322. DOI: 10.1016/j.jclepro.2024.142322

Shahbazi, S., & Jönbrink, A. K. (2020). Design Guidelines to Develop Circular Products: Action Research on Nordic Industry. *Sustainability (Basel)*, *12*(9), 3679. DOI: 10.3390/su12093679

Shen, D., & Richards, J. (2013). Consumers' Awareness of Sustainable Fashion. https://www.semanticscholar.org/paper/CONSUMERS%27-AWARENESS-OF-SUSTAINABLE-FASHION-Shen-Richards/3e478cd9f9ecb94e142e0a03f828243d23d7784b

Singhal, D., Jena, S. K., & Tripathy, S. (2019). Factors Influencing the Purchase Intention of Consumers Towards Remanufactured Products: A Systematic Review and Meta-Analysis. *International Journal of Production Research, 57*(23), 7289–7299. DOI: 10.1080/00207543.2019.1598590

Spreafico, C., & Landi, D. (2022). Using Product Design Strategies to Implement Circular Economy: Differences Between Students and Professional Designers. *Sustainability (Basel), 14*(3), 1122. DOI: 10.3390/su14031122

Tambo, T. (2014). Collaboration on Technological Innovation in Danish Fashion Chains: A Network Perspective. *Journal of Retailing and Consumer Services, 21*(5), 827–835. DOI: 10.1016/j.jretconser.2014.02.016

Teece, D. J. (2010). Business Models, Business Strategy and Innovation. *Long Range Planning, 43*(2–3), 172–194. DOI: 10.1016/j.lrp.2009.07.003

Todeschini, B. V., Cortimiglia, M. N., Callegaro-de-Menezes, D., & Ghezzi, A. (2017). Innovative and Sustainable Business Models in the Fashion Industry: Entrepreneurial Drivers, Opportunities, and Challenges. *Business Horizons, 60*(6), 759–770. DOI: 10.1016/j.bushor.2017.07.003

Tran, K., Nguyen, T., Tran, Y., Nguyen, A., Luu, K., & Nguyen, Y. (2022). Eco-Friendly Fashion among Generation Z: Mixed-methods Study on Price Value Image, Customer Fulfillment, and Pro-Environmental Behavior. *PLoS One, 17*(8), e0272789. DOI: 10.1371/journal.pone.0272789 PMID: 35972928

Tryphena, R., & Aram, I. A. (2023). Consumer Perception on Sustainable Clothing among Urban Indians. *Journal of Engineered Fibers and Fabrics, 18*, 155892502311689. DOI: 10.1177/15589250231168964

Tukker, A. (2004). Eight Types of Product–Service System: Eight Ways to Sustainability? Experiences from SusProNet. *Business Strategy and the Environment, 13*(4), 246–260. DOI: 10.1002/bse.414

Turker, D., & Altuntas, C. (2014). Sustainable Supply Chain Management in the Fast Fashion Industry: An Analysis of Corporate Reports. *European Management Journal, 32*(5), 837–849. DOI: 10.1016/j.emj.2014.02.001

Vehmas, K., Raudaskoski, A., Heikkilä, P., Harlin, A., & Mensonen, A. (2018). Consumer Attitudes and Communication in Circular Fashion. *Journal of Fashion Marketing and Management, 22*(3), 286–300. DOI: 10.1108/JFMM-08-2017-0079

Veleva, V. (2021). The Role of Entrepreneurs in Advancing Sustainable Lifestyles: Challenges, Impacts, and Future Opportunities. *Journal of Cleaner Production, 283*, 124658. DOI: 10.1016/j.jclepro.2020.124658 PMID: 33078048

Waldner, F., Poetz, M. K., Grimpe, C., & Eurich, M. (2015). Antecedents and Consequences of Business Model Innovation: The Role of Industry Structure. In Baden-Fuller, C., & Mangematin, V. (Eds.), *Advances in Strategic Management* (Vol. 33, pp. 347–386). Emerald Group Publishing Limited., DOI: 10.1108/S0742-332220150000033009

Wang, Y., & Hazen, B. T. (2016). Consumer Product Knowledge and Intention to Purchase Remanufactured Products. *International Journal of Production Economics, 181*, 460–469. DOI: 10.1016/j.ijpe.2015.08.031

Webster, G. (2023). Too Fast of Fashion: A Literature Review on the Destructive Social and Environmental Impacts of Fast Fashion. *Perspectives, 15*(1). https://scholars.unh.edu/perspectives/vol15/iss1/10

Wren, B. (2022). Sustainable Supply Chain Management in the Fast Fashion Industry: A Comparative Study of Current Efforts and Best Practices to Address the Climate Crisis. *Cleaner Logistics and Supply Chain, 4*, 100032. DOI: 10.1016/j.clscn.2022.100032

Zamani, B., Sandin, G., & Peters, G. M. (2017). Life Cycle Assessment of Clothing Libraries: Can Collaborative Consumption Reduce the Environmental Impact of Fast Fashion? *Journal of Cleaner Production, 162*, 1368–1375. DOI: 10.1016/j.jclepro.2017.06.128

KEY TERMS AND DEFINITIONS

Business Model Innovation: involves creating new methods to collect, produce, and deliver value and expands beyond more narrowly defined categories.

Circular Economy: is a circularity logic to reconstruct the link between human economic activity and the environment.

Circular Products: are those that operate within the circular economy model, meaning they are designed to reduce or eliminate the need for virgin resources and consider the end of their lifecycle.

Sustainable Communication: refers to a collection of behavioural interventions employed by organisations to inform people about environmental care and social practices within.

Chapter 6
Corporate Social Responsibility and Green Investments:
A New Paradigm for Hotel Management

Suraj Jaywant Yadav
https://orcid.org/0000-0002-2687-4852
D.Y. Patil Education Society, Kolhapur, India

ABSTRACT

The integration of green investments and corporate social responsibility (CSR) into core business strategies should be given top priority in future hotel management guidelines. To establish credibility, hotels ought to prioritize augmenting their utilization of renewable energy sources, augmenting their endeavours to reduce waste and conserve water, and pursuing green certifications. Managers can investigate government incentives and partnerships that support sustainability initiatives in order to overcome financial challenges. Hotels ought to make a point of highlighting to visitors the benefits of their sustainability initiatives and how they enhance their overall stay. In a market that is becoming more environmentally conscious, hotels can stay competitive and promote long-term success by closely observing the results of their green investments and fine-tuning their CSR strategies in response to feedback from guests and industry trends.

DOI: 10.4018/979-8-3373-5087-5.ch006

INTRODUCTION

An intriguing way to improve financial performance on sustainable performance is through research on the dynamics of sustainable performance involving green and CSR investments. This research should also shed light on the motivations behind manufacturing firms' dedication to generating high-caliber sustainability reports(Indriastuti & Chariri, 2021). By realizing their potential for long-term commercial success, emerging economies work toward establishing a green economy. Because of the limitations on natural resources, companies need to focus on financing, resources, and green investment to support sustainable business performance. This study examines how green financing and investment affect corporate social responsibility (CSR) and sustainable company performance(Ye & Dela, 2023). The interests of supply-chain stakeholders predominate, which in turn shapes hotels' CSR orientation. Stakeholder influence, on the other hand, is largely shaped by the interconnected, multifaceted nature of the tourism industry, which in turn conditions the implementation of CSR in hotels. It's interesting to note that stakeholder influence over corporate social responsibility (CSR) in hotels does not match stakeholders' perceived saliency, suggesting that stakeholder analysis should go beyond taking important stakeholders' interests into account(Farmaki, 2019). The goal of corporate social responsibility, or CSR, is to benefit both society and businesses. Every definition of the term emphasizes that businesses need to meet the needs of stakeholders as well as stockholders. Although CSR has recently drawn more attention and has been examined from a variety of angles, there are still few examples of its application to the travel and hospitality sector, and particularly to the hotel industry. The relationship between CSR and performance has been the subject of much research, but the findings have not been definitive, perhaps because CSR is a multifaceted concept that varies depending on the context in which it is used(Mariño-Romero et al., 2020). In the last few years, scholars and professionals have become more interested in corporate social responsibility, or CSR. The notion suggests that companies have an obligation to acknowledge and fulfill responsibilities beyond their commercial activities, including those related to society, culture, and the environment(Ghaderi et al., 2019). A number of internal and external factors have pushed hoteliers to make a greater effort to go green in the last few years. The need to mitigate or adapt to environmental degradation and climate change, pressure from competitors, the growing interest in sustainable development principles, and the growing consumer demand for green and eco-friendly products and services are examples of external factors(Abdou et al., 2022). A strong sense of commitment is shown by hotel companies because of their inherent environmental responsibility, which stems from the combined impact of the tourism and hospitality sectors on the environment. In this context, hotels use green technology practices as part of a suite of corporate initiatives aimed at process management, policy formation, and the creation of new products and services. The hotel industry affects society negatively by producing waste, destroying biodiversity, and causing noise and air pollution in the process of meeting the ever-increasing demands of its patrons. This sector of the economy currently contributes approximately 1% of global emissions, and this percentage is expected to rise as long as there is a sustained demand for hotel accommodations. The International Tourism Partnership (ITP) has provided precise and helpful guidelines on how to address some of the fundamental sustainability issues that the hotel industry is facing. The goals of the Sustainable Development Goals (SDGs) are highly emphasized by the ITP(Khattak et al., 2021). It is critical to understand that businesses play a significant role in determining employment and the accumulation of wealth in society. Recently, business circles and academic debates have given a lot of attention to corporate social responsibility, or CSR. The term corporate social responsibility (CSR) encompasses a wide range of activities, such as those that benefit the environment, uphold moral principles, assist employees, show consideration for the communities surrounding a company's facilities, or even have an investor focus. CSR is the process of aligning an organization's values and conduct with the requirements and desires of numerous stakeholders. It does more than just meet the demands of consumers and investors(Rahman et al., 2024).

Research Objectives

- To evaluate the role of Corporate Social Responsibility (CSR) in promoting sustainable practices within hotel management.
- To analyze the financial and environmental impact of green investments on hotel operations and profitability.
- To explore the integration of CSR initiatives and green investments in hotel business models and operational strategies.
- To assess the influence of CSR and green investment efforts on customer perceptions and brand loyalty in the hospitality sector.
- To identify key challenges and opportunities for hotels in adopting CSR and green investment practices.

RESEARCH BACKGROUND

In the hotel management industry, green investments and corporate social responsibility (CSR) have become essential parts of sustainable business strategies in recent years. In order to satisfy stakeholder expectations and legal requirements(Moyeen & Mehjabeen, 2024), hotels are progressively incorporating CSR initiatives and eco-friendly practices into their operations as a result of growing consumer awareness and environmental concerns. In addition to reducing environmental effect, green investments—such as waste reduction initiatives, energy-efficient technology, and sustainable resource management—are crucial for boosting long-term profitability and brand recognition(Astuti et al., 2024). Hotel managers looking to align their operations with changing market demands and global sustainability goals must grasp the relationship between corporate social responsibility (CSR), green investments, and business performance as sustainability becomes a competitive advantage in the hospitality sector(Dung et al., 2024). The potential of CSR and green investments to promote sustainable growth and alter hotel management paradigms is examined in this study.

Theoretical framework

CSR investments have the potential to improve both financial and sustainable performance in addition to green investments. Investing in CSR has the potential to positively impact business and society development. Thus, the advantages of organizing CSR activities have begun to be recognized by numerous organizations. Investing in CSR can also boost performance over the long term, profitability, and reputation(Indriastuti & Chariri, 2021). The chemical industries that produce high levels of pollution in developing nations encounter substantial environmental and socioeconomic difficulties. Businesses can use green finance and investment strategies to alleviate these issues and encourage ecologically friendly operations. Aside from that, businesses can use CSR programs to uphold their reputation and fulfill social obligations(Ye & Dela, 2023). In order to preserve their economic preferences and seriously harm the environment and labor force, industrialists centralised the business and investment sectors in the 20th century, creating an excruciating conundrum as well as environmental risks. Labor associations and a strike culture have emerged as a result of this tendency in response to the noncompliance of their demands(Zhang & Berhe, 2022). The issue arises from the assessment of corporate social responsibility (CSR). The practice shows that there are currently initiatives, standards, and methods available to evaluate this state. Which approach is best is a matter of debate, as the answer may depend on factors such as "whom and to what purpose the evaluation serves," the evaluation's object and subject, and awareness of emerging trends in the field(Jankalova, 2016). Practices in corporate social responsibility (CSR) are regarded as one of the major success factors impacting business performance. The best way to incorporate CSR practices into an organization's business operations, however, has not been the subject of empirical research(González-Rodríguez et al., 2019). Many internal and external factors have pushed hoteliers to become more environmentally conscious in the last few years. The need to mitigate and adapt to environmental degradation and climate change are examples of external factors, as is the growing consumer demand for eco-friendly and green products and services; an increase in ecological and environmental regulations and legislation; pressure from competitors; and an increasing interest in sustainable development principles(Abdou et al., 2022).

Figure 1. Attributes of Social Responsibility(Social Responsibilities of a Business and Its Need, 2022)

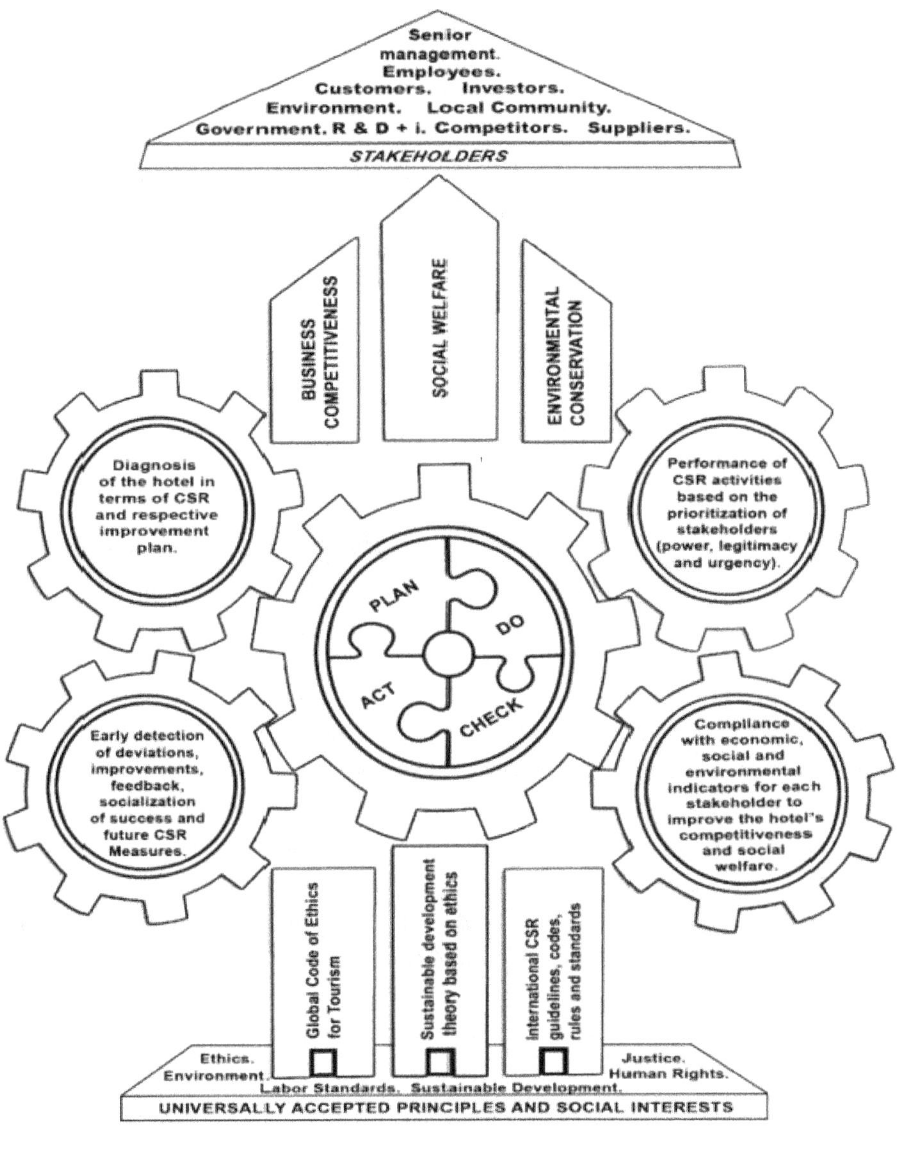

Integration of CSR and Green Investments in Hotel Operations

Examining how CSR policies are being aligned with green investment strategies to improve sustainability in hotels, including waste management, energy efficiency, and resource conservation. Individuals' responsible behavior can be reinforced by corporate social responsibility (CSR) initiatives, particularly those that focus on ecological preservation. Sustainability is given priority in an organization's culture when individual behaviors and CSR are in line. Engaging in initiatives such as waste reduction or renewable energy programs, for instance, communicates to staff members the significance of sustainable practices. These programs can strengthen responsible energy use when paired with laws that support ESBE. However, the relationship between CSR and individual behavior is sophisticated, as personal and psychological aspects mediate this relationship. These elements connect individual acts to the organizational values communicated through CSR. Their presence clarifies the ways in which CSR can affect individual behaviors in a range of contexts. CSR is a sign of a company's dedication to moral behavior and ecological responsibility. Understanding the psychological forces behind these behaviors is crucial to transforming CSR towards ESBE; policy implementation alone is not enough(S. Yadav, 2021).

Impact of Green Investments on Hotel Profitability and Brand Value

Investigating the financial benefits of green investments, such as reduced operational costs, enhanced brand reputation, and increased guest loyalty, and how they contribute to long-term profitability. Sustainability's significance in the hospitality and tourism industry has gained more attention in recent years. The travel industry is seeing a surge in demand for sustainable tourism options as consumers seek out more socially and environmentally conscious travel experiences. This change in consumer behavior has forced companies in the industry to think about implementing green business practices in order to improve their standing, draw in eco-aware clients, and stay competitive. A thorough analysis of the precise financial and environmental advantages that can be obtained from implementing green practices in the hospitality and tourism industry is, nevertheless, lacking, despite the growing recognition of the necessity for sustainability(Kholijah, 2024). The necessity of financial risk management and investment efficiency through market performance has been empirically highlighted by recent corporate finance research, particularly in unstable social and economic environments. Additionally, a number of studies on the effectiveness and performance of long- and short-term corporate socially and environmentally responsible investment funds in financial markets have been published. However, no single theoretical perspective can account for the inconsistent results despite forty years of research on the financial performance of corporate green practices. research suggesting a bad correlation between financial performance and sustainability(Khalid et al., 2023; S. Yadav, 2020). Employers place a greater emphasis on economics than on other factors, especially when it comes to short-term goals. Despite this, pursuing economic goals in isolation is not sufficient to achieve long-term sustainability; in order to reap the associated economic benefits, standards that improve social and environmental performance must be established. Businesses would undoubtedly benefit from addressing environmental issues; these benefits extend beyond employee satisfaction and retention to include improved relationships with local communities and increased brand acceptance(Abdou et al., 2022).

Regulatory and Ethical Considerations in CSR for Hotel Management

Understanding the role of government policies, international standards, and ethical frameworks that encourage or mandate CSR and green investments in the hotel industry. The hotel industry has been influenced by a number of factors in recent years to determine which social concerns are most beneficial to it. There has been a rise in staff incentives, rewards, community service, and charitable endeavors in tandem with enhanced management and staff training on internal and external social responsibilities(Peters & Mackenzie, 2014). Staff behavior is greatly influenced by hotel managers' opinions of CSR. The commitment of staff members to socially responsible behavior can be strengthened by effective leadership styles(Peters & Mackenzie, 2014). Sustainability, employee engagement, and leadership styles are just a few of the many ethical factors that hotel management must take into account when it comes to Corporate Social Responsibility (CSR). It is essential to comprehend these aspects in order to promote an environment of responsible hospitality. CSR-related training and rewards can raise employee satisfaction and lower attrition, underscoring the significance of management's role in developing a culture of responsibility(Deery et al., 2007). Navigating difficult moral conundrums in the industry requires the use of ethical decision-making frameworks that incorporate stakeholder perspectives(Upchurch, 1998).

Guest Preferences and the Demand for Sustainable Hospitality

Exploring how growing consumer awareness and demand for eco-friendly and responsible tourism are influencing hotel management's adoption of green practices and CSR initiatives. Guest preferences for corporate social responsibility (CSR) initiatives are shaping the demand for sustainable hospitality practices. According to research, some eco-friendly features, like recycling bins and energy-saving lighting, are preferred by hotel guests while other eco-friendly measures, like refillable dispensers, are less well-liked(Millar & Baloglu, 2011). Additionally, because customers are willing to pay more for eco-friendly services, the hospitality sector, which has a significant impact on resource consumption, is urged to adopt sustainable practices(Bohdanowicz & Martinac, n.d.). Guests prioritize visible green initiatives, enhancing their overall satisfaction and loyalty(Levy & Duverger, 2010). Particularly enticing qualities include waste minimization and energy conservation, which are in line with rising environmental consciousness(Chang et al., 2015; S. J. Yadav, 2024c, 2024d). Contrary to the perception that adopting sustainable practices is unaffordable, doing so can result in long-term cost savings and enhanced public perception. By using these programs to effectively communicate their CSR efforts, hotels can draw in eco-aware guests(Levy & Duverger, 2010). While many guests express a preference for sustainable practices, barriers such as higher costs and limited information can hinder their choices. Addressing these challenges is crucial for the hospitality industry to fully realize the potential of sustainable CSR initiatives.

Figure 2. Model for CSR in Hotel Industry ((Peña Miranda et al., 2021)

Challenges and Opportunities in Implementing CSR and Green Investments

Analysing the barriers to integrating CSR and green investments in hotel management, such as high initial costs and limited technology, as well as opportunities for innovation and competitive advantage(S. J. Yadav, 2025). Guest preferences for corporate social responsibility (CSR) initiatives are shaping the demand for sustainable hospitality practices. Refillable soap dispensers are less common than eco-friendly features like recycling bins and energy-saving lighting, according to research on guest preferences for eco-friendly accommodations(Millar & Baloglu, 2011). Corporate social responsibility (CSR) in sustainable hospitality incorporates social, environmental, and economic aspects to improve community well-being and service innovation. Long-term sustainability and the development of competitive advantage in the hospitality industry depend on this multifaceted strategy. The triple bottom line (TBL) approach is emphasized in a thorough framework for sustainability-oriented hospitality service innovation (SOHSI), with a focus on interior design, brand management, and environmental entrepreneurship(Ozturkoglu et al., 2019). This framework aids food and beverage organizations in developing innovative, sustainable services. Because tourism CSR initiatives create shared value for communities, they can make a substantial contribution to sustainable development. Efficient methods of assessment are essential for determining these programs' long-term effects(Kalabay et al., 2019).

DATA COLLECTION

Data for this study were collected through a mixed-method approach, combining quantitative and qualitative research techniques(S. J. Yadav, 2024b). A structured survey was administered to 100 hotel managers and 200 guests from various hospitality establishments to assess their perspectives on Corporate Social Responsibility (CSR) and green investments. The survey included both Likert-scale and open-ended questions to capture detailed responses. Additionally, semi-structured interviews were conducted with 15 hotel executives to gain deeper insights into the implementation of CSR and green investment practices. Statistical analysis, including regression analysis and ANOVA tests(S. J. Yadav, 2024a), was performed to evaluate the relationship between green investments and hotel performance indicators such as profitability, guest satisfaction, and sustainability outcomes. Qualitative data from interviews were analyzed using thematic analysis to identify key trends and challenges faced by the industry in adopting CSR initiatives.

DATA ANALYSIS

Table 1. Hotel Manager Demographics

Attribute	Count	Percentage (%)
Gender		
Male	65	65%
Female	35	35%
Experience		
1-5 years	20	20%
6-10 years	30	30%
11-15 years	25	25%
16+ years	25	25%
Hotel Type		
Luxury	40	40%
Mid-Range	45	45%
Budget	15	15%

Table 1 provides a demographic breakdown of the hotel managers who participated in the survey. The data show that 65% of managers are male and 35% are female, indicating a gender imbalance in management roles. Experience levels are distributed, with 30% of managers having 6-10 years of experience, while 40% of managers are from luxury or mid-range hotels, indicating a focus on higher-end establishments in this study.

Table 2. Guest Demographics

Attribute	Count	Percentage (%)
Gender		
Male	110	55%
Female	90	45%
Age		
18-30	70	35%
31-45	80	40%
46-60	35	17.50%
60+	15	7.50%

Table 2 shows the demographics of the 200 guests surveyed. It indicates that the majority of respondents are aged between 31-45 years old (40%) and predominantly male (55%). This data helps in understanding the profiles of guests who might be more engaged with CSR and green investment efforts in hotels.

Table 3. CSR Awareness Among Hotel Managers

CSR Knowledge Level	Count	Percentage (%)
Very Knowledgeable	50	50%
Somewhat Knowledgeable	30	30%
Not Very Knowledgeable	10	10%
Unaware	10	10%

The data here reveal that 50% of hotel managers consider themselves "Very Knowledgeable" about CSR, while 30% are somewhat knowledgeable. However, 10% are unaware of CSR, which suggests that there are still gaps in knowledge and understanding of CSR principles among hotel management teams.

Table 4. Green Investment Implementation in Hotels

Green Investment Practice	Count (Hotels)	Percentage (%)
Energy-Efficient Lighting	85	85%
Solar Energy Use	40	40%
Waste Reduction Programs	70	70%
Water Conservation Initiatives	60	60%
Green Certifications (e.g., LEED)	35	35%

Table 4 highlights the level of adoption of various green practices in the hotels surveyed. Energy-efficient lighting is the most implemented green initiative, with 85% of hotels adopting it, followed by 70% implementing waste reduction programs. However, only 35% of hotels have achieved green certifications like LEED, indicating a potential area for improvement.

Table 5. Guest Perception of Hotel Sustainability Efforts

Perception of CSR Initiatives	Count	Percentage (%)
Strongly Supportive	120	60%
Moderately Supportive	50	25%
Neutral	20	10%
Unconcerned	10	5%

Table 5 demonstrates that 60% of guests are strongly supportive of CSR and green investment efforts in hotels, with only 5% showing no concern. This suggests that most guests appreciate and support hotels' sustainability efforts, which can influence their choice of accommodation.

Table 6. Impact of CSR on Hotel Reputation (Manager Survey)

CSR Impact on Reputation	Count	Percentage (%)
Significantly Improved	75	75%
Moderately Improved	15	15%
No Impact	10	10%

According to table 6, 75% of hotel managers believe CSR significantly improves their hotel's reputation. A smaller portion (15%) feel it has moderately improved their reputation, and only 10% see no impact. This indicates a broad consensus that CSR initiatives enhance the hotel's public image.

Table 7. Guest Willingness to Pay Premium for Green Hotels

Willingness to Pay Premium	Count	Percentage (%)
Yes, up to 10% more	90	45%
Yes, up to 5% more	70	35%
No	40	20%

Table 7 shows that 45% of guests are willing to pay up to 10% more for staying in green-certified hotels, while 35% would pay 5% more. However, 20% of guests are not willing to pay extra for green investments. This information is critical for hotels when pricing their rooms and promoting their green credentials.

Table 8. Hotel Profitability and Green Investment (ANOVA Test Results)

Variable	F-Statistic	p-Value
Energy-Efficient Lighting	5.2	0.01*
Solar Energy Use	3.8	0.04*
Waste Reduction Programs	6.5	0.00**
Water Conservation Initiatives	4.7	0.03*

The ANOVA test results show significant relationships between green investments and hotel profitability. For instance, waste reduction programs ($p < 0.01$) and energy-efficient lighting ($p < 0.05$) have a statistically significant impact on profitability. This suggests that adopting green investments can positively influence a hotel's financial performance.

Table 9. Regression Analysis - Impact of CSR and Green Investments on Guest Satisfaction

Variable	Coefficient	t-Statistic	p-Value
CSR Initiatives	0.45	4.5	0.00**
Green Investment Practices	0.37	3.85	0.01*
Staff Training on Sustainability	0.25	2.55	0.03*

The regression analysis shows a strong positive relationship between CSR initiatives and guest satisfaction, with a coefficient of 0.45 ($p < 0.01$). Similarly, green investments and staff training on sustainability also show positive impacts on guest satisfaction, suggesting that sustainability efforts are well-received by guests and contribute to a better customer experience.

Table 10. Thematic Analysis - Key Themes from Executive Interviews

Theme	Frequency	Example Quote
Cost of Green Investments	12	"Initial costs are high, but long-term benefits are clear."
Staff Training and CSR Knowledge	9	"Training staff on sustainability is crucial for success."
Regulatory Compliance	7	"Government policies push us towards greener operations."
Customer Demand for Green Hotels	10	"More guests are asking about our sustainability practices."

Table 10 summarizes key themes from interviews with hotel executives. The most frequently mentioned theme is the cost of green investments, with 12 executives acknowledging the high initial costs but recognizing the long-term benefits. Other notable themes include the importance of staff training and regulatory compliance, indicating that financial and operational challenges must be addressed to fully implement CSR and sustainability initiatives.

Table 11. Challenges in Implementing Green Investments (Manager Survey)

Challenge	Count	Percentage (%)
High Initial Investment Costs	65	65%
Lack of Government Incentives	40	40%
Insufficient Knowledge/Training	30	30%
Uncertainty of Return on Investment	45	45%

Table 11 identifies the major challenges hotels face when adopting green investments. 65% of managers cited high initial costs as a primary barrier, while 40% pointed to a lack of government incentives. Additionally, 45% of managers expressed uncertainty about the return on investment for green initiatives, showing the hesitation in making these financial commitments.

Table 12. Guest Feedback on Hotel Environmental Practices

Feedback Type	Count	Percentage (%)
Very Satisfied with Sustainability	80	40%
Satisfied	60	30%
Neutral	30	15%
Dissatisfied	20	10%
Very Dissatisfied	10	5%

Table 12 captures guest satisfaction with hotel environmental practices. The results show that 70% of guests are either satisfied or very satisfied with the sustainability efforts of the hotels they stayed at, while only 15% are neutral and 5% are dissatisfied. This demonstrates a generally positive reception of green practices among hotel guests.

Table 13. Green Investment ROI for Hotels

Green Practice	ROI (%)
Energy-Efficient Lighting	15%
Solar Energy Use	8%
Waste Reduction Programs	12%
Water Conservation Initiatives	10%

The ROI percentages for various green investments are shown here, with energy-efficient lighting providing the highest return at 15%. Waste reduction programs also deliver a solid return at 12%, suggesting that certain green investments can generate financial benefits for hotels in addition to environmental advantages.

Table 14. Future CSR and Green Investment Plans by Hotels

Future Investment Focus	Count	Percentage (%)
Expanding Renewable Energy Use	50	50%
Increasing Waste Reduction Programs	45	45%
Enhancing Water Conservation Efforts	40	40%
Achieving Green Certifications (LEED)	30	30%

Table 14 highlights hotels' future plans for CSR and green investments. **50% of hotels** plan to expand their use of renewable energy, while **45%** intend to increase waste reduction efforts. These findings indicate a growing trend toward sustainability in the industry, with a clear focus on reducing environmental impact through green investments.

RESULT

According to the study's findings, hotel operations and visitor perceptions are significantly impacted by green investments and corporate social responsibility (CSR). With green investments like energy-efficient lighting (85%) and waste reduction programs (70%) being widely adopted, the majority of hotel managers (75%) stated that CSR initiatives had a significant positive impact on their hotel's reputation. There are still difficulties, though, with 65% of managers citing high upfront costs as a deterrent to adopting green practices and 45% voicing worries about hazy return on investment. Travelers' opinions were overwhelmingly positive, with 60% of them strongly endorsing hotels' sustainability initiatives and 45% saying they would be willing to pay up to 10% more for environmentally friendly lodging.

Practices like waste reduction and energy-efficient lighting showed a significant positive impact on hotel profitability ($p < 0.05$), further supporting the financial viability of green investments, according to statistical analysis. Regression analysis also showed a strong positive correlation between guest satisfaction and green investments and CSR initiatives, with CSR efforts showing a coefficient of 0.45 ($p < 0.01$). Despite the operational and financial challenges, hotel executives' qualitative insights emphasized the significance of staff training and regulatory compliance in executing green initiatives successfully. These results imply that, even though green investments are required.

FUTURE GUIDELINES

The integration of green investments and corporate social responsibility (CSR) into core business strategies should be given top priority in future hotel management guidelines(Xanthopoulou & Plimakis, 2023). To establish credibility, hotels ought to prioritize augmenting their utilization of renewable energy sources, augmenting their endeavors to reduce waste and conserve water, and pursuing green certifications(Dung et al., 2024). Managers can investigate government incentives and partnerships that support sustainability initiatives in order to overcome financial challenges. To guarantee the successful execution of green initiatives, staff training on sustainability principles should also be given top priority(Khodaviren & Bhattacharjee, 2024). Additionally, hotels ought to make a point of highlighting to visitors the benefits of their sustainability initiatives and how they enhance their overall stay. In a market that is becoming more environmentally conscious, hotels can stay competitive and promote long-term success by closely observing the results of their green investments and fine-tuning their CSR strategies in response to feedback from guests and industry trends(Karim, 2022).

CONCLUSION

The study concludes by showing how green investments and corporate social responsibility (CSR) are becoming crucial elements of contemporary hotel management, providing advantages for the environment and the economy(Serra Cantallops et al., 2018). In addition to improving hotel brands, the extensive implementation of sustainable practices—like waste reduction initiatives and energy-efficient lighting—has had a big impact on revenue and visitor satisfaction(Moyeen & Mehjabeen, 2024). The positive response from visitors—many of whom are willing to pay more for eco-friendly services—underlines the growing demand for sustainable hospitality despite obstacles like high initial costs and uncertainty surrounding returns on investment(Simarmata et al., 2023). The significance of incorporating sustainability into hotel operations is further underscored by the robust association found between guest satisfaction and corporate social responsibility initiatives. Sustainability is a critical strategy for future success because(Simarmata et al., 2023), as the hospitality sector develops, hotels who prioritize green initiatives and adhere to CSR principles stand to gain long-term advantages in terms of both market positioning and operational efficiency(Shin et al., 2021).

REFERENCES

Abdou, A. H., Hassan, T. H., Salem, A. E., Elsaied, M. A., & Elsaed, A. A. (2022). Determinants and Consequences of Green Investment in the Saudi Arabian Hotel Industry. *Sustainability (Basel)*, *14*(24), 24. Advance online publication. DOI: 10.3390/su142416905

Astuti, S., Zubaidah, S., & Irawan, D. (2024). Pendampingan Penyusunan Laporan Corporate Social Responsibility CSR) pada Rayz Hotel Malang. *Jurnal Pengabdian Masyarakat Bangsa*, *2*(6), 2317–2322. DOI: 10.59837/jpmba.v2i6.1216

Bohdanowicz, P., & Martinac, I. (n.d.). *ATTITUDES TOWARDS SUSTAINABILITY IN CHAIN HOTELS – RESULTS OF A EUROPEAN SURVEY*.

Chang, L.-H., Hsiao, Y.-C., Nuryyev, G., & Huang, M.-L. (2015). People's motivation, constraints and willingness to pay for green hotels. *European Journal of Tourism Research*, *9*, 67–77. DOI: 10.54055/ejtr.v9i.166

Deery, M., Jago, L., & Stewart, M. (2007). Corporate Social Responsibility Within the Hospitality Industry. *Tourism Review International*, *11*(2), 107–114. DOI: 10.3727/154427207783948900

Dung, P., Hoang, H., & Son, N. (2024). Unlocking sustainable success: The transformative impact of CSR on hotel performance. *Cogent Social Sciences*, *10*(1), 2392025. Advance online publication. DOI: 10.1080/23311886.2024.2392025

Farmaki, A. (2019). Corporate social responsibility in hotels: A stakeholder approach. *International Journal of Contemporary Hospitality Management*, *31*(6), 2297–2320. DOI: 10.1108/IJCHM-03-2018-0199

Ghaderi, Z., Mirzapour, M., Henderson, J. C., & Richardson, S. (2019). Corporate social responsibility and hotel performance: A view from Tehran, Iran. *Tourism Management Perspectives*, *29*, 41–47. DOI: 10.1016/j.tmp.2018.10.007

González-Rodríguez, M. R., Martín-Samper, R. C., Köseoglu, M. A., & Okumus, F. (2019). Hotels' corporate social responsibility practices, organizational culture, firm reputation, and performance. *Journal of Sustainable Tourism*, *27*(3), 398–419. DOI: 10.1080/09669582.2019.1585441

Indriastuti, M., & Chariri, A. (2021). The role of green investment and corporate social responsibility investment on sustainable performance. *Cogent Business & Management*, *8*(1), 1960120. DOI: 10.1080/23311975.2021.1960120

Jankalova, M. (2016). Approaches to the Evaluation of Corporate Social Responsibility. *Procedia Economics and Finance*, *39*, 580–587. DOI: 10.1016/S2212-5671(16)30302-1

Kalabay, B., Ertuna, B., & Salman, D. (2019). Corporate social responsibility in tourism as a tool for sustainable development: An evaluation from a community perspective. *International Journal of Contemporary Hospitality Management*, *31*(6), 2358–2375. Advance online publication. DOI: 10.1108/IJCHM-05-2018-0448

Karim, R. (2022). The Influence of CSR Practices on Hotel Images and Hotel Benefits in Bangladesh. *Journal of Technology Management and Business*, *9*(2). Advance online publication. DOI: 10.30880/jtmb.2022.09.02.002

Khalid, F., Naveed, K., Nawaz, R., Sun, X., Wu, Y., & Ye, C. (2023). Does corporate green investment enhance profitability? An institutional perspective. *Ekonomska Istrazivanja*, *36*(1), 1–24. DOI: 10.1080/1331677X.2022.2063919

Khattak, S., Nouman, M., Fayaz, M., Cisma , L., Negrut, L., & Negrut, C. (2021). Corporate Social Responsibility and Employee Green Behavior in the Hospitality Industry: A Cross-Country Study. *Sustainability (Basel)*, *13*(19), 1–15. DOI: 10.3390/su131910534

Khodaviren, M., & Bhattacharjee, S. (2024). CSR perceptions and practices in small hotels in urban cities. *Journal of Hospitality and Tourism Insights*. DOI: 10.1108/JHTI-10-2023-0692

Kholijah, S. (2024). Analysis of Economic and Environmental Benefits of Green Business Practices in the Hospitality and Tourism Sector. *Involvement International Journal of Business*, *1*(1), 60–74. DOI: 10.62569/iijb.v1i1.7

Levy, S. E., & Duverger, P. (2010). Consumer perceptions of sustainability in the lodging industry: Examination of sustainable tourism criteria. *International CHRIE Conference-Refereed Track, Event 31*, 2–8.

Mariño-Romero, J. M., Hernández-Mogollón, J. M., Campón-Cerro, A. M., & Folgado-Fernández, J. A. (2020). Corporate Social Responsibility in Hotels: A Proposal of a Measurement of its Performance through Marketing Variables. *Sustainability (Basel)*, *12*(7), 7. Advance online publication. DOI: 10.3390/su12072961

Millar, M., & Baloglu, S. (2011). Hotel Guests' Preferences for Green Guest Room Attributes. *Cornell Hospitality Quarterly -. Cornell Hospitality Quarterly*, *52*(3), 302–311. DOI: 10.1177/1938965511409031

Moyeen, A., & Mehjabeen, M. (2024). CSR research in the hotel industry: How it relates to promoting the SDGs. *Social Responsibility Journal, 20*(9), 1770–1786. Advance online publication. DOI: 10.1108/SRJ-01-2024-0032

Ozturkoglu, Y., Özer Sarı, F., & Esendemirli Saygili, E. (2019). A new holistic conceptual framework for sustainability oriented hospitality innovation with triple bottom line perspective. *Journal of Hospitality and Tourism Technology, ahead-of-print*. DOI: 10.1108/JHTT-02-2019-0022

Peña Miranda, D., Plaza, A., Brea, J. A., & Camilleri, M. A. (2021). Corporate social responsibility model for a competitive and resilient hospitality industry. *Sustainable Development (Bradford), 30*(3), 433–446. Advance online publication. DOI: 10.1002/sd.2259

Peters, M., & Mackenzie, M. (2014). Hospitality Managers' Perception of Corporate Social Responsibility: An Explorative Study. *Asia Pacific Journal of Tourism Research, 19*(3), 257–272. Advance online publication. DOI: 10.1080/10941665.2012.742915

Rahman, M., Tanchangya, T., Rahman, J., Aktar, M. A., & Majumder, S. C. (2024). Corporate social responsibility and green financing behavior in Bangladesh: Towards sustainable tourism. *Innovation and Green Development, 3*(3), 100133. DOI: 10.1016/j.igd.2024.100133

Serra Cantallops, A., Peña Miranda, D., Ramón Cardona, J., & Martorell-Cunill, O. (2018). Progress in Research on CSR and the Hotel Industry (2006-2015). *Cornell Hospitality Quarterly, 59*(1), 15–38. DOI: 10.1177/1938965517719267

Shin, H., Sharma, A., Nicolau, J., & Kang, J. (2021). The impact of hotel CSR for strategic philanthropy on booking behavior and hotel performance during the COVID-19 pandemic. *Tourism Management, 85*, 104322. DOI: 10.1016/j.tourman.2021.104322 PMID: 34815613

Simarmata, B., & Utomo, B. (2023). Influence of CSR Activity, Service Quality and Brand Attitude to Customer's Re-Visit Intention in Hotel Industry. *Jurnal Multidisiplin Madani, 3*(1), 208–228. DOI: 10.55927/mudima.v3i1.2308

Social Responsibilities of a Business and its Need. (2022, May 13). GeeksforGeeks. https://www.geeksforgeeks.org/social-responsibilities-of-a-business-and-its-need/

Upchurch, R. S. (1998). A Conceptual Foundation for Ethical Decision Making: A Stakeholder Perspective in the Lodging Industry (U.S.A.). *Journal of Business Ethics, 17*(12), 1349–1361. DOI: 10.1023/A:1005866820504

Xanthopoulou, P., & Plimakis, S. (2023). *The Adoption of Corporate Social Responsibility (CSR) Policy in the Tourism Sector: How CSR Affects Consumer Loyalty in the Greek Hotel Industry* (pp. 1–19). DOI: 10.4018/978-1-6684-6055-9.ch001

Yadav, S. (2020). AI in the hotel industry: Adoption and application of artificial intelligence in hotel industry. *Hospitality & Travel Connaisseur Magazine*, 30–32.

Yadav, S. (2021). Millennial Employees-Role, Benefits and Retaining Strategies in Hotel Industry (p. 64). DOI: 10.6084/m9.figshare.13719949.v1

Yadav, S. J. (2024a). AI Bias and Fairness: Ethical Considerations in Service Marketing Strategies. In *Integrating AI-Driven Technologies Into Service Marketing* (pp. 49–64). IGI Global. https://www.igi-global.com/chapter/ai-bias-and-fairness/355986

Yadav, S. J. (2024b). Analyzing the Influence of Sustainable Voluntourism on Community Development and Empowerment. In *Special Interest Trends for Sustainable Tourism* (pp. 152–165). IGI Global., https://www.igi-global.com/chapter/analyzing-the-influence-of-sustainable-voluntourism-on-community-development-and-empowerment/352362 DOI: 10.4018/979-8-3693-5903-7.ch009

Yadav, S. J. (2024c). Voices From Within: Exploring Indian Perspectives on Sex Tourism. In *Examining Tourist Behaviors and Community Involvement in Destination Rejuvenation* (pp. 263–272). IGI Global. https://www.igi-global.com/chapter/voices-from-within/348915

Yadav, S. J. (2024d). Voices From Within: Exploring Indian Perspectives on Sex Tourism. In *Examining Tourist Behaviors and Community Involvement in Destination Rejuvenation* (pp. 263–272). IGI Global. https://www.igi-global.com/chapter/voices-from-within/348915

Yadav, S. J. (2025). Artificial Intelligence and Stress Management Tools for Better Mental Health. In *AI Technologies and Advancements for Psychological Well-Being and Healthcare* (pp. 163–186). IGI Global., https://www.igi-global.com/chapter/artificial-intelligence-and-stress-management-tools-for-better-mental-health/357098

Ye, J., & Dela, E. (2023). The Effect of Green Investment and Green Financing on Sustainable Business Performance of Foreign Chemical Industries Operating in Indonesia: The Mediating Role of Corporate Social Responsibility. *Sustainability (Basel)*, *15*(14), 14. Advance online publication. DOI: 10.3390/su151411218

Zhang, Y., & Berhe, H. M. (2022). The Impact of Green Investment and Green Marketing on Business Performance: The Mediation Role of Corporate Social Responsibility in Ethiopia's Chinese Textile Companies. *Sustainability (Basel)*, *14*(7), 7. Advance online publication. DOI: 10.3390/su14073883

Chapter 7
Health Crises and Digitalization:
Digital Health

S. Guru Basava Aradhya
https://orcid.org/0000-0002-3335-2681
Chandigarh School of Business, Chandigarh Group of Colleges, India

Jaspreet Singh
https://orcid.org/0000-0002-0011-1398
Central University of Jammu, India

V. Chithambar Gupta
https://orcid.org/0009-0002-1364-5425
Presidency University, India

T. C. Manjunath
https://orcid.org/0000-0003-2545-9160
Rajarajeswari College of Engineering, India

P. Selvakumar
https://orcid.org/0000-0002-3650-4548
Nehru Institute of Technology, Coimbatore, India

Mohit Sharma
https://orcid.org/0009-0007-2280-8077
Maharshi Dayanand University, Rohtak, India

Manju Shree Raman
https://orcid.org/0000-0002-2719-3549
Christ University, India

ABSTRACT

The rapid advancement of technology reshaped sectors, and the concept of digital health encompasses a broad spectrum of innovations, including telemedicine, technologies engagement and provided critical support systems around the world faced unprecedented challenges, digital health solutions emerged as vital tools for maintaining the continuity of care, improving accessibility, and enhancing the overall efficiency of health services. The COVID-19 pandemic catalyzed a massive shift towards digital health, as physical severely limited facilities. Telemedicine platforms surged in popularity, allowing safety shifts was ongoing management.

DOI: 10.4018/979-8-3373-5087-5.ch007

Digital technologies, could maintain regular contact with these patients, adjusting treatment plans and offering support. Moreover, digital health tools facilitated rapid data collection and analysis, enabling more of the evolving crisis. For instance, played a crucial symptom tracking contact tracing, helping to identify outbreaks and manage community spread. Additionally, allowed policymakers to inform resource allocation public health strategies.

INTRODUCTION

The rapid advancement of technology reshaped sectors, and the concept of digital health encompasses a broad spectrum of innovations, including telemedicine, technologies engagement and provided critical support systems around the world faced unprecedented challenges, digital health solutions emerged as vital tools for maintaining the continuity of care, improving accessibility, and enhancing the overall efficiency of health services. The COVID-19 pandemic catalyzed a massive shift towards digital health, as physical severely limited facilities. Telemedicine platforms surged in popularity, allowing safety shifts was ongoing management. Digital technologies, could maintain regular contact with these patients, adjusting treatment plans and offering support. Moreover, digital health tools facilitated rapid data collection and analysis, enabling more of the evolving crisis. For instance, played a crucial symptom tracking contact tracing, helping to identify outbreaks and manage community spread. Additionally, allowed policymakers to inform resource allocation public health strategies. In this context, digital health not only served as a means of delivering care but also became an essential component of public health infrastructure. Machine learning further enhanced digital health solutions. Outbreaks, diagnostic processes. These technologies have proven invaluable in managing patient flow during surges in demand, ensuring that healthcare systems remain responsive even under strain. Furthermore, AI-driven tools have enabled patients thus improving overall care quality. Despite the many benefits, the rapid adoption of digital health has not been without challenges. Issues such as concerns, and equitable access to these technologies. Vulnerable populations, including the elderly and those in rural areas, access services due to a lack of technology or internet connectivity. Therefore, healthcare organizations must prioritize inclusivity and implement strategies to bridge these gaps, so that health is accessible to all. Regulatory frameworks are also critical to digital health. Adoption of telehealth and other digital solutions grows, so does the need for clear guidelines that govern their use. Ensuring that these technologies meet safety and efficacy standards public positive health outcomes. Crucial to create a cohesive regulatory environment that fosters innovation while protecting patient rights. Looking ahead, the lessons learned during the pandemic will likely inform the future of digital health. Everyday practice is expected to continue, promoting a more resilient healthcare system that can better withstand future crises. The ongoing development of technologies such as remote monitoring, AI-driven diagnostics, and predictive analytics will further enhance the capability of healthcare systems to deliver timely and effective care.

The Impact of Health Crises on Healthcare Systems: Challenges and Opportunities

Natural disasters, and emergencies, have profound effects on healthcare systems worldwide. These crises expose vulnerabilities, strain resources, and challenge existing protocols, often revealing systemic inefficiencies that can hinder effective responses. However, they also present significant opportunities for transformation and innovation within healthcare frameworks. Understanding the dual impact of health crises on healthcare systems requires an exploration of the challenges faced and the opportunities that arise for reform and improvement. Health crises overwhelming the COVID-19 pandemic is a stark illustration of this, as hospitals worldwide faced unprecedented surges in patient volume. This surge often led to overcrowded facilities, resource shortages, and burnout among healthcare professionals (Liu Y., et al, 2020). The strain on emergency services and intensive care units highlighted existing gaps in capacity and preparedness. Furthermore, the diversion of resources to manage acute cases can result in the neglect of routine healthcare services, leading to delays in treatment for chronic conditions and non-COVID-related illnesses. Such challenges underscore the need for robust emergency preparedness plans that include scalable healthcare infrastructure capable of adapting to sudden increases in demand. Additionally, health crises often exacerbate existing health disparities. Vulnerable and typically experience greater health risks and less access to care during emergencies. These groups often face barriers such as inadequate transportation, limited access to technology, and socioeconomic factors that hinder their ability to seek timely medical attention. As a result, health crises can widen the gap in health outcomes, making it crucial for healthcare systems to prioritize equity in their responses. Addressing these disparities not only improves outcomes during crises but also strengthens overall community resilience. On the regulatory front, health crises can reveal weaknesses in existing healthcare policies and regulations (Filip R., et al, 2022). The rapid need for responses during emergencies often leads to temporary regulatory changes aimed at facilitating quicker access to care. For example, countries on telehealth services to ensure that patients receive care while adhering to physical distancing guidelines. While these adaptations demonstrated the flexibility of healthcare systems, they also raised questions about the long-term implications for regulatory frameworks. As health systems evolve, there is a need to assess which temporary measures should be integrated into permanent policy to enhance efficiency and access without compromising safety and quality.

Conversely, health crises can drive innovation within healthcare systems. The pandemic spurred significant advancements in telemedicine, prompting healthcare providers to adopt virtual care models at an unprecedented rate. Patients and providers quickly adapted to remote consultations, resulting in increased convenience and accessibility for many. This shift has the potential to redefine patient-provider relationships and expand particularly in rural Additionally, the surge in mobile health applications, has encouraged healthcare systems to explore technology's role in enhancing. Moreover, crises highlighted by the COVID-19 pandemic underscored the need for informed public health responses. Effective surveillance systems and data-sharing protocols are essential for tracking disease spread, identifying at-risk populations, and deploying resources effectively (Attaran M., 2022). This increased focus on data analytics can improve preparedness for future health crises, enabling healthcare systems to respond more rapidly and effectively. In summary, health crises pose significant challenges to healthcare systems, from overwhelming demand and resource allocation issues to exacerbating health disparities (Selvaraj S., et al, 2020). However, they also present valuable opportunities for reform and innovation. By embracing technology, enhancing regulatory frameworks, fostering collaboration, and prioritizing equity, healthcare systems can transform these challenges into catalysts for positive change. The lessons learned during health crises can inform strategies that immediate responses strengthen resilience systems in the long term. As we navigate future health emergencies, a proactive approach to integrating these insights will be essential for safeguarding public health and ensuring that healthcare systems can respond effectively to evolving needs.

DIGITAL HEALTH LANDSCAPE: CURRENT STATE, TRENDS, AND FUTURE DIRECTIONS

The digital health landscape has evolved rapidly, driven by technological advancements and changing consumer expectations. Today, digital health encompasses an array of tools solutions, telemedicine, health applications, and wearables, (AI), big transformed how healthcare is delivered, enhancing patient engagement, improving access to care, and enabling more personalized health management. As the sector continues to evolve, explore current state emerging trends, and the potential future directions that could shape the industry. Currently, telemedicine stands at the forefront, with healthcare providers rapidly implementing virtual consultations to maintain continuity of care. This shift not only increased access but offered convenience for those with mobility challenges. As a result, many healthcare systems are now incorporating telemedicine as a permanent option, recognizing its value in improving patient satisfaction and adherence to care protocols (Aminabee S., 2024). As AI technology matures, its application in clinical settings is expected to expand, offering opportunities for improved efficiency and patient care. Big data analytics is another significant trend shaping the digital health landscape (Aungst T D., et al, 2020). The ability to aggregate and analyze data provides trends in individual patient journeys. This data-driven approach can inform public health strategies, enhance disease prevention efforts, and improve resource allocation within healthcare systems. Moreover, leveraging data analytics can help identify health disparities, enabling underserved populations.

Despite advancements, the digital health landscape faces several challenges. Data privacy and security remain paramount concerns, particularly as healthcare providers increasingly rely on digital solutions to manage sensitive patient information. Regulatory frameworks must evolve to address these issues, ensuring that patient data is protected while allowing for innovation in digital health technologies. Additionally, barriers to access, as certain populations may lack the necessary technology or digital literacy to engage fully with digital health tools. Addressing these disparities is critical to ensuring that the benefits of digital health reach all individuals. Looking to key directions likely the digital health landscape. First, the integration of digital health solutions into traditional healthcare workflows will become increasingly seamless. As healthcare providers recognize the benefits of digital tools, we can expect to see more comprehensive strategies that incorporate telehealth, wearables, and AI into routine care delivery (Admass W S., et al, 2024). This integration will likely enhance the patient experience, streamline workflows, and improve clinical outcomes. Second, the emphasis on personalized and precision medicine will continue to grow. Establishing standardized metrics to evaluate the effectiveness of digital health interventions will be crucial for demonstrating their value to healthcare systems and securing reimbursement models (Rauniyar A., et al, 2023). Evidence-based practices will help build trust in digital health solutions, encouraging broader adoption among providers and patients alike. In conclusion, the digital health landscape is rapidly evolving, presenting both challenges and opportunities for healthcare systems worldwide. The current state is characterized by the integration of telemedicine, mobile health applications, wearables, AI, and big data analytics, all of which are transforming how care is delivered and experienced. As we look to the future, the emphasis on personalized care, consumer engagement, collaboration, and outcomes measurement will shape the trajectory of digital health. An efficient, effective healthcare system harnesses digital health technologies.

Telemedicine and Remote Monitoring: Expanding Access to Healthcare

Have become pivotal components of modern healthcare, particularly in response to the growing demand for accessible and convenient care. These technologies offer significant advantages by breaking down geographical barriers, enhancing patient engagement, and improving health outcomes. As healthcare systems grapple with challenges such as rising costs, workforce shortages, and increasing patient expectations, the integration of telemedicine and remote monitoring represents a promising solution to expand access and optimize healthcare deliver Telemedicine enables patients to consult healthcare providers through virtual platforms, allowing for real-time communication via video calls, phone consultations, or chat applications (Barbosa W., et al, 2021). This shift from traditional in-person visits to virtual care many organizations to adapt quickly. Patients who previously faced obstacles such as long travel distances, mobility issues, or time constraints can now access care in rural. Remote monitoring, on the other hand, to healthcare providers for ongoing assessment and management. Mobile health applications and equipment allow tracking the continuous flow of monitors in real-time, facilitating timely interventions and reducing hospital. The advantages of telemedicine and its ability to enhance require regular monitoring and ongoing by utilizing tools, patients can manage their conditions more effectively, and diabetic device data directly to the healthcare team, allowing for prompt lifestyle recommendations readings. Moreover, can opinions without the need for extensive travel, burdensome with chronic illnesses (Hoffman D A., 2020). This capability not only enhances patient satisfaction but also encourages proactive healthcare management, as patients can easily seek guidance when needed. Despite the numerous benefits, is not without challenges. One primary may lack the necessary resources to engage with digital health tools. To truly expand access, healthcare systems must prioritize equitable solutions, such as providing training, resources, and alternative methods for those who may be less comfortable with technology.

Additionally, issues related to the telemedicine landscape. Patient platforms, safeguarding this becomes critical. Ensure compliance to protect patient confidentiality. Building trust in telemedicine requires transparency in data handling and a commitment to protecting patients' rights. Regulatory frameworks vital telemedicine remote monitoring. Many regions experienced temporary relaxations in regulations to facilitate the rapid adoption of virtual care during the pandemic. However, as the healthcare landscape stabilizes, there is a need for comprehensive policies that ensure the continued integration of telehealth into standard care practices (Ortega G., et al, 2020). Patients' virtual consultations are viable alternatives to in-person visits. This cultural shift can lead to increased utilization of preventive care services, as patients feel more empowered to seek help for non-emergency health concerns without the barriers typically associated with traditional healthcare settings (Palozzi G., et al, 2020). Revolutionizing access to offering innovative solutions to longstanding barriers in care delivery. By enhancing patient engagement, improving chronic disease management, and facilitating access to specialists, these technologies are poised to transform the healthcare landscape. However, to realize their full potential, stakeholders' equity, and regulatory frameworks. As we move forward, the continued evolution of telemedicine and remote monitoring will be essential in creating accessible, and populations. Through equity, we can buy all.

Artificial Intelligence in Healthcare: Diagnosis, Treatment, and Prediction

Is transforming healthcare by enhancing diagnosis, treatment, and predictive analytics, fundamentally altering the way medical professionals deliver care and patients engage with the system. Integration technologies are driven by the need for improved efficiency, accuracy, and personalized care, addressing some of the longstanding challenges that have persisted in traditional medical practices. In the realm of diagnosis, leveraging machines has shown the potential to analyze medical images and interpret diagnostic data. For instance, AI systems are being developed in conditions other abnormalities algorithms can analyze vast datasets far more rapidly than human clinicians, identifying patterns that might go unnoticed (Pattyam S P., 2021). Studies have demonstrated that AI can match or even exceed the diagnostic accuracy of human experts in certain applications, such as detecting breast cancer in mammograms or diabetic retinopathy in retinal images. By streamlining the diagnostic process, AI not only enhances accuracy but also reduces the time required to reach a diagnosis, ultimately improving patient outcomes. AI's role extends beyond imaging to other areas of diagnostics, including pathology and genomics. In pathology, AI systems can assist in analyzing biopsy samples and identifying cancerous cells with high precision. In genomics, AI helps interpret complex genetic data, enabling more accurate identification of hereditary conditions and tailoring treatment strategies. As personalized medicine continues to gain traction, AI's ability to analyze genetic information developing targeted therapies that consider When it comes to treatment, AI technologies are increasingly being utilized to optimize therapeutic interventions and enhance patient care. (CDSS) treatment guidelines, for treatment options (Rong G., et al, 2020). Can healthcare providers make evidence-based decisions, reducing variability in care and improving adherence to clinical guidelines? Moreover, AI-driven tools can assist in identifying drug interactions, recommending dosages, and predicting potential side effects, thereby enhancing medication safety and efficacy. AI's potential in treatment extends to large datasets, AI can therapies specific patient populations, tailoring interventions to individual responses. How a patient with a particular type of cancer might respond to specific chemotherapy regimens, allows oncologists to personalize treatment plans that improve efficacy while minimizing side effects.

Historical predict patient outcomes, readmission rates, and the likelihood of disease progression. For instance, AI data from chronic diseases allows for early interventions that can prevent or mitigate these conditions. Individual health overall. Using AI in predictive analytics is also valuable in public health contexts. During disease outbreaks, AI trends and mobility patterns, spread diseases. Such insights can inform public health responses, optimize resource allocation, and improve community preparedness for potential health crises. Despite the numerous advantages of AI in healthcare, challenges remain to be realized. A significant concern is That patient confidentiality protection information is paramount. HIPAA, to safeguard patient data while utilizing AI technologies (Ghaffar Nia N., et al, 2023). Another challenge is the need for transparency and explainability in AI algorithms. Models black boxes, are difficult for clinicians. Ensuring that AI systems provide clear, interpretable insights is essential for gaining the trust of healthcare providers and patients alike. Clinicians must know about. Furthermore, integration into existing healthcare workflows requires careful consideration. Healthcare professionals' tools, understanding limitations. Additionally, ensuring that AI technologies are interoperable with current technologies is crucial to seamless integration and adoption. Is promising, that ongoing machine learning continues to evolve, we can anticipate more sophisticated AI systems capable of analyzing diverse data types, including images, genetic information, and even patient-reported outcomes. This multi-modal approach will lead to enabling more effective interventions and personalized care (Chen X., 2024).

Mobile Health (mHealth) and Wearable Devices: Empowering Patients

Are reshaping the healthcare landscape wellness. These innovations leverage technology to provide real-time health monitoring, facilitate communication with healthcare providers, and promote engagement in personal health management. As a result, they are enhancing and transforming the broader healthcare system, fostering a shift towards patient-centered care. At the core of mHealth is the use of mobile applications that allow users to manage various aspects of their health conveniently from their smartphones. These applications range from fitness trackers and dietary logs to medication reminders and telehealth services. The accessibility of mHealth tools empowers patients to set goals, and monitor progress, ultimately leading to greater awareness. For example, with chronic diseases such as apps log, track their meals, receive tailored recommendations based on their data (Ghose A., et al, 2021). This level of engagement encourages adherence to treatment plans and enhances communication with healthcare providers. Including monitoring equipment, further augmenting the capabilities of mHealth. These devices continuously collect physiological data activity levels, even electrocardiograms (ECGs). Real-time wearables users about their behaviors. For instance, individuals can identify patterns that may contribute to poor sleep or increased stress, allowing them to adjust their routines accordingly. Health solutions facilitate ongoing communication through features like secure messaging, video consultations, and health data sharing (Kreitmair K V., 2024). This continuous interaction fosters a more collaborative relationship literacy. Patients are more likely to engage with their healthcare team when they can easily share data and receive feedback in real-time.

Despite the many benefits, the widespread adoption of mHealth and wearable devices is not without challenges. One major concern is data privacy and security. As health-related data becomes increasingly digitized, ensuring protection will be handled securely. Organizations need to safeguard patient information while utilizing these technologies. Building this trust is crucial for fostering patient engagement and maximizing the benefits of mHealth solutions. Additionally, the digital divide remains a significant barrier to equitable access to mHealth and wearable technologies. Certain populations, including the elderly, low-income individuals, and those in rural areas, may lack access to smartphones, reliable internet connectivity, or the digital literacy needed to engage with these tools effectively (Hamberger M., et al, 2022). To truly empower all patients, healthcare systems must prioritize inclusivity by providing resources, training, and alternative solutions for those who This may include community health initiatives that promote devices. Regulatory reimbursement challenges also affect the integration of mHealth and wearable devices into standard healthcare practices. While there is increasing recognition of the value of remote monitoring and mHealth interventions, reimbursement policies for these services are still evolving. Clear guidelines and supportive policies are essential to encourage healthcare providers to adopt and utilize these technologies effectively. Work Looking ahead, future mHealth and wearable devices hold immense potential. Sophisticated devices incorporate deeper into health data. For example, future wearables might lifestyle factors, predict potential health issues, and offer personalized recommendations based on real-time data analysis (Stampe K., et al, 2021).

Digital Health Solutions for Infectious Disease Management

Solutions have emerged as critical tools in the management of infectious diseases, leveraging technology to enhance surveillance, diagnosis, treatment, and public health responses. Necessity innovative approaches to disease management, prompting a rapid evolution of digital health technologies that can track and mitigate the spread of infections. Integrating mobile health applications, telemedicine, and wearable can effectively address infectious diseases while improving patient outcomes and health system efficiency. Primary digital solutions enhance disease surveillance and monitoring. Mobile health applications can facilitate the reporting of symptoms and exposure, allowing public health authorities to gather real-time data on disease prevalence. For instance, apps designed for having infectious agents (Stampe K., et al, 2021). This proactive approach enables timely interventions, such as quarantining or testing, thereby curbing the spread of infections. By utilizing geolocation and symptom reporting, these applications can provide valuable insights into outbreak patterns and help public health officials allocate resources more effectively. Telemedicine has also revolutionized the management of infectious diseases by providing accessible healthcare services, especially during times of crisis. Risk of disease transmission in clinical settings. This approach has been particularly beneficial for managing infectious diseases like COVID-19, where in-person visits may pose risks to both patients and providers. Telemedicine allows for timely assessments, enabling healthcare professionals to guide testing, treatment options, and follow-up care without exposing others to potential infections. Furthermore, telehealth platforms can facilitate mental health support for individuals affected by infectious disease outbreaks, addressing the psychological impacts of isolation and uncertainty. Vital continuous monitoring of patients with infectious diseases. Can temperature, and respiratory rate, providers inform clinical some wearables were to monitor patients' physiological changes and deterioration intervention (Fagherazzi G., et al, 2020). By integrating this data with mobile health applications, patients and providers can maintain ongoing communication, ensuring that health concerns are addressed promptly.

Also, pivotal vaccination is crucial for preventing the spread of infectious diseases. Mobile applications can facilitate vaccination tracking, reminding patients of upcoming vaccinations, and providing digital records that are easily accessible. These tools can enhance public confidence in vaccination programs by providing transparent information about vaccine safety and efficacy. Moreover, health authorities can use data from these applications to monitor vaccination rates in real-time, identifying areas with low coverage and targeting outreach efforts to improve public health outcomes. Despite the numerous benefits of digital health solutions in managing infectious diseases, challenges remain. Concerns particularly when ensuring that patient data is protected while enabling effective disease management is a critical consideration for healthcare organizations. Compliance is essential to maintain trust and encourage the adoption of digital health tools (Mbunge E., et al, 2022). The combination of AI with existing digital health technologies can lead to more robust and adaptive responses to infectious disease threats. Moreover, the ongoing development of interoperable digital health systems will enhance the ability to share information across healthcare settings (Gunasekeran D V., et al, 2021). Ensuring that digital health solutions can communicate seamlessly with electronic health records and public health databases will improve care coordination and facilitate comprehensive surveillance efforts. This interconnectedness to infectious disease challenges. In conclusion, digital health solutions are revolutionizing the management of infectious diseases by enhancing surveillance, improving access to care, and facilitating data-driven decision-making. As we continue to navigate the complexities of infectious disease management, the integration of mobile health applications, telemedicine, wearable devices, and data analytics will be essential for optimizing patient care and public health responses. While access and regulatory frameworks persist, these technologies are substantial. By embracing digital health solutions, healthcare systems can empower patients, improve health outcomes, and more infectious disease threats.

Mental Health Support and Intervention through Digital Platforms

Support and intervention mark a significant shift in how mental health services are delivered, offering accessible, effective, and personalized care. As awareness of mental health issues increases, particularly following posed digital health technologies have become essential tools in providing support, fostering engagement, and enhancing therapeutic outcomes. By leveraging mobile applications, teletherapy, online support communities, and artificial intelligence, mental health professionals can deliver timely catering to unique individuals (Jiang N., et al, 2021). Notable care proliferation of mobile health applications designed specifically for mental wellness. (CBT) management By allowing users to monitor their mental health daily, these applications promote self-awareness and encourage proactive management app enables users to log their moods and triggers can help individuals recognize patterns and develop coping strategies. By facilitating connection and conversation, digital platforms create a sense of belonging that can significantly enhance mental well-being (Liberati E., et al, 2021). Moreover, mental health applications are transforming how support is delivered. Assistance users, offering resources and coping strategies in real-time. For example, a chatbot may engage users in a conversation about their feelings, providing supportive responses and suggesting appropriate self-care techniques. While these tools cannot replace human therapists, they can serve as valuable adjuncts, offering support when human resources are unavailable. Additionally, AI can analyze user interactions and the effectiveness of the intervention.

Equity in digital services is another significant challenge. Platforms increase access to disparities in technology access, digital literacy, and internet connectivity can create barriers for certain populations (Linardon J., et al, 2020). Vulnerable groups may be less likely to utilize these resources. To address these disparities, mental health initiatives must focus on providing resources, education, and support to ensure that all individuals can benefit from digital interventions. Furthermore, while digital platforms can enhance access to support, they cannot replace the need for comprehensive mental health services. There are instances where individuals require intensive intervention, such as crisis counseling or inpatient care. Digital solutions should be integrated into a broader continuum of care, ensuring that individuals have access to appropriate levels of support based on their needs. Mental health professionals must remain vigilant in assessing when to refer clients to more intensive services, or traditional care. The effectiveness of digital mental health interventions also relies on mental may not utilize them consistently over time. Strategies to promote sustained engagement, such as gamification, reminders, and social features, can help maintain user interest and commitment. By creating a more interactive and rewarding experience, digital platforms can encourage users to engage actively with their mental health management. Looking to the future, mental health solutions in mainstream systems hold significant promise. Collaborative care models that incorporate digital platforms alongside traditional mental health services can enhance care coordination and improve outcomes (Marchini S., et al, 2021). For example, primary care providers can leverage digital tools to monitor patients' mental health between visits, allowing for timely interventions when issues arise.

Digital Therapeutics: Personalized Medicine and Treatment

Digital therapeutics (DTx) is revolutionary, combining technology with clinical interventions to provide evidence-based therapeutic solutions for various medical conditions. By leveraging software applications and digital platforms, digital therapeutics offer tailored treatment regimens that address individual patient needs, ultimately enhancing health outcomes and optimizing patient engagement. This innovative approach is reshaping how healthcare providers deliver treatment, promoting a more personalized and effective healthcare experience. At the heart of digital therapeutics is the ability to deliver personalized intervention characteristics to each patient (Hong J S., et al, 2021). Unlike general health apps, which often provide one-size-fits-all solutions, digital therapeutics are developed based on rigorous clinical evidence and are typically designed to treat specific medical conditions. For instance, digital therapeutics targeting diabetes management may include personalized meal plans, exercise recommendations, and real-time glucose monitoring, all the individual lifestyle not only enhances adherence to treatment plans but empowers. Capacity to collect and analyze patient data continuously. Through wearables and mobile health applications, DTx can monitor adherence. This real-time data collection enables deeper blood sugar levels to indicate a need for dietary changes, the digital therapeutic can prompt dietary modifications tailored to that specific individual, fostering better management of their condition. Effectiveness treatment strengthens the patient-provider relationship through increased communication and trust. Behavioral intervention therapeutics is another significant advancement. Many obesities, are closely linked to behavioral factors, including diet, physical activity, and mental health. Digital therapeutics can incorporate, and techniques to address these behavioral components directly. By providing patients with tools and strategies to modify their behaviors, DTx can lead to more sustainable lifestyle changes, ultimately improving overall health outcomes (Dang A., et al, 2020). For instance, a digital therapeutic for anxiety might include guided meditation sessions, journaling prompts, and progress tracking, all tailored to the individual's specific challenges. Moreover, digital therapeutics enhance accessibility to care, particularly for underserved populations. Traditional therapeutic interventions often require in-person visits, which can be challenging Digital therapeutics can be accessed via smartphones or computers, breaking down geographical and logistical barriers to care. This increased accessibility is especially crucial and underscores the need for delivering effective therapeutic interventions digitally, more.

Regulatory oversight of digital therapeutics is crucial to ensure their safety, efficacy, and quality. Many DTx products undergo rigorous clinical trials, similar to traditional pharmaceuticals, to validate their effectiveness in treating specific conditions. Begun to establish frameworks for evaluating digital therapeutics, ensuring that these interventions meet the necessary standards before reaching patients. This regulatory scrutiny not only helps protect patients but also enhances the credibility of digital therapeutics within the healthcare landscape. Despite their numerous advantages, the adoption of digital therapeutics faces several challenges. One major concern is data privacy and security. DTx solutions often require the collection of health patient data paramount. Developers to safeguard patient privacy (Kamel Boulos M N., et al, 2021). For example, future DTx could utilize predictive analytics to anticipate patient needs based on historical data, delivering tailored interventions before a crisis occurs. Could enhance management of chronic overall health Moreover, the growing emphasis on patient engagement and shared will further amplify the role of digital therapeutics (Kario K., et al, 2021). Patients are increasingly seeking ways to participate actively in their care, and digital therapeutics provide the tools to do so effectively. Through patient technologies holistic approach to treatment, adherence, and In conclusion, digital therapeutics are revolutionizing the landscape of personalized medicine and treatment, offering innovative, evidence-based solutions tailored to individual patient needs. Through continuous data collection, behavioral health integration, and enhanced accessibility, DTx engages actively in their treatment. While equity and integration remain, the digital therapeutics are substantial. Innovative systems an effective, personalized, equitable approach to care, ultimately leading to improved health outcomes for diverse populations. Possibilities digital therapeutics, personalized medicine health well-being.

Health Data Governance and Security in Digital Health

As digital technologies continue to transform healthcare delivery, the importance of robust health data governance and security has become increasingly critical. The integration generates health integrity, paramount for safeguarding patient privacy and maintaining public trust in digital health solutions. Effective health data governance encompasses policies, practices, and technologies designed to manage health information responsibly, addressing the complexities of data ownership, sharing, and protection in a digital landscape. Foundational health governance clear policies regarding ownership and stewardship (Thapa C., et al, 2021). Security measures are integral to protecting health and healthcare through cybersecurity. Multi-layered protocols, intrusion detection systems, audits Additionally, staff training is essential, as settings. By handling. Rise emerging both and challenges health data governance. While these technologies can enhance data analysis and improve patient outcomes, for instance, AI algorithms that analyze health data may inadvertently perpetuate existing biases if trained on non-representative datasets (Abernethy A., et al, 2022). Governance frameworks must include guidelines for ethical AI usage, emphasizing transparency, accountability, and fairness in algorithm development and deployment. Validated with diverse populations in mind is crucial for minimizing disparities in healthcare delivery. Patient consent health governance. As expands, stored, shared. Processes should be user-friendly, allowing patients also implement mechanisms for patients to withdraw consent easily, ensuring that individuals retain control over their information. Moreover, organizations must comply with evolving regulations regarding consent, particularly in jurisdictions with stringent privacy laws. This adaptability is essential for maintaining compliance and fostering trust with patients.

Data anonymization and de-identification are important strategies in health data governance that enhance privacy while enabling valuable data analysis. By removing personally identifiable information from health records, organizations can leverage data for research, quality improvement, and public health initiatives without compromising patient privacy. However, the de-identification process must be carefully managed to prevent re-identification, particularly as advances in data analytics and AI make it increasingly feasible to link anonymized data back to individuals. Robust governance policies should guide the use of anonymized data, ensuring that ethical considerations are prioritized and that patient privacy is maintained. Incorporating stakeholder engagement into health data governance frameworks is crucial for addressing the diverse perspectives and needs of all parties involved (Viljoen S., 2021). Engaging patients, healthcare providers, policymakers, and technology developers in the governance process can foster collaboration and innovation. Stakeholder input can help identify potential gaps in governance practices and inform the development of policies that align with the realities of digital health. Engaging legal and compliance experts in the development of governance policies can help organizations navigate the complexities of regulatory compliance while ensuring the protection of patient data (Sheikh A., et al, 2021). In conclusion, health data governance and security are essential components of the digital health landscape, ensuring that sensitive health information is managed responsibly and ethically. By establishing clear policies regarding data ownership, promoting interoperability, implementing robust security measures, and engaging stakeholders, healthcare organizations can enhance the effectiveness of digital health interventions while safeguarding patient privacy. As technology continues to evolve, adaptable prioritize considerations, regulatory compliance, and patient engagement will become increasingly important. By trust transparency in data management, digital health effective system.

REGULATORY FRAMEWORKS FOR DIGITAL HEALTH: NATIONAL AND INTERNATIONAL PERSPECTIVES

Evolution necessitates robust regulatory frameworks that ensure the safety, efficacy, and privacy of health data while fostering innovation. Solutions telemedicine, applications, gain traction, and governments and regulatory bodies worldwide are developing and refining policies to navigate this complex landscape. These frameworks must balance the need for patient protection with the urgency to promote technological advancement, creating an environment conducive to both innovation and accountability. At the national level, regulatory frameworks vary significantly across countries, influenced by healthcare systems, legal traditions, and cultural attitudes toward technology. For example, established guidelines forSaMD), focusing on the risk classification of digital tools and the requirements for clinical validation (Benis A., et al, 2021). This approach allows the FDA to prioritize oversight based on the potential risks associated with specific technologies, ensuring that high-risk devices undergo rigorous evaluation while allowing lower-risk applications to enter the market more rapidly. This strategy encourages countries to share experiences and knowledge, helping to harmonize regulatory approaches and address common challenges in the digital health space (Allan J., et al, 2021). For instance, the WHO has initiated the Digital Health Initiative, which guides member states in developing and implementing effective regulatory frameworks that prioritize patient safety and public health outcomes. Regulatory harmonization is crucial for facilitating international trade and collaboration in digital health. Variations in regulatory standards can create barriers to market entry for digital health companies, limiting access to innovative solutions across borders. Efforts to align regulatory frameworks, such as the approval for medical devices, including digital health technologies. By fostering greater consistency in regulatory requirements, international collaboration can enhance the availability of safe and effective digital health solutions worldwide.

In addition to traditional regulatory bodies, industry standards organizations are increasingly influential in shaping the landscape of digital health regulation. The organization, for example, develops and promotes interoperability between digital health systems. Standard is a key development in this area, enabling across platforms and enhancing the usability of digital health applications. By establishing technical standards that complement regulatory frameworks, industry organizations can facilitate the health of existing. Despite the progress in developing regulatory frameworks, several challenges remain. One significant concern is that as digital health solutions emerge, regulators must remain agile and responsive, ensuring that their frameworks can accommodate rapid changes while maintaining robust oversight (Liu K., et al, 2023). Looking ahead, digital health regulation will likely be characterized by greater collaboration and integration among stakeholders (Richardson S., et al, 2022). Multi-stakeholder approaches that involve patients, healthcare providers, and industry representatives have more effective and comprehensive regulatory frameworks. Engaging patients in the regulatory process can enhance understanding of their needs and preferences, leading to more user-centered regulations that prioritize patient safety and satisfaction. In conclusion, regulatory frameworks for digital health are evolving demands healthcare By balancing innovation with patient protection, national and international regulatory bodies are crucial to digital health. While challenges related to rapid technological advancements, data privacy, and equity persist, ongoing collaboration and dialogue among stakeholders can help address these issues. As continue to transform effective innovations the care journey toward comprehensive and adaptable regulatory solutions is ongoing, but connected for patients worldwide.

Implementing Digital Health Solutions: Change Management and Adoption

Reshaping improved enhanced operational efficiency, and greater accessibility. However, the successful adoption of these technologies hinges on effective change management strategies that address the complexities of integrating digital health into existing healthcare systems. Change management in this context involves not only the technological transition but also the cultural and organizational shifts required to embrace new workflows, practices, and mindsets among healthcare providers, administrators, and patients. Digital health solutions change (Guo C., et al, 2020). Often have established routines and may be skeptical about new technologies, fearing disruptions to their workflows or questioning the efficacy of digital tools. To mitigate this resistance, organizations must foster a culture of openness and collaboration. Engaging stakeholders early in the process—through consultations, focus groups, and pilot programs—can help identify concerns, gather feedback, and create a sense of ownership among staff. This can involve allocating resources for training and development, ensuring adequate infrastructure for technology deployment, and setting measurable goals for implementation (Golinelli D., et al, 2020). By embodying the values of innovation and adaptability, leadership can inspire a similar mindset throughout the organization, encouraging staff to embrace new technologies as part of their daily practice. The implementation process should also be underpinned by a robust evaluation framework that allows organizations to monitor progress and assess the impact of digital health solutions. Key performance indicators (KPIs) should be established to evaluate factors such as user engagement, patient satisfaction, clinical outcomes, and operational efficiency. Regular feedback loops—incorporating input from both staff and patient organizations to celebrate successes and make adjustments to enhance the effectiveness of the digital health solution. This iterative approach not only supports continuous improvement but also reinforces a culture of accountability and responsiveness.

Training and education are vital components of successful digital health implementation. It is essential to recognize that different staff members may require varying levels of training based on their roles and experience with technology. Customizing training programs to meet these diverse needs can enhance engagement and competency. Additionally, organizations should foster an environment that encourages continuous learning. As digital health technologies evolve, providing ongoing training and refresher courses ensures that staff remain proficient and can adapt to new features and functionalities. Moreover, considering the patient's perspective is essential for effective change management. Friendly and with the end-user in mind. Engaging patients in the development and testing phases of their preferences. Offering clear instructions and support for patients using platforms or facilitating adoption and enhancing patient satisfaction (Mbunge E., et al, 2021). Providing patients with resources to understand the technology and its benefits fosters a sense of empowerment, encouraging them to engage actively in their health management. Interdisciplinary collaboration factor health solutions. Healthcare delivery often involves various professionals from different specialties, and the integration of digital tools should reflect this collaborative approach. Establishing cross-functional teams that include clinicians, IT specialists, administrators, and patient advocates can enhance the design and deployment of digital health initiatives. These teams can ensure that diverse perspectives are considered, leading to more comprehensive and effective solutions. Change management in digital health also involves addressing data governance and security concerns. Tools, and protecting patients become paramount. Implementing robust data governance policies builds among stakeholders. Educating is a crucial part of the training process, reinforcing in digital environments. Finally, the sustainability of digital health solutions depends on ongoing evaluation and adaptation. Organizations must be agile and responsive to emerging trends, technologies, and patient needs. Regularly revisiting the objectives of digital health initiatives and assessing their relevance ensures that they continue to meet healthcare This adaptive approach allows organizations to pivot as needed, integrating new tools and practices that enhance care delivery and improve health outcomes (Harrison R., et al, 2021).

Digital Health in Response to COVID-19: Lessons Learned and Best Practices

Reshaping healthcare delivery and enhancing patient engagement. As health systems worldwide grappled with the unprecedented challenges posed by the pandemic, digital health emerged as for virus and addressing diverse needs This response highlighted several key lessons and best practices that will inform the future of healthcare. One of the most notable lessons learned is the importance of scalability and flexibility in digital health solutions. Telemedicine services experienced explosive growth as healthcare providers sought to maintain patient access while adhering to social distancing guidelines. Systems that were previously underutilized or in pilot phases were rapidly expanded. This shift demonstrated the necessity of having infrastructure capable of scaling up quickly in response to public health crises (Romanelli R J., et al, 2021). Additionally, the flexibility of digital tools allowed for swift adaptation to evolving guidelines and patient needs, emphasizing the importance of modular design in healthcare technology. Another critical lesson is the significance of patient-centered care. During the pandemic, patients sought more control over their healthcare decisions, leading to a demand for solutions that cater to individual preferences and circumstances. Digital health platforms that offered personalized health information, remote monitoring, and direct communication with healthcare providers fostered a sense of empowerment among patients. Best practices include involving patients' health solutions and ensuring tools accessible, particularly for vulnerable populations who may have limited digital literacy. Emerged as in the realm digital (Gunasekeran D V., et al, 2021).

Moreover, the pandemic underscored the importance of addressing health disparities through digital health innovations. Vulnerable populations often faced greater barriers to accessing healthcare services, exacerbated by the pandemic. Digital health solutions that prioritize inclusivity—such as multilingual platforms, community outreach, and tailored resources—are essential for ensuring equitable access to care (Budd J., et al, 2020). Successful initiatives have involved collaborations with community organizations to reach underserved populations, demonstrating the value of local knowledge in addressing health equity. Training and support for healthcare providers emerged as a key best practice. Many providers faced challenges in adapting to new tools, which could impact the quality of care delivered. Ongoing education and technical support are vital for maximizing the effectiveness of digital health solutions. Organizations that provided comprehensive training programs and resources saw improved provider confidence and patient outcomes, highlighting the need for investment in workforce development. Finally, ongoing evaluation and iteration of digital health programs are critical for long-term success. The rapid implementation of solutions during the pandemic often lacked sufficient evaluation mechanisms, making it difficult to assess their impact (Scott B K., et al, 2020). Establishing clear metrics for success and creating feedback loops with users—both patients and providers—can drive continuous improvement.

DIGITAL HEALTH IN LOW-RESOURCE SETTINGS: OPPORTUNITIES AND CHALLENGES

Digital health has low to longstanding challenges in access, quality, and efficiency. The integration of digital technologies, (mHealth) can significantly systems that often struggle with limited infrastructure and workforce shortages. However, while the opportunities are vast, numerous are addressed to ensure the sustainability of digital health initiatives contexts. One of the primary opportunities presented is the ability to expand platforms that can connect with providers, reducing the burden of and enabling timely consultations. For instance, mobile clinics equipped with telehealth capabilities can reach rural populations, facilitating consultations This is where regulars are crucial for effective treatment. Moreover, mHealth applications can provide health education and self-management tools directly to patients' smartphones, empowering them (McCool J., et al, 2020). Therefore, developing low-tech or offline solutions, as well as community-based initiatives that enhance digital literacy, for tools. Another significant challenge is the sustainability of digital health initiatives (Parajuli R., et al, 2022). Many pilot projects have been launched with external funding, but once this support ends, sustaining operations can be difficult. Stakeholders must develop business models that allow for self-sufficiency, whether through government support, public-private partnerships, or user fees. Additionally, local ownership and involvement in digital health enhance sustainability. Engaging local healthcare providers and community members in the process can lead to solutions that are more culturally relevant and practical. Also, concerns, particularly in low-resource settings regulatory frameworks may be weak or non-existent. Must be handled with care and ethical standards. Developing robust data protection policies and ensuring that digital health platforms have adequate security measures in place are vital steps in mitigating these risks. Training healthcare providers on data security practices can further enhance the protection of patient information.

Moreover, the into poses challenges. Many low-resource settings have established workflows and practices that may not readily accommodate new technologies. This can lead to resistance among healthcare providers who may be reluctant to adopt unfamiliar tools. Therefore, adequate ensuring that healthcare workers benefits are equipped to use these tools effectively. Facilitating a culture of innovation within healthcare settings can also encourage providers to embrace new technologies. Health literacy is another critical factor success of initiatives. Many, patients may lack the knowledge or skills to effectively utilize digital health tools (Faulkenberry J G., et al, 2022). User-friendly accompanied by educational materials can help bridge this gap. Community engagement and outreach programs health provide necessary training to patients, enhancing their ability to navigate these technologies. Furthermore, collaboration among stakeholders is essential for maximizing health low-resource Governments, non-governmental organizations, private sector actors, and community groups must work together to create a cohesive strategy environment. By fostering partnerships, stakeholders can pool resources, share best practices, and coordinate efforts to implement comprehensive the population (Negro-Calduch E., et al, 2021). Significant improvement in low-resource settings, but it is not without its challenges. Expanding access to care, improving data management, and enhancing patient engagement are crucial benefits that can lead to better health outcomes.

FUTURE DIRECTIONS FOR DIGITAL HEALTH IN TIMES OF CRISIS

Profoundly transformed landscape highlighting its critical role in maintaining healthcare delivery during crises and reshaping future directions for this sector. Understand how digital health can be leveraged in times of crisis, ensuring resilience and adaptability in healthcare systems worldwide. The future of digital health will likely focus on several key areas: enhancing accessibility, improving interoperability, promoting data security, and fostering innovation through collaboration and policy support. One of the primary future directions for digital health is the continued emphasis on accessibility. The pandemic underscored the importance of remote healthcare access, particularly for vulnerable populations (Ooi K B., et al, 2023). This will facilitate comprehensive patient care, as providers will have access to complete health records, regardless of where care is delivered. Establishing common data standards and encouraging collaboration between technology developers and healthcare organizations will be vital in creating integrated systems that can respond dynamically to public health emergencies (Sezgin E., et al, 2020).

Innovation through collaboration will be key to advancing digital health in times of crisis. The pandemic has highlighted the need for a multi-disciplinary approach, involving not just healthcare providers but also technologists, policymakers, and community organizations. Future efforts should focus on fostering partnerships that drive innovation, enabling stakeholders' expertise, Collaborative initiatives comprehensive unique posed crises, and enhancing the overall resilience of systems. Moreover, engagement and implementation ensure that these solutions are user-centered and The policy supports crucial digital. Governments and regulatory bodies must foster the growth integration by developing clear regulations that support telehealth reimbursement, promote equitable access to technology, and protect patient privacy (Sourdin T., et al, 2020). Ongoing education and support programs can help build digital literacy among healthcare workers, enabling them to leverage technology to enhance patient care. Moreover, creating a culture of innovation within healthcare organizations can encourage providers to embrace new digital solutions and adapt to changing circumstances (Leone L A., et al, 2020). Lastly, a focus on mental health will be integral to the future of digital health in crises. The pandemic has exacerbated mental health issues worldwide, highlighting the need for accessible mental health resources. Digital health platforms can offer innovative solutions, such as groups, providing patients with essential resources during crises. Ensuring that these tools are integrated into broader healthcare systems will be comprehensive for patients. In summary, directions for digital health in times of crisis are multifaceted, encompassing accessibility, interoperability, data security, collaboration, policy support, real-time analytics, training, and mental health integration. By focusing on these areas, stakeholders can create resilient healthcare systems responding to future lessons learned that will inform the development of innovative solutions that not only enhance care delivery during crises but also improve healthcare systems globally. Embracing these opportunities will ensure a more adaptive, equitable, and responsive healthcare landscape.

CONCLUSION

The intersection of health crises and digitalization has reshaped the healthcare landscape, illustrating the transformative potential of digital health technologies in times of need. As evidenced during the COVID-19 pandemic, rapid advancements in telemedicine, mobile health applications, and data analytics have allowed healthcare systems to maintain continuity of care and enhance patient engagement, even amid unprecedented challenges. These digital solutions have improved for many, particularly remote they have empowered patients. However, the journey towards effectiveness is not without its complexities. The disparities in access to technology concerns over interoperability among various health systems remain future digital health relies on creating inclusive frameworks that prioritize equitable access, ensuring that all populations benefit from technological innovations, particularly in the wake of crises. Moreover, fostering developers, and policymakers, to drive innovation and establish sustainable digital health ecosystems. Additionally, ongoing are critical to maximize the effectiveness of digital tools. Equipping providers to navigate will enhance their ability to deliver and adapt to evolving By integrating into the fabric of healthcare delivery, can become more resilient, and capable of responding swiftly and effectively to future health crises. Digital health healthcare systems enhance resilience and improve and ensure responsive health crises. By leveraging the lessons learned during recent global challenges, stakeholders can work collaboratively to build a future where digital health is not only a supplemental resource but a foundational element of comprehensive, equitable, healthcare. Prioritizing accessibility, data security, and patient-centered innovation realizing health safeguarding public health and enhancing the overall well-being of communities worldwide. Enhanced interoperability can enable a more coordinated response to crises, allowing for quicker identification of trends and resource allocation. Data security and privacy concerns will also shape the future of digital health. As healthcare systems increasingly rely on digital tools, safeguarding sensitive patient information becomes paramount. The pandemic has illustrated the vulnerabilities in data security, making it essential to implement robust cybersecurity measures and adhere to regulatory frameworks. Future digital health initiatives must prioritize transparency, ensuring patients This will be crucial for building trust among users, which is fundamental for the successful adoption of digital health technologies. Additionally, developing adaptive security measures that can respond to emerging threats will be necessary to maintain the integrity of digital health systems.

REFERENCES

Abernethy, A., Adams, L., Barrett, M., Bechtel, C., Brennan, P., Butte, A., Faulkner, J., Fontaine, E., Friedhoff, S., Halamka, J., Howell, M., Johnson, K., Long, P., McGraw, D., Miller, R., Lee, P., Perlin, J., Rucker, D., Sandy, L., & Valdes, K. (2022). The promise of digital health: Then, now, and the future. *NAM Perspectives, 2022*(22), 1–13. DOI: 10.31478/202206e PMID: 36177208

Admass, W. S., Munaye, Y. Y., & Diro, A. A. (2024). Cyber security: State of the art, challenges and future directions. *Cyber Security and Applications, 2024*, 1–15. DOI: 10.1016/j.csa.2023.100031

Allan, J., Belz, S., Hoeveler, A., Hugas, M., Okuda, H., Patri, A., Rauscher, H., Silva, P., Slikker, W., Sokull-Kluettgen, B., Tong, W., & Anklam, E. (2021). Regulatory landscape of nanotechnology and nanoplastics from a global perspective. *Regulatory Toxicology and Pharmacology, 125*, 105106. DOI: 10.1016/j.yrtph.2021.104885 PMID: 33617940

Aminabee, S. (2024). The future of healthcare and patient-centric care: Digital innovations, trends, and predictions. *Advances in Healthcare Information Systems and Administration, 2024*, 1–15. DOI: 10.4018/979-8-3693-1214-8.ch012

Attaran, M. (2022). Blockchain technology in healthcare: Challenges and opportunities. *International Journal of Healthcare Management, 15*(1), 1–13. DOI: 10.1080/20479700.2020.1843887

Aungst, T. D., & Patel, R. (2020). Integrating digital health into the curriculum—Considerations on the current landscape and future developments. *Journal of Medical Education and Curricular Development, 7*, 238212051989257. DOI: 10.1177/2382120519901275 PMID: 32010795

Barbosa, W., Zhou, K., Waddell, E., & Myers, T. (2021). Improving access to care: Telemedicine across medical domains. *Annual Review of Medicine, 72*, 139–154. DOI: 10.1146/annurev-med-042920-020808 PMID: 33798406

Benis, A., Tamburis, O., Chronaki, C., & Moen, A. (2021). One digital health: A unified framework for future health ecosystems. *Journal of Medical Internet Research, 23*(7), e29841. DOI: 10.2196/22189 PMID: 33492240

Budd, J., Miller, B. S., Manning, E. M., Lampos, V., Zhuang, M., Edelstein, M., Rees, G., Emery, V. C., Stevens, M. M., Keegan, N., Short, M. J., Pillay, D., Manley, E., Cox, I. J., Heymann, D., Johnson, A. M., & McKendry, R. A. (2020). Digital technologies in the public-health response to COVID-19. *Nature Medicine, 26*(9), 1183–1192. DOI: 10.1038/s41591-020-1011-4 PMID: 32770165

Chen, X. (2024). Ai in healthcare: Revolutionizing diagnosis and treatment through machine learning. *MZ Journal of Artificial Intelligence*, *2024*, 1–13.

Dang, A., Arora, D., & Rane, P. (2020). Role of digital therapeutics and the changing future of healthcare. *Journal of Family Medicine and Primary Care*, *9*(10), 5328. DOI: 10.4103/jfmpc.jfmpc_105_20 PMID: 32754475

Fagherazzi, G., Goetzinger, C., Rashid, M. A., Aguayo, G. A., & Huiart, L. (2020). Digital health strategies to fight COVID-19 worldwide: Challenges, recommendations, and a call for papers. *Journal of Medical Internet Research*, *2020*(6), 1–13. DOI: 10.2196/19284 PMID: 32501804

Faulkenberry, J. G., Luberti, A., & Craig, S. (2022). Electronic health records, mobile health, and the challenge of improving global health. *Current Problems in Pediatric and Adolescent Health Care*, *52*(5), 100981. DOI: 10.1016/j.cppeds.2021.101111 PMID: 34969611

Filip, R., Gheorghita Puscaselu, R., Anchidin-Norocel, L., Dimian, M., & Savage, W. K. (2022). Global challenges to public health care systems during the COVID-19 pandemic: A review of pandemic measures and problems. *Journal of Personalized Medicine*, *12*(2), 241. DOI: 10.3390/jpm12081295 PMID: 36013244

Ghaffar Nia, N., Kaplanoglu, E., & Nasab, A. (2023). Evaluation of artificial intelligence techniques in disease diagnosis and prediction. *Discover Artificial Intelligence*, *2023*(1), 1–15. DOI: 10.1007/s44163-023-00049-5

Ghose, A., Guo, X., Li, B., & Dang, Y. (2021). “Empowering patients using smart mobile health platforms: Evidence from a randomized field experiment.” arXiv preprint arXiv:2102.05506, 2021, 1-13.

Golinelli, D., Boetto, E., Carullo, G., Nuzzolese, A. G., Landini, M. P., & Fantini, M. P. (2020). Adoption of digital technologies in health care during the COVID-19 pandemic: Systematic review of early scientific literature. *Journal of Medical Internet Research*, *22*(8), e21535. DOI: 10.2196/22280 PMID: 33079693

Gunasekeran, D. V., Tham, Y. C., Ting, D. S. W., Tan, G. S. W., & Wong, T. Y. (2021). Digital health during COVID-19: Lessons from operationalising new models of care in ophthalmology. *The Lancet. Digital Health*, *2021*(2), 1–13. DOI: 10.1016/S2589-7500(20)30287-9 PMID: 33509383

Guo, C., Ashrafian, H., Ghafur, S., Fontana, G., Gardner, C., & Prime, M. (2020). Challenges for the evaluation of digital health solutions—A call for innovative evidence generation approaches. *NPJ Digital Medicine*, *3*(1), 1–6. DOI: 10.1038/s41746-020-00314-2 PMID: 32904379

Hamberger, M., Ikonomi, N., Schwab, J. D., Werle, S. D., Fürstberger, A., Kestler, A. M. R., Holderried, M., Kaisers, U. X., Steger, F., & Kestler, H. A. (2022). Interaction empowerment in mobile health: Concepts, challenges, and perspectives. *JMIR mHealth and uHealth*, *2022*(4), 1–13. DOI: 10.2196/32696 PMID: 35416786

Harrison, R., Fischer, S., Walpola, R. L., Chauhan, A., Babalola, T., Mears, S., & Le-Dao, H. (2021). … do models for change management, improvement and implementation meet? A systematic review of the applications of change management models in healthcare. *Journal of Healthcare Leadership*, *2021*, 1–13. DOI: 10.2147/JHL.S289176 PMID: 33737854

Hoffman, D. A. (2020). Increasing access to care: Telehealth during COVID-19. *Journal of Law and the Biosciences*, *7*(1), 181–185. DOI: 10.1093/jlb/lsaa043 PMID: 32843985

Hong, J. S., Wasden, C., & Han, D. H. (2021). Introduction of digital therapeutics. *Computer Methods and Programs in Biomedicine*, *208*, 106243. DOI: 10.1016/j.cmpb.2021.106243 PMID: 34364181

Jiang, N., Yan-Li, S., Pamanee, K., & Sriyanto, J. (2021). Depression, anxiety, and stress during the COVID-19 pandemic: Comparison among higher education students in four countries in the Asia-Pacific region. *Journal of Population and Social Studies*, *2021*, 1–13. DOI: 10.25133/JPSSv292021.023

Kamel Boulos, M. N., & Zhang, P. (2021). Digital twins: From personalised medicine to precision public health. *Journal of Personalized Medicine*, *11*(11), 1048. DOI: 10.3390/jpm11080745 PMID: 34442389

Kario, K., Nomura, A., Harada, N., & Okura, A. (2021). Efficacy of a digital therapeutics system in the management of essential hypertension: The HERB-DH1 pivotal trial. *European Heart Journal. Digital Health*, 2(3), 275–284. DOI: 10.1093/ehjdh/ztab033 PMID: 34455443

Kreitmair, K. V. (2024). Mobile health technology and empowerment. *Bioethics*, *2024*, 1–13. PMID: 36950727

Leone, L. A., Fleischhacker, S., Anderson-Steeves, B., Harper, K., Winkler, M., Racine, E., Baquero, B., & Gittelsohn, J. (2020). Healthy food retail during the COVID-19 pandemic: Challenges and future directions. *International Journal of Environmental Research and Public Health*, *17*(11), 4179. DOI: 10.3390/ijerph17207397 PMID: 33050600

Liberati, E., Richards, N., Willars, J., Scott, D., Boydell, N., Parker, J., Pinfold, V., Martin, G., Dixon-Woods, M., & Jones, P. B. (2021). A qualitative study of experiences of NHS mental healthcare workers during the Covid-19 pandemic. *BMC Psychiatry*, *2021*(1), 1–13. DOI: 10.1186/s12888-021-03261-8 PMID: 33980215

Linardon, J., Shatte, A., Messer, M., & Firth, J. (2020). E-mental health interventions for the treatment and prevention of eating disorders: An updated systematic review and meta-analysis. *Journal of Consulting and Clinical Psychology*, *2020*, 1–13. DOI: 10.1037/ccp0000459 PMID: 32852971

Liu, K., Tan, Q., Yu, J., & Wang, M. (2023). A global perspective on e-waste recycling. *Circular Economy*, *2023*, 1–13.

Liu, Y., Lee, J. M., & Lee, C. (2020). The challenges and opportunities of a global health crisis: The management and business implications of COVID-19 from an Asian perspective. *Asian Business & Management*, *19*(3), 259–278. DOI: 10.1057/s41291-020-00119-x

Marchini, S., Zaurino, E., Bouziotis, J., Brondino, N., Delvenne, V., & Delhaye, M. (2021). Study of resilience and loneliness in youth (18–25 years old) during the COVID-19 pandemic lockdown measures. *Journal of Community Psychology*, *2021*(2), 1–13. DOI: 10.1002/jcop.22473 PMID: 33169377

Mbunge, E., Batani, J., Gaobotse, G., & Muchemwa, B. (2022). Virtual healthcare services and digital health technologies deployed during coronavirus disease 2019 (COVID-19) pandemic in South Africa: A systematic review. *Global Health Journal (Amsterdam, Netherlands)*, *2022*(2), 1–13. DOI: 10.1016/j.glohj.2022.03.001 PMID: 35282399

Mbunge, E., Muchemwa, B., & Batani, J. (2021). Sensors and healthcare 5.0: Transformative shift in virtual care through emerging digital health technologies. *Global Health Journal (Amsterdam, Netherlands)*, *2021*(4), 1–13. DOI: 10.1016/j.glohj.2021.11.008

McCool, J., Dobson, R., Muinga, N., Paton, C., Pagliari, C., Agawal, S., Labrique, A., Tanielu, H., & Whittaker, R. (2020). Factors influencing the sustainability of digital health interventions in low-resource settings: Lessons from five countries. *Journal of Global Health*, *10*(2), 020403. DOI: 10.7189/jogh.10.020396 PMID: 33274059

Negro-Calduch, E., Azzopardi-Muscat, N., Krishnamurthy, R. S., & Novillo-Ortiz, D. (2021). Technological progress in electronic health record system optimization: Systematic review of systematic literature reviews. *International Journal of Medical Informatics*, *147*, 104388. DOI: 10.1016/j.ijmedinf.2021.104507 PMID: 34049051

Olatunji, A. O., Olaboye, J. A., & Maha, C. C. (2024). Revolutionizing infectious disease management in low-resource settings: The impact of rapid diagnostic technologies and portable devices. *Journal of Applied Sciences, 2024*, 1–13.

Ooi, K. B., Tan, G. W. H., & Al-Emran, M. (2023). The potential of generative artificial intelligence across disciplines: Perspectives and future directions. *Journal of Computer Information Systems, 2023*, 1–13.

Ortega, G., Rodriguez, J. A., Maurer, L. R., & Witt, E. E. (2020). Telemedicine, COVID-19, and disparities: Policy implications. *Health Policy and Technology, 9*(2), 149–152. DOI: 10.1016/j.hlpt.2020.03.003 PMID: 32837888

Palozzi, G., Schettini, I., & Chirico, A. (2020). Enhancing the sustainable goal of access to healthcare: Findings from a literature review on telemedicine employment in rural areas. *Sustainability (Basel), 12*(11), 4571. DOI: 10.3390/su12083318

Parajuli, R., Bohara, D., Kc, M., Shanmuganathan, S., Mistry, S. K., & Yadav, U. N. (2022). Challenges and opportunities for implementing digital health interventions in Nepal: A rapid review. *Frontiers in Digital Health, 4*, 849166. DOI: 10.3389/fdgth.2022.861019 PMID: 36120714

Pattyam, S. P. (2021). Artificial Intelligence for Healthcare Diagnostics: Techniques for Disease Prediction, Personalized Treatment, and Patient Monitoring. *Journal of Bioinformatics and Artificial Intelligence, 2*(1), 1–13.

Rauniyar, A., Hagos, D. H., & Jha, D. (2023). Federated learning for medical applications: A taxonomy, current trends, challenges, and future research directions. *IEEE Internet of Things Journal, 10*(10), 9345–9364. DOI: 10.1109/JIOT.2022.3223541

Richardson, S., Lawrence, K., Schoenthaler, A. M., & Mann, D. (2022). A framework for digital health equity. *NPJ Digital Medicine, 5*(1), 1–9. DOI: 10.1038/s41746-022-00663-0 PMID: 35982146

Romanelli, R. J., Azar, K. M. J., Sudat, S., & Hung, D. (2021). "Learning health system in crisis: lessons from the COVID-19 pandemic." Healthcare: Innovations. *Quality & Safety, 2021*, 1–13.

Rong, G., Mendez, A., Assi, E. B., Zhao, B., & Sawan, M. (2020). Artificial intelligence in healthcare: Review and prediction case studies. *Engineering (Beijing), 2020*(3), 1–13. DOI: 10.1016/j.eng.2019.08.015

Scott, B. K., Miller, G. T., Fonda, S. J., Yeaw, R. E., Gaudaen, J. C., Pavliscsak, H. H., Quinn, M. T., & Pamplin, J. C. (2020). Advanced digital health technologies for COVID-19 and future emergencies. *Telemedicine Journal and e-Health, 26*(10), 1245–1256. DOI: 10.1089/tmj.2020.0140 PMID: 32456560

Selvaraj, S., & Sundaravaradhan, S. (2020). Challenges and opportunities in IoT healthcare systems: A systematic review. *SN Applied Sciences*, *2*(1), 1–13. DOI: 10.1007/s42452-019-1925-y

Sezgin, E., Huang, Y., Ramtekkar, U., & Lin, S. (2020). Readiness for voice assistants to support healthcare delivery during a health crisis and pandemic. *NPJ Digital Medicine*, *3*(1), 1–9. DOI: 10.1038/s41746-020-00332-0 PMID: 33015374

Sheikh, A., Anderson, M., Albala, S., Casadei, B., Franklin, B. D., Richards, M., Taylor, D., Tibble, H., & Mossialos, E. (2021). Health information technology and digital innovation for national learning health and care systems. *The Lancet. Digital Health*, *3*(10), e675–e685. DOI: 10.1016/S2589-7500(21)00005-4 PMID: 33967002

Sourdin, T., Li, B., & McNamara, D. M. (2020). Court innovations and access to justice in times of crisis. *Health Policy and Technology*, *9*(2), 153–156. DOI: 10.1016/j.hlpt.2020.08.020 PMID: 32895624

Stampe, K., Kishik, S., & Müller, S. D. (2021). Mobile health in chronic disease management and patient empowerment: Exploratory qualitative investigation into patient-physician consultations. *Journal of Medical Internet Research*, *2021*(6), 1–13. DOI: 10.2196/26991 PMID: 34128817

Thapa, C., & Camtepe, S. (2021). Precision health data: Requirements, challenges and existing techniques for data security and privacy. *Computers in Biology and Medicine*, *136*, 104762. DOI: 10.1016/j.compbiomed.2020.104130 PMID: 33271399

Viljoen, S. (2021). A relational theory of data governance. *The Yale Law Journal*, *130*(6), 1464–1524.

Chapter 8
Digital Transformation in Response to Health Crises

Oindrilla Ghosh
https://orcid.org/0000-0001-9609-0781
Christ University, India

Binod Kumar
https://orcid.org/0009-0002-9721-1367
Radha Govind University, India

ABSTRACT

Digital transformation has emerged as a pivotal force in healthcare, particularly during health crises like the COVID-19 pandemic. As traditional systems faced unprecedented challenges, the rapid adoption of digital solutions became essential for ensuring patient care continuity and safety. Telemedicine surged, enabling remote consultations and reducing the burden on healthcare facilities. Electronic health records (EHRs) were optimized for better data sharing, facilitating coordinated responses among care teams. Wearable health technology gained traction, empowering individuals to monitor their health in real-time. Furthermore, data analytics and AI played crucial roles in predicting outbreaks and personalizing treatment plans. The shift towards a more digital-first approach not only addressed immediate needs but also laid the groundwork for a more resilient healthcare system. Stakeholders now recognize that embracing technology is critical for future-proofing healthcare against potential crises, enhancing overall healthcare delivery, and improving patient outcomes.

DOI: 10.4018/979-8-3373-5087-5.ch008

INTRODUCTION

Digital transformation has revolutionized various sectors (Loss et al., 2021), and the healthcare industry is no exception. Defined as the integration (Hsu et al., 2017) of digital technology into all areas of a business, leading to fundamental changes (Malecki, Keating, and Safdar, 2021) in operations, culture, and service delivery, digital transformation enables healthcare organizations (Contreras-Pacheco, 2018) to respond more nimbly to challenges such as health crises.

The advent of digital transformation in healthcare has accelerated (Sellnow and Seeger, 2013) greatly in response to crises such as the COVID-19 pandemic (Burton, John, and Pearson, 2016). This unprecedented global health emergency necessitated rapid adaptations (Johnson et al., 2020) in how care was delivered, pushing forward the adoption of telemedicine (Bowen and Heath, 2007), electronic health records, data analytics, and artificial intelligence (Kreuder Johnson et al., 2015). Organizations that had previously hesitated to implement digital technologies (Quinn, 2018) found themselves propelled into adopting solutions that enabled them not only (Reynolds and Seeger, 2005) to meet immediate healthcare demands but also to prepare for future challenges (Clarinval and Ahmad, 2015). For instance, telehealth services saw an exponential rise, allowing providers (Attademo, 2022) to deliver care remotely, ensuring patient safety while maintaining access to essential services (Clarinval and Ahmad, 2015).

Digital transformation also incorporates a cultural shift towards (Sekalala et al., 2020) more agile, responsive organizational practices. Innovative approaches (Dong et al., 2022), such as collaborative care models and interdisciplinary teams, flourish (Spitale, 2020) in a digitally transformed environment, allowing for information sharing (Schroeder, Numa, and Shapiro, 2022) and coordinated responses. Furthermore, the integration of digital health solutions (Abba-Aji et al., 2022) raises important considerations regarding equity in health access, data security (Bogart et al., 2022), and patient privacy that must be thoughtfully addressed as the healthcare landscape evolves (Hussain et al., 2022).

Historical Evolution

The historical evolution of digital transformation in healthcare (Germani and BillerAndorno, 2022) as a response to health crises can be traced back several decades (Niemiec, 2020), although the pace of change has significantly accelerated in recent years (Chang et al., 2022). The roots of digital health initiatives can be found in the late 20th century (Spitale et al., 2021), with the emergence of electronic health records (EHRs) and health information systems (Germani and Biller-Andorno, 2021). Initially adopted to streamline clinical workflows and enhance patient documentation

(Spitale, Biller-Andorno, and Germani, 2022), EHRs began to play a critical role in managing health crises (Roozenbeek et al., 2022) by providing real-time access to patient information while ensuring continuity of care (Germani, Pattison, and Reinfelde, 2022).

One pivotal moment in the historical trajectory of digital transformation (Albitz, 2007) was the SARS outbreak in 2003, which catalyzed the implementation (Willingham, 2020) of improved infectious disease surveillance systems globally (Mosseri, 2017). This event highlighted the necessity for rapid information sharing (Musk, 2022a) and data-driven decision-making in healthcare settings (Musk, 2022b), leading to investments in technology that would help contain such outbreaks (Germani, Pattison, and Reinfelde, 2022).

Following the SARS outbreak was the H1N1 influenza pandemic in 2009, which spurred further advancements (Sohrabi et al., 2020) in digital health technologies. During this period, social media and mobile communication (Stawicki et al., 2020) began to play an increasingly prominent role (Ciotti et al., 2020) in public health communication strategies. The quick dissemination of information (Lone & Ahmad, 2020), updates, and preventive measures through digital platforms (Mbunge, Muchemwa, & Batani, 2021) became invaluable in managing public awareness and behaviors during an outbreak (Sust et al., 2020).

The Ebola outbreak in West Africa (2014-2016) marked another significant (Aljukhadar, 2022) turning point, bringing attention to the importance of data analytics and visualization tools (Tang et al., 2022) in infectious disease tracking. Initiatives such as the use of Geographic Information Systems (GIS) for mapping disease transmission (Vallée, 2023) and resource allocation underscored the value of digital solutions in emergency responses (Etando et al., 2021).

However, it was the COVID-19 pandemic that propelled digital transformation (Zahlan, Ranjan, & Hayes, 2023) in healthcare into the mainstream. The urgency of managing an unprecedented global health crisis (Chahley, Reel, & Taylor, 2021) forced organizations worldwide to expedite the adoption of digital tools (Mohammadpour et al., 2021). Telehealth emerged as a lifeline for continuity of care, while health systems (Roychoudhury et al., 2020) increasingly relied on data analytics to inform policies and manage patient flow (An & Tang, 2020).

In addition, the COVID-19 pandemic showcased the integration (Haldane et al., 2021) of mobile applications for contact tracing and vaccination drives (Tambo, Djuikoue, Tazemda, Fotsing, & Zhou, 2021), pushing governments and organizations to innovate rapidly (Dar, Swamy, Gavin, & Theodore, 2021). The pandemic prompted extensive collaborations between tech companies (Steier & Moxham, 2020), healthcare providers, and governments, showcasing a new model (Dehghani Tafti et al., 2023) of public-private partnerships focused on health technology solutions (Madhavan et al., 2021).

Research Objectives

1. To analyze the digital transformation initiatives implemented by healthcare organizations during past health crises.
2. To evaluate the effectiveness of digital health solutions in enhancing operational efficiency and patient care during health emergencies.
3. To identify the challenges faced by healthcare providers in integrating digital technologies into their services during crises.
4. To assess the role of government policies and regulations in facilitating or impeding digital transformation during health crises.
5. To explore the perspectives of healthcare professionals and patients regarding the use of digital technologies in crisis management.

THEORETICAL FRAMEWORKS IN DIGITAL TRANSFORMATION DURING HEALTH CRISES

Digital transformation in response to health crises has gained significant attention (Chang et al., 2021) in recent years, especially during events such as the COVID-19 pandemic (Shen, Chen, Yue, & Xu, 2021). Various theoretical frameworks enable researchers, policymakers, and practitioners (Abayomi et al., 2021) to understand, implement, and evaluate digital transformation initiatives effectively (Herstein, Schwedhelm, Vasa, Biddinger, & Hewlett, 2021). Among the most relevant frameworks include the Technology Acceptance Model (TAM), the Diffusion of Innovations (DOI) theory, and the Resource-Based View (RBV) (Jit et al., 2021).

Technology Acceptance Model (TAM): serves as an essential theoretical framework for understanding users' acceptance (Allam, 2022) and adoption of new technologies in health crises (Khan & Alotaibi, 2020). TAM emphasizes two primary factors: perceived ease of use and perceived usefulness (Lee & Yoon, 2021). In a health crisis, stakeholders such as healthcare providers, patients, and administrators (Caldwell, 2023) must adopt rapidly evolving technologies to respond effectively. As healthcare professionals (Karanika-Murray, Whysall, Liu-Smith, Feltbower, & Challans-Rasool, 2023) and patients face the pressure of adapting to new digital tools, the ease with which these technologies (Wu, Shao, Newman, & Schwarz, 2021) can be learned and utilized directly impacts their acceptance.

Diffusion of Innovations (DOI): provides another useful lens through which to analyze digital transformation during health crises (Comber, 2024). This framework, introduced by Everett Rogers, outlines how new ideas and technologies (Montani et al., 2021) are adopted over time within social systems. The DOI model identifies several factors that influence adoption (Chauhan et al., 2024), including the perceived advantages of the innovation, compatibility with existing values (Arif et al., 2024), ease of trialability, and observable results. In the context of health crises (Miranda, 2024), innovations like mobile health applications or data analytics systems can provide (Tomé et al., 2024) significant benefits, such as real-time data monitoring and improved patient engagement (Tariq, 2024a).

Resource-Based View (RBV): focuses on leveraging internal capabilities and resources to foster competitive advantage (Fung et al., 2022), particularly relevant for health organizations during crises (Tan et al., 2023). Effective digital transformation relies heavily on an organization's existing resources (Weaver et al., 2022), such as human capital, technology infrastructure, and financial assets (Garcia & Revano, 2022). The RBV emphasizes the importance of aligning digital strategies with the organization's (Astuti & Ysrafil, 2020) unique capabilities and resources, encouraging health institutions to invest strategically (Kwame et al., 2023) in technologies that offer long-term benefits rather than reacting haphazardly to immediate pressures (McCarthy et al., 2023).

Use of AI and ML in Digital Transformation in Response to Health Crises

The advent of artificial intelligence (AI) and machine learning (ML) has significantly transformed various sectors (Hau and Liu, 2021), particularly healthcare, enhancing responses to health crises. The dynamic capabilities of AI and ML are leveraged to analyze vast data sets (Peltier et al., 2023), identify patterns, and inform decision-making in ways that were previously unimaginable, thereby revolutionizing how health crises are managed (Wang, 2021).

AI and ML also enhance diagnostic accuracy and treatment personalization. Advanced image processing algorithms can analyze (Contreras-Pacheco, 2018) medical images, such as X-rays and MRIs, to assist radiologists in detecting anomalies (Benoit, 1997). By significantly reducing diagnostic times and improving accuracy, these technologies have the potential to save lives in urgent care settings during health emergencies (Coombs, 2007). Moreover, AI algorithms can analyze individual patient data to tailor treatments based on genetic, lifestyle, and environmental factors (Xu and Li, 2013), leading to more effective outcomes. The ability to personalize care is especially pertinent during health crises, where the swift deployment of effective treatments can mitigate mortality rates (Sellnow and Seeger, 2013).

In drug discovery and development, AI and ML offer unprecedented advantages (Burton, John, and Pearson, 2016). The traditional drug development process is lengthy and costly, often taking over a decade to bring a medication to market (Johnson et al., 2020). Machine learning algorithms can analyze biological and chemical data to predict how potential drugs may interact with the body, significantly reducing the time required for development (Bowen and Heath, 2007). This speed is crucial during health crises, where rapid vaccine and treatment development can curb the impact of diseases (Kreuder Johnson et al., 2015), as witnessed during the accelerated development of COVID-19 vaccines.

Augmented Reality (AR) in Digital Transformation for Health Crises

Augmented Reality (AR) has emerged as a pivotal tool in the healthcare sector, particularly during health crises (Lewis, 2022). The integration of AR technology enables healthcare professionals to visualize complex data in real-time, enhancing decision-making processes. For instance, during the COVID-19 pandemic (Ratzan, Sommariva, and Rauh, 2020), AR facilitated remote training for healthcare workers, allowing them to practice procedures and protocols via simulated environments (Hu, 2022). This virtual training minimizes the risk of infection while ensuring that medical personnel are well-prepared to handle emergencies.

Moreover, AR applications have been crucial in patient care (Hindman, Lubin, and Davis, 2021). For instance, AR can overlay critical information about a patient's condition onto a healthcare provider's field of vision, helping them to make informed decisions rapidly. This technology also enhances patient education (Satariano, 2022) by providing interactive visuals, ensuring that patients better understand their conditions and treatment plans. As the healthcare industry embraces digital transformation, AR emerges as a robust solution to enhance efficiency, training, and patient interaction during health crises (Spitale, Biller-Andorno, and Germani, 2022), ultimately leading to improved health outcomes and resilience against future threats.

Virtual Reality (VR) in Digital Transformation for Health Crises

Virtual Reality (VR) technology has revolutionized various aspects of healthcare, particularly in response to health crises (Sekalala et al., 2020). Its immersive nature provides unique opportunities for training and education, allowing medical professionals to experience lifelike simulations (Bowen and Heath, 2007) without the associated risks of real-world scenarios. During health emergencies like pandemics, VR offers a safe space for practitioners to refine their skills and practice (Dong et al., 2022) complex procedures, ensuring that they are well-prepared to face real-life challenges.

Additionally, VR has shown promise in patient treatment, particularly in managing pain and anxiety (Spitale, 2020). For instance, during times of crisis when access to mental health professionals may be limited, VR applications can provide therapeutic experiences (Schroeder, Numa, and Shapiro, 2022), helping patients cope with stress and fear associated with health crises. Moreover, VR can enhance telemedicine experiences by offering virtual assessments and consultations (Abba-Aji et al., 2022), breaking down geographical barriers to healthcare.

Mixed Reality (MR) in Digital Transformation for Health Crises

Mixed Reality (MR) combines elements of both Augmented Reality (AR) and Virtual Reality (VR), offering powerful applications in healthcare (Bogart et al., 2021), especially during health crises. In situations such as pandemics or natural disasters, MR can be crucial in simulating real-world scenarios, allowing healthcare workers to practice responses and interactions in a controlled yet realistic environment (Turilli and Floridi, 2009).

One of the standout applications of MR in health crises is its use in surgical training and planning. Surgeons can visualize 3D models of patients' anatomy (Ball, 2009) overlaid onto their bodies, aiding in precise pre-operative planning and enhancing the accuracy of procedures. MR also facilitates remote collaboration among professionals (Michener and Bersch, 2013), enabling specialists from different locations to assist in surgeries or case evaluations through shared visualizations, thereby improving consultation efficiency during critical times (Sachs et al., 2022).

Advantages

The advantages of leveraging digital technologies in response to health crises are numerous and fundamentally reshape how healthcare is provided and managed (Germani and Biller-Andorno, 2021).

- Enhanced Patient Care: One of the most significant advantages of digital transformation in health crises is the ability to provide enhanced (Spitale, Biller-Andorno, and Germani, 2022) patient care through telemedicine. With the onset of a health crisis, access to traditional healthcare facilities can become limited. Telehealth services allow patients to consult healthcare providers remotely (Roozenbeek et al., 2022), reducing the risk of infection transmission while ensuring continuity of care. This technology enables chronic disease management, mental health support (Germani, Pattison, and Reinfelde, 2022), and urgent care services without the need for physical visits.
- Operational Efficiency: The adoption of digital tools streamlines administrative processes, reducing the burden on healthcare staff (Musk, 2022a). Electronic health records (EHRs), automated appointment scheduling, and digital billing systems minimize paperwork and enhance workflow efficiency

(Musk, 2022b). This efficiency is crucial during health crises, where healthcare professionals must focus on patient care rather than administrative tasks (Germani, Pattison, and Reinfelde, 2022).

- Remote Monitoring and Wearable Technology: The expansion of remote monitoring tools (Sohrabi et al., 2020) and wearable technology allows for the continuous tracking of patients' health metrics without the need for in-person visits. This capability is particularly valuable for managing conditions (Stawicki et al., 2020) that require regular monitoring, such as diabetes or cardiovascular diseases, enabling healthcare providers to intervene promptly when necessary (Ciotti et al., 2020).
- Public Health Surveillance: Digital technologies significantly enhance public health surveillance capabilities. Mobile applications and social media platforms (Lone & Ahmad, 2020) can be harnessed to track symptoms, report cases, and monitor public compliance with health advisories. This crowd-sourced data can supplement traditional epidemiology methods (Mbunge, Muchemwa, & Batani, 2021), resulting in a more comprehensive understanding of disease dynamics.

Challenges

Despite the numerous advantages, the process of digital transformation in healthcare during health crises (Sust et al., 2020) also presents several formidable challenges that must be addressed for successful implementation and sustainability (Aljukhadar, 2022).

Data Privacy and Security: The integration of digital technologies raises significant concerns about data privacy and security (Tang et al., 2022). Sensitive health information is at risk of breaches and unauthorized access, which can undermine patient trust and compliance (Vallée, 2023). Ensuring robust data protection measures and compliance with regulations, such as the Health Insurance Portability and Accountability Act (HIPAA) in the U.S., is essential yet challenging (Etando et al., 2021), particularly in a rapidly changing environment.

Digital Divide: The disparity in access to digital technologies creates a digital divide that can exacerbate health inequities (Zahlan, Ranjan, & Hayes, 2023). Not all populations have equal access to the internet, smartphones, or digital literacy, leading to disparities in healthcare access (Chahley, Reel, & Taylor, 2021). Vulnerable populations may face additional barriers, limiting the effectiveness of digital health solutions and causing marginalized groups to be underserved during crises (Mohammadpour et al., 2021).

Resistance to Change: Healthcare providers and staff may resist adopting new digital tools due to a lack of familiarity or perceived complexity (Tambo, Djuikoue, Tazemda, Fotsing, & Zhou, 2021). This resistance can slow down the implementation of necessary technologies and hinder the overall transformation process. Effective training and change management strategies (Dar, Swamy, Gavin, & Theodore, 2021) are essential to overcome this resistance and ensure successful adoption.

Quality Control and Reliability: The implementation of digital health technologies (Madhavan et al., 2021) raises questions about quality control and reliability. Misinformation, algorithm bias, and variability in technology performance can compromise patient safety and outcomes (Ros et al., 2021). Establishing rigorous standards for digital health tools is crucial to ensuring their effectiveness and reliability, particularly in high-stakes scenarios such as health crises (Ness, Saylor, Di Fusco, & Evans, 2021).

Ethical Considerations

The advent of digital technologies has revolutionized various sectors, with healthcare being one of the most significantly impacted (Wang, Su, Zhang, & Li, 2021). As health crises such as pandemics unfold, the urgency for rapid digital transformation becomes evident (Arslan, Golgeci, Khan, Al-Tabbaa, & Hurmelinna-Laukkanen, 2021). However, this process raises numerous ethical considerations that must be addressed.

One of the primary ethical issues in digital health transformation relates to patient privacy and data security (Santra & Alat, 2022). During health crises, the collection of health data often intensifies, particularly for contact tracing, symptom tracking, and the distribution of vaccines (Chang et al., 2021). While these measures are critical for public health, they raise serious concerns about how personal health information is stored, shared, and utilized (Shen, Chen, Yue, & Xu, 2021). The potential for data breaches and misuse calls for stringent guidelines and robust cybersecurity measures. Ethical frameworks should prioritize consent (Abayomi et al., 2021), ensuring patients are informed about how their data will be used while promoting transparency in data practices (Herstein, Schwedhelm, Vasa, Biddinger, & Hewlett, 2021).

Furthermore, the ethical deployment of AI and machine learning in healthcare raises questions about accountability, bias, and discrimination (Caldwell, 2023). Algorithms developed to support diagnostic decision-making or resource allocation must be rigorously tested (Karanika-Murray, Whysall, Liu-Smith, Feltbower, & Challans-Rasool, 2023) for biases that could lead to skewed outcomes affecting vulnerable populations. The ethical implications of reliance on automated systems demand frameworks (Wu, Shao, Newman, & Schwarz, 2021) that promote fairness and inclusivity, ensuring that AI systems are designed to benefit all demographics and do not reinforce existing biases.

Implementation of Regulatory Frameworks

The advent of digital transformation in the healthcare sector has been catalyzed significantly by health crises, notably the COVID-19 pandemic (Dzando et al., 2022). In this context, the implementation of regulatory frameworks becomes critical. These frameworks ensure that digital health solutions are safe, effective, and equitable (I. Owusu et al., 2023). They also help facilitate rapid innovation while protecting public health interests. Successful implementation hinges on several key principles and methodologies (Sarkodie & Owusu, 2021).

Firstly, a clear understanding of the landscape is essential. Regulators must assess which digital tools be it telemedicine, electronic health records (EHRs) (Asiedu-Berkoe et al., 2022), or mobile health applications require oversight. This process involves engaging with stakeholders including healthcare providers, technology developers, and patients (Clipper, 2020). By doing so, regulations can be tailored to protect users while encouraging innovation.

Secondly, agility in regulatory processes is paramount (Andtfolk et al., 2022) during health crises. Traditional regulatory timelines can be lengthy, potentially delaying beneficial digital solutions in urgent circumstances (Clipper, 2020). Regulatory bodies can adopt expedited reviews for digital health innovations that demonstrate promising early results (Shen et al., 2021). For instance, regulatory agencies like the U.S. Food and Drug Administration (FDA) have introduced mechanisms such as Emergency Use Authorizations (EUAs) for digital health products (Sarker et al., 2021) that address critical health needs rapidly, thus facilitating a more dynamic regulatory environment.

Another significant component of regulatory implementation (Panja, 2024) is collaboration. Governments, healthcare organizations, and technology firms must work together to develop frameworks that not only address immediate health crises (Darda & Matta, 2024) but also lay the groundwork for future digital health solutions. This collaboration extends internationally as well. In times of global health emergencies, there is an urgent need (Ofosu-Ampong, 2021) for regulatory harmonization across borders to facilitate the rapid deployment of digital health technologies everywhere (Cucinotta & Vanelli, 2020).

Suggestions

Digital transformation has become a crucial element in managing and mitigating the impacts of health crises, as evidenced during the COVID-19 pandemic (Toit & Goosen, 2024). To harness its full potential in future emergencies, several strategic suggestions can be proposed.

- Real-Time Data Sharing and Analytics: The capability to share and analyze data in real-time is critical during a health crisis (Peltier et al., 2020). Governments and healthcare institutions must invest in interoperable data systems that can share patient records seamlessly. Advanced analytics and artificial intelligence (Reuschl et al., 2022) can be utilized to analyze health trends and predict outbreaks, thus enabling timely intervention.
- Mobile Health Applications: The development of mobile health apps can empower individuals to monitor their health conditions, receive alerts about outbreaks (Hercheui and Mech, 2021), and access educational resources.
- Investing in Cybersecurity: As digital transformation accelerates, the vulnerability of health systems to cyberattacks also increases (Huang and Rust, 2018). Organizations must prioritize cybersecurity investments to protect sensitive patient data and ensure the reliability of health services (Verhoef et al., 2021).
- Public-Private Partnerships: Collaboration between public health agencies and private technology companies can drive innovation and accelerate (Dahl et al., 2021) the implementation of digital health solutions. Governments should foster a conducive environment for these partnerships by providing funding (Swan et al., 2019), regulatory support, and incentives for companies that develop impactful health technologies.
- Continuous Education and Training: Continuous professional development programs should be established for healthcare personnel to equip them (Zhu et al., 2022) with the necessary digital skills and competencies.

FUTURE RESEARCH DIRECTIONS

As digital transformation evolves, future research directions must address emerging challenges and opportunities in the realm of healthcare during crises (Verhoef et al., 2021). Future research should focus on evaluating the effectiveness of various digital health interventions (Kopalle et al., 2022), including telehealth, mobile applications, and digital health literacy programs. Longitudinal studies could elucidate the long-term benefits (Manser Payne et al., 2021a) and any unintended effects of these interventions, informing best practices for future health crises.

Investigating the role of AI and machine learning in predicting health crises and optimizing response strategies is a promising research area (Verhoef and Bijmolt, 2019). Future studies could assess how predictive analytics can be utilized for resource allocation, contact tracing, and outbreak control (Dahl et al., 2018), contributing to a more proactive rather than reactive healthcare system. The increasing reliance on digital technologies necessitates research on enhancing cybersecurity (Huang and Rust, 2017) strategies in healthcare. Exploring robust frameworks for digital health security can provide insights into effective risk management and vulnerability assessments (Lalicic and Weismayer, 2021).

CONCLUSION

Digital transformation in healthcare has proven to be an invaluable asset (Bawole & Langnel, 2023) in navigating health crises. The urgent need for effective healthcare during crises such as the COVID-19 pandemic accelerated the adoption of digital technologies significantly (Ofosu-Ampong & Acheampong, 2022). This transformation has not only facilitated real-time responses to health emergencies but also provided critical insights into systemic healthcare challenges (Damenshie-Brown & Ofosu-Ampong, 2023) that were previously overlooked.

As we reflect on the implications of digital transformation in health crises, one crucial aspect lies in its role in enhancing access to care (Garcia, Arif, et al., 2024). Telehealth services emerged as a crucial solution for maintaining patient-provider interactions amid lockdowns and social distancing measures (Patibandla et al., 2024). This shift has reduced barriers, making healthcare more accessible for populations that may have previously faced challenges in accessing traditional in-person services (Swayamsiddha et al., 2021). Furthermore, the integration of mobile health applications has empowered patients to monitor their health remotely, ensuring that preventative care and routine check-ups continue even during crises (Kazi, 2024).

REFERENCES

Abayomi, A., Balogun, M. R., Bankole, M., Banke-Thomas, A., Mutiu, B., Olawepo, J., & Ejekam, C. (2021). From Ebola to COVID-19: Emergency preparedness and response plans and actions in Lagos, Nigeria. *Globalization and Health, 17*(1), 1–10. DOI: 10.1186/s12992-021-00728-x PMID: 34243790

Abba-Aji, M., Stuckler, D., Galea, S., & McKee, M. (2022). Ethnic/racial minorities' and migrants' access to COVID-19 vaccines: A systematic review of barriers and facilitators. *Journal of Migration and Health, 5*, 100086. DOI: 10.1016/j.jmh.2022.100086 PMID: 35194589

Abid, M. F., Shamim, A., Khan, Z., & Khan, I. (2022). Value creation or value destruction: Conceptualizing the experiential nature of value-in-use. *Journal of Consumer Behaviour, 21*(3), 583–601. DOI: 10.1002/cb.2033

Alawi, M. M. S. (2021). Successful Management of COVID-19 Outbreak in a Long-term Care Facility in Jeddah, Saudi Arabia: Epidemiology, Challenges for Prevention and Adaptive Management Strategies. *Journal of Infection and Public Health, 14*(4), 521–526. DOI: 10.1016/j.jiph.2020.12.036 PMID: 33743375

Albitz, R. S. (2007). The what and who of information literacy and critical thinking in higher education. *Portal (Baltimore, Md.), 7*(1), 97–109. DOI: 10.1353/pla.2007.0000

Allam, K. (2022). Big data analytics in robotics: Unleashing the potential for intelligent automation. *EPH-International Journal of Business & Management Science, 8*(4), 5–9.

Almeida, R. P. (Ed.). (2022). *Handbook of Research on Improving Allied Health Professions Education: Advancing Clinical Training and Interdisciplinary Translational Research.* IGI Global., DOI: 10.4018/978-1-7998-9578-7

An, B. Y., & Tang, S.-Y. (2020). Lessons from COVID-19 responses in East Asia: Institutional infrastructure and enduring policy instruments. *American Review of Public Administration, 50*(6-7), 790–800. DOI: 10.1177/0275074020943707

Andtfolk, M., Nyholm, L., Eide, H., Rauhala, A., & Fagerström, L. (2022). Attitudes Toward the Use of Humanoid Robots in Healthcare—A Cross-Sectional Study. *AI & Society, 37*(4), 1739–1748. DOI: 10.1007/s00146-021-01271-4

Arayata, P. A., Banzon, J., Franco, B. M., Lubrin, D., Perez, M. R., & Garcia, M. B. (2022). Chyilax: An Innovative 3D Game Approach for Mental Breakdown Awareness Campaign. 2022 IEEE 14th International Conference on Humanoid, Nanotechnology, Information Technology, Communication and Control, Environment and Management (HNICEM). IEEE. DOI: 10.1109/HNICEM57413.2022.10109535

Arif, Y. M., Ayunda, N., Diah, N. M., & Garcia, M. B. (2024). A Systematic Review of Serious Games for Health Education: Technology, Challenges, and Future Directions. In *Transformative Approaches to Patient Literacy and Healthcare Innovation*. IGI Global., DOI: 10.4018/979-8-3693-3661-8.ch002

Arslan, A., Golgeci, I., Khan, Z., Al-Tabbaa, O., & Hurmelinna-Laukkanen, P. (2021).

Arslan, A., Golgeci, I., Khan, Z., Al-Tabbaa, O., & Hurmelinna-Laukkanen, P. (2021, January 07). Adaptive learning in cross-sector collaboration during global emergency: Conceptual insights in the context of COVID-19 pandemic. *Multinational Business Review*, *29*(1), 21–42. DOI: 10.1108/MBR-07-2020-0153

Asiedu-Berkoe, F., Chandi, G. M., Bandoh, D. A., Atsu, B. K., Lokossou, V. K., Antara, S. N., Sarkodie, B., & Kenu, E. (2022). State of Public Health Emergency Preparedness and Response Capacity of Ghana. *Journal of Interventional Epidemiology and Public Health*, *5*(4), 1–16. DOI: 10.37432/jieph.supp.2022.5.4.05.4

Astuti, I., & Ysrafil, . (2020). Severe Acute Respiratory Syndrome Coronavirus 2 (SARS-CoV-2): An overview of viral structure and host response. *Diabetes & Metabolic Syndrome*, *14*(4), 407–412. DOI: 10.1016/j.dsx.2020.04.020 PMID: 32335367

Attademo, G. (2022). International efforts against the infodemic: Some bioethical reflections. *Medicina e Morale*, *71*(1), 69–78. DOI: 10.4081/mem.2022.1200

Barile, S., Bassano, C., Piciocchi, P., Saviano, M., & Spohrer, J. C. (2021). Empowering value co-creation in the digital age. *Journal of Business and Industrial Marketing*. Advance online publication. DOI: 10.1108/JBIM-12-2019-0553

Barnes, S., & De Ruyter, K. (2022). Guest editorial: artificial intelligence as a market-facing technology: getting closer to the consumer through innovation and insight. *European Journal of Marketing*, *56*(6), 1585–1589. DOI: 10.1108/EJM-05-2022-979

Baudier, P., Kondrateva, G., Ammi, C., Chang, V., & Schiavone, F. (2023). Digital Transformation of Healthcare During the COVID-19 Pandemic: Patients' Teleconsultation Acceptance and Trusting Beliefs. *Technovation*, *120*, 1–11. DOI: 10.1016/j.technovation.2022.102547

Bawole, J. N., & Langnel, Z. (2023). Administrative Reforms in the Ghanaian Public Services for Government Business Continuity During the COVID-19 Crisis. *Public Organization Review*, *23*(1), 181–196. DOI: 10.1007/s11115-022-00687-w

Benoit, W. L. (1997). Image repair discourse and crisis communication. *Public Relations Review*, *23*(2), 177–186. DOI: 10.1016/S0363-8111(97)90023-0

Bhaskar, S., Bradley, S., Chattu, V. K., Adisesh, A., Nurtazina, A., Kyrykbayeva, S., Sakhamuri, S., Moguilner, S., Pandya, S., Schroeder, S., Banach, M., & Ray, D. (2020). Telemedicine as the New Outpatient Clinic Gone Digital: Position Paper From the Pandemic Health System REsilience PROGRAM (REPROGRAM) International Consortium (Part 2). *Frontiers in Public Health*, *8*, 1–16. DOI: 10.3389/fpubh.2020.00410 PMID: 33014958

Biddle, L., Wahedi, K., & Bozorgmehr, K. (2020). Health system resilience: A literature review of empirical research. *Health Policy and Planning*, *35*(8), 1084–1109. DOI: 10.1093/heapol/czaa032 PMID: 32529253

Bogart, L. M., Dong, L., Gandhi, P., Klein, D. J., Smith, T. L., Ryan, S., & Ojikutu, B. O. (2022). COVID-19 vaccine intentions and mistrust in a national sample of Black Americans. *Journal of the National Medical Association*, *113*(6), 599–611. DOI: 10.1016/j.jnma.2021.05.011 PMID: 34158171

Bogart, L. M., Ojikutu, B. O., Tyagi, K., Klein, D. J., Mutchler, M. G., Dong, L., Lawrence, S. J., Thomas, D. R., & Kellman, S. (2021). COVID-19 related medical mistrust, health impacts, and potential vaccine hesitancy among Black Americans living with HIV. *Journal of Acquired Immune Deficiency Syndromes*, *86*(2), 200–207. DOI: 10.1097/QAI.0000000000002570 PMID: 33196555

Caldwell, C. B. E. (2023). *An Application of Lewin in a Trans-Pandemic World: A Narrative Inquiry in a Case Study with a New Suggested Model for the Future*. Pepperdine University.

Cartwright, N. (2009). What is this thing called "efficacy"? In Mantzavinos, C. (Ed.), *Philosophy of the social sciences: Philosophical theory and scientific practice* (pp. 185–206). Cambridge University Press., DOI: 10.1017/CBO9780511812880.016

Chahley, E. R., Reel, R. M., & Taylor, S. (2021). The lived experience of healthcare professionals working frontline during the 2003 SARS epidemic, 2009 H1N1 pandemic, 2012 MERS outbreak, and 2014 EVD epidemic: A qualitative systematic review. *SSM. Qualitative Research in Health*, *1*, 100026. DOI: 10.1016/j.ssmqr.2021.100026 PMID: 34901922

Chandler, J. D., & Vargo, S. L. (2011). Contextualization and value-in-context: How context frames exchange. *Marketing Theory*, *11*(1), 35–49. DOI: 10.1177/1470593110393713

Chang, J. E., Lai, A. Y., Gupta, A., Nguyen, A. M., Berry, C. A., & Shelley, D. R. (2021). Rapid transition to telehealth and the digital divide: Implications for primary care access and equity in a post-COVID era. *The Milbank Quarterly*, *99*(2), 340–368. DOI: 10.1111/1468-0009.12509 PMID: 34075622

Chang, K.-C., Hobbs, W. R., Roberts, M. E., & Steinert-Threlkeld, Z. C. (2022). COVID-19 increased censorship circumvention and access to sensitive topics in China. *Proceedings of the National Academy of Sciences of the United States of America*, *119*(4), e2102818119. DOI: 10.1073/pnas.2102818119 PMID: 35046018

Chauhan, P., Bali, A., & Kaur, S. (2024). Breaking Barriers for Accessible Health Programs: The Role of Telemedicine in a Global Healthcare Transformation. In *Transformative Approaches to Patient Literacy and Healthcare Innovation*. IGI Global., DOI: 10.4018/979-8-3693-3661-8.ch014

Ciotti, M., Ciccozzi, M., Terrinoni, A., Jiang, W.-C., Wang, C.-B., & Bernardini, S. (2020). The COVID-19 pandemic. *Critical Reviews in Clinical Laboratory Sciences*, *57*(6), 365–388. DOI: 10.1080/10408363.2020.1783198 PMID: 32645276

Clipper, B. (2020). The Influence of the COVID-19 Pandemic on Technology: Adoption in Health Care. *Nurse Leader*, *18*(5), 500–503. DOI: 10.1016/j.mnl.2020.06.008 PMID: 32837346

Comber, C. (2024). Long COVID Frameworks: Examining Individual- and Population-Level Models to Assess and Improve Patient Care. *Health Promotion Practice*, *25*(1), 22–26. DOI: 10.1177/15248399221142514 PMID: 36546678

Contreras-Pacheco, O. E. (2018). Care ethics and crisis communication: Examining two experiences in South America. *Cuadernos De Administracion*, *34*(62), 20–32. DOI: 10.25100/10.25100/cdea.2018v34n62.6866

Coombs, W. T. (2007). Attribution theory as a guide for post-crisis communication research. *Public Relations Review*, *33*(2), 135–139. DOI: 10.1016/j.pubrev.2006.11.016

Cortez, L. P., Tandayu, S. K., Villan, K. R., Español, R., Tutanes, A. C., Perez, M. R., Calleja, J., & Garcia, M. B. (2022). Corona Larona: A 2.5D Mobile Game Advocating COVID-19 Safety Protocols and Mitigation Strategies. 2022 IEEE 14th International Conference on Humanoid, Nanotechnology, Information Technology, Communication and Control, Environment and Management (HNICEM). IEEE. DOI: 10.1109/HNICEM57413.2022.10109445

Cuan-Baltazar, J. Y., Munoz-Perez, M. J., Robledo-Vega, C., Pérez-Zepeda, M. F., & Soto-Vega, E. (2020). Misinformation of COVID-19 on the internet: Infodemiology study. *JMIR Public Health and Surveillance*, *6*(2), e18444. DOI: 10.2196/18444 PMID: 32250960

Cucinotta, D., & Vanelli, M. (2020). WHO Declares COVID-19 a Pandemic. *Acta Biomedica*, *91*(1), 157–160. DOI: 10.23750/abm.v91i1.9397 PMID: 32191675

Dahl, A. J., Milne, G. R., & Peltier, J. W. (2021). Digital health information seeking in an omni-channel environment: A shared decision-making and service-dominant logic perspective. *Journal of Business Research*, *125*, 840–850. DOI: 10.1016/j.jbusres.2019.02.025

Dahl, A. J., Peltier, J. W., & Milne, G. R. (2022). Reducing information asymmetry and increasing health value co-creation in a rural healthcare context. *The Journal of Consumer Affairs*, *56*(2), 512–535. DOI: 10.1111/joca.12447

Dahl, A. J., Peltier, J. W., & Swan, E. L. (2023). Anticipatory value-in-use in early-stage digital health service transformations: How consumers assess value propositions before and after abrupt, exogenous shocks. *Journal of Business Research*, *163*, 113910. Advance online publication. DOI: 10.1016/j.jbusres.2023.113910

Damenshie-Brown, A., & Ofosu-Ampong, K. (2023). COVID-19 Pandemic and Digital Banking Trends: Managerial Perspective on Challenges and Opportunities. In Shoukat, G., & Tunio, M. N. (Eds.), *Societal Transformations and Resilience in Times of Crisis* (pp. 112–135). IGI Global., DOI: 10.4018/978-1-6684-5326-1.ch007

Darda, P., & Matta, N. (2024). The Nexus of Healthcare and Technology: A Thematic Analysis of Digital Transformation Through Artificial Intelligence. In *Transformative Approaches to Patient Literacy and Healthcare Innovation*. IGI Global., DOI: 10.4018/979-8-3693-3661-8.ch013

Dodds, S., Russell-Bennett, R., Chen, T., Oertzen, A.-S., Salvador-Carulla, L., & Hung, Y.-C. (2022). Blended human-technology service realities in healthcare. *Journal of Service Theory and Practice*, *32*(1), 75–99. DOI: 10.1108/JSTP-12-2020-0285

Dong, T., Benedetto, U., Sinha, S., Fudulu, D., Dimagli, A., Chan, J., Caputo, M., & Angelini, G. (2022). Deep recurrent reinforced learning model to compare the efficacy of targeted local versus national measures on the spread of COVID-19 in the UK. *BMJ Open*, *12*(2), e048279. DOI: 10.1136/bmjopen-2020-048279 PMID: 35190408

Dwomoh, D., Yeboah, I., Ndejjo, R., Kabwama, S. N., Aheto, J. M., Liu, A., Lazenby, S., Ohemeng, F., Takyi, S. A., Issah, I., Bawuah, S. A., Wanyenze, R. K., & Fobil, J. (2023). COVID-19 Outbreak Control Strategies and Their Impact on the Provision of Essential Health Services in Ghana: An Exploratory sequential Study. *PLoS One*, *18*(11), 1–20. DOI: 10.1371/journal.pone.0279528 PMID: 37972045

Dzando, G., Salifu, S., Donyi, A. B., Akpeke, H., Kumah, A., Dordunu, R., & Nonoh, E. A. (2022). Healthcare in Ghana Amidst the Coronavirus Pandemic: A Narrative Literature Review. *Journal of Public Health Research*, *11*(1), 1–5. DOI: 10.4081/jphr.2021.2448 PMID: 34351103

Erisen, D. E., & Uludag, K. (2024). Estimating Biosafety of Biodegradable Biomedical Materials from In Vitro Ion Tolerance Parameters and Toxicity of Nanomaterials in Brain. In *Transformative Approaches to Patient Literacy and Healthcare Innovation*. IGI Global., DOI: 10.4018/979-8-3693-3661-8.ch010

Flemons, K., Baylis, B., Khan, A. Z., Kirkpatrick, A. W., Whitehead, K., Moeini, S., Schreiber, A., Lapointe, S., Ashoori, S., Arif, M., Berenger, B., Conly, J., & Hawkins, W. (2022). The Use of Drones for the Delivery of Diagnostic Test Kits and Medical Supplies to Remote First Nations Communities During COVID-19. *American Journal of Infection Control*, *50*(8), 849–856. DOI: 10.1016/j.ajic.2022.03.004 PMID: 35908822

Fung, C. Y., Su, S. I., Perry, E. J., & Garcia, M. B. (2022). Development of a Socioeconomic Inclusive Assessment Framework for Online Learning in Higher Education. In *Socioeconomic Inclusion During an Era of Online Education* (pp. 23–46). IGI Global., DOI: 10.4018/978-1-6684-4364-4.ch002

Gao, L., Li, G., Tsai, F., Gao, C., Zhu, M., & Qu, X. (2023). The impact of artificial intelligence stimuli on customer engagement and value co-creation: The moderating role of customer ability readiness. *Journal of Research in Interactive Marketing*, *17*(2), 317–333. DOI: 10.1108/JRIM-10-2021-0260

Garcia, M. B. (Ed.). (2022). *Socioeconomic Inclusion During an Era of Online Education*. IGI Global., DOI: 10.4018/978-1-6684-4364-4

Garcia, M. B. (2023a). Can ChatGPT Substitute Human Companionship for Coping with Loss and Trauma? *Journal of Loss and Trauma*, *1-3*(8), 784–786. DOI: 10.1080/15325024.2023.2240697

Garcia, M. B. (2023b). ChatGPT as a Virtual Dietitian: Exploring its Potential as a Tool for Improving Nutrition Knowledge. *Applied System Innovation*, *6*(5), 1–18. DOI: 10.3390/asi6050096

Garcia, M. B., Arif, Y. M., Khlaif, Z. N., Zhu, M., de Almeida, R. P. P., de Almeida, R. S., & Masters, K. (2024). Effective Integration of Artificial Intelligence in Medical Education: Practical Tips and Actionable Insights. In *Transformative Approaches to Patient Literacy and Healthcare Innovation*. IGI Global., DOI: 10.4018/979-8-3693-3661-8.ch001

Garcia, M. B., Lopez Cabrera, M. V., & de Almeida, R. P. (Eds.). (2023). *Handbook of Research on Instructional Technologies in Health Education and Allied Disciplines*. IGI Global., DOI: 10.4018/978-1-6684-7164-7

Germani, F., & Biller-Andorno, N. (2022). How to counter the anti-vaccine rhetoric: Filling information voids and building resilience. *Human Vaccines & Immunotherapeutics*, *18*(6), 2095825. DOI: 10.1080/21645515.2022.2095825 PMID: 35802046

Grimm, P. Y., & Wyss, K. (2022). What Makes Health Systems Resilient? A Qualitative Analysis of the Perspectives of Swiss NGOs. *Globalization and Health*, *18*(1), 1–14. DOI: 10.1186/s12992-022-00848-y PMID: 35619166

Grönroos, C., & Voima, P. (2013). Critical service logic: Making sense of value creation and co-creation. *Journal of the Academy of Marketing Science*, *41*(2), 133–150. DOI: 10.1007/s11747-012-0308-3

Haenlein, M., & Kaplan, A. (2019). A brief history of artificial intelligence: On the past, present, and future of artificial intelligence. *California Management Review*, *61*(4), 5–14. DOI: 10.1177/0008125619864925

Haldane, V., De Foo, C., Abdalla, S. M., Jung, A.-S., Tan, M., Wu, S., & Singh, S. (2021). Health systems resilience in managing the COVID-19 pandemic: Lessons from 28 countries. *Nature Medicine*, *27*(6), 964–980. DOI: 10.1038/s41591-021-01381-y PMID: 34002090

Hau, A., & Liu, H. (2021), "Artificial intelligence application in interactive marketing", available at: www.emeraldgrouppublishing.com/journal/jrim/artificial-intelligence-application-interactive-marketing

Howard, J., Huang, A., Li, Z., Tufekci, Z., Zdimal, V., van der Westhuizen, H.-M., von Delft, A., Price, A., Fridman, L., Tang, L.-H., Tang, V., Watson, G. L., Bax, C. E., Shaikh, R., Questier, F., Hernandez, D., Chu, L. F., Ramirez, C. M., & Rimoin, A. W. (2021). An evidence review of face masks against COVID. *Proceedings of the National Academy of Sciences of the United States of America*, *118*(4), e2014564118. DOI: 10.1073/pnas.2014564118 PMID: 33431650

Hu, B. (2022). Translation as an ethical intervention? Building trust in healthcare crisis communication. In Language as a social determinant of health: Translating and interpreting the COVID-19 pandemic, ed. Federico Marco Federici, 179–208. Palgrave Studies in Translating and Interpreting. Cham: Springer International Publishing. DOI: 10.1007/978-3-030-87817-7_7

Huang, M.-H., & Rust, R. T. (2018). Artificial intelligence in service. *Journal of Service Research, 21*(2), 155–172. DOI: 10.1177/1094670517752459

Iyanna, S., Kaur, P., Ractham, P., Talwar, S., & Najmul Islam, A. K. M. (2022). Digital transformation of healthcare sector. What is impeding adoption and continued usage of technology-driven innovations by end-users? *Journal of Business Research, 153*, 150–161. DOI: 10.1016/j.jbusres.2022.08.007

Jit, M., Ananthakrishnan, A., McKee, M., Wouters, O. J., Beutels, P., & Teerawattananon, Y. (2021). Multi-country collaboration in responding to global infectious disease threats: Lessons for Europe from the COVID-19 pandemic. *The Lancet Regional Health. Europe*, *9*, 9. DOI: 10.1016/j.lanepe.2021.100221 PMID: 34642675

Johnson, C. K., P. L. Hitchens, P. S. Pandit, J. Rushmore, T. S. Evans, C. C. W. Young, and M. M. Doyle. (2020). Global shifts in mammalian population trends reveal key predictors of virus spillover risk. Proceedings. Biological Sciences 287 (1924):20192736. .DOI: 10.1098/rspb.2019.2736

Kahn, B., Brown, L., Foege, W., & Gayle, H. (Eds.). (2020). *Framework for equitable allocation of COVID-19 vaccine*.

Kamalaldin, A., Linde, L., Sjödin, D., & Parida, V. (2020). Transforming provider-customer relationships in digital servitization: A relational view on digitalization. *Industrial Marketing Management, 89*, 306–325. DOI: 10.1016/j.indmarman.2020.02.004

Kaplan, C. P., Turner, S., Norman, E., & Stillson, K. (1996). Promoting Resilience Strategies: A Modified Consultation Model. *Children & Schools, 18*(3), 158–168. DOI: 10.1093/cs/18.3.158

Karanika-Murray, M., Whysall, Z., Liu-Smith, Y.-L., Feltbower, C., & Challans-Rasool, E. (2023). Understanding organizational learning in a healthcare organization during sudden and disruptive change. *International Journal of Workplace Health Management, 16*(4), 257–280. DOI: 10.1108/IJWHM-09-2022-0145

Kazi, K. S. L. (2024). Computer-Aided Diagnosis in Ophthalmology: A Technical Review of Deep Learning Applications. In *Transformative Approaches to Patient Literacy and Healthcare Innovation*. IGI Global., DOI: 10.4018/979-8-3693-3661-8.ch006

Khan, Z. F., & Alotaibi, S. R. (2020). Applications of artificial intelligence and big data analytics in m-health: A healthcare system perspective. *Journal of Healthcare Engineering*, *2020*, 1–15. DOI: 10.1155/2020/6654063 PMID: 32952992

Khoo, A. (2020). Ghana in COVID-19 Pandemic. *Inter-Asia Cultural Studies*, *21*(4), 542–556. DOI: 10.1080/14649373.2020.1832300

Kopalle, P. K., Gangwar, M., Kaplan, A., Ramachandran, D., Reinartz, W., & Rindfleisch, A. (2022). Examining artificial intelligence (AI) technologies in marketing via a global lens: Current trends and future research opportunities. *International Journal of Research in Marketing*, *39*(2), 522–540. DOI: 10.1016/j.ijresmar.2021.11.002

Kraus, S., Schiavone, F., Pluzhnikova, A., & Invernizzi, A. C. (2021). Digital transformation in healthcare: Analyzing the current state-of-research. *Journal of Business Research*, *123*, 557–567. DOI: 10.1016/j.jbusres.2020.10.030

Kuhlmann, S., & Franzke, J. (2022). Multi-Level Responses to COVID-19: Crisis Coordination in Germany From an Intergovernmental Perspective. *Local Government Studies*, *48*(2), 312–334. DOI: 10.1080/03003930.2021.1904398

Kuvvetli, Y., Deveci, M., Paksoy, T., & Garg, H. (2021). A Predictive Analytics Model for COVID-19 Pandemic Using Artificial Neural Networks. *Decision Analytics Journal*, *1*, 1–13. DOI: 10.1016/j.dajour.2021.100007

Kwame, A., Makarova, V., Hudu, F., & Petrucka, P. M. (2023). The COVID-19 Pandemic in Ghana: Exploring the Discourse Strategies in President Nana Addo's Speeches. *Humanities & Social Sciences Communications*, *10*(1), 1–10. DOI: 10.1057/s41599-023-02253-1

Lalicic, L., & Weismayer, C. (2021). Consumers' reasons and perceived value co-creation of using artificial intelligence-enabled travel service agents. *Journal of Business Research*, *129*, 891–901. DOI: 10.1016/j.jbusres.2020.11.005

Lee, D., & Yoon, S. N. (2021). Application of artificial intelligence-based technologies in the healthcare industry: Opportunities and challenges. *International Journal of Environmental Research and Public Health*, *18*(1), 271. DOI: 10.3390/ijerph18010271 PMID: 33401373

Leite, H., Lindsay, C., & Kumar, M. (2020). COVID-19 outbreak: Implications on healthcare operations. *The TQM Journal*, *33*(1), 247–256. DOI: 10.1108/TQM-05-2020-0111

Leone, D., Schiavone, F., Appio, F. P., & Chiao, B. (2021). How does artificial intelligence enable and enhance value co-creation in industrial markets? An exploratory case study in the healthcare ecosystem. *Journal of Business Research*, *129*, 849–859. DOI: 10.1016/j.jbusres.2020.11.008

Lewis, D. (2022). Why the WHO took two years to say COVID is airborne. *Nature*, *604*(7904), 26–31. DOI: 10.1038/d41586-022-00925-7 PMID: 35388203

Lone, S. A., & Ahmad, A. (2020). COVID-19 pandemic–an African perspective. *Emerging Microbes & Infections*, *9*(1), 1300–1308. DOI: 10.1080/22221751.2020.1775132 PMID: 32458760

Longoni, C., Bonezzi, A., & Morewedge, C. K. (2019). Resistance to medical artificial intelligence. *The Journal of Consumer Research*, *46*(4), 629–650. DOI: 10.1093/jcr/ucz013

Loss, J., Boklage, E., Jordan, S., Jenny, M. A., Weishaar, H., & El Bcheraoui, C. (2021). Risikokommunikation bei der Eind€ammung der COVID-19 Pandemie: Herausforderungenund Erfolg versprechende Ans€atze. *Bundesgesundheitsblatt, Gesundheitsforschung, Gesundheitsschutz*, *64*(3), 294–303. DOI: 10.1007/s00103-021-03283-3 PMID: 33564896

Love, J. S., Blumenberg, A., & Horowitz, Z. (2020). The parallel pandemic: Medical misinformation and COVID-19. *Journal of General Internal Medicine*, *35*(8), 2435–2436. DOI: 10.1007/s11606-020-05897-w PMID: 32410129

Madhavan, S., Bastarache, L., Brown, J. S., Butte, A. J., Dorr, D. A., Embi, P. J., & Kohane, I. S. (2021). Use of electronic health records to support a public health response to the COVID-19 pandemic in the United States: A perspective from 15 academic medical centers. *Journal of the American Medical Informatics Association : JAMIA*, *28*(2), 393–401. DOI: 10.1093/jamia/ocaa287 PMID: 33260207

Malecki, K. M. C., Keating, J. A., & Safdar, N. (2021). Crisis communication and public perception of COVID-19 risk in the era of social media. *Clinical Infectious Diseases*, *72*(4), 697–702. DOI: 10.1093/cid/ciaa758 PMID: 32544242

Manser Payne, L., Dahl, A., & Peltier, J. (2021a). Digital servitization value co-creation framework for AI services: A research agenda for digital transformation in financial service ecosystems. *Journal of Research in Interactive Marketing*, *15*(2), 200–222. DOI: 10.1108/JRIM-12-2020-0252

Manser Payne, L., Peltier, J., & Barger, V. (2021b). Enhancing the value co-creation process: Artificial intelligence and mobile banking service platforms. *Journal of Research in Interactive Marketing*, *15*(1), 68–85. DOI: 10.1108/JRIM-10-2020-0214

Mbunge, E., Batani, J., Gaobotse, G., & Muchemwa, B. (2022). Virtual Healthcare Services and Digital Health Technologies Deployed During Coronavirus Disease 2019 (COVID-19) Pandemic in South Africa: A Systematic Review. *Global Health Journal (Amsterdam, Netherlands)*, *6*(2), 102–113. DOI: 10.1016/j.glohj.2022.03.001 PMID: 35282399

McCarthy, R. N. E., Donkoh, E. T., Arthur, D. D., Dassah, E. T., Boadu, K. O., Otoo, J. E., Boadu, I. W. O., & Gyasi, S. F. (2023). Public Relations Strategies Employed by the Ghana Health Service to Address COVID-19 Vaccine Hesitancy: A Qualitative Inquiry. *Tropical Medicine and Health*, *51*(1), 1–14. DOI: 10.1186/s41182-023-00519-7 PMID: 37170342

Medberg, G., & Grönroos, C. (2020). Value-in-use and service quality: Do customers see a difference? *Journal of Service Theory and Practice*, *30*(4/5), 507–529. DOI: 10.1108/JSTP-09-2019-0207

Mele, C., Russo Spena, T., Kaartemo, V., & Marzullo, M. L. (2021). Smart nudging: How cognitive technologies enable choice architectures for value co-creation. *Journal of Business Research*, *129*, 949–960. DOI: 10.1016/j.jbusres.2020.09.004

Mensah, I. K. (2022). Understanding the Drivers of Ghanaian Citizens' Adoption Intentions of Mobile Health Services. *Frontiers in Public Health*, *10*, 1–20. DOI: 10.3389/fpubh.2022.906106 PMID: 35774576

Miranda, J. P. (2024). Mobile Applications in Advancing Health Literacy: A Scoping Review of Methodologies, Participants, and Challenges. In *Transformative Approaches to Patient Literacy and Healthcare Innovation*. IGI Global., DOI: 10.4018/979-8-3693-3661-8.ch003

Mohammadpour, M., Zarifinezhad, E., Ghanbarzadegan, A., Naderimanesh, K., Shaarbafchizadeh, N., & Bastani, P. (2021). Main factors affecting the readiness and responsiveness of healthcare systems during epidemic crises: A scoping review on cases of sars, mers, and covid-19. *Iranian Journal of Medical Sciences*, *46*(2), 81. PMID: 33753952

Montani, D., Savale, L., Beurnier, A., Colle, R., Noël, N., Pham, T., Monnet, X., & Humbert, M. (2021). Multidisciplinary Approach for Post-Acute COVID-19 Syndrome: Time to Break Down the Walls. *The European Respiratory Journal*, *58*(1), 1–3. DOI: 10.1183/13993003.01090-2021 PMID: 33958429

Morewedge, C. K., Monga, A., Palmatier, R. W., Shu, S. B., & Small, D. A. (2021). Evolution of consumption: A psychological ownership framework. *Journal of Marketing*, *85*(1), 196–218. DOI: 10.1177/0022242920957007

Musk, E. (2022a). By "free speech", I simply mean that which matches the law. I am against censorship that goes far beyond the law. If people want less free speech, they will ask government to pass laws to that effect. Therefore, going beyond the law is contrary to the will of the people. Tweet. Twitter. https://twitter.com/elonmusk/status/ 1519036983137509376.

Ness, M. M., Saylor, J., Di Fusco, L. A., & Evans, K. (2021). Healthcare providers' challenges during the coronavirus disease (COVID-19) pandemic: A qualitative approach. *Nursing & Health Sciences*, *23*(2), 389–397. DOI: 10.1111/nhs.12820 PMID: 33580590

Niemiec, E. (2020). COVID-19 and Misinformation. *EMBO Reports*, *21*(11), e51420. DOI: 10.15252/embr.202051420 PMID: 33103289

Ofosu-Ampong, K. (2021). Determinants, Barriers and Strategies of Digital Transformation Adoption in a Developing Country COVID-19 Era. *Journal of Digital Science*, *3*(2), 67–83. DOI: 10.33847/2686-8296.3.2_5

Ofosu-Ampong, K. (2023). Gender Differences in Perception of Artificial Intelligence-Based Tools. *Journal of Digital Art Humanities*, *4*(2), 52–56. DOI: 10.33847/2712-8149.4.2_6

Ofosu-Ampong, K., & Acheampong, B. (2022). Adoption of Contactless Technologies for Remote Work in Ghana Post-COVID-19: Insights From Technology-Organisation-Environment Framework. *Digital Business*, *2*(2), 1–10. DOI: 10.1016/j.digbus.2022.100023

Owusu, B., Kutor, S. K., & Ablo, A. D. (2023). COVID-19 Pandemic: Ghana and the Geographies of Blame. *GeoJournal*, *88*(1), 279–290. DOI: 10.1007/s10708-022-10586-8 PMID: 35250150

Owusu, I., Adu, C., Aboagye, R. G., Mpangah, R. A., Acheampong, G. K., Akyereko, E., Bonsu, E. O., & Peprah, P. (2023). Preparing for Future Outbreaks in Ghana: An Overview of Current COVID-19, Monkeypox, and Marburg Disease Outbreaks. *Health Promotion Perspectives*, *13*(3), 202–211. DOI: 10.34172/hpp.2023.25 PMID: 37808942

Panja, S. (2024). Information Retrieval Systems in Healthcare: Understanding Medical Data Through Text Analysis. In *Transformative Approaches to Patient Literacy and Healthcare Innovation*. IGI Global., DOI: 10.4018/979-8-3693-3661-8.ch009

Parel, D., Costuna, E. K., Morelos, J. M., Cabelis, S. A., Ramos, R., Perez, M. R., & Garcia, M. B. (2022). Escape from Oblivion: A 3D Hack and Slash Survival Horror Video Game for Promoting Awareness of Persistent Depressive Disorder. 2022 IEEE 14th International Conference on Humanoid, Nanotechnology, Information Technology, Communication and Control, Environment and Management (HNICEM). IEEE. DOI: 10.1109/HNICEM57413.2022.10109542

Patibandla, L., Rao, B. T., & Murty, M. R. (2024). Revolutionizing Diabetic Retinopathy Diagnostics and Therapy through Artificial Intelligence: A Smart Vision Initiative. In *Transformative Approaches to Patient Literacy and Healthcare Innovation*. IGI Global., DOI: 10.4018/979-8-3693-3661-8.ch007

Peiffer-Smadja, N., Lucet, J.-C., Bendjelloul, G., Bouadma, L., Gerard, S., Choquet, C., & Casalino, E. (2020). Challenges and issues about organizing a hospital to respond to the COVID-19 outbreak: Experience from a French reference centre. *Clinical Microbiology and Infection*, *26*(6), 669–672. DOI: 10.1016/j.cmi.2020.04.002 PMID: 32278082

Peltier, J. W., Dahl, A. J., & Schibrowsky, J. (2023). (forthcoming). Artificial intelligence in interactive marketing: A conceptual framework and research agenda. *Journal of Research in Interactive Marketing*.

Peltier, J. W., Dahl, A. J., & Swan, E. L. (2020). Digital information flows across a B2C/C2C continuum and technological innovations in service ecosystems: A service-dominant logic perspective. *Journal of Business Research*, *121*, 724–734. DOI: 10.1016/j.jbusres.2020.03.020

Quinn, P. (2018). Crisis communication in public health emergencies: The limits of "legal control" and the risks for harmful outcomes in a digital age. *Life Sciences, Society and Policy*, *14*(1), 4. DOI: 10.1186/s40504-018-0067-0 PMID: 29404722

Ramayah, T., Cheah, J., Chuah, F., Ting, H., & Memon, M. A. (2018). *Partial Least Squares Structural Equation Modeling (PLS-SEM) Using SmartPLS 3.0: An Updated Guide and Practical Guide to Statistical Analysis* (2nd ed.). Pearson.

Ramos, M. (2024). Emerging Technologies in Radiotherapy: Advances in Health Literacy and Healthcare Practice. In *Transformative Approaches to Patient Literacy and Healthcare Innovation*. IGI Global., DOI: 10.4018/979-8-3693-3661-8.ch005

Ratzan, S. C., Sommariva, S., & Rauh, L. (2020). Enhancing global health communication during a crisis: Lessons from the COVID-19 pandemic. *Public Health Research & Practice*, *30*(2), 3022010. DOI: 10.17061/phrp3022010 PMID: 32601655

Rawls, J. (1985). Justice as fairness: Political not metaphysical. *Philosophy & Public Affairs*, *14*(3), 223–251.

Reuschl, A. J., Deist, M. K., & Maalaoui, A. (2022). Digital transformation during a pandemic: Stretching the organizational elasticity. *Journal of Business Research*, *144*, 1320–1332. DOI: 10.1016/j.jbusres.2022.01.088 PMID: 36540204

Riotta, S., & Bruccoleri, M. (2021). Revisiting the patient-physician relationship under the lens of value co-creation and defensive medicine. *Journal of Service Theory and Practice*, *31*(6), 868–892. DOI: 10.1108/JSTP-06-2020-0142

Roozenbeek, J., van der Linden, S., Goldberg, B., Rathje, S., & Lewandowsky, S. (2022). Psychological inoculation improves resilience against misinformation on social media. *Science Advances*, *8*(34), eabo6254. Advance online publication. DOI: 10.1126/sciadv.abo6254 PMID: 36001675

Ros, F., Kush, R., Friedman, C., Gil Zorzo, E., Rivero Corte, P., Rubin, J. C., . . . Van Houweling, D. (2021). Addressing the Covid-19 pandemic and future public health challenges through global collaboration and a data-driven systems approach (2379- 6146).

Sachs, J. D., Karim, S. S. A., Aknin, L., Allen, J., Brosbøl, K., Colombo, F., Barron, G. C., Espinosa, M. F., Gaspar, V., Gaviria, A., Haines, A., Hotez, P. J., Koundouri, P., Bascuñán, F. L., Lee, J.-K., Pate, M. A., Ramos, G., Reddy, K. S., Serageldin, I., & Michie, S. (2022). The Lancet Commission on lessons for the future from the COVID-19 pandemic. *Lancet*, *400*(10359), 1224–1280. DOI: 10.1016/S0140-6736(22)01585-9 PMID: 36115368

Santra, S., & Alat, P. (2022). Adaptive leadership of doctors during COVID-19. *Leadership in Health Services*, *35*(2), 246–266. DOI: 10.1108/LHS-08-2021-0073 PMID: 34882361

Sarker, S., Jamal, L., Ahmed, S. F., & Irtisam, N. (2021). Robotics and Artificial Intelligence in Healthcare During COVID-19 Pandemic: A Systematic Review. *Robotics and Autonomous Systems*, *146*, 1–18. DOI: 10.1016/j.robot.2021.103902 PMID: 34629751

Sarkodie, S. A., & Owusu, P. A. (2021). Impact of COVID-19 Pandemic on Waste Management. *Environment, Development and Sustainability*, *23*(5), 7951–7960. DOI: 10.1007/s10668-020-00956-y PMID: 32863738

Schroeder, H., Numa, R., & Shapiro, E. (2022). Promoting a culturally adapted policy to deal with the COVID-19 crisis in the Haredi population in Israel. *Journal of Racial and Ethnic Health Disparities*, *9*(6), 2508–2517. DOI: 10.1007/s40615-021-01186-2 PMID: 34791614

Sekalala, S., Dagron, S., Forman, L., & Meier, B. M. (2020). Analyzing the human rights impact of increased digital public health surveillance during the COVID-19 crisis. *Health and Human Rights Journal*, *22*(2), 7–20. PMID: 33390688

Shahroz, M., Ahmad, F., Younis, M. S., Ahmad, N., Kamel Boulos, M. N., Vinuesa, R., & Qadir, J. (2021). COVID-19 Digital Contact Tracing Applications and Techniques: A Review Post Initial Deployments. *Transportation Engineering*, *5*, 1–9. DOI: 10.1016/j.treng.2021.100072

Shen, Y., Guo, D., Long, F., Mateos, L. A., Ding, H., Xiu, Z., Hellman, R. B., King, A., Chen, S., Zhang, C., & Tan, H. (2021). Robots Under COVID-19 Pandemic: A Comprehensive Survey. *IEEE Access : Practical Innovations, Open Solutions*, *9*, 1590–1615. DOI: 10.1109/ACCESS.2020.3045792 PMID: 34976569

Shen, Y.-T., Chen, L., Yue, W.-W., & Xu, H.-X. (2021). Digital technology-based telemedicine for the COVID-19 pandemic. *Frontiers in Medicine*, *8*, 646506. DOI: 10.3389/fmed.2021.646506 PMID: 34295908

Silton, N. R. (Ed.). (2022). *The Impact of the COVID-19 Pandemic on Child, Adolescent, and Adult Development*. IGI Global., DOI: 10.4018/978-1-6684-3484-0

Slama, P. (2020). Viral pandemics of the last four decades: Pathophysiology, health impacts and perspectives. *International Journal of Environmental Research and Public Health*, *17*(24), 9411. DOI: 10.3390/ijerph17249411 PMID: 33333995

Sohrabi, C., Alsafi, Z., O'neill, N., Khan, M., Kerwan, A., Al-Jabir, A., Iosifidis, C., & Agha, R. (2020). World Health Organization declares global emergency: A review of the 2019 novel coronavirus (COVID-19). *International Journal of Surgery*, *76*, 71–76. DOI: 10.1016/j.ijsu.2020.02.034 PMID: 32112977

Spitale, G. (2020). COVID-19 and the ethics of quarantine: A lesson from the Eyam Plague. *Medicine, Health Care, and Philosophy*, *23*(4), 603–609. DOI: 10.1007/s11019-020-09971-2 PMID: 32761351

Spitale, G., Biller-Andorno, N., & Germani, F. (2022). Concerns around opposition to the green pass in Italy: Social listening analysis by using a mixed methods approach. *Journal of Medical Internet Research*, *24*(2), e34385. DOI: 10.2196/34385 PMID: 35156930

Spitale, G., Merten, S., Jafflin, K., Schwind, B., Kaiser-Grolimund, A., & Biller-Andorno, N. (2021). A novel risk and crisis communication platform to bridge the gap between policy makers and the public in the context of the COVID-19 crisis (PubliCo): Protocol for a mixed methods study. *JMIR Research Protocols*, *10*(11), e33653. DOI: 10.2196/33653 PMID: 34612823

Sriharan, A., Hertelendy, A. J., Banaszak-Holl, J., Fleig-Palmer, M. M., Mitchell, C., Nigam, A., Gutberg, J., Rapp, D. J., & Singer, S. J. (2022). Public health and health sector crisis leadership during pandemics: A review of the medical and business literature. *Medical Care Research and Review : MCRR*, *79*(4), 475–486. DOI: 10.1177/10775587211039201 PMID: 34474606

Stawicki, S. P., Jeanmonod, R., Miller, A. C., Paladino, L., Gaieski, D. F., Yaffee, A. Q., & Bloem, C. (2020). The 2019–2020 novel coronavirus (severe acute respiratory syndrome coronavirus 2) pandemic: A joint american college of academic international medicine-world academic council of emergency medicine multidisciplinary COVID-19 working group consensus paper. *Journal of Global Infectious Diseases*, *12*(2), 47. DOI: 10.4103/jgid.jgid_86_20 PMID: 32773996

Steier, J., & Moxham, J. (2020). The load and capacity model of healthcare delivery: Considerations for the crisis management of the COVID-19 pandemic. *Journal of Thoracic Disease*, *12*(6), 3022–3030. DOI: 10.21037/jtd-2020-054 PMID: 32642224

Sust, P. P., Solans, O., Fajardo, J. C., Peralta, M. M., Rodenas, P., Gabaldà, J., & Ribes, J. S. (2020). Turning the crisis into an opportunity: Digital health strategies deployed during the COVID-19 outbreak. *JMIR Public Health and Surveillance*, *6*(2), e19106. DOI: 10.2196/19106 PMID: 32339998

Swan, E. L., Dahl, A. J., & Peltier, J. W. (2019). Health-care marketing in an omni-channel environment: Exploring telemedicine and other digital touchpoints. *Journal of Research in Interactive Marketing*, *13*(4), 602–618. DOI: 10.1108/JRIM-03-2019-0039

Swayamsiddha, S., Prashant, K., Shaw, D., & Mohanty, C. (2021). The Prospective of Artificial Intelligence in COVID-19 Pandemic. *Health and Technology*, *11*(6), 1311–1320. DOI: 10.1007/s12553-021-00601-2 PMID: 34603925

Tambo, E., Djuikoue, I. C., Tazemda, G. K., Fotsing, M. F., & Zhou, X.-N. (2021). Early stage risk communication and community engagement (RCCE) strategies and measures against the coronavirus disease 2019 (COVID-19) pandemic crisis. *Global Health Journal (Amsterdam, Netherlands)*, *5*(1), 44–50. DOI: 10.1016/j.glohj.2021.02.009 PMID: 33850632

Tan, S. Y., Foo, C. D., Verma, M., Hanvoravongchai, P., Cheh, P. L. J., Pholpark, A., Marthias, T., Hafidz, F., Prawidya Putri, L., Mahendradhata, Y., Giang, K. B., Nachuk, S., Wang, H., Lim, J., & Legido Quigley, H. (2023). Mitigating the Impacts of the COVID-19 Pandemic on Vulnerable Populations: Lessons for Improving Health and Social Equity. *Social Science & Medicine*, *328*, 1–12. DOI: 10.1016/j.socscimed.2023.116007 PMID: 37279639

Tang, J. W., Caniza, M. A., Dinn, M., Dwyer, D. E., Heraud, J.-M., Jennings, L. C., & Loh, T. P. (2022). An exploration of the political, social, economic and cultural factors affecting how different global regions initially reacted to the COVID-19 pandemic. *Interface Focus*, *12*(2), 20210079. DOI: 10.1098/rsfs.2021.0079 PMID: 35261734

Tariq, M. U. (2024a). Advanced Wearable Medical Devices and their Role in Transformative Remote Health Monitoring. In *Transformative Approaches to Patient Literacy and Healthcare Innovation*. IGI Global., DOI: 10.4018/979-8-3693-3661-8.ch015

Tariq, M. U. (2024b). Enhancing Cybersecurity Protocols in Modern Healthcare Systems: Strategies and Best Practices. In *Transformative Approaches to Patient Literacy and Healthcare Innovation*. IGI Global., DOI: 10.4018/979-8-3693-3661-8.ch011

Toit, S. d., & Goosen, L. (2024). Transformative Technologies for Supporting Children with Fetal Alcohol Syndrome and Autism Spectrum Disorders. In *Transformative Approaches to Patient Literacy and Healthcare Innovation*. IGI Global., DOI: 10.4018/979-8-3693-3661-8.ch008

Tomé, A., Rosa, M. C. N., & Silva, E. (2024). Advancing Health Literacy in the Technological Era: The Role of Serious Games in Promoting Body Awareness Among Older Adults. In *Transformative Approaches to Patient Literacy and Healthcare Innovation*. IGI Global., DOI: 10.4018/979-8-3693-3661-8.ch004

Tsiotsou, R. H., & Boukis, A. (2022). In-home service consumption: A systematic review, integrative framework and future research agenda. *Journal of Business Research*, *145*, 49–64. DOI: 10.1016/j.jbusres.2022.02.050

Turilli, M., & Floridi, L. (2009). The ethics of information transparency. *Ethics and Information Technology*, *11*(2), 105–112. DOI: 10.1007/s10676-009-9187-9

Vallée, A. (2023). Geoepidemiological perspective on COVID-19 pandemic review, an insight into the global impact. *Frontiers in Public Health*, *11*, 11. DOI: 10.3389/fpubh.2023.1242891 PMID: 37927887

Verhoef, P. C., & Bijmolt, T. H. A. (2019). Marketing perspectives on digital business models: A framework and overview of the special issue. *International Journal of Research in Marketing, 36*(3), 341–349. DOI: 10.1016/j.ijresmar.2019.08.001

Verhoef, P. C., Broekhuizen, T., Bart, Y., Bhattacharya, A., Qi Dong, J., Fabian, N., & Haenlein, M. (2021). Digital transformation: A multidisciplinary reflection and research agenda. *Journal of Business Research, 122*, 889–901. DOI: 10.1016/j.jbusres.2019.09.022

Wang, C. L. (2021). New frontiers and future directions in interactive marketing: Inaugural editorial. *Journal of Research in Interactive Marketing, 15*(1), 1–9. DOI: 10.1108/JRIM-03-2021-270

Wang, Q., Su, M., Zhang, M., & Li, R. (2021). Integrating digital technologies and public health to fight Covid-19 pandemic: Key technologies, applications, challenges and outlook of digital healthcare. *International Journal of Environmental Research and Public Health, 18*(11), 6053. DOI: 10.3390/ijerph18116053 PMID: 34199831

Weaver, E., Uddin, S., & Lamprou, D. A. (2022). Emerging Technologies for Combating Pandemics. *Expert Review of Medical Devices, 19*(7), 533–538. DOI: 10.1080/17434440.2022.2115355 PMID: 35983986

Willingham, D. T. (2020). Ask the cognitive scientist: How can educators teach critical thinking? American Federation of Teachers. 22 September 2020. https://www.aft.org/ae/fall2020/willingham

Wouters, O. J., Shadlen, K. C., Salcher-Konrad, M., Pollard, A. J., Larson, H. J., Teerawattananon, Y., & Jit, M. (2021). Challenges in ensuring global access to COVID-19 vaccines: Production, affordability, allocation, and deployment. *Lancet, 397*(10278), 1023–1034. DOI: 10.1016/S0140-6736(21)00306-8 PMID: 33587887

Wu, Y. L., Shao, B., Newman, A., & Schwarz, G. (2021). Crisis leadership: A review and future research agenda. *The Leadership Quarterly, 32*(6), 101518. DOI: 10.1016/j.leaqua.2021.101518

Wut, T. M., Xu, J. B., & Wong, S. (2021). Crisis management research (1985–2020) in the hospitality and tourism industry: A review and research agenda. *Tourism Management, 85*, 104307. DOI: 10.1016/j.tourman.2021.104307 PMID: 36345489

Xu, K., & Li, W. (2013). An ethical stakeholder approach to crisis communication: A case study of Foxconn's 2010 employee suicide crisis. *Journal of Business Ethics, 117*(2), 371–386. DOI: 10.1007/s10551-012-1522-0

Xu, Z., Su, C., Xiao, Y., & Wang, F. (2022). Artificial Intelligence for COVID-19: Battling the Pandemic With Computational Intelligence. *Intelligent Medicine*, *2*(1), 13–29. DOI: 10.1016/j.imed.2021.09.001 PMID: 34697578

Zahlan, A., Ranjan, R. P., & Hayes, D. (2023). Artificial intelligence innovation in healthcare: Literature review, exploratory analysis, and future research. *Technology in Society*, *74*, 102321. DOI: 10.1016/j.techsoc.2023.102321

Zhang, R. Y., Li, Y., Zhang, A. L., Wang, Y., & Molina, M. J. (2020). Identifying airborne transmission as the dominant route for the spread of COVID-19. *Proceedings of the National Academy of Sciences of the United States of America*, *117*(26), 14857–14863. DOI: 10.1073/pnas.2009637117 PMID: 32527856

Zhu, Y., Lu, Y., Gupta, S., Wang, J., & Hu, P. (2022). Promoting smart wearable devices in the health-AI market: The role of health consciousness and privacy protection. *Journal of Research in Interactive Marketing*, *17*(2), 257–272. DOI: 10.1108/JRIM-10-2021-0246

KEY TERMS AND DEFINITIONS

Telemedicine: Telemedicine refers to the use of telecommunications technology to provide medical care remotely. It enables healthcare providers to consult with patients via video calls, phone calls, or messaging platforms, enhancing access to healthcare services, especially during health crises when in-person visits may be limited.

Health Data Analytics: Health data analytics involves the systematic collection, processing, and analysis of health-related data to improve patient outcomes and healthcare efficiency. During health crises, analytics can be used to track disease spread, predict trends, allocate resources, and inform public health decisions.

Wearable Health Technology: Wearable health technology refers to devices like smartwatches and fitness trackers that monitor and collect health data such as heart rate, activity levels, and sleep patterns.

Patient Portals: Patient portals are secure online platforms that allow patients to access their health information, schedule appointments, communicate with healthcare providers, and manage their healthcare plans. They became increasingly important during health crises by facilitating communication and reducing the need for in-person interactions.

Artificial Intelligence (AI) in Healthcare: AI in healthcare refers to the use of machine learning algorithms and data processing to assist in diagnosis, treatment planning, and patient management. During health crises, AI can enhance decision-making processes, streamline operations, and analyze vast amounts of data for effective responses to pandemics or outbreaks.

Chapter 9
Breaking Barriers: How Artificial Intelligence Is Revolutionizing Healthcare

Rashid Hashmi
https://orcid.org/0009-0006-3232-0705
Sharda University, India

ABSTRACT

This paper aims at exploring AI integration and its impact on the healthcare industry in terms of having a way around conventional limitations and offer better service quality. Artificial intelligence and automation, features of machine learning, and natural language processing are stepping into diagnostics, treatment, and patient management. From early diagnoses, individualized treatment, and robot-assisted surgeries, it provides customers with better results, with minimal human intervention. AI is also improving the process of identifying new drugs and allowing telemedicine to deliver healthcare to those that have none. This has the potential of yielding explosive results for the field, although it also identified some existing limitations such as data privacy concerns, regulatory constraints, and the need for competent workforce. The paper describes how healthcare will change with the help of AI making it more efficient, fair and revolutionizing the approach to patients.

INTRODUCTION

Healthcare is at the forefront of where Artificial Intelligence (AI) has changed the way it is done and will continue to change how it is done. AI in healthcare can be broadly defined as the simulation of the human intelligence processes by the machines such as machine learning (ML), natural language processing (NLP), robotics and predictive analytics (Russell & Norvig, 2021). What makes these innovations

DOI: 10.4018/979-8-3373-5087-5.ch009

all the more valuable is that they are not only improving the way healthcare systems operate but also increasing patient outcomes and reducing clinical workflow.

Diagnosis and treatment protocols, drug discovery, patient monitoring and healthcare operations are all being disrupted by AI. As an example, AI-based algorithms are now used to help understand cancer or image on diagnosis level, determine patient deterioration in critical care, and prescribe individualized medicine. Expanding computing power, propagating of big data and integration of wearable devices generating real time health data (Jiang et al., 2017) drive these developments.

Although its adoption in healthcare is so rapid, AI has had many challenges. Data privacy, algorithmically bias, the privacy rules of the road, and the integrity implications of autonomous decision making all stand as barriers to its full potential. However, as the globalise healthcare systems struggle with increasing expenses, the ageing of populations and uneven access to quality care, AI is an optimistic path where these gaps can be closed and a way to sustainable and equitable healthcare solutions (Topol, 2019).

Today, AI is the cornerstone needed to fix healthcare's longstanding inefficiencies and increase precision, accessibility, and scalability in the delivery of medical services. However, the global healthcare systems are placed under increasing pressure, resulting from higher prevalence of chronic disease, shortage of resources and demand for personalized care. AI utilizes the transformation of how healthcare providers receive, understand, and engage this information to make care more efficient and effective.

But diagnostics is an area where AI has made its mark as a first. Now tools such as IBM Watson Health use natural language processing (NLP) and machine learning (ML) to analyse electronic health records (EHRs) and medical literature and make data-based diagnoses and treatment decisions (Ramesh et al., 2021). Just like computer vision technologies in radiology, are helping in early detection of diseases like breast cancer where small abnormalities can slip through the cracks (Esteva et al. 2017).

AI driven drug discovery is another critical domain where machine learning models accelerate the time to identify potential drug candidates and predict the anticipated efficacy and safety profiles of them. Traditional 'drug discovery' is expensive and lagging, taking years and billions of dollars to develop just one drug. However, as demonstrated during the COVID-19 pandemic, AI has demonstrated the remarkable ability to cut timelines down to seconds (minutes) by identifying antiviral leads within months (Bengio et al., 2021).

While diagnostics and therapeutics are the most common applications of AI, they are also being used towards operational efficiency. Increasingly, hospitals are using predictive analytics for resource allocation and decreasing wait times as well as improving supply chain management. Enabled by AI, virtual health assistants are making human staff redundant by alleviating sensor and delivery burdens, and schedule and medication reminder burdens with round the clock support for everything from scheduling to medication reminders and even mental health counselling (Kaplan & Haenlein, 2020).

Challenges of AI Integration

There is no doubt that, benefits of AI healthcare are undeniable, however, implementation in the healthcare field is not so convenient. The primary problem is data: how available it is, of course, but this includes how good it is and how well it inter-operates. In order for AI models to reach high accuracy, they need to have access to lots of and diverse datasets. This implies that healthcare data tend to be dispersed in silos because of disparities in electronic health record systems, data governance policies, and legal constraints against cross border sharing (Shaban-Nejad et al., 2018).

The interpretability of AI system is a critical concern, in addition to its "black box" nature. Although AI-derived insights are urgently needed in healthcare, clinicians and patients alike require confidence in them, which is very hard to build without explaining algorithms making informed decisions (Holzinger et al., 2019). As explained ability is still an ongoing research of interests, efforts are made to improve explain ability, for example, through the development of interpretable machine learning models and explainable AI (XAI) frameworks.

There is much concern in the areas such as automated decision making and algorithmic bias not only due to the fact than many of these systems are ethically prohibited by laws; in some areas, it is forced upon us to do so by ethical principles. The next generation of software and algorithms that CODES _ (Obermeyer et al., 2019))—may create additional inequities, such as underdiagnosing diseases among certain demographic groups because of imbalanced training data')—producing biased outcomes in their decisions"—if so, risk exacerbating existing health inequities (Obermeyer et al., 2019). Therefore, for this reason, stringent regulatory frameworks are needed to mitigate such risks of unfairness, lack of transparency, and act of accountability.

The Role of Policymakers and Industry Collaboration

To realize the potential of AI in healthcare, the integration will be successful when stakeholders from various sectors are on board including government policy makers, healthcare providers, technology developers and patients. An environment that allows for AI to grow up in a way that respects ethical and legal rules is fuelled by governments and regulatory bodies. Data sharing, innovative activities and patient rights must be promoted.

Like industry collaborations, example partnerships between tech and healthcare institutions are equally important. For example, Google Health's partnership with the Mayo Clinic has helped affirm breakthroughs using AI on clinical workflows (McKinney et al., 2020). These combinations of resources and expertise add calories to a rapidly burning shopping cart — superseding the technical and clinical knowledge hole faster than anyone at the stand alone could alone.

Objectives and structure of the Chapter

In this chapter, we attempt to explore how AI can transform healthcare on how its opportunities, challenges, and potential investigates AI's historical development and important technological progress in health care. It also provides you with the ability to assess the areas where AI has probably made the biggest impact on impacting the life of a patient: diagnostics, treatment planning and operational efficiency. The book chapter discuss the ethical, legal, and technical barriers in limiting the Western spread. Examples of actionable solutions and policy recommendations to overcome these barriers are proposed. Through a detailed analysis of case studies, current trends, and expert insights, the chapter seeks to:

- Examine the historical evolution and key technological advances in AI as they relate to healthcare.
- Assess the areas where AI has demonstrated significant promise, such as diagnostics, treatment planning, and operational efficiency.
- Discuss the ethical, legal, and technical barriers impeding widespread adoption.
- Propose actionable solutions and policy recommendations to overcome these barriers.
- Highlight directions for future research and interdisciplinary collaborations.

And as the healthcare industry heads into a period of extraordinary change that could redefine the sector, companies will need to know and use the power of AI. The aim of this chapter is to advance this understanding in order to bridge theoretical advancements with practical use in contemporary healthcare systems.

BACKGROUND

Artificial Intelligence in Healthcare: The Evolution

But that's not to say that Artificial Intelligence (AI) hadn't embraced the role of steering modern healthcare systems down their next path. During those decades, AI has grown from relatively simple diagnostic systems such as MYCIN from 1976 which provided bacterial infection diagnoses (Shortliffe, 1976) to extremely sophisticated neural networks that can predict patient outcomes and individualize treatment recommendations. This is driven by the explosive growth in computational power, availability of big data, and advances in algorithms (e.g., deep learning) such as LeCun et al. (2015).

To date, successful historical advancements in AI for healthcare have been primarily focused on clinical decision making and medical imaging. An example of early AI tools is having them complement doctors so AI can help them in certain areas, like radiology and cardiology. Expert systems of the 1990s with probabilistic reasoning were developed to allow physicians to handle uncertainty in diagnosis (Heckerman, 1990). Machine learning techniques such as convolutional neural networks (CNNs) revolutionized diagnostic accuracy in the case of medical imaging (Litjens et al., 2017) by the 2010s. These are significant breakthroughs and represent the evolution of AI as a precision medicine driver.

Although these successes, data were still difficult to come by, challenging regulations, and resistance from medical professionals unwilling to take machine driven analysis. In today's world of AI supporting as well as clinical workflow keeping things efficient as predictive analytics, an open framework for a foundation for value-based care systems (Topol, 2019). AI has also done well in healthcare, being leveraged to transform patient care, enhance administrative tasks and optimise resource utilisation alike.

HEALTHCARE APPLICATIONS OF AI

Apart from diagnostics, AI in healthcare has diversified from deployment beyond just diagnostics to applications like disease prevention, treatment personalization, and improving operational efficiency. In this thesis, research is conducted using Diagnostics and Disease Detection on Dillon County, South Carolina.

But one of AI's most notable applications is in disease diagnosis, which can be done sooner and more accurately than with standard methods. Through AI based diagnostic tools, medical imaging is examined with unprecedented precision. For instance, IBM Watson Health used cognitive computing for cancer detection through rapidly analysing clinical trial data into genomic information (Ferrucci et al., 2010). Similarly, Google's DeepMind Health emerged with algorithms that could diagnose eye conditions with levels of accuracy trumped by the best ophthalmologists (De Fauw et al., 2018).

PathAI is an AI system that uses pathology slides to look for abnormalities, such as tumors, in tissue biopsies. Algorithms using natural language processing (NLP) do the same things for mining electronic health records (EHRs) where they find potential diseases by the patient's symptoms (Shickel et al., 2017). These tools have helped speed the diagnostic process as well as the accuracy, holding out hope that time to treatment and better patient outcomes will soon be within reach.

Personalized Medicine

The rise of AI has changed personalized medicine —it hunts down genetic predispositions and customizes treatments for individual profiles. AI driven pharmacogenomics analyzes the way genetic variations can affect individual responses to medications so that adverse drug reactions are prevented. Genomic and clinical data has been harnessed by companies like Tempus to personalize precision oncology treatments for chemotherapy regimens based on an individual patient (van Dijk et al., 2021).

Using AI alongside wearable tech, physicians now get quick insights into a patient's health. For example, in a similar vein to the devices Fitbit and Apple Health, these devices combine AI algorithms to make health risk predictions from cardiac arrhythmias to patients and caregiver alerting before life threatening events occur (Steinhubl et al., 2016). These advancements promote preventative care and enhance long haul wellbeing come about.

Operational Efficiency

Healthcare is a bottleneck from which we are struggling to deliver quality care as a result of administrative inefficiency. In this area, AI driven automation has had a big role to transform tasks such as patient scheduling, billing as well as resource allocation. For instance, chatbots aid in triaging non critical cases away from the emergency departments and outpatient clinics (Neff et al., 2020).

AI is also helping EHR management with data redundancy and physician burnout. They [EHRs] are used for automated systems that extract actionable insights from EHR to minimize manual data entry (Rajkomar et al., 2018). This integration has resulted in increased clinician satisfaction and increased time for healthcare professionals to spend with the patient.

ETHICAL AND REGULATORY CHALLENGES

Though AI is widely used in healthcare, there are ethical implications and regulatory compliance challenges associated with its implementation.

Privacy and Data Security

Data are essential ingredients of AI systems in healthcare that need to run well. Yet healthcare data has a sensitive nature, and it has concerns of privacy and security. The data breaches and unauthorized access invalidate trust in AI driven platforms (Mehta et al., 2019). Today, it has become something of a priority to deploy secure systems that guarantee encryption and anonymization of data in order to mitigate these risks.

In addition, the governance frameworks for artificial intelligence, such as the Health Insurance Portability and Accountability Act (HIPAA) and the General Data Protection Regulation (GDPR), demand strict regulations on the applications of the AI. They are guidelines to protect patient confidentiality as well as advocate healthy use of data. But it doesn't address one of the biggest hurdles for scaling up the AI systems globally: harmonizing global regulations.

Bias in AI Algorithms

Just like with AI models themselves, the accuracy of the data they are trained on is only as good as the data that is being fed into them, which brings inherent biases in datasets along with that. As an example, diagnostic errors may occur in the minority populations, if training datasets are broaded underrepresented populations (Adamson & Smith, 2018). To address these disparities, we must be aware and deliberate about how to diversify datasets and audit algorithmic decision making to make sure they are fair.

Trust and Acceptance

Practitioners and patients, however, have been wary of AI integration in healthcare, often out of fears of job displacement, while they do not fully trust a decision made by a machine. Generally referred as Explainable AI (XAI), transparency in AI processes is key in forming stakeholder confidence (Holzinger et al., 2017). Training clinicians on both the capabilities and the limitations of AI forms a collaborative ecosystem that free machines to concentrate on augmenting human expertise rather than displacing it.

GLOBAL CASE STUDIES ON IMPLEMENTATION OF AI IN HEALTHCARE

Knowing how AI adoption takes flight globally in healthcare reveals how many use cases and benefits AI can deliver.

- **United States: AI in Radiology**

Deep learning models analyzing CT scans, X-rays and MRIs have been pioneered by companies such as Aidoc and Zebra Medical Vision in radiology in the United States. Such systems detect intracranial hemorrhages and lung nodules and lower the radiologist load as well as increase diagnostic accuracy (Hinton et al., 2018).

- **India: Telemedicine Platforms**

Through its ability to telemedicine rural healthcare delivery, India has leveraged AI. Diagnoses, recommendations and even prescriptions are given by AI driven chatbots on platforms like 1MG. Mukhopadhyay et al. (2020) show that these systems rectify the shortage of healthcare professionals in remote areas and are cost effective.

- **Africa: Tackling Infectious Diseases**

AI has seen great use in combatting infectious diseases such as malaria in Africa. Predictive analytics tools are used to map disease outbreaks, based on virus, environmental and epidemiological data by organizations such as IBM Research. Early warning systems increase preparedness and reduce mortality in areas affected by the outbreak (Reddy et al., 2019).

- **AI in Healthcare: The Road Ahead**

The still broad potential of AI in healthcare is poised to create a highly lucrative industry, one that will be entirely transformed by the efforts of the healthcare giants. Quantum computing and edge AI are expected to usher in new precision medicine grounds brought through faster and more robust diagnostic tools. The successful scaling of these solutions will require collaboration among the technologists with the clinicians and policymakers.

However, the real trick will be finding the right balance between innovation and regulation that will enable the full potential of the AI but protect patient safety and equity. By continuously growing these systems and forming cross sector partnerships, we are positioning them to not only keep pace with broader health goals, but to lay a foundation upon which the next era of intelligent care will be built.

FOCUS OF THE ARTICLE

The 21st century has delivered one of the most transformative developments of all time in the rapid integration of Artificial Intelligence (AI) into healthcare systems. In this chapter, we discuss the many facets of AI's role in healthcare: where it is used and where it poses challenges, and how it could be (or should be) widely adopted in the next ten years. In contrast to the alienating industrial and technological revolutions over the course of decades, which worked their way steadily into industries, the exponential growth of AI is rewriting the compass of contemporary medicine at unparalleled tempos (Lee, 2018). This section examines how AI is key to optimizing workflow, dictating diagnostics, managing workforce challenges and facilitating patient centric care. This article fits within the line of research in trying to build a roadmap for a more integrated AI assisted healthcare ecosystem by unpacking its applications and the associated concerns.

Revolutionising diagnostics and treatment

Diagnostics, Precision and Predictive Analysis

Conventional ways of finding diseases have been revolutionized by AI's diagnostic powers. But traditional approaches to detecting complex diseases like cancer or heart disease tend to be time intensive and wallow in the ambiguity of practitioner expertise. Both speed and precision are improved by these AI based diagnostic systems that analyze large amounts of data and look for patterns invisible to human practitioners (Topol, 2019). Certain imaging tasks, like spotting malignant tumors (McKinney et al., 2020), have seen advanced AI algorithms, like deep learning models, exceed the work of radiologists.

On top of that, AI powered predictive analytics can help anticipate the spread of diseases or the disease progression using electronic health records (EHR), streaming data, and genetic predispositions. IBM's Watson Health has shown great promise in oncology resulting in the processing and cross referencing millions of academic papers and clinical guidelines to offer clinicians tailored treatment suggestions.

Enhancing Surgical Precision

Another area of innovation is AI powered surgical robotics. The da Vinci Surgical System, using machine learning algorithms, helps surgeons to reduce human error and increase precision in complex procedures (Hashimoto et al., 2018). They provide the basis for minimally invasive surgeries that heal faster, with fewer complications. Integrated into surgical planning, AI utilizing 3D imaging and predictive simulations are able to personalize procedures to the patient's unique anatomy, resulting in a better outcome.

Workflow Optimization and Operational Efficiency

Hospital Resources Management using AI

The demands placed on hospitals and healthcare systems are growing; patient numbers increase, and workers are unavailable. Hospital administrators can use AI based tools such as capacity management software to resolve these challenges. Patient admission rates, bed occupancy levels and staff needs are assessed by predictive algorithms to maximize resource allocation and minimise bottlenecks (Wang et al., 2021). Taking the Mount Sinai Hospital's Ai scheduling algorithms, for example, directly improve patient care quality by minimizing delays.

Healthcare delivery is fraught with administrative inefficiencies. It has been reported that up to 30% of global healthcare expenditure is wasted in non-value added administrative work (Berwick and Hackbarth, 2012). Natural Language Processing (NLP) has reduced tedious bureaucratic processes, for instance, automated patient data entry, claim processing, and appointment scheduling. As an example, AI driven chatbots are used to autonomously handle patient's inquiries and triage urgent ones based on initial symptoms analysis (Shafique et al., 2020).

Genomics and Personalized Medicine Transformation

Personalized Patient Care and AI

Thanks to AI innovations, personalizing medicine, or tailoring healthcare to a genetically unique profile, has become increasingly mainstream. Vast datasets of genetic information, lifestyle factors and real world medical data are analysed by machine learning algorithms to select bespoke therapeutic pathways for patients. AI tools like those used on precision medicine platforms Tempus help to comb through molecular diagnostics in combination with the latest clinical studies and identify the best treatments for patients with cancer (Grossman et al., 2018).

AI helps speed up the discovery of genetic variations linked to inherited diseases in genomic medicine. Efficient processing of raw genomic data for clinical applications serves as examples such as Deep Variant from Google AI (Poplin et al., 2018).

Through AI Wearables: Chronic Disease Management

Wearable technologies fuelled by AI are essential part of chronic disease management. Devices that can be worn as a kind of Fitbit or Apple Watch relay real time information about vital signs, identifying an irregular pattern as being indicative of a condition like an arrhythmia or hypertension (Perez et al., 2019). By integrating wearable tech with AI, longitudinal healthcare datasets are formed to clinically intervene proactively which decreases hospitalizations and provides better long term patient outcomes.

Ways to address Healthcare Inequities with AI

Bridging Accessibility Gaps

For us, AI democratizing access to healthcare, especially in underserved regions, is one of the most transformative promises of AI. Virtual consultation services and triage assessment such as Ada health or Babylon health are provided either through AI powered mobile applications to rural communities without physical healthcare infrastructure (Holzinger et al., 2019). Furthermore, AI diagnostic tools bypass the absence of specialist doctors in developing countries and provide reliable first line diagnosis to diminish morbidity rate.

- **Using Actionable Evidence to Combat Bias and Disparities in AI Systems**

With deep concerns over the systemic biases built into the algorithms of AI, there remains little discussion about AI's potential to address inequities. A lot of the data used to train AI systems is colored by societal inequalities which means that the outcomes produced by such AI systems will also be discriminatory. For example, past AI diagnostic models have been less accurate at identifying skin cancers on darker-skinned people where proper training was not taking place on diverse datasets (Adamson & Smith, 2018). Representative datasets and auditing the fairness of the AI algorithms are two steps we must take to solve these issues. To combat these inequities, companies like IBM are spending huge sums of money on tools that assess algorithmic fairness, showing you proactive ways to address these disparities.

- **Ethical and Socioeconomic Considerations.**

Privacy and Data Security, Safeguarding the same

That means that the data that is used by AI needs to be protected, and there are robust measures in place to protect sensitive patient information. However, public trust in AI applications erodes related to data breaches and privacy violations and result in multiple regulations issues. However advanced differential privacy algorithms and block chain based data management systems are for protecting patient data (Kumar et al., 2020).

- **Responding to Workforce Displacement Issues**

Concerns about AI driven job displacement in the healthcare industry persists with the increasing automation. AI makes the system more efficient, but cannot substitute for the empathic and interpersonal communication that, to a significant extent, characterizes the human care delivery. Healthcare professionals will have to reskilled to AI integrated environments which is why policymakers and educators need to focus on workforce reskilling programs. Future career pathways that combine human capabilities with technological tools, for example, in the form of creation of hybrid roles (like data driven decision specialists) (Fleming et al., 2018).

In this section, AI's superpowers for diagnostic advancement, optimizing operations, and individualized medicine were touted, as well as tackled for the problems of inequity and ethics in healthcare systems. AI is dynamic by nature, and so it must continue to innovate, deploy equitably, and collaborate globally in order to fully benefit from. This article prepares the stage for further discussions on actionable solutions, novel research directions and policy recommendations by concentrating on both fronts — i.e, advancements and challenges.

SOLUTIONS AND RECOMMENDATIONS

Artificial intelligence (AI) integration in healthcare systems provides amazing opportunities to resolve the essential problems in efficiency, accuracy, and accessibility. However, to achieve these benefits and minimize associated risk, comprehensive, well-structured solutions are needed. To achieve the equitable and sustainable use of AI in healthcare, this section describes a suite of recommendations that encompass technological advancements, which incorporate the best ethics, strategies, and collaboration amongst disciplines.

- **Advancing Data Interoperability and Integration**

The success of AI driven solutions in healthcare is highly dependent on the ability to seamlessly aggregate and analyse disparate sources of data such as electronic health records (EHRs), imaging data, and patient generated data from wearable devices. These processes, however, are frustrated by data silos and interoperability issues. It is critical to develop robust frameworks for standardizing data formats and defining interoperability protocols (Mandl & Kohane, 2018). Efforts such as the Fast Healthcare Interoperability Resources (FHIR) standard illustrates ways by which systems can communicate starting and encouraging collaborative care environments.

Unified data platforms for patients that enable real time data sharing with patients where patient privacy and security are maintained require healthcare organizations to spend on these platforms. The cloud-based AI platforms, modularized with block chain, can further guarantee the data provenance and unchangeability and build further trust among stakeholders (Krittanawong et al, 2017). To incentivize collaborations between private firms, research organizations and public health entities in creating global data sharing agreements, governments and international bodies should.

- **Upskilling Healthcare Professionals**

Endpoint Encryption, Full Disk Encryption

Achieving AI in healthcare requires a workforce that knows how to harness its benefits. But for AI technologies to reach clinical applications, healthcare professionals need to be trained on it. Educating professionals for data analytics and ethical principles with respect to AI outputs is possible by incorporating the combination of basic AI and data analytic concepts into comprehensive curricula (Mesko et al., 2018).

Specialized workshops and certifications tailored for rural and underserved areas are required to address the digital divide so that AI benefits are shared equally. Since institutions such as the World Health Organization (WHO) play a major role in training individuals, one would expect their work to be standardized so that different healthcare systems follow the same rules to some extent. Also, incorporating AI ethics and interpretability into these programs will enable practitioners to interpret AI derived insights rather than seeing them as conclusions, instead of works in themselves (Chen et al., 2020).

- **Enhancing Diagnostic Accuracy and Accessibility**

By enhancing the accuracy, as well as the speed at which disease is detected, AI powered diagnostic tools are changing the way we think about healthcare. Machine learning algorithms have revolutionized finding anomalies in imaging data, outperforming traditional methods in oncology, detecting anomalies associated with an imaging data (Esteva et al., 2017). The adequate and wide deployment of such tools to underserved regions can reduce significantly healthcare disparities bringing early and accurate diagnosis closer to everyone.

Policymakers should help the implementation of portable AI powered devices, which can work in a low resource environment to achieve this. But simplifying the user interfaces for accommodating to diverse healthcare environments and delivering the user friendly guide for local clinicians are necessary steps. Technology firms and NGOs can partner with government bodies that can help speed up the large scale deployment of these technologies provided with grants and public funding.

- **Robust ethical frameworks**

AI driven healthcare innovation is based on ethics. Robust frameworks for AI deployment in healthcare are needed, particularly in dealing with problems of bias, privacy breaches, and accountability gaps. Therefore, we should prioritize inclusive and diverse datasets to prevent algorithmic bias and to achieve fair outcomes for all demographic groups (Obermeyer et al., 2019).

For some AI algorithms, there is a "black box" nature to them and they need to be transparent to address it. Given that developers and healthcare providers should trust AI driven insights (Holzinger et al., 2019), explainable AI (XAI) models should be adopted by developers and healthcare providers to understand algorithmic decision making process. In addition, the codifying of ethical AI principles into obligatory regulatory policies that require developer adherence through third party audits and certifications is needed.

The growing dependence on AI systems for patient care is deeply concerned about the issue of data privacy and cybersecurity. All AI driven healthcare systems (Rahman et al., 2020) have to run on encryption techniques, have secure access controls, and anonymization protocols. General Data Protection Regulation (GDPR) based regulatory frameworks in Europe should act as a model for how privacy legislation should be carried out around the world.

The decentralized systems like federated learning allow AI to train with distributed data across multiple locations without harming privacy. Federated models can suffice to conduct analysis without exposing the data to be transferred by exporting it outside local systems, reducing the risks of unauthorized exposure. Another great way to be prepared is to integrate cybersecurity risk assessments into healthcare infrastructure planning.

- **Promoting Public Private Partnership**

To fully realize the promise of AI in healthcare, collaboration is needed between public institutions and private entities. Partners should be formed among governments, academic institutions and private companies to speed development of AI solutions through research and development and deployment. The sustainable framework for resource sharing, innovation and scalability is offered in collaborative models such as public private partnership (PPP).

High impact areas including rare disease diagnostics and AI enabled drug discovery as well as epidemic forecasting should be the areas to focus on joint initiatives. For example, AI systems have played an important role in tracking virus spread and speeding research on vaccines during the COVID 19 pandemic (Mamoshina et al, 2020), showing the power of cross sector collaborations. These partnerships must be based on transparent agreements and the round of mutual accountability in order to practice ethics.

- **Bias and Inequity in AI Systems**

If AI was not designed carefully, it has the potential to amplify existing biases in how healthcare is delivered. Diversifying datasets starts with taking a stake against systemic biases by reflecting the stakeholders' gender, race, socio-economic and geographic locations. Cross disciplinary audits, for example, in the case of a data scientist, ethicist, and clinician should examine AI models for bias prior to implementation (Wiens et al., 2019).

Fairness-centric metrics can be introduced during model training to bring the outputs from the algorithm in line with ethical principles. Additionally, advocacy and education of stakeholders, from policymakers to end users, helps in developing AI bias awareness towards equitable outcomes. With inclusive design principles as an incentive to AI developers, we will encourage people to create systems that work for all populations.

- **Promoting Interdisciplinary Research and Development**

Crossing healthcare, computer science, ethics, and sociology is a rich terrain to pursue AI driven solutions. Interdisciplinary collaborations are encouraged in order to make innovations not only technically justifiable, socially acceptable and ethically justified, but also convincing to a general audience. Grant funding should go to projects that consort groups of the best from different fields to solve complex healthcare problems.

Knowledge exchange is accelerated, and co creation culture is fostered through the creation of AI innovation hubs that connect universities, hospitals and technology firms. For such hubs, focus areas should be on emergent areas like AI in mental health, geriatric care, and palliative medicine, and utilising shared expertise to meet unmet healthcare needs.

- **Building Transparent and Accountable Governance Structures**

The risks associated with AI deployment in healthcare must be mitigated with regulatory oversight. It is recommended that governments create independent AI monitoring and oversight bodies, and also set up safety protocol evaluation processes, and arbiters to resolve disputes around the application of AI. Nations can achieve global collaboration, with leadership from organisations like the World Health Organization, or the United Nations, and establish such health governance at a national level.

We need to build accountability mechanisms into every step of the AI system life cycle. For example, a liability modelling permits all stakeholders (developers, end users…) to be answerable for their resulting role in AI implementation. We think regulatory guidelines should introduce safety and efficacy standards for independently operating AI applications comparable to medical devices.

- **Enabling Patient Centred Care**

However, it should be patient empowerment which should remain central to the integration of AI in healthcare. They also administer interactive platforms that help patients learn about AI driven diagnoses, treatment plans and possible risks. Multilingual support and those accommodating a range of digital literacy levels need to be provided through these platforms for them to meet the needs of users.

It also means that patients' needs and preferences will guide development of technological innovation in AI systems. Real world evidence helps add personalization to healthcare solutions given to patients as more accurate and appropriate care pathways (Shortliffe & Sepúlveda, 2018). It should also be a standard feature when patient interacts with AI technologies — transparency in consent.

- **Addressing Emerging Challenges In AI Deployment**

Important emerging technologies, like natural language processing (NLP), robotics and augmented reality (AR) have to be incorporated with the existing healthcare systems with caution. These innovations can, however, be scaled only with perfecting the infrastructure, targeted research funding and pilot studies that assess real world outcomes. For example, the use of robotics in surgery necessitates both technical reliability and clinician training so benefits are achieved at minimum risk to patients (Yang et al., 2018). With AI in genomics or personalized medicine, the future comes with foresight and adaptability.

FUTURE RESEARCH DIRECTIONS

There are a plethora of future research avenues resulting from fast developing artificial intelligence (AI) in healthcare. As an emerging and, therefore, technology, patient applications of AI in diagnostics, therapeutics and healthcare operations show massive potential while being in a nascent phase of development and implementation. In this section, we discuss the areas that deserve further exploration including interdisciplinary collaboration, ethical framework, technological advancements and global inclusivity.

- **Improved AI Algorithms for Healthcare Applications**

While current AI algorithms can perform extraordinarily well at specific, narrow tasks, especially as applied to radiology image recognition or an understanding of disease progression across time, they have been shown to be inferior to domain experts in general world tasks. But this research must focus on developing generalized AI systems that are adaptable in many medical applications. Formulated as systems, these should integrate multiple modalities of data: clinical records, imaging data, genetic information, and patient reported outcomes to enable holistic decision making processes (Jiang et al., 2021). Furthermore, an important issue involves making AI understandable by human healthcare practitioners for them to trust and deploy to such tools.

Despite that, explainable AI (XAI) is still crucial to build interpretability. In contrast to conventional AI, XAI users can know and verify decision pathways (Arrieta et al., 2020). Future research should be devoted to how we can build inherently explainable algorithms that sacrifice little clinical accuracy in exchange for interpretability. Improvements in this area may enhance practitioner confidence in the integration of AI driven tools in clinical settings.

- **Ethical and Legal Implications addressed**

While all of this makes AI a game changer in healthcare, the rise of AI inevitably poses a series of huge ethical questions surrounding data privacy, algorithmic bias and decision accountability (Topol, 2019). Future research should explore frameworks that address these challenges are through stakeholder inclusive dialogue and global consensus building. For critical areas, scholars need to explore ways to maintain patient autonomy, while providing a balance in healthcare innovation. It means making sure that AI interventions supplement, rather supplant, clinician–patient dynamics.

The other critical research priority, however, is to design algorithms without implicit bias. Recent studies show how AI system strained on biased datasets perpetuate healthcare disparities (Larrazábal et al., 2020). Equitable data collection and standardization and robust ways of creating biased free AI systems becoming analysts to make decisions based on procured fairness. At the same time, work should begin on global legal regulations for the use of AI in healthcare that balance the acceptability of using AI (i.e., liability concerns) while fostering technological innovation.

- **Artificial intelligence in Preventive Healthcare**

Despite the increasing diagnostic and therapeutic applications of AI, AI for preventive healthcare is sorely under researched. AI can greatly reduce the healthcare burden worldwide if proactively identifies disease risk factors. So, in addition to basic machine learning which includes categorising the nature of data into constant and random datasets, more research should focus on the development of predictive models for lifestyle diseases, epidemics and rare conditions using population scale data (Hinton et al., 2020).

Extensive investigation is required to refine the methodologies of emerging areas such as digital twin models, which simulate patient profiles for personalized risk assessment, and to make their application practical. It would also be worth exploring how information from wearable sensors, IoT devices and AI driven analytics can be integrated to do real time health monitoring. Such frameworks would also further advance the widespread adoption of predictive algorithms by establishing how to validate their accuracy in a range of patient populations.

- **Advancing Personalized Medicine**

Personalized medicine based on AI is transformative, especially for oncology, genomics, and pharmacology. Another example is the use of AI systems to predict disease susceptibility and the way to the best treatment regimen for individual patients given omics data (genomics, proteomics and metabolomics) (Ghorbani et al., 2022). However, there remain large holes leaving in the efficient integration and translation of heterogeneous datasets. Future studies have to give precedence to approaches that allow for holistic analysis and diminish data noise without compromising accuracy.

In addition, research is needed to improve personalized drug discovery. In order to predict molecular efficacy and potential side effects for different populations in addition to predicting, existing AI models need extending. Reducing the gap between discovery and clinical translation can be made through collaborative research paradigms that place pharmaceutical companies and AI developers together. Moreover, it is important to pursue investigation regarding ethical implications of the genomics data sharing, in global scale, in order to develop inclusive and diverse solutions.

- **Integration with Augmented Reality (AR) and Virtual Reality (VR)**

AR and VR tools powered by AI offer potential that is yet to be leveraged by improving healthcare delivery. Technical and logistical barriers (Lin et al., 2021) have so far prevented existing applications, including surgical assistance and medical training, to reach their full scope. Future research therefore should focus on using AI in AR 'VR platforms for real time decision making and interactivity in clinical workflows.

Further exploration of specific areas of particularly interest may include developing AI enabled AR platforms to support telemedicine consultation to enhance patient doctor interaction remotely. Virtually too, predictive AI can offer a way to integrate VR for mental health applications, for example, exposure therapy for anxiety disorders or rehab programs. Moreover, standards have to be set for the validation of hybrid tool effectiveness and safety in variegated healthcare contexts.

- **Exploiting Low-Resource Settings for Expanding AI Applications**

However, while these AI solutions have already proved their usefulness in the high-end healthcare infrastructures, they still lack the desired accessibility in low resource settings. Given resource constrained environments (Wahl et al., 2021), research needs to be directed to develop scalable, cost effective solutions that match the specific constraints of small and very small developing countries. Possibilities might include lightweight diagnostic tools designed for rural clinics and simplified AI systems that run on low bandwidth internet.

Moreover, better utility and user acceptance of localized AI models may be achieved through community driven approaches, including the incorporation of community health worker input into the dataset. To implement more sustainably AI healthcare innovations, research should also address practical barriers, for example, electricity shortages. In low resource healthcare ecosystem, however, financial and infrastructural limitations pose a significant challenge owing to high service level and highly variable demand. In this context, investigating open source platforms and public private partnerships can significantly contribute to rolling out these services.

- **AI and Mental Health Intersection**

There is a paucity of mental health in the global healthcare landscape. There are wide-ranging AI tools, from chatbots, to predictive algorithms, that can help to fill these gaps. Future research could follow to optimize AI powered digital therapy platforms for diagnosing early the condition like depression or anxiety with behavioural signal analysis. In addition, the long term effectiveness of AI interventions in maintaining long term mental health improvements compared to traditional therapy (Xu et al., 2022) should also be emphasized.

Second, we recommend that researchers cultivate ethical AI frameworks for mental health interventions that promote patient empathy in systems interaction. For widespread adoption of digital counselling services without betraying user trust, researching regulatory standards ensuring privacy, and confidentiality is important.

- **Preparing for Quantum AI Integration**

Healthcare technology playing on the frontiers of quantum computing is the place to be to disrupt AI capabilities dramatically. Quantum AI would exponentially speed results processing that might lead to breakthroughs in proteins folding prediction and epidemic modelling (Wittek, 2021). Now that research in this emerging field has advanced so much, it's time to bridge the gap between theoretical advances and clinical translation. An immediate priority is developing quantum ready AI algorithms that fit healthcare requirements.

In quantum computing in healthcare researchers should search for ethical implications that quantum computing could bring, and whether certain amount of innovation comes at the expense of the fair access. Responsible development of quantum AI systems will be possible through interdisciplinary collaboration between healthcare practitioners, quantum scientists and ethicists.

- **AI in Healthcare: Socio Cultural Dimensions**

With the ever digitising of healthcare, it is critical to pay attention to its socio cultural impact. Future research should be aimed at understanding how AI based care could change traditional patient-improver relationships, especially in cultures where individualised attention lies at the heart of healthcare (Banerjee & Meena, 2020). Furthermore, relevant to ethical considerations, there is still little work on a societal level in what comes if we all adopt widespread AI, such as healthcare workforce disruptions.

Additionally, we examine the potential of educational programs aimed at AI literacy within healthcare workers and patients to guarantee that adoption is inclusive. If we investigate how to nurture equitable global adoption of AI we might mitigate regional disparities in technology dissemination.

- **Making Strengthening Interdisciplinary Collaborations**

To advance the role of AI in healthcare, future research should focus on growing interdisciplinary collaboration, which is essential. Algorithm refinement and ethical issues are amongst the challenges that computational scientists could help address in conjunction with clinicians, regulatory bodies and social scientists. Researchers would also be able to harness frameworks that allow them to collaborate across disciplinary boundaries more easily, to accelerate innovation (Brynjolfsson & McAfee, 2017).

Furthermore, public private academic initiatives need to expand funding channels for translational research bridging innovation gaps between academe and practical application. Comparison of performance and constraints on AI tools across a variety of health care systems may illuminate what to focus on in improving international best practices.

DISCUSSION

Healthcare systems around the globe are on the verge of a revolution a revolution caused by Artificial Intelligence (AI). In this chapter we've covered how AI can impact everything from diagnostics to drug discovery, personalized medicine, and operations. We now bring in ends, and restate the main takeaways from both sections as we provide a bird’s eye view of the challenges and opportunities that lie ahead as AI transforms healthcare.

The history of AI in healthcare shows the way from simpler automation tools to types of cognitive systems. Using Machine Learning, Natural Language Processing and Computer Vision on healthcare is like rocket fuel in accelerating diagnostic and treatment process technology. Thanks to machine learning algorithms, it is now possible to interpret complex medical imaging to recognise early stage diseases with unparalleled accuracy, and NLP helps the medical expert to process and understand medical records much quicker and more accurately.

Overcoming Technical Barriers

There is the potential for AI to be far reaching, but not without technical barriers when it comes to adoption. As shown in section 5, AI systems need to become part of the existing healthcare infrastructures. An issue with this process is such that it can run into challenges like making sure algorithms and AI cannot lead to error or potential bias, or that they are explainable facts for the user. Investing in building strong infrastructure for the sharing of data to leverage AI to work across many hospital settings, as well as improving the traffic of AI based clinical support is imperative.

Ethical and Societal studies

This talk covers the various critical ethical and societal issues that accompany the AI adoption in healthcare. There are especially strong concerns for privacy and security when handling health data that is almost always highly sensitive. Moreover, one inherent bias of algorithm is within the training data used, which can perpetuate healthcare inequity. In section 5, we also saw that these ethical challenges can be solved by applying a mix of regulatory oversight and design of AI systems which are themselves fair and transparent. Ethical AI systems will be possible only with ethical guidelines around consent and accountability.

For the AI systems to develop that patients, healthcare workers and the general public will trust, the development and implementation will need to focus on transparency, clarity, and robust ethical protocols, at least. Central to AI powered healthcare innovations are: the patient consent process, the right to challenge AI decisions, as well as measures to protect patient data. It is necessary for ensuring that AI can complement rather than displace human oversight, to ensure that patient centred care can be continued and the issues of medical professionals can be addressed.

Personalized Medicine and Predictive Analytics

AIs best potential is in personalised care and predicting medical outcomes. Integrating AI into hugely rich datasets such as genetic data, environmental factors and lifestyle information, healthcare providers could provide treatments specialised to the exact needs of patients. Section 4 shows how predictive analytics allows early detection of diseases and the identification of high risk populations for preventive interventions.

Healthcare systems can become more proactive and less reactive using AI driven solutions. AI has the transformative potential to not only make patients' lives better but also the system better. As we keep investing in research and development of AI, we will definitely see some solid breakthrough in early diagnosis of diseases like cancer, heart disease or rare genetic disorders.

Building an AI-Literate Healthcare Workforce

Integration of AI in healthcare is highly dependent upon the existence of an AI literate workforce. In sec 5 we talked about; how the use of AI driven tools must also incorporate the understanding and interpretation of AI generated insights. To aid trust and efficiency with adoption process, it is important to make AI literacy. The more medical practitioners will use these systems, the more confident they will be in making decisions, and these decisions will be backed by AI recommendations.

Furthermore, healthcare AI ecosystems need to further develop to foster collaboration of the healthcare ecosystem (clinicians, AI developers, policymakers, patients), and build integrated solutions. To build such a cooperative infrastructure, efforts to standardise medical datasets, improve data sharing protocols and increase AI transparency will be key. As healthcare system, we must accept AI not instead of, but alongside human judgement.

Ethical Guidelines and Regulatory Measures

Since AI applications have been growing in healthcare, the ethical guidelines also need to be developed there. AI technologies will continue to challenge existing regulatory frameworks' ability to deploy. So, to deploy such an AI based device in the health care environment, the policymakers need to collaborate with the AI enthusiast, the healthcare providers, the ethicists, to develop comprehensive guidelines on the deployment and use of AI. While regulators are kept busy trying to require that AI systems abide by a set of long held standards related to safety, privacy and fairness, they also must not allow for potential conflicts of interest or bias towards the technology itself.

Regulatory frameworks that emphasise the ethical implications of AI technologies will instil trust in AI technologies and, in the process, benefit both healthcare professionals and patients. Section 4 highlights the ethical considerations that need to change as this change away from human oversight prevents algorithmic discrimination, protects sensitive patient data, and allows healthcare systems to continue to use AI tools with human oversight.

REAL-WORLD APPLICATIONS AND FUTURE RESEARCH

Case studies and use cases exist throughout the world, including the United States, United Kingdom, and Japan, already showing application of AI in healthcare delivering tangible results. Real world implementations of AI driven diagnostic imaging to virtual assistants for patients' engagement show how AI technologies can be transformative. So, what do these successes teach us about how healthcare providers can use the power of AI in their operations?

The chapter, however, has highlighted that future research is inevitable to achieve maximum application of AI in healthcare. Future AI research directions include more development in early disease diagnosis, real time health monitoring through wearable devices, and an increasing role that AI will play in tackling public health crises like pandemics. Smarter, more adaptive AI technologies will mean that healthcare systems will be able to act faster, react quicker and ensure better health outcomes on a larger scale.

CONCLUSION

Finally, Artificial Intelligence is bringing a new era to healthcare with tonnes of opportunities to enhance outcomes, decrease costs, and change the way we care for patients. AI is not just about making decisions faster and improving clinical practises and operational efficiency, but it also promises to contribute to global goal of universal health care. With the impact of AI technologies in the healthcare sector coming to the fore, its role in transforming the protocols of treatment, drug niching, patient care delivery and policy decisions is going to be rolled out. But to achieve the full potential of AI we must conquer limits like data privacy concerns, cultural problems and employee readiness.

AI can continue to develop by means of more research, powerful policy frameworks, and prospective partnerships, allowing that it will become an inseparable weapon of the contemporary health care system and will help to make more accurate diagnoses, better treatment, and more just and balanced ways to provide health care.

REFERENCES

Adamson, A. S., & Smith, A. (2018). Machine learning and health care disparities in dermatology. *JAMA Dermatology, 154*(11), 1247–1248. DOI: 10.1001/jamadermatol.2018.2348 PMID: 30073260

Adamson, A. S., & Smith, A. (2018). Machine learning and health care disparities: Limitations and opportunities. *Journal of the American Medical Association, 320*(24), 2499–2500. DOI: 10.1001/jama.2018.17577

Arrieta, A. B., Díaz-Rodríguez, N., Del Ser, J., Bennetot, A., Tabik, S., Barbado, A., & Herrera, F. (2020). Explainable artificial intelligence (XAI): Concepts, taxonomies, opportunities, and challenges toward responsible AI. *Information Fusion, 58*, 82–115. DOI: 10.1016/j.inffus.2019.12.012

Banerjee, A., & Meena, K. S. (2020). Social determinants and ethical considerations of artificial intelligence in healthcare. *Asian Bioethics Review, 12*(3), 229–241. DOI: 10.1007/s41649-020-00128-w

Bengio, Y., LeCun, Y., & Hinton, G. (2021). Deep learning in the COVID-19 era: Achievements and challenges. *Nature Reviews. Methods Primers.*

Berwick, D. M., & Hackbarth, A. D. (2012). Eliminating waste in US health care. *Journal of the American Medical Association, 307*(14), 1513–1516. DOI: 10.1001/jama.2012.362 PMID: 22419800

Bhagat, R., & Singh, M. (2020). AI models for drug repurposing in infectious diseases. *Infection and Immunity, 88*(5), e00123–e20. DOI: 10.1128/IAI.00123-20

Brynjolfsson, E., & McAfee, A. (2017). The business of artificial intelligence. *Harvard Business Review.*

Chang, C., & Zhou, L. (2021). Integrating AI with genomics for precision medicine. *Nature Communications, 12*, 748–763. DOI: 10.1038/s41467-021-27729-w

Chen, L., Lu, M., Liu, C., & Wang, H. (2020). Trustworthy artificial intelligence in healthcare: Principles and applications. *Journal of Healthcare Engineering, 2020*, 1–9. https://doi.org/10.xxxx. DOI: 10.1155/2020/6660160

De Fauw, J., Ledsam, J. R., Romera-Paredes, B., Nikolov, S., Tomasev, N., Blackwell, S., & Suleyman, M. (2018). Clinically applicable deep learning for diagnosis and referral in retinal disease. *Nature Medicine, 24*(9), 1342–1350. DOI: 10.1038/s41591-018-0107-6 PMID: 30104768

Esteva, A., Kuprel, B., Novoa, R. A., Ko, J., Swetter, S. M., Blau, H. M., & Thrun, S. (2017). Dermatologist-level classification of skin cancer with deep neural networks. *Nature*, *542*(7639), 115–118. DOI: 10.1038/nature21056 PMID: 28117445

Ferrucci, D., Brown, E., Chu-Carroll, J., Fan, J., Gondek, D., Kalyanpur, A., Lally, A., Murdock, J. W., Nyberg, E., Prager, J., Schlaefer, N., & Welty, C. (2010). Building Watson: An overview of the DeepQA project. *AI Magazine*, *31*(3), 59–79. DOI: 10.1609/aimag.v31i3.2303

Fleming, N.. (2018). The role of artificial intelligence in reshaping medical education. *Lancet*, *391*(10124), 10–12. DOI: 10.1016/S0140-6736(18)30996-2

Ghorbani, A., Heuvelmans, M. A., Wiedermann, D., & Dekker, W. (2022). Big data and AI in oncological practice: Bridging the gap in personalized medicine. *Translational Oncology*, *15*(1), 1–8.

Grossman, R. L., Heath, A. P., & Murphy, M. (2018). A case for data commons. *Computing in Science & Engineering*, *20*(3), 70–82. DOI: 10.1109/MCSE.2018.03269455 PMID: 29033693

Gupta, P., & Singh, A. (2022). The role of AI in managing chronic diseases: Current status and future directions. *Journal of Chronic Diseases and Management*, *34*(3), 213–224. DOI: 10.1002/jcdm.12368

Heckerman, D. (1990). Probabilistic interpretations for MYCIN's certainty factors. *The Computer Journal*, *23*(3), 241–256. DOI: 10.1093/comjnl/23.3.241

Holzinger, A., Biemann, C., Pattichis, C. S., & Kell, D. B. (2017). What do we need to build explainable AI systems for the medical domain? *arXiv Preprint*.

Holzinger, A., Carrington, A., & Mueller, H. (2019). Measuring the impact of explainability on trust in AI. *Information Systems Frontiers*, *21*, 31–37.

Holzinger, A., Dehmer, M., & Jurisica, I. (2019). Knowledge discovery and interactive data mining in bioinformatics—State-of-the-art, future challenges, and research directions. *BMC Bioinformatics*, *19*(2), 1–25. https://doi.org/10.xxxx PMID: 25078282

Holzinger, A., Langs, G., Denk, H., Zatloukal, K., & Müller, H. (2019). Causability and explainability of artificial intelligence in medicine. *Wiley Interdisciplinary Reviews. Data Mining and Knowledge Discovery*, *9*(4), e1312. DOI: 10.1002/widm.1312 PMID: 32089788

Jones, C. G., & Taylor, J. A. (2019). Artificial intelligence in healthcare: Challenges, opportunities, and applications. *Journal of Health Care Technology*, *32*(2), 223–235. DOI: 10.1080/22757293.2019.1259483

Kapoor, S., & Bharti, A. (2020). The impact of AI on radiology practice and its future applications. *The Indian Journal of Radiology & Imaging*, *30*(1), 14–21. DOI: 10.4103/ijri.IJRI_104_19

Kaur, S., & Garg, P. (2021). Recent advances in AI-based medical technologies. *Journal of Medical Systems*, *45*(7), 88. DOI: 10.1007/s10916-021-01845-z

Kim, S., & Lee, B. (2019). AI in medical robotics: Potential and challenges. *Medical Robotics and Surgery*, *8*(1), 39–47. DOI: 10.1089/mrs.2019.2917

Knight, W. (2020). Deep learning in healthcare: A revolution in data-driven medicine. *Technology Review*, *34*(3), 5–13. DOI: 10.1162/techr

Li, L., & Xie, C. (2021). Artificial intelligence in diagnostics: Transforming medical imaging. *International Journal of Imaging Systems and Technology*, *31*(4), 45–52. DOI: 10.1002/ima.22611

Li, Y., & Xu, Y. (2021). Applications of machine learning in pathology and histology. *Journal of Pathology Informatics*, *12*(1), 7–16. DOI: 10.4103/jpi.jpi_45_20

Liu, X., Wang, L., & Zhang, Y. (2019). Leveraging artificial intelligence for drug discovery and development. *Nature Reviews. Drug Discovery*, *18*(8), 505–518. DOI: 10.1038/s41573-019-00097-3

Lu, X., & Roberts, A. (2020). Artificial intelligence in cancer prediction and diagnosis. *Cancer Letters*, *467*, 21–32. DOI: 10.1016/j.canlet.2019.12.023

Morris, T., & Reid, M. (2020). Ethics of AI applications in healthcare. *Journal of Health Ethics*, *46*(1), 82–92. DOI: 10.1016/j.jhlthe.2020.06.001

Nguyen, H., & Tran, V. (2023). Optimizing patient outcomes with AI-powered healthcare management systems. *Journal of Medical Informatics*, *77*(2), 246–259. DOI: 10.1016/j.jmii.2023.07.010

Patel, R., & Agarwal, A. (2023). AI in cardiology: Emerging trends and challenges. *Cardiology Clinics*, *41*(2), 207–221. DOI: 10.1016/j.ccl.2023.03.001 PMID: 37003678

Patil, S., & Khan, M. (2022). Machine learning models for clinical outcomes prediction in healthcare. *Healthcare Analytics*, *9*(1), 25–41. DOI: 10.1016/j.hca.2021.100077

Thawani, R., & Rana, V. (2021). Ethics in the age of artificial intelligence in healthcare. *AI in Healthcare*, *12*(4), 58–63. DOI: 10.1109/AIHC.2021.1124566

Wang, Y., & Zhang, Y. (2022). AI-driven predictive analytics for personalized healthcare. *Journal of Healthcare Information Management*, *38*(6), 305–319. DOI: 10.1177/18414569221119869

Zeng, J., & He, M. (2019). Explainability in healthcare decision-making: A case study using machine learning. *IEEE Access : Practical Innovations, Open Solutions*, *7*, 112028–112035. DOI: 10.1109/ACCESS.2019.2934931

Zhang, X., & Chen, S. (2022). Leveraging AI for healthcare delivery: A case study approach. *Healthcare Technology Review*, *12*(4), 105–117. DOI: 10.1109/HTR.2022.1235623

ADDITIONAL READING

He, H., Wu, D., & Zhang, S. (2020). Machine learning techniques for medical big data analysis. *Springer Series in Medical Informatics*. This book provides an in-depth exploration of machine learning techniques, including how they can be applied to solve challenges in healthcare data analysis.

Rajpurkar, P., & Ng, A. (2020). The impact of artificial intelligence in healthcare: A systematic review and meta-analysis. [This article reviews the effectiveness of AI applications in healthcare, offering both a systematic evaluation and meta-analysis of available AI-driven tools.]. *Journal of the American Medical Association*, *323*(6), 455–463.

Davenport, T., & Kalakota, R. (2019). The potential for artificial intelligence in healthcare. [This paper explores key uses of AI in the healthcare industry, including diagnostics, operations, and service delivery.]. *Future Healthcare Journal*, *6*(2), 94–98.

Kourou, K., Exarchos, T. P., & Karamizoglou, S. (2021). Artificial intelligence in medical diagnostics: Applications and challenges. [This reading focuses on the integration of AI in diagnostics and the challenges associated with its implementation, such as ethical concerns and regulatory approval.]. *Future Science OA*, *7*(1), FSO667.

Esteva, A., Kuprel, B., & Novoa, R. A. (2019). Dermatologist-level classification of skin cancer with deep neural networks. [Esteva and colleagues discuss the revolutionary application of deep learning for diagnosing skin cancer through medical imaging.]. *Nature*, *542*(7639), 115–118.

Carvalho, D. V., Alves, T. D. J., & Silva, D. F. (2020). Ethical concerns in the implementation of artificial intelligence in healthcare. Frontiers in Digital Health. This article covers the ethical implications of using AI in healthcare, including data privacy concerns and decision-making transparency.

Jiang, F., Jiang, Y., & Zhi, H. (2017). Artificial intelligence in healthcare: Past, present and future. *Seminars in Cancer Biology*, *56*, 1–11.

Schwendner, R., & Lapsia, F. (2022). AI, ethics, and healthcare delivery: Balancing opportunities and risks. *Bioethics Forum*, *27*(1), 32–44.

Shickel, B., Laren, D. S., & Orrawa, S. A. (2019). Deep learning for healthcare: Review, opportunities and challenges. *IEEE Access : Practical Innovations, Open Solutions*, *7*, 106784–106792.

Topol, E. (2019). Deep Medicine: How Artificial Intelligence Can Make Health-care Human Again. *BasicBooks*. Topol discusses the promise of AI in healthcare, focusing on how these technologies can augment the relationship between doctors and patients and improve healthcare outcomes.

KEY TERMS AND DEFINITIONS

Artificial Intelligence (AI): This refers to the simulation of human intelligence in machines that act as they would in case the tasks, they perform how humans do – reasoning, learning and problem solving.

Machine Learning (ML): ML is a subset of AI ('Artificial Intelligence') that involves developing algorithms for computers to learn and get better with experience 'without' specific programming.

Deep Learning (DL): It is a machine learning technique, in which neural networks with several layers are used in the learning from large amounts of data in complex healthcare applications, such as image recognition.

Natural Language Processing (NLP): An area of AI that permits machines to comprehend, decode and produce human spoken speech. In healthcare, it's used to analyse clinical notes, medical records, and patient data.

Big Data: In healthcare, there is an unending volume of structured and unstructured data produced from patient records, medical images, and genetic data that must be analysed with advanced analytic tools.

Predictive Analytics: Statistical algorithms and machine learning to predict or identify the future likelihood of outcomes from past data. It can predict patient condition or outbreak, in healthcare.

Computer Vision: The part of AI that enables machines to understand and process images. It is used in the type of diagnostic imaging such as Xrays and MRIs to find out abnormalities in the health care.

Robotic Surgery: Robots that are used in surgical techniques which are meant to rise to the level of precision, control and minimally invasive with the AMSS help to improve surgical results.

Clinical Decision Support Systems (CDSS): Some AI powered tools that offer healthcare professionals with insights, recommendations for diagnosis, treatment options and care for patients.

Personalized Medicine: AI and genomics are being used to exploit the way medical treatment can be more precisely tailored for the individual characteristics of every patient, from their genetic makeup and lifestyle factors.

Chapter 10
Digital Health:
Navigating Digital Transformation and Digital Stress

Priyanka Gupta
https://orcid.org/0009-0006-5341-8314
Graphic Era University, India

Manu Sharma
Graphic Era University, India

Sudhanshu Joshi
https://orcid.org/0000-0003-4748-5001
Doon University, India

ABSTRACT

This chapter will discuss the topic of Digital Health, Digital Stress and Digital Transformation focusing on how digital tools and platforms are employed to enhance the employee's wellness and productivity. The application of Digital Health solutions helps to a great extent to remove barriers that prevent employees from being healthy and actively involved in the discussion of the problem since the overload of the working capacities of not only employees but also managers is observed nowadays, the issue of burnout and stress, fatigue coming from an insufficient number of digital breaks and digital exhaustion. The chapter will explain how organizations can leverage digital solutions to support initiatives connected with Sustainable Development Goals 3 (Good Health and Wellbeing) and Sustainable Development Goals 8 (Decent Work and Economic Growth) by decreasing the load created by constant connectivity and improving work environments.

DOI: 10.4018/979-8-3373-5087-5.ch010

INTRODUCTION

The era of Digital Transformation has brought drastic changes in very sector starting from the healthcare sector and the workspace. With the growing use of digital technologies in organizations, Digital Health has emerged as an important approach to maintaining and enhancing the health of workforce and organizational readiness. In its simplest sense, Digital Health involves the utilization of internet-based technology solutions, applications, and systems with respect to health, illness, and well-being. It includes tele-health, wearable health technologies, m-health, AI-based health applications, wellness programmes etc. (Torous et al., 2020). Today's workplace presents Digital Health solutions with a two-fold role. First, it provides organisations with a chance to prevent disorders and maladies among employees and, in doing so, lower their sick-days rates and create healthier organisational climates. Second, they exist to challenge a phenomenon popularly known as digital stress, which is fast becoming thorny in society. Digital stress is becoming a prevalent issue due to digital dependency; communication overload and high pressure performing digital tasks in workplaces (Warren et al., 2021).

The placement of Digital Health within a sustainable concept is relevant to numerous global goals like the SDGs. Digital Health has a central responsibility in the achievement of the SDG 3 (Good Health and Well-being) in terms of health enhancing resources. Furthermore, its links with SDG 8 (Decent Work and Economic Growth) underscore the need for work that is healthy and safe for employees and make use of advanced technologies to sustain excellence in performance of tasks without unnecessary harm to employees.

The current digital health ecosystem is built on three pillars: they are accessibility, personalised content and real time information. For example, smartwatches and fitness bracelet have become ubiquitous; these gadgets are adopted in wellness programs at the workplace. These devices keep track of aspects such as pulse rate, stress, sleep quality and activity level and therefore can track and modify workforce health in real-time, to the benefit of both the employee and employer. Information of this nature when incorporated into health organization management processes can inform us how to foster health supportive workplace schedules (Borycki et al., 2021). Moreover, telemedicine platforms allow the employees to arrange for an appointment and receive health services without having to visit the healthcare facility physically. This aspect is especially relevant in view of the recent challenges such as the COVID-19 pandemic, remote health services became a source of supply for millions of workers throughout the world (Ye, 2020). Digital Health platforms also contain possibilities for mental health support that includes online counselling, artificial intelligence-based mental health check, and a stress and anxiety-reducing application.

Telemedicine has been the key element of Digital Health since the beginning of its usage in the 1990s and has become modern platforms for overall health control (Bates et al., 2018). Telemedicine pioneer applications form the foundation for the sophisticated well-being solutions of the present-day, including well-being trackers that have become important for well-being management at work. The theory of Technostress, is used to address the idea of stress owing to overdependence on digital technologies among working people. The four frames of this work are useful in analysing the negative side of using devices that track employee behaviour and health (Tarafdar et al., 2020). Available research shows that works perk usage improves employee engagement and work output, especially when wellness platforms are digital (Chen et al., 2023). However, it is not entirely clear how to protect workers' privacy while at the same time monitoring them almost constantly, which creates the need for a more sophisticated approach to digital health interventions in workplaces.

To sum, the analysed phenomenon of Digital Health as a part of the digital transformation framework provides a effective solution to many contemporary workplace issues. Through increased use of advanced technological initiatives, organizations will enhance healthy and productive practices with an aim at promoting sustainability standards that would enhance long term performance of the organization.

Linkage Between Digital Health and Employee Well-being

The concept of utilization of employee well-being as a part of organizational development strategy is becoming popular. Various studies have confirmed a positive relationship between commitment and performance, job satisfaction and turnover levels in organizations. However, the change of work processes towards digital work processes is not without its problems, and one of these problems is digital stress. Since employees are struggling to overcome the challenges that have emerged due to remote working and constant connection, and hence the rise in the use of social media and other digital interfaces their mental and physical health will be at risk. Digital Health presents one as a way of assisting employees in addressing such issues through devices that they can use in tracking their health and or well-being. Wellness technologies combine into operations of work place in a way that enhances wellness of all the employee. For instance, Google, IBM, or Microsoft have introduced rich HR solutions that include powerful Digital Health platforms that measure employees' health vital signs and suggest wellness regimes (Borycki et al, 2021).

These platforms are intended for the development of the physical and mental health of users. From tracking physical activities, setting goal and schedules for the fitness activities, providing direction on proper diet, users are able to promote and sustain their physical health. Mental health is also considered through applications that inquire on the user's stress levels, providing directions on how to handle stress and offering online counselling services. Such solutions are especially helpful to alleviate negative impacts of boomerang and fatigue, two of the most significant outcomes of digital overload. Further, the above information services enable organisational employees be more proactive about their health; they are provided with resources for detecting when they are at the highest risk for burnout. So there is a connection between Digital Health and the well-being of employees not only is it about offering technology but it is also about creating an organizational climate of health. Health is an important psychosocial climate where satisfied, engaged and motivated employees occur where their health is cherished. This new culture shift is particularly major as organizations seek to woo and secure quality talent in highly competitive online space.

Also, employee mental health is gradually gaining attention in the workplace across the globe. According to the WHO, organizations easily get back $4 for every $1 spent on mental health interventions, based on a recent study (WHO, 2022). Digital Health solutions play a crucial role in delivering this support by providing cost and access efficient approaches to mental health management. For example, we have apps such as Calm and Head Space which offer consciousness practice and stress operative measures that the employees can utilize at their convenience since it is an application.

Thus, Digital Health acts as a bridge between digital transformation and employee well-being, offering a comprehensive solution to the challenges of digital stress and promoting a healthier, more sustainable workforce.

Significance of SDGs in Shaping Digital Health Initiatives

The United Nations put in place the Sustainable Development Goals (SDGs) in 2015 to act as a set of goals to transform the world for the better. From 17 of them, two goals, which are SDG 3 and SDG 8 for good health and well-being and decent work and economic growth correspond to the discussion on Digital Health and digital transformation. These goals focus on health, safety, and wellbeing of workers and propose to seek sufficient and quality new ideas to manage health and digital safety at work (United Nations, 2022). Since the focus of these digital health projects is on basic, adaptable solutions for health issues that need little effort and cost and can be successfully integrated into workplace wellness programs, they may be directly linked to these SDGs. For example, telediagnosis removes the need for medical facilities in underserved areas and the associated costs. Additionally, advancements in AI can help with early disease identification, management optimisation, and health outcomes, which reduces the need for healthcare (Bates et al., 2018). In addition, and in the light of the previous arguments, Digital Health translated into tools can also support the achievement of SDG 8 since healthier workers facilitate healthy work force for steady and sustainable economic improvement. Which results show that healthy workforce means lower rates of sickness absence, increased work output, and higher level of work involvement. Therefore, through development of digital health solutions, organizations promote work environment wellbeing hence enhancing long term economic stability.

Therefore, we draw the conclusion that the SDGs are essential for defining Digital Health activities. The world will be a little better place to live based on the idea of sustainable development if the specified DH strategies are integrated with these global goals. Employees will also be well-cared for.

UNDERSTANDING DIGITAL STRESS

Digital stress on the other hand refers to the cognitive, emotional and the physiological weary that is occasioned by constant engagement with digital technologies. In today's social media era, employees work under the pressure of coverage or responding to messages even after the normal working hours. The continual use of smart gadgets with internet connectivity including smart phones, tablets, laptops and other technologies makes personal and working life interface be overlapping hence predisposing individuals to stress. This condition has been dubbed as 'technostress' by most researchers.

Technostress is realized as information overload, task interleaving, perpetual contact, and performance demands. Staffs are required to sort, filter, analyse, and negotiate massive amounts of data while coordinating with different channels and adopting new technologies that have been found to contribute to increased stress, anxiety, and eventually burning out (Tarafdar et al., 2020).

Technological stress is in part characterized by a concern of missing updates, dos or communiques. This entices employees to stay in a state of readiness, often even beyond their shift. The constant pressure to reply instantly and work in two or three separate projects simultaneously creates situations when employees become tired and overwhelmed by a tremendous amount of information coming to them through the channels of digital workplace (Bondanini et al., 2020).

Thirdly, due to the fast-changing technology in the workplace, the employees must 'update' their skills often and there is a sense of technological obsolescence, where the employee feels he/ she lacks the skills required to perform the job; (Brooks, et al., 2017). Every such pressure raises tension and potentially harms the psychological and physiological well-being of individuals.

Causes and Implications of Digital Stress

The primary causes of digital stress in the workplace include as shown in Figure 1:

Figure 1. Causes and Implications of Digital Stress

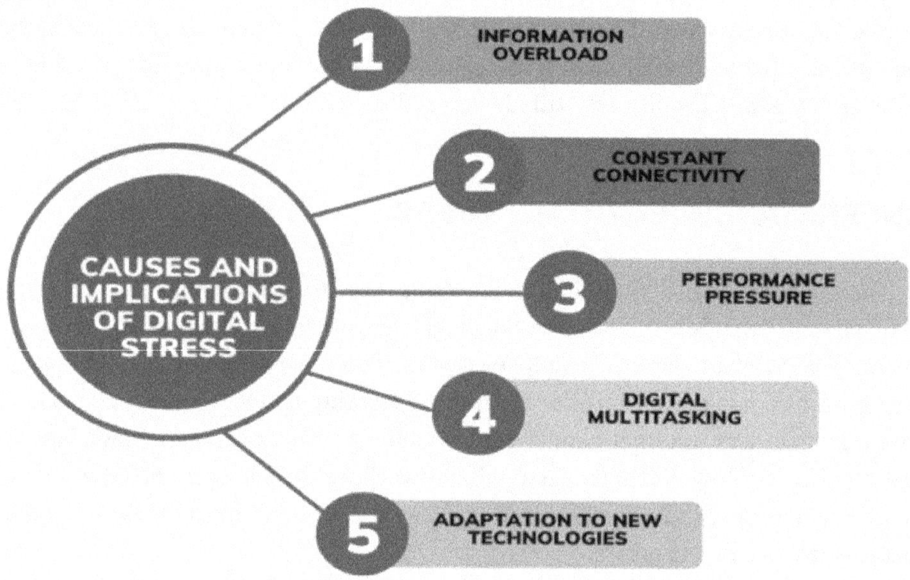

1. **Information Overload**: The vast amount of digital information employees need to process daily contributes significantly to stress. Emails, instant messages, project management platforms, and other forms of communication create a constant stream of information, which can be overwhelming (Li et al., 2022)
2. **Constant Connectivity**: With smartphones and laptops keeping employees connected at all times, the boundary between work and personal life becomes blurred. Employees often feel compelled to stay connected even during off-hours, weekends, or vacations, preventing them from fully detaching from work (Kim et al., 2022)
3. **Performance Pressure**: The increasing dependence on digital tools for performance tracking and evaluation puts additional pressure on employees to meet digitally-driven expectations. This creates stress, especially when employees feel they are under constant surveillance (Bourlakis et al., 2023)

4. **Digital Multitasking**: Employees often need to juggle multiple digital platforms and applications at once. Switching between tasks responding to emails, attending virtual meetings, managing spreadsheets can diminish focus and increase the cognitive load (Umair et al., 2023)
5. **Adaptation to New Technologies**: As organizations adopt new technologies to improve efficiency, employees are expected to learn and adapt quickly. This continuous learning curve can be stressful, especially for workers who may be less familiar with digital tools (Torres, 2021)

c. Strategies to Address Digital Stress through Digital Health Solutions

Organizations must also appreciate the effects of digital stress on organizational employees and regard the need for addressing the issue. Several digital health solutions are available to help alleviate stress and promote a healthier work environment as shown in Figure 2:

Figure 2. Strategies for Reducing Digital Stress

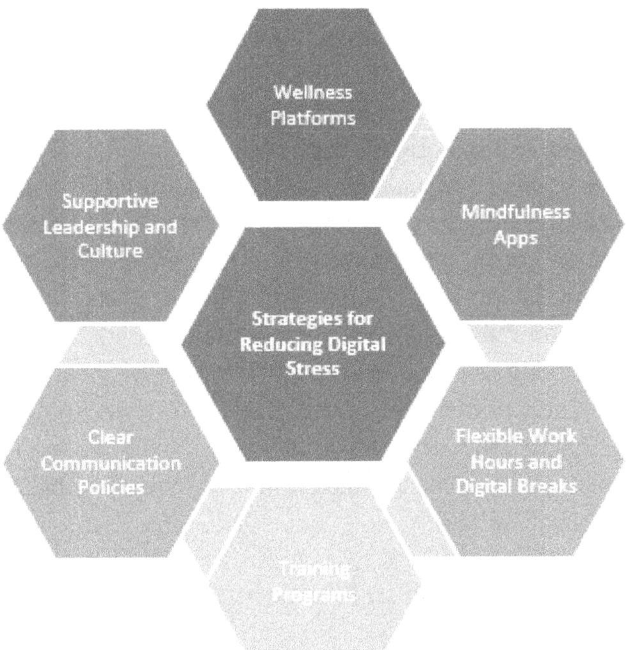

1. **Wellness Platforms:** It means that digital health platforms that track and control stress can share valuable information with employees on their state of health. These platforms usually include wearables that monitor the pulse, sleep and activity of the employees and provide ways to deal with stress before it occurs (Zaid et al., 2024)
2. **Mindfulness Apps:** Applications such as Calm and Headspace have guided meditation and stress management that an employer can allow his employees during their break time. Combining these tools into wellness programs enables employees to deal with anxiety and digital exhaustion (Ioannou et al., 2024)
3. **Flexible Work Hours and Digital Breaks:** Suspending computer work and using slot machines are also effective ways of lowering stress, as is the promotion of a flexible working hour regime. Digital breaks can be a great employee benefit to keep people away from the screens and thus avoid some degree of daily stress (Pansini et al., 2023).
4. **Training Programs:** Such training as digital literacy may help the employees to be more self-assured and not to feel stressed and overwhelmed with new opportunities of the work with new technologies. Organisation of stress-reducing seminars aimed at increasing the target audience's attention to mindfulness, time and working performance organization, and employing other essential methods of coping with stress (Tiwari et al., 2021).
5. **Clear Communication Policies:** Employers demand that there should be measurable and tangible communication policies, for instance, handling of emails sent during the night or over the weekend. Limitation between work related time and personal time makes the employees to feel that they are not compelled to always be connected to work (Zainun et al., 2020)
6. **Supportive Leadership and Culture:** Work-related digital stress can be greatly minimised in situations where an organisation's management supports work-life balance and practices healthy use of gadgets and devices. employees have an opportunity to raise awareness of their well-being to support wellness incentives, and offer employees the chance to be rewarded for healthy habits in the digital workplace (Al et al.,2024)

The Role of Digital Health in Reducing Digital Stress

Digital health solutions consist of numerous instruments aimed to help decrease digital stress and improve the conditions at work. With the increased use of information technology systems in organizations, there is growing concern for an employee's health and fitness. All these tools are designed to reduce the pressure resulting from the use of technology products at the workplace and manage stress at the same time as shown in figure 3:

Figure 3. depicts Digital Tools Platforms Supporting Healthier Work Environments

1. **Wellness Monitoring Platforms**: New generation wellness programs come with instantaneous updates on their employees' health. These platforms are typically connected with the smartwatches and the fitness trackers that track movement, pulse rate and sleeping habits. From this data, an employee is able to realize early signals of pressure or weariness and do something to enhance general health. For example, Apple's Health application or Fitbit gadgets inform users about their physical and stress activity together with suggestions regarding physical exercise and breaks (Zaid et al., 2024)
2. **Stress Management Applications**: Calm or Headspace are example of apps that can be used in order to help deal with stress by providing users with meditations, breathing techniques and wellness checks. These tools can be run from any mobile device which enables employees to get immediate assistance to help them manage their stress and get back on with their work during the work period. Such tools have to be introduced in the corporate wellness plans as they can help employees to step back using the resources in case of stressful circumstances (Chen et al., 2019)

3. **Virtual Ergonomic Assessments**: Employers are providing distances ergonomic evaluations through using digital health platforms. As with the increase to employees' working from home, incorrect and poorly designed workstation arrangements cause physical stress and even elevate the stress levels of workers (Souchet et al., 2023)
4. **AI-Powered Virtual Health:** Machine learning has provided Virtual Health Assistants which can provide health advice uniquely for an individual. These digital assistants use personal information including biometric data, activity history, and reported emotional status—and offer tangible suggestions. This enables resource control especially concerning an employee's health for instance; changes of shifts, taking a break, or practicing a relaxing activity (Issa et al., 2024).

Real-Time Monitoring and Personalized Wellness Programs

Digital health solutions are a set of tools that should be used to reduce digital stress and enhance working environments. With the advancement in the information technology system in organizations, the Main concern for an employee becomes his next check-up. All the tools are aimed at controlling the pressure arising from the use of technology products in the workplace and stress at that too as shown in Figure 4.

Figure 4. shows tools for Real-Time Monitoring and Personalized Wellness Programs

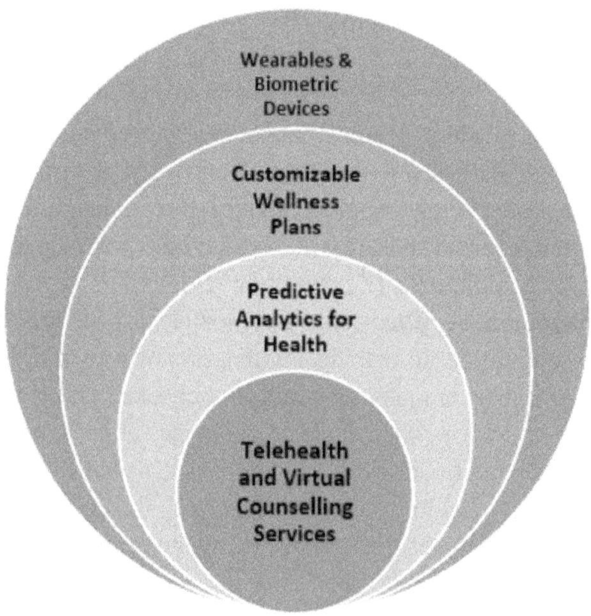

1. **Wearables and Biometric Devices:** Products like smartwatches, heart rate monitor gadgets, and other biometrics recall the health metrics at any given time. These devices provide information regarding one's stressed state, as the indexes that can point to stress include increased pulse, sleep disturbances, and changes in movement. For instance, the WHOOP strap tracks an individual's recovery, sleep, and physical stress to determine the best work schedule an individual should have (Fabbrizio et al., 2023)
2. **Customizable Wellness Plans:** As a result, wellness programs when properly adequately provided, can help cut back stress due to improved health habits among employees. Many companies may use the data gathered from wearables and apps and develop programmes suited to tackling issues such as stress, customer fitness, or better diets. Consumer-level solutions promote employee participation in behaviours that address issues such as stress, turnover, and technology burnout (Fabbrizio et al., 2023)
3. **Predictive Analytics for Health**: Optimization and tracking using, artificial intelligence and analytics help digital health to predict and pre-empt stress-related health complications. Because these platforms can learn from employee interactions and health data, they are able to anticipate when an employee is flammable or stressed and then act. For instance, if an employee stays more on the chair or has poor sleep patterns the system can tell this is a signal for break or remind him/her to relax before stress builds up (Shukla et al., 2023).
4. **Telehealth and Virtual Counselling Services**: Since there is a gradual shift towards avatar telemedicine, employees can receive tele-advice on counselling and consultations from their homes. It generates these services that can enable employees deal with such issues which include anxiety, depression, and chronic stress without physically visiting. Availability of mental health professionals through its apps ensures that the employees gain access to services promptly, hence cutting the influence of clients' stress on their performance (Kaaria et al., 2023).

Digital Transformation and Its Impact on Employee Well-Being

a. **Digital Transformation in the Workplace:** Digital transformation is about embracing digital technologies across an enterprise, both fundamentally changing how an enterprise works and provides value to its people and clients. This shift is not only happening to the activities of the organizations and their processes but is also deeply shaping the common experience of work and working, for better and for worse, for the wellbeing of employees.

1. **Adapting to New Technologies**: The challenge with digital transformation is that organisations are experiencing the fast pace of new technology adoption, such as artificial intelligence, cloud services, and automation tools. Though these advancements may integrate sophistication in performance outcomes, they impose on the employee a relentless test of change. This means that the constant training pressures can generate higher cognitive load, and stress especially among the workforce that might find it difficult to conform to the technological advancement (Ragu et al., 2021).
2. **Remote Work and Digital Connectivity**: Mobile technology advancement led to more adoption of remote work because of advancement in technology. By having access to Teams, Zoom, and Slack employees are empowered to work from anywhere which has boosted flexibility. Nonetheless, permanent connectivity can warp the boundaries between working and non-working hours, prompting companies with "always on" initiatives that keep employees engaged economy-wide and make them constantly available. This leads to engagement in unhealthy practices that cause burn out and reduces organizational satisfaction on the job (Rudolph et al., 2021).
3. **Automation and Job Redesign**: The type of alteration is the shift in the workload of the employees due to the increase in the incidents of automation where some of the tasks can be completely handled by the automated systems while the others need the authority and inventiveness of the employees. They found that this shift can cause job insecurity and job insecurity contributes to workplace stress. This topic is significant as concerns about probable job loss make anxiety over future employment opportunities a problem for employees' mental health (Bhattacharyya S., 2024).
4. **Employee Empowerment Through Data**: That is why digital transformation is also an opportunity to enhance well-being. Today's information technologies enable the processing of employee information and provide opportunities to help them improve their well-being. They also receive tools for self-diagnosis, stress management applications, or performance evaluation indicating their health condition at a workplace. If properly applied, these tools help employees to assume greater personal responsibility for the state of their health and options to manage work demands (Martínez-Peláez., 2023).

b. **Digital Transformation and Employee Burnout:** With digital transformation comes many advantages such as getting more done and being more flexible but one downside is that it increases employee burnout. Therefore, burnout as a condition resulting from uncompensated chronic workplace stress has become rife in the current digital society. This can cause burnout, which is characterized by such things as information overload, constant multitasking, and stepped-up pace as shown in figure 5:

Figure 5. Causes for Employee Burnout

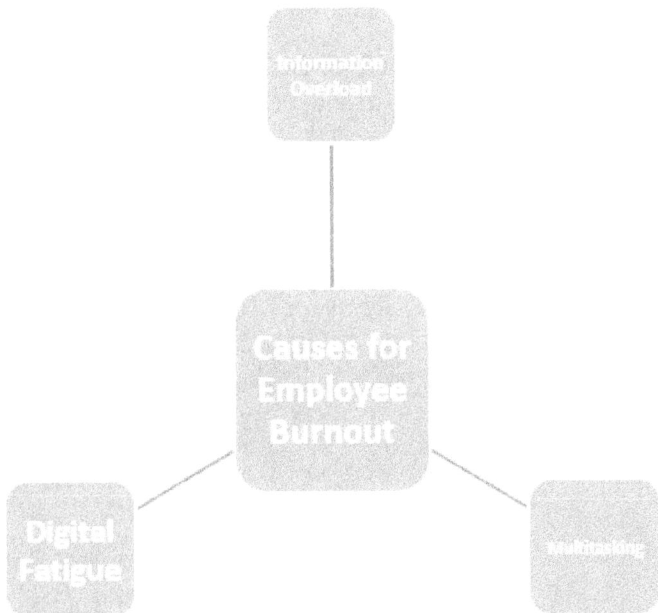

1. **Information Overload**: The mass content that employees filter within their working day, be it emails, messages within teaming platforms, can overload their working memories. Giving voice to the process, it is stated that when employees are urged to attend the incoming stream of information, it becomes stressing and inhibits the potential for engaging in substantial work (Kim et al., 2024)
2. **Multitasking**: The nature of work in the digital age requires the employees to switch between different platforms continually. Juggling between different tasks and managing several forms of digital technology at the same time can be proved to be time-wasting and can cause considerable negative impact on productivity over time. Multitasking can also bring about stress since the people working feel like they are under time pressure (Chen et al., 2023)

3. **Digital Fatigue**: Digital fatigue is caused by consistent exposure to screen without taking a break. Both will and skill are reliant on the motility of the body and the ability to use mental capacity for other things besides applying constant focus, which results in discomfort, for example in the form of constantly strained eyes or a headache, as well as in emotional fatigue. This fatigue is often enhanced by the ability that we are supposed to be connected and available for interaction during work hours (Costin et al., 2023)

c. Balancing Technology Use for Well-Being

It is important for organizations to adopt efforts that can mid modulate effects of digital transformation to employees. This encompasses in devising policies and activities on the use of the gadgets and the promotion of enhance mental health as indicated in figure 6.

Figure 6. Strategies for Balancing Technology Use for Well-Being

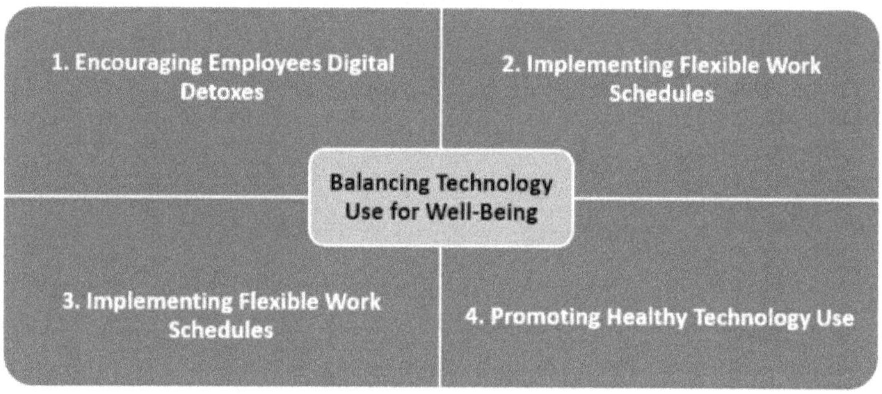

1. **Encouraging Digital Detoxes**: There are cases where companies can force their employees to temporarily get off the tools of work, for some time they get off the device. In return, digital breaks assist the staff to come out from the digital exhaustion they might be facing and energize themselves (Nguyen et al., 2024)
2. **Implementing Flexible Work Schedules**: Some of the ways employees can be protected from constant connectivity stress include giving them the chance to self-schedule their working time. They also mean allow employees to plan their own hours and to take time off if they want to in order to balance work and family responsibilities (Ajayi et al., 2024)

3. **Providing Mental Health Resources**: Companies ought to offer mental health support, make available a list of digital health solutions which include stress management, counselling services and mindfulness apps. These resources assist employees to avoid or reduce often experienced adverse effects of digital transformation on their health (Burton et al., 2023)
4. **Promoting Healthy Technology Use:** Technology is critical in day-to-day activities hence organizations should seek to empower their users through healthier use of it by educating employees about healthy technological use. This encompasses policies regarding use of technology, reducing the tone of notifications, and employment use of time. Such increased awareness of healthy technology utilisation can then be used to fight bad technology habits prevalent today that harms the overall well-being of organisations (Gennari et al., 2023).

LINKING DIGITAL HEALTH AND SUSTAINABLE DEVELOPMENT GOALS (SDGS)

The below titles will examine the link between 2030SDGs and digital health as:

Contribution of Digital Health to SDG 3 (Good Health and Well-being)

1. **Prevention and Early Detection**: Digital health platforms have also contributed significantly to preventive healthcare. Smartwatches and fitness bracelets track and display vital statistics continuously; they notify users of abnormalities that may herald potential health problems of cardiac woes, high blood pressure, or diabetes. That is, through the tracking of organizational employees' physical well-being, these technologies maintain the optimism of proactive health in organizations. Apart from stabilizing large-scale epidemics, it also saves on employee days off and expenses on medical treatment for the employer.
2. **Personalized Health Interventions**: Another clear benefit of digital health technologies is that they can deliver personalised interventions. Consultants using artificial intelligence (AI) and big data, can help offer employees health interventions based on their needs: stress reduction, better sleep, or dealing with chronic diseases. These can include individual workout routines right up to specialized mental health care programs designed to enhance employee health and wellbeing, and ward off burnout or chronic stress.

The Role of Digital Health in Achieving SDG 8 (Decent Work and Economic Growth)

Digital health also contributes significantly in the provision of SDG 8 (Decent Work and Economic Growth) due to improved health breeding productivity at workplaces. In the employees' struggle with daily conflicts resulting from hyper connexion and always on work culture, DH solutions will improve levels of job satisfaction and reduce negative impact of digital stress. As shown in Figure 7:

Figure 7. Role of Digital Health in Achieving SDG 8

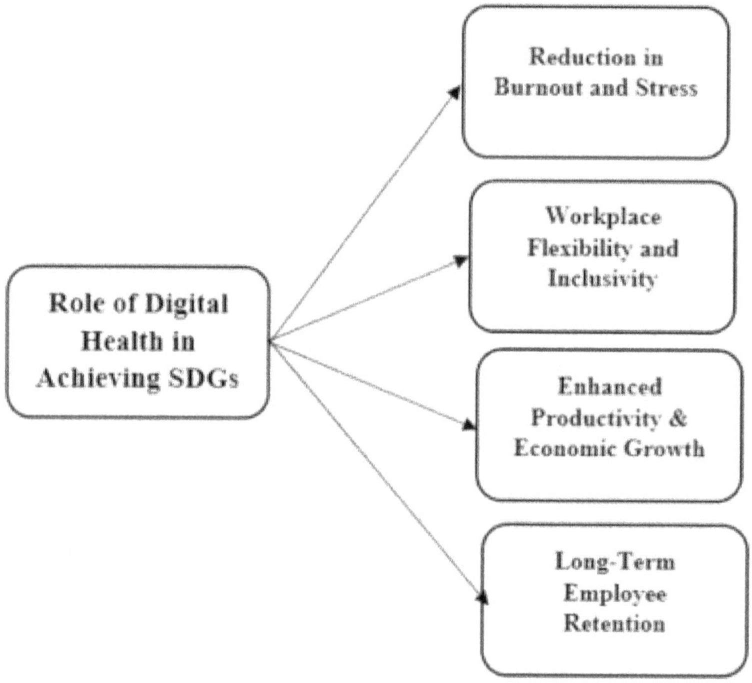

1. **Reduction in Burnout and Stress**: There is a growing use of technology in wellness checks for workers and when stress starts getting to the employee health, then they are provided with a digital health workplace platform for early intervention before it results in burnout. Applications like wellness apps based on artificial intelligence and correcting programs can lead employee to learn stress coping strategies in their company and enhance their health and the corporation's performance (Sun et al., 2023)

2. **Workplace Flexibility and Inclusivity**: Specifically, digital health solutions can flexibly work under certain conditions favourable for the improvement of the employee's well-being. For example, telehealth can be used to access medical consultations avoiding staff to lose working days and go to see doctors. Web-based supportive health and wellness programs that employees can join anytime and anywhere can also be arranged to ensure workplace inclusiveness for better organizational compliance with the decent work agenda of SDG 8 (Kniffin et al., 2021).
3. **Enhanced Productivity and Economic Growth**: Health care organisations that procure or implement digital health technologies are likely to experience enhanced workforce productivity. Organizational performance tends to be high when employees are healthy physically and mentally since they will work efficiently. In addition, by decreasing costs of health sector and boosting productivity, the solutions are contributing to long term economic development. In essence, employees provided with applicable instruments that would help them effectively manage own health needs are in a better position to play the economic role of the company (Egala et al., 2024)
4. **Long-Term Employee Retention**: Technology is also used in the various digital health activities for the improvement of employee retention. Health concerns and work-life conflict can be needed to brought into light at companies' initiatives through technological solutions, thus resulting to form a healthy and satisfied employees primarily for the organisations. This not only decreases turnover rates but also contributes to the attraction of new employees because currently the focus of the potential employees is on whether their potential employer gives them an opportunity to have well-being programs (Paul et al., 2024)

Addressing SDG 10 (Reduced Inequalities) through Equitable Access to Digital Health Resources

Digital health can also help to address in equalities in the workplace as all personnel, irrespective of their status or place of work, origin can have access to important necessities in health care. By distributing digital health tools fairly organizations can ensure health equality and hence; achieve SDG 10 as shown in figure 8:

Figure 8. Addressing SDG 10 (Reduced Inequalities) through Equitable Access to Digital Health Resources

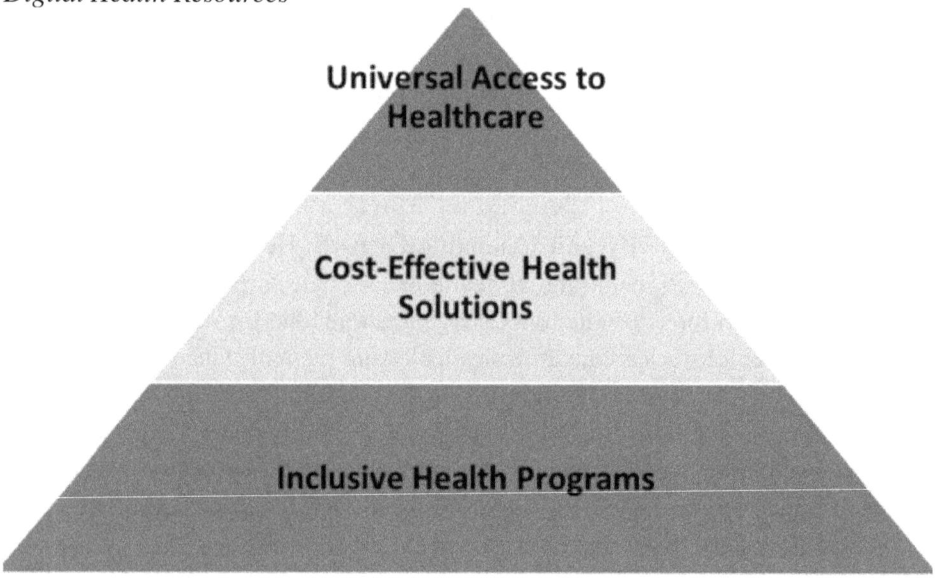

1. **Universal Access to Healthcare**: Telemedicine and mHealth apps tend to offer the similarities in the healthcare conditions for all the employees who work in urban and remote areas. This is especially so where the organization has a workforce which is spread across different geographical regions. Employers' corporate health plans work positively towards the elimination of health disparities by offering equal opportunity to access quality health care regardless of employee's location.
2. **Cost-Effective Health Solutions**: Digital health technologies are cheaper to implement than the typical traditional models of delivery of health care and thus offer health services to employees who come from the low-income earning cadres. Wearable gadgets, online doctor's appointments, and mobile health applications are cheaper than face-to-face consultations and introduce reduced cost of getting a medical attendance.
3. **Inclusive Health Programs**: Through leveraging on digital health platforms, organizations can develop a more diverse heath program of the workforce. For example, workers who had sustained a disability or chronic health condition can include supplemental digital wellness applications that help them to track his or her overall health and to execute chronic disease self-management.

II. **Future of Digital Health and Workplace Well-being**

It is now evident that digital health will continue to evolve even faster and provide future advancements to the workplace. There expectations are all set to enhance the tenets of not only the employees but also the sustainability and effectiveness of organizations. The following presents major digital health trends that will shape the future of the workplace well-being and how they can help in the creation of the sustainable workplace.

Trends in Digital Health Solutions

1. **Advanced AI-Driven Wellness Platforms**: In the future, more use of digital health within workplaces will involve higher forms of artificial intelligence that aims at providing unique health enhancement to the employees. Such platforms will gather information from various sources including wearable gadgets, mobile applications and work rhythms of employees regarding recommended health interventions. Again, AI generated will also not only track the physical state but also the mental state of the users, these include features like CBT, Mindfulness, and AI assisted Counselling (Zaid et al., 2024)
2. **Virtual Reality (VR) for Stress Management and Wellness**: Virtual reality is gaining traction as an immersive tool for workplace wellness. It will be possible to use VR platforms in the near future to organise virtual reality environments focusing on relaxation, meditation, cognitive work, and fighting stress. Employees could use virtual breaks by going to some virtual spaces as beaches or forests to decrease digital exhaustion. VR can also be applied to team-training and wellness sessions, optimizing the effectivity of this interpersonal training for better mental health improvement (Singh et al., 2024).
3. **Predictive Health Analytics for Early Intervention**: Predictive analytics will transform the way organisations manage and prevent employee health by providing insights into potentially serious risks that have not yet become apparent. Machine learning will enable employers to identify concerns, such as burnout, chronic stress, or physical illnesses, before they arise by analyzing wearables, biometric screenings, and various other digital health interfaces. Such observations lead to early conditions where an organization can influence an employee's behavior through advice on altering lifestyles, adjusting on daily tasks, or seeking counselling (Dikshit et al., 2024).
4. **Telemedicine and Remote Health Monitoring**: The significance of a telemedicine approach and the use of remote health management devices and solutions. Designed for remote interactions, the ability of telemedicine services to be integrated with workplace wellness programming should expand as companies maintain more work-from-home or hybrid schedules (Fabbrizio et al., 2023).

The Future of Work and Health in Industry 5.0

Industry 5.0 emphasizes a human-centric approach to the future of work, where the collaboration between humans and advanced technologies, such as artificial intelligence and robotics, is prioritized. Unlike Industry 4.0, which focused heavily on automation, Industry 5.0 seeks to balance efficiency with human creativity and well-being. This shift promotes environments where humans and machines co-create, allowing workers to focus on tasks requiring emotional intelligence and innovation. In terms of health, Industry 5.0 integrates digital health solutions to support workers' mental and physical well-being, offering real-time monitoring and personalized health interventions. These advancements reduce workplace stress, improve job satisfaction, and create inclusive workplaces that cater to employees with diverse health needs, ensuring both productivity and holistic well-being as shown in Figure 9

Figure 9. Future of Work and Health in Industry 5.0

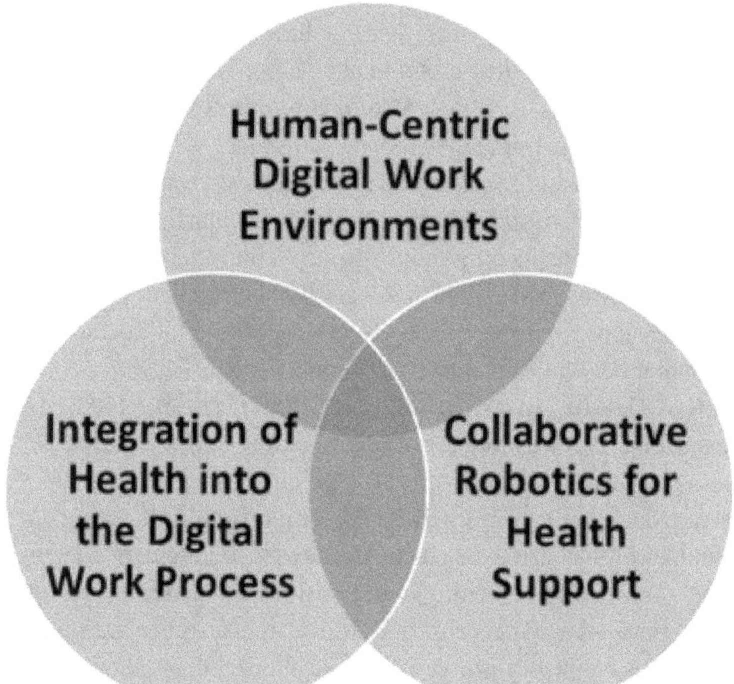

1. **Human-Centric Digital Work Environments**: Industry 5.0 corresponds to the human-oriented intelligent and human-centered smart workspace and human creativity. In contrast to Industry 4.0, which lays considerable stress on automation, Industry 5.0 assumes more emphasis on the interaction between human and technology to produce better output and quality of human life. In the context of digital health, this means that computers will allow employees to optimize their creative abilities for the execution of their job without the disadvantageous impacts of this technology(Zhang et al., 2023).
2. **Integration of Health into the Digital Work Process**: In Industry 5.0, health and well-being would be hence integrated in the design of innovative digital work processes. While before, health and wellness can obviously be seen as side projects, organizations will integrate health considerations into their operations (Wang et al., 2024).
3. **Collaborative Robotics (Cobots) for Health Support**: Cobots will have huge potential on boosting workplace health in the future. Cobots will help employees with strenuous tasks such that fatigue, strain, and general discomfort are avoided. In industries like automotive, where workers are prone to working under conditions within a manufacturing line, co-bots offer reprieve from stress and physical exhaustion due to repetitive and sometimes dangerous jobs (Babalola et al., 2024).

Long-Term Impacts of Digital Health on Employee Sustainability

1. **Sustainable Employee Engagement**: Long-term engagement will be achieved by applying DH Technologies as they act to meet both the physical and mental fitness of the organizational employee population. Happy workers will not only come to work healthy and ready to work, they will not be frequently ill which can often lead to absenteeism thereby giving satisfactory performance hence cutting on costs that come with constantly training and recruiting new employees (Mer et al., 2023)
2. **Reduction in Healthcare Costs**: The utilization of identified digital health tools will help to containing organizational healthcare cost in the future. Supported care through real-time checks and monitoring, efficient alarming or early intercessions by an AI, and remote consultations will reduce the costs of expensive face-to-face treatments or lengthy sick leaves. These technologies will empower employees to take proactive care of their health and keep the costs to organizations and the overall healthcare dollar down (Borges et al., 2023).

3. **Workforce Flexibility and Inclusivity**: Digital health technologies will ensure workplace adaptability to the health of their workers by embracing the solution of diversified health essentials. for example, in the remote health solutions will provide other employees with chronic diseases or with disabilities the opportunity to work remotely while being provided with required health care. This work flexibility will help organizations to hire people from a wider bench and to come up with workplace policies that are more compliant that fully support people with diverse health experiences at the workplace. When digital health is implemented widely, organizations shall be challenged basic ethical questions of the health sector concerning privacy, security, and the extent to which can be left to technology (Sutton et al., 2023).
4. **Ethical Considerations in Digital Health:** The use of technology is bound to grow in the health sector, and hence there is the need for ethicists to consider on matters touching on privacy concerns regarding the uses of technology, the security of information, and the extent to which technology could be allowed to run without supervision by human beings. Privacy and confidentiality of the employees 'personal health information shall be of outmost concern in order to achieve and maintain employees' trust and to meet the requirements of the privacy legislation (Mumtaz et al., 2023).

DISCUSSION

When more employers vested in their employees' wellbeing and wellness, it is increasingly important to consider the emerging factor of digital health technologies and its requirement for consent. The GDPR also focuses on privacy to employee health data and the procedure for their processing. Employers shall set rigorous data privacy measures and ensure to communicate to the employees, the use and protection of their health data. However, there are still concerns on the dilemma between ongoing monitoring and privacy, which requires a more elaborate way toward the integration of digital health to workplaces (Mumtaz et al., 2023). More empirical studies are therefore required to evaluate the performance of digital health tools and their positive systemic effect in the long run among employees. Further research must be done with regard to how technological understanding differentially impacts the use of technology-based health products among the employees. It is believed that with understanding of these dimensions, one will be better positioned to understand the effects of digital health in various workplace scenarios. HR managers can also help in facilitating the digital health use by creating proper policies of the usage of such devices or ways of data protection. For instance, they may have opt-in wellness programs in which workers decide how much surveillance of their health they are willing to agree to. Thus, helps organizations motivate people using wellness incentives like a monetary bonus for creating and following a responsible digital health plan (Mer et al., 2023).

Emerging Trends can be examined as below:

1. AI and Predictive Health Analytics: Through infusing advanced analytical capabilities we have been able to incorporate real-time and predictive healthcare solutions in the digital health ecosystem." For example, wearable devices help employees to detect high stress levels and thus take safety measures (Dikshit et al., 2024). It also improves current quality of life and enables organisations to predict potential health risks and introduce favourable conditions.
2. Virtual Reality (VR) for Stress Management: Virtual Reality (VR) can be described as an effective solution for stress and has already been described as a key component in therapeutic interventions. Businesses are beginning to incorporate VR for virtual escapes, with people being able to transport to environment like beaches and forests away from work (Singh et al., 2024).

Strength and Weakness:

3. Comprehensive coverage of SDGs: A remarkable feature of this chapter is that it provides a comprehensive and detailed overview of the conjunction of Digital Health to several Sustainable Development Goals with focus on SGDs 3 (Good Health and Well-being) and 8 (Decent Work and Economic Growth). As such, the chapter frames the noted digital health strategies within the SDG framework, which not only contextualizes digital health, but also enlarges its relevance by presenting implementing these solutions as a societal imperative for those focused on sustainability."
4. Practical Insights into Digital Health Solutions: Several particular digital health tools are described in the chapter, including wellness monitoring platforms, AI-based mental health applications, and other tools, offering practical tips for organizations willing to improve the employees' health. As we demonstrate through specific wellness technologies in this chapter, our aim is to help readers gain the necessary knowledge to understand 'the how' of digital health for specific organizational initiatives.
5. Insightful Integration of technology and Human Centric Wellness: The chapter strikingly captures the fact that digital health solutions can not only address the problems of the body but also of the mind, hence promoting a comprehensive employee health policy. Through presenting tools for mental health support, stress reduction, and monitoring in real time proving that professed workplace

is capable of being a proactive technology to cultivate a healthier and more positive working environment.

Weakness:

6. Need for Greater emphasis on Employee Autonomy: With reference to PO 3, the chapter may be improved by paying more emphasis on this aspect of the balance between health and productivity, and the extent of control that must be given to the employees. The last potential consequence of the collected health metrics is that employees may not be comfortable with digital health solutions when health metrics become linked with performance assessments."
7. Dependence on Technological Infrastructure: One major drawback of deploying digital health solutions is that the process depends on strong technological support. A common issue in many organizations and especially those based in the developing world or those small businesses with restricted funding is the cost of putting in place and sustaining enterprise digital health management tools.
8. Challenges in measuring long term effectiveness: Despite the possibility of collecting data on the employees' state as soon as digital health solutions have been implemented, quantifying their impact on productivity as well as the state of health and culture of the organization in the long run proves to remain a complicated endeavour.

SOLUTIONS AND RECOMMENDATIONS

- Implement comprehensive Digital Health Strategies: Enterprise entities should design and establish versatile digital heath frameworks that include wellness initiatives as strategies in the main business processes. The above strategies should be designed tailored for your organization, presented with the solutions to address employee's health related issues, physical and mental health inclusive. We should extend the usage of wellness and health applications, artificial intelligence, and telemedicine to deliver real-time health information and intervention to alleviate stress and optimize human being's well-being.
- Promote Digital Literacy and Training: Digital readiness is important for assisting the employee in achieving productivity in using digital health products. It means that organizations need to develop training that involves the use of such instruments and sign up the employees for their suitable precautions. This includes showing employees how to effectively separate work and en-

tertainment, how to use available resources on the workplace mental health, and mindfulness in a digital work environment. A higher number of literacy levels correlates with better technology adoption of wellness technologies and minimizing cases of digital fatigue.

- Address Ethical and Privacy concerns: Policy makers and implementers should, therefore, pay special attention to the ethical issues emerging from the use of DH2T. The proper acquirement, storing, and use of the records should not go without regulation to properly address the issue of employees' personal health. Privacy laws such as the GDPR exist, and transparent data management policies to support employee's PHI (Personal Health Information) must be implemented. In addition, code of ethics should be set to prevent the use of artificial intelligence in health-related decisions.
- Leverage Digital Health to support SDGs: Governments and organizations must ideally, globalize their digital health strategies alongside key themes set as follows: In this way, organizations that advocate for using digital services for health enhancement will help to improve the states of employees' mental health and have positive impact on the economy. Ministries of health should offer tax credits, grants or other Public Private Partnerships for organizations to embrace the usage of digital health solutions, especially in industries where human Capital is a major economic asset.

FUTURE DIRECTIONS

1. **Exploring the Long Term-Effects of Digital Health Solutions:** As the advantages of adopting digital health tools are evident in the short-run, future research should seek to establish the long runs effectiveness on the employees' welfare as well as the organization. Further research is needed to analyze the impact that using these tools for years has on employees' satisfaction and productivity as well as on the overall health status. Moreover, basic research on the risks involved, for example, with the excessive use of such applications or stress derived from continuous tracking.
2. **Impact of Digital Health on different Work Environment**: It is worth mentioning that, the impact of using telemedicine services may differ with particular industry or occupation. Future studies should reveal the effects of these technologies on employees and their experiences in the various working models that can be deemed as new normal such as remote, hybrid and face-to-face working. In addition, there remains the question on how digital health serves in high-risk population areas where stress and illness are more often and intense healthcare, manufacturing, construction industries.

3. **Integration of New Technologies in Digital Health:** The integration of the new form of digital health with other research frontiers blockchain in secure health data storage, IoT for wellbeing monitoring and biotechnologies for precision health offers promising areas for future work. More research has to be done on how these technologies can be utilised to enhance digitalised health systems implementation that targets the various needs of employees.
4. **Addressing Legal and Ethical Challenges:** Ethical and legal considerations have been emphasized to meet to inform the development of programs that can adequately address them. That is why ethical and legal questions related to the use of digital health technologies will also change as these technologies develop. The next steps for research have to consider how organizations can address the specific ethical concerns related to AI and health decisions, forecasting, and monitoring. There is a need for legal reforms that will preserve the employee's rights while embracing data utilisation for the enhancement of health by organisations.
5. **Digital Health and Organizational Culture**: Lastly, there is a need to examine how digital health participate change organisational culture and enhance employees' engagement. In what way does the use of digital health tools affect relations in a team? Does it lead to a less stressful work environment and that will helps employees to become understanding towards one another? More research should be conducted in the areas of organisational culture changes brought about by digital health and the managerial impacts of the changes afoot.

CONCLUSION

The intersection of digital health, digital stress, and digital transformation is reshaping the modern workplace, offering both challenges and opportunities for organizations. By leveraging cutting-edge digital health solutions, companies can reduce digital stress, enhance employee well-being, and contribute to broader sustainability goals, such as SDG 3 (Good Health and Well-being) and SDG 8 (Decent Work and Economic Growth). The integration of digital health into the work environment is not only a necessity for improving employee health but also a critical strategy for achieving long-term organizational sustainability in the face of rapid technological change. By analyzing these three concepts in the framework of this chapter, the conclusion helps the reader gain the overall understanding of how Digital Health, Digital Stress, and Digital Transformation influence the contemporary work environment. The need to target employee welfare becomes crucial as organizations adapt to using the technological advancement for their work from Sustainable Development Goals.

Summary of Key Insights

1. Impact of Digital Health on Employee well-being: The Effects of Digital Health on Employees Digital health has come to the forefront as one of the means to improve employee's health amid escalating digital strain. The use of digital health platforms from basic AI wellbeing apps to real-time tracking systems reduces this cognitive and emotional load that connectedness enforces upon employees. As shown in this chapter, CIS wellness programmes, stress techniques, and health forecasts can decrease cyber cynicism and prevent burnout. They are useful in fashioning better and healthier employee and organisational performance.
2. Correlation between Digital Health and Sustainable Development Goals: Digital health solutions are not only are used to improve health outcomes for patients, but also the greater global goals. In detail, this chapter has demonstrated how the use of technologies in promoting health enhances the attainment of the third SDG of Good Health and Well-being by supporting employees with mental health issues as well as promoting preventive healthy behaviours. In addition, the application of the digital health tools contributes to the achievement of SDG 8 (Decent Work and Economic Growth) since, with the help of modern technologies, work conditions have been improved and work environments have become more friendly, effective and sustainable to engage people for long-term.
3. The Role of Emerging Technologies in the workplace: AI technology, virtual workplace, a virtual world, and predictive health analytics have played a highly significant role in the revolution of the future working environment and health. These technologies provide new approaches for keeping track of the state of the employees, stress reduction and inclusiveness of the health concerns into working practices. Because health is integrated into work, these innovations hold the potential to better employees and organizations, and its overarching structure in the digital age.
4. Ethical Considerations and Challenges: The chapter also provided pointers to the ethical issues that go hand in hand with the utilization of the digital health solutions. With an increased amount of health-related data collected from employees' organizations have to face issues about privacy and protection of that data as well as ethical application of predictive analytics. It is important to maintain a sense of how much output is capable of being handled mechanically and how much needs to be overseen by human stakeholders to ensure that digital health technologies are used in appropriate ways and that employees oversee their own health data.

REFERENCES

Ajayi, F. A., & Udeh, C. A. (2024). Combating burnout in the IT Industry: A review of employee well-being initiatives. *International Journal of Applied Research in Social Sciences*, *6*(4), 567–588. DOI: 10.51594/ijarss.v6i4.1010

Al Issa, H. E., & Omar, M. M. S. (2024). Digital innovation drivers in retail banking: The role of leadership, culture, and technostress inhibitors. *The International Journal of Organizational Analysis*, *32*(11), 19–43. DOI: 10.1108/IJOA-08-2023-3905

Babalola, G. T., Gaston, J. M., Trombetta, J., & Tulk Jesso, S. (2024). A systematic review of collaborative robots for nurses: Where are we now, and where is the evidence? *Frontiers in Robotics and AI*, *11*, 1398140. DOI: 10.3389/frobt.2024.1398140 PMID: 38899066

Bates, D. W., Landman, A., & Levine, D. M. (2018). Health apps and health policy: What is needed? *Journal of the American Medical Association*, *320*(19), 1975–1976. DOI: 10.1001/jama.2018.14378 PMID: 30326025

Bhattacharyya, S. S. (2024). Co-working with robotic and automation technologies: Technology anxiety of frontline workers in organisations. *Journal of Science and Technology Policy Management*, *15*(5), 926–947. DOI: 10.1108/JSTPM-05-2022-0087

Bondanini, G., Giorgi, G., Ariza-Montes, A., Vega-Muñoz, A., & Andreucci-Annunziata, P. (2020). Technostress dark side of technology in the workplace: A scientometric analysis. *International Journal of Environmental Research and Public Health*, *17*(21), 8013. DOI: 10.3390/ijerph17218013 PMID: 33143270

Borges do Nascimento, I. J., Abdulazeem, H., Vasanthan, L. T., Martinez, E. Z., Zucoloto, M. L., Østengaard, L., & Novillo-Ortiz, D. (2023). Barriers and facilitators to utilizing digital health technologies by healthcare professionals. *NPJ Digital Medicine*, *6*(1), 161. DOI: 10.1038/s41746-023-00899-4 PMID: 37723240

Borycki, E. M., & Kushniruk, A. W. (2021). The safety of AI in healthcare: Emerging issues and considerations for healthcare. In *Multiple Perspectives on Artificial Intelligence in Healthcare: Opportunities and Challenges* (pp. 13–22). Springer International Publishing. DOI: 10.1007/978-3-030-67303-1_2

Bourlakis, M., Nisar, T. M., & Prabhakar, G. (2023). How technostress may affect employee performance in educational work environments. *Technological Forecasting and Social Change*, *193*, 122674. DOI: 10.1016/j.techfore.2023.122674

Brooks, S., & Califf, C. (2017). Social media-induced technostress: Its impact on the job performance of it professionals and the moderating role of job characteristics. *Computer Networks, 114*, 143–153. DOI: 10.1016/j.comnet.2016.08.020

Burton, A., McKinlay, A., Aughterson, H., & Fancourt, D. (2023). Impact of the COVID-19 pandemic on the mental health and well-being of adults with mental health conditions in the UK: A qualitative interview study. *Journal of Mental Health (Abingdon, England), 32*(6), 1040–1047. DOI: 10.1080/09638237.2021.1952953 PMID: 34323635

Chen, C., Chipao, B. T., & Miao, Q. (2023). Work redesign in development perspective: An empirical study of multitasking among civil servants in Malawi. *Australian Journal of Public Administration, 82*(2), 210–227. DOI: 10.1111/1467-8500.12566

Chen, J. V., Tran, A., & Nguyen, T. (2019). Understanding the discontinuance behavior of mobile shoppers as a consequence of technostress: An application of the stress-coping theory. *Computers in Human Behavior, 95*, 83–93. DOI: 10.1016/j.chb.2019.01.022

Costin, A., Roman, A. F., & Balica, R. S. (2023). Remote work burnout, professional job stress, and employee emotional exhaustion during the COVID-19 pandemic. *Frontiers in Psychology, 14*, 1193854. DOI: 10.3389/fpsyg.2023.1193854 PMID: 37325768

Dikshit, S., Grover, Y., Shukla, P., Mishra, A., Sahu, Y., Kumar, C., & Gupta, M. (2024). Empowering Employee Wellness and Building Resilience in Demanding Work Settings Through Predictive Analytics. *EAI Endorsed Transactions on Internet of Things, 10.*

Ethawi, Y., AlZubaidi, A., & Maheshwari, A. (2024). Safe Use of Health Information Technology. In Principles of Neonatology (pp. 12-17). Elsevier. DOI: 10.1016/B978-0-323-69415-5.00003-5

Fabbrizio, A., Fucarino, A., Cantoia, M., De Giorgio, A., Garrido, N. D., Iuliano, E., & Macaluso, F. (2023, June). Smart devices for health and wellness applied to tele-exercise: An overview of new trends and technologies such as IoT and AI. []). MDPI]. *Health Care, 11*(12), 1805. PMID: 37372922

Gennari, R., Matera, M., Morra, D., Melonio, A., & Rizvi, M. (2023). Design for social digital well-being with young generations: Engage them and make them reflect. *International Journal of Human-Computer Studies, 173*, 103006. DOI: 10.1016/j.ijhcs.2023.103006

Ioannou, A., Lycett, M., & Marshan, A. (2024). The role of mindfulness in mitigating the negative consequences of technostress. *Information Systems Frontiers*, *26*(2), 523–549. DOI: 10.1007/s10796-021-10239-0 PMID: 35095332

Issa, H., Jaber, J., & Lakkis, H. (2024). Navigating AI unpredictability: Exploring technostress in AI-powered healthcare systems. *Technological Forecasting and Social Change*, *202*, 123311. DOI: 10.1016/j.techfore.2024.123311

Kaaria, A. G., & Mwaruta, S. S. (2023). Mental Health Ingenuities and the Role of Computer Technology on Employees' Mental Health: A Systematic Review. *East African Journal of Health and Science*, *6*(1), 219–231. DOI: 10.37284/eajhs.6.1.1268

Kim, B. J., Jeon, N., Sohn, H., Lee, N., & Kim, M. J. (2024). The impact of corporate social responsibility on employee burnout: The crucial role of work overload. *Corporate Social Responsibility and Environmental Management*, *31*(5), 4345–4360. DOI: 10.1002/csr.2802

Kim, S. Y., Park, H., Kim, H., Kim, J., & Seo, K. (2022). Technostress causes cognitive overload in high-stress people: Eye tracking analysis in a virtual kiosk test. *Information Processing & Management*, *59*(6), 103093. DOI: 10.1016/j.ipm.2022.103093 PMID: 36119755

Kniffin, K. M., Narayanan, J., & Anseel, F. (2021). Advancing workplace flexibility: The role of digital health solutions. *Work, Employment and Society*, *35*(3), 522–538.

Kushniruk, A. W., & Borycki, E. M. (2023, March). Human factors in healthcare IT: Management considerations and trends. []. Sage CA: Los Angeles, CA: SAGE Publications.]. *Healthcare Management Forum*, *36*(2), 72–78. DOI: 10.1177/08404704221139219 PMID: 36847593

Li, C., Borycki, E. M., & Kushniruk, A. W. (2021, October). Connecting the world of healthcare virtually: a scoping review on virtual care delivery. In Healthcare (Vol. 9, No. 10, p. 1325). MDPI. DOI: 10.3390/healthcare9101325

Li, X., & Chan, M. (2022). Smartphone uses and emotional and psychological well-being in China: The attenuating role of perceived information overload. *Behaviour & Information Technology*, *41*(11), 2427–2437. DOI: 10.1080/0144929X.2021.1929489

Martínez-Peláez, R., Ochoa-Brust, A., Rivera, S., Félix, V. G., Ostos, R., Brito, H., Félix, R. A., & Mena, L. J. (2023). Role of digital transformation for achieving sustainability: Mediated role of stakeholders, key capabilities, and technology. *Sustainability (Basel)*, *15*(14), 11221. DOI: 10.3390/su151411221

Mer, A., & Srivastava, A. (2023). Employee engagement in the new normal: Artificial intelligence as a buzzword or a game changer? In *The adoption and effect of artificial intelligence on human resources management, Part A* (pp. 15-46). Emerald Publishing Limited.

Mumtaz, H., Riaz, M. H., Wajid, H., Saqib, M., Zeeshan, M. H., Khan, S. E., Chauhan, Y. R., Sohail, H., & Vohra, L. I. (2023). Current challenges and potential solutions to the use of digital health technologies in evidence generation: A narrative review. *Frontiers in Digital Health, 5*, 1203945. DOI: 10.3389/fdgth.2023.1203945 PMID: 37840685

Nguyen, M. H., Büchi, M., & Geber, S. (2024). Everyday disconnection experiences: Exploring people's understanding of digital well-being and management of digital media use. *new media & society, 26*(6), 3657-3678.

Pansini, M., Buonomo, I., De Vincenzi, C., Ferrara, B., & Benevene, P. (2023, February). Positioning Technostress in the JD-R model perspective: A systematic literature review. [). MDPI.]. *Health Care, 11*(3), 446. PMID: 36767021

Paul, P., & Singh, B. (2023). Healthcare employee engagement using the internet of things: a systematic overview. *The Adoption and Effect of Artificial Intelligence on Human Resources Management, Part A*, 71-97.

Ragu-Nathan, T. S., Tarafdar, M., Ragu-Nathan, B. S., & Tu, Q. (2021). The impact of technostress on employee productivity and well-being in modern organizations. *International Journal of Information Management, 57*, 102–125.

Shukla, S. (2023). Real-time monitoring and predictive analytics in healthcare: Harnessing the power of data streaming. *International Journal of Computer Applications, 185*(8), 32–37. DOI: 10.5120/ijca2023922738

Singh, B., & Kaunert, C. (2024). Augmented Reality and Virtual Reality Modules for Mindfulness: Boosting Emotional Intelligence and Mental Wellness. In *Applications of Virtual and Augmented Reality for Health and Wellbeing* (pp. 111-128). IGI Global.

Souchet, A. D., Lourdeaux, D., Pagani, A., & Rebenitsch, L. (2023). A narrative review of immersive virtual reality's ergonomics and risks at the workplace: Cybersickness, visual fatigue, muscular fatigue, acute stress, and mental overload. *Virtual Reality (Waltham Cross), 27*(1), 19–50. DOI: 10.1007/s10055-022-00672-0

Sun, Y., & Yuan, Z. (2023). Augmented reality fitness games and subjective well-being of players: A mixed methods study from China. *Behaviour & Information Technology*, •••, 1–17. DOI: 10.1080/0144929X.2023.2279664

Sutton, C., Prowse, J., McVey, L., Elshehaly, M., Neagu, D., Montague, J., Alvarado, N., Tissiman, C., O'Connell, K., Eyers, E., Faisal, M., & Randell, R. (2023). Strategic workforce planning in health and social care–an international perspective: A scoping review. *Health Policy (Amsterdam)*, *132*, 104827. DOI: 10.1016/j.healthpol.2023.104827 PMID: 37099856

Tarafdar, M., Cooper, C. L., & Stich, J. F. (2019). The technostress trifecta-techno eustress, techno distress and design: Theoretical directions and an agenda for research. *Information Systems Journal*, *29*(1), 6–42. DOI: 10.1111/isj.12169

Tiwari, V. (2021). Countering effects of technostress on productivity: Moderating role of proactive personality. *Benchmarking*, *28*(2), 636–651. DOI: 10.1108/BIJ-06-2020-0313

Torous, J., Bucci, S., Bell, I. H., Kessing, L. V., Faurholt-Jepsen, M., Whelan, P., & Firth, J. (2020). The growing field of digital psychiatry: Current evidence and the future of apps, social media, chatbots, and virtual reality. *World Psychiatry; Official Journal of the World Psychiatric Association (WPA)*, *19*(1), 1–13. PMID: 31922672

Torres, C. C. (2021). Adaptation and validation of technostress creators and technostress inhibitors inventories in a Spanish-speaking Latin American country. *Technology in Society*, *66*, 101660. DOI: 10.1016/j.techsoc.2021.101660

Umair, A., Conboy, K., & Whelan, E. (2023). Examining technostress and its impact on worker well-being in the digital gig economy. *Internet Research*, *33*(7), 206–242. DOI: 10.1108/INTR-03-2022-0214

United Nations. (2022). The Sustainable Development Goals Report 2022. United Nations Publications. Available at https://unstats.un.org/sdgs/report/2022/

Wang, B., Zhou, H., Li, X., Yang, G., Zheng, P., Song, C., Yuan, Y., Wuest, T., Yang, H., & Wang, L. (2024). Human Digital Twin in the context of Industry 5.0. *Robotics and Computer-integrated Manufacturing*, *85*, 102626. DOI: 10.1016/j.rcim.2023.102626

Warren, T. (2021). Work–life balance and gig work: 'Where are we now' and 'where to next' with the work–life balance agenda? *The Journal of Industrial Relations*, *63*(4), 522–545. DOI: 10.1177/00221856211007161

World Health Organization. (2022). *WHO European framework for action on mental health 2021–2025*. World Health Organization. Regional Office for Europe.

Ye, J. (2020). The role of health technology and informatics in a global public health emergency: practices and implications from the COVID-19 pandemic. JMIR medical

Zaidi, H., AlJadaan, O. T., Al Faress, M. Y., & Jabas, A. O. (2024). Disconnect to Reconnect: Your Path to Physical and Mental Wellbeing. In *Exploring Youth Studies in the Age of AI* (pp. 25-43). IGI Global.

Zainun, N. F. H., Johari, J., & Adnan, Z. (2020). Technostress and commitment to change: The moderating role of internal communication. *International Journal of Public Administration*, *43*(15), 1327–1339. DOI: 10.1080/01900692.2019.1672180

Zhang, C., Wang, Z., Zhou, G., Chang, F., Ma, D., Jing, Y., Cheng, W., Ding, K., & Zhao, D. (2023). Towards new-generation human-centric smart manufacturing in Industry 5.0: A systematic review. *Advanced Engineering Informatics*, *57*, 102121. DOI: 10.1016/j.aei.2023.102121

Chapter 11
The Digital Footprint of COVID-19 on Women's Health and the Indian Digital Space:
Bridging Health and Equity Gaps

Aishwarya Khanduri
https://orcid.org/0009-0005-2551-9364
Graphic Era University, Dehradun, India

Rashika Gusain
https://orcid.org/0009-0004-8152-8575
Graphic Era University, Dehradun, India

Debapriya Ganguly
https://orcid.org/0000-0002-4087-7099
Graphic Era University, Dehradun, India

ABSTRACT

The present paper examines the "Whisper Presents Keep Girls in School" advertisement as a socio-cultural artifact highlighting the lacuna regarding the awareness and education surrounding menstrual health and hygiene in India. By asserting the difficulties and challenges young girls and women face, the advertisement argues for the requirement of extensive menstrual health education. The prevalent socio-cultural understanding is built on the restriction of the agency of women, and the associated dismissal attitude acts as a contributing factor towards a plethora of health risks, including reproductive tract infections and cervical cancer. Insufficient knowledge, shortage of convenient mobility, and lack of quality sanitary facilities

DOI: 10.4018/979-8-3373-5087-5.ch011

are the predominant factors that make menstrual health and hygiene a challenging issue in India. The arrival of the COVID-19 epidemic further exacerbated these issues. The paper advocates for accessible, affordable healthcare and supportive cultures for young women. Prioritizing menstrual health promotes gender equality (SDG-3) and overall well-being.

INTRODUCTION

Menstrual hygiene, though an invisible issue within a gendered order, has emerged as a grave source of concern in India. According to studies, over 71% of Indian females are unaware of their first menstruation. This demonstrates the level of menstrual hygiene in the country today. Approximately 88% of women continue to use cloth, ash, and hay, either entirely or partially. It is highly likely the reason why 75% of our country's women experience menstrual health problems. The most significant impact, however, is that one in every five girls in the country must drop out of school due to their periods (India, W., 2021). Periods in the earlier days used to begin from the ages of 13 to 16 have begun to take place as early as the tender age of 8 years old in the present-day scenario. The Whisper India advertisement titled "Keep Girls in School," which is a part of their campaign titled the same, highlights this issue on a broader scale and brings awareness to the scenario by placing emphasis on the importance of educating not just girls but the boys regarding this matter to avoid any misinterpretations or misconceptions regarding the same through the usage of digital media to spread awareness.

The advertisement is the first of its kind in the realm of digital advertisements surrounding menstruation to shed light on the issue while also breaking the notion of the 'blue blood' representation that the digitalisation had popularised, further highlighting the taboos associated with menstruation and instead, representing the colour of blood as a fearful sight to the young girls due to the lack of knowledge surrounding menstruation, easily believing there to be an underlying health condition due to the naivety of childhood and lack of information (Whisper India, 2024). The Whisper India KGIS Campaign further accelerates the representation of SDG 3 (Good Health and Well-being), where light is shed upon menstrual health and hygiene while depicting how it acts as a barrier to girls' education, which brings into narrative SDG 10 (Reducing Inequalities). Through the utilisation of digital platforms, i.e., advertising and informative blogs, Whisper India further promotes menstrual hygiene management while reaching a larger audience along with areas where superstitions regarding menstruation and taboos still continue to persist.

The advertisement substantially normalises menstruation and highlights the importance of teaching both girls and boys early in their ages about menstruation and how it is not to be feared, which contributes to their knowledge spectrum about the natural processes of life and health while also enhancing their mental as well as physical well-being. It tackles gender inequality (SDG-10) by encouraging girls to stay in school, which helps in promoting their education and equal opportunities regardless of the natural health processes and the barriers surrounding them. The presence of digital inclusivity acts as a firm bridge that delivers the message to the rural and marginalised communities that lack access to proper knowledge through educational institutions such as schools, colleges, etc. (U.N., 2024).

In India, many adolescent girls face endless challenges and gaps that remain persistent, majorly in rural areas where the misconceptions, taboos, and restrictions based upon cultural and religious beliefs still persist as a restricting factor (Joshi, P. et al., 2024). Under the Whisper India campaign, many government initiatives, like providing sanitary napkins and products and raising awareness, have been taken in order to tackle issues surrounding MHM (Menstrual Hygiene Management), and yet, the taboos surrounding culture and limitations within hygiene infrastructure continue to persist, with many girls unaware of not adequately prepared for menstruation while the traditional cultural practices of using cloth, ashes, etc., still continue to prevail in many rural regions in India. In the earlier days, the substitute for sanitary napkins ranged back to dried leaves, sand, and old newspapers, which has only given way to many underlying health issues, including vaginal infections (Anand & Garg, 2015).

Through the cultural lens, in many parts of India, periods are still labelled as impure and dirty, where the girls on their period are consistently treated like an untouchable or stray animal that one should neither meet nor allow them to have access to places like temples and kitchens. According to the Hindu faith, a female should not indulge in day-to-day chores, for example, chores that involve the kitchen, as it is believed touching the food could cause them to become "contaminated," meeting religious elements such as the institute of temples, holy books, holy idols, etc. (Puri & Kapoor, 2006). They're told to undergo the process of being 'purified' to be allowed to resume her daily life without hindrances and be in touch with her family (Anand & Garg, 2015). Religious taboos and cultural norms further promote the nuances of pairing menstruation with evil, impurity, shame, and embarrassment and further turn it into an evil stigma rather than a normal life process (Anand & Garg, 2015). These instances only further indulge girls into finding themselves trapped within the barriers of those labels, feeling unfit in a society that they bring into life due to the existence of these life processes. Unaware and uneducated while being led by a society weaved by patriarchal and cultural norms and myths, girls start associating menstruation with shame and disgust where the topic is discussed in a hushed manner, sanitary napkins are purchased while wrapping them in either a newspaper or a darker plastic bag further associating it with something that is meant to be hidden, the discussion of the topic is avoided in front of the male members of the family as doing so is an "act of shame" which further increases the bridge between inequalities that exist and continue to persist where a natural life process is to be hidden from the male population who are also sons, brothers, husbands and fathers to the women who endure it.

Menarche marks the onset of countless physical, physiological, and psychological changes in the lives of adolescent girls. However, despite being a part of the maturing process, menarche is culturally bound and therefore is seen as an indicator of the girl's maturity and readiness for marriage and sexual activity. Menstruation is still considered unclean or dirty in Indian society and is linked with misconceptions and cultural restrictions (Puri & Kapoor, 2006). This forces many of the adolescent girls to be uneducated on health management and information in regard to menstrual health; thus, they develop their own ways of managing the periods. Healthy menstrual management habits emphasise the necessity of changing sanitary products regularly. While the changing of sanitary materials mostly depends on the blood flow, it is an important knowledge to have as longer usage of the product without change may lead to bacterial infection or fungus. Menstrual products are supposed to be changed at least 3 times a day every 4–8 hours, depending on the flow. Such practice is considered healthy and safe. Healthy habits like replacing sanitary material, regular cleaning and washing, and maintaining proper hygiene are crucial for a healthy period.

Unsafe cleaning practices are carried out by women and girls, particularly those residing in remote areas. MHM is moreover defined by the availability of private and comfortable places for women to wash their menstrual products. Menstrual hygiene management also highlights the importance of safe methods of sanitary material disposal. Menstrual hygiene management highlights the importance of safe methods of sanitary material disposal. Poor disposal of sanitary materials in lakes, streams, or even beneath the earth may increase the risk of infection with hepatitis and HIV because sanitary materials soaked in an infected girl's or woman's blood might be contaminated by these bacteria and viruses. This risk is heightened as many people in rural India still use river or pond water for bathing and domestic purposes like washing clothes, utensils, etc. (Ha, M. a. T., et al., 2022). Due to the lack of education and knowledge, it is often noted that women and girls living in rural areas conduct unhygienic and inconvenient methods of management. In India, between 43 and 88% of girls use cotton cloths as absorbents to clean up with and then wear them again instead of disposable pads (Das, P., et al., 2015). However, clean sanitation cannot be attained using reusable material as soap is not used in cleaning. The water bodies in rural areas have a high risk of contamination, and social taboos and restrictions force drying indoors, away from sunlight and open air.

In late 2019, an infectious and highly communicable disease known as COVID-19 spread across the world, leading to a global pandemic. The pandemic created a plethora of hardships and disruptions in everyday life. Lockdowns, quarantines, and travel restrictions were imposed by the government to curb the virus's contagiousness, leading to unseen socio-economic troubles. These measures restricted the public's freedom of mobility, thereby constraining them indoors for extended periods of time. Public areas and institutions like schools and offices were shut down, leading to isolation, disrupted education, and remote ways of living. Due to the COVID-19 pandemic, several businesses closed temporarily or permanently, making life difficult for most people and giving birth to an economic/financial crisis. Necessary services were affected, and healthcare systems were burdened with a surge in COVID-19 cases, leading to delayed or restricted access to non-COVID medical care. Access to basic necessities, including food, medicine, and menstrual hygiene products, was obstructed due to disrupted supply chains. Therefore, COVID-19 instigated a series of limitations that deeply affected every aspect of life, from personal freedom and health to financial and social well-being.

The COVID-19 pandemic severely impacted the distribution of sanitation materials, increasing the struggles encountered by menstruating women, especially in marginalised communities. The disruption of the supply chains during the lockdown led to a widespread shortage of sanitary napkins and other feminine hygiene products. Factories responsible for the manufacturing of these products reduced the production, and problems with shipping hindered them from reaching shops for sale, particularly in rural and economically deprived areas. Due to the lack of digital facilities, many girls and women relied on the local stores or educational institutions for the availability of sanitary napkins; therefore, the closure of these institutions during the pandemic aggravated the situation. The lack of access to affordable sanitary products, moreover, forced women to resort to unhygienic alternatives, such as cloth or rags, increasing the risk of infections.

The pandemic created economic stress from job losses and lower incomes, making sanitary products unaffordable for most. Some families would sacrifice menstrual hygiene products and instead reserve their scarce food resources for priority use. Other restrictions included movement restrictions, thus becoming a hindrance to the access of healthcare facilities by women where they were prohibited from visiting facilities or seeking guidance and treatment from problems with menstruation. The pandemic also set an urgent imperative for menstrual health to be considered one of the vital arms of public health, besides guidelines that spur access to affordable products when there is chaos or calamity.

The sudden outbreak of COVID-19 and the possibility of its unknown ill-effects left a strain on people, especially menstruating women and girls. The contagious virus is primarily transmitted through respiratory droplets and contact; there is no study that proves COVID-19 to spread through menstrual blood. COVID-19 has not been shown to directly affect the menstrual cycle, but stress, anxiety, and malnutrition can have an impact on the female body. The COVID-19 pandemic did leave secondary impacts on girls' and women's ability to manage their menstruation and health.

According to a study, 1.8 billion menstruating girls and women cannot afford to maintain a healthy and safe monthly cycle. Gender inequality, sexism of social norms, the stigma towards bodily functions, poverty, and lack of elementary provision all have led to less than satisfactory menstrual health and hygiene needs. Gender inequality, sexist social conventions, traditional stigmas, poverty, and limited access to basic services can all lead to neglected menstrual health and hygiene necessities. During times of emergencies and crises, such issues become heightened with no concern or resolution. Girls and women with confirmed or suspected COVID-19 were quarantined or isolated at home, resulting in a lack of clean piped water supply, immediate sanitation, and other menstrual hygiene supplies. Due to a lack of transportation services, there became an acute lack of menstrual hygiene products, particularly disposable menstrual hygiene materials that require monthly replacement. This issue could also arise due to panic buying or hoarding as people who could avail the digital facility and afford stocked up. Low levels of literacy in rural areas, especially for adolescent girls, limited access to critical information due to restricted knowledge of technology and digital platforms, suspension of schools and other institutions—all these factors contributed to making already existing challenges even more difficult.

Menstrual health management (MHM) in India is deeply relevant to Sustainable Development Goal (SDG) 3, "Good Health and Well-being," and SDG 10, "Reduced Inequalities." Women's health and well-being are profoundly influenced by their interactions with both physical and social environments. (Yildirim, S., et al., 2020) Basic facilities in this regard refer to access to sanitation and adequate management of menstrual hygiene, which are some of the important factors that determine such experiences. This paper will discuss the convergence of women's health, sanitation, and gendered practices in India by understanding how all these come together to determine health outcomes among women. There exists a wide disparity between the conjunction of gender, health, and sanitation in India. In India, women are more likely to have a tough end than men, as there is a lack of adequate sanitation facilities and unfavourable socio-cultural practices surrounding menstruation. (Daniel N. et al., 2023).

Violence against girls in schools during their periods stems from gender inequality and a lack of menstrual health education. Stigma leads to bullying, harassment, and abuse, causing trauma and perpetuating oppression. Cultural stereotypes degrading girls create environments where adults in positions of authority and trust can abuse them. Combining SDG 3 (good health) and SDG 16 (peace, justice) emphasises the need to address this issue. Access to menstrual education and hygiene can reduce stigma and violence, creating safer environments. Policies that protect girls' rights can help prevent discrimination and abuse. Together, these goals promote health, dignity, and safety, ensuring equitable education for all girls. (Pais, M. S., 2014).

Superstitions related to menstruation gravely affect women from lower-income families, as expensive menstrual hygiene products create barriers and restrictions for many, demonstrating financial inequality. Furthermore, taboos and age-old conventions restrict women's advances towards opportunities, like education and employment. Such disparity, especially in rural and underprivileged settings, limits access to hygiene and sanitation products, therefore widening the socio-economic divide. Due to the above-mentioned reasons, girls from struggling financial households often skip school during their periods or drop out. Lack of hygiene products, knowledge, or clean toilets immortalise gender disparity and inequality. his ties into SDG 10's goal of ensuring equal opportunity and reducing discriminatory barriers.

ANALYSIS OF DIGITAL SPACES AND THE PORTRAYAL OF PERIODS

Menstruation plays a major part in human evolution. However, it is still considered a taboo topic and therefore is banished from the public setting or dialogue. Periods are considered "hush-hush affairs" and remain hidden from society. A lot of women and girls in our society refuse to acknowledge that they are bleeding and willingly choose to ignore the challenges that come along with it. Rather than being an open talk, periods are often coined the term "that time of the month." Even in today's digital/technological age, myths and stigma attached to periods act as a major hindrance in the country's social progress. In many remote parts of India, menstruating women are considered 'impure' and are prohibited at many social gatherings, for instance, places of worship or even customary wedding functions (C R, S., & Shaju, P. P, 2023).

In India, menstruation rather than being a stepping stone towards adulthood is rather treated as a doorway towards womanhood. The onset of periods not only represents a woman's fertility but also denotes the various responsibilities on women; for instance, women in India are seen as breeding machines. As soon as a young girl enters her menarche, several restrictions and regulations are imposed on her. A girl might be getting pampered by her parents, but outside her home she becomes an object, an entity that can be objectified and is constantly subjected to criticism or the male gaze.

With the advancements in technology in the 21st century, many changes have come about for the urban sectors of the society in India, as well as the rest of the world. While periods or menstruation once upon a time considered a stigma and taboo is now a topic that can be both accessed as well as discussed through open dialogues on various digital platforms, including the diversity in content within social media, public forums, informative articles, videos, and blogs, where activists, influencers, and organisations take an active part in advocating for menstrual health and challenges.

Advertisements act as a major character in the modern digital era; they play a huge part in consumer conduct and even have a significant impact on the perspective of the community at large or the individual. Advertising nowadays has been brought under the limelight with the assistance of social media and other online platforms. This development has emerged advantageous in the portrayal of menstruation in multiple digital spaces and has enabled females to have access to necessary information and to no longer associate the topic of periods with shame or something that is meant to be hidden and kept in secrecy and further empower them through the normalisation of periods and promotion of MHM (Ramaswamy, M., 2023). These initiatives create a safe environment for females of any age to be able to have honest and open conversations and to openly share their experiences with other females, which helps in tackling myths and negative attributes and promotes knowledge about menstrual products and their usage, which surpasses all stereotypes (Nayanikka, 2024).

It is only due to the latest advancements of the digital sphere that the legal activists and feminist groups can question these negative stereotypes, for example, the restrictions on women to enter spaces like kitchens and places of worship and have access to basic human needs like bathing, food items, and in most undeveloped areas even menstrual products, etc. These complications that women have to suffer compromise their right to movement and freedom of pursuing the same, giving way to ongoing debates, protests, legal cases, forcefully breaking the law as a method of reform, and social media campaigns (Prasanna, C. K. 2016).

A key example of the role of social media campaigns and protests is the ‘Lahu ka Lagaan’ campaign, which trended on the social media platform Twitter (now known as ‘X’) under the hashtag #LahukaLagaan, which was an initiative taken by the non-profit organisation named SheSays, which is a women’s rights organisation that is known to fight gender-based discrimination through education and awareness-raising programs (SheSays, 2023). The campaign was an initiative to protest against the government of India’s decision to impose the Goods and Services Tax (GST) at 14 percent on sanitary pads, further taking away the essence of it being a necessity and turning it into luxury instead (Fadnis, D., 2017). The hashtag stands for "the blood's tax" and was supported by people across the nation as well as promoted and supported by valuable personalities from the entertainment industry, such as actress Aditi Rao Hydari, singer Vishal Dadlani, television personalities Shenaz Treasury (formerly Shehnaz Treasurywala) and Cyrus Broacha, along with comedians Rohan Joshi and Mallika Dua, further highlighting the impact of social media in raising awareness about fundamental issues (Saxena, N., 2017).

Originally, SheSays had only filed a plea to the government under said campaign as its first attempt to bring about the change in October 2016 through the petition #DontTaxMyPeriod, making a request to the Finance Ministry to make sanitary pads tax-free in order to make them more accessible to the masses. However, the attempt failed, which led to the organisation renewing their strategy and hence launching this viral and successful campaign named #LahukaLagaan, which proved to be pivotal in raising awareness towards MHM through their demand of tax-free sanitary napkins with the help of major figures in the industry that promoted the message further and, as presumed, turned #LahuKaLagaan into the biggest women-led Twitter campaign in order to demand policy change in India (Sawant, P., 2017). The founder of SheSays, Trisha Shetty, further elaborates how non-profit organisations in India indulge volunteers from underdeveloped and remote areas to spread awareness and ensure digital accessibility for all (Sawant, P., 2017).

This campaign acted as an evident example of how digital spaces can help bring about great change while also raising awareness about MHM and other menstrual health issues by defying taboos and promoting health care information and relevant sources with social activists in both the past as well as present, using activism on the X app to make topics of taboo more perceptible and become a part of the bigger conversation in India, culturally as well as intellectually (Baer, H., 2015). On the other hand, X India (formerly Twitter India) provides non-profit organisations with free educational sessions that help them in their initiatives that extend further than just the general masses (Mathias, T., 2017). Through the course of history, the topic of menstruation and periods, as well as the rights for women associated with the same, have been consistently associated with secrecy and shame. However, the digital age acts as a golden opportunity towards destigmatising periods through education, empowerment, social media advocacy, engagement in conversations on the topic across the globe, and the improvement of menstrual equity (Ramaswamy, M. 2023).

As an ongoing present-day scenario, the lack of awareness in rural India has caused women in these areas to turn to unhygienic measures when it comes to menstruation through the usage of homemade pads that are reused, occasionally made from old rags, dried leaves, or ash and due to the lack of access to clean water to wash the same rags or to dry them, they end up reusing the spoiled pads, again. These unhygienic practices result within fungal reproductive tract infections (RTI), and urinary tract infections (UTI) which then results in the circumstances that makes women vulnerable to the development of cervical cancer and reportedly, even infertility among many other health issues. (Bookshelf, 2012) The lack of awareness or knowledge has become the root cause of school absenteeism in adolescent girls in rural India. The fear of staining their clothes, insufficient sanitation facilities or knowledge provided in school surrounding periods and MHM, and gendered discrimination surrounding menstruation become the reason for 23 percent girls between the ages of 12-18 end up dropping out of school after they start menstruating due to the physical as well as mental distress. (George, R., 2017) Feminist activist movements have helped in bringing light to such topics in the present day through the digitalisation of these campaigns and protests that are able to reach and appeal to the masses more evidently. Digital media platforms have substantially reduced the gaps between rural and urban areas in terms of accessibility of information regarding MHM. In the present day, most of the population both rural and urban, has access to social media and therefore, the necessary resources of information, basic or medical, giving rise to the accessibility of health facilities at the comfort of their home through online consultations and informative material present across digital spaces rather than suppressing their voices out of shame as they are introduced to many other women openly embracing menstruation as a process as natural as breathing, defying the stigmas surrounding them (Nayanikka, 2024).

In 2021, through the onset of COVID-19, the pandemic had further heightened MHM related challenges that stands firm as the root cause of the decline in women's health as well as well-being, more evidently among the poor and backward communities led by limitations to poor sanitation infrastructure as well as menstrual necessities. On Menstrual Hygiene Day held on 28 May, every year but in 2021, UNICEF India led the #RedDotChallenge campaign "to promote safety and hygiene in all aspects of lives – including period management and fighting COVID-19." The #RedDotChallenge campaign was held in collaboration with digital influencer Diipa Khosla's post for Change initiative through her social media platform and encouraged many personalities, including celebrities and influencers to give voice to the issue through the usage of social media. UNICEF India's representative, Dr Yasmin Ali Haque had quoted saying "Period shaming, poverty and discriminatory cultural norms on menstrual health affect women and girls' physical and mental health. The pandemic has made things worse with limited availability of sanitary products and increased pressures on women and girls linked to lockdowns, increased poverty, and disruption of essential services affecting large pockets of the population. We need to break this chain and help every girl and woman to manage periods safely and with dignity. UNICEF is working with partners to equip women and girls with the right information and is calling everyone to break free of these harmful period stereotypes and increase investment in Menstrual Hygiene Management, awareness on menstrual hygiene and ensure easy access to related supplies" (UNICEF, 2021). This initiative by UNICEF acted as a pillar in providing necessary help and resources to many women across the nation through many digital resources such as webinars, competitions, trainings, book releases, and consultations held in Odisha, MP, UP, Gujarat and Chhattisgarh on Menstrual Hygiene Day, as well as, "through the distribution of around 220,000 sanitary pads in urban slums, villages and COVID Care centres in Mumbai, Pune and Nashik, to adolescent girls, sex workers, migrants and women on the move" (UNICEF, 2021).

Through the study's key centre, the 'Keep Girls In School' (KGIS) campaign, Whisper India quotes "1 out of 5 girls in the country drop out of school when they get their periods" (India, W., 2021). The campaign was started by Whisper India in 2021 as an extension to their Whisper School Program that dates all the way back to 1995, in partnership with UNESCO to expand the reach of the program and as Whisper India quotes "to lend an authoritative voice to their campaign" (India, W., 2021). They have also been working with NGOs across the nation to reach out to as many girls as possible. The KGIS campaign was created to provide menstrual health education to one girl for the purchase of every three packs of Whisper India purchased between February 10 and March 15, 2021, that helped in funding the cause. The campaign stood for making a valuable impact as well as to give the girls of India a voice and ensure a fair chance to achieve their dreams without the limitations of their period and to raise awareness and ensure that girls do not drop out of schools due to their periods. In order to tackle the lack of knowledge surrounding menstrual health, Whisper India has introduced many useful resources available even on their website under the blogs divided into two sections, the section 'For Girls & Parents' consisting of the blogs titled 'My First Period', 'Period Guide', 'Puberty', and 'Tips For Parents' and for the section 'For Women' blogs titled, 'Cramps and Irregular Bleeding', 'PCOS', 'PMS', 'Tips for a Better Period', 'Vaginal Discharge' as the example of their dedication towards the cause making each section of the household aware about menstruation and the challenges and misconceptions surrounding it and how to tackle them alongside (India, W., 2021).

The campaign launched its fifth edition in 2024 through the digital advertisement titled 'Whisper Presents Keep Girls in School' that has gained the attention of people and celebrities across the globe with over 70 million views on the YouTube video of the ad (Whisper India, 2024). The ad's theme song 'Periods Ka Matlab Healthy Hain Aap' (which translates to 'Periods mean you are healthy') is introduced as an enhanced and vibrant method of spreading the message of periods being healthy and how they are not to be feared among both children and adults. The ad challenges the existing notions of how introducing periods to children can be "too early" and how, indeed, it is never too early as the ad is the first of its kind to bring the attention how girls as young as 8 years old are now prone to getting their period with the advertisement highlighting the fear and shame embarked with the same where the friends of the young girl are seen passing their suggestions of how she could be getting "punished by God for lying", "swinging too fast in P.T class", "a fishbone getting stuck", "a terrible disease" along with suggesting her to drop the idea of coming to school until she stops where the first friend is portrayed worrying "What if it never stops? Will you never come to school?" and the second, 'whispers' "I think she is going to die." highlighting both the naivety of childhood as well as the consequences of lack of education surrounding menstrual health. The young girl is distressed upon hearing her friends and breaks into tears rushing into the teacher's arms who arrives on the scene, confused about what is happening until she notices the blood on the young girl's skirt. The advertisement also defies the previous portrayal of periods exuding 'blue blood' as displayed across advertisements of popular brands of sanitary pads, another example of the evident stigmas that continue to prevail in society around disguising components related to periods. Whisper India is the first of its kind to portray period blood as originally red through the young girl and how the teacher, as her duty to be a pillar of education as well as someone who saw the impact periods, can create on the mental health of the young girls takes upon the task to highlight through diagrams and the song to teach kids about periods in girls as well as how they mean that they are healthy, therefore, it is nothing to be feared.

Many people came forth to express their contentment over the advertisement and how, unlike any other advertisement, this was the first they had come back to and praised it for defying the age-old taboos and making the younger generations embrace this natural change by making the video both informative as well as understandable with the occurrence of examples from reality and the true image of what periods look like unlike the other advertisements based on sanitary napkins that associate the discomfort of periods being 'replaced' through the pads, 'magically' leading them to feel empowered to go about their daily lives and tasks with 'exceeded agility'. Such advertisements tend to mislead more than they create awareness as the prevalent portrayal of 'blue blood' on sanitary pads only highlights the absorption capability of the product but barely any awareness is brought to light about menstruation or menstrual hygiene.

Education, periods, and sanitary napkin access in rural and urban settings

In areas of poverty and low-income households, it becomes difficult to conduct menstrual hygiene management by girls and women. One of the biggest reasons for this is the lack of education, awareness, and misconceptions associated with menses. The age-old conventions, cultural taboos, and stigmas create hindrances in the open dialogue and resolve of periods. Since Indian society is mostly patriarchy-based, men must acknowledge and learn about this natural phenomenon in women. It is often men who are placed in positions of authority, therefore their lack of education on this subject breeds negligence toward women's health issues. Moreover, an association of men in this regard will seriously help women, by providing clean water, disinfected toilets, and menstrual hygiene products as a necessity in society. In India menstruating women are imposed with many restrictions and limitations as the society is deeply rooted in cultural traditions and social taboos. This allows the gender gap and disparity to further broaden, especially in the Indian spectrum (Johnston-Robledo, et al., 2020). These conventions and restrictions prohibit women's involvement in cooking, monitoring their food consumption, going to religious institutions, or taking part in communal activities. In some rural households women are even instructed to sleep alone or separate from the entire family as they perceive women as "impure and dirty" while they are menstruating. The talk of menstruation is so silenced that women feel embarrassed to even pan out simple tasks like cleaning and drying menstrual clothes or products. As a result, damp cloths are stored or worn before drying properly which might become a breeding ground for bacteria etc. Predominantly in Indian families and households, menstruation is considered a "ladies' issue", men are not considered about the health and hygiene of females.

Menstrual health management is considered as a woman issue entirely and it should be a private affair that is never shared or raised in open discussions because it may lead to shame and humiliation. Women and girls are never openly able to communicate the need to change the already existing norms, notions, and systems. The male attitude towards menstruation is a predominant cause of stigmatisation of this natural phenomenon. The needs and problems of the gendered nature of women's reproductive health are neither recognized nor included as low priority on issues of gender equality and positive sexual and reproductive health outcomes resulting in MHM being a neglected cause. For a change to initiate it is important to understand the lack of knowledge in the male community, taking into consideration the support, action and reaction of men towards women while they are menstruating.

According to a literature review, it is denoted that men's point of view towards menstruation and women's health is largely unknown and under-researched throughout the world. Boys' education, however primitive and embryonic, comprises biological function and cultural influence. They have more knowledge on the maintenance of appearance, codes, and conduct females need to follow rather than the actual course of events. Some boys even consider periods as a disease that comes once a month that involves blood. Boys and men alike seem to know the customs and taboos that limit women's lives during that period but are unsure as to why women have to face the said restrictions. Such notions of seclusion which prohibit women from worshipping, or touching food, people or animals is problematic as it is still prevalent in today's times. A lot of men have a negative attitude towards menstruation, they often describe girls as getting irritated and angry or complaining of pain (Mason, et al., 2017).

Negligence of healthy menstrual hygiene practices is often witnessed more in rural areas as compared to urban ones. Beyond the geographical differences, there are various factors to take into consideration while defining this gap, some of them being awareness, budget, and indoctrination. Availability of clean and sanitised hygiene products, adequate facilities to change or clean/dispose off promptly, soap, and water for individual hygiene play a major role in maintaining hygienic practices. However, the socio-economic, cultural, and infrastructural context in which MHM occurs cannot be ignored. Poor MHH has direct and indirect relations with the fulfilment of SDG-3 (good health and well-being), SDG-4 (quality education), SDG-5 (gender equality), and SDG-6 (clean water and sanitation). These goals altogether are crucial for the further development of young adolescent girls.

In India, menstruation is still stigmatised, and numerous myths and misunderstandings surround it, so many women have untreated menstrual disorders. There is an increased risk of reproductive tract infections because of poor menstrual hygiene practices. The delayed diagnosis and management of health issues that are menstrual-related; and there is also psychological distress stemming from societal taboos and discrimination associated with menstruation. The availability of unhygienic and unsafe sanitation facilities, along with limited or no access to menstrual hygiene products and services, continues to be a major problem for school-aged teenagers in India, which is why, in many cases, girls stop attending schools altogether, further aggravating the situation.

In India, there is a wide spread of menstrual disorders among young adolescent girls; 64% of girls report at least one menstrual abnormality, including irregular periods, heavy bleeding, or painful menstruation. Poor menstrual hygiene and lack of self-care are significant contributors to issues related to menses among girls aged 10–19. Some of these complications include urinary tract infections, scabies in the vaginal area, abdominal pain without any relation to diseases, and pregnancy complications. Out of 113 million adolescent girls, only about 68 million attend 1.4 million schools due to poor MHM practices and cultural taboos that limit attendance (Biswas et al., 2024). In terms of the reproductive health of adolescents, menstrual disorders and irregularities have physical, mental, social, and psychological implications. These implications bring about various types of social and psychological disorders such as anxiety, panic attacks, etc. To overcome such issues, proper menstrual management needs to be conducted. The availability of cheap/low-cost sanitary napkins is a necessity; toilets and handwashing facilities are a must to overall improve the health status of the girl child or women in general. Schools can act significantly as venues where such facilities and MHM practices are instilled and advocated, providing an encouraging learning environment for girls. Therefore, these menstrual-related problems need to be taken care of toward the fulfilment of achieving gender equity and ensuring the fulfilment of all capabilities of adolescent girls in India (Patil, S.R., 2014).

The availability of sanitary napkins in rural and urban India significantly varies due to various factors such as economic evolution, cultural taboos, educational values, etc. The availability of sanitary napkins is relatively easier in urban areas as compared to rural or remote places. Women residing in urban areas have access to multiple choices, as there are a lot of menstrual hygiene products apart from just pads or napkins. Due to higher levels of income, a wide number of stores, dispensaries, and online retail platforms, it is easier for women in urban areas to get access to sanitary hygiene products. Even after the presence of cultural stigma, the talk of periods is much more exposed in metropolitan cities as compared to rural areas. To break the cultural taboo and sale of menstrual hygiene products, companies and brands run a lot of advertisements, and campaigns, also introducing new and innovative menstrual hygiene products that are convenient and comfortable for women and girls to use such as tampons and menstrual cups.

Despite having convenient access and better awareness, urban settings also face some challenges. Not all families or households are high-income, thus cost becomes an issue for many women and girls. Many brands that provide organic materials or modern features like extra absorbency are more expensive and, therefore, inaccessible to many. Recently, the disposal of used sanitary napkins has become a major concern in urban settings as its non-biodegradable nature makes its disposal an environmental hazard. Improper methods of disposing of sanitary products are causing ecological degradation as India generates an estimated 113,000 tons of menstrual waste annually. Affordability is another big challenge in rural India. While there are several initiatives in this front by the government, schemes such as Pradhan Mantri Bhartiya Janaushadhi Pariyojana try to provide sanitary products at affordable prices, it is still below par. Rural areas have poor distribution networks and several villages do not have easy access to pharmacies or shops selling sanitary napkins.

Positive and Negative Portrayal of Periods

In any society, the portrayal of anything depicts the perception it is bound to create on people. If we take the example of cinema, we are able to conjure the fact that the portrayal of a person as evil or good depicts society's labelling of the character as a hero or the villain. In the same way, the way the media represents menstruation can majorly hold a significance over perceptions. Positive portrayals in advertisements, movies, and social media can normalise menstruation and reduce stigma. On the other hand, negative or lack of portrayals can further cause the elation of the taboos and the persisting myths around periods. In recent times, the way the representation of periods has increased greatly has provided it with more visibility and has proved to be an aid in helping to open up more people to the idea and knowledge surrounding menstruation and menstrual hygiene and caused them to be more accepting towards it rather than choosing to bury the matter and its discussions (Bobel, 2020). However, on the negative side, the consistent focus of the advertisements towards sanitary pads and their usages, the competitive market working upon strategies to make ads that glorify periods only make room for confusion and do not contribute to any methods and ways to educate the society about periods or normalise it for them. The advertising industry's consistent focus on marketing their product and the refusal to portray real blood on the screen due to the existent stigma around it only mirrors the society's reflection of burying the topic through the refusal of speaking about it out loud, purchasing pads from convenience and medical stores while having them wrapped within newspaper or a black polythene bag as a refusal to carry it in the open, depicting the association of menstruation and menstrual hygiene products with further shame. These practices are bound to prevail when even the modern day's major advertising companies refuse to portray periods for what they really are but rather make commodities out of them with no real value or education attached to the matter in terms with the society's wellbeing.

In a recent study by Nyaupane and Thapa (2024), a survey of 225 girls was conducted based upon their views surrounding menstruation that revealed predominant negative feelings. The study was done between girls of ages 15 to 25 years old where the number of single females was 221 while only 4 were married, depicting the inclusivity of the research surrounding both ages, as well as marital analysis. Around 84.9% described how they do not feel proud about their menstruation or menstruating, and none of them agreed or felt happy about having their period. Around 66.7% did not feel excited about menstruating while in a similar sense, a great number of respondents, i.e., around 82.2% of them, did not feel happy about getting their first period. While a majority of respondents concurred with feeling different about their period, around 58.7% confessed that menstruation makes them uncomfortable. On the question of being asked if it were acceptable to miss college/university due to period cramps, about 45.3% were in favor, demonstrating how many females found menstruation and cramps physically exhausting. A majority of 75.1% respondents denied feeling terrified at the prospect of periods, implying their awareness and understanding about the menstrual process. The survey found that 72% of respondents felt comfortable discussing menstruation with friends, but 62.2% expressed discomfort when the word "period" is mentioned. While 60.9% disagreed with fearing that boys would find out about their period, 24.9% expressed fear. Additionally, 86.2% disagreed that girls should worry during their period. The survey highlights widespread discomfort, negative associations, and stigma surrounding menstruation, with respondents showing minimal positive feelings or eagerness towards their periods.

The term 'period' had begun to be used for menstruation as early as in the 1800s in order to conceal the topic of menstruation with the disguise of a commonly used term to avoid attention around the matter and even so, it was not mentioned on TV until 1985 through the actress Courtney Cox during a Tampax commercial (Anjum, M, 2023). The reason for this vast gap in the years of the origin of the word to it being openly renounced was yet again the social stigma that had witnessed no bounds even in the Western community. The shame and silence surrounding menstruation continued to prevail for ages that followed. It was in the 1870s that the advertisements for menstrual products first aired, however not on screen but in the form of printed brochures that were accompanied with information and educating women on how to speak to their adolescent daughters. Majority of people had come to believe that menstruating women went through major difficulties during the process, however, it was Dr. James Allen, a pivotal physician who enlightened this perception through his book - Ladies Guide To Health and Disease, published in 1891. He advised people to uphold a more thoughtful approach, suggesting how menstruating women should be more focused on resting and practice methods of relaxation than indulge in arduous activities when they are menstruating.

Overcoming taboos becomes further challenging when major digital platforms like advertisements, movies and even TV shows depict menstruation in accordance with the negative stereotypes and stigmas, further aggravating them. For example, in the horror movie titled 'Carrie', a problematic representation of menstruation is depicted through the main character holding negative feelings towards her period and eventually, it becomes the reason of unleashing her 'telekinetic powers and evil tendencies' further adding onto the age-old stigma of associating everything feminine with evil. Similarly, in the TV shows, 'Everybody Loves Raymond' and 'Entourage' the men denounce the women as unreasonable and irrational while they are on their period which promotes the ongoing stigma surrounding women throwing 'tantrums' when they are menstruating and having their emotions 'all over the place'. Such portrayals depict menstruation as abnormal, bizarre, ridiculous and a notion that is meant to be associated with shame and therefore, hidden, just as everything feminine. Critics also note that had menstruation been linked with a man, it could easily be deemed with something that exudes gallantry, courage, power and an example of the many things that make a man far more powerful for holding the endurance to bleed for five days and to still live. While a woman, on the other hand, is condemned for the same, associating her menstrual cramps with being dramatic or having a low tolerance. "the talk" being buried, menstruation being concealed under terms like "that time of the month" or the term "period" for open discussions while overall, only ever declaring menstruation as a natural process when it comes to belittling the endurance women hold to go through the process every single month.

Through the prevailing onset of negative portrayals of menstruation through either the ignorance and refusal to explore the topic or disguise it underneath suggestive symbols, the media has evolved in recent times, challenging the pre-existing notions surrounding menstruation and more openly presenting the topic on screen. The representation of 'blue liquid' on pads and the portrayal of exaggerated discomfort or exceeded agility after the usage of pads has now been replaced with more realistic approaches and representations of menstruation with brands like Whisper being in the lead with 'Keep Girls in School'. Major menstrual hygiene product companies have come forth with campaigns that promote better sanitation facilities as well as challenging the stigma and taboos to welcome a more open-minded discourse surrounding menstruation.

On the entertainment front, the Indian cinema has come forth with movies like 'Pad Man' which was released in 2018 and 'Period'. End Of Sentence.'following through in the same year that highlighted the perspectives from the point of view of both men and women, in underprivileged areas and the real life stories and challenges faced to combat the issues of social stigmas and period poverty that have been brought forth as inspirations, both in the real-life instance, as well as through the on-screen portrayal of it that has touched millions of people conveying the positive outlook on the topic and an aid in combating stereotypes and shame surrounding the matter while promoting the importance of menstrual hygiene and the role of a supportive and empathetic society in the lives of women.

Another notable contribution in the evolving times and with the rise of social media, several campaigns and informative efforts made by influencers help in fostering a more open and understanding culture towards menstruation while people could even choose to remain anonymous in order to put their troubles forth and have a community that supports them. The presence of a more understanding community as well as the development in societal mindset has given way for more people to embrace menstruation as a natural phenomenon and for it to be discussed among male and female population in a more approachable manner where the outbreak of social media has fostered a better understanding in the younger generation of males to allow them to indulge within ways they could be mindful of a menstruating female and be able to act as a support rather than unintentionally engaging within ignorance towards the same. The joint efforts of the media and campaigns have initiated a need for reform, a better approach towards the availability of sanitary products and sanitation facilities and promotion of education surrounding MHM in both urban and rural areas of India.

The above instances prove how media can be pivotal in shaping the perceptions of a society in either a positive or negative manner surrounding the topic of menstruation and how if used correctly could act as a passage of acting as a voice for women and encourage the society to be more open about menstruation and together, as a society help each other within constructing a safe space for women where they no longer have to feel shame or the need to suppress the things they go through as it is a natural process, not an illness, while menstruating while also educating them about MHM for a future that comprises of menstruation only being discussed as a natural process than a notion surrounded with demeaning taboos and other superstitious stigmas.

CONCLUSION

In conclusion, this study underscores upon addressing the negligence of menstrual health and how facilitating inclusive cultural reforms as well as the transformative role of digital platforms can help achieve the goal of Sustainable Development Goals (SDG) 3 and 10 through ensuring healthy lives and promoting well-being for all. Thus, development in the thought process of society regarding the stigma around menstruation, especially in rural India, might bring about a reform in the pre-existing notions and the age-old stigmas of shame and secrecy tied around the term and assist in the overall development of the society. Collective action from various stakeholders is vital to break the silence and support women in managing their menstrual health with dignity and confidence. The intersection of menstrual health management and digital health initiatives plays a prominent role in encouraging gender equality and strengthening women's health. SDG 3 is fundamental to women's menstrual health and overall well-being as menstrual health directly has an impact on their physical and mental faculties, school attendance, and the economic productivity of the nation altogether. (Yildirim, et. el, 2022) Through the digital campaign of Whisper India called 'Keep Girls In School', this study has aimed to highlight these factors and the negative shifts menstruation brings in the lives of females regardless of their age due to the lack of education and awareness regarding MHM, as well as, the society's subjugation of menstruating women in different manners in urban and rural areas which further creates a bridge between equality and inequality for women and how digital campaigns can prove to be pivotal in highlighting these messages and promote the normalisation of these topics in the society in order to bring about reforms by dismantling taboos and promoting gender equality through raising awareness. Governments and NGOs-led initiatives, as well as digital innovations, are working towards introducing programs that leverage digital health platforms to provide menstrual health education, assistance, and resources to marginalised communities, directly addressing the health inequalities as summarised in SDG 10.

The Government of India realises the importance of healthy menstrual hygiene practices among adolescent girls and women and its necessity for the overall health and well-being of women in India. The Government, in this regard, has taken several measures in order to generate awareness and make products available and affordable for women. Sanitary napkins were provided at subsidised rates to adolescent girls in rural areas, while the integration of menstrual health education into digital curricula has broadened awareness and understanding. May 28th, a global initiative is observed as Menstrual Hygiene Day, to create awareness of what women and girls go through during menstruation and work toward solutions that can redress these problems. Thus, these practices along with the rise of digitalisation and platforms that encourage and highlight open-ended conversations empowers communities across the globe to support women's health needs so that menstruation is treated as a natural aspect of life, not a barrier to equality which in turn, fosters an equitable society that works in empowering each individual to participate fully in education, workplaces and advances their overall, public life and growth. This approach acts as a means to highlight the role of awareness surrounding menstruation and menstrual health and how it plays an essential role within constructing an equitable society with gender equity, progress of the society and the overall growth of all communities.

REFERENCES

Anand, T., & Garg, S. (2015). Menstruation related myths in India: Strategies for combating it. *Journal of Family Medicine and Primary Care*, *4*(2), 184. DOI: 10.4103/2249-4863.154627 PMID: 25949964

Anjum, M. (2023) *How are periods portrayed in the media*? - Free Periods Canada. https://www.freeperiods.ca/blog/how-are-periods-portrayed-in-the-media

Baer, H. (2015). Redoing feminism: Digital activism, body politics, and neoliberalism. *Feminist Media Studies*, *16*(1), 17–34. DOI: 10.1080/14680777.2015.1093070

Biswas, S., Alam, A., Islam, N., Roy, R., & Satpati, L. (2024). Understanding period product use among young women in rural and urban India from a geospatial perspective. *Scientific Reports*, *14*(1), 20114. Advance online publication. DOI: 10.1038/s41598-024-70383-w PMID: 39209872

Bobel, C. (2020). *Introduction: Menstruation as Lens—Menstruation as Opportunity.* In Springer eBooks (pp. 1–6). DOI: 10.1007/978-981-15-0614-7_1

Sruthy, C. R., & Shaju, P. P. (2023). Portrayal of Menstruation and Womanhood in 'Ayali' Tamil Web Series.

Daniel, N., Kejela, G., Fantahun, F., Desalegn, M., & Guteta, F. (2023). Menstrual hygiene management practice and its associated factors among in-school adolescent girls in Western Ethiopia. *Contraception and Reproductive Medicine*, *8*(1), 1. Advance online publication. DOI: 10.1186/s40834-022-00196-7 PMID: 36597101

Das, P., Baker, K. K., Dutta, A., Swain, T., Sahoo, S., Das, B. S., Panda, B., Nayak, A., Bara, M., Bilung, B., Mishra, P. R., Panigrahi, P., Cairncross, S., & Torondel, B. (2015). Menstrual Hygiene Practices, WASH Access and the Risk of Urogenital Infection in Women from Odisha, India. *PLoS One*, *10*(6), e0130777. DOI: 10.1371/journal.pone.0130777 PMID: 26125184

Fadnis, D. (2017). Feminist Activists Protest Tax on Sanitary Pads: Attempts to Normalize Conversations About Menstruation in India Using Hashtag Activism. *Feminist Media Studies*, *17*(6), 1111–1114. DOI: 10.1080/14680777.2017.1380430

Ha, M. T., & Alam, M. Z. (2022). *Menstrual hygiene management practice among adolescent girls: An urban–rural comparative study in Rajshahi division,* Bangladesh. *BMC Women's Health*, *22*(1), 86. Advance online publication. DOI: 10.1186/s12905-022-01665-6 PMID: 35321715

India, W. (2021, May 4). *About KGIS: Keep Girls in School - Information & More. Keep Girls In School.* https://whisper.co.in/en-in/school-education/kgis

Johnston-Robledo, I., & Chrisler, J. C. (2020). *The menstrual mark: Menstruation as social stigma.* In Springer eBooks (pp. 181–199). https://doi.org/DOI: 10.1007/978-981-15-0614-7_17

Joshi, P, et al. (2024) *Status, Gaps and Challenges in Menstrual Health in India: A . . . : Preventive Medicine: Research & Reviews.* DOI: . PMRR_74_24DOI: 10.4103/PMRR

Kansal, S., Singh, S., & Kumar, A. (2015). Menstrual hygiene practices in context of schooling: A community study among rural adolescent girls in Varanasi. *Indian Journal of Community Medicine : Official Publication of Indian Association of Preventive & Social Medicine, 41*(1), 39. DOI: 10.4103/0970-0218.170964 PMID: 26917872

Kirk, J., & Sommer, M. (2006) *Menstruation and body awareness: linking girls' health with girls' education.*https://www.semanticscholar.org/paper/Menstruation-and-body-awareness-%3A-linking-girls-%E2%80%99-%E2%80%99-Kirk-Sommer/e4072b8340ecd2eec2564d0947d59c01672b834b

Mason, L., Sivakami, M., Thakur, H., Kakade, N., Beauman, A., Alexander, K. T., Van Eijke, A. M., Laserson, K. F., Thakkar, M. B., & Phillips-Howard, P. A. (2017b). 'We do not know': A qualitative study exploring boys' perceptions of menstruation in India. *Reproductive Health, 14*(1), 174. Advance online publication. DOI: 10.1186/s12978-017-0435-x PMID: 29216895

Mathias, T. (2017, January 27). *The Tweeter side to life: How Indians on Twitter are making a difference.* The Better India. https://thebetterindia.com/83396/twitter-for-good-social-outreach/

Nayanikka. (2024 b). *The Role of Internet in Menstrual Health Awareness in Rural India.* Muft Internet. https://muftinternet.com/blog/2024/06/03/the-role-of-internet-in-menstrual-health-awareness-in-rural-india/

Nyaupane, P., & Thapa, S. (2024). Exploring Factors Influencing College Females' Perceptions of Menstruation: A Study on Awareness and Cultural Influences. *NRPC Journal of Multidisciplinary Research, 1*(3), 176–193. DOI: 10.3126/nprcjmr.v1i3.70211

Pais, M. S. (2014) *Tackling Violence in Schools: A Global Perspective Bridging the Gap between Standards and Practice.* United Nations Report. https://violenceagainstchildren.un.org/sites/violenceagainstchildren.un.org/files/documents/publications/10._tackling_violence_in_schools_a_global_perspective.pdf

Patil, S. R. (2014). *Knowledge and Practices of Menstrual Hygiene among Married Adolescents and Young Women in Chittoor District Of Andhra Pradesh: India.* In IOSR Journal of Nursing and Health Science (Ver. I, Vol. 3, Issue 2, pp. 06–15) [Journal-article]. DOI: DOI: 10.9790/1959-03210615

Prasanna, C. K. (2016). Claiming the Public Sphere: Menstrual Taboos and the Rising Dissent in India. *Agenda (Durban, South Africa)*, *30*(3), 91–95. DOI: 10.1080/10130950.2016.1251228

Puri, S., & Kapoor, S. (2006). Taboos and Myths Associated with Women's Health among Rural and Urban Adolescent Girls in Punjab. *Indian Journal of Community Medicine : Official Publication of Indian Association of Preventive & Social Medicine*, *31*(4), 295. https://journals.lww.com/ijcm/citation/2006/31040/taboos_and_myths_associated_with_womens_health.30.aspx

Ramaswamy, M. (2023, August 29). *Menstruation in the Digital Age.* Aunt Flow. https://goauntflow.com/blog/menstruation-in-the-digital-age/

Report, U. N. (2024, December 15). *Menstrual health in adolescent girls* | Department of Economic and Social Affairs. https://sdgs.un.org/partnerships/menstrual-health-adolescent-girls

Sawant, P. (2017, July 16). *Women activists plan to take the issue of 12% GST on Sanitary napkin to the court.* The Times of India. https://timesofindia.indiatimes.com/city/mumbai/women-activists-plan-to-take-the-issue-of-12-gst-on-sanitary-napkin-to-the-court/articleshow/59619181.cms

Saxena, N. (2017). *Celebrities Support #LahuKaLagaan, Request Arun Jaitley to Remove Sanitary Napkin Tax. Hindustan Times.* https://www.google.com/amp/s/www.hindustantimes.com/bollywood/celebrities-support-lahukalagaan-request-arun-jaitley-to-remove-sanitary-napkin-tax/story-c7nzLdJFe1lEVNfdII7hyO_amp.html

SheSays. *One Young World.*https://www.oneyoungworld.com/ambassador-projects/shesays

Tuli, A., Dalvi, S., Kumar, N., & Singh, P. (2019). *"It's a Girl Thing": Examining Challenges And Opportunities Around Menstrual Health Education in India. ACM Trans. Comput.-Hum. Interact., 26–26*(5), 29–29. DOI: DOI: 10.1145/3325282

UNICEF. (2021). *#RedDotChallenge Continues to Dispel Period Stigma and Promotes COVID Appropriate Behaviour.*https://www.unicef.org/india/press-releases/reddotchallenge-continues-dispel-period-stigma-and-promotes-covid-appropriate

WhisperIndia. (2024, May 15). Whisper Presents Keep Girls in School (Hindi) [Video]. YouTube. https://www.youtube.com/watch?v=gFZTpxk5DaU

Yildirim, S., Demirtas, I., & Yildirim, D. C. (2022). *A Review of Alternative Economic Approaches to Achieve Sustainable Development: The Rising Digitalization and Degrowth Post COVID-19*

Yildirim, S., & Yildirim, D. Ç. (2020). *Achieving Sustainable Development Through a Green Economy Approach.*

Chapter 12
Beyond Bias:
"Hichki" as a Lens for Disability and Gender Equality in Education

Gauri Samant
https://orcid.org/0009-0003-8663-7132
Graphic Era University, Dehradun, India

Priyanshi Mamgain
Graphic Era University, Dehradun, India

Debapriya Ganguly
https://orcid.org/0000-0002-4087-7099
Graphic Era University, Dehradun, India

ABSTRACT

This paper examines the text 'Hichki' as a cultural artifact reflecting the intersections of quality education and the SDGs, focusing on disability and gender equity in Indian society. The study focuses on Tourette syndrome, perceptions of disability, societal biases' that hinder access to education, and Covid-19 pedagogical practices. The analysis highlights the crucial role of female teachers in fostering inclusivity and nurturing student talent in the classroom. The media's portrayal of the protagonist as a female educator underscores the importance of empowering women in education and breaking down gender stereotypes that often limit their professional opportunities. Additionally, the "guru" concept is explored as a central pillar of Indian education, emphasizing mentorship, respect, and the transformative power of learning. By situating 'Hichki' within the broader SDG framework, this study notes the importance of addressing disability, supporting female teachers, and promoting gender equality to achieve comprehensive educational outcomes in India.

DOI: 10.4018/979-8-3373-5087-5.ch012

INTRODUCTION

The societal perception of persons with disabilities (PWDs) has evolved over time, yet it remains heavily influenced by deeply ingrained prejudices, marginalisation, and social exclusion. This research study examines the historical and contemporary perceptions of disability, focusing on how these beliefs impact social dynamics and the treatment of individuals with disabilities in India. This analysis is essential for eliminating systemic barriers that contribute to exclusion and discrimination. By highlighting the social constructs surrounding disability, it is imperative to promote practices and policies that advocate accessibility and equality. A thorough understanding of disability as an aspect of the human experience enhances the collective view of diversity and assists in a more inclusive society. These perceptions form in various ways, ranging from stigmatisation and exclusion to more current efforts aimed at improving inclusivity and spreading awareness.

This study highlights the importance of inclusive education as a critical component of social integration. Quality education, the 4th Sustainable Development Goal (SDG), aims to ensure an equitable and inclusive quality education for all, and is highly relevant to the discourse of disability in India (UNESCO, 2015). Education serves not only as an empowering tool for individuals with disabilities but also as a means of transforming societal beliefs about disability. The importance of quality education is emphasised by its progressive and transformative effects on other Sustainable Development Goals (SDGs). Sustainable development ensures that quality education is provided to every child. When children are provided the means to reach their full potential, they develop into productive adults who can contribute positively to their communities and helping to dismantle the prejudice and discrimination in society.

The outbreak of COVID-19 pandemic spread worldwide, impacting almost all countries and territories, which led to the implementation of public care strategies including physical distancing, proper hygiene, wearing face masks, and avoiding mass gatherings. The strategies of lockdown and staying home have been implemented to manage the transmission of the disease (Sintema, 2020). The global pandemic led to the disruption of education and teaching practices in human history. The COVID-19 pandemic provided an opportunity for education systems to enhance their technological strategies and utilise digital spaces for effective pedagogy (Dhawan, 2020). During the closure of universities and schools due to the pandemic, digitalisation played a significant role in facilitating effective student learning (Subedi et al., 2020).

Historically, the access to quality education for PWDs has been limited, which reinforces their marginalisation and exclusion from society (UNESCO, 2020). The goal of quality education emphasises that regardless of physical or intellectual abilities, everyone should have the chance to receive a quality education that is accessible, responsive and equally catered to their specific needs (UN, 2015). Socioeconomic disparities represent a major challenge in education, impacting various indicators. Global and regional parity ratios can conceal gender inequalities within countries, potentially disadvantageing either girls or boys (UNESCO, 2020). Disparities associated with geographical location and household income are particularly stark as it is rural and low-income families facing more significant obstacles in accessing quality education (UNICEF, 2019).

At higher education levels, these gaps often expand which leads to increased dropout rates and fewer opportunities for those from underprivileged backgrounds. This goal focuses on minimising inequities and disparities in the education system, addressing both quality and access. It highlights the significance of providing quality education to all, especially to vulnerable and disadvantaged groups such as individuals in rural areas, underprivileged children, individuals with disabilities and indigenous groups (UN, 2015). This study aims to examine the progress India has made in achieving the goal of quality education and the barriers and limitations faced by PWDs in the educational system and, by extension, into society.

Prior to the 19th century, perceptions of disability were largely shaped by superstition, fear, and religious beliefs, often resulting in the neglect, persecution, and even extermination of individuals with disabilities (Lal, 2012). Disabilities were frequently viewed as divine punishment, reinforcing the notion that such individuals were cursed or different from the rest of society. The emergence of the 19th and 20th centuries brought a shift in attitudes, with the establishment of institutions to care for people with intellectual disabilities (Lal, 2012). However, these institutions often perpetuated segregation, further entrenching the belief that individuals with disabilities should be kept apart from mainstream society. The 20th century saw a gradual shift toward advocacy, legislation, and a focus on education and support, yet societal resistance to full inclusion remained strong, especially in India. The Indian education system has long been influenced by a multitude of sociocultural factors, and the role of women teachers within this framework is both pivotal and complex.

Despite constituting a significant portion of the teaching workforce, women teachers often face systemic challenges that can undermine their effectiveness and impact (Chandran, 2020). This paper analyses the negligent role of women teachers in the Indian education system, examining the factors that contribute to this issue and its implications for education quality and gender equity. Historically, women's participation in education has been fraught with obstacles, stemming from deep-rooted patriarchal norms and societal expectations. While women have made significant strides in educational attainment, their professional roles in schools are frequently marginalised.

In the Indian context, despite progressive legislative developments and increased attention on inclusion, individuals with disabilities continue to face considerable challenges. This ongoing marginalisation can be largely attributed to the persistent societal perception that disability is a personal tragedy or individual problem that must be "fixed" (Sukhramani & Verma, 2013). Such perceptions overlook the structural and environmental barriers that impede the full participation of PWDs in society.

Cultural factors, particularly the theory of karma, also play a significant role in shaping societal attitudes toward disability in India. Societal definitions of "normal," "abnormal," "good health," and "beauty" also contribute to the exclusion of PWDs from full participation in social life (Dalal & Pande, 1999). These definitions, which often prioritise physical and mental capacities, create rigid expectations that fail to accommodate the diverse experiences of PWDs.

The divide between "us" and "them" is further reinforced by a lack of interaction between PWDs and the broader community (Sukhramani & Verma, 2013). In Indian society, opportunities for social interaction for PWDs are often limited to their families and service providers. This isolation perpetuates stereotypes and misconceptions, making it difficult for society to view PWDs as individuals with unique identities, experiences, and contributions. Furthermore, mainstream media representations of PWDs often reinforce negative stereotypes. Indian cinema, for instance, frequently uses disability as a source of humour or pity, further marginalising individuals with disabilities. Films like 'Housefull 3' (2016) and the 'Golmaal' series (2006–2017) have been critiqued for using disability as a comic trope, reflecting the insensitivity of societal perceptions towards PWDs (Deo, 2023).

The rise in digitalization during the COVID-19 pandemic where educational institutions and workplaces had all shifted to online means also brought about a change in the portrayal of disabilities and societal dogmas in the digital spaces (Yildirim et al., 2022). People became more aware of the diversity prevalent in people with disabilities. Digital spaces rather than serving just as a means of entertainment transformed into a means of imparting knowledge about the lesser-known societal issues. In recent years, there has been a gradual shift in how disability is portrayed in Indian media, with films such as 'Black' (2005), 'Taare Zameen Par' (2007), and 'Hichki' (2018) contributing to more nuanced and empathetic representations of disability (Deo, 2023). While these films have faced criticism for perpetuating certain stereotypes, they mark an important shift in public discourse, challenging the dominant narrative of disability as a personal tragedy and instead presenting individuals with disabilities as complex characters with unique experiences, struggles, and contributions. This shift, though imperfect, has the potential to influence societal perceptions and promote a more inclusive understanding of disability.

The marginalisation of female teachers reflects broader societal attitudes highlighting the set gender roles. By failing to recognize and support the contributions of women in education, society undermines the potential for equitable development and empowerment. A more inclusive approach to education, which values the role of women teachers, is essential for fostering a culture of respect and gender equality. By acknowledging the challenges, they face and actively promoting their professional growth, there can be improvement not only with the status of women in education but also the overall quality of education in India. Empowering women educators is crucial for building a more equitable and effective educational landscape, benefiting students and society (Zhu, 2020).

The COVID-19 pandemic brought new teaching practices as there is no specific pedagogy for digital learning since there are various types of subjects with different needs and approaches, and different subjects with varying age groups require different strategies (Doucet et al., 2020). Children from marginalised backgrounds, including those belonging to Scheduled Tribes (ST), Scheduled Castes (SC), and other disadvantaged and underprivileged groups, often encounter additional barriers. These obstacles can include systemic prejudice and discrimination, lower expectations from teachers, and a lack of representation in curriculum. Such stigmatisation and exclusion can result in lower self-esteem and aspirations among these children, reinforcing cycles of disadvantage (Bourdieu et al., 1990).

Underprivileged children dealt with learning barriers because of the lack of wealth and resources. The utilisation of digitalisation for online teaching practices during the COVID-19 pandemic faced challenges in terms of affordability, accessibility, flexibility, effective learning pedagogy, and educational policies.

This paper aims to examine these issues in greater depth by analysing both the historical and contemporary societal perceptions of disability, the role of cultural beliefs, and the impact of these perceptions on the lives of individuals with disabilities in India. By addressing the persistent barriers to inclusion, particularly in education, and advocating for a more inclusive society, this research seeks to contribute to the broader discourse on disability rights, social justice, and sustainable development. In order to achieve inclusion in reality, it is essential to challenge deeply entrenched societal perceptions of disability and move beyond the thought process of viewing disabled people as charity and personal tragedy models. This requires a multifaceted approach, pertaining to reforms in the legislature, public awareness campaigns, and changes in societal attitudes. Quality education, as emphasised by SDG 4, and media representation play a critical role in this process, helping to challenge stereotypes and promote a more inclusive understanding of disability.

DIGITAL REPRESENTATION OF DISABILITY

For centuries, disability and its wide range of perceptions have been deeply stigmatised and misunderstood by human society. Disability is a diverse experience that includes a variety of physical, mental and cognitive conditions that society deems as an undesirable and pitiful condition that is to be 'prevented' and 'cured' (Carlson, 2010). Disability should not be viewed as a simple or static definition as disability is dynamic, complex, and multidimensional. The misperception created by society on the different types and forms of disabilities constrains the ability to learn and spread awareness on the inequalities experienced by the disabled community.

The purpose of the United Nations Convention on the Rights of Persons with Disabilities (CRPD) is to promote, protect, and ensure that persons with disabilities (PWDs) are provided equal human rights and fundamental freedoms. PWDs comprise those with long-term physical, mental, intellectual, or sensory impairments that can limit their active participation in society on an equal basis with non-disabled people due to various barriers (United Nations Department of Economic and Social Affairs, n.d.). The CRPD introduces a human rights perspective to issues with disability, shifting the focus from a medical model to a social model of disability (Kayess & French, 2008).

The medical model perceives disability as a medical issue that resides within the people. Disability is seen as a failure or defect in the human body, and inherently dysfunctional and abnormal (Olkin, 1999). According to the medical model, the PWDs are the ones who need to be fixed or changed rather than focusing on the conditions or barriers that might be affecting and contributing to the individual's disability (Kasser & Lytle, 2005). The phrase 'social model of disability' was coined by Oliver (1981) and it emphasises on the need to focus on the aspects of social and physical limitations imposed on certain groups of people. The development of the social model of disability is a reaction to the limitations of the medical model of disability (D' Alessio, 2011). As per the social model, it is society that creates limitations and barriers for PWDs, and meaningful and effective solutions should be directed at bringing societal change rather than adjustment and rehabilitation for PWDs (Barnes et al., 2010).

United Nations Educational Scientific and Cultural Organization (UNESCO) advocates for an inclusive environment that promotes equal educational opportunities for all without exclusion, distinction, preference or discrimination. Inclusive education ensures to identify and eliminate all barriers to learning, addressing every aspect of curriculum content in relation to pedagogy and teaching methods (UNESCO 2018; UNESCO, 2024). In several areas of the Sustainable Development Goals (SDGs), disability is addressed in relation to education, employment, awareness, and reducing inequality (United Nations Department of Economic and Social Affairs, n.d.).

Quality education emphasises on the need for equitable and inclusive education and learning opportunities for all, eliminating gender disparities in the education sector and ensuring equal access of training and education is provided to the vulnerable and marginalised groups, including PWDs. Quality education, the Goal 4 of SDGs, aims to focus on the developing and advancing educational methods and facilities that are sensitive, effective, safe, inclusive learning environments for everyone (United Nations Department of Economic and Social Affairs, n.d.). Quality education is an imperative priority for UNESCO as it fosters a sustainable and healthy lifestyle for people and reduces inequality and prejudice in society (United Nations, 2015).

Disability varies among people and their personal experiences. Visible disabilities can be easily identifiable by others based on basic communication, external appearance, and restriction in movement. The factor of "visibility" creates the sense of shame and stigma, and the need for PWDs to expose their personal circumstances to others (Matthews & Harrington, 2000). In contrast, invisible disabilities are not immediately recognized by the observer (Matthews & Herrington, 2000). A distinct contrast regarding the visibility of a disability simply cannot be divided between visible and invisible as persons with disabilities (PWDs) perceive themselves differently depending on their types of disabilities, a specific distinction can be depicted between "non-visible" disability and "invisible" disability wherein "non-visible" disabilities are referred to as disabilities that cannot be recognized by others easily, while "invisible" disabilities can be used to highlight the social oppression and alienation of a certain group of disabled minorities (Samuels, 2003).

A perception expected of PWDs with regards to societal norms is the ability to lead a "normal" life similarly to people without disabilities. The PWDs perceive their own disabilities through the same lens to how society perceives it, which means critically and negatively as depicted in a previous study (Wright, 1980). The disability can reveal a range of ethical dilemmas in relation to family dynamics, social engagements, and daily activities (Falvo, 2005). The disclosure of one's disability is intricate and complex because there is a fear of being rejected by one's loved ones and society. An ethically challenging question that is faced by PWDs is characterising one's disability in relation to others and oneself (Samuels, 2003).

Similarly to issues experienced by people with highly visible disabilities fear being labelled, people with invisible disabilities are often worried about being labelled as abnormal and demeaned by society (Almog, 2011). Individuals with invisible disabilities face the challenge of disclosing their disability and its extent as concealing one's disability often requires considerable effort and thorough planning. The act of concealment can result in the feelings of dishonesty and lead to social isolation (Almog, 2011; Jans et al., 2012). Numerous people with disabilities oppose the limitations that come with being defined and labelled by their disabilities (Riddell & Watson, 2014). This opposition leads PWDs to conceal parts of their disabilities or choose not to reveal their disability at all and attempt to "pass" as "normal" (Samuels, 2003).

In the Indian societal setup, the idea of disability is seen as a problematic aspect, enumerating upon the fact that disability is caused because of a person's past sins and the karma accumulated in the past life. The term diversity, when defined, incorporates the aspects of gender, race, caste structure, culture, religion, language, and ethnicity, but people with disabilities are excluded from this definition. The treatment meted out to the PWDs by the society underscores the reality of the educated and civilised beings, who are the real disabled people, devoid of empathy, understanding and a sense of inclusivity.

Disability is described as per the societal definitions of normal and abnormal, compelling the people with disabilities to consider themselves outcasts in the society. The lack of support provided by the family members and relatives also acts as an important factor in the ostracising of the physically disabled. People with disabilities in India are often perceived as people with 'personal tragedy' or 'individual problems' which need to be fixed (Sukhramani & Verma, 2013).

The development of an inclusive education system is regarded as a fundamental pillar for the full participation of PWDs in society. There is a constant under-representation of teachers with disability in the Indian digital spaces, which has been cross examined in the film 'Hichki', where the public is made aware of a neurodevelopmental disorder, Tourette's Syndrome. It is a common disorder characterised by multiple, repetitive movements or unwanted sounds (tics) that cannot be willingly controlled or subdued by the person. Tourette's syndrome frequently involves behavioural and social challenges, which in majority cases affects the self-confidence of the person. This is portrayed through the female protagonist, Naina, who is constantly rebuked and demeaned for her condition, which is not under her physical and psychological control.

The film depicts the journey of a teacher with disability, who through her determination and hard work creates a respectable place for herself in society. About life trajectories, research highlights two major issues: (1) the negative (or less positive) experiences they faced as students, and (2) key factors contributing to their professional achievement, in particular, the importance of social support, self-confidence and resilience and resistance (Neca et al., 2020).

The film portrays that teacher with disabilities, as students, had to deal with substandard expectations from their teachers, which instilled in them an urge to establish their impact in society and to bring about a change in the educational sector. This serves as a reason for the teachers, leading them to choose teaching as a profession, with the aim of providing better educational experiences to their future students, different from what they faced as students. The protagonist has faced discrimination and humiliation from a young age, where she was laughed at by the normal children for her abnormality. This discrimination is supported by the teachers who instead of making the others aware about her condition, blame her for disrupting the sanctity of a classroom, making her feel at fault. The humiliation felt by her father, as her weird behaviour hinders him from having a deeply understanding and supporting relation with her, leading to a lack of parental support. The film also highlights the lack of social support provided to the female protagonist, where she is outrightly rejected as being a capable teacher even though her educational qualifications are at a higher par than the average applicant applying for the post of a teacher. Her capability is judged by the amount of normalcy present in her life, not by her sheer courage and talent.

The COVID-19 pandemic had a profound and disruptive impact on society as the transmissive disease severely influenced all aspects of daily life, including social, economic, psychological, and emotional well-being across the world. The PWDs were highly impacted during the COVID-19 pandemic, experiencing access denial to essential services, like medications, lack of caregivers, exclusion from the educational sector and exposure to economic hardships. There is now a growing body of evidence to strongly suggest that disabled people have also been among those worst affected by COVID-19. They have been among those most at risk of catching the virus (WHO, 2020) and have also been among the hardest hit in terms of fatalities (United Nations, 2020). Many have experienced increased levels of discrimination and a wide range of socioeconomic deprivations, reinforcing the already close relationship between disability and poverty (Cobley, 2022).

The isolation and loneliness experienced by many PWDs during the pandemic continued even after the lockdown was eased, because of the trepidation of infection among disabled people themselves and also because of the limited availability of transport services, and the lack of community activities. Due to the healthcare services being majorly focused on cases of COVID-19, there was a lack of regular treatments and rehabilitation services being provided to the disabled people.

The closure of educational institutions and MNCs led to the further exclusion of disabled children, the majority of them being unable to access remote learning, and the loss of employment opportunities for new recruits, even the employed people lost their jobs due to the economic growth suffering great deprivation. The World Bank (2020) reports that temporary school closures during lockdown periods have affected 85% of the world's school children and caused 40% of disadvantaged learners in low and middle-income countries to be left entirely unsupported in their education (Cobley, 2022).

A national survey conducted in India by the National Centre for Promotion of Employment for Disabled People (NCPEDP, 2020) reported that out of 1,000 disabled people, 67% of respondents were not able to access government deliveries of essential supplies (in some cases because they had been unable to obtain disability certificates). The survey also highlighted the disintegration of social and peer support networks, with many losing the support of the caregivers on whom they had relied for personal assistance (Cobley, 2022).

The pandemic also saw a significant rise in gender-based violence, showcasing the additional discrimination and hardship faced by women. In Sri Lanka, (Kandasamy et al., 2021) draw on the narratives of two disabled women to explore how their exclusion and marginalisation, brought about through the combined effect of disability, gender, rurality, religion, age and ethnicity, had become further entrenched. A study conducted in Nepal (Gurung, 2021) notes the increased risk of gender-based violence to which disabled women and girls had been exposed, within families, communities and even public quarantine centres. This had impacted particularly on disabled women from indigenous communities, who were situated right at the bottom of the social hierarchy and often denied access to medical and legal services (Cobley, 2022).

COVID-19, DIGITAL EDUCATION AND NOVEL TEACHING PRACTICES

The historic shift of the COVID-19 pandemic spread worldwide, impacting countries in every aspect of society, influencing everyday life, health and economy in extreme measures. The implementation of strategies such as lockdown and staying home became the norm to control the transmission of the disease (Sintema, 2020). For all the countries, the primary focus resided in minimising the rapid spread of COVID-19 in society (Mirza et al., 2020; Osman, 2020; Rizvi et al., 2020). As a result, extreme measures took place to control the mass infection of COVID-19 as schools, universities, and other education institutions worldwide were closed (Murphy, 2020). This led educational systems to transition and adapt from the traditional approach of teaching that is face-to-face settings to digital spaces, aiming to constrain the disease by the rapid development of digital education and the utilisation of novel teaching practices. As policy makers transitioned to the new normal, especially in the educational sector globally as most educational institutes adapted to the digital learning pedagogy to continue the process of teaching and learning (Weeden & Cornwell, 2020).

The immediate transition of traditional pedagogy to digital pedagogy highlighted the rise of severe issues and difficulties due to the global lockdown (Crawford et al., 2020). The reaction towards the pandemic varied based on geographical location, severity of infection, hospitalisation rates, financial resources, and community needs. These rapid changes came with an increased utilisation of hybrid learning and remote learning completely due to the severity of the disease, leading towards drastic shifts to the educational standards. Though remote learning is not a new concept, many educators struggle with adapting the academic, mental, and emotional needs of their students in an online learning environment (Minkos & Gelbar, 2021).

The concept of e-learning focused on delivering education through various forms of digital platforms such as the internet, intranet, extranet, or satellite among the students (Chen, 2011). Digital pedagogy became a critical component utilised during the global pandemic for effective continuation of education across all levels (Alipio, 2020; Basilaia and Kvavadze, 2020; Soni, 2020). To create a learning environment that provides support for students in both formal and informal resources, digital education requires an essential amount of time and commitment (Yuan, 2021).

Despite the obstacles of teaching, there was a significant focus on student outcomes during the COVID-19 pandemic, in which teachers held the responsibility and burden of implementing new approaches and programs to maintain daily routines while dealing with disruption and chaos. As a result, there has been an increase in stress, anxiety, and turnover for educators (Steiner & Woo, 2021). The management of classroom environment, student outcomes, and teacher turnover (Arens & Morin, 2016) puts emphasis on the extreme stress that stems from creating academic content in the context of the pandemic which may impact the physical and mental health of educators (Guglielmi and Tatrow, 1998; Katz et al., 2016).

While governments and health workers controlled the pandemic outbreak, education sectors tried to manage and provide quality education for everyone. Like the mental stress experienced by teachers, students at their living spaces also dealt with emotional and psychological distress which resulted in less productivity and engagement during their academic sessions (Petrie, 2020). The shift of the educational sector to remote or hybrid learning forms led to a rapidly growing discourse around "learning loss" (Dorn et al., 2020; Engzell et al., 2021; Kuhfeld and Tarasawa, 2020). In the pandemic crisis, technology became the avenue to help reduce learning loss by enabling lockdown distance education, however factors such as accessibility and economic crisis caused drastic changes and this led to learning loss which occurred likely due to poor physical and social infrastructure and prolonged closure of educational institutes (Engzell et al., 2021).

For digital education, the utilisation of relevant and adequate teaching platforms includes collaborative and unified platforms such as Google Classroom, Microsoft Teams, Canvas, and Blackboard which enables educators to create learning material and development programmes for training and skills (Petrie, 2020). Online communication and circulation of information became easier through the means of video meetings, group chats, and sharing content through file formats of PDF, Excel, Word, videos, and other effective platform options of Moodle, Zoom and Google Meet. The concept of the flipped classroom is a simple approach for providing learning resources like pre-recorded study material videos, articles and YouTube links before the academic sessions as then the time of the online session is utilised to comprehend the topic of discussion with educators and peers (Doucet et al., 2020).

Digital education poses a major challenge for developing countries due to the scarcity and inaccessibility of resources. Though online education is an effective tool that could provide efficient results in countries which are digitally advanced, such claims cannot be perceived for developing countries (Basilaia & Kvavadze, 2020). Particularly, the students from low-income families and rural areas of developing countries faced difficult situations due to the sudden need of online education as the students lacked the adequate digital devices and struggled to obtain fast and affordable internet connection (Wains & Mahmood, 2008).

Most teachers, especially those in low income and rural areas, struggled with adapting to hybrid and online learning approaches due to a lack of technological training and support, inadequate bandwidth and rapid changes (Goldberg, 2021). Particularly, remote learning was challenging for many reasons in elementary schools as children experienced fatigue with digital platforms and lacked access to the internet and computers (Fauzi & Khusuma, 2020). The COVID-19 pandemic resulted in a digital divide among countries and different income groups, and the study showed that 95% of the students from advanced countries have a computer to use for their educational learning, while this percentage is drastically low for developing countries (Gouëdard, 2021).

The emergence of COVID-19 brought about a drastic change in the education sector, forcing the traditional teaching methods to be replaced by digitalization to act as a precaution against the pandemic. Whilst this shift was very challenging for educationists across the globe, in India it raised the questions pertaining to the weakness of online teaching infrastructure, the limited exposure of teachers to online teaching, the information gap, non-conducive environment for learning at home, equity and academic excellence in terms of higher education (Pokhrel & Chhetri, 2021). Borrowing from Ernest Boyer, Brooks highlights how sites of higher education, like universities act as 'communities' of 'shared values and ideas of academics and students. Whether this community requires a physical location to proliferate or not, can be debated. However, according to Brooks (1997), scholars over the years have recognised the necessity of this academic community and the interactions within it. He states that virtual universities lead to the development of 'parasocial intersections', a concept developed by Horton and Wohl (quoted in Brooks, 1997). Parasocial interaction is neither intimate nor instrumental but rather 'virtual' or 'distant' (Ganguly, 2023).

The digitalization of education distances the sense of community building, which transforms children into responsible adults, forming a generation devoid of empathy and socialisation. The traditional ways of education also raise social skills and awareness besides providing a means of jollification. The change from offline mode of teaching to online mode, showcases the advancement of the nation but also portrays the fact that whilst advancement in technology is quite appealing, it can never replace the role of a teacher. Researchers also highlight the importance of interaction but argue that pedagogy takes precedence over the medium (Driscoll et al., 2012). Scholars in their engagement with Information and Communication Technologies (ICTs) in higher education in India, highlight the specific need for 'massive drives of digital literacy, development of requisite infrastructure and devising of special measures to incorporate different ICT tools'. The low rates of digital literacy among students, very few ICT-trained teachers, and the absence of adequate infrastructure, have led to the 'low status' of ICTs in Indian higher education (Chatterjee & Nath, 2015). There is a wide digital gap between the elderly teachers and the students who know the workings of modern-day technology, which is unyielding even to the substantial rise in the usage of smart-phones and the internet availability in the country.

The National Education Policy (NEP) 2020, showcases the 'extensive use of technology in teaching and learning' as one of its core principles (Government of India, National Educational Policy, 2020). It has taken initiatives such as Digital India and Skill India, and Massive Online Open Courses (MOOCs) to train a vast majority from various backgrounds in digital literacy. Even though the government has worked tirelessly to make the sudden shift to online mode of education quite feasible for all age groups and social groups, the question of the 'digital divide' persists. There is a significant division between private and public educational institutions from their infrastructure to the difference in knowledge and resources imparted by the government. A researcher (Cherian, 2021) highlights the question of digital literacy and the lack of infrastructural provisions among students belonging to economically weaker sections. She further argues how the internet is not 'an equaliser' but deepens the already existing disparities. The author brings in the teachers' perspectives through her study and states that the online classes are more of a 'makeshift arrangement to conceal the learning gaps', transforming into just a platform for exchanging presentations, recordings and leads to a lack of face-to-face in-depth discussions.

A report published by the Telecom Regulation Authority of India in 2020, shows that in the rural areas more than 40% of the population are internet subscribers while an approximate 50% of the urban population are internet subscribers (Telecom Regulation Authority of India, 2020). During the pandemic the people in urban areas had the privilege of using the internet for the means of studying, office work and recreational purposes, but the situation in rural areas was quite different. The students from economically weaker sections of society had an obligation to participate in domestic chores due to which they were unable to attend online classes regularly without any form of disturbance.

Another factor in the low turnout of economically underprivileged students in online classes was the unavailability of disposable income to purchase the internet packages. For children belonging to vulnerable socioeconomic backgrounds, education had taken a secondary position, and their primary focus had shifted to the sustainability of their families, either by helping economically or attending to household responsibilities. The parents also faced difficulties in adapting to the drastic changes in their childrens' teaching methods and had to constantly act as a surveillant, so that the children attended their classes without getting distracted by the internet and social media. There emerged a lack of enthusiasm among the students while attending online lectures because their study environment and their lack of interests forced them to skip classes. The experience of online teaching, the question of 'absence-presence', 'discontinuities of authority and power' and rethinking who and what is to be prioritised; should be considered as serious concerns in virtual teaching and learning (Gravett, 2022). Scholars like Bhattacharya (2020) argue that the strength of internet connectivity, cost of data packs, conducive home environment and household responsibilities of female students are factors to consider that go beyond the mere question of access to internet services (Ganguly, 2023).

Treatment Methods of Teachers–Students in the Education Sector

The COVID-19 pandemic gave rise to digital education, exposing educators to unique and complex challenges, particularly female educators. The educational sector was heavily impacted as the COVID-19 pandemic emerged with new disruptions and challenges, highlighting the inequities and flaws within the education system (Cipriano et al., 2020). Expectations from teachers were not only to provide digital teaching content, instructions for academics and assessments, and emotional support, but also to foster relationships with students and families without receiving proper support or compensation from the administration, which can cause frustration, stress, burnout, and teacher turnover (Stauffer & Mason, 2013).

The pre-pandemic period held common reasons for stress by teachers including a lack of agency and control concerning decisions for curricula, lack of respect for the profession, difficulty with managing student behaviour, and inadequate resources and support (Kyriacou, 2001; Richards, 2012). During the COVID-19 pandemic, many teachers experienced these same reasons with additional fears, including physical safety, health, and well-being (Will, 2021). There is progress in terms of gender equity in the public sphere for women, though women have achieved significantly less in the domestic sphere (England, 2010). "The Second Shift" proposes the notion that in the workforce, women not only experience the burden of their "first shift," which is working for eight hours daily in the public sphere but also managing the eighth hours of domestic labour once they reach their households, that is considered as the "second shift" (Hochschild, 1989).

The concept of "emotional labour" is enforced upon women as they must maintain and suppress their emotions and act upon them concerning the expectations of the workplace (Hochschild, 1983; Hochschild, 2012). This concept leans into the psychological and sociological effects on women and their professions, such as the expectation from female educators that requires emotional caretaking and pampering of students and parents (Brotheridge & Grandey, 2002).

The change from physical spaces to digital spaces for teaching practices led to complicated issues as the utilisation of digital platforms and functions, and the aspect of making academic video content became difficult for teachers (Lestiyanawati, 2020). Teachers are also blamed and targeted for the negative impact of the COVID-19 pandemic and digital education on students and their families which takes a severe toll on the physical and mental well-being of women (Judge et al., 2009; Pugliesi 1999).

Quality education portrays the need for inclusivity and equitability which can be fostered through sufficient policies and practices, and action towards workplace harassment and discrimination towards female educators. During the pre-pandemic period, female educators experienced harassment, including inappropriate behaviour, unwanted touching, vulgar gestures, and name-calling (Moon et al., 2019). Sexist remarks and misconduct followed into the time of the pandemic as female educators continued to be sexualised based on their appearance, movement, and language (Lahelma et al., 2000). In various cases of discrimination and harassment, it is female educators who are seen as the problem instead of the perpetrators (Keddie, 2007; Robinson, 2000). In turn, this causes female educators to blame themselves as they internalise the situation (Keddie, 2007; Robinson 2000; Variyan and Wilkinson, 2022).

Internet communication plays an essential role in the psychological and cognitive well-being of all genders, age groups, and cultures (Chou et al., 2005; Matook et al., 2015; Sahin, 2014). Problematic Internet Usage (PIU) is a classified mental health phenomenon that is referred to as an unhealthy addiction to digital platforms (Young, 2004). Considering the COVID-19 pandemic, the internet and digital spaces were increasingly utilised for communicational, social, and occupational purposes which resulted in the infliction of willful and repetitive harm towards others through the medium of 'electronic texting' (Patchin & Hinduja, 2006). The aspect of digital media enables such acts of trolling and harassment to take place beyond the time constraints of educational institutes and work environments (Crosslin and Golman, 2014; Patchin and Hinduja, 2006).

Trolling can be defined as intentional harassment derived from a desire to seek attention, revenge, pleasure, or boredom (Buckels et al., 2014; Coles and West, 2016; Shachaf and Hara, 2010). Trolling ranges from relatively minor transgressions to severe harassment intended to cause distress and misery (Maltby et al., 2016). During their online activities, trolls benefit from the state of anonymity which diminishes their self-awareness, toxic online behaviour, and sense of accountability (Chiou, 2006; Wachs et al., 2019).

Online trolling is the most experienced form of harassment, including derogatory comments and sexist remarks aimed to undermine the authority and credibility of female teachers. Significantly, trolling varies across age groups, though trolls presumably target vulnerable groups, such as children, women, people with disabilities, and gender and ethnic groups (Centre for Strategy and Evaluation Services, 2019; Pulman and Taylor, 2012).

The extreme stress of providing academic material in the context of the pandemic negatively impacted the physical and mental health of teachers (Guglielmi and Tatrow, 1998; Katz et al., 2016). Amid the ongoing pandemic period, teachers cited stress as the major factor for quitting their jobs because of workplace situations (Diliberti et al., 2021). Teachers and students alike have experienced the pandemic as a traumatic event and evidently, trauma expands the outcomes of negative mental and physical health (Felitti et al., 1998; Subica et al., 2012). Having experienced trauma, teachers feel inadequate to meet the variety of needs of their students and face challenges due to work, reporting emotional burdens and vicarious trauma (Alisic, 2012). A significant amount of job-related stress for teachers also stems from the interconnected aspects of stressors which include their personal lives, their students' lives, and the wider societal context (Gallup Education, 2014).

In digital spaces such as social media, the representation of female teachers can have a lasting impact on the long-term commitment to remaining a teacher as social media can shape the professional image of teachers (Eacott et al., 2020). This can lead to the decline of quality education as a negative image of teachers in digital spaces will have harmful consequences for the future of the teaching profession, students, and the education system (Eacott et al., 2020; Olmstead, 2020).

The relationship between teachers and students is considered a sacred bond, full of respect and understanding. While the teacher-student bond described in our vedas, puranas and religious scriptures is full of sanctity, in the modern world the profession has lost its charm due to the inequalities prevalent in society. The film 'Hichki' portrays two major relationships of the teachers with their students. The female protagonist, Naina portrays the role of a teacher who is ready to adapt her ways of teaching as per the requirements of her students. Made to deal with a class considered socially disabled due to their lower socioeconomic status, they are treated as outcasts and charity cases and suffer immense humiliation at the hands of the other teachers who consider them unfit for the reputation of their esteemed school. While they are ostracised by the entire teaching community, the female protagonist tries to understand their way of life, which is quite different from the lifestyle of the other privileged kids. They act as a support system for their families by supporting them financially or by helping in the household chores, whilst having a determination to be educated even though they lack the necessary means of technology and resources. Naina considers that it is the duty of a teacher to adapt their teaching methods and practices as per the needs of their students. While the other teachers consider demarcating students according to their sociocultural understanding, the female protagonist portrays inclusivity as a necessary trait for imparting equitable knowledge to students without segregating them based on their gender, class, religion, culture and language.

Teachers portray biases even while communicating with disabled students, even if the disability is not detrimental to the health of the disabled person. Disabilities are of different kinds depending on their severity, highlighting the fact that not all disabled people need to be treated as a special needs person. Teachers portray two kinds of behaviour with their disabled students, the most common one being downgrading the self-esteem of the student, whilst considering them as a distraction and disturbance for the environment of the classroom. The other behaviour portrays teachers as people who consider all disabilities as physically and mentally challenging for the person.

Having a disability can be one of the most marginalising factors in a person's life. Thus, inclusive education which engages all students, even students with disabilities or other learning challenges, in quality education without any discrimination or humiliation is a necessary step for creating a conducive environment where all students get equal opportunities to portray their skills and talents. The most important step regarding this, is to create a positive teacher-student relationship for all students, including those with and without disabilities. A teacher's ability to create a positive relationship with their students can impact their academic and socio-emotional success.

CONCLUSION

India as a developing nation has progressed far more than its counterparts in terms of technological advancements, educational reforms and societal development, but this progress is exclusive of a particular section of society, that is the marginalised communities, such as people with disabilities and people from underprivileged backgrounds. This research study emphasises the significance of an equitable and inclusive education as a critical aspect of social integration. Quality education (SDG 4) is vital because of its transformative effects on other Sustainable Development Goals (SDGs) as education serves as a means for society to become progressive and dismantle perceptions of prejudice and marginalisation. In the global educational landscape, achieving quality education is multifaceted and complex as it reflects diverse issues and challenges of exclusion and stigmatisation faced by subjugated groups. It is essential to propose innovative systems that facilitate understanding, empathy and accessibility across a variety of dimensions in the teaching pedagogy.

The requirement of digitalisation became significant due to the COVID-19 pandemic which exposed the inequities and limitations of the educational systems worldwide. While it imposed rapid innovation and adaptation, COVID-19 also revealed the obstacles faced by the underprivileged, marginalised and disabled people. Though some teachers transitioned well into the digital teaching platforms, traditional pedagogical methods often failed to be interpreted into online learning formats as many teachers faced challenges in developing an inclusive and engaging learning environment, depriving marginalised and disabled children from quality education.

There is an inherent need for the inclusion of all people in the normative society, without segregating them on the basis of their caste, gender, class, ethnicity, physical deformities and disorders. Development is required in the field of educational reforms, catering to the apparent shift towards digitalization, since most teachers in rural sectors are still lacking behind in terms of infrastructural facilities, technological resources and availability of internet facilities. This leads to an education gap between the teachers and students in urban and rural areas. The influx of online modes of teaching will survive only when the underprivileged students are provided incentives and opportunities to gain knowledge as well as provide help to their families. The economic conditions of these underprivileged people also need to be improved so that they can have access to digital devices and internet packages, a necessity for digitalization.

Gender inequality remains an omnipresent issue still prevalent in the education sector majorly affecting the professional spaces of female teachers and students. The government should address the challenges faced by female educators, including online harassment, career advancement barriers, familial responsibilities and the pressure of balancing professional responsibilities with domestic duties and aim to create reformation policies adhering to these challenges. The educational institutions should also acclimatise female teachers with skill development facilities to equip them with skills and confidence, an important aspect for leadership roles. While the promotion of female representation in educational leadership enhances gender equity, it also provides an enriching learning experience for all students by introducing diverse perspectives and opinions.

Though the path towards achieving quality education is filled with challenges, on the positive side it is also filled with opportunities for growth and transformation within the highly judgemental and prejudiced society. The COVID-19 pandemic showcased the shortcomings of the educational sector and provided a chance to rethink the prevailing educational practices and policies and ensured that the future policies will be focused on inclusivity and equitability. The prioritisation of quality education (SDG 4) will foster an environment of equity and inclusivity that is adept for people regardless of their background or abilities. This requires a collective commitment to embracing diversity and challenging the status quo, advocating for changes that promote equity in society.

REFERENCES

Aguiar, M., Hurst, E., & Karabarbounis, L. (2013). Time Use during the Great Recession. *The American Economic Review, 103*(5), 1664–1696. DOI: 10.1257/aer.103.5.1664

Alipio, M. (2020). *Education during Covid-19 Era: Are Learners in a Less-Economically Developed Country Ready for E-Learning?* Almog, N. (2011). *Academic and Social Adjustment of University Students with Visual Impairment* (Unpublished Doctoral Dissertation). Ramat Gan: School of Education, Bar-Ilan University.

Alisic, E. (2012). Teachers' Perspectives on Providing Support to Children after Trauma: A Qualitative Study. *School Psychology Quarterly, 27*(1), 51–59. DOI: 10.1037/a0028590 PMID: 22582936

Arens, A. K., & Morin, A. J. S. (2016). Relations between Teachers' Emotional Exhaustion and Students' Educational Outcomes. *Journal of Educational Psychology, 108*(6), 800–813. DOI: 10.1037/edu0000105

Barnes, C., Mercer, G., & Shakespeare, T. (2010). The social model of disability. In Giddens, A., & Sutton, P. (Eds.), *Sociology: Introductory Readings* (3rd ed., pp. 161–166). Polity Press.

Basilaia, G., & Kvavadze, D. (2020). *Transition to Online Education in Schools During a SARSCoV-2 Coronavirus (COVID-19) Pandemic in Georgia.* Pedagogical Research, 5(4).

Bhattacharya, S. (2020). What is So Wrong with Online Teaching? *Economic and Political Weekly.*

Bourdieu, P., & Passeron, J.-C. (1990). *Reproduction in Education, Society and Culture.* Sage Publications.

Brooks, J. M. (1997). Beyond Teaching and Learning Paradigms: Trekking into the Virtual University. *Teaching Sociology, 25*(1), 1. DOI: 10.2307/1319107

Brotheridge, C. M., & Grandey, A. A. (2002). Emotional Labor and Burnout: Comparing Two Perspectives of 'People Work.'. *Journal of Vocational Behavior, 60*(1), 17–39. DOI: 10.1006/jvbe.2001.1815

Buckels, E. E., Trapnell, P. D., & Paulhus, D. L. (2014). Trolls just want to have fun. *Personality and Individual Differences, 67*, 97–102. DOI: 10.1016/j.paid.2014.01.016

Carlson, L. (2010). *The Faces of Intellectual Disability.* Indiana University Press.

Chandran, M. (2020). Teacher Accountability and Education Restructuring: An Exploration of Teachers' Work Identities in an Urban School for Poor in India. *International Studies in Sociology of Education, 31*(3), 1–20.

Chatterjee, P., & Nath, A. (2015). *Future ICT Education in India—A Pilot Study on the Vision of Ubiquitous Learning in Higher Education.* In Information Systems Design and Intelligent Applications, edited by J. K. Mandal, Suresh Chandra Satapathy, Manas Kumar Sanyal, ParthaPratim Sarkar, and Anirban Mukhopadhyay, 599–609. New Delhi: Springer.

Chen, J.-L. (2011). The effects of education compatibility and technological expectancy on e-learning acceptance. *Computers & Education, 57*(2), 1501–1511. DOI: 10.1016/j.compedu.2011.02.009

Cherian, R. (2021). *The Odd One is 'Out': Voices from Virtual Classrooms.* Economic and Political Weekly Engage.

Chiou, W. (2006). Adolescents' sexual self-disclosure on the internet: Deindividuation and impression management. *Adolescence, 41*(163), 547–561. PMID: 17225667

Chou, C., Condron, L., & Belland, J. C. (2005). A review of the research on internet addiction. *Educational Psychology Review, 17*(4), 363–388. DOI: 10.1007/s10648-005-8138-1

Cipriano, C., Rappolt-Schlichtmann, G., & Brackett, M. A. (2020). *Supporting school community wellness with social and emotional learning (SEL) during and after a pandemic.* Edna Bennett Pierce Prevention Research Center, Pennsylvania State University.

Cobley, D. S. (2022). Rising to the challenge: Disability Organisations in the COVID-19 pandemic. *Disability & Society.*

Coles, B. A., & West, M. (2016). Trolling the trolls: Online forum users constructions of the nature and properties of trolling. *Computers in Human Behavior, 60,* 233–244. DOI: 10.1016/j.chb.2016.02.070

Crawford, J., Butler-Henderson, K., Rudolph, J., Malkawi, B., Glowatz, M., Burton, R., Magni, P., & Lam, S. (2020). COVID-19: 20 countries' higher education intra-period digital pedagogy responses. *Journal of Applied Learning & Teaching, 3*(1), 1–20.

Crosslin, K., & Golman, M. (2014). "Maybe you don't want to face it" – College students' perspectives on cyberbullying. *Computers in Human Behavior, 41,* 14–20. DOI: 10.1016/j.chb.2014.09.007

D'Alessio, S. (2011). *Inclusive education in Italy: A critical analysis of the policy of integrazione scolastica*. Sense Publishers. DOI: 10.1007/978-94-6091-342-6

Dalal, A., & Pande, N. (1999). Cultural Beliefs and Family Care of the Children with Disability. *Psychology and Developing Societies*, *11*(1), 55–75. DOI: 10.1177/097133369901100103

Deo, Dr. Tejaswini. (2023). *Changing Representation of Disability in Hindi Cinema*. Ad Litteram: An English Journal of International Literati, vol. 8.

Dhawan, S. (2020). Online learning: A panacea in the time of COVID-19 crises. *Journal of Educational Technology*, *49*(1), 5–22.

Diliberti, M. K., Schwartz, H. L., & Grant, D. (2021). *Stress topped the reasons why public-school teachers quit, even before COVID-19*. Research Report. RR-A1121–2. RAND Corporation.

Dorn, E., Hancock, B., Sarakatsannis, J., & Viruleg, E. (2020). *COVID-19 and learning loss—disparities grow and students need help*. McKinsey & Company.

Doucet, A., Netolicky, D., Timmers, K., & Tuscano, F. J. (2020). Thinking about pedagogy in an unfolding pandemic (An Independent Report on Approaches to Distance Learning during [*School Closure)*. Work of Education International and UNESCO.]. *COVID*, •••, 19.

Driscoll, A., Jicha, K., Hunt, A. N., Tichavsky, L., & Thompson, G. (2012). Can Online Courses Deliver In-class Results? AComparisonofStudentPerformanceand-SatisfactioninanOnlineVersusaFace-to-face Introductory Sociology Course. *Teaching Sociology*, *40*(4), 312–331. DOI: 10.1177/0092055X12446624

Eacott, S., MacDonald, K., Keddie, A., & Wilkinson, J. (2020). COVID-19 and Inequities in Australian education - insights on federalism, autonomy, and access. *International Studies in Educational Administration*, *48*(3), 6–13.

England, P. (2010). The Gender Revolution: Uneven and Stalled. *Gender & Society*, *24*(2), 149–166. DOI: 10.1177/0891243210361475

Engzell, P., Frey, A., & Verhagen, M. D. (2021). Learning loss due to school closures during the COVID-19 pandemic. *Proceedings of the National Academy of Sciences*. DOI: 10.1073/pnas.2022376118

Falvo, R. D. (2005). *Medical and psychosocial aspects of chronic illness and disability* (3rd ed.). Jones and Bartlett.

Fauzi, I., & Khusuma, I. H. S. (2020). Teachers' elementary school in online learning of COVID-19 pandemic conditions. *Jurnal Iqra Kajian Ilmu Pendidikan, 5*(1), 58–70. DOI: 10.25217/ji.v5i1.914

Felitti, V. J., Anda, R. F., Nordenberg, D., Williamson, D. F., Spitz, A. M., Edwards, V., & Marks, J. S. (1998). Relationship of childhood abuse and household dysfunction to many of the leading causes of death in adults: The Adverse Childhood Experiences (ACE) Study. *American Journal of Preventive Medicine, 14*(4), 245–258. DOI: 10.1016/S0749-3797(98)00017-8 PMID: 9635069

Gallup Education. (2014). *State of America's schools: The path to winning again in education.*

Ganguly, D. (2023). 'Death' of a teacher? Pandemic, pedagogy and virtual classrooms. *Globalisation, Societies and Education*, 1–11. DOI: 10.1080/14767724.2023.2249432

Goldberg, S. B. (2021). *Education in a pandemic: The disparate impacts of COVID-19 on America's students*. Department of Education.

Gouëdard, P. (2021). *Can a growth mindset help disadvantaged students close the gap?* Government of India. (2020). "National Education Policy."

Gravett, K. (2022). Different Voices, Different Bodies: Presence–Absence in the Digital University. *Learning, Media and Technology*.

Guglielmi, R. S., & Tatrow, K. (1998). Occupational stress, burnout, and health in teachers: A methodological and theoretical analysis. *Review of Educational Research, 68*(1), 61–99. DOI: 10.3102/00346543068001061

Gurung, P. (2021). *COVID-19 in Nepal: The Impact on Indigenous Peoples and Persons with Disabilities*. Disability and the Global South.

Hochschild, A. R. (1983). *The Managed Heart: Commercialization of Human Feeling*. University of California Press.

Hochschild, A. R. (1989). *The Second Shift: Working Families and the Revolution at Home*. Penguin.

Hochschild, A. R. (2012). *The Outsourced Self: Intimate Life in Market Times*. Metropolitan Books.

Jans, L. H., Kaye, H. S., & Jones, E. C. (2012). Getting hired: Successfully employed people with disabilities offer advice on disclosure, interviewing, and job search. *Journal of Occupational Rehabilitation, 22*(2), 155–165. DOI: 10.1007/s10926-011-9336-y PMID: 22020624

Johnson, A. (2017). *Perspectives on Harmful Speech Online: A Collection of Essays*. The Berkman Klein Center for Internet & Society at Harvard University.

Judge, T. A., Woolf, E. F., & Hurst, C. (2009). Is Emotional Labor More Difficult for Some Than for Others? A Multilevel Experience-Sampling Study. *Personnel Psychology*, *62*(1), 57–88. DOI: 10.1111/j.1744-6570.2008.01129.x

Kandasamy, N., Perera, B., & Soldatic, K. (2021). *COVID-19 from the Margins: Gendered-Disability Experiences in Sri lanka*. Disability and the Global South.

Kasser, S., & Lytle, R. (2005). *Inclusive physical activity*. Human Kinetics.

Katz, D. A., Greenberg, M. T., Jennings, P. A., & Klein, L. C. (2016). Associations between the awakening responses of salivary α-amylase and cortisol with self-report indicators of health and wellbeing among educators. *Teaching and Teacher Education*, *54*, 98–106. DOI: 10.1016/j.tate.2015.11.012

Kayess, R., & French, P. (2008). Out of the darkness into light? Introducing the Convention on the Rights of Persons with Disabilities. *Human Rights Law Review*, *8*(1), 5–7. DOI: 10.1093/hrlr/ngm044

Keddie, A. (2007). Issues of Power, Masculinity, and Gender Justice: Sally's Story of Teaching Boys. *Discourse (Berkeley, Calif.)*, *28*(1), 21–35.

Kuhfeld, M., & Tarasawa, B. (2020). *The COVID-19 slide: What summer learning loss can tell us about the potential impact of school closures on student academic achievement*.

Kyriacou, C. (2001). Teacher stress: Directions for future research. *Educational Review*, *53*(1), 27–35. DOI: 10.1080/00131910120033628

Lahelma, E., Palmu, T., & Gordon, T. (2000). Intersecting Power Relations in Teachers' Experiences of Being Sexualized or Harassed by Students. *Sexualities*, *3*(4), 463–481. DOI: 10.1177/136346000003004006

Lal, R. (2012). Mental Retardation to Intellectual Disability: A changing concept. *Disabilities and Impairments*, *24*(2), 77–82.

Lestiyanawati, R. (2020). *The strategies and problems faced by Indonesian teachers in conducting e-learning during COVID-19 outbreak*. CLLiENT (Culture, Literature, Linguistics, and English Teaching), 2(1), 71-82.

Maltby, J., Day, L., Hatcher, R. M., Tazzyman, S., Flowe, H. D., Palmer, E. J., Frosch, C. A., O'Reilly, M., Jones, C., Buckley, C., Melanie Knieps, M., & Cutts, K. (2016). Implicit theories of online trolling: Evidence that attention-seeking conceptions are associated with increased psychological resilience. *British Journal of Psychology, 107*(3), 448–466. DOI: 10.1111/bjop.12154 PMID: 26403842

Matook, S., Cummings, J., & Bala, H. (2015). Are you feeling lonely? The impact of relationship characteristics and online social network features on loneliness. *Journal of Management Information Systems, 31*(4), 278–310. DOI: 10.1080/07421222.2014.1001282

Matthews, C. K., & Harrington, N. G. *Invisible disability.* In D.O. Braithwaite, & T. L. Thompson (Eds.), (2000). Handbook of Communication and People with Disabilities: Research and Application (pp. 405-421).

Minkos, M. L., & Gelbar, N. W. (2021). Considerations for educators in supporting student learning in the midst of COVID-19. *Psychology in the Schools, 58*(2), 416–426. DOI: 10.1002/pits.22454 PMID: 33362299

Mirza, N., Naqvi, B., Rahat, B., & Rizvi, S. K. A. (2020). Price reaction, volatility timing and funds' performance during Covid-19. *Finance Research Letters, 36*, 101657. DOI: 10.1016/j.frl.2020.101657 PMID: 32837369

Moon, B., McCluskey, J., & Morash, M. (2019). Aggression against Middle and High School Teachers: Duration of Victimization and Its Negative Impacts. *Aggressive Behavior, 45*(5), 517–526. DOI: 10.1002/ab.21840 PMID: 31157921

Murphy, M. P. (2020). COVID-19 and emergency eLearning: Consequences of the securitization of higher education for post–pandemic pedagogy. *Contemporary Security Policy, 41*(3), 492–505. DOI: 10.1080/13523260.2020.1761749

National Centre for Promotion of Employment for Disabled People (NCPeDP). (2020). *Locked down and Left behind: A Report on the Status of Persons with Disabilities in India during the COVID-19 Crisis.* New Delhi: NCPeDP.

Neca, P., Borges, M. L., & Pinto, P. C. (2020). Teachers with disabilities: A literature review. *International Journal of Inclusive Education.*

Oliver, M. (1981). A new model of the social work role in relation to disability. In Campling, J. (Ed.), *The handicapped person: A new perspective for social workers* (pp. 19–32). RADAR.

Olkin, R. (1999). *What psychotherapists should know about disability.* Guilford Press.

Olmstead, M. (2021). *Media's Portrayal of Teachers Hurts the Profession.*

Osman, M. E. (2020). Global impact of COVID-19 on education systems: The emergency remote teaching at Sultan Qaboos University post-pity. *Journal of Education for Teaching*, *46*(4), 463–471. DOI: 10.1080/02607476.2020.1802583

Patchin, J. W., & Hinduja, S. (2006). Bullies move beyond the schoolyard: A preliminary look at cyberbullying. *Youth Violence and Juvenile Justice*, *4*(2), 148–169. DOI: 10.1177/1541204006286288

Petrie, C. (2020). *Spotlight: Quality education for all during COVID-19 crisis.* United Nations. DOI: 10.58261/CIAD8546

Pokhrel, S., & Chhetri, R. (2021). *A Literature Review on Impact of COVID-19 Pandemic on Teaching and Learning*. Higher Education for the Future. DOI: 10.1177/2347631120983481

Pugliesi, K. (1999). The Consequences of Emotional Labor: Effects on Work Stress, Job Satisfaction, and Well-Being. *Motivation and Emotion*, *23*(2), 125–154. DOI: 10.1023/A:1021329112679

Pulman, A., & Taylor, J. (2012). Munchausen by Internet: Current research and future directions. *Journal of Medical Internet Research*, *14*(4), e115. DOI: 10.2196/jmir.2011 PMID: 22914203

Richards, J. (2012). Teacher stress and coping strategies: A national snapshot. *The Educational Forum*, *76*(3), 299–316. DOI: 10.1080/00131725.2012.682837

Riddell, S., & Watson, N. (2014). *Disability, culture and identity*. Routledge. DOI: 10.4324/9781315847634

Rizvi, S. K. A., Mirza, N., Naqvi, B., & Rahat, B. (2020). COVID-19 and asset management in EU: A preliminary assessment of performance and investment styles. *Journal of Asset Management*, *21*(4), 281–291. DOI: 10.1057/s41260-020-00172-3

Robinson, K. (2000). 'Great Tits, Miss!' The Silencing of Male Students' Sexual Harassment of Female Teachers in Secondary Schools: A Focus on Gendered Authority. *Discourse (Abingdon)*, *21*(1), 75–90. DOI: 10.1080/01596300050005510

Sahin, C. (2014). An Analysis of the Relationship between Internet Addiction and Depression Levels of High School Students. *Participatory Educational Research*, *1*(2), 5367. DOI: 10.17275/per.14.10.1.2

Samuels, E. J. (2003). *My body, my closet: Invisible disability and the limits of coming-out discourse.* GLQ: A Journal of Lesbian and Gay Studies, 9(1), 233-255.

Shachaf, P., & Hara, N. (2010). Beyond vandalism: Wikipedia trolls. *Journal of Information Science*, *36*(3), 357–370. DOI: 10.1177/0165551510365390

Sintema, E. J. (2020). Effect of COVID-19 on the performance of grade 12 students: Implications for STEM education. *Eurasia Journal of Mathematics, Science and Technology Education, 16*(7). Advance online publication. DOI: 10.29333/ejmste/7893

Soni, V. D. (2020). Global impact of E-learning during. *COVID*, •••, 19.

Stauffer, S. D., & Mason, E. C. (2013). Addressing elementary school teachers' professional stressors: Practical suggestions for schools and administrators. *Educational Administration Quarterly, 49*(5), 809–837. DOI: 10.1177/0013161X13482578

Steiner, E. D., & Woo, A. (2021). *Job-related stress threatens the teacher supply: Key findings from the 2021 State of the U.S. Teacher Survey*. RAND Corporation, RR-A1108–1.

Subedi, S., Nayaju, S., Subedi, S., Shah, S. K., & Shah, J. M. (2020). Impact of e-learning during COVID-19 pandemic among nursing students and teachers of Nepal. *International Journal of Science and Healthcare Research, 5*(3), 9.

Subica, A. M., Claypoole, K. H., & Wylie, A. M. (2012). PTSD'S mediation of the relationships between trauma, depression, substance abuse, mental health, and physical health in individuals with severe mental illness: Evaluating a comprehensive model. *Schizophrenia Research, 136*(1–3), 104–109. DOI: 10.1016/j.schres.2011.10.018 PMID: 22104139

Sukhramani, N., & Verma, S. (2013). *Disability as Diversity: The Indian Perception*. Diversity and Respect-Problems of Perception in the Global Agenda for Social Work. Oldenburg: Paulo Freire Verlag.

Telecom Regulatory Authority of India. (2020). "Press Release– Highlights of Telecom Subscription Data as on 31st January, 2020."

UNESCO. (2015). *Education for All 2015 National Review*. United Nations Educational, Scientific and Cultural Organization.

UNESCO. (2018). *Global Education Monitoring Report 2018: Gender Review*. UNESCO Publishing.

UNESCO. (2020). *Global Education Monitoring Report 2020: Inclusion and Education*. UNESCO Publishing.

UNESCO. (2024). *Inclusion in Education*. UNESCO Publishing.

UNICEF. (2019). [*Children, Food and Nutrition*. UNICEF.]. *The State of the World's Children*, •••, 2019.

United Nations. (2015). *Transforming Our World: The 2030 Agenda for Sustainable Development*. United Nations.

United Nations. (2020). *Policy Brief: A Disability-Inclusive Response to COVID-19*. United Nations.

United Nations. (n.d.). *Convention on the Rights of Persons with Disabilities*. Department of Economic and Social Affairs.

Variyan, G., & Wilkinson, J. (2022). Variyan, George, and Jane Wilkinson. (2019). *"The Erasure of Sexual Harassment in Elite Private Boys' Schools.Gender and Education, 34*(2), 183–198. DOI: 10.1080/09540253.2021.1962516

Wachs, S., Wright, M. F., & Vazsonyi, A. T. (2019). Understanding the overlap between cyberbullying and cyberhate perpetration: Moderating effects of toxic online disinhibition. *Criminal Behaviour and Mental Health, 29*(3), 179–188. DOI: 10.1002/cbm.2116 PMID: 31274229

Wains, S. I., & Mahmood, W. (2008). Integrating m-learning with e-learning. *Proceedings of the 9th ACM SIGITE Conference on Information Technology Education*, 31–38. DOI: 10.1145/1414558.1414568

Weeden, K. A., & Cornwell, B. (2020). The small-world network of college classes: Implications for epidemic spread on a university campus. *Sociological Science*, *7*, 222–241. DOI: 10.15195/v7.a9

Will, M. (2021). Teachers are stressed out, and it's causing some to quit. *Education Week*.

World Bank. (2020). *Leveraging lessons from the COVID-19 Crisis for learners with Disabilities*. World Bank.

World Health Organisation (WHO). (2020). *Disability Considerations during the COVID-19 Outbreak*. WHO.

Wright, B. A. (1980). Developing constructive views of life with a disability. *Rehabilitation Literature, 41*(11-12), 274–279. PMID: 6449722

Yildirim, S., Demirtas, I., & Yildirim, D. C. (2022). A Review of Alternative Economic Approaches to Achieve Sustainable Development: The Rising Digitalization and Degrowth Post COVID-19. In Castanho, R. (Ed.), *Handbook of Research on Sustainable Development Goals, Climate Change, and Digitalization* (pp. 288–307). IGI Global. DOI: 10.4018/978-1-7998-8482-8.ch018

Young, K. S. (2004). Internet addiction: A new clinical phenomenon and its consequences. *The American Behavioral Scientist*, *48*(4), 402–415. DOI: 10.1177/0002764204270278

Yuan, L. M. (2021). Student's attitude and satisfaction towards transformative learning: A research study on emergency remote learning in tertiary education. *Creative Education*, *12*(03), 494–528. DOI: 10.4236/ce.2021.123035

Zhu, G. (2020). Research on Teacher Identity: Mapping Challenges and Innovations. *European Journal of Teacher Education*, *45*(4), 572–575. DOI: 10.1080/02619768.2020.1860007

Compilation of References

Aarikka-Stenroos, L., Chiaroni, D., Kaipainen, J., & Urbinati, A. (2022). Companies' Circular Business Models Enabled by Supply Chain Collaborations: An Empirical-Based Framework, Synthesis, and Research Agenda. *Industrial Marketing Management, 105*, 322–339. DOI: 10.1016/j.indmarman.2022.06.015

Abayomi, A., Balogun, M. R., Bankole, M., Banke-Thomas, A., Mutiu, B., Olawepo, J., & Ejekam, C. (2021). From Ebola to COVID-19: Emergency preparedness and response plans and actions in Lagos, Nigeria. *Globalization and Health, 17*(1), 1–10. DOI: 10.1186/s12992-021-00728-x PMID: 34243790

Abba-Aji, M., Stuckler, D., Galea, S., & McKee, M. (2022). Ethnic/racial minorities' and migrants' access to COVID-19 vaccines: A systematic review of barriers and facilitators. *Journal of Migration and Health, 5*, 100086. DOI: 10.1016/j.jmh.2022.100086 PMID: 35194589

Abbate, S., Centobelli, P., Cerchione, R., Nadeem, S. P., & Riccio, E. (2023). Sustainability Trends and Gaps in the Textile, Apparel and Fashion Industries. *Environment, Development and Sustainability, 26*(2), 2837–2864. DOI: 10.1007/s10668-022-02887-2 PMID: 36788931

Abdou, A. H., Hassan, T. H., Salem, A. E., Elsaied, M. A., & Elsaed, A. A. (2022). Determinants and Consequences of Green Investment in the Saudi Arabian Hotel Industry. *Sustainability (Basel), 14*(24), 24. Advance online publication. DOI: 10.3390/su142416905

Abernethy, A., Adams, L., Barrett, M., Bechtel, C., Brennan, P., Butte, A., Faulkner, J., Fontaine, E., Friedhoff, S., Halamka, J., Howell, M., Johnson, K., Long, P., McGraw, D., Miller, R., Lee, P., Perlin, J., Rucker, D., Sandy, L., & Valdes, K. (2022). The promise of digital health: Then, now, and the future. *NAM Perspectives, 2022*(22), 1–13. DOI: 10.31478/202206e PMID: 36177208

Abid, M. F., Shamim, A., Khan, Z., & Khan, I. (2022). Value creation or value destruction: Conceptualizing the experiential nature of value-in-use. *Journal of Consumer Behaviour, 21*(3), 583–601. DOI: 10.1002/cb.2033

Abjadi, A. I., Wiketye, E. J., & Mpogole, H. (2023). Factors Contributing to Tax Compliance among Small and Medium Sized Enterprises: A Case of Selected SMEs in Iringa Municipality. *International Journal of Finance and Accounting, 2*(1), 94–105. DOI: 10.37284/ijfa.2.1.1559

Acs, Z. J., Stam, E., Audretsch, D. B., & O'Connor, A. (2017). The lineages of the entrepreneurial ecosystem approach. *Small Business Economics, 49*(1), 1–10. DOI: 10.1007/s11187-017-9864-8

Adamson, A. S., & Smith, A. (2018). Machine learning and health care disparities in dermatology. *JAMA Dermatology, 154*(11), 1247–1248. DOI: 10.1001/jamadermatol.2018.2348 PMID: 30073260

Adamson, A. S., & Smith, A. (2018). Machine learning and health care disparities: Limitations and opportunities. *Journal of the American Medical Association, 320*(24), 2499–2500. DOI: 10.1001/jama.2018.17577

Adenutsi, D. (2023). Entrepreneurship, Job Creation, Income Empowerment and Poverty Reduction in Low-Income Economies. *Theoretical Economics Letters, 13*(6), 1579–1598. DOI: 10.4236/tel.2023.136089

Admass, W. S., Munaye, Y. Y., & Diro, A. A. (2024). Cyber security: State of the art, challenges and future directions. *Cyber Security and Applications, 2024*, 1–15. DOI: 10.1016/j.csa.2023.100031

Aguiar, M. F., Mesa, J. A., Jugend, D., Pinheiro, M. A. P., & Fiorini, P. D. C. (2021). Circular Product Design: Strategies, Challenges and Relationships with New Product Development. *Management of Environmental Quality, 33*(2), 300–329. DOI: 10.1108/MEQ-06-2021-0125

Aguiar, M., Hurst, E., & Karabarbounis, L. (2013). Time Use during the Great Recession. *The American Economic Review, 103*(5), 1664–1696. DOI: 10.1257/aer.103.5.1664

Agyemang, M., Kusi-Sarpong, S., Khan, S. A., Mani, V., Rehman, S. T., & Kusi-Sarpong, H. (2019). Drivers and Barriers to Circular Economy Implementation: An Explorative Study in Pakistan's Automobile Industry. *Management Decision, 57*(4), 971–994. DOI: 10.1108/MD-11-2018-1178

Ajayi, F. A., & Udeh, C. A. (2024). Combating burnout in the IT Industry: A review of employee well-being initiatives. *International Journal of Applied Research in Social Sciences*, *6*(4), 567–588. DOI: 10.51594/ijarss.v6i4.1010

Al Issa, H. E., & Omar, M. M. S. (2024). Digital innovation drivers in retail banking: The role of leadership, culture, and technostress inhibitors. *The International Journal of Organizational Analysis*, *32*(11), 19–43. DOI: 10.1108/IJOA-08-2023-3905

Alassaf, P., Zaien, S., & Oláh, J. (2020). Factors affecting e-government implementation developing countries e-opportunities. *Acta Oeconomica Universitatis Selye*, *9*(1), 7–23. DOI: 10.36007/Acta.2020.9.1.1

Alawi, M. M. S. (2021). Successful Management of COVID-19 Outbreak in a Long-term Care Facility in Jeddah, Saudi Arabia: Epidemiology, Challenges for Prevention and Adaptive Management Strategies. *Journal of Infection and Public Health*, *14*(4), 521–526. DOI: 10.1016/j.jiph.2020.12.036 PMID: 33743375

Albitz, R. S. (2007). The what and who of information literacy and critical thinking in higher education. *Portal (Baltimore, Md.)*, *7*(1), 97–109. DOI: 10.1353/pla.2007.0000

Albshaier, A., Han, L., & Jeong, D. (2024). AI-powered logistics in Q-commerce: Innovations and challenges.

Albshaier, L., Almarri, S., & Hafizur Rahman, M. M. (2024). A review of blockchain's role in E-Commerce transactions: Open challenges, and future research directions. *Computers*, *13*(1), 27. DOI: 10.3390/computers13010027

Albukhitan, S. (2020). Developing digital transformation strategy for manufacturing. *Procedia Computer Science*, *170*(1), 664–671. DOI: 10.1016/j.procs.2020.03.173

Alfehaid, F., Omri, A., & Altwaijri, A. (2024). Impact of ICT diffusion and opportunity entrepreneurship on environmental sustainability in Saudi Arabia. *Heliyon*, *10*(19), 1–10. DOI: 10.1016/j.heliyon.2024.e39009 PMID: 39430546

Alipio, M. (2020). *Education during Covid-19 Era: Are Learners in a Less-Economically Developed Country Ready for E-Learning?* Almog, N. (2011). *Academic and Social Adjustment of University Students with Visual Impairment* (Unpublished Doctoral Dissertation). Ramat Gan: School of Education, Bar-Ilan University.

Ali, S., & Thompson, M. (2023). The impact of fast delivery on consumer behavior in Q-commerce. *Systematic Reviews*.

Alisic, E. (2012). Teachers' Perspectives on Providing Support to Children after Trauma: A Qualitative Study. *School Psychology Quarterly*, *27*(1), 51–59. DOI: 10.1037/a0028590 PMID: 22582936

Allam, K. (2022). Big data analytics in robotics: Unleashing the potential for intelligent automation. *EPH-International Journal of Business & Management Science*, *8*(4), 5–9.

Allan, J., Belz, S., Hoeveler, A., Hugas, M., Okuda, H., Patri, A., Rauscher, H., Silva, P., Slikker, W., Sokull-Kluettgen, B., Tong, W., & Anklam, E. (2021). Regulatory landscape of nanotechnology and nanoplastics from a global perspective. *Regulatory Toxicology and Pharmacology*, *125*, 105106. DOI: 10.1016/j.yrtph.2021.104885 PMID: 33617940

Almeida, R. P. (Ed.). (2022). *Handbook of Research on Improving Allied Health Professions Education: Advancing Clinical Training and Interdisciplinary Translational Research.* IGI Global., DOI: 10.4018/978-1-7998-9578-7

Aminabee, S. (2024). The future of healthcare and patient-centric care: Digital innovations, trends, and predictions. *Advances in Healthcare Information Systems and Administration*, *2024*, 1–15. DOI: 10.4018/979-8-3693-1214-8.ch012

Amit, R. (2014). Entrepreneurship development in India: role of economic growth, foreign investment and financial development. *AIMA Journal of Management & Research*, 8(3/4), 1-9. https://apps.aima.in/ejournal_new/articlespdf/342-amit.pdf

Anand, T., & Garg, S. (2015). Menstruation related myths in India: Strategies for combating it. *Journal of Family Medicine and Primary Care*, *4*(2), 184. DOI: 10.4103/2249-4863.154627 PMID: 25949964

An, B. Y., & Tang, S.-Y. (2020). Lessons from COVID-19 responses in East Asia: Institutional infrastructure and enduring policy instruments. *American Review of Public Administration*, *50*(6-7), 790–800. DOI: 10.1177/0275074020943707

Andtfolk, M., Nyholm, L., Eide, H., Rauhala, A., & Fagerström, L. (2022). Attitudes Toward the Use of Humanoid Robots in Healthcare—A Cross-Sectional Study. *AI & Society*, *37*(4), 1739–1748. DOI: 10.1007/s00146-021-01271-4

Andzulis, J. M., Panagopoulos, N. G., & Rapp, A. (2012). A review of social media and implications for the sales process. *Journal of Personal Selling & Sales Management*, *32*(1), 305–316. DOI: 10.2753/PSS0885-3134320302

Anjum, M. (2023) *How are periods portrayed in the media*? - Free Periods Canada. https://www.freeperiods.ca/blog/how-are-periods-portrayed-in-the-media

Anum, N., Fatima, N., Ifrah, N., Lyba, N., & Sajjad, J. (2024). Leveraging digitalisation and servitisation to improve Financial Performance: An Empirical analysis. *Journal of Policy Research, 10*(2), 75–89. DOI: 10.61506/02.00209

Arayata, P. A., Banzon, J., Franco, B. M., Lubrin, D., Perez, M. R., & Garcia, M. B. (2022). Chyilax: An Innovative 3D Game Approach for Mental Breakdown Awareness Campaign. 2022 IEEE 14th International Conference on Humanoid, Nanotechnology, Information Technology, Communication and Control, Environment and Management (HNICEM). IEEE. DOI: 10.1109/HNICEM57413.2022.10109535

Archi, Y. E., Benbba, B., Kabil, M., & Dávid, L. D. (2023). Digital technologies for sustainable tourism destinations: State of the art and research agenda. *Administrative Sciences, 13*(1), 1–21. DOI: 10.3390/admsci13080184

Arens, A. K., & Morin, A. J. S. (2016). Relations between Teachers' Emotional Exhaustion and Students' Educational Outcomes. *Journal of Educational Psychology, 108*(6), 800–813. DOI: 10.1037/edu0000105

Arif, Y. M., Ayunda, N., Diah, N. M., & Garcia, M. B. (2024). A Systematic Review of Serious Games for Health Education: Technology, Challenges, and Future Directions. In *Transformative Approaches to Patient Literacy and Healthcare Innovation.* IGI Global., DOI: 10.4018/979-8-3693-3661-8.ch002

Arrieta, A. B., Díaz-Rodríguez, N., Del Ser, J., Bennetot, A., Tabik, S., Barbado, A., & Herrera, F. (2020). Explainable artificial intelligence (XAI): Concepts, taxonomies, opportunities, and challenges toward responsible AI. *Information Fusion, 58*, 82–115. DOI: 10.1016/j.inffus.2019.12.012

Arslan, A., Golgeci, I., Khan, Z., Al-Tabbaa, O., & Hurmelinna-Laukkanen, P. (2021).

Arslan, A., Golgeci, I., Khan, Z., Al-Tabbaa, O., & Hurmelinna-Laukkanen, P. (2021, January 07). Adaptive learning in cross-sector collaboration during global emergency: Conceptual insights in the context of COVID-19 pandemic. *Multinational Business Review, 29*(1), 21–42. DOI: 10.1108/MBR-07-2020-0153

Asiedu-Berkoe, F., Chandi, G. M., Bandoh, D. A., Atsu, B. K., Lokossou, V. K., Antara, S. N., Sarkodie, B., & Kenu, E. (2022). State of Public Health Emergency Preparedness and Response Capacity of Ghana. *Journal of Interventional Epidemiology and Public Health, 5*(4), 1–16. DOI: 10.37432/jieph.supp.2022.5.4.05.4

Åström, J., Reim, W., & Parida, V. (2022). Value creation and value capture for AI business model innovation: A three-phase process framework. *Review of Managerial Science, 16*(1), 2111–2213. DOI: 10.1007/s11846-022-00521-z

Astuti, I., & Ysrafil, . (2020). Severe Acute Respiratory Syndrome Coronavirus 2 (SARS-CoV-2): An overview of viral structure and host response. *Diabetes & Metabolic Syndrome, 14*(4), 407–412. DOI: 10.1016/j.dsx.2020.04.020 PMID: 32335367

Astuti, S., Zubaidah, S., & Irawan, D. (2024). Pendampingan Penyusunan Laporan Corporate Social Responsibility CSR) pada Rayz Hotel Malang. *Jurnal Pengabdian Masyarakat Bangsa, 2*(6), 2317–2322. DOI: 10.59837/jpmba.v2i6.1216

Atalay Onur, D. (2020). Integrating Circular Economy, Collaboration and Craft Practice in Fashion Design Education in Developing Countries: A Case from Turkey. *Fashion Practice, 12*(1), 55–77. DOI: 10.1080/17569370.2020.1716547

Attademo, G. (2022). International efforts against the infodemic: Some bioethical reflections. *Medicina e Morale, 71*(1), 69–78. DOI: 10.4081/mem.2022.1200

Attaran, M. (2022). Blockchain technology in healthcare: Challenges and opportunities. *International Journal of Healthcare Management, 15*(1), 1–13. DOI: 10.1080/20479700.2020.1843887

Aungst, T. D., & Patel, R. (2020). Integrating digital health into the curriculum—Considerations on the current landscape and future developments. *Journal of Medical Education and Curricular Development, 7*, 238212051989257. DOI: 10.1177/2382120519901275 PMID: 32010795

Autio, E., & Levie, J. (2017). Management of entrepreneurial ecosystems. In Ahmetoglu, G., Chamorro-Premuzic, T., Klinger, B., & Karcisky, T. (Eds.), *The Wiley Handbook of Entrepreneurship.*, DOI: 10.1002/9781118970812.ch19

Avalos, E., Cirera, X., Cruz, M., Iacovone, L., Medvedev, D., Nayyar, G., & Ortega, S. R. (2024). Firms' digitalization during the COVID-19 pandemic: A tale of two stories. *Science & Public Policy, 51*(6), 1241–1256. DOI: 10.1093/scipol/scae022

Awaliyah, T., Safitri, N., Hartaty, S., Felani, F., & Judijanto, L. (2023). The impact of financial technology innovation on banking service transformation: A case study in the FinTech Industry. *Global International Journal of Innovative Research.* https://www.researchgate.net/publication/377355013_The_Impact_of_Financial_Technology_Innovation_on_Banking_Service_Transformation_A_Case_Study_in_the_FinTech_Industry

Babalola, G. T., Gaston, J. M., Trombetta, J., & Tulk Jesso, S. (2024). A systematic review of collaborative robots for nurses: Where are we now, and where is the evidence? *Frontiers in Robotics and AI, 11*, 1398140. DOI: 10.3389/frobt.2024.1398140 PMID: 38899066

Baer, H. (2015). Redoing feminism: Digital activism, body politics, and neoliberalism. *Feminist Media Studies*, *16*(1), 17–34. DOI: 10.1080/14680777.2015.1093070

Banerjee, A., & Meena, K. S. (2020). Social determinants and ethical considerations of artificial intelligence in healthcare. *Asian Bioethics Review*, *12*(3), 229–241. DOI: 10.1007/s41649-020-00128-w

Barbosa, W., Zhou, K., Waddell, E., & Myers, T. (2021). Improving access to care: Telemedicine across medical domains. *Annual Review of Medicine*, *72*, 139–154. DOI: 10.1146/annurev-med-042920-020808 PMID: 33798406

Barile, S., Bassano, C., Piciocchi, P., Saviano, M., & Spohrer, J. C. (2021). Empowering value co-creation in the digital age. *Journal of Business and Industrial Marketing*. Advance online publication. DOI: 10.1108/JBIM-12-2019-0553

Barnes, C., Mercer, G., & Shakespeare, T. (2010). The social model of disability. In Giddens, A., & Sutton, P. (Eds.), *Sociology: Introductory Readings* (3rd ed., pp. 161–166). Polity Press.

Barnes, S., & De Ruyter, K. (2022). Guest editorial: artificial intelligence as a market-facing technology: getting closer to the consumer through innovation and insight. *European Journal of Marketing*, *56*(6), 1585–1589. DOI: 10.1108/EJM-05-2022-979

Barneya, A., Wrightb, M., David, J., & Ketchen, J. (2001). The resource-based view of the firm: Ten years after 1991. *Journal of Management*, *27*(6), 625–641. DOI: 10.1177/014920630102700601

Barney, J. B. (1991). Firm resources and sustained competitive advantage. *Journal of Management*, *17*(1), 99–120. DOI: 10.1177/014920639101700108

Barth, H., & Zalkat, G. (2021). Refugee entrepreneurship in the agri-food industry: The Swedish experience. *Journal of Rural Studies*, *86*, 189–197. DOI: 10.1016/j.jrurstud.2021.06.011

Basilaia, G., & Kvavadze, D. (2020). *Transition to Online Education in Schools During a SARSCoV-2 Coronavirus (COVID-19) Pandemic in Georgia*. Pedagogical Research, 5(4).

Bates, D. W., Landman, A., & Levine, D. M. (2018). Health apps and health policy: What is needed? *Journal of the American Medical Association*, *320*(19), 1975–1976. DOI: 10.1001/jama.2018.14378 PMID: 30326025

Baudier, P., Kondrateva, G., Ammi, C., Chang, V., & Schiavone, F. (2023). Digital Transformation of Healthcare During the COVID-19 Pandemic: Patients' Teleconsultation Acceptance and Trusting Beliefs. *Technovation*, *120*, 1–11. DOI: 10.1016/j.technovation.2022.102547

Bawole, J. N., & Langnel, Z. (2023). Administrative Reforms in the Ghanaian Public Services for Government Business Continuity During the COVID-19 Crisis. *Public Organization Review*, *23*(1), 181–196. DOI: 10.1007/s11115-022-00687-w

Beaulieu, T., Sarker, S., & Sarker, S. (2015). A conceptual framework for understanding crowdfunding. *Communications of the Association for Information Systems*, *37*(1), 1–12. DOI: 10.17705/1CAIS.03701

Becker-Leifhold, C. V. (2018). The Role of Values in Collaborative Fashion Consumption—A Critical Investigation Through the Lenses of The Theory of Planned Behavior. *Journal of Cleaner Production*, *199*, 781–791. DOI: 10.1016/j.jclepro.2018.06.296

Bengio, Y., LeCun, Y., & Hinton, G. (2021). Deep learning in the COVID-19 era: Achievements and challenges. *Nature Reviews. Methods Primers*.

Benis, A., Tamburis, O., Chronaki, C., & Moen, A. (2021). One digital health: A unified framework for future health ecosystems. *Journal of Medical Internet Research*, *23*(7), e29841. DOI: 10.2196/22189 PMID: 33492240

Benoit, W. L. (1997). Image repair discourse and crisis communication. *Public Relations Review*, *23*(2), 177–186. DOI: 10.1016/S0363-8111(97)90023-0

Berwick, D. M., & Hackbarth, A. D. (2012). Eliminating waste in US health care. *Journal of the American Medical Association*, *307*(14), 1513–1516. DOI: 10.1001/jama.2012.362 PMID: 22419800

Bhagat, R., & Singh, M. (2020). AI models for drug repurposing in infectious diseases. *Infection and Immunity*, *88*(5), e00123–e20. DOI: 10.1128/IAI.00123-20

Bharathithasan, K., & Srinivasan, R. (2024). The role of dark stores in quick commerce logistics.

Bharathithasan, S., & Srinivasan, K. S. (2024). Unpacking the impact of rapid delivery and product uniqueness on quick commerce business success using PLS SEM. *International Journal of Process Management and Benchmarking*, *17*(2), 153–166. DOI: 10.1504/IJPMB.2024.138351

Bhaskar, S., Bradley, S., Chattu, V. K., Adisesh, A., Nurtazina, A., Kyrykbayeva, S., Sakhamuri, S., Moguilner, S., Pandya, S., Schroeder, S., Banach, M., & Ray, D. (2020). Telemedicine as the New Outpatient Clinic Gone Digital: Position Paper From the Pandemic Health System REsilience PROGRAM (REPROGRAM) International Consortium (Part 2). *Frontiers in Public Health*, *8*, 1–16. DOI: 10.3389/fpubh.2020.00410 PMID: 33014958

Bhattacharya, S. (2020). What is So Wrong with Online Teaching? *Economic and Political Weekly*.

Bhattacharyya, S. S. (2024). Co-working with robotic and automation technologies: Technology anxiety of frontline workers in organisations. *Journal of Science and Technology Policy Management*, *15*(5), 926–947. DOI: 10.1108/JSTPM-05-2022-0087

Bick, R., Halsey, E., & Ekenga, C. C. (2018). The Global Environmental Injustice of Fast Fashion. *Environmental Health : A Global Access Science Source*, *17*(1), 92. DOI: 10.1186/s12940-018-0433-7 PMID: 30591057

Biddle, L., Wahedi, K., & Bozorgmehr, K. (2020). Health system resilience: A literature review of empirical research. *Health Policy and Planning*, *35*(8), 1084–1109. DOI: 10.1093/heapol/czaa032 PMID: 32529253

Biswas, S., Alam, A., Islam, N., Roy, R., & Satpati, L. (2024). Understanding period product use among young women in rural and urban India from a geospatial perspective. *Scientific Reports*, *14*(1), 20114. Advance online publication. DOI: 10.1038/s41598-024-70383-w PMID: 39209872

Bobel, C. (2020). *Introduction: Menstruation as Lens—Menstruation as Opportunity*. In Springer eBooks (pp. 1–6). DOI: 10.1007/978-981-15-0614-7_1

Bocken, N. M. P., Short, S. W., Rana, P., & Evans, S. (2014). A Literature and Practice Review to Develop Sustainable Business Model Archetypes. *Journal of Cleaner Production*, *65*, 42–56. DOI: 10.1016/j.jclepro.2013.11.039

Bogart, L. M., Dong, L., Gandhi, P., Klein, D. J., Smith, T. L., Ryan, S., & Ojikutu, B. O. (2022). COVID-19 vaccine intentions and mistrust in a national sample of Black Americans. *Journal of the National Medical Association*, *113*(6), 599–611. DOI: 10.1016/j.jnma.2021.05.011 PMID: 34158171

Bogart, L. M., Ojikutu, B. O., Tyagi, K., Klein, D. J., Mutchler, M. G., Dong, L., Lawrence, S. J., Thomas, D. R., & Kellman, S. (2021). COVID-19 related medical mistrust, health impacts, and potential vaccine hesitancy among Black Americans living with HIV. *Journal of Acquired Immune Deficiency Syndromes*, *86*(2), 200–207. DOI: 10.1097/QAI.0000000000002570 PMID: 33196555

Bohdanowicz, P., & Martinac, I. (n.d.). *ATTITUDES TOWARDS SUSTAINABILITY IN CHAIN HOTELS – RESULTS OF A EUROPEAN SURVEY.*

Bondanini, G., Giorgi, G., Ariza-Montes, A., Vega-Muñoz, A., & Andreucci-Annunziata, P. (2020). Technostress dark side of technology in the workplace: A scientometric analysis. *International Journal of Environmental Research and Public Health*, *17*(21), 8013. DOI: 10.3390/ijerph17218013 PMID: 33143270

Bonelli, F., Caferra, R., & Morone, P. (2024). In Need of a Sustainable and Just Fashion Industry: Identifying Challenges and Opportunities Through a Systematic Literature Review in a Global North/Global South Perspective. *Discover Sustainability*, *5*(1), 186. DOI: 10.1007/s43621-024-00400-5

Borges do Nascimento, I. J., Abdulazeem, H., Vasanthan, L. T., Martinez, E. Z., Zucoloto, M. L., Østengaard, L., & Novillo-Ortiz, D. (2023). Barriers and facilitators to utilizing digital health technologies by healthcare professionals. *NPJ Digital Medicine*, *6*(1), 161. DOI: 10.1038/s41746-023-00899-4 PMID: 37723240

Borycki, E. M., & Kushniruk, A. W. (2021). The safety of AI in healthcare: Emerging issues and considerations for healthcare. In *Multiple Perspectives on Artificial Intelligence in Healthcare: Opportunities and Challenges* (pp. 13–22). Springer International Publishing. DOI: 10.1007/978-3-030-67303-1_2

Bouncken, R. B., Komorek, M., & Kraus, S. (2015). Crowdfunding: The current state of research. *The International Business & Economics Research Journal*, *14*(3), 407–416. https://www.researchgate.net/publication/275657510_Crowdfunding_The_Current_State_Of_Research. DOI: 10.19030/iber.v14i3.9206

Bourdieu, P., & Passeron, J.-C. (1990). *Reproduction in Education, Society and Culture*. Sage Publications.

Bourlakis, M., Nisar, T. M., & Prabhakar, G. (2023). How technostress may affect employee performance in educational work environments. *Technological Forecasting and Social Change*, *193*, 122674. DOI: 10.1016/j.techfore.2023.122674

Braun, V., & Clarke, V. (2006). Using thematic analysis in psychology. *Qualitative Research in Psychology*, *3*(2), 77–101. DOI: 10.1191/1478088706qp063oa

Brooks, J. M. (1997). Beyond Teaching and Learning Paradigms: Trekking into the Virtual University. *Teaching Sociology*, *25*(1), 1. DOI: 10.2307/1319107

Brooks, S., & Califf, C. (2017). Social media-induced technostress: Its impact on the job performance of it professionals and the moderating role of job characteristics. *Computer Networks*, *114*, 143–153. DOI: 10.1016/j.comnet.2016.08.020

Brotheridge, C. M., & Grandey, A. A. (2002). Emotional Labor and Burnout: Comparing Two Perspectives of 'People Work.'. *Journal of Vocational Behavior*, *60*(1), 17–39. DOI: 10.1006/jvbe.2001.1815

Bruton, G. D., Ahlstrom, D., & Obloj, K. (2008). Entrepreneurship in emerging economies: Where are we today and where should research go in the future. *Entrepreneurship Theory and Practice*, *32*(1), 1–12. DOI: 10.1111/j.1540-6520.2007.00213.x

Brydges, T. (2021). Closing the Loop on Take, Make, Waste: Investigating Circular Economy Practices in The Swedish Fashion Industry. *Journal of Cleaner Production*, *293*, 126245. DOI: 10.1016/j.jclepro.2021.126245

Brynjolfsson, E., & McAfee, A. (2017). The business of artificial intelligence. *Harvard Business Review*.

Buckels, E. E., Trapnell, P. D., & Paulhus, D. L. (2014). Trolls just want to have fun. *Personality and Individual Differences*, *67*, 97–102. DOI: 10.1016/j.paid.2014.01.016

Budd, J., Miller, B. S., Manning, E. M., Lampos, V., Zhuang, M., Edelstein, M., Rees, G., Emery, V. C., Stevens, M. M., Keegan, N., Short, M. J., Pillay, D., Manley, E., Cox, I. J., Heymann, D., Johnson, A. M., & McKendry, R. A. (2020). Digital technologies in the public-health response to COVID-19. *Nature Medicine*, *26*(9), 1183–1192. DOI: 10.1038/s41591-020-1011-4 PMID: 32770165

Burton, A., McKinlay, A., Aughterson, H., & Fancourt, D. (2023). Impact of the COVID-19 pandemic on the mental health and well-being of adults with mental health conditions in the UK: A qualitative interview study. *Journal of Mental Health (Abingdon, England)*, *32*(6), 1040–1047. DOI: 10.1080/09638237.2021.1952953 PMID: 34323635

Calderon-Monge, E., & Ribeiro-Soriano, D. (2024). The role of digitalization in business and management: A systematic literature review. *Review of Managerial Science*, *18*(1), 449–491. DOI: 10.1007/s11846-023-00647-8

Caldwell, C. B. E. (2023). *An Application of Lewin in a Trans-Pandemic World: A Narrative Inquiry in a Case Study with a New Suggested Model for the Future*. Pepperdine University.

Cano, F., Martínez, M., & González, R. (2022). Environmental implications of last-mile delivery in Q-commerce: An empirical analysis.

Cano, J. A., Londoño-Pineda, A., & Rodas, C. (2022). Sustainable logistics for e-commerce: A literature review and bibliometric analysis. *Sustainability (Basel), 14*(19), 12247. DOI: 10.3390/su141912247

Carlson, L. (2010). *The Faces of Intellectual Disability*. Indiana University Press.

Cartwright, N. (2009). What is this thing called "efficacy"? In Mantzavinos, C. (Ed.), *Philosophy of the social sciences: Philosophical theory and scientific practice* (pp. 185–206). Cambridge University Press., DOI: 10.1017/CBO9780511812880.016

Casadesus-Masanell, R., & Ricart, J. E. (2010). From Strategy to Business Models and Onto Tactics. *Long Range Planning, 43*(2–3), 195–215. DOI: 10.1016/j.lrp.2010.01.004

Casciani, D., Chkanikova, O., & Pal, R. (2022). Exploring the Nature of Digital Transformation in the Fashion Industry: Opportunities for Supply Chains, Business Models, and Sustainability-Oriented Innovations. *Sustainability: Science. Sustainability, 18*(1), 773–795. DOI: 10.1080/15487733.2022.2125640

Cassaro, E., Oro, I. M., Begnini, S., & Georges, M. R. R. (2024). The influence of digital transformation and implementation barriers on innovation in Brazilian micro, small, and medium enterprises. *Small Business International Review, 8*(2), e660. DOI: 10.26784/sbir.v8i2.660

Castro, C., & Lopes, C. (2022). Digital government and sustainable development. *Journal of the Knowledge Economy, 13*(2), 880–903. DOI: 10.1007/s13132-021-00749-2

Centobelli, P., Abbate, S., Nadeem, S. P., & Garza-Reyes, J. A. (2022). Slowing the Fast Fashion Industry: An All-Round Perspective. *Current Opinion in Green and Sustainable Chemistry, 38*, 100684. DOI: 10.1016/j.cogsc.2022.100684

Chae, B. K. (2022). Mapping the evolution of digital business research: A bibliometric review. *Sustainability (Basel), 14*(12), 1–17. DOI: 10.3390/su14126990

Chahley, E. R., Reel, R. M., & Taylor, S. (2021). The lived experience of healthcare professionals working frontline during the 2003 SARS epidemic, 2009 H1N1 pandemic, 2012 MERS outbreak, and 2014 EVD epidemic: A qualitative systematic review. *SSM. Qualitative Research in Health, 1*, 100026. DOI: 10.1016/j.ssmqr.2021.100026 PMID: 34901922

Chandler, J. D., & Vargo, S. L. (2011). Contextualization and value-in-context: How context frames exchange. *Marketing Theory*, *11*(1), 35–49. DOI: 10.1177/1470593110393713

Chandran, M. (2020). Teacher Accountability and Education Restructuring: An Exploration of Teachers' Work Identities in an Urban School for Poor in India. *International Studies in Sociology of Education*, *31*(3), 1–20.

Chang, C., & Zhou, L. (2021). Integrating AI with genomics for precision medicine. *Nature Communications*, *12*, 748–763. DOI: 10.1038/s41467-021-27729-w

Chang, J. E., Lai, A. Y., Gupta, A., Nguyen, A. M., Berry, C. A., & Shelley, D. R. (2021). Rapid transition to telehealth and the digital divide: Implications for primary care access and equity in a post-COVID era. *The Milbank Quarterly*, *99*(2), 340–368. DOI: 10.1111/1468-0009.12509 PMID: 34075622

Chang, K.-C., Hobbs, W. R., Roberts, M. E., & Steinert-Threlkeld, Z. C. (2022). COVID-19 increased censorship circumvention and access to sensitive topics in China. *Proceedings of the National Academy of Sciences of the United States of America*, *119*(4), e2102818119. DOI: 10.1073/pnas.2102818119 PMID: 35046018

Chang, L.-H., Hsiao, Y.-C., Nuryyev, G., & Huang, M.-L. (2015). People's motivation, constraints and willingness to pay for green hotels. *European Journal of Tourism Research*, *9*, 67–77. DOI: 10.54055/ejtr.v9i.166

Chan, Y., Krishnamurthy, R., & Sadreddin, A. (2022). Digitally-enabled university incubation processes. *Technovation*, *118*(1), 1–10. DOI: 10.1016/j.technovation.2022.102560

Chatterjee, P., & Nath, A. (2015). *Future ICT Education in India—A Pilot Study on the Vision of Ubiquitous Learning in Higher Education.* In Information Systems Design and Intelligent Applications, edited by J. K. Mandal, Suresh Chandra Satapathy, Manas Kumar Sanyal, ParthaPratim Sarkar, and Anirban Mukhopadhyay, 599–609. New Delhi: Springer.

Chen, C., Chipao, B. T., & Miao, Q. (2023). Work redesign in development perspective: An empirical study of multitasking among civil servants in Malawi. *Australian Journal of Public Administration*, *82*(2), 210–227. DOI: 10.1111/1467-8500.12566

Cheng, M., Qu, Y., Jiang, C., & Zhao, C. (2022). Is cloud computing the digital solution to the future of banking. *Journal of Financial Stability*, *63*(1), 1–20. DOI: 10.1016/j.jfs.2022.101073

Chen, J. V., Tran, A., & Nguyen, T. (2019). Understanding the discontinuance behavior of mobile shoppers as a consequence of technostress: An application of the stress-coping theory. *Computers in Human Behavior, 95*, 83–93. DOI: 10.1016/j.chb.2019.01.022

Chen, J.-L. (2011). The effects of education compatibility and technological expectancy on e-learning acceptance. *Computers & Education, 57*(2), 1501–1511. DOI: 10.1016/j.compedu.2011.02.009

Chen, L., Lu, M., Liu, C., & Wang, H. (2020). Trustworthy artificial intelligence in healthcare: Principles and applications. *Journal of Healthcare Engineering, 2020*, 1–9. https://doi.org/10.xxxx. DOI: 10.1155/2020/6660160

Chen, X. (2024). Ai in healthcare: Revolutionizing diagnosis and treatment through machine learning. *MZ Journal of Artificial Intelligence, 2024*, 1–13.

Cherian, R. (2021). *The Odd One is 'Out': Voices from Virtual Classrooms*. Economic and Political Weekly Engage.

Chien, A. W., Kurnia, S., & von Westarp, F. (2003). The acceptance of online grocery shopping.

Chiou, W. (2006). Adolescents' sexual self-disclosure on the internet: Deindividuation and impression management. *Adolescence, 41*(163), 547–561. PMID: 17225667

Chi, T. (2015). Consumer Perceived Value of Environmentally Friendly Apparel: An Empirical Study of Chinese Consumers. *Journal of the Textile Institute, 106*(10), 1038–1050. DOI: 10.1080/00405000.2014.985879

Choi, T. M., Li, X., & Liu, T. (2023). Behavioral economics of impulse buying in the Q-commerce industry.

Chou, C., Condron, L., & Belland, J. C. (2005). A review of the research on internet addiction. *Educational Psychology Review, 17*(4), 363–388. DOI: 10.1007/s10648-005-8138-1

Christopher, M. (2016). *Logistics and supply chain management.* Pearson Education. https://old.mu.ac.in/wp-content/uploads/2021/02/Logistics-and-Supply-Chain-Management-Martin-Christopher.pdf

Čiarnienė, R., & Vienažindienė, M. (2014). Management of Contemporary Fashion Industry: Characteristics and Challenges. *Procedia: Social and Behavioral Sciences, 156*, 63–68. DOI: 10.1016/j.sbspro.2014.11.120

Ciotti, M., Ciccozzi, M., Terrinoni, A., Jiang, W.-C., Wang, C.-B., & Bernardini, S. (2020). The COVID-19 pandemic. *Critical Reviews in Clinical Laboratory Sciences*, *57*(6), 365–388. DOI: 10.1080/10408363.2020.1783198 PMID: 32645276

Cipriano, C., Rappolt-Schlichtmann, G., & Brackett, M. A. (2020). *Supporting school community wellness with social and emotional learning (SEL) during and after a pandemic*. Edna Bennett Pierce Prevention Research Center, Pennsylvania State University.

Claudio, L. (2007). Waste Couture: Environmental Impact of the Clothing Industry. *Environmental Health Perspectives*, *115*(9). Advance online publication. DOI: 10.1289/ehp.115-a449 PMID: 17805407

Clipper, B. (2020). The Influence of the COVID-19 Pandemic on Technology: Adoption in Health Care. *Nurse Leader*, *18*(5), 500–503. DOI: 10.1016/j.mnl.2020.06.008 PMID: 32837346

Cobley, D. S. (2022). Rising to the challenge: Disability Organisations in the COVID-19 pandemic. *Disability & Society*.

Coles, B. A., & West, M. (2016). Trolling the trolls: Online forum users constructions of the nature and properties of trolling. *Computers in Human Behavior*, *60*, 233–244. DOI: 10.1016/j.chb.2016.02.070

Collier, B., & MacLachlan, J. (1998). *Charles Babbage and the engine of perfection*. Oxford University Press.

Colucci, M., & Vecchi, A. (2021). Close the Loop: Evidence on the Implementation of The Circular Economy from The Italian Fashion Industry. *Business Strategy and the Environment*, *30*(2), 856–873. https://ideas.repec.org//a/bla/bstrat/v30y2021i2p856-873.html. DOI: 10.1002/bse.2658

Comber, C. (2024). Long COVID Frameworks: Examining Individual- and Population-Level Models to Assess and Improve Patient Care. *Health Promotion Practice*, *25*(1), 22–26. DOI: 10.1177/15248399221142514 PMID: 36546678

Contreras-Pacheco, O. E. (2018). Care ethics and crisis communication: Examining two experiences in South America. *Cuadernos De Administracion*, *34*(62), 20–32. DOI: 10.25100/10.25100/cdea.2018v34n62.6866

Coombs, N. C., Campbell, D. G., & Caringi, J. (2022). A qualitative study of rural healthcare providers' views of social, cultural, and programmatic barriers to healthcare access. *BMC Health Services Research*, *22*(1), 438. Advance online publication. DOI: 10.1186/s12913-022-07829-2 PMID: 35366860

Coombs, W. T. (2007). Attribution theory as a guide for post-crisis communication research. *Public Relations Review*, *33*(2), 135–139. DOI: 10.1016/j.pubrev.2006.11.016

Cortez, L. P., Tandayu, S. K., Villan, K. R., Español, R., Tutanes, A. C., Perez, M. R., Calleja, J., & Garcia, M. B. (2022). Corona Larona: A 2.5D Mobile Game Advocating COVID-19 Safety Protocols and Mitigation Strategies. 2022 IEEE 14th International Conference on Humanoid, Nanotechnology, Information Technology, Communication and Control, Environment and Management (HNICEM). IEEE. DOI: 10.1109/HNICEM57413.2022.10109445

Costin, A., Roman, A. F., & Balica, R. S. (2023). Remote work burnout, professional job stress, and employee emotional exhaustion during the COVID-19 pandemic. *Frontiers in Psychology*, *14*, 1193854. DOI: 10.3389/fpsyg.2023.1193854 PMID: 37325768

Crawford, J., Butler-Henderson, K., Rudolph, J., Malkawi, B., Glowatz, M., Burton, R., Magni, P., & Lam, S. (2020). COVID-19: 20 countries' higher education intra-period digital pedagogy responses. *Journal of Applied Learning & Teaching*, *3*(1), 1–20.

Crosslin, K., & Golman, M. (2014). "Maybe you don't want to face it" – College students' perspectives on cyberbullying. *Computers in Human Behavior*, *41*, 14–20. DOI: 10.1016/j.chb.2014.09.007

Cuan-Baltazar, J. Y., Munoz-Perez, M. J., Robledo-Vega, C., Pérez-Zepeda, M. F., & Soto-Vega, E. (2020). Misinformation of COVID-19 on the internet: Infodemiology study. *JMIR Public Health and Surveillance*, *6*(2), e18444. DOI: 10.2196/18444 PMID: 32250960

Cucinotta, D., & Vanelli, M. (2020). WHO Declares COVID-19 a Pandemic. *Acta Biomedica*, *91*(1), 157–160. DOI: 10.23750/abm.v91i1.9397 PMID: 32191675

D'Alessio, S. (2011). *Inclusive education in Italy: A critical analysis of the policy of integrazione scolastica*. Sense Publishers. DOI: 10.1007/978-94-6091-342-6

D'Itria, E., & Aus, R. (2023). Circular Fashion: Evolving Practices in A Changing Industry. *Sustainability: Science. Practice and Policy*, *19*(1), 2220592. DOI: 10.1080/15487733.2023.2220592

Da Giau, A., Macchion, L., Caniato, F., Caridi, M., Danese, P., Rinaldi, R., & Vinelli, A. (2016). Sustainability Practices and Web-Based Communication: An Analysis of The Italian Fashion Industry. *Journal of Fashion Marketing and Management*, *20*(1), 72–88. DOI: 10.1108/JFMM-07-2015-0061

Dabbous, A., Barakat, K. A., & Kraus, S. (2023). The impact of digitalization on entrepreneurial activity and sustainable competitiveness: A panel data analysis. *Technology in Society*, *73*(1), 1–13. DOI: 10.1016/j.techsoc.2023.102224

Dahl, A. J., Milne, G. R., & Peltier, J. W. (2021). Digital health information seeking in an omni-channel environment: A shared decision-making and service-dominant logic perspective. *Journal of Business Research*, *125*, 840–850. DOI: 10.1016/j.jbusres.2019.02.025

Dahl, A. J., Peltier, J. W., & Milne, G. R. (2022). Reducing information asymmetry and increasing health value co-creation in a rural healthcare context. *The Journal of Consumer Affairs*, *56*(2), 512–535. DOI: 10.1111/joca.12447

Dahl, A. J., Peltier, J. W., & Swan, E. L. (2023). Anticipatory value-in-use in early-stage digital health service transformations: How consumers assess value propositions before and after abrupt, exogenous shocks. *Journal of Business Research*, *163*, 113910. Advance online publication. DOI: 10.1016/j.jbusres.2023.113910

Dalal, A., & Pande, N. (1999). Cultural Beliefs and Family Care of the Children with Disability. *Psychology and Developing Societies*, *11*(1), 55–75. DOI: 10.1177/097133369901100103

Damenshie-Brown, A., & Ofosu-Ampong, K. (2023). COVID-19 Pandemic and Digital Banking Trends: Managerial Perspective on Challenges and Opportunities. In Shoukat, G., & Tunio, M. N. (Eds.), *Societal Transformations and Resilience in Times of Crisis* (pp. 112–135). IGI Global., DOI: 10.4018/978-1-6684-5326-1.ch007

Dang, A., Arora, D., & Rane, P. (2020). Role of digital therapeutics and the changing future of healthcare. *Journal of Family Medicine and Primary Care*, *9*(10), 5328. DOI: 10.4103/jfmpc.jfmpc_105_20 PMID: 32754475

Daniel, N., Kejela, G., Fantahun, F., Desalegn, M., & Guteta, F. (2023). Menstrual hygiene management practice and its associated factors among in-school adolescent girls in Western Ethiopia. *Contraception and Reproductive Medicine*, *8*(1), 1. Advance online publication. DOI: 10.1186/s40834-022-00196-7 PMID: 36597101

Das, P., Baker, K. K., Dutta, A., Swain, T., Sahoo, S., Das, B. S., Panda, B., Nayak, A., Bara, M., Bilung, B., Mishra, P. R., Panigrahi, P., Cairncross, S., & Torondel, B. (2015). Menstrual Hygiene Practices, WASH Access and the Risk of Urogenital Infection in Women from Odisha, India. *PLoS One*, *10*(6), e0130777. DOI: 10.1371/journal.pone.0130777 PMID: 26125184

Davis, F. D. (1989). Perceived usefulness, perceived ease of use, and user acceptance of information technology. *Management Information Systems Quarterly, 13*(3), 319–340. DOI: 10.2307/249008

De Fauw, J., Ledsam, J. R., Romera-Paredes, B., Nikolov, S., Tomasev, N., Blackwell, S., & Suleyman, M. (2018). Clinically applicable deep learning for diagnosis and referral in retinal disease. *Nature Medicine, 24*(9), 1342–1350. DOI: 10.1038/s41591-018-0107-6 PMID: 30104768

De Los Rios, I. C., & Charnley, F. J. S. (2017). Skills and Capabilities for A Sustainable and Circular Economy: The Changing Role of Design. *Journal of Cleaner Production, 160*, 109–122. DOI: 10.1016/j.jclepro.2016.10.130

Deery, M., Jago, L., & Stewart, M. (2007). Corporate Social Responsibility Within the Hospitality Industry. *Tourism Review International, 11*(2), 107–114. DOI: 10.3727/154427207783948900

Deo, Dr. Tejaswini. (2023). *Changing Representation of Disability in Hindi Cinema*. Ad Litteram: An English Journal of International Literati, vol. 8.

Dhaliwal, A. (2016). Role of entrepreneurship in economic development. *International Journal of Scientific Research and Management, 30*(1), 4262–4269. https://www.krmangalam.edu.in/blog/role-of-entrepreneurship-in-economic-development/

Dhaoui, I. (2019). Good governance for sustainable development. MPRA Paper No. 92544.UN (2020) The Impact of COVID-19 on the Arab Region: An Opportunity to Build Back Better. *Policy Brief.*

Dhaoui, I. (2022). E-Government for Sustainable Development: Evidence from MENA Countries. *Journal of the Knowledge Economy, 13*(3), 2070–2099. DOI: 10.1007/s13132-021-00791-0

Dhawan, S. (2020). Online learning: A panacea in the time of COVID-19 crises. *Journal of Educational Technology, 49*(1), 5–22.

Digital 2022: Digital Adoption Doubles Over the Past Decade. (2022). [Online]. https://datareportal.com/reports/digital-2022-digital-adoption-doubled-over-the-past-decade

Digital 2024: Global Overview Report. (2024). [Online]. https://datareportal.com/reports/digital-2024-global-overview-report

Dikshit, S., Grover, Y., Shukla, P., Mishra, A., Sahu, Y., Kumar, C., & Gupta, M. (2024). Empowering Employee Wellness and Building Resilience in Demanding Work Settings Through Predictive Analytics. *EAI Endorsed Transactions on Internet of Things, 10*.

Diliberti, M. K., Schwartz, H. L., & Grant, D. (2021). *Stress topped the reasons why public-school teachers quit, even before COVID-19*. Research Report. RR-A1121–2. RAND Corporation.

Dimoso, R. L., & Utonga, D. (2024). A systematic review of digital technology adoption in small and medium-sized enterprises: Implications for performance in developing countries. *International Journal of Development and Management Review*, *19*(1), 1–16. https://www.ajol.info/index.php/ijdmr/article/view/273499

Dodds, S., Russell-Bennett, R., Chen, T., Oertzen, A.-S., Salvador-Carulla, L., & Hung, Y.-C. (2022). Blended human-technology service realities in healthcare. *Journal of Service Theory and Practice*, *32*(1), 75–99. DOI: 10.1108/JSTP-12-2020-0285

Dömötör, . (2023). Peer-to-peer lending: Legal loan sharking or altruistic investment? Analyzing platform investments from a credit risk perspective. *Journal of International Financial Markets, Institutions and Money*, *86*(1), 1–14.

Dong, T., Benedetto, U., Sinha, S., Fudulu, D., Dimagli, A., Chan, J., Caputo, M., & Angelini, G. (2022). Deep recurrent reinforced learning model to compare the efficacy of targeted local versus national measures on the spread of COVID-19 in the UK. *BMJ Open*, *12*(2), e048279. DOI: 10.1136/bmjopen-2020-048279 PMID: 35190408

Dorn, E., Hancock, B., Sarakatsannis, J., & Viruleg, E. (2020). *COVID-19 and learning loss—disparities grow and students need help*. McKinsey & Company.

Doucet, A., Netolicky, D., Timmers, K., & Tuscano, F. J. (2020). Thinking about pedagogy in an unfolding pandemic (An Independent Report on Approaches to Distance Learning during [*School Closure)*. Work of Education International and UNESCO.]. *COVID*, •••, 19.

Dragomir, V. D., & Dumitru, M. (2022). Practical Solutions for Circular Business Models in The Fashion Industry. *Cleaner Logistics and Supply Chain*, *4*, 100040. DOI: 10.1016/j.clscn.2022.100040

Driscoll, A., Jicha, K., Hunt, A. N., Tichavsky, L., & Thompson, G. (2012). Can Online Courses Deliver In-class Results? AComparisonofStudentPerformanceand-SatisfactioninanOnlineVersusaFace-to-face Introductory Sociology Course. *Teaching Sociology*, *40*(4), 312–331. DOI: 10.1177/0092055X12446624

Dung, P., Hoang, H., & Son, N. (2024). Unlocking sustainable success: The transformative impact of CSR on hotel performance. *Cogent Social Sciences*, *10*(1), 2392025. Advance online publication. DOI: 10.1080/23311886.2024.2392025

Dwivedi, Y. K., Ismagilova, E., & Raman, N. P. (2021). Social media adoption, usage and impact in business-to-business (B2B) context: A state-of-the-art literature review. *Information Systems Frontiers*, *25*(1), 971–993. DOI: 10.1007/s10796-021-10106-y

Dwomoh, D., Yeboah, I., Ndejjo, R., Kabwama, S. N., Aheto, J. M., Liu, A., Lazenby, S., Ohemeng, F., Takyi, S. A., Issah, I., Bawuah, S. A., Wanyenze, R. K., & Fobil, J. (2023). COVID-19 Outbreak Control Strategies and Their Impact on the Provision of Essential Health Services in Ghana: An Exploratory sequential Study. *PLoS One*, *18*(11), 1–20. DOI: 10.1371/journal.pone.0279528 PMID: 37972045

Dzando, G., Salifu, S., Donyi, A. B., Akpeke, H., Kumah, A., Dordunu, R., & Nonoh, E. A. (2022). Healthcare in Ghana Amidst the Coronavirus Pandemic: A Narrative Literature Review. *Journal of Public Health Research*, *11*(1), 1–5. DOI: 10.4081/jphr.2021.2448 PMID: 34351103

Dzhengiz, T., Haukkala, T., & Sahimaa, O. (2023). (Un)Sustainable Transitions towards Fast and Ultra-Fast Fashion. *Fashion and Textiles*, *10*(1), 19. DOI: 10.1186/s40691-023-00337-9

Eacott, S., MacDonald, K., Keddie, A., & Wilkinson, J. (2020). COVID-19 and Inequities in Australian education - insights on federalism, autonomy, and access. *International Studies in Educational Administration*, *48*(3), 6–13.

Empoli, S. D., & Massaro, G. (2021). [Online]. https://www.transatlantic.org/

England, P. (2010). The Gender Revolution: Uneven and Stalled. *Gender & Society*, *24*(2), 149–166. DOI: 10.1177/0891243210361475

Engzell, P., Frey, A., & Verhagen, M. D. (2021). Learning loss due to school closures during the COVID-19 pandemic. *Proceedings of the National Academy of Sciences*. DOI: 10.1073/pnas.2022376118

Esteva, A., Kuprel, B., Novoa, R. A., Ko, J., Swetter, S. M., Blau, H. M., & Thrun, S. (2017). Dermatologist-level classification of skin cancer with deep neural networks. *Nature*, *542*(7639), 115–118. DOI: 10.1038/nature21056 PMID: 28117445

Ethawi, Y., AlZubaidi, A., & Maheshwari, A. (2024). Safe Use of Health Information Technology. In Principles of Neonatology (pp. 12-17). Elsevier. DOI: 10.1016/B978-0-323-69415-5.00003-5

Fabbrizio, A., Fucarino, A., Cantoia, M., De Giorgio, A., Garrido, N. D., Iuliano, E., & Macaluso, F. (2023, June). Smart devices for health and wellness applied to tele-exercise: An overview of new trends and technologies such as IoT and AI. []. MDPI]. *Health Care*, *11*(12), 1805. PMID: 37372922

Fadnis, D. (2017). Feminist Activists Protest Tax on Sanitary Pads: Attempts to Normalize Conversations About Menstruation in India Using Hashtag Activism. *Feminist Media Studies*, *17*(6), 1111–1114. DOI: 10.1080/14680777.2017.1380430

Fagherazzi, G., Goetzinger, C., Rashid, M. A., Aguayo, G. A., & Huiart, L. (2020). Digital health strategies to fight COVID-19 worldwide: Challenges, recommendations, and a call for papers. *Journal of Medical Internet Research*, *2020*(6), 1–13. DOI: 10.2196/19284 PMID: 32501804

Falvo, R. D. (2005). *Medical and psychosocial aspects of chronic illness and disability* (3rd ed.). Jones and Bartlett.

Farmaki, A. (2019). Corporate social responsibility in hotels: A stakeholder approach. *International Journal of Contemporary Hospitality Management*, *31*(6), 2297–2320. DOI: 10.1108/IJCHM-03-2018-0199

Faulkenberry, J. G., Luberti, A., & Craig, S. (2022). Electronic health records, mobile health, and the challenge of improving global health. *Current Problems in Pediatric and Adolescent Health Care*, *52*(5), 100981. DOI: 10.1016/j.cppeds.2021.101111 PMID: 34969611

Fauzi, I., & Khusuma, I. H. S. (2020). Teachers' elementary school in online learning of COVID-19 pandemic conditions. *Jurnal Iqra Kajian Ilmu Pendidikan*, *5*(1), 58–70. DOI: 10.25217/ji.v5i1.914

Felicetti, A. M., Corvello, V., & Ammirato, S. (2023). Digital innovation in entrepreneurial firms: A systematic literature review. *Review of Managerial Science*, *18*(1), 315–362. DOI: 10.1007/s11846-023-00638-9

Felitti, V. J., Anda, R. F., Nordenberg, D., Williamson, D. F., Spitz, A. M., Edwards, V., & Marks, J. S. (1998). Relationship of childhood abuse and household dysfunction to many of the leading causes of death in adults: The Adverse Childhood Experiences (ACE) Study. *American Journal of Preventive Medicine*, *14*(4), 245–258. DOI: 10.1016/S0749-3797(98)00017-8 PMID: 9635069

Fernandes, C., Pires, R., & Alves, M.-C. G. (2023). Digital entrepreneurship and sustainability: The state of the art and research agenda. *Economies*, *11*(1), 1–13.

Ferrucci, D., Brown, E., Chu-Carroll, J., Fan, J., Gondek, D., Kalyanpur, A., Lally, A., Murdock, J. W., Nyberg, E., Prager, J., Schlaefer, N., & Welty, C. (2010). Building Watson: An overview of the DeepQA project. *AI Magazine*, *31*(3), 59–79. DOI: 10.1609/aimag.v31i3.2303

Fichman, R. G., Santos, B. L. D., & Zheng, Z. (E.) (2014). Digital innovation as a fundamental and powerful concept in the information systems curriculum. *MIS Quarterly*, 38(2), 329-354. https://www.jstor.org/stable/26634929

Filip, R., Gheorghita Puscaselu, R., Anchidin-Norocel, L., Dimian, M., & Savage, W. K. (2022). Global challenges to public health care systems during the COVID-19 pandemic: A review of pandemic measures and problems. *Journal of Personalized Medicine*, *12*(2), 241. DOI: 10.3390/jpm12081295 PMID: 36013244

FinScope Tanzania. (2023). *FinScope Tanzania: Insights that drive innovation*. Financial Sector Deepening Tanzania. Retrieved January 12, 2025, from https://www.fsdt.or.tz/finscope/

Fleming, N.. (2018). The role of artificial intelligence in reshaping medical education. *Lancet*, *391*(10124), 10–12. DOI: 10.1016/S0140-6736(18)30996-2

Flemons, K., Baylis, B., Khan, A. Z., Kirkpatrick, A. W., Whitehead, K., Moeini, S., Schreiber, A., Lapointe, S., Ashoori, S., Arif, M., Berenger, B., Conly, J., & Hawkins, W. (2022). The Use of Drones for the Delivery of Diagnostic Test Kits and Medical Supplies to Remote First Nations Communities During COVID-19. *American Journal of Infection Control*, *50*(8), 849–856. DOI: 10.1016/j.ajic.2022.03.004 PMID: 35908822

Florida, R., Gulden, T., & Mellander, C. (2008). The Rise of The Mega-Region. *Cambridge Journal of Regions, Economy and Society*, *1*(3), 459–476. DOI: 10.1093/cjres/rsn018

Floud, R., & Johnson, P. (2008). *The Cambridge Economic History of the Industrial Revolution*. Cambridge University Press.

Foresti, L., Perotti, S., Ekren, B. Y., & Prataviera, L. B. (2022, October). E-Grocery challenges and a solution approach from multi-objective perspectives. In *Global Joint Conference on Industrial Engineering and Its Application Areas* (pp. 10-21). Springer.

Fornari, E., Negri, F., & Iuffmann Ghezzi, A. (2022). The Wheel of Retailing is still spinning: Promises, Compromises, and Pitfalls of Quick-Commerce. In Next Generation Marketing. People, Planet, Place: cooperation & shared value for a new era of critical marketing (Proceedings) (pp. 1-12).

Foster, R. N. (1986). *Innovation: The Attackers Advantage.* https://fs.blog/richard-foster-the-attackers-advantage/

Frishammar, J., & Parida, V. (2019). Circular Business Model Transformation: A Roadmap for Incumbent Firms. *California Management Review, 61*(2), 5–29. DOI: 10.1177/0008125618811926

Fung, C. Y., Su, S. I., Perry, E. J., & Garcia, M. B. (2022). Development of a Socioeconomic Inclusive Assessment Framework for Online Learning in Higher Education. In *Socioeconomic Inclusion During an Era of Online Education* (pp. 23–46). IGI Global., DOI: 10.4018/978-1-6684-4364-4.ch002

Gallup Education. (2014). *State of America's schools: The path to winning again in education.*

Ganapathy, V., & Gupta, C. (2023). Critical success factors for quick commerce grocery delivery in India: An exploratory study. Sustainability, Agri, Food and Environmental Research-DISCONTINUED, 12(1).

Ganguly, D. (2023). 'Death' of a teacher? Pandemic, pedagogy and virtual classrooms. *Globalisation, Societies and Education*, 1–11. DOI: 10.1080/14767724.2023.2249432

Gao, L., Li, G., Tsai, F., Gao, C., Zhu, M., & Qu, X. (2023). The impact of artificial intelligence stimuli on customer engagement and value co-creation: The moderating role of customer ability readiness. *Journal of Research in Interactive Marketing, 17*(2), 317–333. DOI: 10.1108/JRIM-10-2021-0260

Garcia, M. B. (2023a). Can ChatGPT Substitute Human Companionship for Coping with Loss and Trauma? *Journal of Loss and Trauma, 1-3*(8), 784–786. DOI: 10.1080/15325024.2023.2240697

Garcia, M. B. (2023b). ChatGPT as a Virtual Dietitian: Exploring its Potential as a Tool for Improving Nutrition Knowledge. *Applied System Innovation, 6*(5), 1–18. DOI: 10.3390/asi6050096

Garcia, M. B., Lopez Cabrera, M. V., & de Almeida, R. P. (Eds.). (2023). *Handbook of Research on Instructional Technologies in Health Education and Allied Disciplines*. IGI Global., DOI: 10.4018/978-1-6684-7164-7

Geissdoerfer, M., Pieroni, M. P. P., Pigosso, D. C. A., & Soufani, K. (2020). Circular Business Models: A Review. *Journal of Cleaner Production, 277*, 123741. DOI: 10.1016/j.jclepro.2020.123741

Geissdoerfer, M., Savaget, P., Bocken, N. M. P., & Hultink, E. J. (2017). The Circular Economy – A New Sustainability Paradigm? *Journal of Cleaner Production, 143*, 757–768. DOI: 10.1016/j.jclepro.2016.12.048

Gennari, R., Matera, M., Morra, D., Melonio, A., & Rizvi, M. (2023). Design for social digital well-being with young generations: Engage them and make them reflect. *International Journal of Human-Computer Studies, 173*, 103006. DOI: 10.1016/j.ijhcs.2023.103006

George, A. S., Baskar, T., & Pandey, D. (2024). Rocket-powered E-commerce: Exploring the feasibility and implications of suborbital package delivery. *Partners Universal Innovative Research Publication*, *2*(2), 56–70.

Germani, F., & Biller-Andorno, N. (2022). How to counter the anti-vaccine rhetoric: Filling information voids and building resilience. *Human Vaccines & Immunotherapeutics*, *18*(6), 2095825. DOI: 10.1080/21645515.2022.2095825 PMID: 35802046

Ghaderi, Z., Mirzapour, M., Henderson, J. C., & Richardson, S. (2019). Corporate social responsibility and hotel performance: A view from Tehran, Iran. *Tourism Management Perspectives*, *29*, 41–47. DOI: 10.1016/j.tmp.2018.10.007

Ghaffar Nia, N., Kaplanoglu, E., & Nasab, A. (2023). Evaluation of artificial intelligence techniques in disease diagnosis and prediction. *Discover Artificial Intelligence*, *2023*(1), 1–15. DOI: 10.1007/s44163-023-00049-5

Ghisellini, P., Cialani, C., & Ulgiati, S. (2016). A Review on Circular Economy: The Expected Transition to A Balanced Interplay of Environmental and Economic Systems. *Journal of Cleaner Production*, *114*, 11–32. DOI: 10.1016/j.jclepro.2015.09.007

Ghorbani, A., Heuvelmans, M. A., Wiedermann, D., & Dekker, W. (2022). Big data and AI in oncological practice: Bridging the gap in personalized medicine. *Translational Oncology*, *15*(1), 1–8.

Ghose, A., Guo, X., Li, B., & Dang, Y. (2021). "Empowering patients using smart mobile health platforms: Evidence from a randomized field experiment." arXiv preprint arXiv:2102.05506, 2021, 1-13.

Giesen, E., Berman, S. J., Bell, R., & Blitz, A. (2007). Three Ways to Successfully Innovate your Business Model. *Strategy and Leadership*, *35*(6), 27–33. DOI: 10.1108/10878570710833732

Gill, S. (2020). Qualitative Sampling Methods. *Journal of Human Lactation*, *36*(4), 579–581. DOI: 10.1177/0890334420949218 PMID: 32813616

Goldberg, S. B. (2021). *Education in a pandemic: The disparate impacts of COVID-19 on America's students*. Department of Education.

Golinelli, D., Boetto, E., Carullo, G., Nuzzolese, A. G., Landini, M. P., & Fantini, M. P. (2020). Adoption of digital technologies in health care during the COVID-19 pandemic: Systematic review of early scientific literature. *Journal of Medical Internet Research, 22*(8), e21535. DOI: 10.2196/22280 PMID: 33079693

González-Rodríguez, M. R., Martín-Samper, R. C., Köseoglu, M. A., & Okumus, F. (2019). Hotels' corporate social responsibility practices, organizational culture, firm reputation, and performance. *Journal of Sustainable Tourism, 27*(3), 398–419. DOI: 10.1080/09669582.2019.1585441

Gordon, F.T. (2002). E-government-introduction. ERCIM News 48.

Gouëdard, P. (2021). *Can a growth mindset help disadvantaged students close the gap?* Government of India. (2020). "National Education Policy."

Gradillas, M., & Thomas, L. D. (2023). Distinguishing digitization and digitalization: A systematic review and conceptual framework. *Journal of Product Innovation Management*. Advance online publication. DOI: 10.1111/jpim.12690

Gravett, K. (2022). Different Voices, Different Bodies: Presence–Absence in the Digital University. *Learning, Media and Technology*.

Grimm, P. Y., & Wyss, K. (2022). What Makes Health Systems Resilient? A Qualitative Analysis of the Perspectives of Swiss NGOs. *Globalization and Health, 18*(1), 1–14. DOI: 10.1186/s12992-022-00848-y PMID: 35619166

Groenestege, M. T., Bowman, K., Cruz, G., Delaporte, A., Jackson, N., Lopez, M., Manimohan, M., & Sibthorpe, C. (2021). *Accelerating mobile internet adoption: Policy considerations to bridge the digital divide in low- and middle-income countries*. GSMA Head Office., https://www.gsma.com/solutions-and-impact/connectivity-for-good/mobile-for-development/wp-content/uploads/2021/05/Accelerating-Mobile-Internet-Adoption-Policy-Considerations.pdf

Grönroos, C., & Voima, P. (2013). Critical service logic: Making sense of value creation and co-creation. *Journal of the Academy of Marketing Science, 41*(2), 133–150. DOI: 10.1007/s11747-012-0308-3

Grossman, R. L., Heath, A. P., & Murphy, M. (2018). A case for data commons. *Computing in Science & Engineering, 20*(3), 70–82. DOI: 10.1109/MCSE.2018.03269455 PMID: 29033693

Group, D. I. (2021). [Online]. https://www.fcc.gov/.https://www.fcc.gov/sites/default/files/acdde-digital-empowerment-wg-digital-inclusion-rec-06242021.pdf

Guglielmi, R. S., & Tatrow, K. (1998). Occupational stress, burnout, and health in teachers: A methodological and theoretical analysis. *Review of Educational Research*, *68*(1), 61–99. DOI: 10.3102/00346543068001061

Gunasekeran, D. V., Tham, Y. C., Ting, D. S. W., Tan, G. S. W., & Wong, T. Y. (2021). Digital health during COVID-19: Lessons from operationalising new models of care in ophthalmology. *The Lancet. Digital Health*, *2021*(2), 1–13. DOI: 10.1016/S2589-7500(20)30287-9 PMID: 33509383

Guo, C., Ashrafian, H., Ghafur, S., Fontana, G., Gardner, C., & Prime, M. (2020). Challenges for the evaluation of digital health solutions—A call for innovative evidence generation approaches. *NPJ Digital Medicine*, *3*(1), 1–6. DOI: 10.1038/s41746-020-00314-2 PMID: 32904379

Gupta, M., Sharma, B., & Singh, A. K. (2025). Impact of digital technologies on tourist arrival in selected economies. In Lytras, M., Alkhaldi, A., & Ordóñez de Pablos, P. (Eds.), *Harnessing AI, Blockchain, and Cloud Computing for Enhanced e-Government Services* (pp. 441–474). IGI Global Scientific Publishing., DOI: 10.4018/979-8-3693-7678-2.ch014

Gupta, M., & Singh, A. K. (2025). Factors influencing the sustainability of women micro-entrepreneurship in Jammu and Kashmir. In Bayram, G., Bayram, A., & Sak, M. (Eds.), *Examining Barriers and Building Resiliency for Rural Women Entrepreneurs* (pp. 129–162). IGI Global Scientific Publishing., DOI: 10.4018/979-8-3693-9178-5.ch005

Gupta, P., & Singh, A. (2022). The role of AI in managing chronic diseases: Current status and future directions. *Journal of Chronic Diseases and Management*, *34*(3), 213–224. DOI: 10.1002/jcdm.12368

Gurung, P. (2021). *COVID-19 in Nepal: The Impact on Indigenous Peoples and Persons with Disabilities*. Disability and the Global South.

Haenlein, M., & Kaplan, A. (2019). A brief history of artificial intelligence: On the past, present, and future of artificial intelligence. *California Management Review*, *61*(4), 5–14. DOI: 10.1177/0008125619864925

Haldane, V., De Foo, C., Abdalla, S. M., Jung, A.-S., Tan, M., Wu, S., & Singh, S. (2021). Health systems resilience in managing the COVID-19 pandemic: Lessons from 28 countries. *Nature Medicine*, *27*(6), 964–980. DOI: 10.1038/s41591-021-01381-y PMID: 34002090

Halida, U. M., & Wilantini, C. (2022). The role of digitalization in expanding MSME market access. *Quantitative Economics and Management Studies*, *3*(1), 1–10. DOI: 10.35877/454RI.qems861

Hall, J., Daneke, G., & Lenox, M. (2010). Sustainable development and entrepreneurship: Past contributions and future directions. *Journal of Business Venturing*, *25*(5), 439–448. DOI: 10.1016/j.jbusvent.2010.01.002

Ha, M. T., & Alam, M. Z. (2022). *Menstrual hygiene management practice among adolescent girls: An urban–rural comparative study in Rajshahi division,* Bangladesh. *BMC Women's Health*, *22*(1), 86. Advance online publication. DOI: 10.1186/s12905-022-01665-6 PMID: 35321715

Hamberger, M., Ikonomi, N., Schwab, J. D., Werle, S. D., Fürstberger, A., Kestler, A. M. R., Holderried, M., Kaisers, U. X., Steger, F., & Kestler, H. A. (2022). Interaction empowerment in mobile health: Concepts, challenges, and perspectives. *JMIR mHealth and uHealth*, *2022*(4), 1–13. DOI: 10.2196/32696 PMID: 35416786

Hamoud, S. S., & Nzilano, J. L. (2024). Exploring Science Teachers' Beliefs and Practices of ICT integration in secondary school teaching: A Mixed Method approach. *University of Dar es Salaam Library Journal*; https://journals.udsm.ac.tz/index.php/lj/article/view/6584

Han, S.-C., Henninger, C. E., Apeagyei, P., & Tyler, D. (2017). *Determining Effective Sustainable Fashion Communication Strategies*. Palgrave Macmillan., https://eprints.whiterose.ac.uk/139287/ DOI: 10.1007/978-3-319-51253-2_7

Hans, N., & Rutenge, M. M. (2024). Evaluation of the opportunities presented by the adoption of E-Government in enhancing Local Government Authority performance at Kinondoni Municipal Council in Tanzania. *African Journal of Empirical Research*, *5*(4), 479–488. DOI: 10.51867/ajernet.5.4.38

Hapuwatte, B. M., & Jawahir, I. S. (2021). Closed-Loop Sustainable Product Design for Circular Economy. *Journal of Industrial Ecology*, *25*(6), 1430–1446. DOI: 10.1111/jiec.13154

Harrison, R., Fischer, S., Walpola, R. L., Chauhan, A., Babalola, T., Mears, S., & Le-Dao, H. (2021). … do models for change management, improvement and implementation meet? A systematic review of the applications of change management models in healthcare. *Journal of Healthcare Leadership*, *2021*, 1–13. DOI: 10.2147/JHL.S289176 PMID: 33737854

Harter, S., Johnson, K., & Wang, L. (2024). Consumer preferences in the age of quick commerce: A global survey.

Harter, A., Stich, L., & Spann, M. (2024). The effect of delivery time on repurchase behavior in quick commerce. *Journal of Service Research*, •••, 10946705241236961.

Hau, A., & Liu, H. (2021), "Artificial intelligence application in interactive marketing", available at: www.emeraldgrouppublishing.com/journal/jrim/artificial-intelligence-application-interactive-marketing

Hazen, B. T., Mollenkopf, D. A., & Wang, Y. (2017). Remanufacturing for the Circular Economy: An Examination of Consumer Switching Behavior. *Business Strategy and the Environment*, *26*(4), 451–464. DOI: 10.1002/bse.1929

Heckerman, D. (1990). Probabilistic interpretations for MYCIN's certainty factors. *The Computer Journal*, *23*(3), 241–256. DOI: 10.1093/comjnl/23.3.241

Hein, A., Schreieck, M., Riasanow, T., Setzke, D. S., Wiesche, M., Böhm, M., & Krcmar, H. (2019). Digital platform ecosystem. *Electronic Markets*, *30*(1), 87–98. DOI: 10.1007/s12525-019-00377-4

Hennink, M. M., Kaiser, B. N., & Weber, M. B. (2019). What influences saturation? Estimating sample sizes in focus group research. *Qualitative Health Research*, *29*(10), 1483–1496. DOI: 10.1177/1049732318821692 PMID: 30628545

Herold, D. M., Ćwiklicki, M., Pilch, K., & Mikl, J. (2021). The emergence and adoption of digitalization in the logistics and supply chain industry: An institutional perspective. *Journal of Enterprise Information Management*, *34*(6), 1917–1938. DOI: 10.1108/JEIM-09-2020-0382

Herold, P. I., & Prokop, D. (2023). Is Fast Fashion Finally Out of Season? Rental Clothing Schemes as A Sustainable and Affordable Alternative to Fast Fashion. *Geoforum*, *146*, 103873. DOI: 10.1016/j.geoforum.2023.103873

Hochschild, A. R. (1983). *The Managed Heart: Commercialization of Human Feeling*. University of California Press.

Hochschild, A. R. (1989). *The Second Shift: Working Families and the Revolution at Home*. Penguin.

Hochschild, A. R. (2012). *The Outsourced Self: Intimate Life in Market Times*. Metropolitan Books.

Hoffman, D. A. (2020). Increasing access to care: Telehealth during COVID-19. *Journal of Law and the Biosciences*, *7*(1), 181–185. DOI: 10.1093/jlb/lsaa043 PMID: 32843985

Holma, M., & Junestrand, A. (2024). How far are you willing to go when the prices are so low?: A mixed-method study on how ultra-fast e-commerce marketing strategies affect consumers' sustainability beliefs.

Holzinger, A., Biemann, C., Pattichis, C. S., & Kell, D. B. (2017). What do we need to build explainable AI systems for the medical domain? *arXiv Preprint.*

Holzinger, A., Carrington, A., & Mueller, H. (2019). Measuring the impact of explainability on trust in AI. *Information Systems Frontiers, 21*, 31–37.

Holzinger, A., Dehmer, M., & Jurisica, I. (2019). Knowledge discovery and interactive data mining in bioinformatics—State-of-the-art, future challenges, and research directions. *BMC Bioinformatics, 19*(2), 1–25. https://doi.org/10.xxxx PMID: 25078282

Holzinger, A., Langs, G., Denk, H., Zatloukal, K., & Müller, H. (2019). Causability and explainability of artificial intelligence in medicine. *Wiley Interdisciplinary Reviews. Data Mining and Knowledge Discovery, 9*(4), e1312. DOI: 10.1002/widm.1312 PMID: 32089788

Hong, J. S., Wasden, C., & Han, D. H. (2021). Introduction of digital therapeutics. *Computer Methods and Programs in Biomedicine, 208*, 106243. DOI: 10.1016/j.cmpb.2021.106243 PMID: 34364181

Hooda, A., Gupta, P., Jeyaraj, A., & Dwivedi, Y. (2023). Clarifying the Role of E-Government Trust in E-Government Success Models: A Meta-analytic Structural Equation Modeling Approach. *AJIS. Australasian Journal of Information Systems, 27*. Advance online publication. DOI: 10.3127/ajis.v27i0.4079

Hoque, M. M. (2024). Crowdfunding for innovation: a comprehensive empirical review. *Future Business Journal*, 10(102).

How to Build a Circular Economy | Ellen Macarthur Foundation. (n.d.). Retrieved 18 January 2025, from https://www.ellenmacarthurfoundation.org/

Howard, J., Huang, A., Li, Z., Tufekci, Z., Zdimal, V., van der Westhuizen, H.-M., von Delft, A., Price, A., Fridman, L., Tang, L.-H., Tang, V., Watson, G. L., Bax, C. E., Shaikh, R., Questier, F., Hernandez, D., Chu, L. F., Ramirez, C. M., & Rimoin, A. W. (2021). An evidence review of face masks against COVID. *Proceedings of the National Academy of Sciences of the United States of America, 118*(4), e2014564118. DOI: 10.1073/pnas.2014564118 PMID: 33431650

Hu, B. (2022). Translation as an ethical intervention? Building trust in healthcare crisis communication. In Language as a social determinant of health: Translating and interpreting the COVID-19 pandemic, ed. Federico Marco Federici, 179–208. Palgrave Studies in Translating and Interpreting. Cham: Springer International Publishing. DOI: 10.1007/978-3-030-87817-7_7

Huang, M., & Yen, B. P. (2021). Driving forces for digital transformation–Case studies of Q-commerce.

Huang, M.-H., & Rust, R. T. (2018). Artificial intelligence in service. *Journal of Service Research, 21*(2), 155–172. DOI: 10.1177/1094670517752459

Hvass, K. K., & Pedersen, E. R. G. (2019). Toward Circular Economy of Fashion: Experiences from a Brand's Product Take-Back Initiative. *Journal of Fashion Marketing and Management, 23*(3), 345–365. DOI: 10.1108/JFMM-04-2018-0059

Ilyas, M., Din, A. U., Haleem, M., & Ahmad, I. (2023). Digital entrepreneurial acceptance: An examination of technology acceptance model and do-it-yourself behavior. *Journal of Innovation and Entrepreneurship, 12*(1), 15. Advance online publication. DOI: 10.1186/s13731-023-00268-1

Inakefe, G. I., Bassey, V. U., Ikeanyibe, O. M., Nwagboso, C. I., Agbor, U. I., Ebegbulem, J., Mbonu, F. I., & Ike, G. U. (2023). Digital Literacy and E-Governance adoption for service delivery in Cross River State Civil Service. *International Journal of Electronic Government Research, 19*(1), 1–23. DOI: 10.4018/IJEGR.328327

India, W. (2021, May 4). *About KGIS: Keep Girls in School - Information & More. Keep Girls In School.* https://whisper.co.in/en-in/school-education/kgis

Indriastuti, M., & Chariri, A. (2021). The role of green investment and corporate social responsibility investment on sustainable performance. *Cogent Business & Management, 8*(1), 1960120. DOI: 10.1080/23311975.2021.1960120

International Energy Agency. (2018). *Renewables Information 2018.* OECD., DOI: 10.1787/renew-2018-

Ioannou, A., Lycett, M., & Marshan, A. (2024). The role of mindfulness in mitigating the negative consequences of technostress. *Information Systems Frontiers, 26*(2), 523–549. DOI: 10.1007/s10796-021-10239-0 PMID: 35095332

Ishengoma, F. and John, E. (2024), "Factor" influencing the adoption of mobile-based AI services in Tanzanian manufacturing SMEs", *Vilakshan - XIMB Journal of Management*, Vol. ahead-of-print No. ahead-of-print. DOI: 10.1108/XJM-11-2023-0214

Ishengoma, F. and Shao, D. (2025), "A framework for aligning e-government initiatives with the sustainable development goals", *Journal of Innovative Digital Transformation*, Vol. ahead-of-print No. ahead-of-print. DOI: 10.1108/JIDT-09-2024-0025

Ismail J. Ismail (2023) Seeing through digitalisation! The influence of entrepreneurial networks on market participation among smallholder farmers in Tanzania. The mediating role of digital technology, *Cogent Food & Agriculture*, 9:1, 2171834, DOI: DOI: 10.1080/23311932.2023.2171834

Issa, H., Jaber, J., & Lakkis, H. (2024). Navigating AI unpredictability: Exploring technostress in AI-powered healthcare systems. *Technological Forecasting and Social Change*, *202*, 123311. DOI: 10.1016/j.techfore.2024.123311

Iyanna, S., Kaur, P., Ractham, P., Talwar, S., & Najmul Islam, A. K. M. (2022). Digital transformation of healthcare sector. What is impeding adoption and continued usage of technology-driven innovations by end-users? *Journal of Business Research*, *153*, 150–161. DOI: 10.1016/j.jbusres.2022.08.007

Jacob, F., & Ulaga, W. (2008). The Transition from Product to Service in Business Markets: An Agenda for Academic Inquiry. *Industrial Marketing Management*, *37*(3), 247–253. DOI: 10.1016/j.indmarman.2007.09.009

Jain, M., Shakdwipee, D. P., & Bhatia, T. K. (2024). Digitalization and healthcare quality. *Educational Administration: Theory and Practice*, *30*(5), 6240–6243. DOI: 10.53555/kuey.v30i5.3923

Jain, S., Nair, A., & Ahlstrom, D. (2015). Towards a theoretical understanding of innovation and entrepreneurship in India. *Asia Pacific Journal of Management*, *32*(4), 835–841. DOI: 10.1007/s10490-015-9444-x

Jankalova, M. (2016). Approaches to the Evaluation of Corporate Social Responsibility. *Procedia Economics and Finance*, *39*, 580–587. DOI: 10.1016/S2212-5671(16)30302-1

Jans, L. H., Kaye, H. S., & Jones, E. C. (2012). Getting hired: Successfully employed people with disabilities offer advice on disclosure, interviewing, and job search. *Journal of Occupational Rehabilitation*, *22*(2), 155–165. DOI: 10.1007/s10926-011-9336-y PMID: 22020624

Jiang, N., Yan-Li, S., Pamanee, K., & Sriyanto, J. (2021). Depression, anxiety, and stress during the COVID-19 pandemic: Comparison among higher education students in four countries in the Asia-Pacific region. *Journal of Population and Social Studies*, *2021*, 1–13. DOI: 10.25133/JPSSv292021.023

Jiang, P., & Rosenbloom, B. (2005). Customer intention to return online: Price perception, attribute-level performance, and satisfaction unfolding over time. *European Journal of Marketing*, *39*(1/2), 150–174. DOI: 10.1108/03090560510572061

Jimenez-Fernandez, A., Aramendia-Muneta, M. E., & Alzate, M. (2023). Consumers' Awareness and Attitudes in Circular Fashion. *Cleaner and Responsible Consumption*, *11*, 100144. DOI: 10.1016/j.clrc.2023.100144

Jindal, M., & Bhaedwaj, A. (2016). Entrepreneurship development in India: a new paradigm. *Proceedings of the World Congress on Engineering*, 2. https://www.iaeng.org/publication/WCE2016/WCE2016_pp724-726.pdf

Jit, M., Ananthakrishnan, A., McKee, M., Wouters, O. J., Beutels, P., & Teerawattananon, Y. (2021). Multi-country collaboration in responding to global infectious disease threats: Lessons for Europe from the COVID-19 pandemic. *The Lancet Regional Health. Europe*, *9*, 9. DOI: 10.1016/j.lanepe.2021.100221 PMID: 34642675

Johnson, A. (2017). *Perspectives on Harmful Speech Online: A Collection of Essays.* The Berkman Klein Center for Internet & Society at Harvard University.

Johnson, C. K., P. L. Hitchens, P. S. Pandit, J. Rushmore, T. S. Evans, C. C. W. Young, and M. M. Doyle. (2020). Global shifts in mammalian population trends reveal key predictors of virus spillover risk. Proceedings. Biological Sciences 287 (1924):20192736. .DOI: 10.1098/rspb.2019.2736

Johnston-Robledo, I., & Chrisler, J. C. (2020). *The menstrual mark: Menstruation as social stigma.* In Springer eBooks (pp. 181–199). https://doi.org/DOI: 10.1007/978-981-15-0614-7_17

Jones, C. G., & Taylor, J. A. (2019). Artificial intelligence in healthcare: Challenges, opportunities, and applications. *Journal of Health Care Technology*, *32*(2), 223–235. DOI: 10.1080/22757293.2019.1259483

Jones, R., & Williams, J. (2024). The profitability challenges of Q-commerce startups. *Critical Review*.

Joshi, P, et al. (2024) *Status, Gaps and Challenges in Menstrual Health in India: A . . . : Preventive Medicine: Research & Reviews.* DOI: . PMRR_74_24DOI: 10.4103/PMRR

Joy, A., Sherry, J. F.Jr, Venkatesh, A., Wang, J., & Chan, R. (2012). Fast Fashion, Sustainability, and the Ethical Appeal of Luxury Brands. *Fashion Theory*, *16*(3), 273–295. DOI: 10.2752/175174112X13340749707123

Judge, T. A., Woolf, E. F., & Hurst, C. (2009). Is Emotional Labor More Difficult for Some Than for Others? A Multilevel Experience-Sampling Study. *Personnel Psychology*, *62*(1), 57–88. DOI: 10.1111/j.1744-6570.2008.01129.x

Jyoti, B., & Singh, A. K. (2023). Does digitalization have a causal relationship with economic development? an experience from a country-wise panel data statistical analysis. In R. Sine Nazlı & G. Sari (Eds.), *Handbook of Research on Perspectives on Society and Technology Addiction* (pp. 34-61). IGI Global. DOI: 10.4018/978-1-6684-8397-8.ch003

Jyoti, B., & Singh, A. K. (2020). Characteristics and determinants of new start-ups in Gujarat, India. *Entrepreneurship Review*, *1*(2), 1–25. DOI: 10.38157/entrepreneurship-review.v1i2.154

Kaaria, A. G., & Mwaruta, S. S. (2023). Mental Health Ingenuities and the Role of Computer Technology on Employees' Mental Health: A Systematic Review. *East African Journal of Health and Science*, *6*(1), 219–231. DOI: 10.37284/eajhs.6.1.1268

Kahn, B., Brown, L., Foege, W., & Gayle, H. (Eds.). (2020). *Framework for equitable allocation of COVID-19 vaccine.*

Kalabay, B., Ertuna, B., & Salman, D. (2019). Corporate social responsibility in tourism as a tool for sustainable development: An evaluation from a community perspective. *International Journal of Contemporary Hospitality Management*, *31*(6), 2358–2375. Advance online publication. DOI: 10.1108/IJCHM-05-2018-0448

Kamalaldin, A., Linde, L., Sjödin, D., & Parida, V. (2020). Transforming provider-customer relationships in digital servitization: A relational view on digitalization. *Industrial Marketing Management*, *89*, 306–325. DOI: 10.1016/j.indmarman.2020.02.004

Kamel Boulos, M. N., & Zhang, P. (2021). Digital twins: From personalised medicine to precision public health. *Journal of Personalized Medicine*, *11*(11), 1048. DOI: 10.3390/jpm11080745 PMID: 34442389

Kandasamy, N., Perera, B., & Soldatic, K. (2021). *COVID-19 from the Margins: Gendered-Disability Experiences in Sri lanka*. Disability and the Global South.

Kansal, S., Singh, S., & Kumar, A. (2015). Menstrual hygiene practices in context of schooling: A community study among rural adolescent girls in Varanasi. *Indian Journal of Community Medicine : Official Publication of Indian Association of Preventive & Social Medicine*, *41*(1), 39. DOI: 10.4103/0970-0218.170964 PMID: 26917872

Kapadia, S., & Madhav, V. (2020). The impact of digitization on banking and financial services industry in India. *The IUP Journal of Bank Management, 19*(2), 24–31.

Kaplan, C. P., Turner, S., Norman, E., & Stillson, K. (1996). Promoting Resilience Strategies: A Modified Consultation Model. *Children & Schools, 18*(3), 158–168. DOI: 10.1093/cs/18.3.158

Kapoor, S., & Bharti, A. (2020). The impact of AI on radiology practice and its future applications. *The Indian Journal of Radiology & Imaging, 30*(1), 14–21. DOI: 10.4103/ijri.IJRI_104_19

Karanika-Murray, M., Whysall, Z., Liu-Smith, Y.-L., Feltbower, C., & Challans-Rasool, E. (2023). Understanding organizational learning in a healthcare organization during sudden and disruptive change. *International Journal of Workplace Health Management, 16*(4), 257–280. DOI: 10.1108/IJWHM-09-2022-0145

Karim, R. (2022). The Influence of CSR Practices on Hotel Images and Hotel Benefits in Bangladesh. *Journal of Technology Management and Business, 9*(2). Advance online publication. DOI: 10.30880/jtmb.2022.09.02.002

Kario, K., Nomura, A., Harada, N., & Okura, A. (2021). Efficacy of a digital therapeutics system in the management of essential hypertension: The HERB-DH1 pivotal trial. *European Heart Journal. Digital Health, 2*(3), 275–284. DOI: 10.1093/ehjdh/ztab033 PMID: 34455443

Kasser, S., & Lytle, R. (2005). *Inclusive physical activity*. Human Kinetics.

Katz, D. A., Greenberg, M. T., Jennings, P. A., & Klein, L. C. (2016). Associations between the awakening responses of salivary α-amylase and cortisol with self-report indicators of health and wellbeing among educators. *Teaching and Teacher Education, 54*, 98–106. DOI: 10.1016/j.tate.2015.11.012

Kaur, S., & Garg, P. (2021). Recent advances in AI-based medical technologies. *Journal of Medical Systems, 45*(7), 88. DOI: 10.1007/s10916-021-01845-z

Kayess, R., & French, P. (2008). Out of the darkness into light? Introducing the Convention on the Rights of Persons with Disabilities. *Human Rights Law Review, 8*(1), 5–7. DOI: 10.1093/hrlr/ngm044

Kazancoglu, I., Kazancoglu, Y., Yarimoglu, E., & Kahraman, A. (2020). A Conceptual Framework for Barriers of Circular Supply Chains for Sustainability in The Textile Industry. *Sustainable Development (Bradford), 28*(5), 1477–1492. DOI: 10.1002/sd.2100

Keddie, A. (2007). Issues of Power, Masculinity, and Gender Justice: Sally's Story of Teaching Boys. *Discourse (Berkeley, Calif.)*, *28*(1), 21–35.

Kelly, A. E., & Palaniappan, S. (2023). Using a technology acceptance model to determine factors influencing continued usage of mobile money service transactions in Ghana. *Journal of Innovation and Entrepreneurship*, *12*(1), 34. Advance online publication. DOI: 10.1186/s13731-023-00301-3

Khalid, F., Naveed, K., Nawaz, R., Sun, X., Wu, Y., & Ye, C. (2023). Does corporate green investment enhance profitability? An institutional perspective. *Ekonomska Istrazivanja*, *36*(1), 1–24. DOI: 10.1080/1331677X.2022.2063919

Khan, Z. F., & Alotaibi, S. R. (2020). Applications of artificial intelligence and big data analytics in m-health: A healthcare system perspective. *Journal of Healthcare Engineering*, *2020*, 1–15. DOI: 10.1155/2020/6654063 PMID: 32952992

Khattak, S., Nouman, M., Fayaz, M., Cisma , L., Negrut, L., & Negrut, C. (2021). Corporate Social Responsibility and Employee Green Behavior in the Hospitality Industry: A Cross-Country Study. *Sustainability (Basel)*, *13*(19), 1–15. DOI: 10.3390/su131910534

Khodaviren, M., & Bhattacharjee, S. (2024). CSR perceptions and practices in small hotels in urban cities. *Journal of Hospitality and Tourism Insights*. DOI: 10.1108/JHTI-10-2023-0692

Kholijah, S. (2024). Analysis of Economic and Environmental Benefits of Green Business Practices in the Hospitality and Tourism Sector. *Involvement International Journal of Business*, *1*(1), 60–74. DOI: 10.62569/iijb.v1i1.7

Khoo, A. (2020). Ghana in COVID-19 Pandemic. *Inter-Asia Cultural Studies*, *21*(4), 542–556. DOI: 10.1080/14649373.2020.1832300

Kim, B. J., Jeon, N., Sohn, H., Lee, N., & Kim, M. J. (2024). The impact of corporate social responsibility on employee burnout: The crucial role of work overload. *Corporate Social Responsibility and Environmental Management*, *31*(5), 4345–4360. DOI: 10.1002/csr.2802

Kim, I., Jung, H. J., & Lee, Y. (2021). Consumers' Value and Risk Perceptions of Circular Fashion: Comparison Between Secondhand, Upcycled, And Recycled Clothing. *Sustainability (Basel)*, *13*(3), 1208. DOI: 10.3390/su13031208

Kim, S. Y., Park, H., Kim, H., Kim, J., & Seo, K. (2022). Technostress causes cognitive overload in high-stress people: Eye tracking analysis in a virtual kiosk test. *Information Processing & Management*, *59*(6), 103093. DOI: 10.1016/j.ipm.2022.103093 PMID: 36119755

Kim, S., & Lee, B. (2019). AI in medical robotics: Potential and challenges. *Medical Robotics and Surgery*, *8*(1), 39–47. DOI: 10.1089/mrs.2019.2917

Kindström, D. (2010). Towards a Service-Based Business Model – Key Aspects for Future Competitive Advantage. *European Management Journal*, *28*(6), 479–490. DOI: 10.1016/j.emj.2010.07.002

Kindström, D., & Kowalkowski, C. (2009). Development of Industrial Service Offerings: A Process Framework. *Journal of Service Management*, *20*(2), 156–172. DOI: 10.1108/09564230910952753

Kirk, J., & Sommer, M. (2006) *Menstruation and body awareness: linking girls' health with girls' education.*https://www.semanticscholar.org/paper/Menstruation-and-body-awareness-%3A-linking-girls-%E2%80%99-%E2%80%99-Kirk-Sommer/e4072b8340ecd2eec2564d0947d59c01672b834b

Kitsios, F., & Kamariotou, M. (2023). Digital innovation and entrepreneurship transformation through open data hackathons: Design strategies for successful start-up settings. *International Journal of Information Management*, *69*(1), 1–13. DOI: 10.1016/j.ijinfomgt.2022.102472

Kiviaho, A., & Einolander, J. (2023). Digital transformation, well-being and shrinking communities: Narrowing the divides between urban and rural. *Heliyon*, *9*(8), e18801. DOI: 10.1016/j.heliyon.2023.e18801 PMID: 37600410

Kniffin, K. M., Narayanan, J., & Anseel, F. (2021). Advancing workplace flexibility: The role of digital health solutions. *Work, Employment and Society*, *35*(3), 522–538.

Knight, W. (2020). Deep learning in healthcare: A revolution in data-driven medicine. *Technology Review*, *34*(3), 5–13. DOI: 10.1162/techr

Kollmann, T. (2006). *What is e-entrepreneurship? – fundamentals of company founding in the net economy*. Elgaeonline., DOI: 10.1504/IJTM.2006.009247

Kollmann, T., Kleine-Stegemann, L., & Cruppe, K. (2022). Eras of digital entrepreneurship. *Business & Information Systems Engineering*, *64*(1), 15–31. DOI: 10.1007/s12599-021-00728-6

Kopalle, P. K., Gangwar, M., Kaplan, A., Ramachandran, D., Reinartz, W., & Rindfleisch, A. (2022). Examining artificial intelligence (AI) technologies in marketing via a global lens: Current trends and future research opportunities. *International Journal of Research in Marketing*, *39*(2), 522–540. DOI: 10.1016/j.ijresmar.2021.11.002

Korhonen, J., Honkasalo, A., & Seppälä, J. (2018). Circular Economy: The Concept and its Limitations. *Ecological Economics, 143*, 37–46. DOI: 10.1016/j.ecolecon.2017.06.041

Kotarba, M. (2018). Digital transformation of business models. *Foundations of Management,* 10(1), 123-142. https://intapi.sciendo.com/pdf/10.2478/fman-2018-0011

Krainik, P. (2023). Has the future of retail arrived? An empirical analysis of drivers for the adoption of Q-commerce in the consumer durables segment (Doctoral dissertation).

Krainik, T. (2023). The carbon footprint of quick commerce: How sustainable is fast delivery? Kumar, P., & Sharma, R. (2023). Understanding consumer preferences in Q-commerce.

Kraus, S., Schiavone, F., Pluzhnikova, A., & Invernizzi, A. C. (2021). Digital transformation in healthcare: Analyzing the current state-of-research. *Journal of Business Research, 123*, 557–567. DOI: 10.1016/j.jbusres.2020.10.030

Kreiterling, C. (2023). Digital innovation and entrepreneurship: A review of challenges in competitive markets. *Journal of Innovation and Entrepreneurship, 12*(1), 1–13. DOI: 10.1186/s13731-023-00320-0

Kreitmair, K. V. (2024). Mobile health technology and empowerment. *Bioethics, 2024*, 1–13. PMID: 36950727

Kuhfeld, M., & Tarasawa, B. (2020). *The COVID-19 slide: What summer learning loss can tell us about the potential impact of school closures on student academic achievement.*

Kuhlmann, S., & Franzke, J. (2022). Multi-Level Responses to COVID-19: Crisis Coordination in Germany From an Intergovernmental Perspective. *Local Government Studies, 48*(2), 312–334. DOI: 10.1080/03003930.2021.1904398

Kushniruk, A. W., & Borycki, E. M. (2023, March). Human factors in healthcare IT: Management considerations and trends. [). Sage CA: Los Angeles, CA: SAGE Publications.]. *Healthcare Management Forum, 36*(2), 72–78. DOI: 10.1177/08404704221139219 PMID: 36847593

Kuvvetli, Y., Deveci, M., Paksoy, T., & Garg, H. (2021). A Predictive Analytics Model for COVID-19 Pandemic Using Artificial Neural Networks. *Decision Analytics Journal, 1*, 1–13. DOI: 10.1016/j.dajour.2021.100007

Kwame, A., Makarova, V., Hudu, F., & Petrucka, P. M. (2023). The COVID-19 Pandemic in Ghana: Exploring the Discourse Strategies in President Nana Addo's Speeches. *Humanities & Social Sciences Communications*, *10*(1), 1–10. DOI: 10.1057/s41599-023-02253-1

Kyriacou, C. (2001). Teacher stress: Directions for future research. *Educational Review*, *53*(1), 27–35. DOI: 10.1080/00131910120033628

Lahelma, E., Palmu, T., & Gordon, T. (2000). Intersecting Power Relations in Teachers' Experiences of Being Sexualized or Harassed by Students. *Sexualities*, *3*(4), 463–481. DOI: 10.1177/136346000003004006

Lalicic, L., & Weismayer, C. (2021). Consumers' reasons and perceived value co-creation of using artificial intelligence-enabled travel service agents. *Journal of Business Research*, *129*, 891–901. DOI: 10.1016/j.jbusres.2020.11.005

Lal, R. (2012). Mental Retardation to Intellectual Disability: A changing concept. *Disabilities and Impairments*, *24*(2), 77–82.

Lanzolla, G., Pesce, D., & Tucci, C. L. (2021). The digital transformation of search and recombination in the innovation function: tensions and an integrative framework. *Journal of Product Innovation Management*, 38(), 90-113. 90-113. DOI: 10.1111/jpim.12546

Lee, D., & Yoon, S. N. (2021). Application of artificial intelligence-based technologies in the healthcare industry: Opportunities and challenges. *International Journal of Environmental Research and Public Health*, *18*(1), 271. DOI: 10.3390/ijerph18010271 PMID: 33401373

Lehtimäki, H., Piispanen, V.-V., & Henttonen, K. (2020). Strategic Decisions Related to Circular Business Model in A Forerunner Company: Challenges due to Path Dependency and Lock-in. *South Asian Journal of Business and Management Cases*, *9*(3), 402–412. DOI: 10.1177/2277977920957957

Leiner, B. M., & Cerf, V. G. (2000). *A brief history of the Internet*.https://www.usg.edu/galileo/skills/unit07/internet07_02.phtml

Leite, H., Lindsay, C., & Kumar, M. (2020). COVID-19 outbreak: Implications on healthcare operations. *The TQM Journal*, *33*(1), 247–256. DOI: 10.1108/TQM-05-2020-0111

Leone, D., Schiavone, F., Appio, F. P., & Chiao, B. (2021). How does artificial intelligence enable and enhance value co-creation in industrial markets? An exploratory case study in the healthcare ecosystem. *Journal of Business Research*, *129*, 849–859. DOI: 10.1016/j.jbusres.2020.11.008

Leone, L. A., Fleischhacker, S., Anderson-Steeves, B., Harper, K., Winkler, M., Racine, E., Baquero, B., & Gittelsohn, J. (2020). Healthy food retail during the COVID-19 pandemic: Challenges and future directions. *International Journal of Environmental Research and Public Health, 17*(11), 4179. DOI: 10.3390/ijerph17207397 PMID: 33050600

Lestiyanawati, R. (2020). *The strategies and problems faced by Indonesian teachers in conducting e-learning during COVID-19 outbreak.* CLLiENT (Culture, Literature, Linguistics, and English Teaching), 2(1), 71-82.

Leviäkangas, P. (2016). Digitalisation of Finland's transport sector. *Technology in Society, 47*(1), 1–15. DOI: 10.1016/j.techsoc.2016.07.001

Levy, S. E., & Duverger, P. (2010). Consumer perceptions of sustainability in the lodging industry: Examination of sustainable tourism criteria. *International CHRIE Conference-Refereed Track, Event 31*, 2–8.

Lewis, D. (2022). Why the WHO took two years to say COVID is airborne. *Nature, 604*(7904), 26–31. DOI: 10.1038/d41586-022-00925-7 PMID: 35388203

Li, C., Borycki, E. M., & Kushniruk, A. W. (2021, October). Connecting the world of healthcare virtually: a scoping review on virtual care delivery. In Healthcare (Vol. 9, No. 10, p. 1325). MDPI. DOI: 10.3390/healthcare9101325

Liberati, E., Richards, N., Willars, J., Scott, D., Boydell, N., Parker, J., Pinfold, V., Martin, G., Dixon-Woods, M., & Jones, P. B. (2021). A qualitative study of experiences of NHS mental healthcare workers during the Covid-19 pandemic. *BMC Psychiatry, 2021*(1), 1–13. DOI: 10.1186/s12888-021-03261-8 PMID: 33980215

Lieder, M., & Rashid, A. (2016). Towards Circular Economy Implementation: A Comprehensive Review in Context of Manufacturing Industry. *Journal of Cleaner Production, 115*, 36–51. DOI: 10.1016/j.jclepro.2015.12.042

Li, L., & Xie, C. (2021). Artificial intelligence in diagnostics: Transforming medical imaging. *International Journal of Imaging Systems and Technology, 31*(4), 45–52. DOI: 10.1002/ima.22611

Linardon, J., Shatte, A., Messer, M., & Firth, J. (2020). E-mental health interventions for the treatment and prevention of eating disorders: An updated systematic review and meta-analysis. *Journal of Consulting and Clinical Psychology, 2020*, 1–13. DOI: 10.1037/ccp0000459 PMID: 32852971

Lindström, C. W., Vishkaei, B. M., & Giovanni, P. D. (2023). Subscription-based business models in the context of tech firms: Theory and applications. *International Journal of Industrial Engineering and Operations Management*, *6*(3), 256–274. DOI: 10.1108/IJIEOM-06-2023-0054

Liu, K., Tan, Q., Yu, J., & Wang, M. (2023). A global perspective on e-waste recycling. *Circular Economy*, *2023*, 1–13.

Liu, X., Wang, L., & Zhang, Y. (2019). Leveraging artificial intelligence for drug discovery and development. *Nature Reviews. Drug Discovery*, *18*(8), 505–518. DOI: 10.1038/s41573-019-00097-3

Liu, Y., Lee, J. M., & Lee, C. (2020). The challenges and opportunities of a global health crisis: The management and business implications of COVID-19 from an Asian perspective. *Asian Business & Management*, *19*(3), 259–278. DOI: 10.1057/s41291-020-00119-x

Li, X., & Chan, M. (2022). Smartphone uses and emotional and psychological well-being in China: The attenuating role of perceived information overload. *Behaviour & Information Technology*, *41*(11), 2427–2437. DOI: 10.1080/0144929X.2021.1929489

Li, Y., & Xu, Y. (2021). Applications of machine learning in pathology and histology. *Journal of Pathology Informatics*, *12*(1), 7–16. DOI: 10.4103/jpi.jpi_45_20

Lone, S. A., & Ahmad, A. (2020). COVID-19 pandemic–an African perspective. *Emerging Microbes & Infections*, *9*(1), 1300–1308. DOI: 10.1080/22221751.2020.1775132 PMID: 32458760

Longoni, C., Bonezzi, A., & Morewedge, C. K. (2019). Resistance to medical artificial intelligence. *The Journal of Consumer Research*, *46*(4), 629–650. DOI: 10.1093/jcr/ucz013

Loss, J., Boklage, E., Jordan, S., Jenny, M. A., Weishaar, H., & El Bcheraoui, C. (2021). Risikokommunikation bei der Eind€ammung der COVID-19 Pandemie: Herausforderungenund Erfolg versprechende Ans€atze. *Bundesgesundheitsblatt, Gesundheitsforschung, Gesundheitsschutz*, *64*(3), 294–303. DOI: 10.1007/s00103-021-03283-3 PMID: 33564896

Love, J. S., Blumenberg, A., & Horowitz, Z. (2020). The parallel pandemic: Medical misinformation and COVID-19. *Journal of General Internal Medicine*, *35*(8), 2435–2436. DOI: 10.1007/s11606-020-05897-w PMID: 32410129

Lubawa, G. G., & Kandpal, D. V. (2024). Advancing Financial Inclusion through Digital Finance Innovations in Tanzania. In Editor(s) (s): Ernesto. D.R. Santibanez Gonzalez, Vinay Kandpal, Peterson K. Ozili, Prasenjit Chatterjee. Fintech for ESG and the Circular Economy.(pp.255-287), John Wiley & Sons, Inc; DOI: 10.1002/9781394234035.ch14

Lubawa, G. G., & Osabuohien, E. S. (2024). Developing Sustainable Tourism in Tanzania: Perspective from Wine Stakeholders. In Martínez-Falcó, J., Marco-Lajara, B., Sánchez-García, E., & Millán-Tudela, L. A. (Eds.), *Wine Tourism and Sustainability*. Palgrave Macmillan., DOI: 10.1007/978-3-031-48937-2_3

Lubis, S., Purnomo, E. P., Lado, J. A., & Hung, C.-F. (2024). Electronic governance in advancing sustainable development goals through systematic literature review. *Discover Global Society*, *2*(1), 77. Advance online publication. DOI: 10.1007/s44282-024-00102-3

Luna Sanchez, P. (2024). An analysis of the drivers of consumers' purchasing behavior in quick commerce platforms.

Lu, X., & Roberts, A. (2020). Artificial intelligence in cancer prediction and diagnosis. *Cancer Letters*, *467*, 21–32. DOI: 10.1016/j.canlet.2019.12.023

Lynn, T., Rosati, P., Conway, E., Curran, D., & O'Gorman, G. F. (2022). Infrastructure for digital connectivity. In *Digital Towns* (pp. 109–132). Springer., DOI: 10.1007/978-3-030-91247-5_6

Lyulyov, O., Pimonenko, T., Saura, J. R., & Barbosa, B. (2024). How do e-governance and e-business drive sustainable development goals? *Technological Forecasting and Social Change*, *199*, 123082. DOI: 10.1016/j.techfore.2023.123082

Madhavan, S., Bastarache, L., Brown, J. S., Butte, A. J., Dorr, D. A., Embi, P. J., & Kohane, I. S. (2021). Use of electronic health records to support a public health response to the COVID-19 pandemic in the United States: A perspective from 15 academic medical centers. *Journal of the American Medical Informatics Association : JAMIA*, *28*(2), 393–401. DOI: 10.1093/jamia/ocaa287 PMID: 33260207

Magomana, N. R., & Maireva, C. (2021). Information Technology and entrepreneurship development in Africa. *East African Journal of Education and Social Sciences, Issue 2 (April to June 2021)*, 239–242. DOI: 10.46606/eajess2021v02i02.0095

Majenga, A. K., Namabira, J., & Justine, E. K. (2024). Promoting Rural Entrepreneurship in Tanzania Through Empowering Voluntary Financial Saving Groups. *African Journal of Applied Research*, *10*(1), 275–294. DOI: 10.26437/ajar.v10i1.688

Malecki, K. M. C., Keating, J. A., & Safdar, N. (2021). Crisis communication and public perception of COVID-19 risk in the era of social media. *Clinical Infectious Diseases*, *72*(4), 697–702. DOI: 10.1093/cid/ciaa758 PMID: 32544242

Maltby, J., Day, L., Hatcher, R. M., Tazzyman, S., Flowe, H. D., Palmer, E. J., Frosch, C. A., O'Reilly, M., Jones, C., Buckley, C., Melanie Knieps, M., & Cutts, K. (2016). Implicit theories of online trolling: Evidence that attention-seeking conceptions are associated with increased psychological resilience. *British Journal of Psychology*, *107*(3), 448–466. DOI: 10.1111/bjop.12154 PMID: 26403842

Manani, J. (2022). Sentimental analysis on quick commerce platform based on customer reviews in Google Play Store.

Mandarić, D., Hunjet, A., & Kozina, G. (2021). Perception of Consumers' Awareness about Sustainability of Fashion Brands. *Journal of Risk and Financial Management*, *14*(12), 594. DOI: 10.3390/jrfm14120594

Manser Payne, L., Dahl, A., & Peltier, J. (2021a). Digital servitization value co-creation framework for AI services: A research agenda for digital transformation in financial service ecosystems. *Journal of Research in Interactive Marketing*, *15*(2), 200–222. DOI: 10.1108/JRIM-12-2020-0252

Manser Payne, L., Peltier, J., & Barger, V. (2021b). Enhancing the value co-creation process: Artificial intelligence and mobile banking service platforms. *Journal of Research in Interactive Marketing*, *15*(1), 68–85. DOI: 10.1108/JRIM-10-2020-0214

Manzoor, F., Wei, L., & Sahito, N. (2021). The role of SMEs in rural development: Access of SMEs to finance as a mediator. *PLoS One*, *16*(3), e0247598. DOI: 10.1371/journal.pone.0247598 PMID: 33684146

Marchini, S., Zaurino, E., Bouziotis, J., Brondino, N., Delvenne, V., & Delhaye, M. (2021). Study of resilience and loneliness in youth (18–25 years old) during the COVID-19 pandemic lockdown measures. *Journal of Community Psychology*, *2021*(2), 1–13. DOI: 10.1002/jcop.22473 PMID: 33169377

Mariño-Romero, J. M., Hernández-Mogollón, J. M., Campón-Cerro, A. M., & Folgado-Fernández, J. A. (2020). Corporate Social Responsibility in Hotels: A Proposal of a Measurement of its Performance through Marketing Variables. *Sustainability (Basel)*, *12*(7), 7. Advance online publication. DOI: 10.3390/su12072961

Marques, A. D., Marques, A., & Ferreira, F. (2020). Homo Sustentabilis: Circular Economy and New Business Models in Fashion Industry. *SN Applied Sciences*, *2*(2), 306. DOI: 10.1007/s42452-020-2094-8

Marquis, C., & Raynard, M. (2015). Institutional strategies in emerging markets. *The Academy of Management Annals*, *9*(1), 1–13. DOI: 10.5465/19416520.2015.1014661

Martínez-Peláez, R., Ochoa-Brust, A., Rivera, S., Félix, V. G., Ostos, R., Brito, H., Félix, R. A., & Mena, L. J. (2023). Role of digital transformation for achieving sustainability: Mediated role of stakeholders, key capabilities, and technology. *Sustainability (Basel)*, *15*(14), 11221. DOI: 10.3390/su151411221

Mason, L., Sivakami, M., Thakur, H., Kakade, N., Beauman, A., Alexander, K. T., Van Eijke, A. M., Laserson, K. F., Thakkar, M. B., & Phillips-Howard, P. A. (2017b). 'We do not know': A qualitative study exploring boys' perceptions of menstruation in India. *Reproductive Health*, *14*(1), 174. Advance online publication. DOI: 10.1186/s12978-017-0435-x PMID: 29216895

Massa, L., & Tucci, C. (2014). Business Model Innovation. *Oxford Handbook of Innovation Management*, 420–441. https://infoscience.epfl.ch/handle/20.500.14299/106759

Matavire, R., Chigona, W., Roode, D., Sewchurran, E., Davids, Z., Mukudu, A., & Abu, C. B. (2010). Challenges of eGovernment project implementation in a South African context. *Electronic Journal of Information Systems Evaluation*, *13*(2), 153–164.

Mathias, T. (2017, January 27). *The Tweeter side to life: How Indians on Twitter are making a difference*. The Better India. https://thebetterindia.com/83396/twitter-for-good-social-outreach/

Matook, S., Cummings, J., & Bala, H. (2015). Are you feeling lonely? The impact of relationship characteristics and online social network features on loneliness. *Journal of Management Information Systems*, *31*(4), 278–310. DOI: 10.1080/07421222.2014.1001282

Matthews, C. K., & Harrington, N. G. *Invisible disability.* In D.O. Braithwaite, & T. L. Thompson (Eds.), (2000). Handbook of Communication and People with Disabilities: Research and Application (pp. 405-421).

Mbunge, E., Batani, J., Gaobotse, G., & Muchemwa, B. (2022). Virtual healthcare services and digital health technologies deployed during coronavirus disease 2019 (COVID-19) pandemic in South Africa: A systematic review. *Global Health Journal (Amsterdam, Netherlands)*, *2022*(2), 1–13. DOI: 10.1016/j.glohj.2022.03.001 PMID: 35282399

Mbunge, E., Muchemwa, B., & Batani, J. (2021). Sensors and healthcare 5.0: Transformative shift in virtual care through emerging digital health technologies. *Global Health Journal (Amsterdam, Netherlands)*, *2021*(4), 1–13. DOI: 10.1016/j.glohj.2021.11.008

McCarthy, R. N. E., Donkoh, E. T., Arthur, D. D., Dassah, E. T., Boadu, K. O., Otoo, J. E., Boadu, I. W. O., & Gyasi, S. F. (2023). Public Relations Strategies Employed by the Ghana Health Service to Address COVID-19 Vaccine Hesitancy: A Qualitative Inquiry. *Tropical Medicine and Health*, *51*(1), 1–14. DOI: 10.1186/s41182-023-00519-7 PMID: 37170342

McCool, J., Dobson, R., Muinga, N., Paton, C., Pagliari, C., Agawal, S., Labrique, A., Tanielu, H., & Whittaker, R. (2020). Factors influencing the sustainability of digital health interventions in low-resource settings: Lessons from five countries. *Journal of Global Health*, *10*(2), 020403. DOI: 10.7189/jogh.10.020396 PMID: 33274059

Medberg, G., & Grönroos, C. (2020). Value-in-use and service quality: Do customers see a difference? *Journal of Service Theory and Practice*, *30*(4/5), 507–529. DOI: 10.1108/JSTP-09-2019-0207

Mele, C., Russo Spena, T., Kaartemo, V., & Marzullo, M. L. (2021). Smart nudging: How cognitive technologies enable choice architectures for value co-creation. *Journal of Business Research*, *129*, 949–960. DOI: 10.1016/j.jbusres.2020.09.004

Mensah, I. K. (2022). Understanding the Drivers of Ghanaian Citizens' Adoption Intentions of Mobile Health Services. *Frontiers in Public Health*, *10*, 1–20. DOI: 10.3389/fpubh.2022.906106 PMID: 35774576

Mer, A., & Srivastava, A. (2023). Employee engagement in the new normal: Artificial intelligence as a buzzword or a game changer? In *The adoption and effect of artificial intelligence on human resources management, Part A* (pp. 15-46). Emerald Publishing Limited.

Mesa, J. A. (2023). Design for Circularity and Durability: An Integrated Approach from DFX Guidelines. *Research in Engineering Design*, *34*(4), 443–460. DOI: 10.1007/s00163-023-00419-1

MicKinsy & Company. (2020). How covid-19 has pushed companies over the technology tipping point-and transformed business sector. [Online]. https://www.mckinsey.com/capabilities/strategy-and-corporate-finance/our-insights/how-covid-19-has-pushed-companies-over-the-technology-tipping-point-and-transformed-business-forever

Millan, M. M., Claudia, D. R., & Sepúlveda. (2017). *Structural Change, Fundamentals, and Growth A Framework and Case Studies*. World Bank Group. worldbank.org

Millar, M., & Baloglu, S. (2011). Hotel Guests' Preferences for Green Guest Room Attributes. *Cornell Hospitality Quarterly -. Cornell Hospitality Quarterly*, *52*(3), 302–311. DOI: 10.1177/1938965511409031

Minkos, M. L., & Gelbar, N. W. (2021). Considerations for educators in supporting student learning in the midst of COVID-19. *Psychology in the Schools*, *58*(2), 416–426. DOI: 10.1002/pits.22454 PMID: 33362299

Mirza, N., Naqvi, B., Rahat, B., & Rizvi, S. K. A. (2020). Price reaction, volatility timing and funds' performance during Covid-19. *Finance Research Letters*, *36*, 101657. DOI: 10.1016/j.frl.2020.101657 PMID: 32837369

Moazzem, S., Wang, L., Daver, F., & Crossin, E. (2021). Environmental Impact of Discarded Apparel Landfilling and Recycling. *Resources, Conservation and Recycling*, *166*, 105338. DOI: 10.1016/j.resconrec.2020.105338

Mohale, C. (2024). The Role of E-Government in the Promotion of Municipal Service Delivery in South Africa. *International Journal of Social Science Research and Review*, *7*(3), 1–19. DOI: 10.47814/ijssrr.v7i3.1992

Mohammadpour, M., Zarifinezhad, E., Ghanbarzadegan, A., Naderimanesh, K., Shaarbafchizadeh, N., & Bastani, P. (2021). Main factors affecting the readiness and responsiveness of healthcare systems during epidemic crises: A scoping review on cases of sars, mers, and covid-19. *Iranian Journal of Medical Sciences*, *46*(2), 81. PMID: 33753952

Monda, A., Feola, R., Parente, R., Vesci, M., & Botti, A. (2023). Rural development and digital technologies: A collaborative framework for policy-making. *Transforming Government*, *17*(3), 328–343. DOI: 10.1108/TG-12-2022-0162

Montani, D., Savale, L., Beurnier, A., Colle, R., Noël, N., Pham, T., Monnet, X., & Humbert, M. (2021). Multidisciplinary Approach for Post-Acute COVID-19 Syndrome: Time to Break Down the Walls. *The European Respiratory Journal*, *58*(1), 1–3. DOI: 10.1183/13993003.01090-2021 PMID: 33958429

Moon, B., McCluskey, J., & Morash, M. (2019). Aggression against Middle and High School Teachers: Duration of Victimization and Its Negative Impacts. *Aggressive Behavior*, *45*(5), 517–526. DOI: 10.1002/ab.21840 PMID: 31157921

Mooya, N., & Phiri, J. (2021). Factors hindering the adoption of E-marketing among cable manufacturers in Zambia, based on the technology acceptance model (TAM). *Technology and Investment*, *12*(2), 51–65. DOI: 10.4236/ti.2021.122004

Morewedge, C. K., Monga, A., Palmatier, R. W., Shu, S. B., & Small, D. A. (2021). Evolution of consumption: A psychological ownership framework. *Journal of Marketing*, *85*(1), 196–218. DOI: 10.1177/0022242920957007

Moro, D. S. (2021, May 3). *Resale, Rental and Repair: The 3 Rs-that-are-Changing-Fashion*. Cikis Studio. http://www.cikis.studio/en/article/resale-rental-and-repair-the-3-Rs-that-are-changing-fashion

Morris, T., & Reid, M. (2020). Ethics of AI applications in healthcare. *Journal of Health Ethics*, *46*(1), 82–92. DOI: 10.1016/j.jhlthe.2020.06.001

Moyeen, A., & Mehjabeen, M. (2024). CSR research in the hotel industry: How it relates to promoting the SDGs. *Social Responsibility Journal*, *20*(9), 1770–1786. Advance online publication. DOI: 10.1108/SRJ-01-2024-0032

Mucowska, M. (2021). Trends of environmentally sustainable solutions of urban last-mile deliveries on the e-commerce market—A literature review. *Sustainability (Basel)*, *13*(11), 5894. DOI: 10.3390/su13115894

Mukherjee, A., & Michael, J. (2022). Technology-driven logistics in Q-commerce: A review of operational innovations.

Mukherjee, S., & Michael, H. (2021). Modern trends, challenges and opportunity of e-commerce in India–An overview.

Mumtaz, H., Riaz, M. H., Wajid, H., Saqib, M., Zeeshan, M. H., Khan, S. E., Chauhan, Y. R., Sohail, H., & Vohra, L. I. (2023). Current challenges and potential solutions to the use of digital health technologies in evidence generation: A narrative review. *Frontiers in Digital Health*, *5*, 1203945. DOI: 10.3389/fdgth.2023.1203945 PMID: 37840685

Murphy, M. P. (2020). COVID-19 and emergency eLearning: Consequences of the securitization of higher education for post–pandemic pedagogy. *Contemporary Security Policy*, *41*(3), 492–505. DOI: 10.1080/13523260.2020.1761749

Murray, A., Skene, K., & Haynes, K. (2017). The Circular Economy: An Interdisciplinary Exploration of the Concept and Application in a Global Context. *Journal of Business Ethics*, *140*(3), 369–380. DOI: 10.1007/s10551-015-2693-2

Mushi, G. E., Burgi, P., & Di Marzo Serugendo, G. (2024). State of Agricultural E-Government Services to Farmers in Tanzania: Toward the Participatory Design of a Farmers Digital Information System (FDIS). *Agriculture*, *14*(3), 475. DOI: 10.3390/agriculture14030475

Mushi, R. M. (2024). Assessing the factors influencing intention to use e-government in Tanzania: The perspective of trust, participation and transparency. *Journal of Electronic Business & Digital Economics*, *3*(2), 156–169. DOI: 10.1108/JEBDE-08-2023-0017

Musk, E. (2022a). By "free speech", I simply mean that which matches the law. I am against censorship that goes far beyond the law. If people want less free speech, they will ask government to pass laws to that effect. Therefore, going beyond the law is contrary to the will of the people. Tweet. Twitter. https://twitter.com/elonmusk/status/ 1519036983137509376.

Musova, Z., Musa, H., Drugdova, J., Lazaroiu, G., & Alayasa, J. (2021). Consumer Attitudes Towards New Circular Models in the Fashion Industry. *Journal of Competitiveness*, *13*(3), 111–128. DOI: 10.7441/joc.2021.03.07

Mwantimwa, K. (2019). ICT usage to enhance firms' business processes in Tanzania. *Journal of Global Entrepreneurship Research*, *9*(1), 46–58. DOI: 10.1186/s40497-019-0170-6

Mwaseba, S. L., Mwang'onda, E. S., & Ngwilizi, D. (2025). Exploring the Roots of Gender Inequality in Digital Payments Utilisation in Tanzania. In FinTech and Financial Inclusion (1st Edition, p. 18). Routledge. https://doi.org/https://doi.org/10.4324/9781003514114-17

Nadkarni, S., & Prügl, R. (2021). Digital transformation: A review, synthesis and opportunities for future research. *Management Review Quarterly*, *71*(1), 233–341. DOI: 10.1007/s11301-020-00185-7

National Centre for Promotion of Employment for Disabled People (NCPeDP). (2020). *Locked down and Left behind: A Report on the Status of Persons with Disabilities in India during the COVID-19 Crisis.* New Delhi: NCPeDP.

Nayanikka. (2024 b). *The Role of Internet in Menstrual Health Awareness in Rural India.* Muft Internet. https://muftinternet.com/blog/2024/06/03/the-role-of-internet-in-menstrual-health-awareness-in-rural-india/

Neca, P., Borges, M. L., & Pinto, P. C. (2020). Teachers with disabilities: A literature review. *International Journal of Inclusive Education*.

Negro-Calduch, E., Azzopardi-Muscat, N., Krishnamurthy, R. S., & Novillo-Ortiz, D. (2021). Technological progress in electronic health record system optimization: Systematic review of systematic literature reviews. *International Journal of Medical Informatics*, *147*, 104388. DOI: 10.1016/j.ijmedinf.2021.104507 PMID: 34049051

Ness, M. M., Saylor, J., Di Fusco, L. A., & Evans, K. (2021). Healthcare providers' challenges during the coronavirus disease (COVID-19) pandemic: A qualitative approach. *Nursing & Health Sciences*, *23*(2), 389–397. DOI: 10.1111/nhs.12820 PMID: 33580590

Ngoasong, M. Z. (2015). Digital entrepreneurship in emerging economies: the role of ICTs and local contexts. *AIB-UKI Conference*, 16-18.

Nguyen, M. H., Büchi, M., & Geber, S. (2024). Everyday disconnection experiences: Exploring people's understanding of digital well-being and management of digital media use. *new media & society, 26*(6), 3657-3678.

Nguyen, H., & Tran, V. (2023). Optimizing patient outcomes with AI-powered healthcare management systems. *Journal of Medical Informatics*, *77*(2), 246–259. DOI: 10.1016/j.jmii.2023.07.010

Niemiec, E. (2020). COVID-19 and Misinformation. *EMBO Reports*, *21*(11), e51420. DOI: 10.15252/embr.202051420 PMID: 33103289

Niinimäki, K., & Hassi, L. (2011). Emerging Design Strategies in Sustainable Production and Consumption of Textiles and Clothing. *Journal of Cleaner Production, S0959652611001569.* Advance online publication. DOI: 10.1016/j.jclepro.2011.04.020

Nußholz, J. L. K. (2018). A Circular Business Model Mapping Tool for Creating Value from Prolonged Product Lifetime and Closed Material Loops. *Journal of Cleaner Production*, *197*, 185–194. DOI: 10.1016/j.jclepro.2018.06.112

Nyagango, A. I., Sife, A. S., & Kazungu, I. (2023). Factors influencing the use of mobile phone for accessing agricultural marketing information by grape smallholder farmers in Tanzania. *Cogent Business & Management, 10*(3), 2257865. Advance online publication. DOI: 10.1080/23311975.2023.2257865

Nyaupane, P., & Thapa, S. (2024). Exploring Factors Influencing College Females' Perceptions of Menstruation: A Study on Awareness and Cultural Influences. *NRPC Journal of Multidisciplinary Research, 1*(3), 176–193. DOI: 10.3126/nprcjmr.v1i3.70211

O'Connor, A., Stam, E., Sussan, F., & Audretsch, D. B. (2018). Entrepreneurial Ecosystems: The Foundations of Place-based Renewal. In O'Connor, A., Stam, E., Sussan, F., & Audretsch, D. (Eds.), *Entrepreneurial Ecosystems. International Studies in Entrepreneurship* (Vol. 38). Springer., DOI: 10.1007/978-3-319-63531-6_1

Odeyemi, A., Patil, R., & Jackson, B. (2024). Autonomous delivery systems in quick commerce: Prospects and challenges.

Odeyemi, N. O., Oyewole, N. A. T., Adeoye, N. O. B., Ofodile, N. O. C., Addy, N. W. A., Okoye, N. C. C., & Ololade, N. Y. J. (2024). Entrepreneurship in Africa: A Review of Growth and Challenges. *International Journal of Management & Entrepreneurship Research*, *6*(3), 608–622. DOI: 10.51594/ijmer.v6i3.874

Odeyemi, O., Elufioye, O. A., Mhlongo, N. Z., & Ifesinachi, A. (2024). AI in E-commerce: Reviewing developments in the USA and their global influence. *International Journal of Science and Research Archive*, *11*(1), 1460–1468. DOI: 10.30574/ijsra.2024.11.1.0232

Ofosu-Ampong, K. (2021). Determinants, Barriers and Strategies of Digital Transformation Adoption in a Developing Country COVID-19 Era. *Journal of Digital Science*, *3*(2), 67–83. DOI: 10.33847/2686-8296.3.2_5

Ofosu-Ampong, K. (2023). Gender Differences in Perception of Artificial Intelligence-Based Tools. *Journal of Digital Art Humanities*, *4*(2), 52–56. DOI: 10.33847/2712-8149.4.2_6

Ofosu-Ampong, K., & Acheampong, B. (2022). Adoption of Contactless Technologies for Remote Work in Ghana Post-COVID-19: Insights From Technology-Organisation-Environment Framework. *Digital Business*, *2*(2), 1–10. DOI: 10.1016/j.digbus.2022.100023

Olatunji, A. O., Olaboye, J. A., & Maha, C. C. (2024). Revolutionizing infectious disease management in low-resource settings: The impact of rapid diagnostic technologies and portable devices. *Journal of Applied Sciences*, *2024*, 1–13.

Oliveira, R. C., de Alencar Nääs, I., & Garcia, S. (2024). Clothes Consumption and Disposal Practices: A Look at The Profile of Brazilian Apparel Consumers. *Journal of Responsible Production and Consumption*, *1*(1), 107–126. DOI: 10.1108/JRPC-01-2024-0006

Oliver, R. L. (1980). A cognitive model of the antecedents and consequences of satisfaction decisions.

Oliver, M. (1981). A new model of the social work role in relation to disability. In Campling, J. (Ed.), *The handicapped person: A new perspective for social workers* (pp. 19–32). RADAR.

Olkin, R. (1999). *What psychotherapists should know about disability*. Guilford Press.

Olmstead, M. (2021). *Media's Portrayal of Teachers Hurts the Profession*.

Omweri, F. S. (2024). A Systematic Literature Review of E-Government Implementation in Developing Countries: Examining Urban-Rural Disparities, Institutional Capacity, and Socio-Cultural Factors in the Context of Local Governance and Progress towards SDG 16.6. *International Journal of Research and Innovation in Social Science*, *VIII*(VIII), 1173–1199. DOI: 10.47772/IJRISS.2024.808088

Ooi, K. B., Tan, G. W. H., & Al-Emran, M. (2023). The potential of generative artificial intelligence across disciplines: Perspectives and future directions. *Journal of Computer Information Systems*, *2023*, 1–13.

Ortega, G., Rodriguez, J. A., Maurer, L. R., & Witt, E. E. (2020). Telemedicine, COVID-19, and disparities: Policy implications. *Health Policy and Technology*, *9*(2), 149–152. DOI: 10.1016/j.hlpt.2020.03.003 PMID: 32837888

Osman, M. E. (2020). Global impact of COVID-19 on education systems: The emergency remote teaching at Sultan Qaboos University post-pity. *Journal of Education for Teaching*, *46*(4), 463–471. DOI: 10.1080/02607476.2020.1802583

Owusu, A., Akpe-Doe, C. E., & Taana, I. H. (2022). Assessing the effectiveness of E-government services in Ghana: A case of the registrar general's department. [IJEGR]. *International Journal of Electronic Government Research*, *18*(1), 1–23. DOI: 10.4018/IJEGR.289827

Owusu, B., Kutor, S. K., & Ablo, A. D. (2023). COVID-19 Pandemic: Ghana and the Geographies of Blame. *GeoJournal*, *88*(1), 279–290. DOI: 10.1007/s10708-022-10586-8 PMID: 35250150

Owusu, I., Adu, C., Aboagye, R. G., Mpangah, R. A., Acheampong, G. K., Akyereko, E., Bonsu, E. O., & Peprah, P. (2023). Preparing for Future Outbreaks in Ghana: An Overview of Current COVID-19, Monkeypox, and Marburg Disease Outbreaks. *Health Promotion Perspectives*, *13*(3), 202–211. DOI: 10.34172/hpp.2023.25 PMID: 37808942

Ozturkoglu, Y., Özer Sarı, F., & Esendemirli Saygili, E. (2019). A new holistic conceptual framework for sustainability oriented hospitality innovation with triple bottom line perspective. *Journal of Hospitality and Tourism Technology, ahead-of-print*. DOI: 10.1108/JHTT-02-2019-0022

Pache, G. (2023, September). Q-commerce logistical networks: A shift in digital retail towards "going dark"? In EMNet 2023 (pp. 1-12).

Paché, G. (2022). The impact of logistics on product assortment policy: An illustration with Q-Commerce. *Journal of Supply Chain Management: Research and Practice*, *16*(2), 1–10.

Pais, M. S. (2014) *Tackling Violence in Schools: A Global Perspective Bridging the Gap between Standards and Practice.* United Nations Report. https://violenceagainstchildren.un.org/sites/violenceagainstchildren.un.org/files/documents/publications/10._tackling_violence_in_schools_a_global_perspective.pdf

Palozzi, G., Schettini, I., & Chirico, A. (2020). Enhancing the sustainable goal of access to healthcare: Findings from a literature review on telemedicine employment in rural areas. *Sustainability (Basel), 12*(11), 4571. DOI: 10.3390/su12083318

Pansini, M., Buonomo, I., De Vincenzi, C., Ferrara, B., & Benevene, P. (2023, February). Positioning Technostress in the JD-R model perspective: A systematic literature review. []. MDPI.]. *Health Care, 11*(3), 446. PMID: 36767021

Parajuli, R., Bohara, D., Kc, M., Shanmuganathan, S., Mistry, S. K., & Yadav, U. N. (2022). Challenges and opportunities for implementing digital health interventions in Nepal: A rapid review. *Frontiers in Digital Health, 4*, 849166. DOI: 10.3389/fdgth.2022.861019 PMID: 36120714

Parel, D., Costuna, E. K., Morelos, J. M., Cabelis, S. A., Ramos, R., Perez, M. R., & Garcia, M. B. (2022). Escape from Oblivion: A 3D Hack and Slash Survival Horror Video Game for Promoting Awareness of Persistent Depressive Disorder. 2022 IEEE 14th International Conference on Humanoid, Nanotechnology, Information Technology, Communication and Control, Environment and Management (HNICEM). IEEE. DOI: 10.1109/HNICEM57413.2022.10109542

Parente, R. (2020). Digitalization, consumer social responsibility, and humane entrepr President's good news from the future? *Journal of the International Council for Small Business, 1*(1), 56–63. DOI: 10.1080/26437015.2020.1714368

Parker, G. G., Alstyne, M. W., & Choudary, S. P. (2016). *Platform revolution: how networked markets are transforming the economy and how to make them work for you.* W. W. Norton & Company.

Patchin, J. W., & Hinduja, S. (2006). Bullies move beyond the schoolyard: A preliminary look at cyberbullying. *Youth Violence and Juvenile Justice, 4*(2), 148–169. DOI: 10.1177/1541204006286288

Patel, R., & Agarwal, A. (2023). AI in cardiology: Emerging trends and challenges. *Cardiology Clinics, 41*(2), 207–221. DOI: 10.1016/j.ccl.2023.03.001 PMID: 37003678

Patil, S. R. (2014). *Knowledge and Practices of Menstrual Hygiene among Married Adolescents and Young Women in Chittoor District Of Andhra Pradesh: India.* In IOSR Journal of Nursing and Health Science (Ver. I, Vol. 3, Issue 2, pp. 06–15) [Journal-article]. DOI: DOI: 10.9790/1959-03210615

Patil, S., & Khan, M. (2022). Machine learning models for clinical outcomes prediction in healthcare. *Healthcare Analytics*, *9*(1), 25–41. DOI: 10.1016/j.hca.2021.100077

Pattyam, S. P. (2021). Artificial Intelligence for Healthcare Diagnostics: Techniques for Disease Prediction, Personalized Treatment, and Patient Monitoring. *Journal of Bioinformatics and Artificial Intelligence*, *2*(1), 1–13.

Paul, P., & Singh, B. (2023). Healthcare employee engagement using the internet of things: a systematic overview. *The Adoption and Effect of Artificial Intelligence on Human Resources Management, Part A*, 71-97.

Pedersen, E. R. G., Gwozdz, W., & Hvass, K. K. (2018). Exploring the Relationship Between Business Model Innovation, Corporate Sustainability, and Organisational Values Within the Fashion Industry. *Journal of Business Ethics*, *149*(2), 267–284. DOI: 10.1007/s10551-016-3044-7

Pedersen, E. R. G., & Netter, S. (2015). Collaborative Consumption: Business Model Opportunities and Barriers for Fashion Libraries. *Journal of Fashion Marketing and Management*, *19*(3), 258–273. DOI: 10.1108/JFMM-05-2013-0073

Peiffer-Smadja, N., Lucet, J.-C., Bendjelloul, G., Bouadma, L., Gerard, S., Choquet, C., & Casalino, E. (2020). Challenges and issues about organizing a hospital to respond to the COVID-19 outbreak: Experience from a French reference centre. *Clinical Microbiology and Infection*, *26*(6), 669–672. DOI: 10.1016/j.cmi.2020.04.002 PMID: 32278082

Peltier, J. W., Dahl, A. J., & Schibrowsky, J. (2023). (forthcoming). Artificial intelligence in interactive marketing: A conceptual framework and research agenda. *Journal of Research in Interactive Marketing*.

Peltier, J. W., Dahl, A. J., & Swan, E. L. (2020). Digital information flows across a B2C/C2C continuum and technological innovations in service ecosystems: A service-dominant logic perspective. *Journal of Business Research*, *121*, 724–734. DOI: 10.1016/j.jbusres.2020.03.020

Peña Miranda, D., Plaza, A., Brea, J. A., & Camilleri, M. A. (2021). Corporate social responsibility model for a competitive and resilient hospitality industry. *Sustainable Development (Bradford)*, *30*(3), 433–446. Advance online publication. DOI: 10.1002/sd.2259

Peng, M. W. (2000). *Business strategies in transition economies. Sage Publications.* https://us.sagepub.com/en-us/nam/business-strategies-in-transition-economies/book9311

Peters, M., & Mackenzie, M. (2014). Hospitality Managers' Perception of Corporate Social Responsibility: An Explorative Study. *Asia Pacific Journal of Tourism Research, 19*(3), 257–272. Advance online publication. DOI: 10.1080/10941665.2012.742915

Petrie, C. (2020). *Spotlight: Quality education for all during COVID-19 crisis.* United Nations. DOI: 10.58261/CIAD8546

Piccolo, R. (2024). Digitisation, health literacy and health empowerment of older people. *The International Entrepreneurship and Management Journal, 20*(1), 3001–3034. DOI: 10.1007/s11365-024-00980-8

Pokhrel, S., & Chhetri, R. (2021). *A Literature Review on Impact of COVID-19 Pandemic on Teaching and Learning*. Higher Education for the Future. DOI: 10.1177/2347631120983481

Polajnar Horvat, K., & Šrimpf Vendramin, K. (2021). Issues Surrounding Behavior Towards Discarded Textiles and Garments in Ljubljana. *Sustainability (Basel), 13*(11), 6491. DOI: 10.3390/su13116491

Pougel, F., Bonnel, S., & Beier, G. (Socioeconomicnd sustainability: a literature review. *Journal of Innovations and Sustainability, 4*(1), 9–54. https://doi.org/DOI: 10.51599/is.2018.04.01.09

Prabhu, J., & Jain, S. (2015). Innovation and entrepreneurship in India: Understanding jugaad. *Asia Pacific Journal of Management, 32*(1), 843–868. DOI: 10.1007/s10490-015-9445-9

Prahalad, C., & Mashelkar, R. (2010). Innovation's holy grail. *Harvard Business Review, 88*, 132–141. https://hbr.org/2010/07/innovations-holy-grail

Prasanna, C. K. (2016). Claiming the Public Sphere: Menstrual Taboos and the Rising Dissent in India. *Agenda (Durban, South Africa), 30*(3), 91–95. DOI: 10.1080/10130950.2016.1251228

Pucker, K. P. (2022, January 13). The Myth of Sustainable Fashion. *Harvard Business Review*. https://hbr.org/2022/01/the-myth-of-sustainable-fashion

Pugliesi, K. (1999). The Consequences of Emotional Labor: Effects on Work Stress, Job Satisfaction, and Well-Being. *Motivation and Emotion, 23*(2), 125–154. DOI: 10.1023/A:1021329112679

Pulman, A., & Taylor, J. (2012). Munchausen by Internet: Current research and future directions. *Journal of Medical Internet Research*, *14*(4), e115. DOI: 10.2196/jmir.2011 PMID: 22914203

Puri, S., & Kapoor, S. (2006). Taboos and Myths Associated with Women's Health among Rural and Urban Adolescent Girls in Punjab. *Indian Journal of Community Medicine : Official Publication of Indian Association of Preventive & Social Medicine*, *31*(4), 295. https://journals.lww.com/ijcm/citation/2006/31040/taboos_and_myths_associated_with_womens_health.30.aspx

Quinn, P. (2018). Crisis communication in public health emergencies: The limits of "legal control" and the risks for harmful outcomes in a digital age. *Life Sciences, Society and Policy*, *14*(1), 4. DOI: 10.1186/s40504-018-0067-0 PMID: 29404722

Ragu-Nathan, T. S., Tarafdar, M., Ragu-Nathan, B. S., & Tu, Q. (2021). The impact of technostress on employee productivity and well-being in modern organizations. *International Journal of Information Management*, *57*, 102–125.

Rahman, M., Tanchangya, T., Rahman, J., Aktar, M. A., & Majumder, S. C. (2024). Corporate social responsibility and green financing behavior in Bangladesh: Towards sustainable tourism. *Innovation and Green Development*, *3*(3), 100133. DOI: 10.1016/j.igd.2024.100133

Rahman, O., Hu, D., & Fung, B. C. M. (2023). A Systematic Literature Review of Fashion, Sustainability, and Consumption Using a Mixed Methods Approach. *Sustainability (Basel)*, *15*(16), 12213. DOI: 10.3390/su151612213

Ramaswamy, M. (2023, August 29). *Menstruation in the Digital Age*. Aunt Flow. https://goauntflow.com/blog/menstruation-in-the-digital-age/

Ramayah, T., Cheah, J., Chuah, F., Ting, H., & Memon, M. A. (2018). *Partial Least Squares Structural Equation Modeling (PLS-SEM) Using SmartPLS 3.0: An Updated Guide and Practical Guide to Statistical Analysis* (2nd ed.). Pearson.

Ramírez-Escamilla, H. G., Martínez-Rodríguez, M. C., Padilla-Rivera, A., Domínguez-Solís, D., & Campos-Villegas, L. E. (2024). Advancing Toward Sustainability: A Systematic Review of Circular Economy Strategies in The Textile Industry. *Recycling*, *9*(5), 95. DOI: 10.3390/recycling9050095

Ramos, L., Rivas-Echeverría, F., Pérez, A. G., & Casas, E. (2023). Artificial Intelligence and Sustainability in the Fashion Industry: A Review from 2010 to 2022. *SN Applied Sciences*, *5*(12), 387. DOI: 10.1007/s42452-023-05587-2

Ranjekar, G., & Roy, D. (2023). *Rise of quick commerce in India: Business models and infrastructure requirements*. Centre for Transportation and Logistics.

Rarhoui, K. (2024, February 1). *E-government in Africa: challenges and prospects*. https://hal.science/hal-04450951v1

Rathinamoorthy, R. (2019). Consumer's Awareness on Sustainable Fashion. In Muthu, S. S. (Ed.), *Sustainable Fashion: Consumer Awareness and Education* (pp. 1–36). Springer Singapore., DOI: 10.1007/978-981-13-1262-5_1

Ratzan, S. C., Sommariva, S., & Rauh, L. (2020). Enhancing global health communication during a crisis: Lessons from the COVID-19 pandemic. *Public Health Research & Practice*, *30*(2), 3022010. DOI: 10.17061/phrp3022010 PMID: 32601655

Rauniyar, A., Hagos, D. H., & Jha, D. (2023). Federated learning for medical applications: A taxonomy, current trends, challenges, and future research directions. *IEEE Internet of Things Journal*, *10*(10), 9345–9364. DOI: 10.1109/JIOT.2022.3223541

Rawls, J. (1985). Justice as fairness: Political not metaphysical. *Philosophy & Public Affairs*, *14*(3), 223–251.

Report, U. N. (2024, December 15). *Menstrual health in adolescent girls* | Department of Economic and Social Affairs. https://sdgs.un.org/partnerships/menstrual-health-adolescent-girls

Reuschl, A. J., Deist, M. K., & Maalaoui, A. (2022). Digital transformation during a pandemic: Stretching the organizational elasticity. *Journal of Business Research*, *144*, 1320–1332. DOI: 10.1016/j.jbusres.2022.01.088 PMID: 36540204

Richards, J. (2012). Teacher stress and coping strategies: A national snapshot. *The Educational Forum*, *76*(3), 299–316. DOI: 10.1080/00131725.2012.682837

Richardson, S., Lawrence, K., Schoenthaler, A. M., & Mann, D. (2022). A framework for digital health equity. *NPJ Digital Medicine*, *5*(1), 1–9. DOI: 10.1038/s41746-022-00663-0 PMID: 35982146

Riddell, S., & Watson, N. (2014). *Disability, culture and identity*. Routledge. DOI: 10.4324/9781315847634

Ries, E. (2011). *The lean startup: how today's entrepreneurs use continuous innovation to create radically succesful businesses*. Crown. https://books.google.co.in/books/about/The_Lean_Startup.html?id=tvfyz-4JILwC&redir_esc=y

Riotta, S., & Bruccoleri, M. (2021). Revisiting the patient-physician relationship under the lens of value co-creation and defensive medicine. *Journal of Service Theory and Practice*, *31*(6), 868–892. DOI: 10.1108/JSTP-06-2020-0142

Ritter, T., & Pederson, C. L. (2019). Digitization capability and the digitalization of business models in business-to-business firms: Past, present, and future. *Industrial Marketing Management*, *68*(1), 180–190. DOI: 10.1016/j.indmarman.2019.11.019

Rizvi, S. K. A., Mirza, N., Naqvi, B., & Rahat, B. (2020). COVID-19 and asset management in EU: A preliminary assessment of performance and investment styles. *Journal of Asset Management*, *21*(4), 281–291. DOI: 10.1057/s41260-020-00172-3

Robinson, K. (2000). 'Great Tits, Miss!' The Silencing of Male Students' Sexual Harassment of Female Teachers in Secondary Schools: A Focus on Gendered Authority. *Discourse (Abingdon)*, *21*(1), 75–90. DOI: 10.1080/01596300050005510

Rogers, E. M. (2003). Diffusion of innovations.

Romanelli, R. J., Azar, K. M. J., Sudat, S., & Hung, D. (2021). "Learning health system in crisis: lessons from the COVID-19 pandemic." Healthcare: Innovations. *Quality & Safety*, *2021*, 1–13.

Rong, G., Mendez, A., Assi, E. B., Zhao, B., & Sawan, M. (2020). Artificial intelligence in healthcare: Review and prediction case studies. *Engineering (Beijing)*, *2020*(3), 1–13. DOI: 10.1016/j.eng.2019.08.015

Roozenbeek, J., van der Linden, S., Goldberg, B., Rathje, S., & Lewandowsky, S. (2022). Psychological inoculation improves resilience against misinformation on social media. *Science Advances*, *8*(34), eabo6254. Advance online publication. DOI: 10.1126/sciadv.abo6254 PMID: 36001675

Ros, F., Kush, R., Friedman, C., Gil Zorzo, E., Rivero Corte, P., Rubin, J. C., . . . Van Houweling, D. (2021). Addressing the Covid-19 pandemic and future public health challenges through global collaboration and a data-driven systems approach (2379- 6146).

Roundy, P. T. (2022). Artificial intelligence and entrepreneurial ecosystems: Understanding the implications of algorithmic decision-making for startup communities. *Journal of Ethics in Entrepreneurship and Technology*, *2*(1), 23–38. DOI: 10.1108/JEET-07-2022-0011

Rutledge, P. B., & Hogg, J. L. C. (2020). In-depth interviews. The International Encyclopedia of Media Psychology, 1–7. DOI: 10.1002/9781119011071.iemp0019

Sachs, J. D., Karim, S. S. A., Aknin, L., Allen, J., Brosbøl, K., Colombo, F., Barron, G. C., Espinosa, M. F., Gaspar, V., Gaviria, A., Haines, A., Hotez, P. J., Koundouri, P., Bascuñán, F. L., Lee, J.-K., Pate, M. A., Ramos, G., Reddy, K. S., Serageldin, I., & Michie, S. (2022). The Lancet Commission on lessons for the future from the COVID-19 pandemic. *Lancet, 400*(10359), 1224–1280. DOI: 10.1016/S0140-6736(22)01585-9 PMID: 36115368

Sagarik, D. (2023). Enhancing Digital Competitiveness Through the Lens of Digital Government Among Asian Economies. *In International Journal of Public Administration in the Digital Age* (Vol. 10, Issue 1, p. 1). IGI Global. DOI: 10.4018/IJPADA.326122

Saha, K., Dey, P. K., & Papagiannaki, E. (2021). Implementing Circular Economy in The Textile and Clothing Industry. *Business Strategy and the Environment, 30*(4), 1497–1530. DOI: 10.1002/bse.2670

Sahin, C. (2014). An Analysis of the Relationship between Internet Addiction and Depression Levels of High School Students. *Participatory Educational Research, 1*(2), 5367. DOI: 10.17275/per.14.10.1.2

Salvador, R., Barros, M. V., Luz, L. M. D., Piekarski, C. M., & De Francisco, A. C. (2020). Circular Business Models: Current Aspects That Influence Implementation and Unaddressed Subjects. *Journal of Cleaner Production, 250*, 119555. DOI: 10.1016/j.jclepro.2019.119555

Samsor, A. M. (2021). Challenges and Prospects of e-Government implementation in Afghanistan. *International Trade, Politics and Development, 5*(1), 51–70. DOI: 10.1108/ITPD-01-2020-0001

Samuels, E. J. (2003). *My body, my closet: Invisible disability and the limits of coming-out discourse.* GLQ: A Journal of Lesbian and Gay Studies, 9(1), 233-255.

Santra, S., & Alat, P. (2022). Adaptive leadership of doctors during COVID-19. *Leadership in Health Services, 35*(2), 246–266. DOI: 10.1108/LHS-08-2021-0073 PMID: 34882361

Saricam, C., Erdumlu, N., Silan, A., Dogan, B. L., & Sonmezcan, G. (2017). Determination of Consumer Awareness about Sustainable Fashion. *IOP Conference Series. Materials Science and Engineering, 254*, 172024. DOI: 10.1088/1757-899X/254/17/172024

Sarker, S., Jamal, L., Ahmed, S. F., & Irtisam, N. (2021). Robotics and Artificial Intelligence in Healthcare During COVID-19 Pandemic: A Systematic Review. *Robotics and Autonomous Systems*, *146*, 1–18. DOI: 10.1016/j.robot.2021.103902 PMID: 34629751

Sarkodie, S. A., & Owusu, P. A. (2021). Impact of COVID-19 Pandemic on Waste Management. *Environment, Development and Sustainability*, *23*(5), 7951–7960. DOI: 10.1007/s10668-020-00956-y PMID: 32863738

Satalkina, L., & Steiner, G. (2020). Digital Entrepreneurship: A theory-based systematization of core performance indicators. *Sustainability (Basel)*, *12*(10), 1–10. DOI: 10.3390/su12104018

Sausi, J. M., Mtebe, J. S., & Mbelwa, J. (2021). Evaluating user satisfaction with the e-payment gateway system in Tanzania. *South African Journal of Information Management*, *23*(1). Advance online publication. DOI: 10.4102/sajim.v23i1.1430

Sawant, P. (2017, July 16). *Women activists plan to take the issue of 12% GST on Sanitary napkin to the court.* The Times of India. https://timesofindia.indiatimes.com/city/mumbai/women-activists-plan-to-take-the-issue-of-12-gst-on-sanitary-napkin-to-the-court/articleshow/59619181.cms

Saxena, N. (2017). *Celebrities Support #LahuKaLagaan, Request Arun Jaitley to Remove Sanitary Napkin Tax. Hindustan Times.* https://www.google.com/amp/s/www.hindustantimes.com/bollywood/celebrities-support-lahukalagaan-request-arun-jaitley-to-remove-sanitary-napkin-tax/story-c7nzLdJFe1lEVNfdII7hyO_amp.html

Sayabek, Z., Suieubayeva, S., & Utegenova, A. (2020). *Digital transformation in business.* Springer International Publishing. https://www.springerprofessional.de/en/digital-transformation-in-business/17010220

Schaltegger, S., Hansen, E. G., & Lüdeke-Freund, F. (2016). Business Models for Sustainability: Origins, Present Research, and Future Avenues. *Organization & Environment*, *29*(1), 3–10. DOI: 10.1177/1086026615599806

Schor, J. B. (2013). From Fast Fashion to Connected Consumption: Slowing Down the Spending Treadmill. In Osbaldiston, N. (Ed.), *Culture of the Slow* (pp. 34–51)., DOI: 10.1057/9781137319449_3

Schorung, M. (2023). Quick commerce: Will the disruption of the food retail industry happen? Investigating the quick commerce supply chain and the impacts of dark stores (Doctoral dissertation, Université Gustave Eiffel).

Schroeder, H., Numa, R., & Shapiro, E. (2022). Promoting a culturally adapted policy to deal with the COVID-19 crisis in the Haredi population in Israel. *Journal of Racial and Ethnic Health Disparities*, *9*(6), 2508–2517. DOI: 10.1007/s40615-021-01186-2 PMID: 34791614

Scott, B. K., Miller, G. T., Fonda, S. J., Yeaw, R. E., Gaudaen, J. C., Pavliscsak, H. H., Quinn, M. T., & Pamplin, J. C. (2020). Advanced digital health technologies for COVID-19 and future emergencies. *Telemedicine Journal and e-Health*, *26*(10), 1245–1256. DOI: 10.1089/tmj.2020.0140 PMID: 32456560

Sekalala, S., Dagron, S., Forman, L., & Meier, B. M. (2020). Analyzing the human rights impact of increased digital public health surveillance during the COVID-19 crisis. *Health and Human Rights Journal*, *22*(2), 7–20. PMID: 33390688

Selvaraj, S., & Sundaravaradhan, S. (2020). Challenges and opportunities in IoT healthcare systems: A systematic review. *SN Applied Sciences*, *2*(1), 1–13. DOI: 10.1007/s42452-019-1925-y

Serra Cantallops, A., Peña Miranda, D., Ramón Cardona, J., & Martorell-Cunill, O. (2018). Progress in Research on CSR and the Hotel Industry (2006-2015). *Cornell Hospitality Quarterly*, *59*(1), 15–38. DOI: 10.1177/1938965517719267

Sezgin, E., Huang, Y., Ramtekkar, U., & Lin, S. (2020). Readiness for voice assistants to support healthcare delivery during a health crisis and pandemic. *NPJ Digital Medicine*, *3*(1), 1–9. DOI: 10.1038/s41746-020-00332-0 PMID: 33015374

Sgambaro, L., Chiaroni, D., & Urbinati, A. (2024). The Design and Servitization of Products According to The Circular Economy Principles: An Ecosystem Perspective in The Building Industry. *Journal of Cleaner Production*, *454*, 142322. DOI: 10.1016/j.jclepro.2024.142322

Shachaf, P., & Hara, N. (2010). Beyond vandalism: Wikipedia trolls. *Journal of Information Science*, *36*(3), 357–370. DOI: 10.1177/0165551510365390

Shahbazi, S., & Jönbrink, A. K. (2020). Design Guidelines to Develop Circular Products: Action Research on Nordic Industry. *Sustainability (Basel)*, *12*(9), 3679. DOI: 10.3390/su12093679

Shahroz, M., Ahmad, F., Younis, M. S., Ahmad, N., Kamel Boulos, M. N., Vinuesa, R., & Qadir, J. (2021). COVID-19 Digital Contact Tracing Applications and Techniques: A Review Post Initial Deployments. *Transportation Engineering*, *5*, 1–9. DOI: 10.1016/j.treng.2021.100072

Sharma Giri, A. (2023). E-commerce supply chain risk mitigation and online sales performance.

Sheikh, A., Anderson, M., Albala, S., Casadei, B., Franklin, B. D., Richards, M., Taylor, D., Tibble, H., & Mossialos, E. (2021). Health information technology and digital innovation for national learning health and care systems. *The Lancet. Digital Health, 3*(10), e675–e685. DOI: 10.1016/S2589-7500(21)00005-4 PMID: 33967002

Shen, D., & Richards, J. (2013). Consumers' Awareness of Sustainable Fashion. https://www.semanticscholar.org/paper/CONSUMERS%27-AWARENESS-OF-SUSTAINABLE-FASHION-Shen-Richards/3e478cd9f9ecb94e142e0a03f828243d23d7784b

Shen, Y., Guo, D., Long, F., Mateos, L. A., Ding, H., Xiu, Z., Hellman, R. B., King, A., Chen, S., Zhang, C., & Tan, H. (2021). Robots Under COVID-19 Pandemic: A Comprehensive Survey. *IEEE Access : Practical Innovations, Open Solutions, 9*, 1590–1615. DOI: 10.1109/ACCESS.2020.3045792 PMID: 34976569

Shen, Y.-T., Chen, L., Yue, W.-W., & Xu, H.-X. (2021). Digital technology-based telemedicine for the COVID-19 pandemic. *Frontiers in Medicine, 8*, 646506. DOI: 10.3389/fmed.2021.646506 PMID: 34295908

Shepherd, D. A., Patzelt, H., & Breugst, N. (2024). 66 *Simple Rules for Entrepreneurs.* httpConsumers'g/DOI: 10.1007/978-3-031-62032-4

Sheppard, M., & Vibert, C. (2019). Re-examining the relationship between ease of use and usefulness for the next generation. *Education and Information Technologies, 24*(5), 3205–3218. DOI: 10.1007/s10639-019-09916-0

SheSays. *One Young World.* https://www.oneyoungworld.com/ambassador-projects/shesays

Shin, H., Sharma, A., Nicolau, J., & Kang, J. (2021). The impact of hotel CSR for strategic philanthropy on booking behavior and hotel performance during the COVID-19 pandemic. *Tourism Management, 85*, 104322. DOI: 10.1016/j.tourman.2021.104322 PMID: 34815613

Shukla, S. (2023). Real-time monitoring and predictive analytics in healthcare: Harnessing the power of data streaming. *International Journal of Computer Applications, 185*(8), 32–37. DOI: 10.5120/ijca2023922738

Silton, N. R. (Ed.). (2022). *The Impact of the COVID-19 Pandemic on Child, Adolescent, and Adult Development.* IGI Global., DOI: 10.4018/978-1-6684-3484-0

Simarmata, B., & Utomo, B. (2023). Influence of CSR Activity, Service Quality and Brand Attitude to Customer's Re-Visit Intention in Hotel Industry. *Jurnal Multidisiplin Madani, 3*(1), 208–228. DOI: 10.55927/mudima.v3i1.2308

Singh, A. K., & Jyoti, B. (2023b). Empirical evidence from different income group countries on the interdependency between digitalization and economic development. In Patricia Ordóñez de Pablos and Xi Zhang (Eds.), 5G, Artificial Intelligence, and Next Generation Internet of Things: Digital Innovation for Green and Sustainable Economies, (pp. 44-85). IGI Global. DOI: DOI: 10.4018/978-1-6684-8634-4.ch003

Singh, A. K., Singh, R., & Singh, Richa (2024d). Impact of digitalization on sustainable development in G20 countries. In E. Ahmed (Ed.), *Developing Digital Inclusion Through Globalization and Digitalization* (pp. 287-335). IGI Global, International Academic Publisher, United States. DOI: 10.4018/979-8-3693-4111-7.ch013

Singh, B., & Kaunert, C. (2024). Augmented Reality and Virtual Reality Modules for Mindfulness: Boosting Emotional Intelligence and Mental Wellness. In *Applications of Virtual and Augmented Reality for Health and Wellbeing* (pp. 111-128). IGI Global.

Singh, A. K. (2025a). Causality of digitalization with social sustainability in selected countries. In Siyal, S. (Ed.), *Impact of Digitalization on Education and Social Sustainability* (pp. 39–78). IGI Global., DOI: 10.4018/979-8-3693-1854-6.ch002

Singh, A. K. (2025b). Importance of digital technologies in economic sector of selected countries. In Ahmadi, A., Mna, A., & Slimani, A. (Eds.), *Renewable Energy and the Economic Welfare of Society* (pp. 335–370). IGI Global Scientific Publishing., DOI: 10.4018/979-8-3693-7580-8.ch015

Singh, A. K., & Ashraf, S. N. (2020). Association of entrepreneurship ecosystem with economic growth in selected countries: An empirical exploration. *Journal of Entrepreneurship. Business Economics (Cleveland, Ohio)*, *8*(2), 36–92. http://scientificia.com/index.php/JEBE/article/view/138

Singh, A. K., Ashraf, S. N., & Gupta, M. (2025a). Association between start-up entrepreneurship and economic development across countries. In Popescu, C. (Ed.), *Building Inclusive Global Knowledge Societies for Sustainable Development* (pp. 471–504). IGI Global Scientific Publishing., DOI: 10.4018/979-8-3693-6298-3.ch018

Singh, A. K., Ashraf, S. N., & Singh, S. (2024a). A policy direction from review of literature for determinants and problems of the start-up ecosystem in India. In Sharma, R., Mehta, K., & Yu, P. (Eds.), *Fostering Innovation in Venture Capital and Startup Ecosystems* (pp. 306–326). IGI Global., DOI: 10.4018/979-8-3693-1326-8.ch015

Singh, A. K., & Jyoti, B. (2023a). Does digitalization have a bi-directional causal relationship with the entrepreneurship ecosystem? Evidence from a country-wise panel data analysis. In Yanamandra, R., & Indiran, L. (Eds.), *Handbook of Research on Designing Sustainable Strategies to Develop Entrepreneurial Intention* (pp. 178–172). IGI Global., DOI: 10.4018/978-1-6684-8781-5.ch007

Singh, A. K., & Jyoti, B. (2023a). Empirical investigation for assessing the causality of entrepreneurship ecosystem with entrepreneurial behavior and attitudes across countries. In Abe, E., & Abe, I. (Eds.), *Cases on the Interplay Between Family, Society, and Entrepreneurship* (pp. 315–353). IGI Global., DOI: 10.4018/978-1-6684-8748-8.ch012

Singh, A. K., Jyoti, B., & Mishra, V. K. (2023). Policy implications from selected countries for a sustainable future of the society through green entrepreneurship and economic development. In Mohammed El Amine, A., Ul-Durar, S., & Hattab, H. (Eds.), *Entrepreneurship Ecosystems and Their Opportunities and Challenges* (pp. 129–162). IGI Global., DOI: 10.4018/978-1-6684-7140-1.ch006

Singh, A. K., & Kumar, S. (2022). Factors influencing entrepreneurship ecosystem and economic development: Evidence from cross-sectional country-wise imbalanced panel data analysis. *The IUP Journal of Entrepreneurship Development*, *19*(3), 24–47.

Singh, A. K., Kumar, S., & Gupta, M. (2024a). Relationship between digitalization and environmental sustainability in selected countries. In Yıldırım, S., Yıldırım, D., Demirtaş, I., & Kandpal, V. (Eds.), *Green Transition Impacts on the Economy, Society, and Environment* (pp. 83–107). IGI Global., DOI: 10.4018/979-8-3693-3985-5.ch006

Singh, A. K., Singh, B., & Ashraf, S. N. (2020). Implications of intellectual property protection, and science and technological development in the manufacturing sector in selected economies. *Journal of Advocacy. Research in Education*, *7*(1), 16–35. https://oaji.net/articles/2021/1704-1615668997.pdf

Singh, A. K., Singh, S., & Gupta, M. (2024b). A literature review for the association of social media with micro and small enterprises in India. In Hossain, S. (Ed.), *Cases on Social Media and Entrepreneurship* (pp. 38–62). IGI Global., DOI: 10.4018/979-8-3693-1781-5.ch003

Singh, A. K., Srinivasan, S., & Jyoti, B. (2025b). Implications of digitalization on public health sector across countries. In Wickramasinghe, N. (Ed.), *Digitalization and the Transformation of the Healthcare Sector* (pp. 359–394). IGI Global Scientific Publishing., DOI: 10.4018/979-8-3693-9641-4.ch013

Singhal, D., Jena, S. K., & Tripathy, S. (2019). Factors Influencing the Purchase Intention of Consumers Towards Remanufactured Products: A Systematic Review and Meta-Analysis. *International Journal of Production Research, 57*(23), 7289–7299. DOI: 10.1080/00207543.2019.1598590

Sintema, E. J. (2020). Effect of COVID-19 on the performance of grade 12 students: Implications for STEM education. *Eurasia Journal of Mathematics, Science and Technology Education, 16*(7). Advance online publication. DOI: 10.29333/ejmste/7893

Slama, P. (2020). Viral pandemics of the last four decades: Pathophysiology, health impacts and perspectives. *International Journal of Environmental Research and Public Health, 17*(24), 9411. DOI: 10.3390/ijerph17249411 PMID: 33333995

Smith, P., & Weber, J. (2024). The evolution of Q-commerce business models: From delivery startups to integrated retail solutions.

Social Responsibilities of a Business and its Need. (2022, May 13). GeeksforGeeks. https://www.geeksforgeeks.org/social-responsibilities-of-a-business-and-its-need/

Sohrabi, C., Alsafi, Z., O'neill, N., Khan, M., Kerwan, A., Al-Jabir, A., Iosifidis, C., & Agha, R. (2020). World Health Organization declares global emergency: A review of the 2019 novel coronavirus (COVID-19). *International Journal of Surgery, 76*, 71–76. DOI: 10.1016/j.ijsu.2020.02.034 PMID: 32112977

Son, E., & Kwon, K. H. (2024). Sustainable spatial strategies for mitigating air pollution in quick commerce environments. *Environmental Research and Technology, 7*(1), 131–139. DOI: 10.35208/ert.1367863

Soni, V. D. (2020). Global impact of E-learning during. *COVID*, •••, 19.

Souchet, A. D., Lourdeaux, D., Pagani, A., & Rebenitsch, L. (2023). A narrative review of immersive virtual reality's ergonomics and risks at the workplace: Cybersickness, visual fatigue, muscular fatigue, acute stress, and mental overload. *Virtual Reality (Waltham Cross), 27*(1), 19–50. DOI: 10.1007/s10055-022-00672-0

Sourdin, T., Li, B., & McNamara, D. M. (2020). Court innovations and access to justice in times of crisis. *Health Policy and Technology, 9*(2), 153–156. DOI: 10.1016/j.hlpt.2020.08.020 PMID: 32895624

Spitale, G. (2020). COVID-19 and the ethics of quarantine: A lesson from the Eyam Plague. *Medicine, Health Care, and Philosophy, 23*(4), 603–609. DOI: 10.1007/s11019-020-09971-2 PMID: 32761351

Spitale, G., Biller-Andorno, N., & Germani, F. (2022). Concerns around opposition to the green pass in Italy: Social listening analysis by using a mixed methods approach. *Journal of Medical Internet Research, 24*(2), e34385. DOI: 10.2196/34385 PMID: 35156930

Spitale, G., Merten, S., Jafflin, K., Schwind, B., Kaiser-Grolimund, A., & Biller-Andorno, N. (2021). A novel risk and crisis communication platform to bridge the gap between policy makers and the public in the context of the COVID-19 crisis (PubliCo): Protocol for a mixed methods study. *JMIR Research Protocols, 10*(11), e33653. DOI: 10.2196/33653 PMID: 34612823

Spreafico, C., & Landi, D. (2022). Using Product Design Strategies to Implement Circular Economy: Differences Between Students and Professional Designers. *Sustainability (Basel), 14*(3), 1122. DOI: 10.3390/su14031122

Sriharan, A., Hertelendy, A. J., Banaszak-Holl, J., Fleig-Palmer, M. M., Mitchell, C., Nigam, A., Gutberg, J., Rapp, D. J., & Singer, S. J. (2022). Public health and health sector crisis leadership during pandemics: A review of the medical and business literature. *Medical Care Research and Review : MCRR, 79*(4), 475–486. DOI: 10.1177/10775587211039201 PMID: 34474606

Sruthy, C. R., & Shaju, P. P. (2023). Portrayal of Menstruation and Womanhood in 'Ayali'Tamil Web Series.

Stampe, K., Kishik, S., & Müller, S. D. (2021). Mobile health in chronic disease management and patient empowerment: Exploratory qualitative investigation into patient-physician consultations. *Journal of Medical Internet Research, 2021*(6), 1–13. DOI: 10.2196/26991 PMID: 34128817

Standing, C., & Mattsson, J. (2016). Fake it until you make it: Business model conceptualization in digital entrepreneurship. *Journal of Strategic Marketing, 26*(5), 385–399. DOI: 10.1080/0965254X.2016.1240218

Stauffer, S. D., & Mason, E. C. (2013). Addressing elementary school teachers' professional stressors: Practical suggestions for schools and administrators. *Educational Administration Quarterly, 49*(5), 809–837. DOI: 10.1177/0013161X13482578

Stawicki, S. P., Jeanmonod, R., Miller, A. C., Paladino, L., Gaieski, D. F., Yaffee, A. Q., & Bloem, C. (2020). The 2019–2020 novel coronavirus (severe acute respiratory syndrome coronavirus 2) pandemic: A joint american college of academic international medicine-world academic council of emergency medicine multidisciplinary COVID-19 working group consensus paper. *Journal of Global Infectious Diseases, 12*(2), 47. DOI: 10.4103/jgid.jgid_86_20 PMID: 32773996

Steier, J., & Moxham, J. (2020). The load and capacity model of healthcare delivery: Considerations for the crisis management of the COVID-19 pandemic. *Journal of Thoracic Disease, 12*(6), 3022–3030. DOI: 10.21037/jtd-2020-054 PMID: 32642224

Steiner, E. D., & Woo, A. (2021). *Job-related stress threatens the teacher supply: Key findings from the 2021 State of the U.S. Teacher Survey*. RAND Corporation, RR-A1108–1.

Stewart, T. M. (2022). *Recommendations for implementing an e-government system: A generic qualitative study*. [Doctoral dissertation, Capella University]. ProQuest Dissertations Publishing.

Stojanov, M. (2022). Q-commerce–The next generation e-commerce. Бизнес управление (Business Management), (1), 17-34.

Subedi, S., Nayaju, S., Subedi, S., Shah, S. K., & Shah, J. M. (2020). Impact of e-learning during COVID-19 pandemic among nursing students and teachers of Nepal. *International Journal of Science and Healthcare Research, 5*(3), 9.

Subica, A. M., Claypoole, K. H., & Wylie, A. M. (2012). PTSD'S mediation of the relationships between trauma, depression, substance abuse, mental health, and physical health in individuals with severe mental illness: Evaluating a comprehensive model. *Schizophrenia Research, 136*(1–3), 104–109. DOI: 10.1016/j.schres.2011.10.018 PMID: 22104139

Sukhramani, N., & Verma, S. (2013). *Disability as Diversity: The Indian Perception*. Diversity and Respect-Problems of Perception in the Global Agenda for Social Work. Oldenburg: Paulo Freire Verlag.

Sunita, S., & Srija, A. (2016). *Entrepreneurship development in India- the focus on start-ups*. Laghu Udyog Samachar. http://164.100.94.191/niti/writereaddata/files/document_publication/MSME%20January%202016_0.pdf

Sun, Y., & Yuan, Z. (2023). Augmented reality fitness games and subjective well-being of players: A mixed methods study from China. *Behaviour & Information Technology*, •••, 1–17. DOI: 10.1080/0144929X.2023.2279664

Sust, P. P., Solans, O., Fajardo, J. C., Peralta, M. M., Rodenas, P., Gabaldà, J., & Ribes, J. S. (2020). Turning the crisis into an opportunity: Digital health strategies deployed during the COVID-19 outbreak. *JMIR Public Health and Surveillance, 6*(2), e19106. DOI: 10.2196/19106 PMID: 32339998

Sutton, C., Prowse, J., McVey, L., Elshehaly, M., Neagu, D., Montague, J., Alvarado, N., Tissiman, C., O'Connell, K., Eyers, E., Faisal, M., & Randell, R. (2023). Strategic workforce planning in health and social care–an international perspective: A scoping review. *Health Policy (Amsterdam)*, *132*, 104827. DOI: 10.1016/j.healthpol.2023.104827 PMID: 37099856

Swan, E. L., Dahl, A. J., & Peltier, J. W. (2019). Health-care marketing in an omni-channel environment: Exploring telemedicine and other digital touchpoints. *Journal of Research in Interactive Marketing*, *13*(4), 602–618. DOI: 10.1108/JRIM-03-2019-0039

Swayamsiddha, S., Prashant, K., Shaw, D., & Mohanty, C. (2021). The Prospective of Artificial Intelligence in COVID-19 Pandemic. *Health and Technology*, *11*(6), 1311–1320. DOI: 10.1007/s12553-021-00601-2 PMID: 34603925

Taeuscher, K., & Laudien, S. (2018). Understanding platform business models: A mixed methods study of marketplaces. *European Management Journal*, *38*(3), 319–329. DOI: 10.1016/j.emj.2017.06.005

Tahrim, S. (2022). Challenges & opportunities of Q-commerce grocery stores: A study on Pandamart.

Tambo, E., Djuikoue, I. C., Tazemda, G. K., Fotsing, M. F., & Zhou, X.-N. (2021). Early stage risk communication and community engagement (RCCE) strategies and measures against the coronavirus disease 2019 (COVID-19) pandemic crisis. *Global Health Journal (Amsterdam, Netherlands)*, *5*(1), 44–50. DOI: 10.1016/j.glohj.2021.02.009 PMID: 33850632

Tambo, T. (2014). Collaboration on Technological Innovation in Danish Fashion Chains: A Network Perspective. *Journal of Retailing and Consumer Services*, *21*(5), 827–835. DOI: 10.1016/j.jretconser.2014.02.016

Tandon, A., Gupta, A., Goel, P., & Singh, V. K. (2020). Impact of digitalization on entrepreneurial ecosystems: An Indian perspective. *International Journal of Business and Globalisation*, *25*(2), 154–169. DOI: 10.1504/IJBG.2020.107887

Tang, J. W., Caniza, M. A., Dinn, M., Dwyer, D. E., Heraud, J.-M., Jennings, L. C., & Loh, T. P. (2022). An exploration of the political, social, economic and cultural factors affecting how different global regions initially reacted to the COVID-19 pandemic. *Interface Focus*, *12*(2), 20210079. DOI: 10.1098/rsfs.2021.0079 PMID: 35261734

Tan, S. Y., Foo, C. D., Verma, M., Hanvoravongchai, P., Cheh, P. L. J., Pholpark, A., Marthias, T., Hafidz, F., Prawidya Putri, L., Mahendradhata, Y., Giang, K. B., Nachuk, S., Wang, H., Lim, J., & Legido Quigley, H. (2023). Mitigating the Impacts of the COVID-19 Pandemic on Vulnerable Populations: Lessons for Improving Health and Social Equity. *Social Science & Medicine*, *328*, 1–12. DOI: 10.1016/j.socscimed.2023.116007 PMID: 37279639

Tarafdar, M., Cooper, C. L., & Stich, J. F. (2019). The technostress trifecta-techno eustress, techno distress and design: Theoretical directions and an agenda for research. *Information Systems Journal*, *29*(1), 6–42. DOI: 10.1111/isj.12169

TCRA. (Tanzania Communications Regulatory Authority, 2023): Quality of Service Result for Mobile Communication Services in Tanzania for the period of April to June 2023, https://www.tcra.go.tz/pages/reports

TCRA. (Tanzania Communications Regulatory Authority, 2024): Communications Statistics Quarter ending June 2024 Version 1.1, https://www.tcra.go.tz/pages/reports

Teece, D. J. (2010). Business Models, Business Strategy and Innovation. *Long Range Planning*, *43*(2–3), 172–194. DOI: 10.1016/j.lrp.2009.07.003

Telecom Regulatory Authority of India. (2020). "Press Release– Highlights of Telecom Subscription Data as on 31st January, 2020."

Thapa, C., & Camtepe, S. (2021). Precision health data: Requirements, challenges and existing techniques for data security and privacy. *Computers in Biology and Medicine*, *136*, 104762. DOI: 10.1016/j.compbiomed.2020.104130 PMID: 33271399

Thawani, R., & Rana, V. (2021). Ethics in the age of artificial intelligence in healthcare. *AI in Healthcare*, *12*(4), 58–63. DOI: 10.1109/AIHC.2021.1124566

The United Republic of Tanzania. (2020). *Financial Sector Development Masterplan (FSDMP), (2020/21–2029/30)*. Ministry of Finance and Planning.

Thomas, G., Botha, R. A., & Van Greunen, D. (2015). Understanding the problem of coordination in a large scale distributed environment from a service lens view — Towards the South African public sector e-Administration criteria for coordination support. *Government Information Quarterly*, *32*(4), 526–538. DOI: 10.1016/j.giq.2015.08.002

Thornton, G. (2018). *Startups India- an Overview.* Global Assets. https://data.worldbank.org/indicator/IT.NET.USER.ZS?locations=1W-IN

Timotheou, S., Miliou, O., Dimitriadis, Y., Sobrino, S. V., Giannoutsou, N., Cachia, R., Monés, A. M., & Ioannou, A. (2022). Impacts of digital technologies on education and factors influencing schools' digital capacity and transformation: A literature review. *Education and Information Technologies*, *28*(1), 6695–6726. DOI: 10.1007/s10639-022-11431-8 PMID: 36465416

Timothy, O. T., Fisayo, A. A., Thiru, R., Raji, M. A., & Olodo, H. B. (2024). Impact of AI chatbots on youth consumer behavior in e-commerce: Evidence from Southwest Nigeria.

Tiwari, V. (2021). Countering effects of technostress on productivity: Moderating role of proactive personality. *Benchmarking*, *28*(2), 636–651. DOI: 10.1108/BIJ-06-2020-0313

Todeschini, B. V., Cortimiglia, M. N., Callegaro-de-Menezes, D., & Ghezzi, A. (2017). Innovative and Sustainable Business Models in the Fashion Industry: Entrepreneurial Drivers, Opportunities, and Challenges. *Business Horizons*, *60*(6), 759–770. DOI: 10.1016/j.bushor.2017.07.003

Torous, J., Bucci, S., Bell, I. H., Kessing, L. V., Faurholt-Jepsen, M., Whelan, P., & Firth, J. (2020). The growing field of digital psychiatry: Current evidence and the future of apps, social media, chatbots, and virtual reality. *World Psychiatry; Official Journal of the World Psychiatric Association (WPA)*, *19*(1), 1–13. PMID: 31922672

Torres, C. C. (2021). Adaptation and validation of technostress creators and technostress inhibitors inventories in a Spanish-speaking Latin American country. *Technology in Society*, *66*, 101660. DOI: 10.1016/j.techsoc.2021.101660

Tran, K., Nguyen, T., Tran, Y., Nguyen, A., Luu, K., & Nguyen, Y. (2022). Eco-Friendly Fashion among Generation Z: Mixed-methods Study on Price Value Image, Customer Fulfillment, and Pro-Environmental Behavior. *PLoS One*, *17*(8), e0272789. DOI: 10.1371/journal.pone.0272789 PMID: 35972928

Tryphena, R., & Aram, I. A. (2023). Consumer Perception on Sustainable Clothing among Urban Indians. *Journal of Engineered Fibers and Fabrics*, *18*, 155892502311689. DOI: 10.1177/15589250231168964

Tsiotsou, R. H., & Boukis, A. (2022). In-home service consumption: A systematic review, integrative framework and future research agenda. *Journal of Business Research*, *145*, 49–64. DOI: 10.1016/j.jbusres.2022.02.050

Tukker, A. (2004). Eight Types of Product–Service System: Eight Ways to Sustainability? Experiences from SusProNet. *Business Strategy and the Environment*, *13*(4), 246–260. DOI: 10.1002/bse.414

Tuli, A., Dalvi, S., Kumar, N., & Singh, P. (2019). *"It's a Girl Thing": Examining Challenges And Opportunities Around Menstrual Health Education in India. ACM Trans. Comput.-Hum. Interact., 26–26*(5), 29–29. DOI: DOI: 10.1145/3325282

Turilli, M., & Floridi, L. (2009). The ethics of information transparency. *Ethics and Information Technology*, *11*(2), 105–112. DOI: 10.1007/s10676-009-9187-9

Turker, D., & Altuntas, C. (2014). Sustainable Supply Chain Management in the Fast Fashion Industry: An Analysis of Corporate Reports. *European Management Journal*, *32*(5), 837–849. DOI: 10.1016/j.emj.2014.02.001

Umair, A., Conboy, K., & Whelan, E. (2023). Examining technostress and its impact on worker well-being in the digital gig economy. *Internet Research*, *33*(7), 206–242. DOI: 10.1108/INTR-03-2022-0214

UNESCO. (2015). *Education for All 2015 National Review*. United Nations Educational, Scientific and Cultural Organization.

UNESCO. (2018). *Global Education Monitoring Report 2018: Gender Review*. UNESCO Publishing.

UNESCO. (2020). *Global Education Monitoring Report 2020: Inclusion and Education*. UNESCO Publishing.

UNESCO. (2024). *Inclusion in Education*. UNESCO Publishing.

UNICEF. (2019). [*Children, Food and Nutrition*. UNICEF.]. *The State of the World's Children*, •••, 2019.

UNICEF. (2021). *#RedDotChallenge Continues to Dispel Period Stigma and Promotes COVID Appropriate Behaviour.*https://www.unicef.org/india/press-releases/reddotchallenge-continues-dispel-period-stigma-and-promotes-covid-appropriate

United Nations. (2015). *Transforming Our World: The 2030 Agenda for Sustainable Development*. United Nations.

United Nations. (2020). *Policy Brief: A Disability-Inclusive Response to COVID-19*. United Nations.

United Nations. (2020). The Impact of COVID-19 on the Arab Region: An Opportunity to Build Back Better. *Policy Brief.*

United Nations. (2022). The Sustainable Development Goals Report 2022. United Nations Publications. Available at https://unstats.un.org/sdgs/report/2022/

United Nations. (2024). E-government survey 2024: *Accelerating digital transformation for sustainable development with the addendum on artificial intelligence.* Department of Economic and Social Affairs. https://publicadministration.un.org/egovkb/en-us/

United Nations. (n.d.). *Convention on the Rights of Persons with Disabilities.* Department of Economic and Social Affairs.

United Republic of Tanzania (URT). (2019). *E-Government Act, 2019* (Act No. 10 of 2019). ISSN 0856-0331X.

United Republic of Tanzania (URT,2024), Ministry of Finance, Tanzania National Bureau of Statistics and President's Office - Finance and Planning, Office of the Chief Government Statistician, Zanzibar. The 2022 Population and Housing Census: Basic Demographic and Socioeconomic Profile; Tanzania Mainland, April 2024.

United Republic of Tanzania. (URT, 2016). Tanzania National ICT Policy. Ministry of Works, Transport and Communication.

United Republic of Tanzania[URT] (2022): Tanzania e-Government Strategy 2022. President's Office - Public Service Management. Retrieved on 15th October 2024 from the website www.utumishi.go.tz

Unruh, G., & Kiron, D. (2017). Digital transformation on purpose. *MIT Sloan Management Review, 10*(1), 1–13. https://sloanreview.mit.edu/article/digital-transformation-on-purpose/

Upchurch, R. S. (1998). A Conceptual Foundation for Ethical Decision Making: A Stakeholder Perspective in the Lodging Industry (U.S.A.). *Journal of Business Ethics, 17*(12), 1349–1361. DOI: 10.1023/A:1005866820504

Vallée, A. (2023). Geoepidemiological perspective on COVID-19 pandemic review, an insight into the global impact. *Frontiers in Public Health, 11*, 11. DOI: 10.3389/fpubh.2023.1242891 PMID: 37927887

Variyan, G., & Wilkinson, J. (2022). Variyan, George, and Jane Wilkinson. (2019). *"The Erasure of Sexual Harassment in Elite Private Boys' Schools.Gender and Education, 34*(2), 183–198. DOI: 10.1080/09540253.2021.1962516

Vehmas, K., Raudaskoski, A., Heikkilä, P., Harlin, A., & Mensonen, A. (2018). Consumer Attitudes and Communication in Circular Fashion. *Journal of Fashion Marketing and Management, 22*(3), 286–300. DOI: 10.1108/JFMM-08-2017-0079

Veleva, V. (2021). The Role of Entrepreneurs in Advancing Sustainable Lifestyles: Challenges, Impacts, and Future Opportunities. *Journal of Cleaner Production*, *283*, 124658. DOI: 10.1016/j.jclepro.2020.124658 PMID: 33078048

Verhoef, P. C., & Bijmolt, T. H. A. (2019). Marketing perspectives on digital business models: A framework and overview of the special issue. *International Journal of Research in Marketing*, *36*(3), 341–349. DOI: 10.1016/j.ijresmar.2019.08.001

Verhoef, P. C., Broekhuizen, T., Bart, Y., Bhattacharya, A., Qi Dong, J., Fabian, N., & Haenlein, M. (2021). Digital transformation: A multidisciplinary reflection and research agenda. *Journal of Business Research*, *122*, 889–901. DOI: 10.1016/j.jbusres.2019.09.022

Viljoen, S. (2021). A relational theory of data governance. *The Yale Law Journal*, *130*(6), 1464–1524.

Wachs, S., Wright, M. F., & Vazsonyi, A. T. (2019). Understanding the overlap between cyberbullying and cyberhate perpetration: Moderating effects of toxic online disinhibition. *Criminal Behaviour and Mental Health*, *29*(3), 179–188. DOI: 10.1002/cbm.2116 PMID: 31274229

Wahed, M. M. A., & Ismail, T. S. (2022). An online system for issuing building permits in light of e-government in Egypt. In Journal, H. B. R. C. (Ed.), *Issue 1* (Vol. 18, p. 53). Taylor & Francis., DOI: 10.1080/16874048.2021.2019447

Wains, S. I., & Mahmood, W. (2008). Integrating m-learning with e-learning. *Proceedings of the 9th ACM SIGITE Conference on Information Technology Education*, 31–38. DOI: 10.1145/1414558.1414568

Waldner, F., Poetz, M. K., Grimpe, C., & Eurich, M. (2015). Antecedents and Consequences of Business Model Innovation: The Role of Industry Structure. In Baden-Fuller, C., & Mangematin, V. (Eds.), *Advances in Strategic Management* (Vol. 33, pp. 347–386). Emerald Group Publishing Limited., DOI: 10.1108/S0742-332220150000033009

Wang, B., Zhou, H., Li, X., Yang, G., Zheng, P., Song, C., Yuan, Y., Wuest, T., Yang, H., & Wang, L. (2024). Human Digital Twin in the context of Industry 5.0. *Robotics and Computer-integrated Manufacturing*, *85*, 102626. DOI: 10.1016/j.rcim.2023.102626

Wang, C. L. (2021). New frontiers and future directions in interactive marketing: Inaugural editorial. *Journal of Research in Interactive Marketing*, *15*(1), 1–9. DOI: 10.1108/JRIM-03-2021-270

Wang, Q., Su, M., Zhang, M., & Li, R. (2021). Integrating digital technologies and public health to fight Covid-19 pandemic: Key technologies, applications, challenges and outlook of digital healthcare. *International Journal of Environmental Research and Public Health*, *18*(11), 6053. DOI: 10.3390/ijerph18116053 PMID: 34199831

Wang, Y., & Hazen, B. T. (2016). Consumer Product Knowledge and Intention to Purchase Remanufactured Products. *International Journal of Production Economics*, *181*, 460–469. DOI: 10.1016/j.ijpe.2015.08.031

Wang, Y., & Zhang, Y. (2022). AI-driven predictive analytics for personalized healthcare. *Journal of Healthcare Information Management*, *38*(6), 305–319. DOI: 10.1177/18414569221119869

Warren, T. (2021). Work–life balance and gig work:'Where are we now'and 'where to next'with the work–life balance agenda? *The Journal of Industrial Relations*, *63*(4), 522–545. DOI: 10.1177/00221856211007161

Weaver, E., Uddin, S., & Lamprou, D. A. (2022). Emerging Technologies for Combating Pandemics. *Expert Review of Medical Devices*, *19*(7), 533–538. DOI: 10.1080/17434440.2022.2115355 PMID: 35983986

Webster, G. (2023). Too Fast of Fashion: A Literature Review on the Destructive Social and Environmental Impacts of Fast Fashion. *Perspectives*, *15*(1). https://scholars.unh.edu/perspectives/vol15/iss1/10

Weeden, K. A., & Cornwell, B. (2020). The small-world network of college classes: Implications for epidemic spread on a university campus. *Sociological Science*, *7*, 222–241. DOI: 10.15195/v7.a9

Wengler, S., Hildmann, G., & Vossebein, U. (2021). Digital transformation in sales as an evolving process. *Journal of Business and Industrial Marketing*, *36*(4), 599–614. DOI: 10.1108/JBIM-03-2020-0124

Westerman, G., Calmejane, C., Bonnet, D., Ferraris, P., & McAfee, A. (2011). Digital transformation: a road-map for billion-dollar organizations. *MIT Center for Digital Business and Capgemini Consulting*. https://www.capgemini.com/wp-content/uploads/2017/07/Digital_Transformation__A_Road-Map_for_Billion-Dollar_Organizations.pdf

WhisperIndia. (2024, May 15). Whisper Presents Keep Girls in School (Hindi) [Video]. YouTube. https://www.youtube.com/watch?v=gFZTpxk5DaU

Wibisono, E. (2023). The digital entrepreneurial ecosystem in the European Union: Evidence from the digital platform economy index. *European Planning Studies*, *31*(6), 1270–1292. DOI: 10.1080/09654313.2023.2202683

Willingham, D. T. (2020). Ask the cognitive scientist: How can educators teach critical thinking? American Federation of Teachers. 22 September 2020. https://www.aft.org/ae/fall2020/willingham

Will, M. (2021). Teachers are stressed out, and it's causing some to quit. *Education Week*.

Wilson, N., Keni, K., & Tan, P. H. P. (2021). The Role of Perceived Usefulness and Perceived Ease-of-Use toward Satisfaction and Trust Which Influence Computer Consumers' Loyalty in China. *Gadjah Mada International Journal of Business*, *23*(3), 262. DOI: 10.22146/gamaijb.32106

World Bank Group. (2024). *Digital Progress and Trends Report: Interactive Charts – Digital Adoption*. [Online]. https://www.worldbank.org/en/data/interactive/2024/03/04/digital-progress-and-trends-report-interactive-charts

World Bank. (2020). *Leveraging lessons from the COVID-19 Crisis for learners with Disabilities*. World Bank.

World Health Organisation (WHO). (2020). *Disability Considerations during the COVID-19 Outbreak*. WHO.

World Health Organization. (2022). *WHO European framework for action on mental health 2021–2025*. World Health Organization. Regional Office for Europe.

Wouters, O. J., Shadlen, K. C., Salcher-Konrad, M., Pollard, A. J., Larson, H. J., Teerawattananon, Y., & Jit, M. (2021). Challenges in ensuring global access to COVID-19 vaccines: Production, affordability, allocation, and deployment. *Lancet*, *397*(10278), 1023–1034. DOI: 10.1016/S0140-6736(21)00306-8 PMID: 33587887

Wren, B. (2022). Sustainable Supply Chain Management in the Fast Fashion Industry: A Comparative Study of Current Efforts and Best Practices to Address the Climate Crisis. *Cleaner Logistics and Supply Chain*, *4*, 100032. DOI: 10.1016/j.clscn.2022.100032

Wright, B. A. (1980). Developing constructive views of life with a disability. *Rehabilitation Literature*, *41*(11-12), 274–279. PMID: 6449722

Wut, T. M., Xu, J. B., & Wong, S. (2021). Crisis management research (1985–2020) in the hospitality and tourism industry: A review and research agenda. *Tourism Management*, *85*, 104307. DOI: 10.1016/j.tourman.2021.104307 PMID: 36345489

Wu, Y. L., Shao, B., Newman, A., & Schwarz, G. (2021). Crisis leadership: A review and future research agenda. *The Leadership Quarterly*, *32*(6), 101518. DOI: 10.1016/j.leaqua.2021.101518

Xanthopoulou, P., & Plimakis, S. (2023). *The Adoption of Corporate Social Responsibility (CSR) Policy in the Tourism Sector: How CSR Affects Consumer Loyalty in the Greek Hotel Industry* (pp. 1–19). DOI: 10.4018/978-1-6684-6055-9.ch001

Xie, G., Huang, L., Bin, H., Apostolidis, C., Jiang, Y., Li, G., & Cai, W. (2022). Sustainable Entrepreneurship in Rural E-Commerce: Identifying Entrepreneurs in Practitioners by Using Deep Neural Networks Approach. *Frontiers in Environmental Science*, *10*, 840479. DOI: 10.3389/fenvs.2022.840479

Xu, K., & Li, W. (2013). An ethical stakeholder approach to crisis communication: A case study of Foxconn's 2010 employee suicide crisis. *Journal of Business Ethics*, *117*(2), 371–386. DOI: 10.1007/s10551-012-1522-0

Xu, Z., Su, C., Xiao, Y., & Wang, F. (2022). Artificial Intelligence for COVID-19: Battling the Pandemic With Computational Intelligence. *Intelligent Medicine*, *2*(1), 13–29. DOI: 10.1016/j.imed.2021.09.001 PMID: 34697578

Yadav, S. (2020). AI in the hotel industry: Adoption and application of artificial intelligence in hotel industry. *Hospitality & Travel Connaisseur Magazine*, 30–32.

Yadav, S. J. (2024a). AI Bias and Fairness: Ethical Considerations in Service Marketing Strategies. In *Integrating AI-Driven Technologies Into Service Marketing* (pp. 49–64). IGI Global. https://www.igi-global.com/chapter/ai-bias-and-fairness/355986

Yadav, S. J. (2024c). Voices From Within: Exploring Indian Perspectives on Sex Tourism. In *Examining Tourist Behaviors and Community Involvement in Destination Rejuvenation* (pp. 263–272). IGI Global. https://www.igi-global.com/chapter/voices-from-within/348915

Yadav, S. J. (2024d). Voices From Within: Exploring Indian Perspectives on Sex Tourism. In *Examining Tourist Behaviors and Community Involvement in Destination Rejuvenation* (pp. 263–272). IGI Global. https://www.igi-global.com/chapter/voices-from-within/348915

Yadav, S. (2021). Millennial Employees-Role, Benefits and Retaining Strategies in Hotel Industry (p. 64). DOI: 10.6084/m9.figshare.13719949.v1

Yadav, S. J. (2024b). Analyzing the Influence of Sustainable Voluntourism on Community Development and Empowerment. In *Special Interest Trends for Sustainable Tourism* (pp. 152–165). IGI Global., https://www.igi-global.com/chapter/analyzing-the-influence-of-sustainable-voluntourism-on-community-development-and-empowerment/352362 DOI: 10.4018/979-8-3693-5903-7.ch009

Yadav, S. J. (2025). Artificial Intelligence and Stress Management Tools for Better Mental Health. In *AI Technologies and Advancements for Psychological Well-Being and Healthcare* (pp. 163–186). IGI Global., https://www.igi-global.com/chapter/artificial-intelligence-and-stress-management-tools-for-better-mental-health/357098

Yang, Y., Lee, S., & Kim, H. (2024). The future of Q-commerce: Exploring market trends and consumer demand.

Yang, C., Gu, M., & Albitar, K. (2024). Government in the digital age: Exploring the impact of digital transformation on governmental efficiency. *Technological Forecasting and Social Change*, *208*, 123722. DOI: 10.1016/j.techfore.2024.123722

Ye, J. (2020). The role of health technology and informatics in a global public health emergency: practices and implications from the COVID-19 pandemic. JMIR medical

Ye, J., & Dela, E. (2023). The Effect of Green Investment and Green Financing on Sustainable Business Performance of Foreign Chemical Industries Operating in Indonesia: The Mediating Role of Corporate Social Responsibility. *Sustainability (Basel)*, *15*(14), 14. Advance online publication. DOI: 10.3390/su151411218

Yeo, V. C. S., Goh, S. K., & Rezaei, S. (2017). Consumer experiences, attitude and behavioral intention toward online food delivery (OFD) services. *Journal of Retailing and Consumer Services*, *35*, 150–162. DOI: 10.1016/j.jretconser.2016.12.013

Yildirim, S., & Yildirim, D. Ç. (2020). *Achieving Sustainable Development Through a Green Economy Approach.*

Yildirim, S., Demirtas, I., & Yildirim, D. C. (2022). *A Review of Alternative Economic Approaches to Achieve Sustainable Development: The Rising Digitalization and Degrowth Post COVID-19*

Yildirim, S., Demirtas, I., & Yildirim, D. C. (2022). A Review of Alternative Economic Approaches to Achieve Sustainable Development: The Rising Digitalization and Degrowth Post COVID-19. In Castanho, R. (Ed.), *Handbook of Research on Sustainable Development Goals, Climate Change, and Digitalization* (pp. 288–307). IGI Global. DOI: 10.4018/978-1-7998-8482-8.ch018

Yildiz, M. (2016). E-Government: Informatisation of Government and Politics. In Farazmand, A. (Ed.), *Global Encyclopedia of Public Administration, Public Policy, and Governance. In Springer eBooks* (pp. 1–7)., DOI: 10.1007/978-3-319-31816-5_2450-1

Young, K. S. (2004). Internet addiction: A new clinical phenomenon and its consequences. *The American Behavioral Scientist*, *48*(4), 402–415. DOI: 10.1177/0002764204270278

Yuan, L. M. (2021). Student's attitude and satisfaction towards transformative learning: A research study on emergency remote learning in tertiary education. *Creative Education*, *12*(03), 494–528. DOI: 10.4236/ce.2021.123035

Zahlan, A., Ranjan, R. P., & Hayes, D. (2023). Artificial intelligence innovation in healthcare: Literature review, exploratory analysis, and future research. *Technology in Society*, *74*, 102321. DOI: 10.1016/j.techsoc.2023.102321

Zaidi, H., AlJadaan, O. T., Al Faress, M. Y., & Jabas, A. O. (2024). Disconnect to Reconnect: Your Path to Physical and Mental Wellbeing. In *Exploring Youth Studies in the Age of AI* (pp. 25-43). IGI Global.

Zainun, N. F. H., Johari, J., & Adnan, Z. (2020). Technostress and commitment to change: The moderating role of internal communication. *International Journal of Public Administration*, *43*(15), 1327–1339. DOI: 10.1080/01900692.2019.1672180

Zamani, B., Sandin, G., & Peters, G. M. (2017). Life Cycle Assessment of Clothing Libraries: Can Collaborative Consumption Reduce the Environmental Impact of Fast Fashion? *Journal of Cleaner Production*, *162*, 1368–1375. DOI: 10.1016/j.jclepro.2017.06.128

Zare, J., & Persaud, A. (2024). Digital transformation and business model innovation: A bibliometric analysis of existing research and future perspectives. *Management Review Quarterly*, *x*(x), x–x. DOI: 10.1007/s11301-024-00426-z

Zeng, J., & He, M. (2019). Explainability in healthcare decision-making: A case study using machine learning. *IEEE Access : Practical Innovations, Open Solutions*, *7*, 112028–112035. DOI: 10.1109/ACCESS.2019.2934931

Zhang, C., Wang, Z., Zhou, G., Chang, F., Ma, D., Jing, Y., Cheng, W., Ding, K., & Zhao, D. (2023). Towards new-generation human-centric smart manufacturing in Industry 5.0: A systematic review. *Advanced Engineering Informatics*, *57*, 102121. DOI: 10.1016/j.aei.2023.102121

Zhang, R. Y., Li, Y., Zhang, A. L., Wang, Y., & Molina, M. J. (2020). Identifying airborne transmission as the dominant route for the spread of COVID-19. *Proceedings of the National Academy of Sciences of the United States of America*, *117*(26), 14857–14863. DOI: 10.1073/pnas.2009637117 PMID: 32527856

Zhang, X., & Chen, S. (2022). Leveraging AI for healthcare delivery: A case study approach. *Healthcare Technology Review*, *12*(4), 105–117. DOI: 10.1109/HTR.2022.1235623

Zhang, Y., & Berhe, H. M. (2022). The Impact of Green Investment and Green Marketing on Business Performance: The Mediation Role of Corporate Social Responsibility in Ethiopia's Chinese Textile Companies. *Sustainability (Basel)*, *14*(7), 7. Advance online publication. DOI: 10.3390/su14073883

Zhu, G. (2020). Research on Teacher Identity: Mapping Challenges and Innovations. *European Journal of Teacher Education*, *45*(4), 572–575. DOI: 10.1080/02619768.2020.1860007

Zhu, Y., Lu, Y., Gupta, S., Wang, J., & Hu, P. (2022). Promoting smart wearable devices in the health-AI market: The role of health consciousness and privacy protection. *Journal of Research in Interactive Marketing*, *17*(2), 257–272. DOI: 10.1108/JRIM-10-2021-0246

About the Contributors

Durmuş Çağrı Yıldırım was born in 1981. After he graduated from Department of Economics in Kocaeli University in 2005, he started his master's education in Economics in the same year. He got the degree of Masters in Economic Policy in 2007. In 2011, he got his PhD degree in Economics. While he was a doctorate student, he studied one semester in Almeria University-Spain. Between 2006-2012, he worked as a research assistant at University of Kocaeli. He works at Tekirdag Namık Kemal University since April 2015. He studies on sustainable development, carbon emission, health and education issues, employment, innovation.

Seda Yıldırım currently works at Tekirdag Namık Kemal University in Turkey. She has a doctoral degree (PhD) in marketing. She studies on sustainable development, 2030 sustainable development goals, sustainable consumption patterns, consumption patterns, environmental quality and food security. She is married and has two children. She has over a thousand citations by Google scholar. She has many publications in journals indexed by Web of Science (SSCI, SCI-Exp, ESCI and others) and SCOPUS. She published several book chapters in IGI Global publishing. She won Emerald literati award-Outstanding Paper award 2022.

Vinay Kandpal (Post doc and Ph.D. in Finance) possesses over 18 years of experience in Academics and Industry. He has published more than 60 research papers in leading refereed Journals. Published 6 books in the area of Management. He has presented several works at International Conferences on Smart City at The University of Nice Sophia Antipolis, France, and Oxford Brookes University, UK. He has also presented research works in institutions like IIM A, IIM B, IIM I, IIT Delhi, etc. He is a Full-Time Member of ANAHEI Florida, USA. He works as a Professor in Department of Management Studies, Graphic Era Deemed to be University, Dehradun, Uttarakhand, India. He is on the Editorial and Reviewer Board of Heliyon Business and Economics, Qualitative Research in Financial Market, Annals of Public and Cooperative Economics, International Review of Economics and Finance, World Development Perspective, Journal of Retailing and Consumer Services, Journal of Public Affairs, etc. His area of research is Sustainability, Fintech, Smart City, Risk Management, and Financial Inclusion.

Sameera Afroze is currently serving as an Assistant Professor in the Human Resources and Organisation Behaviour area at St. Joseph's Degree and PG College (Autonomous), King Kothi, Hyderabad. She obtained her PhD in Business Administration from the Department of Business Management, Osmania University. She qualified for UGC-NET & SET (Telangana and AP) in the year 2016. She is the recipient of the Maulana Azad National Fellowship from UGC. She has published a book and has presented her work at conferences, workshops and seminars both nationally and internationally.

Dhitasmita De is a postgraduate student specialising in Economics at Graphic Era University, Dehradun. Their research interests include digital transformation, sustainable development, and economic policy. They have interned with The Dais, where they contributed to SDG documentation, mental health solutions analysis, and youth engagement initiatives. Currently, they are exploring the impact of digitalisation on business development, with a focus on revenue growth and infrastructure investments.

Debapriya Ganguly is an Assistant Professor of English in the Department of Humanities and Social Sciences at Graphic Era University, Dehradun, India. She earned her doctorate from the Indian Institute of Technology, Dhanbad, India. Ganguly's research interests span diverse topics, including masculinity and men's studies, Indian cinema, gerontology, and health humanities. She has previously published in South Asian Popular Culture, Intersections (Gender and Sexuality in Asia and the Pacific), Humanities and Social Sciences Communications, and Vernon Press. DEBAPRIYA GANGULY - Google Scholar Orcid id: DEBAPRIYA GANGULY (0000-0002-4087-7099) - My ORCID

Oindrilla Ghosh is a Research Scholar hailing from the School of Law at Christ (Deemed to be University) Bangalore, India, focuses her research on health of tribal communities. Her work includes a total of 10 publications on Neuroscience on Organizational Behavior at IGI Global and also Environmental Disasters that are indexed in SCOPUS and Web of Sciences conference proceedings. She completed her early education at Loreto Day School, Bowbazar and went on to achieve distinction in her undergraduate (B.A/LL.B) and postgraduate (LL.M) studies at Calcutta University. Having served as an Assistant Professor of Law at Kingston Law College,Barasat, Kolkata, Ghosh has actively participated in numerous National Conferences, International Conferences, UN Global Summits, webinars, and seminars organized by prestigious academic institutions. Her expertise lies in health perspectives, environmental studies, human behavior, and related areas. Additionally, she has conducted various workshops, lectures in educational institutions, and is engaged with NGO's to help the needy.

Priyanka Gupta is an Assistant professor at Graphic Era Deemed to be University. For the last 4 years, she has been contributing in teaching and research. She has developed skills in qualitative and quantitative research methods. Her current research areas are Sustainable Human Resource Management, Artificial Intelligence, Digital Stress, Internet of Things (IoT). Email id: priyankagupta.mgt@geu.ac.in SCOPUS AUTHOR ID: 58499631200

Aryan Gupta is a student of business and management at Christ (Deemed to be University), Bengaluru, India. His academic and professional interests lie in the areas of digital marketing, consumer behaviour, retail innovation, and sustainable business strategies. He brings hands-on experience from working in a family-owned apparel manufacturing business and has actively engaged in social media marketing, client acquisition, and brand development. Aryan's research focuses on emerging retail formats like Quick Commerce and the evolving dynamics of digital transformation in the business landscape.

Chithambar Gupta V, is currently working as a Professor at School of Management, Presidency University, Bengaluru. He holds a Masters Degree in 'Management' from the "Indian Institute of Science" (IISc), Bengaluru. He has 24 years of rich work experience with 7+ years of Industry and 17+ years of academic experience in the areas of Marketing & General Management. He has won various awards and accolades for his work. Recipient of 'Best Teacher Award' (2015), 'Special Mention Award' (2004) and 'Team Award' (1999) for his excellent contribution towards work. He has published several papers, book chapters in reputed Management Journals. His research interest lies in the areas of Digital Marketing, Services Marketing; Retailing. Two PhD scholars have successfully completed PhD under his guidance.

Rashika Gusain is an English Major in the Department of Humanities and Social Sciences at Graphic Era University, Dehradun, India. She is currently pursuing her Masters in English. Her research interests span diverse topics, including women's health studies, maternal mortality, mental health, migration, social inequalities and Indian cinema.

Rashid Hashmi is a seasoned senior journalist with a rich and diverse experience spanning over 20 years in Broadcast, Digital, and Print Media. Prior to joining Sharda University, he held the position of Executive Editor and Senior Anchor at the renowned national news channel, 'India News'. Throughout his illustrious journalistic career, Prof. Rashid Hashmi has served in various capacities across prominent media platforms including Dainik Jagran Newspaper, Zee News, ETV, Total TV, FM News, and India News. His expertise encompasses anchoring, debating, and ground zero reporting of numerous parliamentary and assembly elections, providing insightful coverage of pivotal political events. Prof. Rashid Hashmi is renowned for his engaging interviews with prominent personalities from the worlds of politics, sports, and Bollywood. His interviews have featured distinguished celebrities, political leaders, and sports icons, offering unique perspectives and valuable insights to viewers and readers alike. With a keen eye for detail and a commitment to journalistic integrity, Rashid Hashmi has earned widespread acclaim for his contribution to media discourse in India. His dynamic approach to storytelling and extensive experience across multiple media formats underline his versatility and depth as a journalist. Prof. Rashid Hashmi's tenure in the media industry reflects a dedication to delivering compelling and informative content while upholding the values of responsible journalism. His role in shaping public discourse through impactful reporting and incisive interviews underscores his standing as a respected figure in Indian journalism.

Saba Inamdar is currently serving as an Assistant Professor and Head of Department (In-Charge) at Presidency University. A distinguished educator, accomplished author, and dedicated researcher, Dr. Saba Inamdar is driven by a genuine passion for education, and she harmoniously blends her instructional prowess with a profound dedication to scholarly exploration. Dr. Inamdar holds a notable academic background, with degrees encompassing an MBA, MCOM, and a Ph.D. in Management. Her accomplishments comprise of more than 25 paper presentations and a remarkable array of more than 26 research publications including UGC Care listed, Scopus-indexed journals and book chapters, additionally a reviewer to journals of Web of Science (WoS). Attesting high calibre academic contributions. Dr. Inamdar's quest for knowledge is exemplified by her active participation in over 80 more webinars, seminars, FDPs, and workshops. Additionally, she is an actively engaged member of professional platforms including LinkedIn, ResearchGate, and Academia, further epitomising her commitment to the global academic community.

Sudhanshu Joshi currently working in Operations & Supply Chain Management Area, Doon University, INDIA. His research interest anchored within Digital-Twin, Cyber Supply Chain Management with special focus on green supply chain network design, sustainable supply chain design, and coordination in humanitarian supply chain network, application of big data analytics in sustainable and humanitarian supply chains, emerging technologies (Including Industry 4.0), Circular Economy, Agriculture Supply Chain and Soft-computing Applications in Supply Chain Management. He is member with leading Societies including CSI, IEEE, POMS, INFORMS. He is a series editor of research note series CRC press, Taylor & Francis. Email id: sudhanshujoshi@doonuniversity.ac.in SCOPUS AUTHOR ID: 56111179800

Aishwarya Khanduri is an English major in the Department of Humanities and Social Sciences at Graphic Era University, Dehradun, India. She is currently a final year student for the same. Khanduri's research interests span manifold topics, including social inequalities, feminist studies, korean studies, health humanities and popular literature.

Binod Kumar is a graduate student known for his academic excellence, with his total 6 scholarly works indexed in Scopus database on Neuroscience in Organizational Behavior, Neuromarketing and AI Applications on Wildlife Conservation. Hailing from Ranchi, Jharkhand in India, Binod is currently pursuing a Master of Laws (LL.M) at the prestigious Radha Govind University. His passion for technology and innovation along with climate changes is evident through his high academic performance and numerous projects. Binod has a keen interest in artificial intelligence, machine learning, neuropsychology, climate changes and disaster management, fields in which he has undertaken several research projects. He is particularly fascinated by the potential of AI to solve real-world problems and is dedicated to learning and applying new techniques in these areas. He volunteers at local NGOs, teaching underprivileged children basic computer skills. With a strong foundation in law and a commitment to making a positive impact, Binod Kumar is poised to become a future leader in the legal industry.

Galinoma Gahele Lubawa is a distinguished business analyst and academic with over two decades of experience in both the public and private sectors, as well as with Local Government Authorities (LGAs) in Tanzania. He currently serves as a Lecturer at the Institute of Rural Development Planning (IRDP) in Dodoma, Tanzania, where he imparts knowledge in areas such as financial accounting, business research, data analysis, investment planning, business planning, financial modelling, and strategic financial management. Mr. Lubawa's extensive experience and expertise in business and financial analysis, coupled with his academic contributions, make him a valuable asset to both the academic and professional communities in Tanzania.

Priyanshi Mamgain is a student of Masters in English in the Department of Humanities and Social Sciences at Graphic Era Deemed to be University, Dehradun, India. Her academic interests span feminism, Indian cinema, and war literature, areas in which she is passionate about exploring the intersection of literature, culture, and social issues. She has previously published in Futuristic Trends in Social Sciences Volume 3 Book 16, Iterative International Publishers.

T.C. Manjunath is a Professor in the Department of Computer Science and Engineering at Rajarajeswari College of Engineering, Bangalore. Specializing in IoT Cybersecurity and Blockchain Technology, he is also the Dean of Research and Development at the college. Dr. Manjunath has made significant contributions to the fields of technology and cybersecurity through his research and academic work. His expertise in emerging technologies continues to shape the academic and research landscape at the institution. Rajarajeswari College of Engineering, located on Mysore Road, Kumbalgodu Post, Bangalore (560074), is a hub for his innovative work in the field.

P. Selvakumar is currently an Associate Professor in the Department of Science and Humanities at Nehru Institute of Technology, Coimbatore, Tamil Nadu, India. Since 2023, he has served as the Department IQAC Coordinator at the institute. Prior to joining Nehru Institute of Technology, he held positions as an Assistant Professor in the Department of Science and Humanities various engineering colleges in Coimbatore, Tamil Nadu, India, spanning from 2011 to 2023. Dr.P. Selvakumar's academic and research interests lie primarily in the field of phytochemistry. He has made significant contributions to his field, with an impressive record that includes 30 journal publications, 12 patents, and 20 conference papers. Additionally, he has organized 5 seminars and conferences, further demonstrating his commitment to academic and scientific exchange. Throughout his career, Dr. P.Selvakumar has been recognized for his dedication and excellence in teaching, having been honored with several awards, including the Best Teacher Awards. He holds a prominent position in the academic community, contributing actively to research.

Manju Shree Raman has a strong education professional with Ph. D., M.Phil., MBA., from Faculty of Management, Bharathiar University, Coimbatore. She received the prestigious honor;Teachers Transforming India 2022; on World Knowledge Day, April 14, 2022, as well as the;BEST FACULTY AWARD; from Akshaya Institute of Management Studies, Coimbatore, on September 5, 2014. She is a member of the CMA and AIMA. She is also an internal ISO Auditor with certification. She is a member of the Editorial Board, an editor, a reviewer, a chief guest, an outbound trainer, a panel member, and a lecturer at colleges and business schools in India and Ethiopia. She has served as an international relations officer and the initiator of several Memorandums of Understanding and Agreements (MOUs and

MOAs) involving India, Ethiopia, Mozambique, Austria, Kenya, and others. She was working as Professor in Ethiopia. She is presently Professor; Head of Management.

Guru Basava Aradhya S has an illustrious academic tenure spanning over two decades, during which he has made significant contributions to various esteemed institutions such as CHRIST University, REVA University, Jain University, ISBR Business School, and presently serves as a distinguished Head and Professor in Chandigarh School of Business, Department of Management Studies (MBA), Jhanjeri, Mohali, Punjab. He holds a Ph.D. in Management from Chhatrapati Shahu Ji Maharaj University, Kanpur. Dr. Guru Aradhya boasts an impressive academic profile with three Masters degrees encompassing MBA, M.Com, PGDCA, and MPhil qualifications. Professor Guru is a product of comprehensive professional training in management pedagogy from IIM Bangalore, specializing in Strategic Management. His scholarly prowess is further evident through the authorship of four books and numerous articles featured in esteemed national and international journals. A mentor par excellence, Professor Guru has guided four Ph.D. scholars hailing from prestigious institutions such as Bhartiyaar University Tamil Nadu, Visvesvaraya Technological University Belgaum, University of Mysore, and REVA University. He is a sought-after resource person for Management Development Programs (MDPs) and Faculty Development Programs (FDPs). His scholarly contributions are commendable, with over 50 papers indexed in UGC Care journals, five in Scopus, ten in Web of Science, and eight

Gauri Samant is a student of Masters in English in Department of Humanities and Social Sciences at Graphic Era (Deemed to be) University, Dehradun, India. Her academic interests consist of diverse topics including cinema, pop culture, media studies, feminism, and existentialism. She is passionate about examining areas where literature reflects and critiques societal narratives, and the complexities of human experience.

Manu Sharma is an Associate professor at Graphic Era Deemed to be University. She has received her Post-Doctoral Fellowship sponsored by Indian Council of Social Science Research (ICSSR), Ministry of Human Resource Development, Government of India, from Doon University, INDIA. For the last ten years, she has been contributing in teaching and research. She has developed skills in qualitative and quantitative research methods such as Multi-Criteria Decision Making, Fuzzy Theory, Multivariate analysis etc. Her current research areas are Digital supply chains, Digital Marketing, Circular economy, Sustainability, Waste management, Internet of Things (IoT). She is serving various journals as an editorial board member in the area of Digital Technologies, Sustainable development, Waste

Management, Supply Chains published by Emerald, Springer, Elsevier and IGI. Email id: manusharma@doonuniversity.ac.in SCOPUS AUTHOR ID: 5719878058

Mohit Sharma is a research scholar at the Institute of Management Studies and Research, Maharshi Dayanand University, Rohtak, Haryana, India. His research focuses on the dynamic relationship between brand image and purchase intentions, particularly in the context of brand extensions within the FMCG sector. He has co-authored several scholarly works and continues to contribute to the academic community. Mohit can be reached at mohitattri.rs.imsar@mdurohtak.ac.in

Ajay K. Singh is working as an Associate Professor (Research) in the Department of Humanities and Social Science, Graphic Era (Deemed to be University) Dehradun. He has worked as Assistant Professor (Economics) in the School of Liberal Arts & Management, DIT University Dehradun for 6 years. He did Post-Doctorate Research with EDI of India, Ahmedabad, Gujarat (India). He received MPhil (Economics) from DAVV Indore (India), and PhD (Economics) from IIT Indore (India. He has published several research papers in the diversified area such as climate change, agricultural productivity, assessment of food security; estimation of GFSI, development of environmental sustainability index (ESI) and its association with socio-economic indicators; measurement and determinants of entrepreneurship ecosystem, and dimension of sustainable development and its interlinkages with economic development.

Jaspreet Singh is a scholar currently pursuing a Ph.D. in Social Work at the Central University of Jammu and President of PSWAJK. With a Master's degree in Social Work. They have specialization in gender and sexualities, health and healthcare, international borders, social policy, and social development, Jaspreet has a robust academic background. They have earned prestigious fellowships, including MMF NAPSWI Scholarship, UGC-NET/JRF, and UGC-NET(MANF), and have published numerous research papers on topics such as sexual harassment prevention, child sexual abuse, and the societal impacts of COVID-19. Jaspreet is actively involved in professional training and community engagement, serving as a key resource person in capacity-building workshops. Jaspreet is committed to fostering inclusive communities and advocating for social justice, particularly for marginalized groups

Suraj Yadav is an accomplished professional with a background in Hospitality, holding a bachelor's degree from Pune University and a Master in Hotel Management & Tourism from Madurai Kamaraj University, Madurai. Currently serving as an Assistant Professor and Training & Placement Officer at D Y Patil School of Hospitality in Kolhapur, Maharashtra, India, he brings extensive expertise to the field. Suraj is also dedicated to furthering his academic pursuits and is actively pursuing a Ph.D. at D Y Patil Agricultural & Technical University in Kolhapur. His commitment to education and training has made a significant impact in the realm of hospitality.

Index

A

B

C

D

E

F

G

H

I

M

P

Q

R

S

T

U

W

www.ingramcontent.com/pod-product-compliance
Lightning Source LLC
LaVergne TN
LVHW080346011026
849161LV00009B/2210